STAGE LIGHTING

Stage Lighting: The Fundamentals is written specifically for introductory stage lighting courses. The book begins with an examination of the nature of light, perception, and color, then leads into a conversation of stage lighting equipment and technicians. Lamps, luminaries, controls/dimming, and electricity form the basis of these chapters. The book also provides a detailed explanation and overview of the lighting design process for the theatre and several other traditional forms of entertainment. Finally, the book explores a variety of additional areas where lighting designers and technicians can find related future employment, such as concert and corporate lighting, themed design, architectural and landscape lighting, and computer animation.

New for this edition:

- enlarged full-color illustrations, photographs, light plots and examples of lighting design;
- updated information on LED lighting and equipment;
- expanded discussion of the practical use of color as a designer;
- expanded discussion of psychological/perceptual effects of color;
- new discussion of color mixing through light sources that make use of additive mixing;
- expanded discussion of industry professions;
- expanded discussion and illustrations relating to photometrics;
- expanded discussion and examples of control protocols and new equipment; and
- updated designer profiles along with the addition of still more designer profiles.

Richard Dunham is a scenic and lighting designer as well as a professor and head of design at the University of Georgia. He is a United States Institute for Theatre Technology (USITT) Fellow and former lighting commissioner from 1998 to 2006. His professional credits include numerous productions throughout the East Coast, New York City, and the Midwest, as well as being Lighting Certified (LC) and a member of Illuminating Engineering Society of North America (IESNA) and associate member of the International Association of Lighting Designers (IALD).

STAGE LIGHTING

The Fundamentals

SECOND EDITION

RICHARD DUNHAM

Routledge
Taylor & Francis Group

NEW YORK AND LONDON

Second edition published 2019 by Routledge
711 Third Avenue, New York, NY 10017

and by Routledge
2 Park Square, Milton Park, Abingdon, Oxon, OX14 4RN

Routledge is an imprint of the Taylor & Francis Group, an informa business

First published 2011 by Pearson

Library of Congress Cataloging-in-Publication Data
Names: Dunham, Richard, author.
Title: Stage lighting : the fundamentals / Richard Dunham.
Description: Second edition. | New York, NY : Routledge, 2018. |
    Includes bibliographical references and index.
Identifiers: LCCN 2018013410 | ISBN 9781138672161 (hardback : alk. paper) |
    ISBN 9781138672178 (pbk. : alk. paper) | ISBN 9781315454696 (ebook)
Subjects: LCSH: Stage lighting.
Classification: LCC PN2091.E4 D87 2018 | DDC 792.02/5—dc23
LC record available at https://lccn.loc.gov/2018013410

ISBN: 978-1-138-67216-1 (hbk)
ISBN: 978-1-138-67217-8 (pbk)
ISBN: 978-1-315-45469-6 (ebk)

Typeset in Adobe Garamond and Frutiger
by Apex CoVantage, LLC

Photos are courtesy of the author, Richard Dunham, unless otherwise credited.

Printed in Canada

CONTENTS

PREFACE

IT IS IMPORTANT to note that *Stage Lighting: The Fundamentals* is the first of a two-part companion set of lighting design books, the second book being *Stage Lighting: Design Applications and More*. The chapters that form the basis for the material presented in this book are based on the printed segment of the first edition (*Stage Lighting: Fundamentals and Applications*) while the chapters on more specialized applications that were previously presented online in the first edition are now in print in the second book (*Stage Lighting: Design Applications and More*). This book, *Stage Lighting: The Fundamentals*, is focused primarily on materials typically found in introductory to intermediate courses, while *Stage Lighting: Design Applications and More* is focused on a variety of specialized lighting applications that are more characteristic of topics presented in more advanced lighting classes. That book may also be used by more advanced readers as a personal reference. Both books have also been updated with new materials to reflect current trends in the industry and are now printed in color. Regardless of the reader's level of lighting expertise, they will most likely find materials that speak to their interests and needs in both books.

Before going any further, I want to express my continued thanks to the many instructors and colleagues who have made the first edition of the book so successful. More importantly, I'm thankful for the conversations and suggestions we have had that aided me in making improvements in this second edition. Focal Press/Routledge–Taylor & Francis Group reflects a new partnership that I feel will allow the book to continue to grow in both popularity and usefulness to students and future lighting designers. In addition to updating, the most significant changes between the first and second editions relate to moving the former online chapters into a second volume and printing both books in color. This also allowed me to move *Stage Lighting: The Fundamentals* towards more introductory materials while shifting some of the more advanced concepts to the applications topics in the second book. Several additional upgrades and revisions provided in the second edition of both books include the following: printing the majority of the images and figures in full color, updating a number of technology sections to reflect current trends and equipment (especially in the area of LEDs, which are overtaking the lighting industry), updating several design processes (i.e., significant changes have been made in the recommended practices of architectural lighting since the printing of the first edition), reorganization and consolidation of several topics to fit the manner in which instructors are using the book, additions to the books' resources (glossary, bibliography, manufacturer contacts, and periodical listings), and the inclusion of nearly a dozen additional professional profiles that provide introductions to lighting professionals who aren't necessarily designers but who represent other avenues of employment for future lighting specialists (along with updates to the majority of the designer profiles that appeared in the first edition).

Lighting design is one of the most influential design specializations existing in today's society. Light gives us the primary means by which we sense our environment. It plays a fundamental role in our perception of the world and how we observe it. Light can hide or reveal an object and its features, modify the perceived shape of an object, suggest motion, distort or enhance an object's colors or texture, and can be used to create or alter moods. These are only a few of the many ways that light can manipulate our perception of the world. This book has been written primarily for the beginning to intermediate level student. While a certain amount of technology must be understood before moving on to concepts involving design, the majority of this book is focused on the design process. Other topics presented in this volume are based primarily on theatrical lighting and include the properties of light, effects of lighting, the control and manipulation of light, theatrical lighting equipment, designing for traditional forms of entertainment, projection, and a brief introduction to a variety of lighting applications beyond theatrical lighting. Although it is assumed that this and its partner book will be used primarily in theatrical lighting classes, the books should also be useful to those in the electrical engineering and architectural or interior design lighting fields as well. The books speak to a broader audience—one that is seeking the fundamentals of lighting regardless of lighting discipline and where we are encouraged to crossover between the many lighting specialties.

I believe that the future of lighting design lies in a designer's ability to understand and deliver designs in light—period. Whether designing for an opera or a building, the basic principles of lighting hold true despite the differences in equipment and specific design applications that exist between the disciplines. Many theatrical designers already move naturally among any number of genres of entertainment lighting—and while most were trained predominantly in theatrical design, there is immense potential for designing in a number of additional areas of lighting as well. Likewise, designers with an electrical engineering background are bringing more theatrical elements into their designs as well. All you need to succeed can be found in a positive attitude in making the shift, becoming familiar with the equipment and practices of the specialty, looking for opportunities to observe and learn a new discipline, and being able to modify your techniques in order to suit the new avenue of design. Regardless of individual preferences, more and more lighting designers are finding themselves crossing back and forth among a variety of lighting applications as a means of maintaining a successful career. As an added benefit, these additional areas of lighting also frequently offer larger design fees and other incentives for a project (such as permanence) that many theatrical organizations or projects cannot provide.

The theme of both books lies in providing a link between many of these lighting disciplines. While there is a solid introduction to theatrical lighting design (especially design process) in this book, it is my hope that you can use both books as references that focus on lighting design and the design methodology that connects these fields rather than simply focusing on the equipment and technological emphasis that are characteristic of many lighting books. The topic of crossover to this degree had not really been attempted in a lighting text before the first edition of this text. Additionally, a detailed discussion of the design process spans several chapters and forms another critical element of this book. While the book outlines a reasonably specific process, it should not be thought of as the only process. It is simply a place for the beginner to receive fairly detailed instructions that can then be tweaked as their skills and processes evolve. In keeping with the more universal applications of lighting, a variety of specific lighting disciplines are introduced in Chapter 16. Many of these are presented in considerable detail and as individual chapters in *Stage Lighting: Design Applications and More*. Those chapters focus on essential design issues and equipment differences that are unique to working in a variety of different areas of lighting design. Questions relating to special considerations, luminaires, control and equipment needs, and design concerns that are characteristic of a particular lighting specialty are also raised in those chapters. While technology cannot be avoided, it's been my goal to present the technical material as it becomes relevant and best pertains to the design needs of a "total" lighting designer. Because equipment is constantly in a state of evolution, I have chosen to dedicate many figures to illustrations that present design concepts rather than the traditional photographs of lighting equipment and production shots. Instead, in order to remain current, I provide an appendix with a listing of lighting equipment manufacturers along with a link to their websites, where up-to-date product information is always available.

Finally, the most important element of both books is to simply demonstrate the profound effect that light and a lighting designer can have on our lives. My hope is that not only can I provide the spark of inspiration that will allow readers to have a deeper appreciation of the art and tools of lighting, but also that these books will equip them with enough information to use these tools to develop effective art while "painting with light."

ACKNOWLEDGMENTS

AS WITH ANYTHING of this magnitude, there are many people who have provided help in producing this project. You don't have to work very long in this business to discover that many professionals in our line of work are truly giving and willing to share their knowledge and experiences freely. This extends from the designers who have worked on common projects with me, to fellow educators, to the Tony Award nominees and winners who form the mainstay of Broadway lighting design. Colleagues who have been using the first edition of the book have also been a great source of suggestions as we have worked on the second edition of this project. Additionally, our equipment manufacturers and professional organizations are another group of contributors who are truly interested in sharing their expertise and knowledge with us as well. It is impossible to mention every one of them here, but there are a number of individuals that deserve a special mention and thank you. First, my editors and the rest of the staff at Focal Press/Routledge and Taylor & Francis Group: Stacey Walker (acquisitions editor, who first approached me regarding the second edition) and Meredith Darnell (editorial assistant) and Lucia Accorsi (editorial assistant) who have kept this project on track since we first began to work on the second edition nearly three years ago. Also, to my initial editors and staff at Pearson Education/Allyn & Bacon who brought the first edition of the book to life. I am most appreciative of all of these individuals and their helpful suggestions as we have gone through the process of producing both editions of the books. I also want to thank all of the designers and manufacturers who shared materials with me or who were kind enough to be interviewed and let me feature them in the sidebars. These are among some of the busiest people in the business and I appreciate their willingness to share their knowledge with the next generation of lighting designers. Also, I want to thank the many students that I have had the pleasure of teaching, and in some cases learning from, over the 30-plus years that I have been involved in lighting education. Nobody is an expert in all areas, and the breadth of these books makes this an even more relevant issue. This is especially important for those topics that are featured in *Stage Lighting: Design Applications and More*—and to that point I enlisted several colleagues and friends who graciously read and offered comments and corrections on materials I have presented on various specialty areas of the lighting industry. Many, but not all, of these individuals are featured in the sidebars, but to make sure that none are missed I want to publicly acknowledge and thank the following individuals for their support and comments: Marilyn Lowey, Jim Moody and Jeff Ravitz (concert and spectacle lighting), Bill Klages, (film and television lighting), Bob Shook and the late Bill Warfel (display, landscape, and architectural lighting), Tom Ruzika (themed/specialty design), and finally Mike Hussey and John Kundert-Gibbs (virtual lighting). These folks are all at the top of their respective specialties. I also want to thank those colleagues who reviewed portions of the manuscript as I went through the revision/updating process; I am appreciative of the comments and suggestions that came from these individuals for both editions of the books. It's difficult to be a sole writer on a project as large as this, and the books are much improved through the comments and input that I received from all of these individuals. Finally, as in the first edition, a very special thank you to my family (my very supportive wife, Joelle and our children, Chelsea, and Richy) as well as our many friends and extended family who once again had to deal with the fact that "the books" were always somewhere in my list of priorities over the last several years.

Richard Dunham, Spring 2018

ABOUT THE AUTHOR

Richard E. Dunham, LC, IESNA (professor and head of design at the University of Georgia) has been involved in lighting design for close to 40 years—more than 30 in lighting education. He has hundreds of design credits in both academic and professional lighting/scenic design with credits in drama, dance, musical theatre, opera, concert/music festivals, and various architectural projects. Several lighting credits include designing for the Brunswick Music Theatre (Maine State Music Theatre), Music Theatre North, Springer Opera House, Atlanta Lyric Theatre, and many New York metropolitan and Off/Off-Off Broadway productions with companies like Broadhollow Theatres, The Circle Repertory Lab, and Jean Cocteau Repertory Theatres. He is a USITT Fellow, and has served on the board of directors and has been active in the leadership of the lighting commission of USITT for many years—most notably as lighting co-commissioner from 1998 to 2006. He is a frequent presenter at conferences and has authored articles on theatre design and technology, edited the second edition of *Practical Projects for Teaching Lighting Design: A Compendium*, was on the editorial committee of the second volume of the compendium that was published in 2016, and has won two Herbert D. Greggs Honor Awards for his articles. He also coordinated the latest revision of the *RP-2 Recommended Practice for Lighting Design Graphics* (2006). In architectural lighting, he holds the LC certification granted by the National Council for Qualifications for the Lighting Profession (NCQLP) and is a member of IESNA and an associate member of IALD. He can be contacted through his website (rdunhamdesigns.com).

PART ONE

LIGHT:
THE MEDIUM

CHAPTER 1

THE NATURE OF LIGHT

BEFORE YOU CAN learn to design with light it is important to gain a basic under-standing of the nature of light. Unlike other areas of design, light isn't tangible: it appears to be mysterious and can cause unpredictable results, yet it has an impact on everything it touches. Light is controlled in ways that require at least some understanding of optics and electricity—topics that easily intimidate many people. As lighting designers, light itself is our medium, and we can usually convey our design ideas only through indirect methods such as with pencils, paints, or computer simulations. This is very different when compared to other artistic disciplines where the media are tangible. You can't easily draw or render light as you would in a rendering of a scenic or costume design or with a sketch of a building, where a viewer can easily gain an understanding of a structure and color schemes that are created by a designer. The effects of light are in many ways a mystery until the lights are turned on and a subject is illuminated. Because of this, it is important to develop an understanding of the actual medium of light. What is it? How does it behave? How might we control it? What is its effect on other objects? With experience, you can predict many of the answers to these questions, but even then, you can't be completely sure of your design choices until you see them actually revealed in light.

In this chapter I examine the physical properties of light, its makeup, and how it moves through space. I will also provide you with several methods that we use to describe light. Finally, I examine how light functions within our daily lives. These fundamental principles hold true not only in lighting dramas and other entertainment programs, but also for lighting buildings and natural settings where the sun and other light sources can be observed.

WHAT IS LIGHT?

Quite simply, light is a form of energy. Specifically, it is a form of radiant energy that is associated with a given portion of the **electromagnetic spectrum.** Radiant energy is a form of energy given off by radiant bodies (heat/light sources) such as stars, like our sun. Radiant energy moves away from its source at a constant speed while light is but one form of radiant energy which has a speed of 186,000 miles/second. Most of us know this as the "speed of light."

The Electromagnetic Spectrum

The electromagnetic spectrum represents all forms of radiant energy. Some researchers identify the electromagnetic spectrum with a particle-based theory while others refer to a wave-theory approach. Regardless of the theory, the general principles are the same. In each case, energy is thought to pulsate outward from a source at the speed of light in oscillations that create a wavelike effect and form patterns that can be measured. In fact, the variables that we generally use to describe radiant energy are based on wave theory. Most commonly we make distinctions between different forms of radiant energy through measurements of either **frequency** (f) or **wavelength** (λ). Wavelength is the distance between similar points in a waveform over the time that a wave completes one cycle, while frequency refers to the number of oscillations or cycles that a waveform completes over a given time. These variables are inversely proportional to one another: as frequency increases, the wavelength gets shorter, or as frequency decreases, the wavelength gets longer. The strength or amplitude of the waves is commonly called the **intensity (I).** In visible light we often refer to this as the brightness of the light. Figure 1.1 illustrates the relationship between intensity, frequency, and wavelength.

In lighting, we generally use a measurement of wavelength to make a distinction between different types of light. The range of wavelengths produced by radiant sources is extreme. At one end of the electromagnetic spectrum we find electrical waves with wavelengths measured in miles. The 60-cycle electrical currents that are used in our homes may have a wavelength of more than 3,000 miles. Many other forms of **electromagnetic radiation (ER)** are associated with wavelengths so small that a special unit, the **angstrom (Å),** has been introduced to measure them. One angstrom is equal to 1/254,000,000 of an inch. At the opposite end of the electromagnetic spectrum from electricity are cosmic rays, which may have wavelengths as small as 1/10,000 Å. The electromagnetic spectrum is a collection of different types of radiant energy that can be specified through their varied wavelengths.

The Visible Spectrum

What concerns us as lighting designers is a very limited range of wavelengths contained within the electromagnetic spectrum that we commonly refer to as the **visible spectrum.** This is a collection of wavelengths that can be sensed by the human eye. Those energy forms that lie outside of our perception with wavelengths that are longer than we can sense include infrared, radar, television and radio waves (with increasingly longer wavelengths). Energy forms with progressively shorter wavelengths that also lie outside the realm of our visibility include ultraviolet, x-ray, gamma and cosmic rays. Figure 1.2 illustrates the relationship between wavelength and the individual classifications of energy that make up the electromagnetic spectrum.

The visible spectrum can be further broken down into smaller components representing individual colors—each color representing a specific wavelength of radiant energy. We have all witnessed the rainbow effect produced through the refraction and separation of light into these individual colors by a prism, a storm cloud, or water spray from a hose or fountain. Every color represents light of a different wavelength or frequency. The range of wavelengths generally found within the visible spectrum extends from approximately 400 (violet) to 700 (red) nanometers. A nanometer is one-billionth of a meter. A second manner of expressing wavelength has already been introduced through the measurement known as an angstrom. An angstrom is 1/10 of a nanometer. In this case, the visible spectrum would be expressed as having wavelengths in the approximate range of 4,000–7,000 Å.

THE EYE AND SEEING

Our observation of the world around us is based solely on the manner in which we sense our environment. We can't directly observe anything without the aid of various senses. If you think back to a basic biology class you will probably remember that the human body is equipped with five sensory devices. The senses that these manage include sound, touch, smell, taste, and sight. Each sense consists of a series of sensory organs that convert physical phenomena into nervous impulses that our brains process in a way that helps us to observe the world around us. Our skin allows us to feel, our ears allow us to hear, and our eyes allow us to see.

The visible spectrum represents the range of wavelengths to which the human eye can sense light. If we were sensitive to light relating to a different range of wavelengths, our visible spectrum would shift to a different portion of the electromagnetic spectrum. An infrared camera, such as the ones used in defense or security systems, is sensitive to a different portion of the electromagnetic spectrum than the human eye. Hence, in a situation such as a dark night where we cannot see the movements of people like prowlers or soldiers, the camera is able to "see" for us.

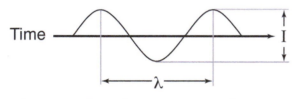

λ = wavelength over one cycle
I = intensity/amplitude over one cycle

Figure 1.1a Wave relationships. a. Relationship of intensity (I), wavelength (λ), and cycle or frequency (f)

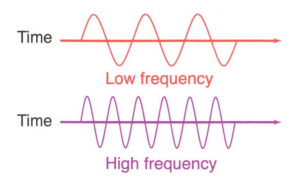

Low frequency

High frequency

Figure 1.1b Frequency (f) and wavelength (λ) are inversely proportional

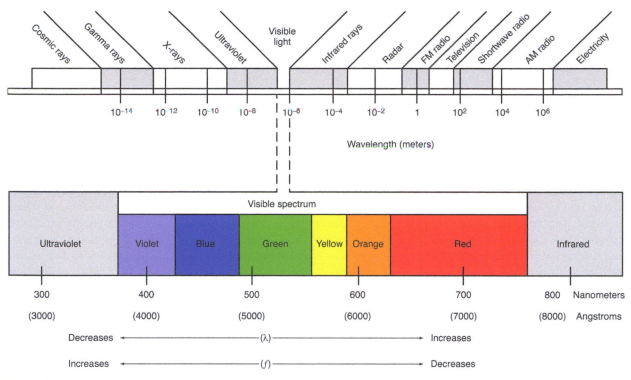

Figure 1.2 The electromagnetic and visible spectrums

THE CONTROLLABLE QUALITIES OF LIGHT

It is important at this point to introduce a vocabulary that enables us to define and describe light. One of the most difficult tasks for a lighting designer is in describing the lighting envisioned for a project. Light is our medium and it cannot be illustrated effectively through an indirect means such as with a model or rendering. A scenic designer can illustrate to a reasonable degree of success a final design and color palette for a project through the use of markers, pencils, or paints. Likewise, in addition to renderings, a costumer can present swatches or scraps of fabric to indicate the materials from which a costume will be created. This isn't so with a lighting design, where light itself is the medium and where nobody can get a true sense of the outcome of a design until the actual lights (**luminaires**) are placed in the performance space, colored, and balanced through setting specific brightness levels for each light. Because of this, several descriptive qualities have been defined to help us communicate with one another about light. These are generally not thought of in terms of quantitative elements but are used instead to help us set up a comparison between various lights and lighting effects. While absolutes may come into the discussion, most of these qualities are used solely within a descriptive or comparative basis. These qualities are also universal and can be translated to any field of lighting, whether working in traditional theatre or lighting an office tower,

garden, or the latest Rolling Stones tour. While there may be slight variations in terminology between lighting disciplines, most designers have come to refer to four primary qualities for describing light. Any light, no matter how produced or modified can be described through these four attributes. The variation of any one of these qualities will make a distinction between any given example of light. These qualities include **intensity, distribution, color,** and **movement.** As a whole, these are essentially the same qualities that Stanley McCandless described in 1932 when he first wrote *A Method of Lighting the Stage*.

Intensity

The most easily described quality of light is intensity, which refers to the brightness of the light. While it might be described very specifically and can be evaluated through measurements such as the candela or footcandle, it is more often described through a comparative basis. "This light is brighter than that light," "this light is approximately half the intensity of another light," or "that light is as bright as the moon" are examples of this type of comparison. The human eye can perceive light at an extreme range of intensities. In World War II, soldiers learned that a German scout plane nicknamed "Bed Check Charlie" could see the tip of a lit cigarette from several miles away. If they were spotted, soldiers could anticipate a visit from a bomber sometime later that night. At the other extreme, the intensity of a light can be so bright that it becomes harmful and could even cause damage to our eyes. Examples of this would include looking directly into the sun or being exposed to the bright light that accompanies welders as they strike an arc. In most theatrical venues we are generally concerned only with the relative appearance of the light and whether there is enough visibility to see what has to be seen at any given moment on the stage. In video and film lighting, the intensity isn't as flexible, and there is a minimum threshold of intensity that a **director of photography** must provide to maintain a proper exposure for a setting. We have all taken photographs of last Friday night's party or some other special event to find that the results that our phone or camera captured produced only shadowy silhouettes that we think we recognize as our friends. Even with today's mobile phone cameras we often find that images can suffer from poor lighting and are either under or overexposed. Architectural lighting designers speak of a minimum amount of illumination for a given **visual task** or job. These tasks require a minimum number of **footcandles** or **lumens** of illumination. For example, the lighting levels required for a personal home are much lower than those needed at a retirement home, where elderly residents often have trouble seeing, while a meeting room requires higher intensity levels than a restaurant seating area—although none of these settings would require the illumination levels needed for an assembly line producing high-tech products. Regardless of whether describing a specific level of illumination (i.e., footcandles) or simply describing intensity on a comparative basis, intensity becomes one of the most important ways of helping us distinguish between different types of light and lighting.

Another important element of intensity relates to the principle whereby the intensity of a light drops off dramatically as the distance from the source is increased. This is expressed through a concept/formula known as the **Inverse Square Law.** This law will be presented in more detail in Chapter 7, but simply states that the illuminance of a light source is inversely proportional to the square of the distance from the source. A quick examination of this principle can be demonstrated by playing a flashlight on a wall and noting the apparent brightness and coverage of the light while varying the distance that the flashlight is held from the wall.

Distribution

The second controllable quality of light is known as distribution. McCandless described this as "form." Most lighting designers relate distribution to two specific properties of light: angle (or direction) and quality.

Angle refers to the direction from which the light is coming. Where are you hanging the light source? How does it play upon the subject? Where are the highlights?

Where do the shadows fall? A light coming from behind the subject presents a completely different image and associated mood than a light coming from in front of the subject. A couple walking hand-in-hand into a sunset presents a much more dramatic image than if the sun were directly overhead. Dracula would most likely not appear so scary if we chose to light him in any other way than through a silhouette. The angle of the light helps to define or reveal the form of an object. Light directly from the front tends to flatten a subject and will cause the subject to appear two-dimensional, while from the side it tends to sculpt and etch the subject away from its background. **Backlight** tends to push objects forward, while **downlight** tends to squash the subject. A light from below generally appears unnatural and can be used to create effects that clue audiences into peculiarities within a production. Architects can use these principles to make a room appear larger or smaller.

Quality refers to the texture and characteristic features of the light. Some lighting may be harsh and crisp—representing strong parallel rays—while other lighting will reflect a soft diffuse quality. Are the edges of the light and shadows sharp and well-defined or are they soft and fuzzy? Compare a clear sunny day in summer with the cold gray light associated with a December afternoon. Is the light even in distribution, or are there patterns? A typical contemporary classroom lighting scheme will most likely result in a soft, even wash of light over the entire room with some form of fluorescent fixtures. In comparison, a warehouse set in 1930 would probably be lit with single-bulb fixtures with simple shades that would produce cones of light throughout the structure. A walk on a sunny day through an open field exposes you to a very different kind of light than the textured light that you would expect once you move into a wooded area, where the trees create patches of light and shadow along your path. Lighting designers can create their own textured light by inserting patterns known as **gobos** into the fixtures that illuminate a space. While gobos were first utilized in entertainment designs, they have now become elements of architectural and display lighting as well.

Color

The third controllable quality of light is color, which is considered by many to be the most dynamic of the controllable qualities of light. Light will have an associated color that is determined through the specific collection of wavelengths present within its makeup. Hence, you might have a lavender light, a red light, or a blue light—each one distinguished from the others by those wavelengths of light found within its composition. However, color is actually a perception based on how specific wavelengths of the light stimulate the photo sensors in our eyes. Light, more importantly, has a major impact on the color of any objects that it falls on, and the resultant color is a factor of both the object's surface color and that of the light that strikes the object. All objects selectively absorb or reflect various wavelengths of light—which becomes the means by which we determine the color of any object. The use of a light containing some or all of the wavelengths of light that are naturally reflected by an object will generally result in enhancing that object's color. On the other hand, the use of a colored light with limited or no common wavelengths with that of an object will result in a distortion and graying of that object's color. Color is produced through the spectral makeup of the light source itself, through the removal of specific wavelengths of the light through filtering, or by the selective absorption of a light's wavelengths by a surface. While it is generally agreed that color is the easiest quality of light to observe, it is also commonly acknowledged that due to the unpredictability of its results, it is perhaps the hardest quality to master and control.

Movement

The final quality of light is movement, which refers to changes in the light from moment to moment. This might be represented in a number of different ways: First, the actual movement of the light source. This is quite common and can be illustrated by a candle or flashlight carried across a room, where you actually see the source move from one location to another. A second form of movement involves observing the movement of the light without actually observing the light source directly. Two examples of this include watching the effect of a followspot on a rock musician and the use of a progression of lamps to light actors as they move from one stage position to another. In the first example, you see the effect of the light following the musician, but you can't see the actual spotlight because it is located somewhere behind you at the rear of the auditorium or arena. In the second example, lights slowly come up along the path that the actors walk such that the individual lights precede the arrival of the actors to specific locations on the stage. For even more effect, the individual lights could also slowly dim down once the actors move beyond their positions to other locations along the path. The last element of movement relates simply to changes within the lighting over time. This is the one that theatrical lighting designers deal with most often as they create **cues** for a production. For all practical purposes this would come about through making changes in any of the other three controllable qualities of light. Lights suddenly getting brighter or dimmer, shifting to another color, or slowly moving to a different angle all form examples of this kind of movement. The movement may be nearly instantaneous (i.e., flipping a light switch on or off) or could involve long transitions like sunset sequences that are so subtle that a viewer isn't aware of the lighting changes being made from one moment to another. Movement can also be thought of as a transition in lighting. While there are occasions where the lighting for an environment may be static, most of us consider transitions in lighting to be just as important as the images that a designer creates for a given project.

In summary, all lighting conditions reflect the manipulation of these four qualities. Whether you light a building, a museum display, an opera, or any other form of entertainment, each moment that a viewer observes can be associated with a given combination of intensity, color, and distribution in the lighting. Movement can most often be directly related to the transitions between different "**moments**" (also called "**looks**," "**states**," or "**cues**"). Each of these terms refers to names that a designer may use to refer to a static view of the lighting. Movement provides the fluid, dynamic quality required in a lighting design—a quality that many of us believe is just as important as the combination of fixtures, colors, and intensities that one sees at any given time. If mounted correctly, the lighting can greatly enhance a production or project. If done incorrectly, it can quickly become an interruption or distraction for the viewers.

Sidebar 1.1 DESIGNER PROFILE

A creative force in the New York theatre since the mid-1970s, Ken Billington is one of Broadway's most successful lighting designers. He remembers his first attraction to stage lighting from when he was in the fourth grade. From that point on, all Ken "wanted to do was lighting," but it wasn't until he was in junior high school that he realized that there were actual "lighting designers" in the world and that it was a proper design discipline. Finishing high school, he went directly to Manhattan to study at The Lester Polakov Studio and Forum of Stage Design, apprenticing with both Peggy Clark and Tharon Musser. In fact, he often claims that he went to "Musser U" and credits that legendary designer with his first big break.

Ken has designed a hundred Broadway shows, 70 off-Broadway shows, and operas for companies worldwide, as well as for concerts, theme park

Ken Billington

Credit: photo courtesy Ken Billington

shows, and architecture. He is often associated with lighting large musicals and spectaculars, with design credits that include the original *Sweeney Todd*, *White Christmas*, *Footloose*, and *Chicago* (the longest-running American musical in history). For 27 seasons, he designed the Christmas and Easter shows at the Radio City Music Hall and has lit a range of celebrated personalities, including Ann-Margret, Shirley MacLaine, Carol Channing, Liberace, and Hugh Jackman. Ken's designs have enhanced such extraordinary projects as *Fantasmic* at Disneyland, the lavish aquatic show at Seaworld Parks (Orlando, Florida; San Diego, California; and San Antonio, Texas), productions at Busch Gardens (Williamsburg, Virginia), and spectacular ice shows, including *Stars on Ice*. His television work includes many PBS theatre, concert specials, and several episodes of the NBC series *Smash*. His architectural designs have highlighted such New York landmarks as Feinstein's 54 Below and Tavern on the Green. Ken has been honored with most of the awards presented for lighting design in the theatre, including a Tony Award for *Chicago* and the Distinguished Lighting Designer Award from the United States Institute for Theatre Technology (USITT). In 2016, Ken became only the third lighting designer to be inducted into the Theatre Hall of Fame.

Ken considers himself primarily a "Broadway" designer, but his career embraces many creations beyond the New York stage. "I have done as many as five Broadway shows in a year," he says, "and only one the following year, but that year might include six shows that tryout and hope to come to New York. As a freelance designer, you have no idea where the jobs will come from each year." He expanded his career beyond the theatre, he declares,

> ❝by using "common sense" to apply what I know about stage lighting in other areas of lighting design. The basics of lighting—angle, color, intensity, and *concept*—remain the same in all venues. The manner of execution may differ, and you may need a different technical language as you move from collaboration with a stage electrician to working with a contractor, but the final product is the same: *designed* lighting.❞

Ken's experience has underscored his belief that lighting is a collaborative process, and the challenges, rewards, and personal friendships that come with being part of a creative team are what keep him excited about his art: "I can't paint or draw a picture, but I can paint with light. It is the same for any artist. *Why* do you do this? And, of course, it's always thrilling to sit in a theatre and see what you have created on paper come to life."

In order to remain current in his always-evolving craft, he reads the trade magazines, attends conventions, and makes himself available to sales people who come to his studio, talking directly to company reps about innovations in technology. He maintains, however, that the best way to remain up-to-date is simply going out and admiring what his colleagues are doing and observing the current trends for himself. He remains an enthusiastic theatregoer. When asked what he considers Rule Number One in lighting design, Ken is firm: "Concept! No matter what the project, big or small—if there is no concept, you will usually get yourself and the production into trouble." Ken also believes in hands-on training:

> ❝The best way to learn how to light is by *lighting*, no matter what the project. You might do a great job or just an okay job, but remember that even if you really screw up, the worst that will happen is that you'll get fired—they don't take you out back and shoot you. No matter what the project, learn from it—look at what worked and what did not work and file it away and remember it for the future.❞

FUNCTIONS OF LIGHTING

There are numerous functions associated with lighting. Light is used to reveal. Many of the functions of lighting relate specifically to the manner in which light is used to reveal an object(s) or setting. While most lighting designers agree in principle with many of the named lighting functions discussed in the following sections, sometimes designers may combine several of these functions into larger groups or associate a different term with a given function. In these cases, what is important is the performance of the function rather than the specific name used by a given individual. In reality, lighting designers combine and modify the controllable qualities of light to produce the varied functions that we find within any specific lighting. I will discuss the functions of lighting from a more traditional theatrical or entertainment background first and then go on to relate several other functions of lighting that are more specific to other practices. Again, it is important to be aware that many of the functions are characteristic of all types of lighting design.

Visibility

Most lighting designers would argue that the most important element of lighting is **visibility.** Many even refer to it as the primary function of lighting. After all, isn't this why we created artificial light in the first place? Visibility simply refers to the principle of using light to reveal or illuminate objects. In the early days of lighting, the job of the designer was nothing more than to create enough light so that the audience or occupants of a space could see. In many ways this philosophy of lighting was based on the premise that more was better and that the more footcandles or lumens of light placed on a stage or in a room, the better visibility that you had. Since the 1950s or '60s, theatrical designing moved towards a concept that we call **selective visibility,** which simply refers to revealing to an audience only what needs to be seen. Hence, a less-revealing image on stage might be more appropriate for the dramatic action than a fully illuminated stage. In selective visibility, areas of low intensity, shadows, silhouettes, and high contrast can become effective elements in a lighting designer's arsenal of tools. An image of Dracula appearing from the shadows is much more terrifying than seeing him come to his next victim in full light. Until recently, architectural lighting has been known for being largely dependent on the quantity rather than the quality of its lighting, and most recommended practices of the past carefully specified the minimum number of footcandles that were required for a given **task** or environment. Finally, while it may appear obvious that the level of illumination plays a dominant role in the visibility of an object, it is not the only control that has an effect on whether you see something or not. The angle of the light also determines how much or little of an object is revealed to you. The color of the light might help an object either blend in or pop out from its background and will also enhance or gray the object's color. These are just a few of the additional elements that can have an effect on visibility.

Mood

Another function of lighting relates to creating **mood.** Mood refers to the observer's emotional response to the lighting. Lighting can be foreboding or inviting, carefree and light, energetic versus passive, or tragic and oppressive. In all of these and many more moods, the light provides an atmosphere or ambiance for the environment that is being lit. Other than visibility, mood is probably the function of lighting that has the next most important impression or effect on a viewer. Studies have shown that light can have a profound effect on individuals and their moods. In entertainment lighting, we often produce extreme ranges of mood for a given theatrical production or special event. These moods may also be changed many times throughout a two- or three-hour performance. Mood changes may occur quickly or may be so subtle that the audience isn't necessarily aware that the changes have even taken place. A well-lit production will have lighting that reflects the varied moods of a piece while also following the rhythm of the changes that occur throughout the script. In architectural lighting, more subtle choices are used to produce environments for more productive offices, more welcoming reception areas, and to provide calming effects for patients in medical facilities. Lighting has also been used to influence sales volumes and turnover rates in retail markets. As an example, consider the lighting associated with a fine restaurant like a favorite bistro versus any number of fast-food restaurants. The soft, amber lighting associated with a bistro is very different from the harsh, bright, fluorescent lighting that is characteristic of most fast-food restaurants, where turnover is key to a successful business. In this case, the lighting helps create an environment that prevents patrons from becoming too comfortable in fast-food establishments.

Establishing a Scene

Some functions of lighting are related specifically to the discipline that you are designing within, while others are consistent with almost any kind of lighting. For instance, in a theatrical production it would be critical for the lighting to help establish or communicate specific information about the play or environment that is being created. Time of day, season, and geographical location are all parts of this function. Many refer to this as **establishing a scene.** In short, the lighting, as well as all the other elements of the scene, must combine to create a single cohesive environment that creates a "true" world of the play. A play that requires a night scene must be lit in some fashion that would be suggestive of night. This could be a night with lights on or lights off, lights that would suggest a specific interior lighting (i.e., a chandelier versus a fireplace or table lamp), or even lights that are suggestive of a specific type of light source or historical period (electric versus gas or candlelight). All of these form specific design considerations that lighting designers should consider as they light the given night scene. Establishing a scene is much more important for an entertainment lighting designer, who is concerned with creating a world for a performance, than an architectural lighting designer who is simply lighting a particular space. In reality, though, even the architectural designer must create a design that deals in some manner with establishing a scene that is consistent with producing the proper response or ambience for a building or environment. An example would be in creating the appropriate lighting for a five-star restaurant versus an office suite. There is an appropriate and unique approach to lighting each of these projects.

Modeling

Another common function of lighting is in **modeling** or sculpting. Some designers refer to this as "revelation of form." This function relates to using light for enhancing the three-dimensional qualities of an object. We can best distinguish form through carefully observing the **highlights** and **shadows** of an object. Highlights represent the flashes of reflected light from areas that are directly illuminated by a light source, while shadows may be represented by either the area of an object that is not lit or the area of darkness or shadow that is cast by a lit object (**cast shadow**). Areas that are raised are prone to highlights, while recessed surfaces usually fall into shadow areas. However, this revelation of highlight and shadow is dependent on both the angle and number of lights that strike an object. As an object is lit from different directions more, or less, of its surface textures and associated form are revealed to the observer. As a rule, the best light for revealing an object's form or three-dimensional qualities is to its side. Angles that come from either behind or in front of an object tend to create more of a two-dimensional or profile-like image of the subject. The vertical angle of the light source(s) also has an effect on how the object is revealed to an observer. As an experiment, try shining a light on a piece of molding (like a cornice) from different angles. The light can change your perception of which parts of the molding are inset or raised. In fact, when lit from straight front, the individual shapes might even be masked and may not reveal any depth at all.

Focus

Focus is a lighting function that relates to drawing attention to various elements within an environment. Architectural designers often refer to this as **accent lighting.** It is actually common to have several different layers of attention or focus established for a stage or given space. The single most important focus is generally referred to as the **primary focus** of a scene or environment. While a given subject may be less prominent than the primary focus, it may well appear more prominent than the rest of the environment, which results in creating a **secondary focus** for a scene. One role of a lighting designer is to help point out where a viewer or audience member's attention should be directed at any given time. In a typical theatrical application the audience members' view is confined to the stage, while in a building, occupants have the potential to look wherever they wish. The signage at an airport should be lit in a manner that allows passengers to easily navigate between locations such as gates, ticket counters, and baggage claim areas. On a stage, what should the audience be watching at any given moment? Who in the band has the solo? How do you bring attention to a specific scenic element of a setting? Techniques that a lighting designer can use to control focus include many familiar tricks. One example is simply blacking out an entire stage except for those areas where the focus must be directed. Highlighting an actor delivering a monolog within a single spotlight or pulling lights down to a single light on a significant prop like an empty wheelchair form examples of this type of directed focus. In a more subtle manner a designer may simply boost or raise the intensity of the light around an area to which they want to direct your focus. Brightening the lights around furniture clusters such as tables or seating areas is a common practice for lighting relatively long conversations that take place in specific locations. Another example of this is when an entrance is pointed up by boosting the level of a **special** that is focused on the door from which an actor will enter. It is important to understand that we use relative brightness to help direct focus. While I have spoken of raising the intensity of light on a subject, an equally valid and at times even preferred technique involves lowering the intensity of the areas surrounding the point to which we want to draw focus.

An architectural lighting designer uses the same concepts to draw an occupant's attention to various details in a room or building. Directing track lighting onto wall hangings or photographs, placing more light around a hotel lobby's reservations desk, or creating focusable lighting for product displays in a department store all form examples of using light to direct focus. The eye will usually focus on the element within our vision that is different from other objects in view. Lighting designers can also use color to establish focus.

Placing a single white light on the lead singer while the rest of a band is bathed in magenta-colored light is an example of this. A designer does not necessarily have to make use of extreme color differences to make use of this principle. A night scene in which the entire stage is cast in blue light, with bluish lavender moonlight streaming through the French doors where Dracula is to appear, can be just as effective of a use of contrast in color.

Composition

Composition is a function of lighting that relates to combining all of the elements of a stage or room together into a complete visual package. We see nothing until it is revealed to us through light, and one of the lighting designer's primary responsibilities lies not only in choosing what to reveal to us but also how it is revealed to us. While other collaborators give us the primary elements of a composition, such as the scenery and costumes, the actors or characters, and the furniture, the lighting designer can reveal these objects in an infinite number of ways. By comparison, the lighting designer often makes the largest single contribution in determining the overall composition of a stage or environment. The same objects or space can appear quite differently with just a couple of simple alterations to the lighting of the environment. The lighting also determines how all of the individual objects and designs tie together as a whole; it becomes a unifying element for most design projects.

Style

Style represents yet another function of lighting. It relates to creating visual traits that allow a characteristic overall visual quality to be connected to a given production. In reality, style is specifically determined through the collaboration and discussions of the entire production team. While we may discuss the style of any given production, we may also use style to compare and contrast a project with other productions or projects. An architect may refer to postmodernism, while a director might speak about absurdism. In each case, style is representative of various visual qualities that are characteristic of each school or movement. The scenic designer, director, costume designer, and lighting designer must share a common understanding of the style of a production in order to realize a successful unified project. Most importantly, once the style is agreed upon, a production should remain consistent in the manner in which it approaches style. A number of designers will discuss theme as an element of style. How is the play constructed? Does the playwright use a specific type of delivery? Are there social and visual themes within a production? A lighting design must help reinforce the visual quality associated with the remaining elements

of a project. One manner in which style becomes most readily identified is through establishing the degree of realism in a production. How literal is the world that we are creating? Could this be a naturalistic environment? Are there any symbolic elements? Are there any recurring themes to be reinforced or emphasized? Are we simplifying our image so that it contains only those elements that are absolutely essential to the action? Are period realism and historical accuracy important to the piece? Should there be a limited color palette? How are the traditional elements of design (line, form, texture, etc.) characterized within a given project? Are particular conventions used in the production? All of these questions form examples of issues that will help a design team define a project's style.

Staging the Story

In the case of entertainment design we also need to consider the actual techniques of production as another function of lighting. A number of designers refer to this as **staging the story**. In principle, this simply means taking the script and finding a proper mechanism for presenting it to an audience. In a production making use of a single box setting, a design team may simply use the act curtain and a series of blackouts to make distinctions between various scenes. Lighting transitions have become one of the most important means of enabling us to quickly shift the reality of a play from one location to another. A very different approach would be required for a production containing 20 independent scenes in which each scene requires a different location. Do we need to observe the entire space, or can we break it up through using smaller locations such as platforms? Is a unit set part of the design solution? Can tightly confined specials be used to define the spaces required by the action of the play? What scenic mechanisms might we utilize to move from one scene to another? What theatrical **conventions** will be used throughout the production? Are there specific lighting techniques or equipment available that will help us present the play to an audience? How are transitions handled? The answers to these and other similar questions will help establish the style of both the production and its lighting.

Rhythm

A final function of light that relates primarily to entertainment lighting is **rhythm**. Rhythm in lighting relates essentially to movement and transitions; it may be very subtle and unobserved or dramatic and very apparent to the audience. Rhythm can relate to transitions based simply on the logistical needs of making the production workable for an audience (staging the story), or more importantly, rhythm can follow the dramatic tensions of a production. Do changes from one scene to another occur in a natural, fluid manner, or are they disruptive to the flow of the show? We've all witnessed those times where the lighting isn't quite in sync with the actors, scene changes, or other elements of a production. A second form of rhythm relates to the changes that occur as a result of various movement patterns (blocking) with the actors, changes in mood, focus, or any other requirements that make a dramatic comment on the play through the lighting. As tensions mount and are resolved, the lighting should underscore the associated emotional changes throughout a production. Often, the lighting will build as a scene moves towards its climax. A well-designed production will be dynamic and will have lighting that follows the rhythm of the rest of the show. In fact, it has been demonstrated that lighting that remains too static may have a negative impact on audience members. Even contemporary architectural lighting applications now make allowances for rhythm when lighting many projects. Not only is rhythm varied throughout the day in offices and other workplaces, but it also can become a major design element for large exterior objects such as building facades and towers, landscape architecture, and even bridges. In these cases, the lighting of a structure may change color through intervals of as little as 30 seconds to as long as 30 minutes or longer. Rhythm can also be observed in something as simple as the spacing intervals and patterns that are created when laying out a group of luminaires, such as an arrangement of ceiling fixtures.

FOR FURTHER READING

DiLaura, David L., Kevin W. Houser, Richard G. Mistrick, and Gary R. Steffy. eds. *Illuminating Engineering Society– The Lighting Handbook Tenth Edition: Reference and Application*. New York: Illuminating Engineering Society, 2011.

Illuminating Engineering Society of North America. *IESNA Lighting Education 150 (Intermediate Level)*. New York: Illuminating Engineering Society of North America, 1993.

Illuminating Engineering Society of North America. *IESNA Lighting Ready Reference*. 4th ed. New York: Illuminating Engineering Society of North America, 2003.

McCandless, Stanley. *A Method for Lighting the Stage*. 4th ed. New York: Theatre Arts Books, 1958.

McCandless, Stanley. *A Syllabus of Stage Lighting*. 5th ed. New Haven, CT: Yale University, 1941.

Rae, Mark. ed. *IESNA Lighting Handbook*. 9th ed. New York: Illuminating Engineering Society of North America, 2000.

CHAPTER 2

LIGHT AND PERCEPTION

THE IMPORTANCE OF light in the perception of our world cannot be overstated. Light, by its very nature, allows us to see and therefore perceive the environment around us. Because we observe the world through images that are created through the stimulation of our optic nerves and nerve impulses, we have to account for the fact that what we sense is actually an indirect means of observation. Therefore, images can be interpreted very differently from one person to another. This, to some degree, is due to our personal backgrounds, which add interpretive elements to these observations that are based on our past experiences. In addition, we may simply experience different degrees of stimulation from one individual to another. For instance, we learn to define the color that we call "red" based on our experiences of what our parents taught us was the color red. After a time, we learned to associate the color red with a given experience of sight. However, if we are given a more complex color, such as an orange-red or an orange-orange-red, we may have trouble distinguishing the point at which the orange-red shifts into becoming an orange-orange-red as we add more yellow to the color. In this case, we define the new color based on our personal experience, and one person's experience may be quite different from that of another's. The color hasn't changed—only our perception of that color. Another manner in which we might perceive different experiences in light comes from sensing the light in different ways from others. For example, some people are color-blind. Their experience of the world is considerably different from those of us who have normal color vision. Other people are light sensitive and may find even moderate levels of brightness to be painful, while others have acute night vision. All of these factors relate to people sensing light in different ways. In most cases, our sense of sight actually undergoes changes throughout our lives. Young people might have to wear contacts or glasses, people in their late 40s to 50s may need reading glasses, and the elderly often have difficulties with night vision. While some of these experiences are determined by the actual physical properties of light and our eyes, others are related to our psychological perception of light and the environment.

Possibly more important than the way that we experience light through our senses is the manner in which light is used to modify or reveal an object. In the last chapter I discussed the importance of light and vision. To be seen, an object must be capable of reflecting some degree of light. This is in addition to assuming that it can be sensed through a sensory device like an eye or camera. Without a surface to reflect upon, light will continue to expand outward unnoticed. We have all seen the effect of a car's headlights becoming observable in the mist of a foggy night while on a clear night it is often impossible to distinguish the edges of the beams that the fog so clearly defines. Through light, we can reveal an object in any number of different ways. We can use varied degrees of brightness to allow differing degrees of visibility. The angle between the viewer and light source might be modified to create very different revelations of an object. The color of the light could also be changed to create a significantly different response in the way that the subject is seen by an observer. Everyone knows that a white T-shirt under red light will appear red even though we know that the color of the shirt remains white. All of these represent examples of light being used to modify a viewer's perception of an object.

In this chapter I examine many of the ways in which light can be used to shape a viewer's perception of the world around them. The chapter begins with a look at the eye and how it functions, then moves into discussions of several fundamental principles of composition and visibility, and how light can affect our perception in both positive and negative ways. What are appropriate techniques that a lighting designer may use to reveal a subject to an audience? What are several aspects of control that we can use to create a given response in a viewer? Are there issues that may negatively affect an observer's experience? How much of a subject or setting does a designer have to reveal to an audience? Each of these questions and many like them relate to how our vision is impacted by light and its manipulation. Effective lighting designers will learn to take command of the immense range of possibilities that are both available and acceptable for completing the task of visibility. At the same time, they must remain sensitive to the repercussions that might also come from lighting an object or environment inappropriately.

PHYSIOLOGY OF THE EYE

In order to understand the eye and vision, we often make a comparison between the eye's anatomy and the manner in which a camera is constructed. Figure 2.1 illustrates the principal components of an eye. The primary structure of the eye is the **sclera,** which is most recognizable as the white portion of the eye that surrounds all of the other components. The eye is an assembly of essentially three primary component groups. Each of these is responsible for a step that is required for vision. Each is also directly comparable to a part of the optical system found in any camera. The first group controls the amount of light that enters the eye. Basic components of this group include the **cornea,** which is the clear outer layer of the eye; a layer of fluid (**aqueous humor**) directly behind the cornea (**anterior chamber**); the **iris,** which is the area of the eye that has color; and the black dot at the center of the eye that we call the **pupil.** Finally, a lens is located directly behind the iris, and a second area of fluid is found between the lens and the back surface of the eye (**vitreous humor).** The cornea and anterior chamber function much like a lens to focus the light on the back surface of the eye where the optical sensors are located (much like the film or sensor plate in a digital or video camera). The size of the pupil is controlled by a set of muscles in the iris that regulate the amount of light entering the eye. The more light that the eye is exposed to, the smaller the pupil becomes. The lens is controlled by a second set of muscles (**ciliary muscles**) that modify the shape and thickness of the eye, enabling it to focus on different objects and at different distances.

The second primary component group of the eye includes the **retina,** the interior wall at the back of the eye. This is the portion of the eye where optical sensors are located and where the eye attempts to focus its images. A special portion of the retina known as the **fovea** is located near the center of the retina. This area has a much higher concentration of photosensitive cells and is responsible for much of our ability to distinguish both colors and detail. A second area of the retina is the **optic disk,** which forms the location where the nerve endings of the photoreceptors are bundled together to form the **optic nerve.** The optic nerve carries nerve impulses to the brain where they are processed into images.

The third and final group of primary eye components includes the photoreceptors, specialized cells that convert light exposure to a neural impulse that is sent to the brain. A typical human eye contains approximately 128 million photoreceptors. There are two types of photoreceptors, each with a different function. The first, the **rods,** are sensitive to light across a wide range of wavelengths and luminous levels. The rods are predominantly responsible for our sight both at low levels of illumination and for distinguishing our peripheral vision, which is often referred to as **scotopic vision.** The second type of receptors, **cones,** are responsible for both our color and detail vision within light levels associated with typical interior and exterior illuminances. This type of vision is known as **photopic vision.** The fovea contains cones, while the remainder of the retina contains both cones and rods. Rods and scotopic vision are associated with night vision, and cones and photopic vision with day vision.

The structure of the eye and its various photoreceptors ultimately determine an individual's sight. When the structure of the eye is abnormal, and the lens doesn't focus the light properly on the retina, an individual can be either near- or farsighted and must wear corrective lenses. The structure of your eye may change throughout

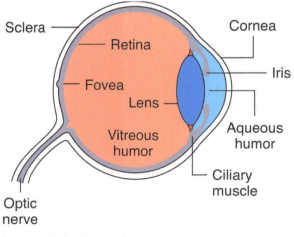

Figure 2.1 Physiology of the eye

your lifetime as the lens slowly ages, becoming more rigid and less pliable. LASIK surgery reshapes the lens in order to refocus the light properly onto the retina. Some of us are light sensitive and find a bright sunny day to be a painful sensation while others have problems seeing objects in the dark. Color blindness is another condition in which the eyes don't perform normally. The causes of these problems are often related to a physical impairment of the eye.

In addition to any problems with the eye itself, there are a number of psychological effects that can have an additional impact on your vision. Some of these can improve your sight, while others can create problems. More importantly, these effects usually relate to your perception of light and vision, not necessarily to the actual amount of light that your eyes sense. In any case, a lighting designer must be aware of these effects in order to create designs that will compensate for any of these issues. Later portions of this chapter discuss several of the most important issues related to light and perception.

COMPOSITION

Since light is the primary means by which we sense an environment, it is through its revelation of composition that we can comprehend a space. Without light, our perception of an environment is severely impaired. Whether you are lighting a stage, exhibit hall, or office, the entire environment is seen as a total composition. The architectural or scenic units, people and their clothing, as well as furniture and building materials are all elements that are revealed through the lighting. Light provides us with a means of indicating depth; it modifies the colors and textures of the other elements, reveals form, and indicates areas of focus or interest within the composition of a stage or room. Elements that are more important will usually be treated with higher light intensities, while the degree of overall visibility can be established by setting threshold levels that illuminate the environment as a whole. At any given time, there will always be a complete composition for an environment— and much of the way that it is revealed to us is through the basic task of illumination.

While many environments incorporate relatively constant lighting treatments, entertainment lighting generally makes use of ever-changing compositions and a very dynamic lighting style. Unlike a painting, which has a static composition, the stage is constantly evolving into new compositions. Where is the focus at this particular moment? How bright does the room absolutely have to be? Is there an area we wish to take an audience's attention away from? Can a certain color be enhanced at a particular time? All of these questions relate to how the composition and lighting might change from one moment to another. The idea of creating dynamic lighting was for many years limited to the entertainment field, but today's architects and illuminating engineers also recognize the need for creating dynamic environments for their clients. Although it is generally subtle in comparison to theatrical venues, the lighting of buildings, trade shows, and exhibits can also employ active lighting elements for many projects.

VISIBILITY

Visibility refers to allowing the viewers' eyes and mind to be stimulated to such a degree that they can make an observation. Visibility, however, is a relative term, and we need to examine it in terms of specific contexts. In the most basic sense, it refers to the effect of providing enough visual information so that viewers can establish a meaning from what you have presented them with. In a way, visibility becomes a means of communication. If done well, the message is received—but if done poorly, the message becomes confused or is lost. Historically, there have been two basic approaches for creating visibility through light. The first is based on providing good uniform illumination over a widely dispersed area, where **quantity of light** is considered a major component of visibility. The second relates to the quality of the visual experience and refers to visibility in terms of what needs or doesn't need to be seen by an observer—a concept that we refer to as **quality of light.** In other words, we increase visibility to a point where we reveal only enough of a subject to bring meaning to an audience and therefore become more selective in what we do or don't reveal. Most lighting designers refer to this as **selective visibility**—revealing only what is necessary to bring meaning to a viewer. Directors of the 1940s and '50s were frequently trained to believe that the audience had to see the actors' faces in order to hear them, a concept that by today's standards is severely limited. Today, shadows, distorted colors, and even low intensities have become common techniques for manipulating lighting to express mood and style associations, which can actually produce a more effective image than simply bringing visibility to an environment.

Illuminating engineers generally refer to the demand for successful vision or the ability to see accurately as **visual acuity.** This essentially refers to being able to manipulate the visual stimulus and environment in such a way that a given visual task can be completed. Visual acuity is actually a function of factors such as the size of the object, distance between the object and viewer, surface reflectivity of the object, and amount of illumination present, as well as sensitivity of the optic sensors. For example, small text has a more limiting effect on visual acuity than large text. A reading lamp, on the other hand, might be used to help raise the visual acuity of a page. A general rule has been to associate more critical tasks with the need for more illumination.

Hence, working in a classroom demands brighter conditions than eating in a restaurant, while performing surgery in a hospital operating room would require still higher levels of illumination. However, a number of consequences have also been associated with maintaining overly consistent levels of illumination within a given environment—especially when those levels are maintained at either relatively high or low intensity levels. A number of these effects are examined a bit later in this chapter.

INTENSITY OR BRIGHTNESS

While visibility may be modified through any one of the controllable qualities of light, we often associate the most important element of visibility with the control of intensity or brightness. For now, we'll primarily examine the effects of intensity on vision. The other controllable qualities and their effects on vision will be addressed throughout later portions of this chapter. The eye is an amazing mechanism in that it can observe an incredible range of light intensities. While at one extreme we might observe light so bright that it could damage our eyes (such as in looking at the sun or a welder's arc) we can also observe light in intensities as low as that of a candle flame or match strike from more than 10 to 15 miles away (once again using the example of the military scout plane to spot enemy troops at night). Additionally, we can perceive relatively small variations in intensity across our field of vision. This extreme range of sensitivity is characteristic of the human eye and cannot be found in equipment such as cameras or other optical sensors. A camera is usually not as sensitive to these variations and will recognize only the broader extremes of illumination levels within a given camera frame. When we work with cameras, we often refer to their **contrast ratio,** which refers to the range of intensities between the brightest and darkest elements of a camera's view. The reason many of us shoot so many "bad" photographs is due most commonly to the limited sensitivity and contrast ratios of the film and/or cameras that we are using. Fortunately, technology continues to improve: cameras are ever more sensitive to light and offer a wider range of contrast ratios. The personal digital camera that I currently own (and quite possibly my smartphone camera) probably has better light sensitivity than many of the commercial cameras that were available just a few years ago.

Relative Intensity

In many cases, what is more important to a theatrical lighting designer is the perceived, rather than the actual or absolute, brightness of an object or light source. We have learned that simply adding more light to an environment doesn't always produce better visibility. An object's perceived brightness is a function of several items, not just the amount of light focused onto it. Other factors include the distances between the source, object, and viewer; the reflectivity of the object; and the sensitivity of the optical device (eye or camera). In the early days of television and film lighting, cameras weren't nearly as sensitive as they currently are, and directors of photography were much more concerned with creating minimum intensity thresholds so that the cameras could simply process the information necessary to create an image. The film speeds that you would select on a single-lens reflex film camera help you adjust the camera's light sensitivity to a given film or digital sensor plate. If you set the ASA (American Standard Association) setting incorrectly you will end up with photographs that are either over or underexposed. Even though cameras are vastly improved, it is still quite common for designers working in the video and film industries to use a light meter to ensure that both even and minimal intensity levels are created for a shoot.

As a whole, we consider the brightness of a subject compared with that of both the surrounding environment and other objects—the relative intensities of these objects. What is important is that an object often receives focus if it is lit more brightly than the objects that surround it. On the other hand, our attention might also be drawn to the darkest part of a stage—like the upstage entrance tunnel of a cave in a production of *Swiss Family Robinson.* In both cases, the eye is attracted to the most different element of the scene, and the relative intensities of the objects play a more significant role in determining the focus than the actual intensities. We also refer to **brightness perception** when we consider all of the variables that result in determining the overall brightness of a particular subject. The amount of light falling on the object, our optical sensitivity, and the degree of reflectivity are all factors in determining the perceived intensity of an object.

Psychological Responses

Finally, there is the element of psychological response to the intensity of light. Most importantly, this plays a role in the determination of the mood of the occupants in a lit environment. As a whole, well-lighted environments produce an emotional response in the occupants that is positive and healthy. Poorly lit rooms and corridors can produce gloomy environments that tend to have a negative impact on the inhabitants' moods. Studies have indicated an association between people's mood and the hours of sunlight exposure that they receive in a typical day. A condition known as **Seasonal Affective Disorder (SAD)** is a form of depression that affects people during the winter who live in latitudes where they aren't exposed to enough sunlight in a typical day. Elevated brightness has been associated with increases in an individual's heart and respiration rates, while studies have shown that increased productivity and more friendly work environments have been created through modifications in the lighting intensities of a workplace. Finally, psychiatric hospitals and elderly care facilities are just a few of the many social service clinics that make use of intensity to alter the behavior of their patients.

INTENSITY AND OTHER PERCEPTUAL ISSUES

Some of the most common design problems in lighting design can be related to intensity issues. First, everyone's visual system is slightly different: People will often have varying responses to a given design. Some individuals are light sensitive while others may struggle with issues of depth perception. Some may have good night adaptation while others may have issues related to color blindness. Even among people who have what we would consider to be normal vision we often see large variations in individual responses to the same visual stimuli. Due to this, we typically design for the individuals that require the most stringent visual requirements. For example, our eyes degenerate over time, and our vision generally becomes more impaired as we get older. Therefore, in most cases, we should design the lighting for the oldest occupants who will be seeing a play or making use of a given room. Older patrons struggle more with dimly lit scenes than people in their 20s and 30s. Likewise, we also design lighting based on the most critical task to be performed in a room or building. An operating room requires brighter lighting than a stairway in an apartment building. In following this practice, we can fulfill the lighting needs for all the people using an environment, since most individuals will be comfortable with the minimum intensity levels set by the most demanding needs.

While individual reactions may be responsible for much of how we both respond to and perceive light, there are many other factors that can also have a significant impact on how we sense light. Many of these relate specifically to how our eyes function and compensate for varying conditions within an environment. Some of these factors are due to the physical properties of our visual systems, while others are related to our psychological responses to the brightness of a given object or environment. Many of these effects can have a negative impact on our visual experience, so a designer must be both aware of and sensitive to these effects in order to produce the most effective design for a client or production. Several visual effects that are specifically related to the intensity of a given light include mood alterations, overstimulation, glare, color perception, and adaptation.

Mood Alteration

Intensity is a key element in creating mood. The contrasts that you observe in the brightness levels found in many buildings quickly demonstrate the association that intensity plays upon mood. Bright offices create productive atmospheres, while funeral homes are lit in soft warm tones in order to create a somber reflective mood. A fast-food restaurant will be lit in a way that produces a less-inviting environment than a formal sit-down restaurant. Low lighting levels can create mysterious and foreboding moods while brightly lit scenes are associated with celebratory or comic moods. On stage, we have traditionally used higher intensities for comic plays, while tragedies have characteristically been lit with low intensities and shadows. Think back to the lighting levels found in the *Batman* and *Pirates of the Caribbean* films. Each can be associated with a very different overall mood and lighting—even though both films had both comic and scary moments. The lighting and moods of the *Batman* films were generally darker and more sinister than those found in the *Pirates of the Caribbean* films. On the other hand, the intensity of the lighting for each of these is very different than that for much more upbeat films like *Baywatch or Going in Style*. Mood is very dependent upon the intensity of the light that illuminates a given environment. As a reminder, intensity may also be used to draw focus to specific elements within a stage picture. Light can creep up on locations that the action will be shifting to, while brightness can be used to draw customers to specific displays in a department store. In each case, the designer uses brightness not only to create a mood, but also to also draw focus.

Overstimulation

A common occurrence in theatrical design relates to overstimulating various combinations of rods or cones within the eye. This may happen through exposing the eye to disproportionally high levels of light in a given color range or through simply leaving the environment unchanged for extended periods of time. In these cases, upon the removal of the stimulus or light, the eye is tricked and continues to provide sensory information that gives an appearance that the environment remains unchanged. We refer to these illusions as **afterimages.** An example of this phenomenon is the old trick of looking onto a neutral surface after staring at a colored box or single dot for a given amount of time. Once your view is shifted to the neutral surface, an afterimage of the box or dot is commonly observed to be floating on the neutral background. A variation of this effect may happen on stage during blackouts where a brightly lit scene is suddenly plunged into darkness. In most cases, many audience members perceive a momentary glow or afterimage of the scene for several seconds into the blackout.

Glare

Glare refers to the presence of distracting light within a viewer's field of vision. This may come about through a number of ways. The first is nothing more than the result of seeing an unusually high level of reflectance off of an object. The sometimes painful experience that you might have when looking at white-beach sand or newly fallen snow on a bright sunny afternoon are examples of this type of glare. Another type of glare occurs when an observer is forced to look directly into a light source. Common examples of this include the oncoming headlights of an approaching car at night, or when a person might look directly into a spotlight or the sun. How often have you struggled with the glare of the sun while driving due west around sunset? As a rule, the farther that the source of glare is located from the subject, the less effect or distraction that it will present to the overall scene. As designers we usually try to avoid glare and choose lighting angles that place our light sources either out of the observer's view or within the peripheral vision of the observer. In theatrical lighting, a designer must be especially mindful of glare when working in thrust and arena theatres where audience members could easily look directly into the lenses of lighting fixtures that light the opposite side of the stage. On the other hand, there are times when glare may be considered a positive element of a scene. We often refer to this positive element of glare as **sparkle** or **glitter.** In the case of architectural lighting we may occasionally want to create a limited amount of glare simply to add visual interest and perhaps some focus to a scene or project. An example would be the lamps and crystals that form a chandelier. In this case, the chandelier may or may not be the primary light source of a room, but it certainly takes on a primary focus simply through the glitter that occurs from the reflections of its lamps and crystals.

Color Perception

An object's color is often perceived differently when viewed under light sources of different intensities and colors. Colors will generally appear more saturated if viewed under light of a lower intensity. Under increased levels of illumination red-colored objects tend to have colors that shift towards the shorter yellow wavelengths, while violet-colored objects shift toward the blue wavelengths. Conversely, under lower intensities red objects will appear redder while violet objects will appear even more violet. (See Figure 2.2 for examples.) Colors found near the center of the spectrum are less affected than those at the extreme ends of the spectrum. In addition, we lose our ability to differentiate colors as the intensity of the light is lowered. When we view a full spectrum or wide variety of individual wavelengths of light, we perceive the combination of wavelengths as white light—a condition that we see as normal. One of the most interesting concepts of color perception lies in the wide range of deviation in what our mind will accept as white light. In exterior settings, white light tends to take on a cooler

Figure 2.2a Effects of decreasing intensity on color perception. a. Color chips under high-intensity light

Figure 2.2b Same color chips under medium-intensity light

Figure 2.2c Same color chips under low-intensity light

quality that has an overall blue tint, while interior light sources are most commonly associated with lamps that produce an overall warm amber-like tint. In each case, we still accept the associated light as being white.

At this point, our discussion has been limited to the effects of brightness on color, but there are a number of additional effects related to color and perception that are due to the color of the light itself. These are discussed in Chapter 3.

Adaptation

While the eye can see an immense range of brightness, the eye quickly narrows its response to a limited range of brightness perception. We refer to this as **adaptation.** Adaptation allows the eye to become more efficient and sensitive within a relatively narrow range of brightness. The eye tends to accept this range as normal and is inclined to ignore anything with brightness levels that lie outside of this range. Unfortunately, being stimulated by the same intensity of light over a long period of time can have negative impacts on vision. One of the most commonly experienced problems is **visual fatigue.** In this case, viewers are subjected to an unchanging visual environment, and their eyes grow tired through the overuse of some of the optical sensors. Viewers might experience effects like eyestrain, headaches, and blurriness that negatively impact their vision due to visual fatigue. We commonly correct for this while reading or doing detailed paperwork through simply glancing across the room and away from our work for a minute or so once we feel the effects of fatigue setting in. A common practice used in theatre to avoid this condition involves creating subtle shifts in the lighting over an extended period of time. Many of us call these "**blood pressure**" cues. Care must also be taken when a dark scene follows a bright scene to ensure that the dark scene doesn't appear excessively dark. The effects of maintaining a bright scene generally require that the brightness be continually raised in order that the perceived brightness appears unchanged throughout the scene. Many times, the most effective lighting of bright scenes will occur immediately following dark scenes, during which audience members' eyes have undergone adaptation based on the lower intensity of the dark scene. It takes much less light to give the appearance or perception of a brightly lit scene in these cases. Another effect of adaptation is often experienced when walking into a darkened room after returning from outside during a bright, sunny day. In this case, most people find it nearly impossible to see anything until after their eyes have grown accustomed to the dark. The opposite effect commonly occurs as people get up in the middle of the night and turn on the lights in order to make their way to the bathroom or kitchen. In both cases, the experience not only limits your vision but may also bring painful sensations to your eyes. On stage, a lighting designer must be careful to not overlight a bright scene that immediately follows a dark scene because the sudden brightness can cause the same painful experience as turning on the bathroom lights in the middle of the night.

Defining Form and Shape

Light is the primary medium through which we determine the form and shape of objects. It also helps us to determine the relative positions of objects from one another. While we could use our sense of touch to feel our way around a collection of objects, it is much quicker to observe them and the surrounding environment through our sense of sight. As light strikes a surface it is reflected back toward the viewer, where it creates a series of impulses that are interpreted by the mind. These visual clues not only allow us to identify an object, but also to judge spatial relationships based on prior experiences and memory. Light travels only in straight paths and its direction can easily be determined through careful study of the shadows and highlights that it produces on objects. We see those areas where light strikes the surface as **highlights,** while those that are not lit are seen as **shadows**. In many ways, shadows are simply

the absence of light, while highlights are restricted to those surfaces directly in the path of the light. We use highlights and shadows to help distinguish depth and form within objects. In a complete void, where there is no chance of scattered reflections, a single light source will produce characteristic highlights and shadows that allow us to determine an object's directional relationship with the light source. We often take these relationships between highlights and shadows for granted, and have learned to analyze this information based on our daily experiences. In order to demonstrate this principle you only need to play a flashlight on an object from a variety of positions to observe the changing relationships between the shadows and highlights and how these are readily linked to the angle from which the light is coming and the viewing angle of the observer. For instance, a basketball will appear as a circle or disk, not a sphere, if viewed from straight on and lit by light directly from a frontal orientation. This image and its associated highlights and shadows will change considerably as the light is moved around the ball.

We must also consider the relationship of the viewer to the object or subject as well as the correlation between the positions of the object and light source. One of the most obvious day-to-day illustrations of this phenomenon in the natural world is in the observation of the phases of the moon (Figure 2.3). In this case, at different times of the month we observe more or less of the reflected highlights and shadows of the moon's surface. When the moon is full, the sun is behind the earth and we observe an image of the moon that looks like a complete circle because all of the surfaces that we see are exposed to the sun's light. However, at either quarter-moon phase, we see only part of the moon's exposed surface (actually only a quarter of the total

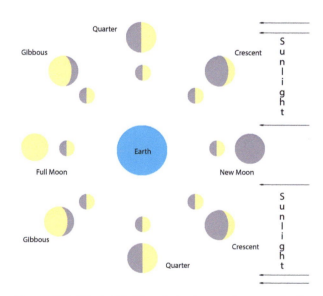

Figure 2.3 Effect of light and viewing angle on perception of an object's shape

surface) because the earth is oriented in such a manner that we observe half of the moon in highlight while the other half is left in shadow—despite the fact that the sun still fully illuminates the same amount of the moon's surface. In most cases, things aren't as simple as in the moon phases example, and having a single light source is more often the exception than the rule. In addition to the influences of several light sources, there are additional impacts such as reflections that will further complicate the lighting of an environment.

Designers can use the relative angle between an object and a light source to either enhance or diminish the three-dimensional qualities of an object. Most designers relate this principle to the controllable quality of distribution. In fact, angle becomes a major determinant in how we perceive the form of an object. Figures 2.4–2.10 provide illustrations of how light plays on a subject from a variety of angles that are common to theatrical lighting. Light from the front tends to flatten a subject. This is due to the fact that from a **flat angle** (relatively straight on) the entire surface appears to be equally well lit and there is no contrast between the shadow and highlight areas. This results in the object appearing mostly two-dimensional rather than three-dimensional. As the direction of the light rotates to the sides and back, the viewer will see a more modeled three-dimensional quality that designers commonly call **revealing form.** What has happened is that

the light now reveals those surfaces and shadows that the eye uses to define depth. The effects of several principal lighting angles are summarized in the following sections.

Front Light

Front light is popular because it reveals details of a subject. Most designers associate front light with visibility. It is used for tasks such as lighting an actor's face, making the lettering of a large piece of signage readable, or simply providing enough illumination for people to clearly see the walls and background of a setting. Front light is an overall naturalistic angle but can be distorted through either raising the angle until it becomes so steep that unnatural shadows form in areas like the eye sockets, or lowering it to the point that it produces unnatural highlights from underneath the subject (**uplight**). As stated earlier, a significantly flat front light angle can cause a subject to appear two-dimensional.

Light from a **front diagonal** is considered to be one of the most naturalistic angles that a lighting designer can use. The reason for our attraction to this angle isn't so much in when a light is used as a single light source as in when it is combined with a second light. One of the most familiar lighting combinations places two different lights on opposing 45° diagonals so that

Figure 2.4 Flat front light

Figure 2.5 Low front light (uplight)

Figure 2.6 Front diagonal (approximately 45°)

Figure 2.7 Sidelight

the two fixtures mirror one another. Through this, the front of the subject is under a significant influence of two lights—producing one zone on the subject that is lit with an equal mixture of light from both sources while also creating two additional areas that are lit predominantly under the influence of one light or the other. The front diagonal provides a good combination between the visibility desired by a front light and the modeling capabilities of a sidelight.

Sidelight

Sidelight may come from either side of the subject and helps to reveal its depth and form. It can take on qualities that may appear either dramatic or naturalistic depending on how it might be colored or mixed with other combinations of light. Sidelight is the most productive angle for modeling or creating dimensionality in a subject. Sidelight may come from a variety of vertical angles. The steeper-angled high side is generally more naturalistic than light shining on a subject as a direct sidelight. An even further dramatic quality can be achieved through using low sidelight that may even be angled upward. In this case, the light reveals areas such as the undersides of a subject that would normally fall into shadow. Dance lighting, because of its emphasis on the body and form, makes heavy use of a variety of sidelight angles.

Downlight and Backlight

Several additional lighting angles are important because of their ability to bring drama to a setting while creating still other influences on the appearance of an object or subject. The **downlight** creates one of the most dramatic angles available to a lighting designer. The dramatic quality is primarily due to the excessive shadows that are created from the overhead light source. Flashes of highlight on the very top surfaces of the subject are also characteristic of this angle. While it creates a strong sense of dimension or modeling, it also tends to produce shadows that aren't very naturalistic. A viewer will typically see the eye sockets of a subject develop into deep shadows (raccoon eyes) under strong downlights. A certain harshness or distortion is often characteristic of this lighting angle. Downlight may also give the perception of a shortening or squashing appearance in a subject. **Backlight** comes from behind the subject and can create a silhouette. It can also produce a rimming effect around the subject by casting an outline of highlight around its edges, or a halo-like appearance. It has been known to cause performers' hair to glow. A look at concert videos where performers have extremely large hairstyle treatments clearly illustrates this effect. Backlight also has the ability to help separate a subject from its background and can seemingly push the subject forward towards the viewer. A **back-diagonal** source forms an angle that is a combination of the back and sidelight angles.

Figure 2.8 Downlight

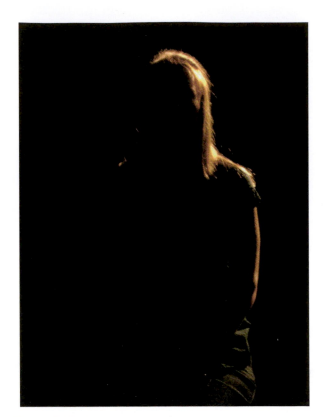

Figure 2.10 Back diagonal light

Figure 2.9 Backlight

Sidebar 2.1 DESIGNER PROFILE

Marilyn Lowey

Credit: photo courtesy Todd Kaplan

Marilyn Lowey's lighting specialties tend to be along the lines of spectacle performances and productions. However, her experience and impressive list of credits span a considerable breadth of the lighting industry. Areas that she frequently designs within include concerts, arena spectacles, ice shows, large revue shows and stadium projects, and theme park shows. She holds a BFA from Emerson College and an MFA from Carnegie Mellon University. She is the recipient of an Emmy Award as well as other awards and nominations for lighting projects that she has designed. Several notable concert credits include designing for Neil Diamond, Diana Ross, Liza Minnelli, Harry Connick, Jr., Whitney Houston, and Stevie Wonder. Her lighting of spectacle events and live theme park productions include *Siegfried and Roy, Champions on Ice, Disney on Ice*, and a number of shows for Universal Studios at Orlando and Los Angeles (*Phantom of the Opera, Beetlejuice Rockin' Graveyard Revue, Universal Studio's Islands of Adventure Lost Continent Attractions, Star Trek—The Adventure*, and *The Flintstones Live*). Television credits include lighting specials for many of the previously mentioned artists plus special events like the *Disney Hall Opening Gala, The Opening Ceremonies of the World Cup Cricket Games, Olympic & World Figure Skating, Nickelodeon Kids' Choice Awards,* and the *MTV: New Year's Eve Show.* Her industrial clients include Nissan, Sony, Anheuser-Busch, Buick, Calvin Klein, Epson, and Apple Computers. Finally, she has also compiled a list of impressive architectural lighting credits, including the Mandalay Bay Theatre and Arena (Las Vegas), the Bellagio Hotel lobby lounge, Golden Nugget Showroom, IBM Facilities, Disneyland Hotel, Lloyds Art Gallery, and several private residences.

Marilyn received solid training in her formal education but made it a point to also learn from other experiences as well: "I always worked every summer from my senior year in high school through grad school in summer stock . . . beginning as an apprentice and climbing up the ladder to the role of lighting designer." While at college, she also worked at a lighting shop in order to understand how gear was rented and what equipment was available outside of college. She came to work on the projects that she now designs through taking the opportunity to light as many different types of projects as she could: "I went after every project that I heard about and began lighting everything. After a period of time, I developed clients and continued working in the many avenues in which lighting was needed." By working in so many different areas, she has also found that her work tends to remain more stable:

> ❝It's difficult to say what amount of my work comes from particular areas. What happens is that each discipline has its peak period while others are in slower times. Recessions hit the disciplines at different times and the work at any given time is reflected in that way.❞

When discussing the differences between lighting for different types of projects, she states that "Lighting for me is learning how to see. Once I realized how to see, I could light any discipline easily . . . it's the givens and parameters that will change between the disciplines."

Her movement into lighting outside of theatrical design came through her employment by Imero Fiorentino Associates (IFA) in New York City. It was through this association that she was introduced to different aspects of the entertainment industry and where she received her initial break. Stig Edgren, a lighting designer at IFA during that time, had an abundance of work and gave her several projects, which began her career in this part of the entertainment industry: "One of the more significant differences between working in these areas of lighting is that there is more money for equipment . . . and the more expensive gear at that." On the other hand, she also speaks of the importance of working with other people in this part of the business and states, "The lighting is easy—the people will kill you!" On the other hand, "I love lighting all the areas of design that I presently work in. I felt that theatre was too slow for me and a bit self-indulgent for me at that period of my life. I was also more interested in the larger-scale work." On the downside, she hates having to work all the nights that this type of lighting often requires.

She closes by sharing:

> ❝The lighting business has changed since I selected it as my career and is now flooded with potential designers where everyone thinks that they can light a show. This in some ways has caused the quality of the lighting in some areas of the industry to be lower than we might like.❞

Equipment is changing at an ever-increasing pace and she likes to talk to shops and manufacturers to learn what is new. She also receives calls from vendors about using new equipment as it becomes available for beta testing and will sometimes work this gear into the productions that she is working on. When asked what she considers to be the most essential principle of lighting for these events she shares that:

> ❝Art takes time no matter what discipline of lighting you are working within. Despite this, you had better be both fast and good in this type of work. Go the distance and do whatever it takes to make it perfect for yourself and the client.❞

Silhouettes and Grazing

Designers may also discuss two other forms of light that refer to the direction in which the light illuminates an object. The first, **silhouette lighting** (Figure 2.11), relates not to lighting the object itself but to lighting the background behind an object. Under this type of lighting the object is seen as a dark outline or silhouette against its background. This technique is quite popular in theatrical lighting, where unlit subjects/objects are placed in front of a well-lighted cyclorama (cyc). The second, **grazing** (Figure 2.12), occurs when a light is played on a surface of an object at an extreme angle. This angle is commonly used to enrich or enhance the textures of a surface. Ceiling or ground/floor-mounted lights that are mounted relatively close to a wall or scenic surface can enhance the shadows formed by the downward/upward direction of the light and will make the unevenness of the rocks and cracks or mortar in a masonry wall much more interesting. Grazing techniques are commonly used for lighting building facades where a designer wants to initiate interest in a section of wall.

Shape and Texture

Light may also have shape. This can best be described as the area or volume to which the light is confined or projected. In a spotlight, the shape of the light is generally

Figure 2.12a Grazing lighting. a. A stone wall lit from straight-on

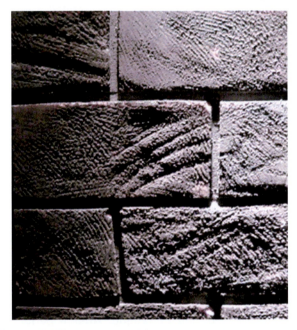

Figure 2.12b Same wall lit from a grazing light

in the form of a cone. The apex forms at the **luminaire,** while the light spreads outward away from it in a conical volume (imagine a performer within a single spotlight). Other styles of fixtures produce light in different shapes or distribution patterns. If the light from a spotlight is cast directly onto a wall you will observe a circle if the angle is dead on—but the shape becomes an ellipse if the angle is skewed. Light can be shaped to a rectangle as it enters a room through a doorway or window. This

Figure 2.11 Silhouette lighting: a tree silhouetted against a fence

might form a skewed trapezoid if the position of the light is shifted to the side or above the opening. Light may also be defined through a combination of several different fixtures that together define a particular shape in light. Examples of this would be using several lights to create a pathway across a stage, or a roadway that is lit by hundreds of light fixtures that together produce a linear path of illumination along an interstate or highway.

While what I have written up to this point relates only to the overall shape of a light source, there can also be shape within the light itself. When light passes through the slats of a louver door or Venetian blind, the resultant shape will be divided into slivers of light. An outdoor location will typically have textured light as a result of light passing through overhead trees and branches. A popular technique for initiating texture and pattern into a light is by using **gobos**. Gobos are simple template patterns etched into pieces of metal or glass that are inserted into lighting fixtures in order to create shadow projections. Gobos may also be called **patterns, templates,** and **cookies.** While a single gobo might be used to project the image of a window with all of its decorative mullions, a group of a half-dozen or more units with leaf-breakup patterns can be used to create a tree canopy over an entire stage. Gobos may be custom manufactured or purchased from catalogs that contain hundreds of patterns. Figure 2.13 illustrates the effect of a breakup gobo on a subject and the surrounding floor.

KEY AND FILL LIGHT

In practice, most objects are typically under the influence of several light sources—each with varying intensities and qualities that may make it difficult to identify the specific source of each light. The fewer the number of light sources, the more stark the associated lighting will appear. From our perspective, we almost always see light sources coming from above. The sun is generally high in the sky, most rooms are lit from ceiling fixtures, and even the sky itself becomes a source of illumination through the effects of atmospheric scattering and diffusion. Because of this, we tend to view lighting from above as a natural condition. Light that isn't consistent with this is often thought to be more dramatic or may be directly linked to a low elevation source like a fireplace, candle, or table lamp.

In a performance situation we usually prefer that stray light, or **spill,** be quickly absorbed once it passes beyond a subject. In theatre, we color most of our masking fabrics, walls, and floors black to absorb and prevent reflections of excess light. We usually refer to the light that is primarily responsible for lighting a scene as the **key light.** Many times this is in the form of a single source. In theatres there is usually little ambient light due to all the non-reflective surfaces, and a single key light will often produce extreme contrasts between the

Figure 2.13 Light shaped by gobos

Figure 2.14 Combination of lighting angles on a subject: two opposing front diagonals (approximately 45° to each side and vertical)

highlight and shadow areas of a subject. On the other hand, a subject may also be under the influence of light as a result of diffusion or scattered reflections that add light to the areas of a subject that would normally be shadowed. We refer to this as **fill light,** and it can be thought of as the ambient light that exists within an environment. Fill light is typically diffuse and often cannot be readily associated with a directional angle: it is simply present. In video and film design, fill light specifically refers to the light that is provided by additional fixtures that softens the shadows and "fills in" those areas of a subject that would otherwise be cast into dark shadow. Figure 2.14 illustrates the effect of a key and fill light combination on a subject.

Movement and Light

Movement refers to changes within the light and composition from moment to moment. As discussed in Chapter 1, this may present itself in one of three manners. First, a light source might move in full view of the observer, as in the case of a lantern being carried around in the dark. Another variation of this type of movement comes from seeing a sequence of lights turned on and off in order to produce particular patterns. The most obvious examples of this are lights associated with **chase** or **ropelights** and marquees. Other familiar examples are found in sales displays and restaurant or casino signage. The flashing beacons of emergency and maintenance vehicles also rely heavily on this principle. A second form of movement involves observations of the movement of the light without seeing the light source itself move. A followspot located at the rear of an auditorium is an example of this type of movement. Another example of this is illustrated by the use of progressive specials that light the path of a moving actor. Third, the most common form of lighting movement simply relates to changes taking place in the lighting over time. The changes might be so subtle that the observer isn't fully aware of them; in some cases, they might appear to operate on a subconscious level. Sunset sequences often display this type of subtlety. Other examples might include foreshadowing by slowly creeping the lights up around an actor for a monolog or slowly building the intensities of a scene to alter the mood for an impending sequence or action. In other cases, such as in flipping a light switch to the "on" position, the movement might appear to be nearly instantaneous. While there are occasions where the lighting for an environment may be static, most of us consider the lighting transitions themselves to be just as important as the actual images or cues that a lighting designer creates.

Cues and Transitions

While there are applications in which light will remain static over a period of time, this is generally the exception rather than the rule in entertainment lighting. Static lighting is for the most part limited to architectural and display applications, although even these may incorporate dynamic properties for the design of a particular project. In most entertainment venues, lighting is expected to take on a dynamic role—and changes in lighting add to the drama and theatricality of an event. In entertainment lighting we refer to the individual moments as **cues**. A cue simply reflects a snapshot that is a record of a specific combination of lighting and compositional qualities of an environment at a given time. You may also hear designers referring to cues as **moments**, **states**, or **looks**. In reality, the lights in a typical lighting design for most performance events are undergoing some form of change or transition throughout much of a performance.

The period of time (or **timing**) when one cue changes into another becomes a major component of a successful lighting design. This is called a **transition** and we commonly refer to each change between cues as a **crossfade.** If done poorly, this can be distracting; if done well, transitions play a major factor in enhancing the effectiveness of actors as they proceed toward the climax of a given scene. Cue timing is generally measured in seconds and is often referred to as a **count.** A five-count cue would take place over five seconds. With the computers that we now use for lighting control, we can create subtle effects that may take minutes or even hours to complete. At the same time, we can create other sequences so complex that an observer may have to see the sequence run a number of times to fully comprehend the extent of a cue. Today's light boards are capable of completing a number of operations simultaneously while giving separate timings to each of the components of a cueing sequence. In fact, it is quite common to have lights fading down at one rate while other lights fade up to a different rate (what is known as a **splitfade**). It's also possible to draw the focus to one performer, lower the lights around the rest of the set, and maintain a sunset sequence—and have it all run on a series of completely different time intervals. Even with all this, you can run even more overlapping cues if you think that it might be necessary.

Finally, you can create implied or perceived motion in objects simply by applying changes to other lighting variables, such as in the angle from which different lights strike an object. By switching back and forth between a front and backlight, an object will be perceived to swing forward and backward. The same object can be made to look as if it is swinging side to side if you alternate between lights that are oriented directly to the sides of the object. It can also appear to rise and sink if lit alternately between an up light and down light. In sidelighting, we can use light to seemingly either push or draw the performers across a stage. Ballet and other forms of dance lighting make frequent use of this phenomenon. What's important through all of this is that all of these effects result from our perception being led by the visual clues that are being provided by the lighting.

For Further Reading

DiLaura, David L., Kevin W. Houser, Richard G. Mistrick, and Gary R. Steffy. eds. *Illuminating Engineering Society–the Lighting Handbook Tenth Edition: Reference and Application.* New York: Illuminating Engineering Society, 2011.

Illuminating Engineering Society of North America. *IESNA Lighting Education 100 (Fundamental Level).* New York: Illuminating Engineering Society of North America, 1993.

Illuminating Engineering Society of North America. *IESNA Lighting Education 150 (Intermediate Level).* New York: Illuminating Engineering Society of North America, 1993.

Illuminating Engineering Society of North America. *IESNA Lighting Ready Reference.* 4th ed. New York: Illuminating Engineering Society of North America, 2003.

Palmer, Richard H. *The Lighting Art: The Aesthetics of Stage Lighting Design.* 2nd ed. Englewood Cliffs, NJ: Prentice Hall, 1994.

CHAPTER 3

COLOR AND ITS EFFECTS

OF ALL THE controllable qualities of light, color produces one of the greatest impacts on how we see an object and the surrounding environment. Many say that color is the most difficult element for a young designer to learn to control in a lighting design. Some of the reasons for this profound impact come from the fact that color has both physiological and psychological effects on how we view a scene or object. It has the ability to completely alter the observed color of a subject, change the perceived distance of objects, and can even cause objects to blend in or pop out from their backgrounds. Additionally, the color of light has been associated with the ability to affect our heart and breathing rates, influence our productivity, and to alter our moods. With light and color having such an impact on how we view the world, I have chosen to dedicate a whole chapter to color and its effects. The first portion of the chapter provides essential color theory, while later elements of the chapter address specific design considerations, techniques, and equipment that a designer may use to manipulate color.

WHAT IS COLOR?

Color is a perception. It simply refers to how we see an object and how we have come to associate specific visual responses with the naming of given colors. Color is therefore dependent on memory associations. As children our parents taught us what was red, blue, or any other color, and we have learned that these basic color names can be associated with a given visual response. We refer to these color names as **hues**, which is the generic description or name for a given color. As long as we aren't color blind these hues become a familiar way of communicating color information from one person to another. Basic hues such as red, orange, or purple are easily understood, while hues like fuchsia, ultramarine, or sepia may be harder to understand for people who are less familiar with describing hues. On the other hand, a color like sandy rose will most likely cause a problem in color understanding no matter who is discussing this particular hue.

In practice, the color that we actually see is a function of three factors: the color of the light itself, the ability of the optical sensor such as an eye or camera to distinguish between different colors, and the color of the objects being observed. A change in any one of these will result in our perceiving a different color. Each of these effects is described more specifically throughout this chapter, but for now, here is one familiar example that illustrates the effect of changing just one of these elements. I'm sure that you have worn a white shirt while you have either ridden an amusement-park ride or attended a club where there were a variety of different colored lights. It should come as no surprise that as you walked under the lights you saw your shirt change to whatever color the light was at any given time. This is a basic example of the color of the light changing your perception of the color of the shirt. In reality, the shirt never changed color—but your perception of it did. While this is a drastically simple example of how colored light can alter the appearance of an object, the effect is always present. We are constantly seeing less obvious shifts in an object's color due to the constant lighting changes that exist in our world.

THE VISIBLE SPECTRUM

In further examination of the electromagnetic spectrum that I discussed in Chapter 1, we are now going to consider only the narrow band of wavelengths that can be sensed or experienced by our eyes. This very narrow portion of the electromagnetic spectrum is known as the **visible spectrum** and simply represents a range of wavelengths to which our eyes are sensitive (see Figure 1.2 in Chapter 1). Within the visible spectrum, the wavelengths can be further differentiated through the varying color responses that they elicit from our eyes. Most light sources like the sun or a lamp contain elements of all the individual wavelengths of the visible spectrum, with the combined result producing an overall color that is perceived as white light. In reality, this white light is actually a mixture of all the other colors, or wavelengths. The visible spectrum can be observed through a prism that through refraction breaks a light source into its component wavelengths. The familiar rainbow of red, orange, yellow, green, blue, and violet is the product of each hue being separated from the others as an effect of their ever-decreasing wavelengths. Red is associated with the longest wavelengths while violet is associated with the shortest wavelengths.

Hue may not give enough information for communicating a color from one person to another. While I may describe the color of an object as red, what distinguishes the red of an apple from the red of an old book cover? The red of a rose versus the "rosy" red cheeks of cold? All of these descriptions carry a degree of vagueness and may mean different things from one person to another. Because of this, we have additional ways of describing color. **Saturation** refers to the purity of a color. The more saturated the color, the more specific and limited the range of wavelengths associated with it. A saturated color cannot have a diverse range of wavelengths; instead, saturated colors contain a very limited range of wavelengths of light. Saturation may also be referred to as **chroma.** We often describe the opposite effect of saturation as a **tint.** In tints, a color is combined with either white light or a mixture of other wavelengths to produce a softer, less saturated variation of the hue, so that a greater variety of wavelengths are present in the light. We also describe color through referencing its overall lightness or darkness based on a gray scale ranging from black to white. We describe this component of color as **value.**

Primary Colors

The eye contains a collection of photoreceptors called **cones** and **rods.** While the rods aid the eye in night vision, the cones provide the color reception. You can refer back to Chapter 2 to review the physical properties of the eye. The cones are separated into three specific types, each one sensitive to a different range of color frequencies or wavelengths of light—red, blue, and green. The cones detect and respond to varying levels or intensities of each of these three colors and help us sense and create an understanding of a given stimulus of light. These colors have become known as the **primary colors**

of light because they are used in various combinations to produce every other color. A close examination of your computer monitor or television screen will illustrate a composite use of these primaries to produce colored lighting effects.

CIE Chromaticity Chart

The relationships between the many varied colors of light can be related to one another through a chart called the **CIE Chromaticity Chart** (Figure 3.1). While this chart illustrates the wavelengths of color radiation given off by various temperatures of black body radiation, the importance to us as lighting designers lies in its depiction of the relationships that exist between each of the three primary colors of light. You can use this chart to make a fairly accurate prediction of the color that will result from a specific combination of colored light. This is done by locating the point that lies within the center of all the plotted positions for each of the individual colored sources. If two sources are represented, the resultant color will lie at the midpoint of a line drawn between the points representing the two colors. If three sources are indicated, the resultant color will be in at the middle of the field of a triangle that is created by connecting the points that represent the three colors. Points associated with colors that fall towards the outside extremes of the chart are associated with colors that have higher saturations and can be seen as more pure, while colors plotted near the center of the chart indicate tints and white light that contain a wider selection of individual colors or wavelengths. Colors falling between the primary colors will be shifted more or less toward one of the two primaries, such as red-orange or red-violet, or could fall equally between the primaries— thus representing a given **secondary color** of the two initial colors.

As described earlier, white light is a combination of many different wavelengths of light. We are typically under the influence of light created by the sun, which we see as normal "white" light. In reality, even though we perceive the light of the sun to be white, it is actually changing color throughout the day. In the early mornings sunlight tends to have a yellow tint; at midday we often associate an overall cool or bluish color to it; and as sunset approaches, the color once again shifts toward more saturated hues of yellow, red, and orange. The light associated with the sun may also be influenced by the time of year and physical location of the observer. Regardless, we all tend to register each of these conditions as white light.

Color Temperature

Since sunlight is constantly undergoing color shifts, we need a way to describe the associated color that we

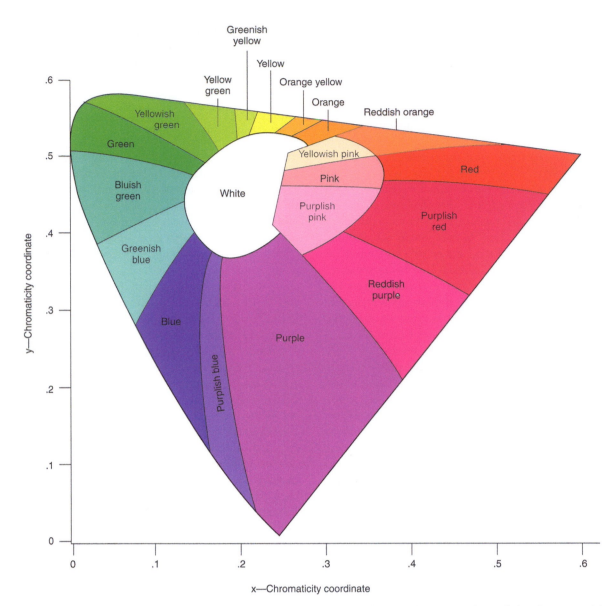

Figure 3.1 CIE Chromaticity Chart: The most saturated hues are located along the outer edges of the diagram, with the primary colors (red, blue, and green) falling approximately at the corners and the secondary colors (magenta, cyan, and amber) at approximately the midpoints between these. White light is found at the center with tints found between the white and the basic hue of the tint.

Credit: Based on a variation of the 1976 CIE Chromaticity Diagram by Photo Research, Inc.

perceive as white light. This is done through a referencing technique that we call **color temperature.** Color temperature compares the sum of all the individual wavelengths of a given light source with the color emitted from a black body radiation of a given temperature (measured in degrees Kelvin). All materials emit radiation, or glow, when heated; as the temperature rises, the glow shifts from red to yellow, yellow to white, white to blue, etc. In this way, every color of radiant energy can be equated to a referenced temperature on the Kelvin scale, where absolute zero (where no molecular action occurs) equates to 0°. All light sources—the sun, the

arc from a welder's flame, the light bulbs (lamps) in our homes and businesses, and the light sources used on our stages—can be described through their color temperatures. The general range of color temperatures to which we are typically exposed is from about 2,000° to 13,000° Kelvin. Low color temperatures have an abundance of red or orange/yellow colored wavelengths while higher color temperatures are associated with an increased presence of blue and violet wavelengths. Light sources with low color temperatures (approximately 3,000°) will appear relatively warm and have an overall reddish tint, while sources with higher color temperatures

(4,000–5,000° and higher) will appear cooler and have more white or blue in their colors. Several approximate color temperatures for everyday light sources include candles (2,000°), 50-watt incandescent lamps (2,500°), stage and studio lamps (3,250°), cool fluorescent lamps (4,000°), arc sources (6,000°), and skylight (7,000° or even higher).

Color Rendering

The sun is generally considered to be a full-spectrum light source in which each of the individual wavelengths of the visible spectrum are present. In full-spectrum lighting all of these wavelengths combine to collectively create a variation of white light. The natural color of any object is due to the fact that its surface selectively absorbs and reflects different wavelengths of light. For example, a red sweater reflects primarily red light, while it tends to absorb other wavelengths or colors of light; a green shirt reflects green light; and a purple shirt will reflect some combination of blue and red light. An object appears most attractive when it is illuminated with lighting that contains some of the wavelengths that it naturally reflects. In these situations, it is said that the lighting **enhances** an object. The red object will look good not only under red light but also under white light because the white light contains red light as one of its components. A white light source that contains a diverse range of wavelengths will usually make most objects look relatively good, while light that has a very narrow or limited spectral composition will make many objects appear dull and gray. Many of the early LED luminaires that only made use of red, blue and green LEDs often produced this effect despite being able to produce variations of white light. Taking this further, white objects reflect all colors of light and will take on the color of any light that is shone on them, while black surfaces tend to absorb all wavelengths of light and will generally appear black no matter what color of light strikes them.

While color temperature refers to the cumulative color of the light, many light sources produce light with very different spectral compositions despite having an overall appearance of whiteness. In other words, the actual wavelengths present in a white light source may vary considerably from one source to another. In fact, light sources may share the same color temperature while still having very different spectral compositions. In this case, while they may for all effective appearances appear the same, they will, in fact, produce very different effects on the materials that they illuminate. If a source contains a lot of red wavelengths within its composition, a subject with a fair amount of red in its color will be enhanced, while another source that contains mostly blue wavelengths will tend to mask, or **gray,** the red color of the subject. The predominantly blue source will enhance blue objects, while the predominantly red source will gray a blue object. The ability to reflect or absorb a variety of wavelengths is generally referred to as **color rendering.** This principle is readily seen in the high-pressure sodium lighting that is characteristic of interstate highways. In this case, the illumination has a pinkish-yellow tint produced through the given color temperature of the roadway lamps. However, these lamps also have very narrow spectral compositions, which results in poor color rendering for many of the colors that we see. Many of the colors that we would normally see under daylight conditions become masked and it is hard to determine the original color of objects like cars under the effects of sodium lighting. In fact, many colors simply turn to varying shades of gray and black under these conditions. Make a note to observe the changes in color that you see in the objects in your car the next time that you travel on roadways that provide different types of illumination. This effect is even more drastic in low-pressure sodium lighting, which is found along some roadways and is identified by its dark yellow coloring (similar to bug lamps).

One of the problems in choosing light sources in architectural and display lighting relates to the diversity in the spectral composition of the light. Many light sources such as fluorescent lamps have an overall high concentration of blue light within their spectral composition. When these lamps are used to light sales displays such as the meat at your local grocery store, the meat often doesn't look very attractive—most likely appearing dull and gray. It would look better if the light source contained an element of red light to help enhance the bright red color of the blood that the meat contains. By enhancing the color of the blood, the meat takes on a fresh appearance. If a store's products have a wide range of colors, the light source that you choose should have a wide distribution of colors in its spectral composition. We can address these issues through making a comparison of a property known as the **Color Rendering Index (CRI)** for each light source. Color rendering refers to how well a source can render or accurately depict an object's color. Sources with high CRIs will have more individual wavelengths present within their associated light and will enhance a larger range of individual colors. The maximum CRI value that a source can have is 100, which is a point where color rendering is considered to be ideal. High CRIs are generally associated with daylight or incandescent light sources. A typical fluorescent lamp will have a CRI rating of 40–50. If we go back to the meat example, we would find that a lamp with a CRI rating of 80 or 90 or better would make the meat look the best. Unfortunately, the expense of using lamps with higher CRI ratings also increases as the CRI gets higher: at some point, you must weigh the factors of appearance versus cost as part of a design solution.

ADDITIVE AND SUBTRACTIVE MIXING

There are two different methods by which color may be created: **additive color mixing** and **subtractive color mixing** (see Figure 3.2). Colors are modified through either the addition or removal of specific wavelengths of light. These systems produce variations in color through very different means, and each has a different group of primary and secondary colors. Each system also has a unique color wheel that illustrates the relationships between the principal hues. In each color wheel the three primary colors are located equally distant around the perimeter of the circle while the **secondary colors** are placed at points midway between the primaries. A **complementary color** is a color that lies directly across the color wheel from a color and forms a pair between the two colors.

Additive Mixing

Additive color mixing comes about when different wavelengths of light are combined or added together.

The process can occur with two different colored light sources and their associated light illuminating a common surface. The overlapping light combines to produce a third and different color. Earlier I identified red, blue, and green as primary colors that activate specific groups of cones in eye. All colors of light are determined through various combinations of these three. We refer to the combination of equal mixtures of any two primary colors as secondary colors: magenta (red and blue), cyan (blue and green), and amber (green and red). An equal mixture of all three primaries produces white light. A combination of all three colors with a bit more red produces pink light. The relationships between all of these colors are indicated by the additive light color wheel, which is illustrated in Figure 3.2a. The color triangle (Figure 3.3) is a variation of the CIE Chromaticity Chart and color wheel; it is commonly used as a reference to the relationships between the primary and secondary colors of light. It also helps to illustrate how complementary colors interact with one another. The primary colors are located at each of the corners of the triangle, while the secondary colors lie at the midpoint along each of the triangle's sides. These positions also correspond to the complementary relationships between each of the colors. White light is located in the center of the triangle. An unequal mixture or combination of

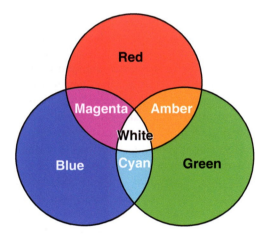

Figure 3.2a The Color Wheels. a. Light color wheel (additive)

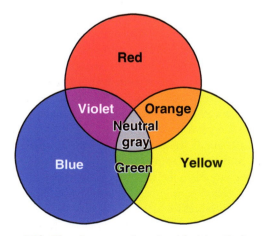

Figure 3.2b The pigment color wheel (subtractive)

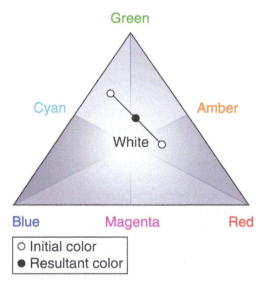

Figure 3.3 The color triangle. The color that results from mixing two different colors can be determined by locating the approximate position of the initial colors on the triangle and drawing a line between them. If colors are balanced, the resultant color will be located midway along the line. If unbalanced, the color is found along the line based on the relative proportions of the two initial colors. Additional colors may also enter into consideration, in which case the central point of any field defined by the initial colors (e.g., a triangle for three colors) is identified with the resultant color.

the primary colors will produce **tertiary** or **intermediate colors**. Additive color mixing within the luminaires themselves has become especially popular now that we are using many LED light sources in a number of theatrical luminaires. These will be discussed in more detail later in the chapter.

Subtractive Mixing

Subtractive color mixing comes about through a process where various wavelengths of light are removed by an object or material. All materials selectively absorb or reflect different wavelengths of light (selective absorption or selective reflection). An object appears to be a given color such as blue because it absorbs the wavelengths of all colors except blue—which it instead reflects. This is the basic color system that most of us have been instructed in since elementary school, and the primary colors include the familiar colors of red, blue, and yellow. These are often called the primary colors of pigment. Just as in the case of additive mixing, if you combine equal portions of any two primary colors you will produce a secondary color, which in this case will produce the colors of orange, violet, and green. Finally, if you combine an equal mixture of all three primaries you will create a muddy warm brown color that we often refer to as **neutral gray.** The pigment color wheel (Figure 3.2b) is based on subtractive mixing and illustrates the relationships between each of these colors.

FILTERING LIGHT

Subtractive mixing also occurs when we filter light. In general, the sunlight that we experience naturally throughout the day comes directly from its source unaffected, the exception being atmospheric conditions such as cloud cover or when there are physical obstructions to the light such as branches or architectural structures. When we go outside, sunlight falls directly upon us; or indoors, we might read a book directly under the light of a table lamp. In both cases, the light leaves its source and is not altered in any way. However, many times we may want to change either the quality or color of the light to better suit our purposes. In the theatrical and entertainment worlds it is much more common to modify or change the color of the light than to keep the color the same as originally produced by a lamp. **Filtering** refers to placing an object in front of a light source that will selectively filter, or remove, various frequencies or wavelengths of light from the source. The remaining wavelengths will pass through the material and continue onward to interact with the environment. Some wavelengths are absorbed or removed, while others are **transmitted** or permitted to pass through the material. Wavelengths that are absorbed are converted into heat. Through this technique, the color of a light source can be altered through selectively choosing which wavelengths of color pass through a filter and continue on to a target. Historically, many devices have been used to filter light, including colored glass, plastic, fabrics, and even fluids like wines and oils.

Filtering also takes place when light strikes an object. We perceive an object's color through sensing those wavelengths that the object has selectively reflected back to us. All other wavelengths are once again absorbed and converted into heat. The reason we might wear a dark sweater in the winter is because most wavelengths of light are absorbed and converted into heat, warming the individual. On the other hand, a white T-shirt reflects nearly every wavelength of light and therefore undergoes little absorption, which keeps the wearer relatively cool during the summer. All materials go through a selective absorption or reflection of these visible wavelengths, which will ultimately determine the color that we perceive for a given object.

COLOR MEDIA

Color media is the term for materials that we use to filter or modify the color and/or quality of the light that is produced by a lighting fixture. The media may be made from a number of different materials such as glass or plastic, or even fluids or silks. The media is usually placed in some type of holder that is positioned at the front of a lighting instrument. Light from the fixture then passes through the color media, where it is altered and continues to travel towards its intended target. The most common type of color media, by far, is the colored plastic filters that we call **gel**. Light passes through the material where certain wavelengths are filtered out while others continue to pass through to the other side. Due to this filtering effect, many designers also refer to gel as **filters.** In fact, "filters" is a more accurate name for color media. Gel was originally made from a specific material (animal gelatin) that was tinted to produce a variety of different colored filters. As lighting fixtures improved and lamps of higher intensities were developed, gel could no longer stand up to the extreme temperatures produced by the newer lamps and would melt or burn out (fade in its center where the heat and light were concentrated) resulting in inconsistent coloring of the light. Along with more efficient light sources, engineers also developed filters in plastic media such as acetate and Mylar that could survive the higher temperatures. Today, even though we rarely use actual gelatin media, we often refer to all these filters collectively as gel—regardless of the actual material.

Plastic Media

Plastic media is by far the most common form of filter in the entertainment lighting industry due to its overall low costs and ease of replacement. The media is purchased in 20 × 24 inches sheets or in rolls that let you cut it to any size needed. The material that is used to manufacture these sheets may be acetate or Mylar, plastics that were developed to withstand the higher temperatures of contemporary lighting fixtures. Some gel systems have the color applied to the surfaces of clear sheets of plastic like acetate, while others, such as Mylar, have the color embedded into the plastic through the manufacturing process. By far the most important advantage of these filters lies in the range of color options. There are four primary filter manufacturers—Apollo, Gam, Lee, and Rosco—which each produce approximately a hundred or more different colored filters. Each company produces booklets with samples of the colored filters called **swatch books** that contain every color filter manufactured in a given system (several, like Rosco, produce three or four different color systems).

While plastic is the most popular filtering material, it does have a drawback in that it will fade or burn out over time. The rate of **burnout** is related to issues such as the intensity of the light source (the brighter the light, the quicker a gel will burn out), the hanging position of the fixture (lights pointed upward will result in more heat passing through a filter and loss of gel life), and the color saturation of the filter (the more saturated the filter, the quicker it will burn out because more wavelengths are absorbed and converted into heat). In most theatrical venues burnout isn't a problem, and gels can be used and reused over many different productions. If burnout becomes an issue—through using very saturated colors or through being used over an extended period of time, such as at a theme park installation—the designer may either replace the gel as needed or might consider more permanent (though often more expensive) filtering materials such as glass.

With so many different colors available, there have been issues in trying to name and reference each individual color. While each manufacturer has given a name to every one of its colored filters, the name assigned to any particular filter will often not give a clear indication of the actual color that it will create. It is also impossible to indicate all these names on the light plot and paperwork. Therefore, each manufacturer has also referenced each filter with a numbering system so that specific colors of filters or gels can be quickly indicated with simple two- or three-digit numbers. While designers in the past often chose to use a single manufacturer's gels on a given project, today's designers often use a variety of gel selections that represent color choices from several different manufacturers. In order to keep the color designations straight we often place a letter in front of the gel number that corresponds with the manufacturer of the specified filter (i.e., R-33 for Rosco #33, L-120 for Lee #120, G-160 for Gam #160, and AP-7900 for Apollo #7900). It is important to note that each of these color systems is completely independent from one another: While you may find the same name or even number in two or more of the different filter systems, these filters may, in fact, be quite different. Even those that at first glance appear to look quite similar may respond quite differently to light.

Figure 3.4 Several prominent gel swatch books

Sidebar 3.1 SPECTRAL ANALYSIS OF GEL

To illustrate the response of light under the influence of a given gel, manufacturers provide a spectral analysis for each filter. This is presented as a graph on a sheet of paper that is mounted directly behind each filter in a swatch book. This analysis provides two essential types of information for a designer.

First, a percentage identifies the overall transmission of the filter. This tells you how much light passes through the gel and is available to illuminate your subject. In many cases, a filter will reduce the light by a significant amount. Pastel or lightly tinted colors frequently have transmission rates in the 70–80% range, while colors of even medium saturation quickly drop down to transmission rates in the 30–40% range. The transmission rates of heavily saturated colors like the deep blues often have transmissions of less than 10%, meaning that more than 90% of the light is being absorbed and converted into heat!

Second, the graph displays the individual transmission values of specific wavelengths of light as affected by the given filter. The individual wavelengths of the visible spectrum are identified by wavelength (usually in nanometers) and plotted along the horizontal axis while the individual transmission rates of each wavelength are plotted along the vertical axis. The importance of this graph lies in how each wavelength responds to different colors of the visible spectrum when using that filter. Tints generally reflect an overall high transmission across many of the wavelengths (Figure 3.5a), while highly saturated colors (Figure 3.5b and c) generally have low transmission rates across the spectrum while spiking in several specific wavelengths or areas of the spectrum. A saturated red filter will have its highest transmission values in the 700–800 nanometer range while a saturated blue will have its peak transmission in the 400–500 range.

A designer can use these graphs to help predict how a filter will affect the surface color of any object that it strikes. If you want to enhance a green object, choose a filter with a fair to good amount of transmission in the green portion of the spectrum, choose high red transmission if the object is red, or choose high blue transmission if the object is blue. If you want a wide range of colors to appear unaltered, choose a filter that is more of a tint with a high degree of transmission across the

c. Hidden colors

Figure 3.5c Blue filters often contain a hidden amount of transmission in the red portion of the spectrum. Here, Rosco 80 (Primary Blue) illustrates transmission in not only the blue but also the red area of the spectrum.

Credit: transmission data courtesy of Lee Filters, GamColor, and Rosco

a. A tint

Figure 3.5a Spectral analysis of gels. a. Spectral distribution graph for Lee 153 (Pale Salmon). Note the relative high transmission levels for most wavelengths throughout the spectrum and slightly higher ones yet within the red portions of the spectrum. The overall transmission rate is relatively high at 64.9%.

b. A saturated filter

Figure 3.5b Spectral distribution graph for GamColor 250 (Medium Red XT). Note the lack of transmission across most of the spectrum with a strong spike of transmission in the red wavelengths. The overall transmission rate is only 7.7%

entire spectrum. A designer can also use the transmission curves to predict what colors a given filter will have a negative impact upon. Any color that is found to correspond with a wavelength of an overall low transmission rate will generally be darkened or grayed. Even colors that appear to be strongly dominant in a given color may contain some hidden transmissions in other parts of the spectrum. One of the strange effects of deep blue lighting is in that many blue filters also have a high degree of transmission in the red portion of the spectrum, resulting in many objects that contain any red dye taking on a reddish glow despite the overall blue color of the lighting. Costumes, paint, and even **maskings** such as legs and borders may demonstrate this effect—which has surprised designers who have not carefully planned their color selections. If this effect is undesirable, then the designer needs to carefully choose a filter with very limited, if any, transmission in the particular portion of the spectrum where these problems have been encountered. These spectral distribution charts are also posted on the manufacturers' websites. Rosco even provides an indication of where the filter is located on the CIE Chromaticity Diagram.

It should be noted that as a general principle you should avoid placing or stacking several layers of gel in an instrument. While this practice may occasionally prove desirable—such as in the case of bringing two relatively unsaturated colors together to produce a new color—this practice typically causes problems. This is particularly true if the colors are saturated and unrelated to one another. If you think about how a filter works, it should become apparent why stacking gels usually doesn't work. For instance, if you were to try to combine a red and blue gel together to produce a purple colored light, you would find that the red filter would eliminate all the light except the red light and that the blue gel would filter out all colors except the blue light—including the red light transmitted by the red filter. The outcome of mixing these filters therefore results in effectively eliminating all of the light through absorption. This not only creates virtually no light transmission but also produces the added effect of a large heat conversion that will most likely result in simply melting the gels together and causing them to burn out. Because of this, it is best to select a single gel to produce a color than to try to combine several gels in the same unit. Over time, especially with more saturated gels, the media will eventually break down and fade or burn out. Several methods of slowing down or preventing this include placing a **heat shield** or **color extender** on a fixture. Heat shields are a special variety of clear gel that are placed in a second slot of a fixture's color holder (between the lens and the gel). This creates a gap between the gel and the fixture that allows additional air to circulate and cool the gel while also filtering out some of the harmful infrared or ultraviolet heat. Not all lighting instruments are designed to hold a second filter. A color extender looks like a top hat and works in much the same way but has internal slots that allow the gel to be placed further away from the lamp. Another technique involves running a pouncing wheel over the gel to create a number of small holes in the gel's surface to help dissipate the heat buildup. The effect of these holes is not distinguishable in the light output.

Glass Media

In the past, glass provided a very favorable form of color filter. However, due to problems such as color consistency (keeping colors consistent from one manufacturing run to another), limited color selection, breakage, and expense, glass has been replaced by gel products. However, if a filter is to be used over a long-term project such as an architectural installation or a themed environment where the filters will be subjected to years of service, glass once again becomes a viable alternative to gel.

Many early glass filters were in the form of **roundels,** circular glass filters that are installed in many **striplight** fixtures. These fixtures contain a series of lamps mounted side-by-side in a single bank. The lamps are wired into circuits that allow every third or fourth lamp to be controlled together—independent from the other lamps, which are also wired into their respective circuits. These fixtures are often used for color toning, and each circuit is typically equipped with a different set of colored filters. In many cases, these striplights were installed permanently in theatres, and color was created through using roundels to color each of the independent light sources. Many secondary and elementary school stages are equipped with several rows of these striplights (often called **border lights**) that hang across the entire width of the stage. Due to expense, roundels were made in only a few colors (typically red, blue, green, amber, and white). By using combinations of these colors, it is possible to create almost any color that a designer might want. While roundels may be used in striplights even today, most designers now specify colors for striplights from gel choices. In addition to providing color filtering, the roundels may also provide some form of patterning or diffusion that modifies the softness and focus of the lamps. Striplights are also commonly used to light linear scenic pieces like drops and **cycloramas (cycs)**.

Manufacturers have recently introduced new glass filters that are inserted into the optical train of a lighting instrument rather than being placed at the front end of a fixture. These filters are being referred to as **variegated glass filters** and in general are used primarily to alter the physical quality of the light. While they may provide color filtering, the majority of their effects are in creating various diffusion patterns and textures in the light. The variegated glass may also be used in combination with traditional color filters to make further changes in the light. These filters are inserted into the area of the fixture known as the **gate,** which corresponds approximately with the focal point of the fixture, and are manufactured so that they will slip into the same pattern holders and slots as a gobo. Some manufacturers even refer to these filters as glass gobos. You may also use these products in combination with traditional steel gobos to produce even more sophisticated patterns. Due to their placement within a fixture, color media other than glass will not hold up to the extreme temperatures of the gate.

Dichroic Filters

A special version of glass filter is the **dichroic filter.** These filters work on the principle of reflecting unwanted wavelengths of light rather than absorbing them. A red dichroic filter will allow red light to pass through it while the majority of the remaining light is reflected backwards away from the filter. In this case, the reflected light will appear cyan (the complementary color to red). Dichroic filters need to be oriented correctly within the light path to work properly. An angle that isn't acute enough may result in scattered reflections of the light rather than allowing the desired wavelengths to pass through the filter. Advantages to dichroic filters lie in their color permanence and increased purity or saturation of a produced color. Dichroic filters can produce some of the most vivid strongly saturated colors that are available to a lighting designer. Because of this, it has become popular to include a selection of dichroic filters in the color wheel of many automated fixtures that are rigged for lighting spectacle events like concert and themed activities.

While dichroic filters are expensive, their costs continue to drop—and more designers are choosing to use dichroic filters for applications where a filter may be used for many months or years. They are especially attractive for themed environments and architectural applications. Dichroics may also be used in gobo designs where crushed pieces of dichroic glass are mounted on a slide to produce effects like water reflections or stained-glass imagery. The range of colors that are available is still quite limited when compared to traditional filters, but continues to improve with every passing year. Manufacturers like Rosco and Apollo Design are producing a solid collection of colors in dichroic filters.

Diffusion

Technically speaking, diffusion isn't an actual color media: it primarily alters the quality rather than the color of the light that passes through it. Many designers and manufacturers refer to **diffusion media** as **frost.** The materials of which diffusion media or frost are made are usually derived from plastics and are therefore manufactured by the same companies that make color media. In fact, manufacturers typically combine their diffusion and color filter media in the same swatch books. As a rule, diffusion softens the beam of light that passes through it. Various degrees of diffusion can be created through a wide selection of frost materials. (Note that diffusion cannot be used to sharpen or harshen a light; it can only produce a softening effect.) The frost selected may be very light or quite heavy depending on the individual needs of a design. There are even frosts that can spread or diffuse the light differently in different orientations. Uses of frost include softening the edges of lights that won't quite focus softly enough, increasing the spread, evening out and eliminating any shadows between two or more adjoining light sources, and knocking down any hot spots that exist between comparable lights. As a

side effect, frosts will often lower the intensity of a light and can cause a large amount of ambient or spill light.

Frost is often combined with color filters. It should always be placed on the side of the color media that is away from the light source; not doing so may cause excessive heat to form and the two sheets of media could melt together. This will occur even more quickly if you try stacking several layers of frost together. In order to remedy problems like this, most gel manufacturers have designed a limited selection of media that combine a color filter with a diffusion treatment in a single product. This color selection is for the most part restricted to primary colors and several other colors that are typically used to light cycs and drops. Finally, diffusion media can also be used to change fundamental qualities such as the color temperature of any light passing through it. In the film and video industry it is imperative that light from different sources be modified to share common traits such as color temperature. Many of these filters are known as **color correction** and are used for applications including converting fluorescent lighting to daylight or incandescent color temperatures, shifting daylight (where crews actually gel over the windows of an on-location set) to tungsten color temperature so that the two light sources will be compatible with one another, or reducing the higher color temperatures of arc light to match incandescent light sources. Correcting for color temperature is also common in architectural applications of lighting design.

CREATING COLOR THROUGH LIGHT

The color that we perceive for any object is actually the result of several variables. Most importantly we need to consider the following: the actual color of the object (those wavelengths of light that are reflected or absorbed), the color of the light (what wavelengths are present), and the color sensitivity of the viewing device (those wavelengths that an eye or camera responds to). The color that we ultimately see is known as the **perceived color** of an object. Changes in any variable can alter the perceived color quite significantly. We don't really have to consider the response of the eye since, for most practical purposes, we all have similar responses to color. However, this does become a factor when comparing color perception between devices such as film and video cameras because different cameras and films may respond to light quite differently from one another. The two primary questions that a lighting designer needs to answer in regard to color perception are: What does this object look like under different colored light sources, and what do all these different colored objects look like under a given color of light? An often forgotten fact is that all colors that an audience sees on stage are only perceived colors. The colors that the audience observes have all undergone some form of color manipulation, unless the scene has been lit with unfiltered light only—and even then, lights at lower intensities will reflect some form of color shift that will make the light and resultant colors of objects appear warmer in color.

To add further complications to color perception, not all light sources are alike. Incandescent lighting is considered full-spectrum lighting because it essentially contains each of the colored wavelengths of visible light despite, having an overall white appearance. This is important because it allows most colors to be enhanced. Other light sources, however, do not contain an abundance of each of the colored wavelengths and therefore will not provide good color rendering of all colors. This is especially true of LED sources, where the colors are created by additively mixing the light from different colored LEDs and where holes will appear in the spectral coverage of the light source. Under LED lighting, some objects' colors will appear grayed or distorted despite the fact that the light may appear to be coming from a white light source. This issue in perception, known as **metamerism,** although it has always been present, had not been a significant factor in most instances until

we started using LEDs for illumination. Metamerism is simply an effect in which objects that appear to share the same color under one light source will appear differently when lit under a different light source. This is all due to the simple effect that the spectral compositions of the two light sources are different. With this now becoming a factor in LED luminaries, designers are making more use of a metamerism index that relates the percentage of reflectance that a particular light source has within a variety of different wavelengths. Figure 3.6 demonstrates the significant effect that different colored lights can have on an object's perceived color.

Color Prediction Through Filters

I have found that you can get a pretty good indication of the perceived color of an object by simply thinking of the light in terms of its primary and secondary color components. By thinking of what colored wavelengths are present in a light and how each is affected by filtering and reflection, you can get a pretty good indication of how an object's color might be changed under the influence

Figure 3.6a Perceived color and light. a. A sample of fabric lit under white light

Figure 3.6c The same sample under red light

Figure 3.6b The same sample under blue light

Figure 3.6d The same sample under green light

of a given color of light. Figure 3.7 illustrates this principle by showing different colored shirts illuminated by a magenta light source. In the first case (Figure 3.7a), the light leaving the fixture contains white with equal proportions of red, blue, and green (the primaries). To create a magenta light, a filter is placed in front of the light to filter out green and allow blue and red wavelengths to continue on to the shirt. The shirt, being red, will absorb the blue light and reflect the red light, resulting in us seeing the shirt as red. This is an easily predictable result. The same is true if we don't change the magenta lighting but instead switch to a white shirt as shown in Figure 3.7b. In this case the magenta lighting goes on to strike the white shirt, which reflects both the blue and red light, thus appearing magenta in color. In addition, if we switch to a green shirt, the magenta light will strike the shirt, which will absorb both the blue and red light. This results in the shirt reflecting no light, giving it a dark or black appearance as illustrated in Figure 3.6c.

If you think of white light and objects as either having all three wavelengths present or being capable of reflecting all three wavelengths, and black as both absorbing and lacking all three wavelengths, you can make some predictions as to how a colored light will theoretically affect the colors of any materials that you may be lighting. This same approach can be used to demonstrate why combining filters will typically be ineffective.

In Figure 3.8a the initial light from the source provides red, blue, and green wavelengths. Upon passing through the first filter, the blue light is filtered away and the red and green continue towards the second filter. In passing through the second filter, the red light is absorbed while the green light passes on toward its target. The second example (Figure 3.8b) illustrates why we shouldn't combine filters. In this example, the first (red) gel filters out each of the wavelengths except red, while the green gel proceeds to absorb the remaining red light—resulting in no light continuing beyond the two filters.

Through experience and careful study of the spectral graphs that accompany the color samples in a swatch book, you can make educated guesses regarding the perceived color of various combinations of filters and colored objects. But even if you use these techniques for

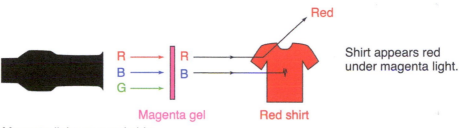

a. Magenta light on a red shirt

Figure 3.7a Effects of colored light. a. The shirt appears red because red wavelengths of magenta light are reflected while the blue ones are absorbed

b. Magenta light on a white shirt

Figure 3.7b The shirt appears magenta because both red and blue wavelengths of magenta light are reflected

c. Magenta light on a green shirt

Figure 3.7c The shirt appears black because both red and blue wavelengths are absorbed

a. Combining an amber and green filter

Figure 3.8a Combining color filters. a. Light coming from the fixture contains red, blue, and green primaries. Upon passing through the amber gel, the blue is absorbed, while the red and green continue on to the green gel, where the red is absorbed. Only green light passes completely through both sets of filters.

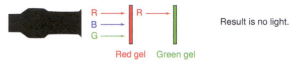

b. Combining a red and green filter

Figure 3.8b Again, the fixture provides red, blue, and green light, which is filtered to only red light once passing through the red gel. The red light continues on to the green gel, where it, too, is absorbed resulting in all light being filtered out by the gels.

predicting the effects of different colored objects and light sources, there are still surprises that come about due to various combinations of fabrics, dyes, and filters. Because of this, there really is no substitute for experimenting with the actual materials and filters and trying various combinations through using mechanisms like **light labs** or **mock-ups**. For instance, the black dyes that are often used in theatrical draperies commonly contain a lot of red pigment. When lighted with a deep blue light (i.e., a night scene) many blue gels contain hidden red wavelengths in their composition that causes the black fabrics to display a deep burgundy or maroon glow.

You also need to consider angle when looking at the effect of colored light on an object. This is particularly noticeable if an object is lit by lights that are colored quite differently from one another (see Figure 3.9). If the two sources come from essentially the same direction, the object will provide a common surface on which the light from both sources will mix quite evenly, producing a third color through additive mixing. However, if the lights are positioned in such a manner that they are directly opposed to one another, they will strike very few common surfaces. You will see that some surfaces of the object will be colored by the first source, while others will be lit by the second source. In effect, the shadows of the first light source will be filled by the color of the second source, while the shadows of the second light source will be filled by the color of the first light source. Finally, if the lights are mounted as mirror images in such a manner that they are both slightly to the sides and front of the subject, the resultant colors will begin with different

a. Effect of extreme angles on color mixing

Figure 3.9a Angle and color mixing. a. Spotlights 1 and 2 are positioned at opposing angles to the sphere or subject. The areas to each side indicate those areas that are under the influence of only one light, while the central area will most likely represent some form of shadow area where there is no or little light from either spotlight and therefore virtually no color mixing.

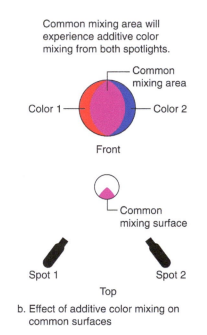

b. Effect of additive color mixing on common surfaces

Figure 3.9b Spotlights 1 and 2 are brought closer toward the front of the subject, which once again results in the two side areas being lit by only a single source, but this time much of the light overlaps in a common mixing area where additive mixing produces a third color that is derived from the two spotlight colors.

colors to each side of the subject that will slowly grade or blend into an equal mix of both colors on those surfaces that are under the influence of both light sources.

Sidebar 3.2 CHANGING COLOR

One of the most significant problems of traditional filters lies in the fact that only one filter can be used in a fixture at a given time. Until the last 30 or so years, the only way to change the color of light coming from a given direction remotely was to hang a second fixture containing the second color next to the first light. The color was then created by selecting which fixture was used at any given time—which also provided a way to use additive color mixing to produce a host of new colors by adjusting the intensity proportions between the two fixtures. This is commonly called **double-hanging**.

In recent years, manufacturers have created accessories that hold a variety of filters that are taped together into some form of a scroll. The scroll can then be rolled back and forth to specific positions that correspond to different colors. These devices, called **automated color changers** or **scrollers,** slide into the color attachment of a lighting instrument and allow a single fixture to have its color changed numerous times throughout a production. Scrollers can substantially reduce the number of fixtures required for a project. Earlier models of automated color changers often contained 10–20 different filters in a scroll, or **gelstring,** while more recent models can contain 30 or more colors. There are other variations of scrollers that produce colored light through the movement of two different scrolls that lie in front of one another. These later-generation scrollers have an enormous range of color selection (nearly 500 colors) and allow the light to be mixed in various combinations by using the relative positions of the two scrolls. Another more recent means of generating colors places dichroic filters on disks. On these disks, the density of yellow, cyan, magenta, and possibly green filters (one per disk) becomes progressively more dense as they are rotated or inserted into the optical train of a lighting fixture. These devices allow a designer to dial in an almost infinite range of colors. The positioning of gelstrings or dichroic disks in each type of color accessory is controlled via commands that come from a typical lighting console. All of these effectively allow designers many more color selections or even the possibility of actually mixing the color of light that they feel is appropriate for any given circumstance or moment. Many of these devices are found in luminaires such as automated or moving lights, which greatly reduces the need to double- or triple-hang lights. They have also become popular accessories in many architectural/display applications.

CMY, RGB, and LED Color Mixing

CMY is an acronym for cyan, magenta, and yellow. Some refer to **CMY color mixing** as **CYM color mixing**. This subtractive mixing process is used for luminaires with a single source of white light. A combination of cyan, magenta, and yellow dichroic filters are moved in front of the light to subtract specific colors or wavelengths from the light in order to mix the desired color. CMY mixing is often utilized in automated or moving lights to produce a wide variety of different colors. Many of these fixtures use incandescent light sources as well as short-arc lamps that also produce variations of white light.

LED light sources, also known as solid-state lighting, make use of the principles of additive color mixing. Currently there are several ways in which these sources can be used to produce light on stage. One makes use of either single or several white LED sources to produce white light of a given color temperature. The actual color temperature is dependent on the phosphors used to produce the LEDs. Variations of these may include either warm or cool white light that is then filtered like traditional lighting instruments with gel or other color media. Electronic Theatre Controls (ETC) makes use of a retrofit lamp housing that replaces the popular Source Four® incandescent lamp with LED light sources. A second type of LED light source provides a cluster or array of LEDs of several different colors. The individual colors typically fall within the primary or secondary wavelengths and are mixed in various intensity combinations to produce light of almost any imaginable color. The earliest versions of these sources combined red, blue, and green LEDs and were known as tri-color luminaires. This form of additive color mixing is often referred to as **RGB color mixing**. Unfortunately, though you could theoretically mix almost any color (as described earlier in additive mixing), each of the individual LED colors has a very narrow spectral response, which results in a condition where there are a number of missing wavelengths of the visible spectrum within these light outputs. This results in many colors not responding well to the limited number of wavelengths present in the LED light and the effect that many colors will appear gray or distorted on the stage (with low CRI values). Many tri-color LED fixtures can be found at the lower end of the LED luminaire market. These are commonly found in small contemporary worship facilities as well as club or bar installations. You can often spot them through the unnatural white light that they produce and their often fluorescent-like quality.

In order to improve color response, many manufacturers now add LEDs of additional colors to fill in those wavelengths that form the missing portions of the visible spectrum. The most common combinations that manufacturers are currently offering include RBGA (red, blue, green, and amber) and RBGW (red, blue, green, and white) LED arrays of LEDs. One variation, the Selador™ series of LED luminaires by ETC, uses seven different colors of LEDs that provide superior color rendering in the light output of these units—but this results in a significant increase in cost. Each color is controlled by an individual channel, and the luminaire includes red, red-orange, amber, green, cyan, blue, and indigo colored LEDs. An even more recent innovation in LED luminaires that is less cost prohibitive makes use of RGB-L (red, green, blue and lime) LEDs that also provide improved color rendering. Though it might be difficult to individually address each of these channels/colors to determine the correct proportions in intensity to produce a specific color, most of the latest generation light consoles allow designers to select a color by making reference to a specific gel number or through using a color picker that is very similar to what is found in a computer paint or graphic program like Adobe Photoshop. These light consoles automatically determine the proper combination of LED intensities to produce a given color. I will make a comparison of the spectral output of these LED systems in more detail in Chapter 5.

Red Shift/Amber Drift

Another effect that needs to be considered is the color of the light source itself. As stated earlier, different light sources have different color temperatures. Most color systems for the stage (filtering systems) are based on incandescent light sources that have a color temperature of around 3,250° K. This is fine when the lamp is operating at full capacity, but in most stage applications we like to dim the lights, which lowers the color temperature of the lamp—and the light output of the lamp shifts to producing a much larger proportion of red and yellow wavelengths of light. We call this effect **red shift** or **amber drift,** and it can have a dramatic impact on any colors and filters used with light sources that are run at lower intensity levels. Art directors in film and video need to be extremely conscious of color temperatures; for this reason they use special filters to correct color temperatures for a variety of situations. In fact, film productions usually run lamps at full intensity (hot) so that they don't have to contend with the effects of red shift.

COMPLEMENTARY TINT SYSTEM

Over time, designers have come to use several of the principles outlined throughout this chapter to produce fairly naturalistic lighting for a number of environments and stages. This is typically done through combining several light sources that strike a subject from different angles. The basic theory is generally referred to as **Complementary Tint Theory** and is often credited to

a pioneer in the field of stage lighting named Stanley McCandless. Most designers in the entertainment business simply call it the **McCandless System** or **McCandless Method** of stage lighting. While this system or variations of it were so widely adopted that theatres were even wired to accommodate its needs, McCandless himself suggested that this was only one way of producing effective lighting designs. In brief, McCandless felt that very naturalistic lighting could be produced if two lighting fixtures containing complementary colored tints were hung on opposing 45° angles from one another. The two lights are hung 45° to both the front and each side of the subject (splitting centerline) with a vertical angle of 45° for each light. Tinted pairs that form complementary colors with one another are then used to color the two spotlights. A pink light might be combined with another fixture that is gelled with a cyan tint, or an amber colored spotlight might be combined with a pale lavender unit as a second example of a complementary pair. The pair of lights form a **key/fill** relationship on each side of a subject's face, which aids in creating shadows and modeling while also mixing to a variation of white light on the central portion of the face. Figure 3.10 illustrates the mounting positions for a McCandless lighting system.

Figure 3.10 A McCandless hang for naturalistic lighting: two lighting instruments are gelled in complementary tints that are hung at 45° to either side of a subject along with a 45° vertical angle

PSYCHOLOGICAL AND PHYSIOLOGICAL EFFECTS OF COLOR

Color can be an extremely effective tool for creating an overall mood or emotional effect in an environment. This is primarily due to the effectiveness that it can have in shaping moods and other psychological responses of a viewer. After intensity, color is the next most likely element of a lighting design to shape the mood that will be produced through a given lighting condition. One of the most distinguishing ways of characterizing light is by its sense of warmth. Light that has an overall abundance of red, yellow, and orange wavelengths is said to be **warm,** while light that is dominated by blue, green, and lavender wavelengths is said to be **cool.** Warm and cool light will produce distinct psychological responses in most observers. Most people tend to associate warm colors with conditions of higher energy, tension, and excitement, while cool colors tend to generate a more peaceful and tranquil response. On the whole, there are fairly consistent emotional responses that can be observed in a viewer when we examine color associations and mood. For instance, red brings about arousal and draws our attention or focus. It also creates relatively strong responses and can be associated with emotions like passion, conflict, and anger. Yellow forms that area of the spectrum to which we are most sensitive and tends to be perceived overall as white light. Green tends to react poorly with skin tones and is associated with unnatural feelings. It also tends to provide an overall neutral response. Blue helps create the illusion of distance and is associated with tranquility and more peaceful emotions (particularly in tints or medium saturations). Finally, violet typically produces a more solemn or melancholy response.

Sidebar 3.3 PSYCHOLOGICAL RESPONSES TO COLOR

White   Typically used to enhance or enrich the colors of any object that it is lighting, white is a combination of all other colors. More importantly, we typically think of white light as actually being pale tints of the other colors. It, therefore, is frequently associated with positive emotions and softens the intensity and emotional response to the colors that the tints are associated with.

Red   Associated with feelings of warmth, passion, energy, and excitement, red can also elicit negative feelings of lust, evil, or aggression. It often gives the perception of causing objects to appear closer to us and can command our attention. It also has been shown to cause tension and to elevate our respiration and heart rates.

Pink   Often associated with femininity, pink is a color that is connected to feelings of warmth and sexuality. It is a pleasing color that is often used in comedic and other scenes that generate positive emotional responses.

Yellow   This color is thought to generate some of the strongest psychological responses; yellow is most often associated with positive feelings and an overall sense of optimism. It has also been known to elevate self-esteem and can be used to reflect a sense of confidence and optimism. However, too much of it can produce negative effects and responses such as visual fatigue and emotional outbreaks of frustration and anger.

Orange   Like yellow and red, orange is associated with feelings of warmth and passion. It is also often connected to feelings of safety, fun, and assurance. At times, it may even produce a sensual feeling.

Green   Often associated with balance and harmony, green is found in the middle of the spectrum. It can produce a tranquil, comfortable, and peaceful state. However, it can also be associated with negative feelings such as stagnation and boredom.

Blue   This color is associated with calmness and elicits peaceful or serene moods. It can suggest a more reflective attitude and can help resolve tensions. Its calming effect is often used to suggest darkness while visibility is still required on stage. Blue colored objects also have the tendency to appear more distant than they may actually be.

Violet   On the whole, violet produces restful, peaceful emotional responses. Though it can be associated with a calming effect, it can also be suggestive of a more mysterious or foreboding mood. It is often associated with the court or royalty as well as with spirituality.

Gray   Essentially a lack of color, gray frequently does not produce an emotional response. It is a neutral color that can suggest little emotion and as such can produce a depressing effect. It can also be used to tone down the emotional response/emotional effect of other colors.

Black	Black is frequently associated with darker emotions that may even be connected to a sense of evil. It is a lack of color and light, and as such can be associated with total absorption and darkness. It is often used to communicate feelings of mystery, oppression, and formalism.

We tend to have more positive responses to colors that aren't as strongly saturated. Pink produces a more pleasant association than red. A golden color can be associated with light sources that are based on our daily experience (sunlight, candlelight, or a table lamp) and is seen as natural, while a light with a strong orange or red color is more unnatural and can take on a greater symbolic interpretation—many times in a negative frame of reference such as in the implication of hell or anger. A medium blue color could be associated with romantic moonlight, while a deep blue might help create the mystery of a scene set near Count Dracula's crypt. Warm colors tend to attract our attention while cool colors tend to be submissive and draw a more neutral response. We choose to paint emergency vehicles red because of the attention-getting power of the red color. Understanding these properties allows a designer to use color to draw focus to particular elements of a scene. Another practical observation lies in the tendency of warm colors to advance or jump toward us while cool colors tend to recede into the background or distance. A look at a distant landscape horizon clearly illustrates this principle of distancing.

In the manufacturing and healthcare industries the overall color temperature of the light that illuminates a space is often used to modify the behavior of the occupants. Psychiatric hospitals incorporate lighting to create non-threatening environments for their patients, while hospital birthing rooms are often illuminated in warm incandescent lighting that suggests the warmth that you would find at home. Relief of anxiety, productivity, sense of contentment, and overall degree of comfort are all psychological feelings that have been shown to be correlated with the lighting of a given environment. Architects are working to create additional ways of incorporating daylight into building designs because it has been discovered that the number of hours of natural daylight exposure that we experience has an impact on our overall moods.

Color Contrast

Color can be relative. It is easy to compare a red colored light to a blue one to determine which of the two colors is warm or cool. However, a designer can make use of the relative warmth or coolness of any two colors to make a design statement. Is this blue cool in comparison to that blue? Is this pink warm compared to that pink? In fact, most colors will be warm when compared to some colors and cool when compared to others. We refer to these changes and relative comparisons of warmth and coolness as **color contrast.** What we acknowledge isn't so much the degree of color contrast (large or small) but that color contrast is simply present in a given scene. Designers can use this to their advantage in a number of ways. First, in a broad sense, color can be used to draw focus through simply placing a single object in a different colored light from everything else on stage. The eye has a natural tendency to be drawn to whatever is different in a given composition. A concert stage washed in red light with a single amber spotlight on the lead vocalist will bring attention to this performer. A room bathed in deep blue light with light-lavender moonlight streaming through the window will bring attention to the area lit by the window. Second, it is possible that a scene might work best in an overall single hue, but in order to make it more interesting and more modeled, some form of contrast will need to be added. By using variations of a basic hue where small differences in relative warmth or coolness are found, a designer can go a long way towards creating a scene that has believable overall coloring without necessarily using a distinctly warm versus cool color scheme. In going back to the example of the moonlight streaming through the window, it can be seen that variations of several distinctly cool colors will most likely produce a much more effective scene than simply picking warm and cool colors.

Adaptation and Afterimages

A final effect of color relates to two generally negative principles called **color adaptation** and **afterimages.** These occur when the eye has been overstimulated in some way. If the lighting remains unchanged for an extended period of time it is possible for color adaptation to become an issue. Fatigue may play upon the viewers' eyes or colors may appear to shift in hue and value. The effect is especially pronounced if there are strong color saturations in the lighting of a scene. For a night scene that is lit under predominantly blue lights, the blue cones of the eye will become desensitized and sluggish. If the scene is followed by a day scene that is lit under essentially white lighting, the day scene will often initially appear to be too gold or yellow in color. This is due to the fact that the red and green cones are fully sensitive while the blue ones aren't as reactive. For the second scene, the eye simply misses some of the blue light sensitivity that would normally balance the color to its normal white appearance. In time, the blue cones once again become fully functional and the gold quality will eventually fade away. Afterimages come about through a similar phenomenon in which the eyes remain stimulated even though the source of the stimulation has been removed. In this case, the cones will overcompensate once the initial image is removed—causing an afterimage to appear on a neutral surface. These images often appear to be colored in the complementary tint of the original image. You can create an experience that produces an afterimage by simply staring at a colored object for a period of 30–60 seconds, then shifting your sight to a neutral piece of paper or white wall. You will experience the temporary sensation of seeing a second object in the complementary hue of the original object. A similar effect can occur when a scene that is dominated by lighting with a strongly saturated color is immediately followed by a blackout. In this case, the audience quite commonly experiences an afterimage in the initial moments of the blackout. A designer may even make use of this phenomenon to add to the dramatic impact of the final image for a scene.

Practical Use of Color

One of the fundamental concepts that a lighting designer must ultimately master is the use of color in a lighting design. It generally takes time and experience before you learn to feel comfortable with making appropriate color assignments. The primary reason for this lies in the dramatic impact that color can have on our perception of a scene. Young designers often choose colors that are either too pastel, which adds little interest or contrast to a design, or so saturated that they significantly distort a project. More importantly, you need to play the middle of the road—by knowing when pastels are appropriate versus when saturated hues might be required to successfully light a project. Color choices need to always be made within the context of the project. What worked in one situation may not be successful at all in a similar situation; every choice comes down to a consideration of whether the color is appropriate for a specific image. There are a wealth of filter choices available for your color consideration—not only through the hundreds, if not thousands, of colors of gel that are available but also through the additional possibilities of color mixing devices such as those that are used in automated fixtures. Experimentation is the one technique that you can use to best come to grips with the color selection process. The use of a light lab or software simulations like CAST Software's wysiwyg, Design and Drafting's LD Assistant, or West Side Systems' Virtual Light Lab can greatly assist in this process. Even shining light through a sample from a swatch book to view the results of the filtered light on the skin, costume fabrics, and painted colors of a set rendering or paint elevation will give you some indication of how these materials will react under a specific filter. There are designers who like to peer through a filter to see its effect on sample materials, but I prefer to shine sunlight or an incandescent drafting lamp through a filter to observe how the light reacts to my skin, paint elevations, and costume swatches. If you use this method, try to be sure that the color temperature of the light source is compatible with that of the fixtures that you will be using in your design (i.e., don't use a florescent drafting lamp).

Although I discuss color considerations later in this book, and provide several specific design applications, there are a couple of practical considerations that I want to explore at this point in my discussion. As a general rule, lighting designers are typically trying to enhance the colors of a subject as they light a scene or object. This requires that—to some degree—the colors that are present in the costumes, scenery, or any other portions of the stage must also be present within the light that is being used to light a scene. If these colors aren't present, or if there is a high presence of the complement of these colors, the lighting might produce a dulling or graying effect on these objects. Keep in mind that the more lights and varied colors that you initiate on stage at any given time generally increases the amount of graying within a scene. However, you can overcompensate for this effect and cause some colors to be so enhanced that they might "zing" or become neon-like in their appearance. This, too, is usually considered an undesirable effect of choosing the wrong colors. Sidebar 3.4 provides a list of several practical issues that lighting designers tend to consider as they select colors for a given project. While these may tend to be true in most situations, be forewarned that none of these statements are absolute: in some cases, it might even be appropriate to use a completely conflicting technique for a given production. Stick to the principle that all design decisions are relative and must be made within the context of the given project. Also remember that your color decisions commonly change from one moment to another and that a stage composition doesn't remain static.

Sidebar 3.4 DESIGNER CONSIDERATIONS FOR COLOR AND LIGHT

1. Use colors that enhance the skin tones of the performers. For White performers these tend to be tints in the pink and lavender hues. Care must be taken when using amber gels because the green within the amber tends to emphasize the arteries that lie just below the skin's surface, which can produce an overall sickly

color on the performer. Green light should generally be avoided because of both its unnatural color and, once again, the effect that it has on the arteries of performers. Dark complexions such as those found in African Americans and performers from areas of the world such as India are generally enhanced by lavender tints, while colors with strong elements of red may give an unnatural glowing quality to the skin tones of these performers. The yellow tint in the complexions of many Asian performers will also react differently to color than other subjects and this, too, must be considered when choosing gels for a production or event. In projects where there is a constant mixture of individuals reflecting a diverse range of ethnic backgrounds, the best choices of color will reflect various tints that have a wide range of colored light.

2. In addition to the obvious effect of colored light on the skin tones of various ethnic groups, a designer should also consider the social effects of color on a given design. Color often represents different meanings from one society to another. For instance, in Western tradition black is a color often reserved for mourning, while in Eastern societies white is commonly associated with death. In Western society, social implications of color include examples like white light being associated with purity while red light is often associated with anger, passion, or even demonic events.

3. Any natural colors found in the environment should be enhanced through choosing lighting that reflects a spectral composition that augments these natural colors. Fabrics, paints, and other colors that are characteristic of the individual design areas like costume, props, or scenic pieces will look best if lit with similar colors. The principle is also true in architectural and display lighting where the product should be made to look its best through selecting colors that have an enhancing effect on the natural colors of the subject. In some cases, especially in the areas of theatrical design and themed environments, materials may be painted or colored with colors that can be purposefully modified by changing the color of the light that illuminates the material at any given time. With this technique, some design elements may be quite visible under one lighting condition while becoming hidden under another. Alternate wallpaper treatments can be masked or revealed by using this lighting technique.

4. Color can be used to mold an object or to increase its dimensionality by the use of progressively more saturated variations of a color in light sources that wrap around the subject from front to back. Colors from the front that are too saturated will distort an object.

5. Additive color mixing will have an increased effect as the angles between two separate light sources (with different colors) becomes less pronounced. In other words, there will be more surfaces that are commonly illuminated by both sources, resulting in a larger display of color mixing between the two colors on these surfaces.

6. In examining overall hues, keep in mind that warm colors tend to advance, while cool colors tend to recede, and warm colors can generally attract focus—although it needs to be understood that all colors must be considered on a relative basis. The illusion of distance on stage can be amplified by lighting downstage areas and objects with predominantly warm colors while the upstage areas and drops, cyc, etc., are lit primarily with cool colors.

7. With motivational lighting (light that is linked to an apparent light source), the color of the light needs to reflect the natural color properties of the source of illumination. For example, the light lavender of moonlight, the golden glow of a candle, the red glow of embers, or the warm amber of a late afternoon sun are all based on the color of each source of light.

8. Lighting color plays a dominant role in developing the mood and character for an environment or setting. Light airy moods are generally associated with warm colors, while somber moods tend to be associated with cool colors. The depiction of psychological energy can also be associated with color choices: warm colors are characteristic of more energetic feelings and tension while cool colors are more often associated with tranquility and more peaceful, reflective moments. The argument of using pink light for comedy comes out of these observations.

9. In many theatrical applications lighting forms the dominant manner of producing colored backgrounds for the stage. This is done through creating large washes of evenly colored light on large scenic surfaces like drops, a **cyclorama (cyc)** or **skydrop.** In this case, filter colors are chosen that can either mix a large range of colors (i.e., the primary colors) or will work together to amplify a given range of color that is found in the scenic elements of these backgrounds.

Even after discussing several general principles for color selection, the importance of experimentation needs to be re-emphasized in the process of working with color. Color can be unpredictable and there is no better way of gaining an understanding of the hidden properties of a gel than trying it out on a sample of the materials that will actually be illuminated. Many fabrics with colors such as navy blue and black are dyed with chemicals that contain hidden colors that aren't immediately apparent under white lighting conditions.

Another practical consideration to keep in mind is the relativity that exists in the color applications of lighting. What was an appropriate color choice for one setting or project might be completely wrong in another situation. To help designers sort through some of the effects that many gels might produce, most gel manufacturers provide a set of tables that suggest many applications for which a given color of gel might be appropriate. Finally, if worse comes to worse, gel is relatively cheap and can be changed fairly easily if you should decide that you have made the wrong choice. In fact, next to changing intensities, color is the most easily changed variable of the controllable qualities of light. The significance of color to the lighting's overall design is a major impact on any project; through time and experience you will learn how to control color and make it an effective element of your designs.

Sidebar 3.5 DESIGNER PROFILE

Mark Stanley

Credit: photo © Rosalie O'Connor Photography

Mark Stanley is best known for his dance lighting. He has been associated with many of America's premier dance companies and continues to actively light dance companies that include The New York City Ballet, Joffrey Ballet, San Francisco Ballet, and Boston Ballet, among others. His reputation has also led him to designing internationally for companies like the Royal Danish Ballet, Royal Ballet, London, the National Ballet of Canada, and the Stuttgart Ballet. While he has frequently designed for ballet, he has also designed for leading modern dance companies and choreographers like Susan Marshall, Pilobolus, Alvin Ailey Dance Theater, and David Gordon. He has also designed for opera and drama, with credits at venues that include the Paper Mill Playhouse, Kennedy Center, Radio City Music Hall, Long Wharf Theatre, and New York City Opera. He also heads the lighting program at Boston University.

Mark began his lighting training through earning a BA in Theatre from the College of William and Mary. His MFA is in Lighting Design from the University of Wisconsin, where he studied under the legendary Gilbert Hemsley. His interest in lighting dance is best recounted through his own words:

"Some of my earliest exposure to lighting design was in the dance world. Visiting companies like Nicholas Dance Theatre and Paul Taylor came to my undergrad school. It was something I connected with from the very beginning. During graduate school, and then through assisting Gilbert Hemsley, I was introduced to the world of opera and that became my primary area of focus early in my professional career. In 1986 I was offered the opportunity to work with the New York City Ballet and since that time dance has been a major component of my design work."

Like many other lighting designers, Mark works in other areas of lighting as well and says that while the proportions of his work change from year to year, at this point, dance lighting accounts for about 80% of what he does, with the other 20% being made up of opera, special events, and an occasional play or musical. More importantly Mark claims:

"There are no traditional areas of lighting anymore. Careers are made up of everything from lighting theatre to car shows, from opera to corporate events and cruise ships. The fundamentals are the same, even though some of the techniques might change. But the crossover is important."

To remain current, he suggests, "See as many productions and the work of other designers as possible. Read reviews. Explore ideas with other designers and try to work with as many new people as you can."

When asked about what additional training he had to do to cross over into dance lighting he replied:

"Every area of lighting has techniques and approaches that are unique, but it is all built on the same fundamentals. For lighting dance, an understanding of its history, the breadth of the form, the process and discipline of the dancers, and the vocabulary of the choreographers are all important. Basically, it's exposure and immersion in the art form, and getting your head wrapped around the idea of lighting abstract images and ideas that aren't grounded in a text."

Mark claims to have had a lot of great mentors along the way—starting with a TD at the Arlington, Virginia, Recreation Department back when he was only in the seventh grade. However, his big break came as a result of his association with Gilbert Hemsley:

"The single biggest influence on my career and me was Gilbert Hemsley—both as a teacher and professional designer whom I assisted. He not only opened doors, but opened my eyes and thinking in ways that were profound. His death was a great personal loss to me and to the theatre community. It was a tough way to get a break."

What Mark likes most about lighting dance is the challenge of creating lighting that moves through time and space in a graphic, abstract environment. "It's also great working with creating a complete idea from scratch with a choreographer rather than starting with an existing text or libretto." Lighting dance also often requires you to wear several hats:

"Many times you need to have production management skills, scenic design skills, and technical direction skills. Frequently you are the only designer on the production team and you need to think of more than just the lighting. It also requires you to conceive of an entire environment for the world of the dance."

Finally, dance lighting requires you to be focused on the critical components of the design: "By working in a non-text format, and generally in 30–40 minute periods of time, your design ideas must be concise and clear." What he likes least is that there is never enough time:

"The dance world works on such tight budgets and schedules that there is often little time to explore. You need to come to the table prepared and focused and there is rarely a chance for trying something really new or working through an idea or design choice."

He suggests the following as an essential rule for lighting in the dance discipline:

"Choose a single quality of light as the basis for your ideas and build layers. Don't try to do too much. Don't forget that even though there isn't a text to a dance, there is still a beginning, middle, and end, and that you have to help connect them to one another in your design."

FOR FURTHER READING

Bellman, Willard F. *Lighting the Stage: Art and Practice*. 3rd ed. Louisville, KY: Broadway Press, 2001.

DiLaura, David L., Kevin W. Houser, Richard G. Mistrick, and Gary R. Steffy. eds. *Illuminating Engineering Society–the Lighting Handbook Tenth Edition: Reference and Application*. New York: Illuminating Engineering Society, 2011.

Illuminating Engineering Society of North America. *IESNA Lighting Education 100 (Fundamental Level)*. New York: Illuminating Engineering Society of North America, 1993.

Illuminating Engineering Society of North America. *IESNA Lighting Education 150 (Intermediate Level)*. New York: Illuminating Engineering Society of North America, 1993.

Illuminating Engineering Society of North America. *IESNA Lighting Ready Reference*. 4th ed. New York: Illuminating Engineering Society of North America, 2003.

Palmer, Richard H. *The Lighting Art: The Aesthetics of Stage Lighting Design*. 2nd ed. Englewood Cliffs, NJ: Prentice Hall, 1994.

Warfel, William B. *The New Handbook of Stage Lighting Graphics*. New York: Drama Book Publishers, 1990.

Warfel, William B. and Walter R. Klappert. *Color Science for Lighting the Stage*. New Haven, CT: Yale University Press, 1981.

PART TWO

LIGHT:
THE TOOLS

CHAPTER 4

ELECTRICITY

DEVELOPING A BASIC understanding of electricity is essential to the success of any lighting designer. While the actual pulling of cable, wiring, and installation are often delegated to the electrics crews, a designer still needs to have an understanding of basic electrical theory, power distribution, electrical safety, and fundamental electrical calculations. This knowledge is essential for making the specifications that are required to complete a lighting project. More importantly, most lighting designers begin their careers working as **stage electricians** (the crew members who actually install and operate the lighting for a production) who use much of this material on a regular basis. This holds true whether the application is for a temporary installation such as for a stage or touring production or for a permanent lighting installation like a building, garden, or exhibit.

Due to electricity's potential for causing injuries and even death, it is imperative that proper safety procedures be taken throughout the installation and operation of any lighting design. A designer is responsible for the safety of not only the crews, but also the performers and audience as well. If a designer isn't present for the installation of a design, then the crew and **master electrician** (head of the electrics crew) are responsible for the proper installation of the equipment and safety of the theatre personnel and audience. In the case of permanent installations, the safety requirements become even more stringent to protect a building's occupants. These installations are guided by a number of safety codes as well as the requirement that all designs must be certified and installed by licensed professionals. While regulations may vary somewhat from municipality to municipality, the basis of most electrical standards and safety are found in the National Electric Code (NEC). All lighting specifiers and designers should have an understanding of those portions of the NEC that are directly applicable to their niche of the industry. In today's practices, many theatrical designers are being used as consultants on architectural projects; it is common for a designer to make design recommendations that are given to licensed electrical engineers who then work out the detailed specifications of a project. In architectural practices, the codes are strictly enforced and the designs and installations are always inspected by municipal authorities at various stages of a project's completion. Though theatrical lighting typically is not subject to inspections, stage electricians are still bound by various elements of the NEC and have a responsibility to use safe practices in order to protect themselves, other crew and performance personnel, and their audiences. In either case, it is important for designers to apply safe practices throughout their designs because they could be held liable for any decisions that fall outside the codes and common practices. One area that gets a bit sticky relates to the fact that lighting designers are frequently not present for the load-in of their shows—often their first appearance is the first focus call (typically because producers/organizations are not willing to pay the additional costs of lodging and per diem for bringing the lighting designer in before this point). This means that a designer cannot monitor whether a plot has been installed safely and correctly. Because of this, many designers now place liability disclaimers on their light plots. Making sure that you are covered by a company's liability coverage or having your own liability insurance policy is another way to cover yourself if, heaven forbid, an accident should happen.

This chapter is not meant to present a complete guide to electricity; you should refer to the books listed in the Further Reading portion of this chapter for more in-depth information. More importantly, this chapter is an introduction to those elements of electrical theory that are most applicable to a lighting designer's needs. I begin with an introduction to general electrical theory and the means by which we measure electricity and relate these elements to one another. I then present information related to how power is created and distributed, and go on to describe basic electrical equipment. Finally, I deal with several applications that are fairly common to stage electrics as well as provide some troubleshooting and safety guidelines for working as a stage electrician.

Sidebar 4.1 DESIGNER PROFILE

John Martin

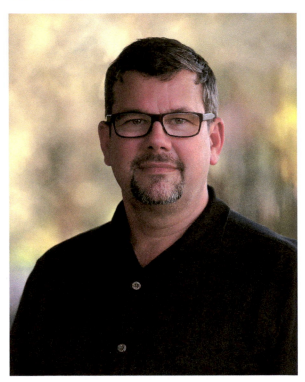

Credit: photo courtesy Ralph Stier

John Martin's involvement in lighting spans a variety of credits in both theatrical events and themed venues. In the past 10 years his focus has been architectural lighting design. At a young age he focused his creative interests in lighting and has been happy ever since. John's formal education includes a BA from University of California, Irvine, and a MFA from the University of California, San Diego, the first generally in drama and the latter specifically in theatrical lighting design. Shortly after finishing graduate school he became involved in environmental themed projects. This experience led to his work in architectural lighting. Currently, he is an Associate Principal for KGM Architectural Lighting where he continues to design a variety of projects.

When John speaks of education he relates:

"I believe that theatre training programs share a good deal with what used to be called a "liberal arts" education—learning to think and articulate through the lens of literature. It creates a new kind of businessperson, one that is capable of collaborating with others to bring vision to reality. Theatre taught me how to make things: start with the core idea in the script, overcome restraints of budget, time, and space, and culminate with an aesthetic response that goes beyond the collection of the individual parts."

A big break following grad school was joining a World Expo team (similar to a World's Fair) in South Korea. It was a short seven weeks leading up to the opening. Next was a small park in Japan where he spent months on the construction site translating paper designs into the final realized product. During this time, he received an NEA/TCG Young Designer's Fellowship. This exposed him to a whole new set of mentors and experiences by traveling throughout the United States, with stops in South America and the United Kingdom. Upon completing the grant, a friend invited him to interview for a position with Universal Studios' creative team. For more than three years John worked on Orlando's Islands of Adventure park—including the exterior lighting for Port of Entry and Marvel's Super Hero Island. The park won a Thea Award from the Themed Entertainment Association.

Commenting on such a variety of work, he advises young designers: "Networking, networking, networking. This is a business of people making things. Find the people that share your interests and develop with them. Be open to the possibilities that come up and seize them with the best energy possible." He chooses not to point to a single event or individual who helped him. Instead, he states that there were many generous people who helped him out along the way and that each project presented the introductions needed to branch out into different areas of the industry.

An important aspect of both themed and architectural lighting is the extended timeline of a project. While a theatrical production may take one to three months of involvement, a themed or architectural project will typically take one to three years to complete (or more). Because of this, projects may go through several different designers before they are finally realized: "Core ideas and presentation are very important in these designs—napkin sketches have their place in the design process but articulated narratives and color renderings are much more successful for getting the funding for a project." On the other hand, one of the frustrations of working in these areas is that "with the longer time frames of these jobs, the project may be completely designed and never get built—this makes putting one's gusto into the next job all the harder." He also notes that the contracting community is not typically sensitive to the lighting needs of a project. This is in stark contrast to a technical theatre staff.

Regardless of what he is lighting, John's most important advice is to make something compelling and relevant: "No matter what project you light, two things are consistent—collaborating with a client and taking fixed resources and making them into something aesthetic." He also speaks of several important lifestyle choices that have influenced his career:

> "The earlier part of my career had a good deal of exciting travel. Once I had a family I sought out other options. Architectural work fits well with my choice to spend time with my family. There is a normalcy to the job and there are many opportunities to collaborate. I work in a large office and cannot think of any other time in my past where there have been 20 lighting designers in one room that can go home to their own beds at night. The collegiate atmosphere is very fulfilling, sharing ideas with younger designers trained in architecture and interior design."

His final recommendations are: "Develop a healthy passion. Lighting is my first love but so are compelling spaces and life partners. Community comes in many forms. We should always focus on the global good and pay it forward."

BASICS OF ELECTRICITY

Most theories of electricity refer to the concept of creating an electrical flow of electrons from one place to another. This flow begins at the atomic level and can result in a relative electron flow through both small and great distances. The following sections address many of the issues relating to the fundamental qualities and nature of electricity.

Atomic Theory

Most scientists recognize the concept of **particle theory,** in which all substances are made up of small particles called **atoms.** These, in turn, are made up of even smaller particles that are associated with given charges. **Protons** carrying a positive charge are found in the central cluster (**nucleus**) of the atom along with neutrally charged particles called **neutrons.** Orbiting this cluster are additional particles called **electrons** that carry negative charges. The most basic form of any material is called an **element** and can be identified through a specific atomic structure as defined by the number of protons that are contained in each atom. Most atoms have an overall neutral charge and contain the same number of protons and electrons. The familiar model of the solar system, with the sun at its center and a number of orbiting planets, is a good model for the basic concept of an atom. As atoms become more complex, the numbers of protons and electrons increase, and the electrons shift to positions (or "energy shells") that are farther away from the nucleus and contain progressively more and more electrons. Each energy shell becomes progressively more stable as additional electrons continue to fill its empty orbital or shell positions. Materials with a completely filled outer shell are the most stable materials found in nature. If an energy shell only has one or two electrons in its outermost shell it can become unstable, and these electrons might be dislodged or shared between adjoining atoms that have a similar structure.

Electrical Potential

Inducing electrons to form an electron flow may be achieved through a number of different means, but what is characteristic to all and the first requirement of electron flow is the fact that an excess of electrons or charge is introduced between two different points or locations. This gathering of electrons or electrical charge is known as **electrical potential.** All forces in nature work to reach a neutral level of energy, or what scientists often call a "state of equilibrium" in which all forces are in balance. An example of this principle would be that (given enough time) all mountains will erode as valleys fill in to create flat planes. Another example is that if a ball is released from the top of one of two adjoining hills, it will roll and come to rest at some point in the lowest area between the higher elevations. Electrical charges also strive to reach a state of equilibrium through a basic principle: electrons always try to create a neutrally charged environment. This becomes the driving force in creating electrical flow. How might excess electrical charge be created? Storm clouds could cause a gathering of electrons that are discharged as lightning; a battery can provide electrical potential through chemical reactions; and a generator can convert a source of energy (such as gas) and motion into electrical potential.

A second requirement for electrical flow is that a path must be established between those points where an excess of electrical potential exists and the point of neutrality. If a path doesn't exist, there will be no electrical flow unless the potential difference becomes so great that the electricity actually jumps from one place to another. Lightning is an example where electricity literally jumps from cloud to cloud or from a cloud to the ground. More commonly, we create electrical pathways by introducing materials and objects like wires into an electrical system. If a wire breaks at any point in an electrical system, the electricity will fail to complete its journey and the task of turning on lights, operating a motor, or heating a toaster cannot be achieved. While some scientists believe that electrical flow actually represents a shifting of electrons from atom to atom along these paths, most believe that the electrons nudge one another, which displaces the energy without actually shifting electrons from one atom to another. This is similar to the chain reaction that might occur when a person near the back of a line shoves the person directly in front of them, who then falls into the person in front of them, and so on progressively down the line. The waveforms that are created through this progressive movement of electrons are quite long and form a particular type of **electromagnetic radiation** or energy.

Conductors and Insulators

Wires are made of metals, which are generally very good **conductors** of electricity because they readily allow electrons to flow through them. Virtually all materials will conduct electricity if you apply enough power to them, even the human body: the results may not be pleasant but the fact remains that you can still get an electrical flow to pass through nearly any material. One of my most vivid memories as a teenager includes a demonstration in which a youth leader had 20 of us stand in a circle and instructed us to tightly hold each other's hands. At one point the leader broke into the circle and gave the teen on each side of him a single lead from a 12-volt car battery. One lead was conveniently equipped with a switch, and the two teens holding the leads from the battery were instructed not to touch one another. As one might imagine, when the leader pressed the switch we all felt the effects of electricity passing through our bodies until someone had the good sense to let go. A human chain became the wire for our leader's circuit, and when that one person let go, the human wire failed along with the electrical force that was traveling through it. **Do not try this demonstration**: with what we now know about shocks and heart rhythms,

and how we are now mindful of anything that could possibly be construed as abusive behavior, you would be setting yourself up for a lawsuit. What's important is what the demonstration taught me about electrical flow.

Just as all materials demonstrate some form of conductivity, they also display some form of **resistance** to electrical flow. In this case, there are characteristics of a material's composition that form a barrier to electrical flow. If a material has an overall high resistance to electrical flow we refer to it as an **insulator.** We cover wires with insulation to prevent accidental contact between the individual conductors and any other objects. The reason some materials are better insulators than others lies in their atomic structures, which cause them to be more resistant to electron movement.

As a rule, metals form the best conductors. Gold and silver provide the least amount of resistance and are used in high-quality wiring components like those found in critical applications such as in the space program and high-end audio/video industries. These metals are too expensive for most general purposes, so other metals like copper and aluminum have become the most popular conductors for common wiring practices. Popular insulators that have been used in the electrical market include rubber, nylon, porcelain, Bakelite, and asbestos. Asbestos and Balelite are no longer used due to their potential for causing cancer and other toxic risks, although they can still be found on occasion in older equipment that was manufactured prior to the 1980s. If you run into any equipment with asbestos you should take extreme care to protect yourself and others from inhaling the fibers and dust that are associated with this material. In all practicality, these units should be either retrofitted or retired.

GROUNDING

Electricity, like any other form of energy, constantly strives to reach the lowest energy level possible. For all practical purposes this is the natural surface of the earth, which corresponds to a zero-voltage potential. More commonly we refer to this as the earth or absolute **ground** and all electricity strives to flow to it. One of the most common accidents connected with electricity results from an accidental path being provided for an electrical flow from one place to another. This may happen between areas of high and low potential or the actual earth ground itself. A short-circuit, an electrical shock, or even a lightning strike are all results of instances where electricity was presented with a pathway to a lower electrical potential. All electricity attempts to flow towards the ground, and when you grab a live wire, the shock that you receive is simply due to your body becoming the pathway that the electricity uses to flow to the ground. If this happens in buildings it can produce heat and sparks that might produce a fire.

In order to protect ourselves, electrical codes now insist that we provide a special safety path or wire that forms a path of least resistance for any electrical potential that may be let loose within an electrical device. If for some reason a device becomes electrically unstable, this path provides for the safe conduction of electricity away from the device and the user, and in turn helps to prevent shocks and fires from occurring. This emergency path is called the **ground** and will always connect an electrical device to an actual earth ground in some way. The grounding device with which you are most likely familiar is the third prong that is common to most wall outlets and appliances that have appeared over the last 40 or 50 years. This third prong is connected to a wire that extends from the device back through all the branch circuits to the main circuit box of a building. At the circuit box, the wire is joined with all the other grounding wires of the building, which are ultimately connected to a heavier wire that leads to a stake or rod that is driven into the actual ground outside of the building. Most wires associated with a grounding function can be quickly identified by color: these wires' insulation is color-coded green or the wire is left bare. Most ground wires in the United States are identified with green insulation, but large-capacity ground wires will often have black insulation with green tape applied near their ends. Grounding hardware (such as screws) is also often colored green as a means of identification. These pathways provide a safe electrical service for the occupants of a building. At this time, virtually every electrical project imaginable must provide grounding in order to comply with current electrical codes and regulations. Even in theatrical practices, where codes have been lax, most equipment is now provided with grounding features, and stage electricians need to make every effort possible to provide grounding for every situation.

Units of Measurement and Essential Formulas

A system of measurements has been developed as a way of both quantifying and describing specific characteristics of a circuit while also allowing electricians to make comparisons between circuits. These characteristics may be measured through a variety of meters and can be related to one another through several different formulas. The following sections describe several of these components and then relate them to one another through two different formulas.

Units of Measure

VOLTAGE (E) The first measurement that we use to describe electricity refers to a measurement of the potential difference that exists between two different points. This is known as **voltage (E)**

and is measured through a unit known as a **volt**. We may also refer to voltage as electromotive force (EMF), which is nothing more than a measurement of the energy difference between electrons at one location and electrons at another. Typical voltages with which we are quite familiar are the 12-volt systems in our cars, the 1.5-volt batteries that are common to handheld devices like flashlights and personal CD/MP3 players, and the 120-volt systems that power most of our households.

AMPERAGE (I) The second measurement of electrical flow refers to the rate of electrons flowing through a point at any given time. This is called **amperage (I),** and its unit of measurement is the **ampere**. Most wiring devices and appliances carry product warnings that refer to their electrical capacity. This is simply a statement that specifies either how much amperage a device may draw or the maximum amperage that the device may safely conduct. If a user exceeds these specifications, problems such as heated wires, short-circuits, and ultimately fires can develop. The practice of plugging too many appliances into a household extension cord is a common example of this type of safety problem. The basic rule is to never exceed the amperage specifications of a device.

RESISTANCE (R) All materials have an ability to either conduct or resist electrical flow. While some materials such as metals have a low resistance and become conductors, others resist electrical flow and are known as insulators. The basic measurement of electrical resistance **(R)** is measured in ohms (Ω) or kilo-ohms (1,000 ohms). A large-diameter wire will conduct more electrons per unit time than a smaller diameter wire—in much the same way an interstate with four lanes will carry a larger volume of cars than a two-lane highway. Just as in traffic, if you suddenly try to reduce the size of a wire or number of lanes, you create problems as more traffic tries to get through a point than intended for a given location.

POWER (P) While I have provided several ways in which we can describe an electrical circuit, I haven't talked about the concept of how the electromotive force can be used to perform a task for us. How does this electromotive force accomplish the task? How can we determine if one manner is more efficient than another? How does energy change from electrical potential to performing a practical task? This is what physicists would refer to as "work." The most common manner of relating how an electrical force is performing work or consuming power is through a measurement known as the **watt.** The watt is simply a measurement of the rate of doing work and can be thought of in terms of how much power a task might be consuming. Many appliances are rated in watts, which simply refers to how much energy the device translates from electricity to some other form of energy. The most common everyday example of this is in the varying wattages of light bulbs. The higher the wattage, the more light that a lamp will produce, but with a side effect of also consuming more power.

Power Formula (West Virginia) and Ohm's Law

In order to relate each of these components of electricity to one another we have several essential laws or formulas that correlate each measurement to the others. The most common law is known as the **Power Formula** and relates the power (P) or wattage to the voltage (E) and amperage (I). If you can determine two of the three variables you can easily calculate the final unknown. Many designers and electricians also use a variation of this formula, which they refer to as the **West Virginia Formula** due to the way in which its units are expressed in regard to one another. Both formulas follow:

Power Formula	West Virginia
Power = Amperage × Voltage	Wattage = Voltage × Amperage
$P = I \times E$	$W = V \times A$

A second popular formula relates the resistance of a circuit to the remaining measurements. This relationship is represented by **Ohm's Law** and is indicated here:

Ohm's Law
$$I = E / R$$
Amperage = Voltage / Resistance
$$A = V / R$$

By using various combinations of these two formulas, all of the components of an electrical circuit can be related to one another.

Common Electrician Calculations

The most practical use of these formulas is in making load determinations for any circuits that are used in a lighting application. As stated earlier, a primary safety consideration in an electrical circuit is to not overload or exceed the rated capacity of any electrical device. If a wire is rated for 100 amps then you cannot safely extend this to incorporate a load of 110 amps. If a lighting fixture's safety label says not to exceed a 60-watt lamp, then placing a 75-watt lamp within the fixture could present

a fire hazard. The simplest use of this determination is to add up the wattages of all the lamps or devices contained in a circuit and make sure that the combined wattage does not exceed the rated wattage of the circuit. A circuit containing three 20-watt lamps and four 100-watt lamps has a total load of 460 watts: (3 × 20) + (4 × 100). If a circuit is rated for 2,400 watts and you were asked how many 500-watt lamps it could safely support, you would simply divide 2,400 by 500 to determine the number of lamps. In this case, the result is 4.8 lamps, or four lamps. You should always round the number of lamps downward since rounding up will always create an overloaded condition.

FUNDAMENTAL CIRCUITS

Electricity does not occur unless there is an energy flow. A stored potential is of no use unless we can set the electrons into motion to create work. In order for the flow to occur we must provide three elements: first, an area where an excess charge or potential is stored or created; second, an area of lower potential that the excess energy will seek; and third, a device or material that connects the two areas by creating a pathway for the electrical flow. Most importantly, since electricity attempts to create a stable or neutral condition, the pathway must also form a return path back to the source. An electrical device requires both a connection that supplies the excess electrical flow and a second one that forms a return path back to the source. Through all of this, a complete circle is created for the electron flow, which we refer to as a basic electrical **circuit.** If you remove any one of these elements you interrupt the flow of the electrons and there will be no electricity. The mechanism with which we are most familiar for conducting electricity is the **wire,** and if a wire becomes broken at any point there will be no electrical flow.

Series Circuits

While I have already described a fundamental circuit, most circuits are more complex than this. We use a circuit to identify how components are connected to one another, while also tracing the electrical path from the source through the circuit and back again. There are essentially only two variations of a basic electrical circuit, regardless of how complex the individual wiring or number and type of devices that it might contain. These are the series and parallel circuits. A **series circuit** simply connects the leads of each device together in a daisy-chain fashion that stretches between the leads of a power source. Figure 4.1a illustrates a series circuit containing seven lamps. Because all lamps in a series circuit share the power equally, there are two side effects that might be considered undesirable. First, if a single lamp burns out, the pathway for the electricity is interrupted for all the lamps and they all go out. Second, assuming that all the lamps are the same wattage, as more lamps are added to the circuit, the lamps will glow equally bright but become progressively dimmer as the additional lamps are introduced to the circuit. A common example of a series circuit is found in the miniature lights that we use during the holidays. These can cause all sorts of frustration when a single lamp's failure renders a whole string inoperable. While these strings are designed to plug into a wall outlet of 120 volts, each individual lamp is only rated for 1–3 volts, which is why there are usually 50–150 of them in a given string. If you were to shorten the length of the string from the manufactured 100 lamps to 50 you would probably discover that the lamps would glow about twice as bright as normal—until they burned out from the excessive voltage. They might even burst from the initial surge of power.

It is extremely important to ensure that an electrical device is connected to a power source that matches its designed voltage requirements—especially considering the fact that different areas of the world use different operating voltages. An appliance that is designed

Figure 4.1a Circuit variations. a. A series circuit. If the circuit is broken at any point (including a lamp burnout), all the lamps go out.

Figure 4.1b A parallel circuit. All lamps remain on except the affected lamp when there is a burnout because an electrical pathway is kept available.

to work on the 120-volt United States standard will be damaged or destroyed if connected to the 240-volt service that is typical throughout much of Europe. While most equipment is rated for a single voltage, some gear, such as many of the moving lights used on world tours, is equipped with switches or other mechanisms that permit the voltage to be matched to a particular electrical service.

Parallel Circuits

The second type of circuit is the **parallel circuit,** illustrated in Figure 4.1b. The parallel circuit differs from a series circuit in that each device is wired directly to the power source, which provides two advantages. First, since each device has a direct pathway to the power source, the power flow can continue independently of any other device in a circuit. If any one of the lamps were to go out or be removed from a parallel circuit, the remaining lamps would continue to burn unaffected. A second advantage is that each device has access to the full power supply so that the lamps will glow at full intensity regardless of the number of lamps in the circuit at any given time. The parallel circuit forms the primary type of circuit that we use in most lighting applications. A typical application of the parallel circuit is found in the wiring of multiple lighting fixtures. All of the lights burn equally bright, and as one light burns out the remaining fixtures remain lit at the same brightness that they've always had. In practice, many circuits make use of both parallel and series elements. While all of the light fixtures in the previous example may have been wired in parallel, they are typically under the control of a single switch. The switch is located at a place in the circuit that allows the power to be cut off from all the fixtures, therefore becoming a series element in this circuit. Note that the switch should also be located along the segment of the wiring that provides power to the circuit as opposed to being along the return path. While it would still work (you've still interrupted the

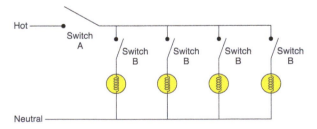

Figure 4.2 The effect of switch location on combination circuits: Switch A (wired in series) will control all of the lamps, while any switch labeled B (wired in parallel) will control only the lamp that is wired to that part of the branch circuit as long as Switch A is also closed. Fuses and circuit breakers are frequently placed in the location of Switch A.

power flow), for obvious reasons, it is safer to place switching devices near the source of the power. If an electrician wanted to control one group of lights in the above circuit separately, they would only have to add a switch to that portion of the circuit. We refer to these circuits as **combination circuits.** Figure 4.2 illustrates a combination circuit, in which all the lamps are under the influence of Switch A while they are also individually controlled using the B switches. Protective electrical devices like fuses and circuit breakers should also be located near the power source and are wired as series components in most electrical circuits.

DIRECT CURRENT VERSUS ALTERNATING CURRENT

Electrical power may be produced in a variety of manners. It can be created by rubbing surfaces together (static electric), sun activity (photoelectric), chemical reactions (batteries), or by moving wires through magnetic fields (electromagnetism). Each of these and other types of electrical power production can be measured using the properties that were discussed earlier.

Direct Current (DC)

We refer to power production as comprising two different forms of voltage. In the first type, **direct current (DC)**, the voltage remains constant through time. A device such as a battery produces electricity with a voltage that remains steady and relatively constant—although over time the voltage will gradually drop as a battery's life weakens. DC power is produced by relatively inefficient methods and cannot be transported over great distances due to voltage drops and wire resistance, which has led to it becoming a very limited power source in contemporary society. It is also much easier to convert **alternating current (AC)** to DC power through electronic components like diodes than to convert DC power to AC power (see the next section for a definition of AC). The benefit of DC power lies in its portability for personal devices that can make use of batteries. However, battery life is always a factor—even when considering rechargeable batteries. It's fascinating to note the interest that hybrid and electric cars are creating in the auto industry as batteries get smaller/more efficient and gas prices increase while the ranges of these cars becomes greater.

Alternating Current (AC) and Power Generation

The most important means of electrical power creation is through **generators** and **electromagnetism.** A generator is nothing more than a device that allows mechanical motion to be transferred into electrical potential or power. Whether a power plant is nuclear, hydro-electric, or steam based doesn't really matter. What is common to each is that a force is created by elements like water or steam that pass through a turbine, which translates the spinning motion to a generator, which converts the force into electrical power. A generator functions in much the same way as an AC motor—with the exception that the motor translates the electrical impulses back into mechanical motion and energy.

Generators operate on the principle that you can produce a current in a wire by moving that wire through a magnetic field. The orientation of the wire within the magnetic field becomes an important element in determining both the direction and magnitude of any current that is created or **induced** in the wire. The basic action simply results from the tendency of electrons to be attracted or repelled by the two poles of a magnetic field. In a basic generator we take a wire and form it into a coil, which is then rotated around a central axis (**armature**) that extends through the associated magnetic field. If the armature is rotated to an orientation that coincides with the coil being closest to the poles of the magnetic field, the electrons will be attracted to one end of the coil while being repelled by the opposite side of the coil. If the coil is rotated through half a revolution, the electrons would be acted on by the magnetic force in the same manner, but since the coil is now reversed, the relative charges now accumulate in the opposite manner as found in the earlier position. In this way the electrons have moved the same amount but in the opposite direction from the first point. As the armature is rotated, the movement of the electrons shifts from a maximum potential in one direction to a maximum potential in the opposite direction at these two points within the spin or cycle. As the armature continues to complete a full rotation we are brought back to the same position as when we began and a maximum flow of electrons shift to the initial direction. Furthermore, at the points that coincide with a quarter turn, the electrons come to a point where they are under an equal influence from both poles of the magnetic field, which results in a condition where there is no net movement of electrons from one side of the coil to the other. Between these points, electrons will slowly either increase or decrease their flow and collection to one of the two sides of the coil, depending on the relative position of the coil in the magnetic field.

Alternating Current (AC)

A single revolution of a generator will produce a variety of voltages that begin with a maximum voltage in one direction that gradually decreases to zero at the 90° orientation, then once again builds to a maximum potential in the opposite direction at the 180° point of rotation, then decreases back to zero at the 270° interval,

Figure 4.3 DC voltage compared with AC voltage: note how DC voltage remains constant over time, while AC voltage changes not only in level but also in relative direction of flow over time

and finally increases once again to a maximum as the rotation comes to a complete revolution of 360°. A single rotation or revolution of a generator is typically called a **cycle,** and the type of electricity that is produced in this manner is commonly known as AC because of both the varying direction and voltage associated with it. In order to make power generation more efficient we increase the size of the coils to include miles of wire and spin the armature through many revolutions per second. In the United States the standard for power generation is 60 cycles per second, meaning that the armature and associated voltages are undergoing changes and revolutions 60 times every second. Figure 4.3 illustrates these changing voltages at various orientations in an armature's revolution.

Phases

In AC wiring, the wire that runs from the power source is called the **hot wire** because it is providing the energy to the circuit, while the wire that provides the return path is termed the **neutral**. To make power production more efficient we generally wind three identical yet separate coils on an armature of a generator so that in a single revolution we can provide three times the power production of a single coiled generator. All three coils will be oriented slightly differently on the armature so that each produces its maximum and minimum associated voltages at points in the revolution that are slightly skewed from one another. Each of these separate power sources or hot wires are known as a **phase**, and together they form a type of electrical service that we typically call **three-phase power (3ϕ)**. Each phase lags slightly behind the other phases but produces full-strength power, as illustrated in Figure 4.4.

Transformers

In the early days of commercial power, electricity was provided through DC services and could not travel over long distances because of its relatively low voltage. It

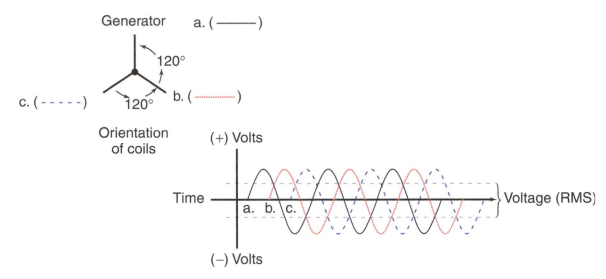

Figure 4.4 Three-phase power generation: A three-phase generator places three separate coils and power taps on the same armature of a generator, each oriented 120° from one another. By using the offset orientation, each of the three generated currents/voltages produced through a cycle will be at a different point in the rotation at any given time and therefore at a different voltage as well. The result is that three separate voltages can be drawn from a single generator and a resultant overall higher average voltage (208 voltage RMS) is produced.

was too difficult to raise the voltage to a point where it could be easily transported from one location to another. However, with the development of AC power, it was discovered that with sufficient voltage increases, electricity could be distributed over long distances with little effort. This set the stage for the emergence of AC power for electrical transmission because its voltage could be easily regulated due to its electromagnetic nature. In short time, the standard for distributing commercial power quickly shifted to AC. The importance of alternating power lies in the fact that it contains rapidly moving electrons that can be used to modify the voltage of a current through simply making use of electromagnetic principles. The devices that we use to regulate AC voltage are called **transformers** and we use them to either increase or decrease the voltage of a given circuit.

Transformers work in much the same manner and principles of electromagnetism as a generator does. In the case of a transformer, two or more coils are wrapped around a ferrous (iron) metal core. The core is critical because of its ability to take on magnetism. The two coils are electrically insulated from one another and lead to separate circuits. If AC power is provided to one of the coils, the pulsating energy of the moving electrons can create a reaction that produces a pulsating magnetic field that corresponds to the strength or voltage of the AC power. This pulsating magnetic field then influences the second coil in such a way that an electrical current and corresponding voltage are produced in it as well.

This is an **induced current.** More importantly, the strengths of the two currents are proportional to one another and are directly related to the relative number of turnings that are found in each coil. The coil that is associated with the supply of electrical power is called the **primary coil,** while the coil associated with the induced current is the **secondary coil.** If a primary coil has fewer windings than the secondary coil, the voltage will be increased, or stepped up, and we call the transformer a **step-up transformer.** Conversely, a **step-down transformer** has more windings on the primary coil than the secondary, and the voltage is reduced or stepped down. In the United States, we make use of a number of transformers to help distribute power from a power plant to customers. While most of our appliances are designed for 120-volt operation, the voltage of the power that is provided to us actually changes several times as it makes its way to our homes and businesses from a power-generation plant. In other countries many appliances are designed to operate on a 240-volt (rather than 120-volt) standard. Also, while our generators in the United States create power based on a 60 cycles/second standard, other countries have other standards, such as 50 cycles/second power, which is common in South America and Europe.

POWER DISTRIBUTION

The whole networked system of wiring that delivers power from a generating plant to a customer is referred to as the **power grid.** In the United States, we have grown so accustomed to the flawless performance of our power grid that we tend to take its operation for granted. When we experienced a widespread blackout of the entire Northeast during the summer of 2003 it caused major disruptions in our activities for a day or two before normal conditions were once again restored. I experienced this blackout: modern conveniences like traffic lights, gas pumps, and refrigeration were just a few of the necessities that failed for a day or so while we were out of power.

At a typical power plant in the United States the initial voltage of the power produced at a generator is on the order of several thousand volts (actual voltages here and across the power grid frequently vary from utility to utility). Immediately outside of most power stations you will find a large metal structure called the **transmission substation,** which is composed of heavy metal cables, insulators, and mast-like structures. A principal component of these structures is a number of step-up transformers that boost the voltage up to a point where it can be easily transmitted or conducted over long distances—this voltage can be as high as 155,000 to 765,000 volts. The electricity is then fed to **transmission lines** that are used to carry the power across the countryside and over long distances. The transmission towers that carry this power are generally found in more remote locations; they contain three separate wires, each corresponding to one of the three power phases (hot wires) created by the generators. Often, we refer to each of these hot wires or phases as **legs.** It should be obvious that these lines are very dangerous and that you should stay clear of them. We generally consider them to be unsafe in populated areas. Because of this, these lines will terminate at a second substation just outside of a populated area where the voltage is stepped down by transformers to voltages that are still high but not as threatening to a neighborhood. At this point **subtransmission lines** may distribute the power to smaller distribution stations that send power to a couple of central locations before stepping the power down even more before going into specific neighborhoods. Most of these voltages are typically less than 10,000 volts, with the most common being on the order of 7,200 volts. Additional equipment at these substations helps regulate the voltage and might also allow the power to be split up or distributed to several different locations. These lines will then lead to additional substations where the voltage is once again stepped down, to something on the order of 500–750 volts. These lines can be observed on the typical utility or power poles that you normally see along a roadway or street. These, too, carry three wires that represent each phase of the power. Many contemporary communities bury these cables as opposed to distributing the power through overhead wires. Finally, one last transformer steps the voltage down to the 120- or 240-volt standard that we use in our households. These final transformers are the cylinder-shaped devices that are mounted on utility poles or, in the case of underground wiring, the green metal vaults that are sprinkled throughout a neighborhood. Each transformer will generally service two or three buildings and will have several wires leading from it to each property. A residential or small commercial service will provide two of the three phases of power to an individual building, while other buildings will be provided with two phases from other combinations of the three phase power. A device that breaks either one or two phases off of a three-phase service is called a **tap.** A commercial property that has more demanding power needs will often be provided with all three phases of power and might also have increased service voltages. Transformers within the building can then be used to regulate the power and step it down as required. You can often see many of these transformers near the service entrances of schools and commercial buildings.

Electrical Services

Electrical power can be provided to a customer in one of several configurations. The actual configuration or **service** is dependent on the number of wires that are brought into a building at the **service entrance.** The electric meter is provided at the service entrance and is the point at which the responsibility for the electricity and electrical equipment shifts from the utility company to a customer. An electrical service is specified by the maximum capacity that it can handle, which is typically expressed in amps. In homes of the 1940s and 1950s it was common to have an electrical service of only 75–100 amps. The service for the home that I built only a few years ago has a 200-amp service, illustrating how contemporary homes demand much more power. Services that are provided in a theatre or commercial building typically run on the order of 400–800 amps and can actually run considerably higher. In each power configuration, the electrical distribution is based primarily on the number of legs of power brought into the building, regardless of service capacity. Several typical service arrangements are 150 amp single-phase, 200 amp single-phase, 100 amp three-phase, and 400 amp three-phase. The service may also be expressed according to voltage: 120/240-volt, single-phase, three-wire; 120/208-volt, three-phase, four-wire; or 277/480-volt, three-phase, four-wire.

As a shorthand method of indicating phase, we may also use the Greek letter ϕ to indicate power phases. This might be used to indicate specific legs of power (e.g., Aϕ, Bϕ, or Cϕ) or it could be expanded to describe the particular service (i.e., 120/240-volt–3ϕ). It is important to note that the voltage may change across different legs of power and that it will also vary to some degree from one service type to another. Figure 4.5 illustrates several service configurations and their associated voltages. In order to provide a safe circuit, an independent grounding system and wire should also be included in each of these service arrangements. The service can often be identified by the number and type of wires leading into a building from a transformer. Any insulated wires are usually the hot wires, while the neutral is often the metal cable that is used to support the hot cables. The neutral also commonly terminates at or near the

a. Two-wire system (service)

Figure 4.5a Electrical service configurations. a. This form of power distribution provides a single hot wire to a customer and was characteristic of residential distribution prior to around 1950. A ground is added as an additional element of each circuit but is independent from the actual distribution system.

b. Three-wire system (service)

Figure 4.5b This power distribution provides two separate hot power sources along with a neutral and is the most popular form of distribution for current residential customers. A ground is added as an additional element of each circuit but is independent from the actual distribution system.

c. Four-wire system or service
(Three-phase or Wye power distribution)

• Connection
⌐ Not connected

Figure 4.5c This form of distribution contains three hot wires and a neutral (three-phase or Wye power distribution) and is characteristic of the power that is provided for commercial and industrial installations. A ground is added as an additional element of each circuit but is independent from the actual distribution system.

transformer, where it is often run to an earth ground. In this manner, a consideration in many installations is the link between the grounding system and the neutral. At one point in time it was a common practice to share connections between the neutral and ground systems in some wiring installations. This is no longer considered safe, and current codes discourage it because it defeats the purpose of an isolated ground. If an electrical service is installed properly, there should be no voltage between the neutral and the ground of any building.

TWO-WIRE SYSTEM (SERVICE)   A two-wire system provides a single hot wire or leg and a neutral to a customer. This system was popular in homes built before the 1960s but due to the increased power needs of air conditioning, water heaters, heat pumps, and other large appliances it is no longer considered sufficient for most homes. The voltage between both of these wires is around 120 volts, although I have personally seen it drop to as low as 95–98 volts. The utility is responsible for maintaining a consistent voltage between the two wires, and if the voltage drops too much it may cause problems in the operation of sensitive electronic equipment. **Surges** or **spikes** (sudden increases in voltage) can also cause problems that could create safety hazards or might damage equipment.

THREE-WIRE SYSTEM (SERVICE)   A three-wire system provides two hot wires or legs and a common neutral. The electrical potential between either one of the hots and the neutral will be 120 volts, while the voltage between the two hots will be 240 volts. This is due to the fact that even though each phase only represents a 120-volt potential they are oriented in opposition with one another, resulting in the total potential difference between the two hots becoming 240 volts. This is the most popular service available for today's residential power services. Small appliances and lights typically operate on the 120-volt power, while large appliances like ovens, water heaters, or air conditioners will use the 240-volt power.

WYE OR FOUR-WIRE SYSTEM (SERVICE)   Most commercial operations need more efficient power. The most popular power configuration for providing these needs is known as the **wye** or **four-wire system.** In this configuration a utility provides three different hot wires and a common neutral. These three phases are the same phases associated with the power produced by the generators at the power plant, and each leg's alternating voltage lags slightly behind each of the others. Large motors are typically connected to all three legs of the power supply in order to create more efficient work or motion. The efficiency of this arrangement results in an overall higher average voltage over a given cycle when comparing voltages across any two hot wires, despite the fact that the net voltage is still balanced. This voltage is called the **Root Mean Square Voltage, RMS voltage,** or **VRMS.** The voltage that can be observed between any single phase and the neutral is 120 volts, while the voltage between any two hots, due to this shifted orientation, will be on the order of 208 volts.

In order to produce a truly safe condition, electrical engineers design circuits so that the neutral carries no net potential as electricity flows back to its power source. In systems where more than one leg of power is provided we try to orient the phases in such a way that the sum of the voltage of all the phases equals a net of zero potential on the neutral. In the case of services with two hot wires, the phases are oriented in direct opposition with one another, while the skewed orientation of a three-phase system accomplishes the same task. We also strive to **balance** an electrical system so that the demands of the entire service are evenly distributed on each of the legs to ensure that the neutral will not carry any excess current. In any AC distribution system, an electrical device should always be connected between the hot and neutral wires of a circuit. Bringing two hots in direct contact with one another, the neutral, or ground will result in creating a **short-circuit,** which commonly results in shocks, sparks, and a possible fire. A short-circuit can be thought of as an accidental flow of electricity. If you've ever cut through a power cord you have most likely witnessed the effects of a short-circuit.

ELECTRICAL HARDWARE

As stated earlier, every device has a natural ability to either conduct or resist electrical flow. This innate ability results in every material or object having some natural capacity for conducting electricity. If we exceed this level there will be consequences such as heat buildup or sparks due to the natural resistance of the material. All electrical components are rated by their capacity, in amps, that specifies how much electricity they can safely conduct. This rating is usually stamped or labeled on the product in some way. Switches, outlets, and lamp fixtures are but a few of the devices that have their capacities indicated somewhere on their bodies.

Wire

The most common conductor is wire, which can be made of a solid piece of metal (**solid core**) or smaller strands of metal that are woven together much like a fibrous rope (**stranded**). Solid core wire conducts electricity better than stranded wire but is not as flexible and can easily break if flexed too often. Because of this, solid core wire is used in permanent installations, while stranded wires are used in situations where the wires are moved around, such as in theatre or film production. While metal forms the conductive path, we have to take measures to prevent unwanted power from flowing from it, and we cover each conductor with a highly resistant material called **insulation.** In any circuit, every wire has a unique purpose, and we color-code the insulation as a means of quickly identifying a wire's purpose. The most important electrical coding includes red or black for hot wires, white for a neutral wire, and green for a ground wire. If a third phase is contained in a service, the last leg will often be color-coded blue. The color code is modified for connecting hardware such as screws and clamps, where brass or brown forms a hot connection, silver is used for neutral connections, and green is used for ground connections. Nearly all switches, lighting hardware, and receptacles use these coding practices. With so much electrical equipment now coming from Asia and Europe, one must also note that the color coding of these wires may be different. One popular color coding scheme incorporates brown insulation for hot wires, light blue for the neutrals, and green and yellow striped insulation for ground wires.

The capacity of a wire for conducting electricity is related to its thickness or diameter. The thicker the wire, the more electron flow that can occur and the greater capacity that a wire will have. This is similar to a larger diameter pipe being associated with a larger volume of water flow. We size wire according to its diameter or **gauge**. The smaller the diameter of the wire, the larger the number of the gauge. A #10 gauge wire is thicker than an #18 gauge wire. Each gauge is specified with a maximum capacity rating that increases as the gauge number goes down. The most common gauges found in entertainment and architectural practices are #12 and #14, which are rated for loads of 20 and 15 amps, respectively. In areas where we have a significant power flow we use large-gauge wires called **feeders** that deliver high-capacity power (i.e., 100 or more amps) to a panel or device. These typically have diameters that are approximately the size of a finger and are called 0, 00, or 000—each one getting progressively larger. While we are predominantly concerned with wire, on some large-capacity applications we actually use metal bars called **bus bars** rather than wires to move the electricity from one location to another. This is quite common in large-capacity dimmer racks and distribution panels.

Figure 4.6a Common electrical connectors. a. Displayed from left to right, beginning with the back row: Polar Edison male, ground lift, grounded Edison male, grounded Edison female, male twist-lock (30 amp), and a three-fer block. In the front row is a 20-amp male three-pin connector (opened), while all the connectors are surrounded by a two-fer.

Figure 4.6b Power Con. LED luminaires typically use this special connector to daisy-chain power between separate LED units.

Cables

It is rare that we need to run single wires in lighting applications. More commonly, we combine several insulated wires together to form a **cable.** The most common cable contains three wires and is used to carry a hot, neutral, and ground wire. Each wire typically has its own insulation that is then molded into a single sheath or jacket along with the other wires and insulators. Standard coloring of the insulation allows anyone to identify the purpose of a given wire (red or black for hot, white for neutral and green or bare without insulation for a ground wire). While the ends of a cable may be wired directly to a device, it is more common to include **connectors** that allow the connecting and disconnecting of the cables to occur with relative ease. Just like wire, connectors are also rated for specific capacities. There are two types of connectors, **male** and **female.** A male connector should always be placed on the device or wire that will be receiving the power, while the female should always be reserved for the location or tap that will provide the power source. Household plugs form an example of these connectors. Several of the most common connectors include the standard household Edison plug, the pin connector, and the twist-lock connector. A photograph of these plugs is found in Figure 4.6. In each case, the connector provides specific contacts associated with the hot, neutral, and ground wires for each connector. In the twist-lock and Edison connectors, the ground wires are mounted to blades that are shaped quite differently from the other two (often with a green mounting screw), while in the pin connector the ground is mounted on the center pin. The neutral for a twist-lock or Edison connector is associated with the larger of the two remaining blades (these will also frequently have silver screws), while the pin connector's

neutral is reserved for the outside pin that is mounted closest to the ground. The final blade or pin in both cases is reserved for the hot connection and is often the smallest or most distant pin from the others. Figure 4.7 illustrates the proper wiring connections for a male pin connector which is one of the most popular connectors used in entertainment lighting applications.

In entertainment lighting we make constant changes in the wiring from show to show, and using permanent wiring practices would be both tedious and wearing on the equipment. Because of this, a number of pre-wired cables and connectors are used that allow us to quickly connect and disconnect electrical devices. A **jumper** or **cable** is a variation of cable that contains

Figure 4.7 Wiring of a three-pin connector for the stage (male connector illustrated)

three conductors and a male and female connector. These come in a variety of lengths from 3 feet to 200 feet and function in the same manner as an extension cord. Lengths of these cables are normally measured in 5- or 10-foot intervals such as 5, 10, 15, 25, and 50 feet. An **adapter** is a short length of cable that has different types of connectors on each end and allows a cable to be adapted from one system of connectors to another (as in twist-lock to pin connector or pin connector to Edison). Most cables are designed for use on a single circuit and contain a single hot, neutral, and ground wire. No cable or adapter will have either male or female connectors on both ends. In newer devices, such as with LED luminaires, it is common to daisy-chain the power from one unit to another through cables that have special fittings called **Power Con** connectors.

While we might occasionally wire each device directly to its power source, it's more common to combine several devices together by wiring them into a single circuit. In architectural installations, objects may be permanently wired together, as in the case of wiring several ceiling lights or connecting all the convenience outlets of a room to a common circuit. However, in entertainment lighting the need for both speed and constant modification has produced several specialty devices that allow two or more lights and/or cables to be plugged into a common circuit. These devices typically join two or more female plugs to a single male connector. Most electricians refer to these specialized accessories as **two-fers** (two females) or **three-fers** (three females). Occasionally electricians need to service many circuits through a given cable. In this case there are two options. The first uses cables that are manufactured with a number of independent conductors whose ends terminate in a given number of male and female connectors that correspond to the number of circuits contained in the cable. This is called a **multi-cable** or **multi** and will

often contain six or more independent circuits. A popular multi-cable used in many road houses and the touring industry, called **Socapex**, typically contains six independent circuits. These specialized cables terminate in threaded connectors to which special fittings that split the circuits into the individual cables and connectors are attached. These are then used to either plug the instruments into the Socapex cable (**break-out**) or the Socapex into the power source/dimmers (**break-in**).

An alternative to using a multi is to create a **bundle**, which combines individual cables that run along common areas like an electric by tying the individual cables together so that they effectively become a single entity. Each of the individual circuits/cables begins at the dimmer racks and drops out of the bundle or terminates at the location of the associated lighting instrument that they feed. Bundles are frequently used to provide pre-wired electrics for touring productions.

Making determinations of the load that is placed on a given cable is an important safety concern for any stage electrician. Figure 4.8 illustrates how the same three lights may be wired in such a way that the wiring is safe in two of the wiring scenarios but unsafe and overloaded in the final example.

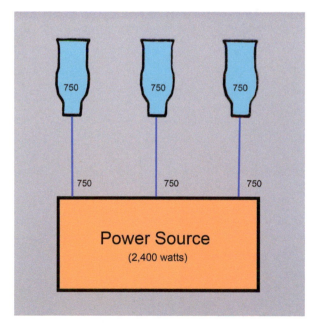

Figure 4.8a Load Distribution on Cables. Just keeping the load below a dimmer's rating doesn't guarantee that you haven't overloaded a circuit. The same three 750 watt lighting instruments are wired to a 2400 watt dimmer in three different manners. Two are safe while the final one has a cable overloaded. The capacity of 12 AWG cable is 20 amps or 2400 watts at 120 volts while the capacity of 14 AWG cable is 15 amps or 1800 watts at 120 volts. a. Safe with 12 or 14- AWG cables

Figure 4.8b Safe with 12 or 14- AWG cables

Figure 4.8c Safe with 12 AWG gauge cables but over-loaded with 14- AWG cables.

Data Cables

Traditionally, most lighting instruments had cables that provided power to their associated lamps and only the intensity of the lamp could be changed. This was (and still is) done primarily through varying the voltage in the circuit, which ultimately affects the intensity or brightness of the lamp. Newer lighting equipment, such as moving or automated lights, make use of additional control functions such as being able to change position/

focus, color, gobo patterns, etc. These functions are controlled remotely through a second set of cables that provide the control data or information to the lighting equipment. These cables, known as **data cables**, are of a relatively small gauge (approximately #22 or so) and carry low-voltage control signals (12–24 volts) that provide specific instructions for the various operations of the fixture. Control cables will ultimately make a connection between the lighting devices and the light board or control console. The cables have special fittings/plugs and are typically around the thickness of a mic cable. These are discussed in more detail in Chapter 7.

6. Be sure that all connections between cables, connectors and hardware are tight. In the case of pin connectors, be sure that all three pins fit snuggly together. If they are loose, use a pin splitter to spread the individual pins to a point where a solid connection is formed between the male and female pins.
7. Be absolutely sure of which connections go to each of the hot, neutral, and ground wires before making your connections—and follow all standard electric color codes when wiring your devices.
8. Periodically check your cables for stress, loose connectors, aging or damaged insulation, etc. to ensure that they are in their best working order.

Switches

A **switch** is a device that is used to control the flow of power through an electrical circuit. A switch is wired in series along the hot wire of the circuit and just like a fuse or circuit breaker, it should be located somewhere in the circuit ahead of all of the devices that it is controlling. The common wall switch used in electrical lighting is the most common switch available; when it is closed, it completes the circuit, allowing power to flow throughout the circuit. If it is moved to the open position, it puts a break in the line that interrupts the flow of power. Most switches that we are familiar with are considered **light duty** and are rated for 15 or 20 amps only, while many of the switches found in commercial and entertainment applications are considered heavy-duty and may carry up to several hundred amps. There are a number of different kinds of switches available to lighting designers. Some provide power to a single load, while others can be assigned to multiple loads. A **three-way switch** allows a single circuit to be controlled through several switches placed at different locations. Finally, there are specialized switches that may be activated by a timer, photosensitivity, or even through motion detection. In each case the switch becomes the mechanism by which power is made available to a circuit.

Circuit Protection

Another major group of electrical components comprises circuit-protection devices such as **fuses** and **circuit breakers.** These are designed to be the weakest link in a circuit and are meant to trip or blow if the circuit should become exposed to a short-circuit or is overloaded. Every fuse or circuit breaker is rated by a capacity that specifies the actual power requirements or **load** of all the devices that may be assigned to a given

circuit. A breaker or fuse is designed to stop the power flow by causing a physical break in the wiring if its capacity is exceeded by the current in the circuit. The protection device should be wired in series on the hot wire of a circuit, as close to the power source as possible. This ensures that as many of the components as possible are protected from any overload conditions. A typical distribution panel contains a central power source along with a number of fuses or circuit breakers that are wired to the numerous branch circuits.

Most circuit protection devices react to either a heat buildup or significant change in the electromagnetic activity of a circuit. They may trip in an immediate catatonic sense due to a sudden overload like a short-circuit or could simply fail due to excessive heating through having too many devices drawing power from a source at a particular time. Many electricians refer to this second condition as a **slow blow,** characterized by a condition in which everything appears to be working fine but that over time causes a breaker to trip for no apparent reason. Slow blows are most often due to conditions such as excessive resistance being created in a circuit through extra-long jumpers, cables being undersized, loose connections, or a slight overload in the capacity assignment or load of a circuit. While **circuit breakers** may be reset, **fuses** need to be replaced once they blow. Figure 4.9 illustrates several fairly common circuit-protection devices. Fuses come in a variety of sizes and shapes, and while many small-capacity fuses are of a plug or screw-type style, larger-capacity fuses are of a cartridge style with either ferrule or knife-blade conductors. Ferrule fuses will generally be used in applications under 100 amps while knife-blade fuses are common for capacities of 100, 150, 200, 400, and 800 amps or more. Circuit breakers are manufactured in a variety of sizes that cover the entire range of load capacities. Some respond

Figure 4.9 Circuit protection devices: These electrical fuses include a buss, cartridge, and knife-blade fuses along with a plug fuse. A 50-amp single-phase circuit breaker is shown at the extreme right.

to thermal monitoring, while most use magnetic detection. Several of the advantages of using circuit breakers include their ability to be reset and their faster detection and reaction to an overload condition. Magnetic breakers can be reset more quickly than thermal breakers because there is no need to wait for the breaker to cool down. Another variation of circuit protection is the **Ground Fault Circuit Interrupter (GFCI),** which detects any flow of electricity between the neutral and the earth ground. If it detects a flow, it trips in much the same manner as a circuit breaker. These devices are typically installed in areas where there is a good chance of a person coming in contact with a live wire and equipment or materials that may be associated with moisture or an earth ground. By code, these devices are often required in wet environments such as kitchens, bathrooms, and exterior locations. In the Cirque du Soleil production of *O* at the Bellagio Casino in Las Vegas the entire production takes place in and around a large pool, and specially designed dimmers that incorporate GFCI protection were developed and installed throughout the facility that houses this production.

Dimmers

A **dimmer** is a control device that is used for adjusting the intensity of any lights that are contained in a circuit. In most cases, a dimmer varies the voltage to control the brightness of the lamps. In theatrical applications we use dimmers to help control the mood and focus of the lighting. We also use them to make adjustments in the balance of a stage as well as for making adjustments in intensity throughout a performance. These devices are also popular in restaurants and residences, as well as for other architectural applications where a more artistic quality and mood are desired for an environment. Dimmers also provide a sound means of achieving energy management by allowing a space to be sufficiently lit without using the lamps or luminaires at their full power. Additionally, lamp life can be increased significantly by as little as a 10–20% drop in voltage or intensity—something that most individuals can't distinguish. Dimmers are examined in more detail in Chapter 7.

COMPANY SWITCHES AND DISTRIBUTION PANELS

Once an electrical service enters a facility, the electricity splits off into a number of different directions as it is conducted through a series of devices and wires that distribute the power throughout a building. Figure 4.10 illustrates the electrical distribution pattern of a typical stage lighting system once the power has already been brought into the theatre or stage (service power or **company switch**). Most stages will provide at least one company switch in order to accommodate the electrical needs of touring companies.

Theatrical Distribution

In most cases, a performance facility is wired in the same manner as any other commercial building, with the exception that the theatrical lighting systems will be powered from separate distribution panels. In the case of a permanent installation, the lighting system is wired directly to a distribution panel that has been specifically designated for the lighting system. However, in many productions, such as in touring, it is common to package an individualized system based on the specific needs pertaining to that tour. In this case, the touring company provides the entire lighting system, which is simply connected or tied into a theatre's power supply. Broadway theatres typically operate in this manner. A **company switch** or **road-tap** is a specialized distribution panel or **disconnect box** that is used to make these connections. This provides the majority of the power that a touring system will connect to. Most company switches are located somewhere backstage; traditional locations are in the wings of a theatre, along an upstage wall, or below the stage in the trap room. It is becoming common to place company switches above the wings on a catwalk as a means of getting the lighting gear and cable out of the way, which has the added benefit of reducing the length of cable runs that will have to be run from the electrics to the dimmers. These disconnect boxes typically provide 200–800 amps of three-phase power to a stage. Extreme care must be taken when wiring a company's **feeders**

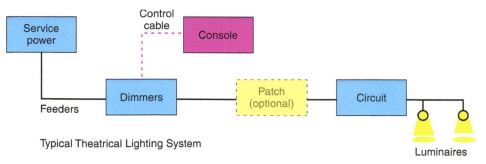

Typical Theatrical Lighting System

Figure 4.10 A typical electrical distribution for theatrical power systems

Figure 4.11 A typical company switch/disconnect: two road house disconnects (two 400-amp services). The 400-amp box on the left is open to reveal its fuses and cam-lock connections. Note lockout procedures with locks on power switches and cover panels.

(the heavy duty cables that provide power to the dimmers) to the connections contained within these panels. Disconnect boxes typically don't contain any branch circuits and simply provide the hardware that will allow for the connection of the feeders that will lead to the touring equipment. Fuses for each leg of power and a main switch or a single heavy-duty breaker are the only other features contained in many of these boxes. Some touring facilities make things even easier and have special **cam-lock** fittings on these boxes that allow the touring company's feeders to be plugged directly into the box. Many road houses provide several company switches that are located throughout a backstage area. Figure 4.11 shows a typical company switch with the front panel opened. To prevent accidents, many companies place locks on these panels and switches. The wiring of a company switch is a dangerous job and should be reserved for an experienced electrician. In many municipalities only a licensed electrician may perform this service.

Sidebar 4.6 TAPPING INTO COMPANY SWITCHES

Many experienced stage electricians will at some point in their career have to do the "company tie-in" in which feeder cables from a portable dimming system are connected to a company switch. Here are some guidelines:

1. If you have any question at all about what you are doing—STOP. Get somebody who knows how to safely complete the electrical

connections and tie-in process. In some cases, only a licensed electrician will be allowed to complete the tie-in process (check your local regulations).

2. Company switches should be governed by lock-out and tagging rules—meaning that these panels have padlocks on them so that they can be opened or powered up only when everyone is aware that it is completely safe and nobody is working on them. If a box is tagged, the tag will provide more information regarding how it might be powered up and who should work on it.

3. Always make sure that the circuit box is actually dead (off) before working on it; then check it with a meter to make sure that it is actually off.

4. If you are using camlock connectors, your job is easy. Just plug the cam connectors into the plugs mounted on the distribution panel matching the associated color codes in the order as outlined in number 7. Be sure to give each connector a twist upon inserting the connectors to engage the locking mechanism that prevents the connectors from pulling out.

5. Once an electrical box is opened, be absolutely sure of what each connection or bus bar represents: hot phase, neutral, or ground. Make sure that you know which side of the switch and connections represent the load versus power source for each connection; some boxes have the power source at the top while others have it at the bottom. Use a meter to ensure that you are working on dead circuit components.

6. Run the feeders into the box through the provided knockout holes, taking care to allow plenty of slack for making your electrical connections while also avoiding contact with any of the terminal strips or bus bars. Use tie-line to form a strain-relief for these cables on the outside of the box so that the weight of the cables will not be placed on the electrical connections.

7. Using the terminals provided in the box, attach each of the feeder cables to their appropriate connection points, making sure that all the connections are tight and that there are no stray strands of wire protruding from your connections. The order that must be followed is: ground wire first, neutral second, then the hots last.

8. Make a final check your wiring to make sure that you have everything wired correctly before you close or replace the cover to the box. Also make sure that your dimmers or other electrical devices are turned off before throwing the switch and applying power to the system.

Though this is often not possible, try to throw the power and check all of your connections with a meter before adding the actual load of your dimmer racks.

9. When striking a company switch, reverse the order in which you added the feeders: remove the hots first, neutral second, and ground last. Once again, use a meter to ensure that there is no power to the components that you are working on.

In a typical theatrical lighting system we want to control a number of lights independently of one another and must therefore provide numerous dimmers so that the lights can be individually controlled. We also run a number of individual circuits to many locations throughout a theatre to provide permanent wiring for many of the most popular hanging positions of a theatre. Some of these locations may include anywhere from 30 to 50 or more individual circuits—each allowing additional lights to be added to the design through a process that is as simple as plugging the light's connector into a pre-existing receptacle. We refer to each of these pathways as a **circuit.** Contemporary theatres often wire each circuit to its own dimmer (**Dimmer per Circuit, or DPC**) but many theatres can't afford this practice and instead make use of a relatively high number of circuits that are then assigned or connected to a limited number of dimmers. In these cases, theatres make use of another specialized piece of electrical hardware called a **patchbay** or **patch panel** that allows the circuits to be assigned to individual dimmers through some form of quick-connection device.

TROUBLESHOOTING ELECTRICAL PROBLEMS

Troubleshooting electrical problems can at times be daunting—especially when a problem is discovered during a dimmer check and there is little time to solve the problem before the house must open. To make matters even more difficult, the problems are almost always located in a component that can be reached only by either dropping a pipe in or bringing a lift or ladder out. On a positive note, most electrical problems (barring burned out lamps) typically occur primarily during the hang and focus of a show. Once the package is pretty well assembled there is little to go wrong—especially if the electricians were careful to install the equipment properly.

When solving electrical problems, the best approach is to use logic to isolate the problem into various elements that can be checked independently of one another. A test lamp (a 25-watt bulb and carnival socket wired to a connector of the style used by your theatre)

can simplify much of your troubleshooting efforts: just plug the test lamp into various points along the circuit path. Sidebar 4.7 provides several troubleshooting techniques for common issues.

Sidebar 4.7 A GUIDE TO ELECTRICAL TROUBLESHOOTING

Respond to each question/statement. If the answer is yes, work down through the list of suggested problems. If no, go down to the next question. The most common issues are found at the top. Tracing the entire circuit should generally be saved as a last resort to fixing a problem—though it is also one of the most common issues that will cause a lamp to not function.

1. Is there more than one lamp in a given circuit not functioning?
   Yes:

   a. Is the correct channel pulled up on the console?
   b. Is the circuit(s) patched to the correct channel?
   c. Are lamps plugged into the correct circuit?
   d. Check the circuit receptacle with test lamp to determine if you have power at the start of the circuit. If yes, trace each cable and junction in sequence from the power source towards the non-working lamps and test for continuity and loose connections.

No: skip to Step 5.

2. Is the lamp one of several units that are still functioning on the same circuit?
Yes:

   a. Check the lamp for burnout
   b. Trace the cables from the last working unit towards the non-working unit and use a test light to determine continuity at each junction/connection along the cable path. Be on the lookout for connectors that have come undone as well as shorts and loose wires/connections within individual connectors.

3. Is there power to the lighting instrument? Use a test lamp to determine this.
Yes:
   a. Check lamp for burnout.
   b. Check connector for loose wires or poor connections
   c. Check socket and internal wires for continuity

---

4. Is the channel/dimmer powered up on light board?

Yes:

    a. Is the dimmer patched/addressed correctly?

    b. Determine if there is power at the dimmer/circuit outlet.

    c. Beginning at the source, trace the cable and use a test light to determine continuity at each junction/connection along the cable path to the non-working fixture. Be on the lookout for shorts and loose wires/connections.

5. Is a circuit breaker blown at the dimmer or circuit panel?

Yes:

    a. Reset the breaker. If the breaker blows again, stop, determine the cause and fix the problem before resetting the breaker again.

    b. Test the bad circuit on a non-dim circuit to determine if problem is in the circuit or the dimmer.

    c. If problem is in the circuit, beginning at the source, trace the cable and use a test light to determine continuity at each junction/connection along the cable path to the non-working fixture. Be on the lookout for shorts and loose wires or connections.

6. Swap dimmer modules to determine if you have a bad dimmer. Test the new module with another circuit that has no problems before placing the original circuit on the dimmer.

7. Check control cables for positive connection to dimmers

8. Find someone with more experience in troubleshooting these problems.

Sidebar 4.8 ELECTRICAL SAFETY

When you're working with electricity, safety is extremely important not only for yourself, but also for the other occupants of a facility. An accident can occur without warning and the consequences can be extreme—even fatal. When you are working as an electrician and entrusted with wiring an electrical device there are several general rules that should be followed.

1. If you have any question about what you are doing, stop and get somebody who knows how to safely complete the electrical connections.

2. Always make sure that any electrical device that you will be working on is **dead** (off) before working on it, then check it with a meter to make sure that its actually off. If the device has a plug or connector, make sure that you disconnect it from its power source.

3. Provide grounding whenever possible and avoid removing any grounding device unless it is absolutely necessary.

4. Strip only enough insulation off a wire to allow a good solid connection between the wire and any electrical hardware. There should never be an excess of exposed conductor in any connection. Use crimp-style electrical connectors when possible.

5. Always check to make sure that every connection is secure and tight and that there are no loose strands of wire extending beyond the connections. Wires secured by screws should be wrapped clockwise around a screw before being tightened down.

6. Never cross any wires or make a connection directly between phases, a hot leg and the ground, or a hot leg and the neutral. This produces a short-circuit. Always observe proper color codes when making any connection.

7. Be sure that all components of a circuit are properly rated and not overloaded. A circuit is only as strong as its weakest component. If the wire is rated for only 15 amps and you place a 20-amp breaker or fuse on the circuit, the wire will most likely melt and cause a fire before the fuse will blow.

8. Be leery of excessively long cable runs. This, along with additional connections (i.e., connecting several long cables together) will increase the resistance in a circuit, which can cause overloads and unsafe heating of the wires. If you must complete a longer cable run, shift to using a cable with lower gauge (thicker) wires.

9. Always check your wiring, test your connections, and—especially in those cases where there is a substantial amount of power involved—verify your wiring with a meter before adding power to the circuit.

FOR FURTHER READING

Bellman, Willard F. *Lighting the Stage: Art and Practice.* 3rd ed. Louisville, KY: Broadway Press, 2001.

Cadena, Richard. *Electricity for the Entertainment Electrician and Technician.* 2nd ed. Oxford and Boston: Focal Press, 2014.

DiLaura, David L., Kevin W. Houser, Richard G. Mistrick, and Gary R. Steffy. eds. *Illuminating Engineering Society–the Lighting Handbook Tenth Edition: Reference and Application.* New York: Illuminating Engineering Society, 2011.

Illuminating Engineering Society of North America. *IESNA Lighting Education 100 (Fundamental Level).* New York: Illuminating Engineering Society of North America, 1993.

Illuminating Engineering Society of North America. *IESNA Lighting Education 150 (Intermediate Level).* New York: Illuminating Engineering Society of North America, 1993.

Illuminating Engineering Society of North America. *IESNA Lighting Ready Reference.* 4th ed. New York: Illuminating Engineering Society of North America, 2003.

Lindsey, Jack L. *Applied Illumination Engineering.* 2nd ed. Liburn, GA: The Fairmont Press, Inc., 1997.

NFPA (National Fire Protection Association). *NFPA 70: National Electrical Code (NEC) 2008.* Quincy, MA: National Fire Protection Association, 2017.

CHAPTER 5

LAMPS AND OTHER LIGHT SOURCES

A LIGHT SOURCE IS nothing more than an object or device that produces light. The most prevalent light source that we are familiar with is the sun. When lighting designers discuss **lamps,** they are usually referring to a device that produces some manner of artificial light. A number of different light sources have been used throughout history. A torch or campfire, candles or lanterns, arcs or electrical sparks, incandescent lamps, and now LEDs all form examples of light sources that have been used throughout recorded time. What is most important about light sources is the particular quantity and quality of light that a given source can create. While there are a number of natural ways of creating light—such as in the atomic reactions of the sun, the discharge of a spark, a chemical reaction, or burning a material to produce a flame—there are essentially only four ways in which we commercially produce light in today's society. These techniques involve light production through **incandescence,** an **arc,** a **gaseous discharge,** or **solid-state sources**.

For now, incandescence is by far the most common form of light production and is represented by the common light bulb. In incandescence a metal material is heated to the point that it glows and gives off electromagnetic radiation. Because of the significance of this light source, a large portion of the chapter is devoted to incandescent lighting. While incandescent sources are the most popular way of creating light, they also have several significant drawbacks such as their overall inefficiency and high level of heat production. Incandescent lamps are actually only about 5–10% efficient—meaning that approximately 90% of the energy that they consume is wasted as heat. In fact, there are a number of movements throughout the United States and other countries to "ban the bulb" as communities struggle to switch to more efficient sources like compact fluorescent and LED lights. In the last several years, solid-state (LED) lighting has had significant growth and in short time will most likely overtake incandescent lighting in popularity.

Due to the inefficiencies of the incandescent lamp, alternative methods of light production have been developed. An arc source creates a very bright light in comparison to incandescent sources and is nothing more than an electrical spark jumping between two electrodes. A gaseous discharge source places an arc in an atmosphere of a specific mixture of gases that glow. Two special versions of sources that are popular in architectural applications include the **fluorescent lamp** and the **high-intensity discharge (HID) lamp.** Both are discussed later in this chapter. In some applications, these alternative sources have become even more popular than incandescent lamps. For instance, in architectural applications, the fluorescent lamp has taken on a very significant role in commercial/industrial illumination. Due to issues related to energy management and quality of light, there are distinct differences between the sources that we use for architectural and theatrical applications. Many of these considerations are examined throughout this chapter. Two good references relating to the historical development of light sources include Brian Bowers' *Lengthening the Day: A History of Lighting Technology* and Maureen Dillon's *Artificial Sunshine: A Social History of Domestic Lighting.* Frederick Penzel's *Theatre Lighting Before Electricity* provides an especially good history of theatrical lighting. (See "For Further Reading" for information on these resources.)

LUMENS, WATTS, AND LAMP LIFE

Lamp selection is often based on making comparisons between various properties of the lamps that we might be considering for a given application. One common practice for comparing light sources refers to the **lumen output** that is created by a lamp and is determined by measuring the actual amount of light produced by a lamp. The most common way of measuring this until recently is by rating a lamp according to its **wattage,** or ability to do work. However, it should be noted that although lumen output generally corresponds to wattage, the principle doesn't always hold true: some lamps are more efficient than others. Due to this, manufacturers are now starting to specify lamps by lumen output rather than wattage. As a general rule, though, lamps of a higher wattage usually appear brighter and generally produce more light than lamps of comparatively lower wattages. We also consider how long a lamp will last before burning out as another criteria before selecting a lamp for a given task. We measure this in **lamp life.** Simply put, lamp life is a means of determining the average number of hours that a lamp will burn before failing. This is based on trials in which a number of lamps are tested until they either actually fail or their light output drops to below 80%. Obviously, if you are specifying exterior spotlights for a church steeple, where the lamps are going to be hard to replace, it would be more practical to use lamps with longer lamp lives. Another general rule relates to the fact that lower-wattage lamps tend to have longer lives than those with higher wattages. Therefore, it can also be concluded that brighter lamps tend to have shorter lamp lives. It's like life: those who live hard and fast tend to burn out before those who live more moderately (though there are exceptions). Some special-duty stage and studio lamps have a lamp life of as few as 50 hours while most theatrical lamps can average several hundred hours. Household lamps are rated for up to 1,000 hours, while fluorescent lamps typically have lamp lives that can extend to approximately 10,000 hours. Some extended-service lamps, such as the familiar mercury street or utility lamp, can have lamp lives up to 24,000 hours or more. In addition to lamp life, it is also important to consider how quickly the light output from a lamp drops off over time. This refers to the efficiency of the lamp and is called **lumen maintenance.** Some lamps progressively cloud or darken over time, which can have a serious impact on the amount of light actually being produced. As time progresses, this effect on lumen output becomes greater and greater. Other lamps stay essentially clear throughout their lives and maintain a more consistent light output as they age.

Lamps are designed for specific operating voltages. In incandescent lighting the actual light production is directly proportional to the amount of resistance and voltage that are applied to the lamp. If a lamp is subjected to a higher voltage than for which it was designed, it will glow brighter but will also burn out much quicker. If the voltage is high enough it might fail instantaneously or even explode. On the other hand, a lamp that is often dimmed or that runs at only 80% intensity will have its lamp life increased significantly. In theatrical applications, where lamps are seldom run continuously or at full intensity, lamp life can often be extended two or three times beyond the lamp life ratings that are specified by the manufacturers.

LAMPS AND COLOR

Regardless of light source, we also make reference to the **color temperature** of a lamp as a way of comparing its overall spectral composition with that of other light sources. As you may recall, color temperature is based on a color reference to a particular Kelvin temperature. However, in addition to the overall color temperature, a designer might also have to consider the specific spectral composition of a light source to predict its effect on different objects. Light sources that emit a wide distribution of spectral wavelengths tend to enhance objects across a wider range of colors. This ability is referenced in a comparative manner by assigning numbers that represent a lamp's **Color Rendering Index (CRI).** As a light source's CRI increases, its ability to render a wider selection of colors also increases. A CRI of 100 represents a source capable of producing full-spectrum light. Comparisons of a light source's CRI and its individual spectral responses to various wavelengths of light can be used along with color temperature to identify the best light source for a given project.

INCANDESCENT LAMPS

At present, incandescent lamps still form the most common means of producing light in the world today. However, this is rapidly changing as more and more industries are moving towards **solid-state lighting,** with LEDs forming the most common solid-state sources. The original lamps produced by Edison and others worked on the principle of incandescence, and while we have gone on to create thousands of variations on the basic design, the overall principle of its operation has not changed much from his original concept. Incandescent lamps remain popular due to the ease and low cost with which they can be manufactured. Additionally, not only are they functional, but they can also be created in a variety of shapes and sizes for any number of decorative applications. On the other hand, they are inefficient as energy sources and as much as 90% of the energy that they consume is wasted as heat.

The basic principle in which an incandescent lamp works is by heating a highly resistant material or wire (**filament**) with electricity to the point that it begins to radiate or glow with visible energy. This process is known as **incandescence.** Due to the high resistance of the wire, the filament will first glow red and then glow progressively brighter as the voltage is increased until it gives off white light. The primary components of a lamp are illustrated in Figure 5.1. We usually refer to the whole assembly as a **lamp** rather than a light bulb. The **bulb** is the actual glass envelope of a lamp. If a filament were to be exposed to the natural air while energized with electricity it would oxidize rapidly and burn out. The bulb prevents this natural reaction from occurring so quickly by providing either a vacuum or a gas-filled environment that is oxygen-deprived. The filament, often made of tungsten, is the resistant wire that is heated by the electric current. It is often wrapped into a tight coil as a means of compacting the surface area upon which the light is actually produced. The smaller and more compact the coil, the more effective the lamp. The filament must be located at a specific location within a bulb to maximize the efficiency of the lamp, and a set of **support wires** is used to hold the filament in this proper position and orientation. A set of **lead-in wires** is used to provide the electrical connections to each side of the filament. Finally, a **base** provides the electrical connections between the lamp and the socket as well as the physical mounting of the lamp in a way that ensures its proper position and orientation in a lighting instrument.

Each of the lamp components can be modified in a number of ways to produce a variety of qualities and orientations of light that would be characteristic of a particular style of lamp. Ultimately, there is no single combination of components that make for the most efficient light source: every combination relates to a lighting solution that is more effective for one situation over another. Hence, there are literally thousands of individual lamp types, each with a different combination of filament, base, size, bulb, etc. Even if all the components of a lamp's construction are kept the same, variations in wattage, color temperature, efficiency, and overall lumen output can also be made from one lamp to another. The following pages address only a few of the key variations that may occur in the primary lamp components.

Filaments

The filament is the most important element of a lamp because it is the component that actually produces the light. One of the objectives of lamp manufacturing is to make the filament and resulting lamp as small as possible. Optical devices like lenses and reflectors work best when light is concentrated at an infinitely small point. A light source that can concentrate a majority of its light at this point will make the associated lens or reflector all the more efficient and powerful. This is generally referred to as creating a **point light source.** Today's lamps are much smaller than lamps from 30 to 40 years ago because of this trend. The importance of this principle will become even more apparent through the optics discussion that you will find in the next chapter.

Filaments have been made more efficient by coiling the tungsten wire into a tight **coil (C)** as opposed to simply stringing it between its support wires—**straight (S).** This provides a more concentrated light source by producing a greater amount of filament surface area at a given point or location. More recent lamps have effectively made use of a **coiled-coil (CC)** filament design that takes an already coiled wire and then coils this, too, into a secondary coil. As a lamp manufacturer varies the specific shape and orientation of the filament, the associated light is produced in different orientations. This allows the lumen output of the lamp to be increased in one direction or another. Figure 5.2 illustrates many of the more popular filament configurations that have been used in lamp designs over the years. A couple designs of special significance include the following: the **C-7** or **corona** filament, which is typical of many everyday or general-purpose (bare bulb) lamps that produce light in a spherical pattern extending outward in nearly all directions; the **C-5** or **barrel** filament, which produces light in a torus or donut-shaped pattern that extends around the filament; the **C-13** or **monoplane,** which produces light primarily in two opposing directions; the **C-13D** or **biplane,** which further concentrates the filament in a set of two offset planes that result in even more light being produced in two directions; and the CC or coiled coil, which produces very concentrated light in a comparatively small space that expands outward in most directions. The **4C-8** filament was used as the basis of a lamp design that was developed in the early 1990s as part of the more efficient revolutionary design of the

Figure 5.1 Components of an incandescent lamp

Bulb

Vacuum or gas-filled

Filament

Filament support

Lead wire

Base (neutral)

Contact button (hot)

C-7
(Corona)

C-5
(Barrel)

C-13
(Monoplane)

(top views)

C-13D
(Biplane)
the two filament
planes are slightly
offset from one another

CC-8
(Coiled coil)

4C-8
(HPL)

Figure 5.2 Common filament styles

enhanced **ellipsoidal reflector spotlight**: the Source Four® by Electronic Theatre Controls (ETC). This filament orients four coiled filament elements in a tight vertical box-like arrangement that produces a highly concentrated light in most directions. A couple of specialty lamps make use of multiple filaments within a single bulb. Examples of these include the three-way lamps commonly found in many table or floor lamps and a variety of studio lamps used in video or film settings where multiple brightness settings are created through applying power to one or more filaments of a lamp at any given time.

Bulbs

The most dominant part of many lamps is the glass enclosure, or bulb, that encases the filament and its associated support and lead wires. The bulb contains the atmosphere for a filament. It is important that this environment prevents the natural oxidation of the filament; gases such as nitrogen and argon are typically added into the bulb to slow down this process. A bulb's shape and size may be based fully on function or could be based on a decorative element. We may also characterize a bulb based on its finish or color. In stage and studio applications designers prefer to have **clear** finishes, which ensures that there is very little change in the quality of the native light. Although this is useful in applications where designers want the light to initially be as pure as possible, in some situations clear lamps may become a distraction and can lead to glare. In these cases, lamps with alternative finishes are often used. The most popular finishes for lamps in these applications are **frosted** finishes that soften and diffuse the light of a lamp. A limited number of colored lamps (red, white, blue, yellow, and green) are also created by manufacturers for decorative applications like carnival and amusement marquees, advertising signage, and Christmas lights. Incandescent lamps with light pastel tints have also been introduced to the consumer market by lighting manufacturers such as Philips and General Electric to create more personal lighting throughout a home or office. Finally, a number of specialized lamps like those found in candelabra and chandelier fixtures are shaped and finished in highly decorative manners.

An important element of lamp designation refers to the overall shape and size of the bulb. We usually refer to a bulb type with a combination of a letter or two and a number. The letters are given first and refer to the bulb's shape, while the number refers to the size of the bulb. The size is expressed in units that are equivalent to 1/8-inch intervals of the diameter of the bulb at its widest point. In other words, if a bulb is 2 inches in diameter it would be associated with the number 16. A lamp with a diameter of 1 1/4 inches would be assigned a value of 10. More importantly, the shape of the bulb and filament type determine the distribution pattern of the light associated with a particular lamp. Figure 5.3 provides an illustration of a number of popular bulb shapes. The shape that most people are familiar with is the **arbitrary (A)** shape, which is typically used in most household fixtures. The **globe (G)** lamp is shaped like a sphere and is often used in bathroom vanity or mirror applications. Each of these lamps is designed to disperse the light in a fairly even pattern away from the source. The **tube (T)** lamp is often used to disperse light in a more cylindrical or linear fashion, while **parabolic aluminized reflector (PAR)** and **reflector (R)** lamps act as spotlights and direct the light in a conical shape that

Figure 5.3 Common bulb configurations

is primarily in a single direction. A lamp can be readily identified with simple combinations such as T-12, meaning a tube-shaped lamp that is 1 1/2 inches in diameter, or G-25, which indicates a globe-shaped lamp that is 3 1/8 inches in diameter.

R and PAR lamps are special types of lamps in that they include not only the elements of a lamp but also several optical features that allow them to further enhance their light in a more efficient directional or spotlight-like manner. The R lamp contains a reflector and diffuse lens that allows the light to be concentrated in a pool with a soft edge that spreads gently away from the lamp while the PAR lamp contains a pre-defined lens (as well as reflector) that allows the light to be more concentrated and focused with nearly parallel light rays as it leaves the lamp. Both units are unique in that they are in a sense complete lighting fixtures within a single lamp. Each lamp is manufactured with a unique set of optical properties that cannot be modified. However, there are a number of different optical configurations. When designating PAR lamps from one another designers and manufacturers use abbreviations that designate the approximate beam or distribution pattern of the lamp. Popular lamps include the Wide Flood (WFL), Medium Flood (MFL), Narrow Spot (NSP), and Very Narrow Spot (VNSP). While most of these lamps provide a circular or conical distribution pattern there are also variations that have an oval or elliptical pattern.

Popular size variations of these lamps include R-40, PAR-38, PAR-56, and the PAR-64 (which has been a popular unit for concert lighting).

Bases

The last of the primary components of a lamp is the base. The base provides the means by which a lamp is mounted within a **luminaire** (lighting instrument) as well as the manner by which the lamp might be oriented. It also forms the electrical contacts that will ultimately connect the lamp's filament to a source of power. Most lamps have their bases at one end while some T lamps may have bases mounted at each end of their tubular-shaped bulbs. Just as there are different bulb sizes, there are also different base sizes. The smallest bases are primarily associated with decorative lamps and are called **miniature** or **candelabra** bases. Miniature bases are approximately 3/8 inch in diameter, while candelabra bases are around 1/2 to 5/8 inch in diameter. The most common base size is the **medium base,** which is 1 inch in diameter, while for large lamps, a 1 1/2–inch base called a **mogul base** may be used. There are numerous base styles and a variety of ways for mounting a lamp to a socket and associated lighting fixture. Figure 5.4 illustrates several of the more common base styles that are used in stage/studio and architectural applications. Often the bases are designed to ensure that a lamp

Figure 5.4 Common lamp bases

Candelabra

Medium screw

Mogul screw

Bi-pin or 2-pin

Mogul end prong

Medium pre-focus

Small fin

Large fin

Bi-post

Mogul pre-focus

Pre-focus bottom view

will be properly oriented once it is put into a lighting instrument. This is extremely important for those lamps that make use of filaments that create a directional light source. A **screw base**, like the ones typically found in residential lamps, does not require precise orientation and its threads simply need to hold the lamp in place while providing the electrical connections for the lamp. Spotlights that require a very directional light output will make use of lamps with bases such as the **bayonet, pre-focus, bi-pin** or **2-pin,** and **bi-post** configuration. Through using bases like these, a lamp can be placed in a fixture with confidence that the filament will be set in its proper orientation and that the majority of the light will be directed either to the reflector or through the lens and front of the fixture.

TUNGSTEN-HALOGEN OR QUARTZ LAMPS

The **tungsten-halogen lamp (TH LAMP)** is a specialized version of an incandescent lamp. These lamps first appeared in the 1970s and began a trend toward creating smaller light sources for stage and studio applications. The lamps are also popular in many floodlighting applications in architectural lighting. Tungsten-halogen lamps substitute a halogen gas for the traditional gases that are enclosed in a bulb and have paved the way for the manufacturing of much smaller lamps by refining the atmospheric requirements and thickening the glass bulbs. In a traditional lamp, the filament slowly breaks down as molecules of tungsten slowly drift away from the filament, becoming weaker and weaker over time. In most cases, the filament material is redeposited on the coolest portion of a lamp (the bulb), resulting in the black, cloudy deposits that appear on the surface of many lamps. Tungsten-halogen lamps, on the other hand, make use of the **tungsten-halogen process,** in

which tungsten particles are redeposited on the hottest portion of the lamp, which coincides with the filament. These lamps therefore create a recycling effect that increases the lamp's life while also preventing the tungsten buildup on the bulb that has such a negative impact on the performance of traditional incandescent lamps. Due to this, TH lamps maintain a more consistent light output throughout their life while also lasting longer. The primary issue that ultimately results in the failure of these lamps is that the tungsten particles cannot be redeposited evenly over the filament, so eventually a weakness will develop that results in the filament breaking and the lamp failing. Stage and studio lamps of this style have become so popular that **retrofit** versions of TH lamps have been created for nearly every lamp configuration for older lighting instruments while most new luminaires have been designed around the smaller TH lamps right from the beginning. Most headlamps in today's cars use TH lamp technology (although these, too, are now giving way to LED designs). While this is not technically correct, some individuals may also refer to TH lamps as **quartz lamps.**

Sidebar 5.1 LIGHT CENTER LENGTH (LCL)

When making comparisons between lamps it is quite possible to have a lamp that will physically mount in a socket of a luminaire and appear to operate normally while still being completely inappropriate for that fixture. This most commonly relates to the problem of placing a lamp's filament at the appropriate location in a luminaire and the fact that despite having the same base, lamps come in a variety of lengths which can place the filament at inappropriate heights within a luminaire. In fixture design, a lamp is chosen based on its ability to locate the filament along the primary optical path of any lenses and reflectors that are used in that fixture. If a lamp's filament is placed too high or low, the efficiency of the fixture is compromised. This was a particular problem in the 1970s and '80s when newer lamp styles were introduced as replacements or **retrofits** for fixtures that dated back to earlier times. In fact, many retrofit lamps are still in common use today. As a means of specifying these filament placements a critical measurement called the **light center length (LCL)** has been added to a lamp's specification. The LCL is simply a measurement from the center of the lamp's filament to a specified location on the lamp's base. This base location will vary depending on the type of base but remains consistent between all bases of a given style. For instance, the LCL for a pre-focus base is taken from the fins at the top of the base to the center of the filament, while the LCL for a screw base is taken from the center of the filament to the contact button at the bottom of the base. If you replace a lamp with any type of lamp other than a direct substitution of the one that you are removing, you need to make sure that the two lamps share a common LCL. Several retro-fit lamps are shown in the top row of Figure 5.5 and are characterized by the porcelain spacer that is found between the base and bulb.

The increased operating temperatures of TH lamps require several additional precautions. The most significant being that these lamps should not be handled with bare hands or fingers. If you handle the lamps, the deposits of oil from your fingertips will actually become etched into the glass bulb once the lamp is powered up. This etching often causes a weakness to develop in the bulb and the lamp will eventually melt through and burn out. Occasionally, a lamp may even fail in an explosive manner. If you should accidentally touch a quartz lamp, take care to wipe your finger marks from the bulb with alcohol before applying any power to the lamp. Quartz lamps are also fragile. When hot, they will not survive sudden shocks or bumps that might occur if anyone should be careless as they handle a lit fixture.

ANSI Codes

We use three-letter codes to refer to any given lamp with a specific combination of components. This code has been devised by the **American National Standards Institute** and is known as the **ANSI** code. This code is consistent between manufacturers and is a convenient

Figure 5.5 Several popular TH lamps

way to quickly identify a particular type of lamp. Although some properties will ultimately vary to some degree due to quality and individual manufacturing techniques, the primary characteristics of each type of lamp will remain the same between different manufacturers. Essential properties such as base, bulb, and filament styles and sizes are dictated by an assigned ANSI code, Examples of popular stage/studio lamps include EGG, EHG, EHD, FEL, BTL and HPL. While there are similarities between lamps that share similar codes, the codes themselves do not provide a clear indication of individual components for a given lamp. Each of the major lamp manufacturers provide catalogs (many online) that allow a designer to further compare specifications like color temperature and lumen output of a given lamp from one manufacturer to another.

ARC LIGHT SOURCES

An arc source quite literally produces an **arc** or spark of electricity that jumps between two differently charged contacts or electrodes. Light sources of this type are created in much the same manner as a welder produces an arc to fuse metal together. The spark that is created by the electricity flowing across the gap between the two electrodes is the light source. Arc light is extremely bright and can damage your eyes if you are exposed to it without eye protection. In addition to being one of the brightest light sources available, arc light produces light that has a much higher color temperature than standard incandescent lighting. It is easily distinguished from other light sources not only by its brightness but also by its characteristic bluish-white tint. Many arc sources have color temperatures around 6,000° K as compared to 3,000°–3,600° K range of incandescent lamps. Due to the visible contrast between arc and traditional lamps, arc sources are often used in fixtures such as followspots and moving lights where the light needs to cut through or be noticeable in comparison to the other sources that are lighting a stage.

Limelight

In the early days of theatrical spotlighting a special spotlight was created called a **limelight.** This fixture contained a block of lime that was heated with a gas flame to a point where it created a bright source of light for the stage. The flame required constant monitoring, and operators were used not only to manage the flame but also to shift the spotlight to accommodate the movements of the principal performers. These fixtures formed what may have been considered some of the earliest appearances of followspots. The limelight produced an overall quality of light that was very flattering to the actors' skin and costumes and allowed a director to add some focus to a performer without adding distortion. The limelight was so popular that when electricity appeared it didn't take long for its basic principle of operation to be adapted so that electricity became the means of producing the flaming light source.

Carbon-Arc

Some of the most common arc lighting fixtures for many years made use of two pencil-shaped electrodes or rods (a positive and negative) made of a carbon material with an outer sheathing of copper that were burned for producing light. These were often called **carbon-arc spotlights.** The electrodes were oriented in an end-to-end configuration so that the two tips were separated by a gap of approximately 1/2 inch; the location of this gap was set to coincide with the focal point of any reflectors and lenses that were contained within the fixture. In order to begin the electrical flow and resulting spark, the electrodes are briefly brought together and then gently separated. This is what we commonly call **striking** an arc. By maintaining the proper distance between the two rods, the flame or arc stays lit between the electrodes. While the arc remains lit the rods slowly burn down; an operator or mechanical device must continually feed the rods together as a means of making up for the material that has been burned away. This process of maintaining the arc is called **trimming.** A typical set of carbon rods was expendable and would only last for about 30–45 minutes before having to be replaced. Additionally, an operator would have to ensure that the position of the arc remained at the focal point of the fixture and that the gap between the electrodes didn't become too close or far apart. If the rods get too close together they can cause excessive amounts of material to be burned and splattered over the optical components of the fixture, or the rods may become fused together and extinguish the flame. If the gap becomes too wide, the arc simply fizzles out. While arc lamps cannot be dimmed electrically, operators learned to gently pull the rods farther apart to cause the light output of the lamp to drop by about 10–20%. This became known as **backing off the rods** or running the fixture at **ballet dim.** Most arc sources require that the power be converted to a DC voltage before being administered to the electrodes through the use of a special power supply or **ballast.** Carbon-arc remained one of the most popular arc sources for film projectors and followspots for many years in the entertainment industry but in recent times is found primarily in lighting archives.

Short-Arc and High-Intensity Discharge (HID) Lamps

A significant side effect of carbon-arc sources is the carbon monoxide that is given off as a byproduct of the illumination process. Over the years, many operators became victims of carbon monoxide poisoning due to the poor ventilation that was once common to many projection rooms and spotlight booths. Additionally, the constant need for monitoring and maintaining the rods and flame made the operation of carbon-arc fixtures relatively tricky. As a result, engineers developed other ways of producing arc sources without actually having to burn materials like carbon.

Short-Arc Lamps

Modern arc sources commonly used in followspots, projectors, and other high-intensity fixtures of today more commonly make use of a **short-arc lamp** (Figure 5.6). This is a specialized lamp that is made of extremely heavy glass with permanent electrodes that are built right into the lamp. The lamp is filled with a variety of gases that are kept under high pressure. Most importantly, these sources produce the same high-quality arc that is characteristic of the earlier carbon-rod fixtures without the need for constant rod adjustments and side effects like producing carbon monoxide. These lamps last much longer than carbon rods and often have lamp lives that extend to 100 hours or more. On the other hand, the lamps are usually quite expensive and require a warm-up period that can take three to five minutes from striking the arc to having the lamp come up to full power. On initial power-up these lamps have a low-intensity, very bluish-purple color until they complete the warm-up process. This warm-up period exists even if the arc has just been used or been powered down. A number of concert encores have been screwed up because

Figure 5.6 Components of a high-intensity discharge (HID or short-arc) Lamp

Bulb (coated with film)

Electrode
Arc tube
Electrode

Supports
Base (neutral)
Contact button (hot)

spot operators using these short-arc sources have powered down too soon when a band has come out to do a second or third encore. Another issue that plagued earlier versions of these sources, such as the xenon-arc lamp, was that the lamps were under such high pressure that they would occasionally explode. Heavy-duty lamp housings were added to these fixtures as a means of protecting operators from this. Several more recent versions of short-arc lamps make use of other gases and materials that work under less threatening pressures. The most common short-arcs used in today's applications include HMI (hydrargyrum medium-arc iodide or halogen metal iodide) and HTI (tubular metal halide) metal halide lamps, which produce a very intense light for the number of watts that they consume. They also have a relatively high color temperature in the range of 6,000° K. Metal halide lamps are commonly found in commercial movie projectors, today's followspots, and many moving or automated lighting fixtures.

High-Intensity Discharge (HID) Lamps

Short-arc lamps are special variations of a broader class of light sources called **HID lamps.** We tend to use the name "short-arc" more commonly with stage and studio lamps, while architectural practices refer to these light sources as HID lamps. Initially, fixtures containing these sources were used to light large open spaces. HID lamps have become quite popular in larger architectural applications such as warehouses, arenas, and manufacturing plants. Luminaires employing this technology produce a bright, widely distributed wash of light that is much more efficient than incandescent or fluorescent light sources. In general, the mounting height of these lamps is also relatively high in comparison to more traditional light sources. Lighting fixtures typically used in gymnasiums and warehouse stores like Home Depot or Bed, Bath, and Beyond form common examples of facilities that make use of HID light sources. Probably the most common application of HID lighting is found in roadway and parking lighting. With increasing energy costs, the basic design of these units has been modified to produce small HID fixtures that are used in display lighting, such as the fixtures found in many recently renovated supermarkets and retail stores. Several of the most popular HID sources used today include the familiar bluish-green **mercury lamp,** the pinkish-amber **high-pressure sodium lamps,** and the crisp, white light of **metal halide lamps.** The mercury lamp is most commonly seen along highways and building exterior applications; many of the security lamps installed on the properties of personal residences also make use of mercury light sources. The roadway lighting typically associated with interstates and urban areas uses primarily high-pressure sodium light sources. Their pinkish-orange tint makes them easily identifiable. Metal halide lamps

are more expensive to operate but produce a more diverse spectrum of light and are commonly found in retail spaces. Metal halide and mercury lamps are quite similar—both use mercury as an interior gas for the arc's conduction—but metal halide lamps differ from mercury lamps through the introduction of additional materials (metal halides) into the gas to improve the lumen output and color rendering of the lamps. Sodium lamps make use of a sodium vapor. The pinkish-orange tinted high-pressure sodium lamp has become the most popular source for roadway lighting due to its great energy efficiency. There are also **low-pressure sodium lamps,** which are marked by their strong yellow color (similar to a bug light). These are even more energy efficient but have limited applications due to their extremely narrow spectral composition and poor CRIs. All HID lamps require a ballast and cannot be ignited instantly. Just as with stage and studio short-arc lamps, these lamps glow dimly when first ignited and then slowly build to full brightness over a warm-up period. In fact, most HID lamps have warmup periods that can take up to 10 or more minutes to come up to full lumen output. If the lamp is extinguished, it will take an additional period to cool down and then five or more minutes from the re-strike until the source once again comes up to full power. Due to the mercury that a number of these lamps contain and their lower efficiency, many of these lamps are now being replaced with other sources like LEDs.

In stage and studio applications HID lamps are typically limited to being used in followspots, moving lights, and high-intensity fixtures like large studio luminaires. You may also see many of these sources used in fixtures that are used as sky trackers or search lights for bringing attention to malls, car dealerships, sports attractions, and other special events. In film, these light sources are often used on location shoots to fill in shadows on large interior or exterior settings. Several of the most popular HID lamps in use today are specific variations of the metal halide lamp and include the **HMI (halogen metal iodide)** that has color temperatures that make it comparable to daylight, the **CSI (compact source iodide),** the **CID (compact iodide daylight),** and **xenon** lamp. Each lamp has a specific mixture of material components that produces light associated with a particular color temperature, spectral composition, and lumen output.

GASEOUS DISCHARGE LAMPS

The most common form of gaseous discharge lamp is the **fluorescent lamp** (Figure 5.7). For many years, due to both its ability to produce uniform washes and its comparable high power efficiency, architectural practices have used fluorescent rather than incandescent lamps as a primary light source. In fact, the need for power conservation toward the end of the 1990s has resulted

Figure 5.7 Components of a gaseous discharge (fluorescent) lamp

in a trend in which even more fluorescent fixtures have become attractive alternatives to the incandescent sources that were traditionally used in many residential and hospitality applications. The **compact fluorescent lamp (CFL)** is an adaptation of these lamps that for a period of time was becoming a popular alternative light source for many residential lamps. Modifications of these lamps have appeared in all areas of fixture design and include table and floor lamps as well as downlights and wall washer designs. It is hard to enter a hotel these days where compact fluorescent lamps can't be found in nearly every lighting application. There's even a new trend to replace the once-efficient HID lighting installations of factories and warehouse stores with even more efficient next-generation fluorescent sources and LEDs.

Fluorescent Lamps

The **fluorescent lamp** works on the principle of energizing an enclosure or field of low-pressure gas between two electrodes or cathodes. However, unlike an arc source that uses an arc to produce light, this arc is of relative low intensity and instead energizes another material that begins to glow or create light. In the case of fluorescent lighting, the gas for the electron flow has traditionally been mercury, and the material that glows is phosphorous. The electron flow through the excited gas causes radiation to be emitted primarily in the ultraviolet rather than visible portion of the spectrum. This energy is then used to excite the powdered phosphorous material to a point where it will fluoresce (give off light). A similar effect can be seen on a moonlit night as the glowing waves of plankton spread away from a boat's wake or across the breakers that form along a beach. While fluorescent sources don't usually create strong enough intensities to be considered for theatrical applications, they are often the source of choice for many commercial operations where distances between a fixture and task are relatively close, there are extended hours of operation, and there are concerns about energy conservation. In addition to relatively low light output, another disadvantage of fluorescent tubes relates to the negative impact that cold temperatures can have upon their operation. The fluorescent tubes that are commonly found in gas stations often pulsate and sputter when exposed to winter temperatures. Fluorescent lamps also don't react well to dimming (which will be discussed later).

A fluorescent lamp cannot be turned on by simply applying power to a lamp; in most cases, fluorescent lamps require that cathodes be used to stimulate their electrical arcs. There are both cold and hot cathode systems, but due to energy efficiency, most fluorescent lamps make use of hot cathode or rapid-start technology. In the majority of fluorescent luminaires a transformer-like device called a **ballast** is wired in series with the lamp to regulate the current and voltage of the lamp while also providing the initial burst of voltage that is needed to start the ignition process. A starter element may also be required with some fluorescent lamps. HID lamps also make use of a ballast. Ballasts are specified or matched to a given lamp and are not interchangeable between different wattages of fluorescent lamps. It should also be noted that the power load of a circuit containing fluorescent lamps must not only include the wattage of the lamps but also any ballasts that are in a circuit. However, the power requirements for a fluorescent lamp are also much smaller than for a comparable incandescent lamp that would be used for producing the same amount of light. A typical installation consists of a single ballast being shared between two lamps, although there are also fixtures that make use of a single lamp and associated ballast. In addition to their overall energy efficiency, fluorescent lamps also have lamp lives that are as high as 10,000–20,000 hours, which is up to 20 times longer than comparable incandescent lamps. In areas where it is difficult to change lamps, the fluorescent source becomes a popular design choice.

The most popular form of fluorescent lamps are in the shape of tubes that vary in lengths of up to 8 feet. The thickness or diameter of the tube is also considered, with the most popular lamps being variations of the T-12, T-8, and T-5 lamps. These numbers refer to a tubular construction with a diameter expressed in 1/8-inch intervals. The T-8 lamp therefore is 1 inch in diameter. The T-12 was the primary workhorse of fluorescent lighting for many years while the T-8 and T-5 are now the most popular configurations. The T-5 lamp is especially popular in applications like compact florescent lamps. The lamps also don't necessarily have to be in the straight tube or linear shape of traditional fluorescent fixtures. U-shaped and circular-shaped lamps are also popular. In fact, many compact fluorescent lamp designs shape the lamp into a coil. On the whole, most fluorescent lamps have a strong spectral response in the green area of the spectrum and are therefore not the most flattering form of illumination. However, by varying the mixtures of the gases and fluorescent materials, manufacturers have been able to create a range of fluorescent lamps with a variety of different light qualities and CRIs. The most popular versions include "cool white" and "warm white," which refer to the spectral composition of the light produced by each lamp. The "cool white" lamp produces a bluer light, while the "warm white" lamp has better spectral responses in the warm portions of the spectrum. Additional variations of these lamps include "daylight," "cool deluxe," and "warm deluxe" lamps that make use of phosphors that have different responses to a wider selection of lighting wavelengths. On the other hand, while incandescent lamps have a CRI of nearly 100, most fluorescent lamps have CRIs on the order of 50–90. There are also specialty fluorescent lamps used in areas such as television production, display, and advertising work that can achieve much better color rendering, but their associated prices also increase significantly as better CRIs are obtained.

LOW-VOLTAGE LAMPS

In the last 50 years there hasn't been a strong demand for low-voltage lighting in the area of general illumination. As a rule, low-voltage sources were more commonly associated with applications in which power supply became an issue (e.g., portable devices such as in transportation—cars, planes, utility equipment, etc.) or in situations where a specific lighting effect was required. For a number of years, the most common use of low-voltage lighting in entertainment applications was in the use of **aircraft landing lights (ACLs)** for concerts. These are very narrow-beamed PAR lamps that have been adapted from their designated use in airplanes. However, in the last 20 or so years we have seen a significant appearance of low-voltage lighting systems migrating into the entertainment and architectural fields of lighting. In general, low-voltage lamps operate on a relatively low DC voltage, the most common voltage being 12 volts—although 24-volt sources are also in use. The advantage of low-voltage systems lies in their ability to make a smaller lamp and filament, therefore becoming a more efficient lamp through a closer approximation to a point light source. On stage these sources have typically been confined to mini-strip units where numerous lamps are wired together into alternating circuits that provide for the creation of several even washes of colored light. The individual lamps that are utilized in these fixtures are **MR (miniature reflector) lamps.** Much like their larger R and PAR lamp cousins, these lamps come in a variety of sizes and pre-engineered beam patterns. Several common configurations of the MR lamp include the MR-11, MR-13, and MR-16 lamps (Figure 5.8). In architectural applications, these lamps are popular in decorative display and track lighting fixtures. They are also a dominant source for landscape lighting luminaires.

A significant difference between low-voltage light sources and traditional lamps is that the voltage provided to the lamps must be reduced to a comparatively small percentage of the standard 120-volt line-voltage that is typically used to control our lighting fixtures. If a low-voltage lamp were to be plugged directly into a standard wall outlet it would quickly blow out due to the excessive voltage. Low-voltage lamps, therefore,

Figure 5.8 A MR-16 low-voltage lamp

require that a transformer be incorporated into the circuit to reduce the voltage to a point that is within the safe operating range of a lamp. While a single-source fixture may have its own transformer, there are applications where a transformer may be used to power several different fixtures or lamps at the same time. In stage and studio applications this would be true of many fixtures that use multiple low-voltage light sources like the brute or mini-strip fixtures that have already been mentioned, while in low-voltage landscape lighting a single transformer is often used for powering 20 or more fixtures.

SOLID-STATE LIGHT SOURCES

In the last 20 or so years there have been a number of advances in lamp technology, but the area that is getting the most attention is in **solid-state light sources**. These are sources where solid-state electronic components convert electrical potential into light. The most familiar form of solid-state lighting comes in the form of LEDs, which are revolutionizing the entire lighting industry. Though these sources at first gave very limited lumen output and weren't used for much more than power indicators, they have advanced significantly in not only the amount of light that they produce, but also in other capacities such as being able to produce white light, color rendering ability, and efficiency. The architectural and display/exhibit lighting communities have been rapidly shifting towards these efficient light sources for a number of years. In fact, due to the "ban the bulb" movement, it is becoming more and more difficult to find traditional incandescent lamps for common residential lighting applications. LED sources can even be found as replacements to traditional fluorescent tubes and street lamps. However, up to the last 15 or so years, the entertainment industry has been reluctant to adopt these sources due to their lower light output when compared to the conventional sources that are typically used in stage and studio applications.

In the first edition of *Stage Lighting: Fundamentals and Applications* I indicated that though we were using various forms of colored LEDs to provide wash illumination, the industry at that time hadn't produced a line of white LEDs that were suited to the spotlighting needs of stage design—primarily due to lower light outputs. Now, the industry not only has white LED sources capable of fulfilling our needs, but still further innovations in LED technologies have been made that will most likely make LEDs the source of choice in the not-too-distant future. Not only the theatrical community, but also the film and video industries, are migrating towards LED sources. The following sections discuss basic concepts of how LEDs function, several of the advantages and disadvantages of this technology, and several variations of LED technology that are being applied to the lighting industry. While these discussions are limited to examining LEDs as a light source, Chapter 6 will examine a variety of luminaires that make use of the new LED technology and Chapter 8 will discuss how this technology is making big changes in the role of projection. Though LEDs form the most significant area of solid-state sources, there have been other significant developments in solid-state lighting as well. The one receiving the most attention for stage applications is the **plasma lamp,** which is discussed at the end of this section.

LEDs

LEDs are a relatively new form of light source. We recognize them primarily from their initial use as indicator lights for electronic devices: beginning in the 1970s, virtually all power indicators in this equipment made use of a red LED to indicate that the power for a device was on. As time went on we saw variations in LEDs that produced yellow, green, and even blue light for monitoring electronic devices. We saw them appear in CB radios to indicate transmission strength, while the audio industry used them to monitor signal strength in sound gear like mixers and amplifiers. In the last 20 years, a newer generation of LEDs (High-Output LEDs) have been developed in which the light output is sufficient enough to be used as a light source. These newer-generation LEDs have made their way into a variety of applications such as flashlights, traffic signals, car head and signal lamps, holiday lights, video/advertising signage, and finally into actual luminaire designs. They first appeared in industries where throw distances were not that significant (display/exhibit and limited applications of architectural lighting), then moved into specialty applications in stage and club design, to the point where they are now being considered as a primary light source in entertainment design.

LEDs (Figure 5.9) are solid-state devices that produce light through a process in which electricity is applied to a crystal or diode material. The diodes are typically made up of two contacts (an anode and cathode) that come together on a common surface formed by a semi-conductor chip. Diodes allow electricity to flow in a single direction only, and when electricity is applied to the circuit (a low-voltage DC current) atoms move across the semi-conductor chip in a manner that produces light in a limited range of wavelengths (colors) as a product of the reaction. The reaction and components are contained in an epoxy lens that helps focus the light in a given direction. In some cases, the lens may also contain a specific mixture of phosphors that allow a specific color of light to be created in part by a phosphoric process (blue and white LEDs are often produced in this manner). By varying the construction and materials of a diode (and/or phosphors), different colored light outputs can be achieved. More importantly, since the components are solid-state, there are no filaments or other components to burnout—which means that an LED can last for an exceptional amount of time (current estimates place most lamp lives for LEDs at between 50,000 and 300,000 hours). The only downside is that the light output of LEDs will gradually diminish over time.

In addition to their long life cycles, LEDs can provide a number of other advantages to their users. First, the devices are extremely small—about the size of a pencil eraser in most cases, which means that they come much closer to creating the point light source that we desire than traditional incandescent sources provide. Their size also allows for many more of them to be mounted in a given area, which becomes a factor when designing fixtures with more than one LED light source.

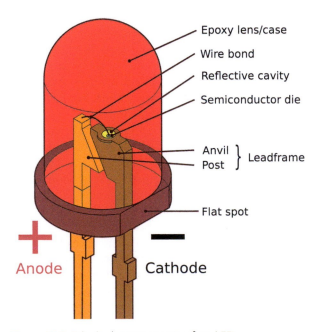

Figure 5.9 Principal components of an LED

One of the most important advantages of LEDs lie in their efficiency. For the amount of energy that they consume, they produce an especially large amount of light and very little energy is wasted as heat. As an example, a 9-watt LED replacement lamp produces an amount of light comparable to a 60-watt general duty incandescent lamp. Other advantages of LEDs include their extreme durability and ruggedness, their ability to produce light in a very narrow range of wavelengths, little heat/wasted energy, no warm-up or cooling periods, and low power consumption. They also have the ability to respond quickly to dimming instructions and voltage changes like pulsating. While a traditional halogen lamp will have a lamp life in the hundreds of hours, LEDs have life spans in the neighborhood of 50,000 hours or more.

With all of these advantages, we must then ask why LEDs haven't been used in more applications. This answer lies predominantly in the intensity factor: despite all their advantages, until recently LEDs have not been capable of producing enough light to compete with other light sources. However, as technology improves, so does the intensity of LEDs—and as a rule, the intensity of these sources increases by 20-fold every 10 years. More remarkably, this is done at the same time that these sources become even more power efficient. Currently, the most significant disadvantages of LED lighting are the initial costs of the technology (a traditional spotlight will retail for around $275 while a comparable LED unit can cost closer to $1,800 or more), limited voltage requirements (voltage must be kept within a fairly narrow range), compromised CRIs (light output of white LEDs often fail to cover the full spectrum), low intensity operation (LEDs tend to bump on and off at somewhere around 10–20% intensity), and sensitivity to temperature. Low temperatures can inhibit the atomic flow while high temperatures can cause damage—an especially important consideration in clustered LEDs where heat sinks and cooling fans might have to be designed into these units. Another concern is related to the ability of these units to maintain consistent color output, especially if units were purchased over a period of time where LEDs may have come from different sources or manufacturing runs (**binning**). This can be addressed by providing methods to recalibrate the LEDs in more expensive units. As LEDs have become brighter, they have found their way into an increasing number of applications. This trend should continue well into the future as more and more lighting fields are finding ways to use LEDs as a light source—including the entertainment lighting industry. The development of white LED technologies over the last several years has been exceptional and there now are a number of companies manufacturing LED spotlights in addition to a range of other luminaires that utilize LED sources. ETC has even introduced an LED housing that is used to convert its popular Source Four units to a LED light

Figure 5.10 ETC Source 4WRD™ LED retrofit lamp housing
Credit: photo courtesy of Electronic Theatre Controls (ETC)

source (Figure 5.10). This conversion isn't complex and doesn't take much longer than simply replacing a lamp.

Several popular uses of LEDs include traffic lights, various chase and effects lighting equipment, video walls, decorative architectural applications like along stair and platform edges or cove lighting, and a number of display and exhibit lighting applications. As a source, LEDs may be viewed directly (e.g., a video wall where a composite image is produced through a matrix of LEDs) or indirectly, where the emitted light is cast onto another surface. A very popular use of LEDs is when they are mounted in clusters that contain at least one LED of each of the three primary colors (red, blue, and green) called **tri-colored luminaires**. Video walls and many electronic signs and billboards form the ultimate example of clustering LEDs into a composite lighting system that is capable of forming photographic and video images (these are examined in detail in Chapter 8).

Unfortunately, the spectral output of LEDs is very narrow. Though you can theoretically additively mix a seemingly infinite number of colors as well as white light with just three colors of LEDs (light's primary colors of red, blue, and green), there are large holes in the spectral composition of the produced light that often results in less than satisfactory color rendering with these fixtures (see Figure 5.11). As a solution, LEDs of additional colors like amber, white, or cyan are added to improve a luminaire's color rendering through filling in the missing elements of the fixture's spectral composition. Several variations of this technology have been incorporated into fixtures that mimic both striplights and PAR-64 luminaire designs. The voltage or intensity of each LED color is varied so that the overall mixture combines to produce colored light through additive mixing (RGB mixing if using

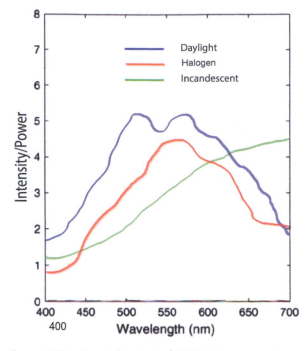

Figure 5.11a Spectral output of LED light sources a. Incandescent, halogen, and daylight light sources

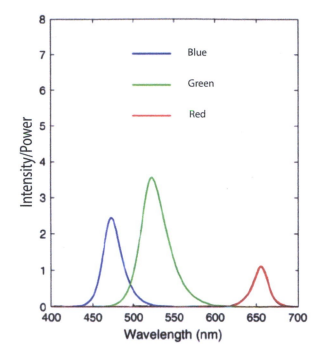

Figure 5.11b A three-color LED light source

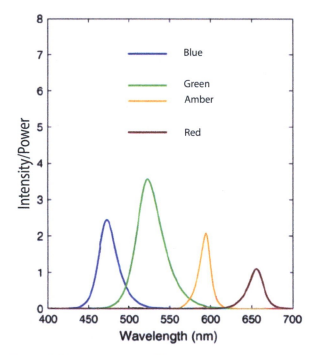

Figure 5.11c A four-color LED light source

Figure 5.11d A seven-color LED light source

tri-colored luminaires). Many of these fixtures produce an unnatural, high-color temperature version of white light when using LEDs of just the three primary colors. By creating an even more sophisticated array of additional multi-colored LEDs, a fixture can be created that has the potential for producing almost any conceivable color of light while the unnatural white and color rendering ability of the three-colored fixtures can also be improved upon

significantly. Figure 5.11 illustrates a comparison between the spectral outputs of a tricolor LED source with an incandescent source and a fixture with additional LED colors. ETC manufactures a series of luminaires (Selador™ Series) that make use of seven different LED colors that produce exceptionally good color response in anything that they light. See Sidebar 5.2 to learn more about one of the innovators of the Selador Color Mixing System.

Rob Gerlach

Credit: photo courtesy of Rob Gerlach

Robert (Rob) Gerlach is the co-inventor of the Selador product line and x7™ LED color system that is now found in many of ETC's LED luminaires. The Selador system was introduced in 2004 and pioneered the use of seven different colored LEDs in a system that could effectively mix nearly any color imaginable. More importantly, since the system made use of LEDs of seven different colors, as opposed to the tri-colored (red, blue, and green) LEDs of the time, the system provided much more subtle color blending and extremely high color rendering—the additional colored LEDs filling in the holes in the spectral coverage that the tri-colored units were limited by. In 2009, Selador was acquired by ETC and Rob joined its team to continue his research towards developing LED products that are brighter and even more colorful than those that are currently available.

Rob specializes in research, design, and evaluation of LED-based luminaires. He is particularly interested in the development of theatrical luminaires with a special interest in color-mixing fixtures: "Over my career in this industry, my expertise has become more and more focused on advanced color mixing and control, color theory and metrics, color metamerism, and psycho-physiological interactions with color and light." He had no formal training or background in lighting, per se, before leaping into the business of designing and building LED fixtures: "I had a MBA and a BA in Classical Music Composition and only had a life-long, deeply registered fascination with color and light." Starting as a preschool-aged child, he would go to the theatre and spend half his time gazing at the lights, whether they were turned on or not: "I spent countless hours playing with colored lamps in my parents' basement and examining natural light all around me, picking up by intuition many of the principles that I could attach labels to many years later."

The early days of Rob's research were marked primarily by his individual drive to seek out alternative methods of creating better color responses in fixtures using LED illumination:

"Upon attaching myself to LEDs for exploring novel approaches to color mixing (at a certain point, I couldn't avoid thinking about this), I dove into as much self-guided education as I could generate. In 2001, while attending Lightfair, I found the perfect business partner for me and my little venture. This partnership was with lighting designer Novella Smith, who helped me work through the three years of development that we needed before we had a product ready to bring to market. It was also in 2001 that I received a life-giving grant from USITT, which provided essential funding to develop the first large-scale, theatrical LED fixtures. Early prototype units helped prove my gut-feelings about additive color mixing to myself as much as to anyone else. Up to that point, no fixture existed that could do the work I needed."

Rob continues to explain:

"As important as the funds were from the USITT grant, the stamp of approval that USITT gave for my research gave me vital access to a whole industry of professionals who otherwise might not have given me any notice. Interaction with them was an invaluable education on the craft of lighting design, the artistic process, and the working structure of the entertainment industry. They imparted to me a secondhand familiarity with the basic lighting tools that I hadn't ever actually used in practice, coming as an outsider to the profession."

It took three and a half years before Selador was ready to go to market. During that interim period, Rob was a featured presenter at USITT's 2003 conference, wrote articles in the industry's trade magazines, and spoke numerous times around the country about additive color mixing:

"It was agonizing to have no product to promote on these occasions, but these, too, were learning experiences for me, and they helped generate a budding, latent demand for better color from LED luminaires. I couldn't work where I do today without the profound influence of my co-founder and business partner, Novella Smith. Raising a new company together can feel an awful lot like child-rearing, compounded when that company is built around a new technology. It put strain on us and on our families that we couldn't have imagined at the beginning. There were many times when I was convinced that Selador was doomed to failure. I'm sure Novella experienced some of those moments, but she and I worked very hard to make our families and our relationship top priorities. Novella pulled me through some impossible struggles, and she gave me critical market awareness as a career lighting designer herself."

In discussing his shift from being an independent business to being acquired by ETC, Rob shares some valuable insights:

"My current work is narrower now than it used to be, and that's a tremendous luxury. Previously I had many things to manage, including overseeing a purchasing, manufacturing, and logistics operation (which I never enjoyed doing and never did very well), directing all aspects of research and development of new products, and keeping a company running with balanced books. I especially hated the managing-the-books part—probably because it took eight years of working on Selador before I got my first, real paycheck."

That paycheck came the day they sold all of the Selador product rights to ETC:

"Now I get to do just the parts of the job that I truly love: checking out new advancements in technology; working in super-secret labs with marvelous, unique tools for high-level color mixing and analysis; providing periodic input on new product development while leaving the daily management of an R&D team to people who do it much better than I can; and going around the world with beloved colleagues, sharing fun presentations about color with fantastically gracious audiences."

At times, Rob also gets to help out with university research or can insert bits of advice into standards development and similar work that is less about producing products and more about enhancing the overall industry: "These extra opportunities are particularly fulfilling for me. I love deciphering why things work the way they work and how to best apply this knowledge for user benefits."

In closing, Rob shares that

"In the categories of color and human vision, color control and quantification, and the language of color communication, we have long distances to travel before we can start to claim that we've tackled the most important challenges. Doing this work requires that I stay constantly abreast of new advances in technology, and that can be a little exhausting; it's not always easy to predict where relevant improvements or solutions will pop up. By the time new technology shows up in competitors' offerings, it's far too late to be just learning about it. I need to have eyes on technologies that have not yet been fully proven and must be ready to leap onto some of them quite early, occasionally without knowing that they will survive into maturity."

As a final bit of advice Rob states:

"I believe that to be truly innovative, one must be humble enough to never presume to know the best answer—not without seriously questioning it. This can be a lot harder than it sounds, particularly when working with large teams or well-established organizations. I've been unusually lucky to consistently work with some of the very best souls in the industry, who allow this sort of questioning to occur as a common part of the development process. Above all, I try to remind myself and my industry to frequently set aside market research and science assumptions and to simply engage our own eyeballs in adoring the miracle of color and light. It can invoke surprising truth. My eyeballs led me onto my unique path, and there are many unique paths waiting to be seen and explored."

Some LED sources make use of the same color mixing principle and combine several variations of white LEDs (warm and cool) to create either a variety or specific color temperature of white light. Variations of these white LED designs and colored LED sources are now being engineered into spotlight designs where the endless possibilities of color mixing will most likely render the use of gel obsolete. Also of significance are the small multi-colored LED emitters that are found in materials like LED tapes (Figure 5.12) where a single solid-state component contains elements that provide various combinations of RGB or more colored LED lighting. These tapes, though fragile, are appearing in all sorts of applications such as lining architectural features like cove and platform edges, backlighting panels and decorative pieces, and edging scenic units—they are even being worked into costume pieces.

Now, with the introduction of successful white LEDs in spotlight designs, LEDs are pretty much posed to become the primary source of illumination in the future. Several examples of these LED luminaires are examined in Chapter 6. For now though, even though the technology is constantly improving and the costs keep dropping, the costs of these luminaires often remain beyond the means of many production organizations. One additional concern relates to how facilities are managing the transition from conventional sources to LED technologies. Traditional sources are dimmed through using dimmers and varying the AC voltage of a circuit while most LED luminaires achieve their dimming internally and need only a standard line-voltage supplied to them (120 volts in the United States). This can cause problems when we want to use some combination of conventional and LED luminaires and the theatre does not have enough non-dim accommodations to run all of the LED gear. In many cases, this can be solved by going to the dimmer racks and swapping out the dimmer modules for non-dim modules or by changing the profile characteristics of the associated

circuits/dimmers, but this may not always be possible. New theatres will more than likely be set up to run almost entirely on LED lighting, but when renovating an existing facility where it is known that conventional fixtures will remain an important part of the lighting inventory for some time, some sort of balance will have to be determined in order to provide proper circuiting for both the conventional and LED lighting. Touring productions are probably least affected since all they need is a company switch that is sufficient to cover their total load while all of their touring equipment can be tailored to the LED technology. Additionally, LED or solid-state lighting requires that more data lines/ports be available to send control information to each of the LED fixtures. Despite these issues, many people in the industry feel that we are currently experiencing the next major innovation in the lighting industry and that LEDs represent that future. Figure 5.13 illustrates two popular styles of LED luminiares.

Figure 5.13a Cluster LED luminaires. a. A LED PAR Luminaire, ETC Selador Desire D60X LED PAR

Credit: photo courtesy ETC Lighting

Figure 5.12 City Theatrical's QolorPIX™ LED Tape

Credit: photo courtesy of City Theatical

Figure 5.13b A LED Wash Luminaire, Philips Color Kinetics ColorBlaze Striplight

Credit: photo courtesy Philips Lighting

Plasma Lamps

Plasma lamps represent another form of solid-state lighting, although some feel that these are more properly characterized as gaseous discharge light sources. The reason for this is that the plasma that forms the actual light source is a gaseous substance contained in a heavy quartz bulb that has no electrodes or filaments. These lamps are activated by radio frequencies/waves (RF) rather than directly by electricity. In actuality, the cloud is a mix of noble gases such as argon and xenon along with various materials such as metal halides, mercury, and salts that become energized and form the light as a result of the RF stimulation. The actual light source is quite small. It is surrounded by a ceramic insulator and series of fins that form a heat sink to help dissipate the heat that is produced by the lamp (Figure 5.14). This entire assembly is often referred to as a "puck." A separate power supply containing the RF transmitter is used to focus the radio waves onto the emitter, which then energizes the lamp. The light output of these sources is very similar to short-arc sources and they have characteristically high CRIs (90 or better). These lamps are very efficient at producing light of this quality while at the same time their life span is quite high—somewhere in the range of 10,000 hours or more. Plasma lamps were first developed around 2000 and have seen a very limited use in theatrical and stage design, with just a few manufacturers creating luminaires that make use of plasma light sources. One area where they seem to be making an appearance is in automated lighting, where their qualities of the produced light are very similar to those sources that are currently used in these fixtures.

NON-TRADITIONAL LIGHT SOURCES

Though the incandescent lamp has been the most popular light source for most theatrical luminaires, in recent years there has been an increasing interest in using alternative light sources in theatrical production. Energy efficiency has driven the architectural markets towards fluorescent and LED sources while the need for higher intensities and specific light qualities has led to the acceptance of a number of short-arc sources for uses in retail lighting as well as for exterior applications like street and roadway lighting. Theatrical and other entertainment lighting designers are also making use of these HID and other non-traditional light sources for various stage applications.

Ballasted Fixtures

In theatrical applications, non-traditional sources are usually used to introduce a different quality of light to a stage. Qualities like color temperature and color rendering can vary considerably from one light source to another. One of the most significant differences of non-traditional fixtures is that most of these units make use of arc sources—with the added requirement that a ballast is required for each unit. This also means that electrical dimming of these sources isn't possible and that some form of mechanical mechanism (**dowser**) must be provided for producing any dimming effect in the light. Lighting instruments that may have ballasts include HMI sources in Fresnels, ellipsoidal reflector spotlights, and followspots. Light sources like xenon or other short-arcs may also be used for various specialized effects. Most moving lights make use of HMI sources, which provide a bright high color temperature light that will cut through traditional stage lights and bring focus to a given entertainer. Both high-pressure sodium and mercury sources have been used in productions of major operas and other theatrical events to bring a unique lighting quality to a setting. In architectural and film production, ballasted fixtures are often preferred in order to avoid the **red shift** and associated changes in color temperature that dimming can cause to an incandescent lamp. Intensity, in these cases, is controlled by varying the wattage of the source or by placing filters or **scrims** over the front of the fixtures.

Blacklight

Blacklight (also known as ultraviolet or UV light) is a special form of light that exists primarily outside of our visual spectrum. More specifically, blacklight is a form of ultraviolet radiation that has the ability to cause bleached materials or materials that have fluorescent properties to radiate or glow in brilliant colors under what appears to be a deep bluish-violet light. Through the use of special ultraviolet paints, objects that appear normal under traditional lighting can glow in iridescent or, even more often, psychedelic colors. Though used on stage, blacklight is most commonly used for effects in specialty applications such as in fun houses or Halloween displays. You might also ask your parents or grandparents about the blacklight posters that were once so popular in

Figure 5.14 The Plasma LiFi Puck by Luxim Corporation

Credit: photo courtesy Luxim Corporation

college dorm rooms. Blacklight works best when it is the only light source being used; its effect is quickly compromised once other light sources are introduced to an environment. Consumer-grade blacklights can often be found at novelty stores like Spencer's Gifts but in most instances are ineffective on many stages.

Blacklight is generally produced in one of two manners. The first, and least effective, is through special blacklight tube lamps that fit standard fluorescent luminaires. These can come in a variety of lengths such as the popular 4-foot tube version. The tubes are specially constructed and can be recognized by their black or purplish color. The light that they produce is relatively low in intensity and objects must typically be fairly close for them to produce the best effects. Often an entire bank of these must be run across a stage to maintain a uniform quality for the effect. A second variety is much more powerful: one or two of the units can frequently light an entire stage. These are blacklight cannons, which for all practical purposes are HID luminaires that make use of a mercury vapor light source (which produces a byproduct of a lot of ultraviolet light) and a heavy ultraviolet filter (that filters out virtually all light from the visible spectrum). An even newer innovation (Figure 5.15) makes use of LEDs to produce blacklight effects.

Figure 5.16 A contemporary strobe luminaire (Martin's Atomic 3000 DMX)

Credit: photo courtesy Martin Lighting

Strobes

Other non-traditional sources include **strobe lights,** which are specialty lamps that can be set to a rapid on-off firing sequence to produce a stop-motion effect. Most strobes are equipped with a high-intensity xenon lamp that creates a bright high-color temperature flash. Older models had an independent control unit that allowed an operator to manipulate both the speed and intensity of the flashes. Contemporary strobes (Figure 5.16) are controlled through control signals (**DMX**) that allow a designer to pre-program the intensity, rate, and duration of the flashes. More importantly, while these fixtures can still be used to produce standard strobe effects, they can

Figure 5.15 Two styles of LED blacklight fixtures (VioStorm Series by Wildfire Lighting)

Credit: photo courtesy Wildfire Lighting

also be programmed to produce more random effects like lightning flashes or explosions. There are even variations of strobe units that have multiple lamps. Care must be used when using these fixtures because the rapid flashing has been known to trigger epileptic seizures in people who are exposed to them.

Neon

Neon is a form of decorative lighting in which neon gas is placed in a glass tube that is bent into designer-determined shapes. It is a special form of gaseous discharge lighting. When turned on, the gas is energized by a transformer, which then causes the entire tube to glow and give off light. We frequently see neon used in outlining applications or in signage such as those typically found in bars and nightclubs. Though neon has been used on stage, due to the glass, it is extremely fragile and therefore not well-suited for stage applications. It is also quite costly because the tubes are typically hand-crafted to specific shapes needed by a given design. Most people collectively refer to neon as any form of lighting produced in this manner, however, neon gas gives off an intense red-orange light while other gases such as argon with a bit of mercury could be used along with various phosphor coatings to produce a number of additional colors such as yellow, green, blue, and white. Due to costs and fragility, there are now a number of alternate solutions to neon that can produce very convincible neon-like effects. Several of these alternatives include cold-cathode and fiber-optic treatments along with plastic tubes that have LEDs contained throughout their length.

Fiber Optics

Fiber optics have not made a strong appearance in theatre applications due to the relatively low intensity of the light that they produce. However, beautiful stardrops and other effects have been made possible through this innovation. Fiber optics have even been worked into scenic, prop, and costume designs. There are two variations of fiber-optic cable that are popular in entertainment applications. The first, **end-emitting fiber**, conducts light through its length until it emerges at the end of the fiber with relatively no light being emitted from its sides. This is the type of fiber used in stardrops. It is also used to conduct light to a point where a lens or head then projects the light onto an object (such as in a retail item or museum artifact). The second, **side-emitting fiber**, conducts light along its length and also radiates light outward along its sides and glows like a neon tube. Side-emitting fiber is used quite effectively to simulate neon signs. It is also used to line objects like the edges of pools. In either case, the fibers are joined together at one end, where a manifold connects the bundle of fibers

to a light source. The source is called an **illuminator**. In addition to the light source, many illuminators also house devices like color wheels and patterned disks that produce color variations and shimmering effects in the light. The majority of the heat produced in these systems is confined to the illuminator.

Architectural and display applications have made use of this technology for many years. Stars have been created in plaster ceilings and poster board displays. Model theatres have been created that use fiber optics for creating illumination. Side-emitting fibers have been especially effective as a decorative element for lining objects like steps, buildings, and ceiling perimeters, while museums may use end-emitting systems and specialized heads to direct light to heat-sensitive areas of a display. Particularly interesting uses of fiber optics have been as tools for making design presentations and in educational lighting. Here, model theatres are outfitted with miniature fiber-optic heads and a control system that allows a set designer's model to be lit on a miniature scale. LightBox (Figure 5.17) is a particularly successful product that uses this technology.

Lasers

Lasers are a special form of light. While they may combine several different wavelengths, they still represent a fairly narrow range, if not a single wavelength, of light. More importantly, although most light is emitted as a scattered form of energy, a laser produces its light in a very narrowly defined direction. This degree of directionality makes it an ideal source for defining lines, which is precisely why we use it for line-referencing

Figure 5.17 A miniature fiber-optic model theatre for Syracuse University using the LightBox Model Lighting System by Thematics. Scenic models are placed within the structure and are lit by miniature fiber-optic heads that are scaled optically to actual stage luminaires. The system can be colored and is controlled by a standard console that allows the actual cues to be pre-programmed and simulated.

Credit: photo courtesy Syracuse University

applications in the surveying or construction industries. Additionally, a laser emits light in a synchronized manner. Rather than creating a random or continuous emission of light, a laser emits its energy in such a way that corresponding wavelengths and the waveform of each individual wave are in sync or in step with one another. This produces a cumulative effect that results in a higher overall amplitude for the light and associated energy of a laser. This cumulative effect is responsible for the energy of lasers and is called **stepping.** The principle is quite similar to that of AC power creation, with the exception being that with a laser we are trying to maximize, rather than neutralize, the strength of the combined wavelengths. For all practical appearances a laser will appear as a bright dot of light on any object that it happens to be played upon. However, if the air is charged with particles like dust or haze, the laser becomes clearly visible as a line of light. This effect is what originally made lasers so popular in the entertainment field. Lasers are often played on theatrical fog and haze for a number of spectacle productions like concert events. In outdoor settings, clouds and even smoke from fireworks are used as projection surfaces for laser effects.

Even up to now, lasers have not played a great role in lighting for illumination. This is in part due to the extremely concentrated effect of these light beams. However, this intense concentration of energy is precisely what makes them so attractive to industries that use laser technology for various cutting or precision measurement applications. Engineers often refer to lasers as being "coherent forms of light." The medical and manufacturing communities have been using lasers effectively for medical or machining procedures for a number of years, using them to cut and shape metal, take bearings for surveying, remove damaged tissue in surgery, and to create straight reference lines for hanging pictures or ensuring that a course of masonry remains level. Several years ago I even had a cavity treated with the use of a dental laser. Despite all the beneficial uses of lasers, the lighting industry to this point has only come to use them as a means of creating effects or for spotting purposes. On a small scale, these effects can be on the order of a single point of light (comparable to laser pointers that are used in classroom or business presentations) while grander schemes include aerial displays during pop concerts and other spectacle events where the laser effects can be seen for miles around. Just outside of Atlanta, Georgia, is Stone Mountain Park, which houses one of the largest aerial laser shows in the world. This 30- to 40-minute production is performed nightly over the summer and contains numerous laser effects and fireworks that are choreographed to popular music. The closing show that occurs nightly at Epcot Center in Disney World (*IllumiNations*) also incorporates a number of laser effects that are projected throughout the lagoon and surrounding areas of the park. This presentation culminates in a grand finale of fireworks and laser image of a rotating globe that is projected onto the signature sphere that houses the Spaceship Earth attraction.

Laser devices should always be considered dangerous due to the extreme concentration of energy that is associated with these light sources. Even relatively small laser pointers bear warnings that speak of the potential damage that a laser can bring to a person's eyesight. Commercial lasers always require that some form of protective measures be taken to guard against accidental exposure of the laser to both the operator and other individuals. In entertainment applications there are specific guidelines that operators must follow in order to protect not only the audience but the performers as well. In many circumstances a laser may not be used unless the operator is licensed. Some practical considerations of laser operation include ensuring that the laser paths are far enough off the ground that nobody can look directly into a laser beam or that a laser reflection won't be directed onto an unsuspecting victim. A popular concert effect at one time involved directing laser beams several feet above the heads of an audience, which worked fine until audience members got the brilliant idea of standing on each other's shoulders to "touch the light."

There are several notable laser effects that are used in the entertainment industry. The first, a **scanner,** makes use of the principle of rapidly moving the beam of a laser from place to place. The eye cannot distinguish this rapid movement and does not see the laser as the single point of light that it actually is. Instead, through perception, we connect the points and see the image as a series of lines that lie along the path of the laser. In this manner, we use the laser and scanning to actually trace or draw basic images. A similar effect can be seen at raves or club gatherings where glow-activated tubes and balls are placed on a string and twirled around. If spun fast enough the path of the tube will appear as a circle rather than as a single object moving in the path of a circle. The second type of laser display creates **interference patterns.** These images are less predictable and are more organic in nature. Here, the laser is distorted by passing it through an irregular piece of material such as glass or plastic so that the individual waves become either scattered or knocked out of phase with one another. This produces colored patterns of light that are capable of being transported over long distances. In either case, a laser can bring very dramatic effects to a production.

FOR FURTHER READING

Bowers, Brian. *Lengthening the Day: A History of Lighting Technology.* Oxford: Oxford University Press, 1998.

DiLaura, David L., Kevin W. Houser, Richard G. Mistrick, and Gary R. Steffy. eds. *Illuminating Engineering Society—the Lighting Handbook Tenth Edition: Reference and Application.* New York: Illuminating Engineering Society, 2011.

Dillon, Maureen. *Artificial Sunshine: A Social History of Domestic Lighting*. London: National Trust Enterprises, Ltd., 2002.

Elenbaas, W. *Light Sources*. New York: Crane, Russak and Company, Inc., 1972.

Friedel, Robert and Paul Israel. *Edison's Electric Light: Biography of an Invention*. New Brunswick, NJ: Rutgers University Press, 1986.

Gerlach, Robert. "LEDs To Light the Theatre," *Theatre Design and Technology (TD &T)*, 39 (4):11–22.

Gordon, Gary. *Interior Lighting for Designers*. 5th ed. Hoboken, NJ: John Wiley and Sons, Inc., 2014.

Illuminating Engineering Society of North America. *IESNA Lighting Ready Reference*. 4th ed. New York: Illuminating Engineering Society of North America, 2003.

Lindsey, Jack L. *Applied Illumination Engineering*. 2nd ed. Liburn, GA: The Fairmont Press, Inc., 1997.

Millerson, Gerald. *The Technique of Lighting for Television and Film*. 3rd ed. New York and London: Focal Press, 2013.

Penzel, Frederick. *Theatre Lighting Before Electricity*. Middletown, CT: Wesleyan University Press, 1978.

Rhiner, James L. *A Complete Guide to the Language of Lighting*. Elk Grove Village, IL: Halo Lighting Division, McGraw-Edison Company, 1983.

CHAPTER 6

LUMINAIRE FUNDAMENTALS

W HEN WE REFER to **luminaires** we are discussing the actual lighting fixtures. We also refer to luminaires as **lighting units, instruments,** and **lamps.** While all of these names are technically correct, you may find one term used more commonly throughout different regions of the world or in various specialty areas of lighting. For instance, luminaires with a permanent mounting like those used in architectural practices are frequently called **fixtures.** In entertainment lighting we often prefer to use "lighting instruments" or "units."

In the purest sense, luminaires are the devices that we use to both produce and control light. A luminaire can be as simple as a ceiling or table lamp, as large as the rotating light of a lighthouse, or as sophisticated as the moving lights that you see in concerts. By definition, luminaires contain several specific elements that provide critical functions in producing light. First, the luminaire must contain a light source. This is often nothing more than a **lamp.** Once the light is produced, we add mechanisms to make the light more controllable and efficient. Most luminaires contain a **reflector** that allows the light to be gathered or directed in a particular direction. Many also use **lenses** as an additional way of focusing the light into a more controlled beam. Finally, a luminaire has a **housing** or **body** that holds the hardware and optical assembly together while also providing electrical connections and various means for hanging it and mounting accessories to the unit. All luminaires represent a specific combination of lenses, reflectors, and light sources that ultimately determine the unique quality of light that is associated with a given fixture. Therefore, we choose a particular lighting instrument or luminaire because we want to produce a particular quality of light.

Since luminaires create the light, many lighting designers believe that their consideration represents the single most important factor in the design process. In this chapter I discuss the components of a luminaire based on the functions that each provides to a unit, offer an introduction to **photometrics,** and examine the principal luminaires associated with entertainment lighting. I also examine the means by which we control or manipulate light. What makes one luminaire different from another one? What is the quality of light associated with a particular luminaire? What type of optical control might a luminaire provide? In entertainment lighting there are only a few basic lighting instruments that a designer needs to become familiar with while there are thousands of designs in architectural practices. Because of this, a designer must also be able to interpret graphs and tables to understand the unique qualities of a particular luminaire.

BASIC PRINCIPLES OF OPTICS

The primary reason that there is such a diverse collection of luminaires (most notably in architectural lighting) is due to the fact that each luminaire design provides a unique combination of light source and optical control. In this segment I examine the primary optical components that are used to control the light once it has been produced by a light source. **Reflection** and **refraction** form the basis of this discussion, which then expands to illustrate how these principles are used in the design of different luminaires.

Reflection and Reflectors

Reflection is a physical principle by which light is bounced or reflected from a surface. The basic principle of reflection is governed by the **Law of Reflection** (Figure 6.1), which states that the angle of incidence is equal to the angle of reflection ($\angle i = \angle r$; when considering an angle that is normal or perpendicular to the reflective surface). In essence, this simply means that when light bounces off a surface, it does so at an angle that is complementary (or equal) to the angle at which it first struck the surface. Materials that have shiny mirrored surfaces create reflections that follow the Law of Reflection quite specifically, and we call these reflections **specular reflections.** Other materials don't provide as good of a surface for reflection and create either a **spread reflection,** where most of the light is reflected off the surface in the same general direction, or a **diffuse reflection,** where the light is scattered in numerous directions. A crumpled piece of aluminum foil or light reflecting off the surface of water can create spread reflections, while most objects made of un-mirrored materials or with an uneven surface characteristically produce diffuse reflections. In reality, most surfaces are associated with diffuse reflections.

As you may recall from Chapter 5, most light sources produce light in many, if not nearly all, directions. This isn't efficient since we usually want to direct light to a specific location. Sources that create light in many directions waste energy because only a small amount of their total light output falls where we actually want it. A **reflector** uses the principles of reflection to gather or redirect this otherwise unutilized light so that it can help support the primary direction in which the light is desired. Some reflectors have matte finishes (with surfaces that are dulled or painted white to diffuse the light) while others are made from polished mirror-like materials that create specular reflections that redirect the most light possible.

A fundamental element of reflector design lies in the principle that the shape of a reflector determines the behavior of the light that it reflects. Every reflector is designed around an optical point known as the **focal point.** The focal point is a point along the optical path of a lens or reflector that coincides with the location from which light rays will either be directed from or toward when using a reflector or lens. This point is infinitely small and exists only in theory. However, if a light source (i.e., the lamp) is located at the focal point of a reflector, the light that leaves the lamp in the direction of the reflector will be reflected or redirected in a way that is dictated by the shape of the reflector. There are several notable reflector shapes, and each produces a characteristic directional effect on any light that strikes it (Figure 6.2). In each case, it is important to understand that focal points are infinitely small, and while only a small amount of the total light follows the path exactly, in reality, a source that is centered around the focal point will for the most part follow the suggested reflection pattern. Smaller sources permit a larger portion of a lamp's total output to be concentrated around the focal point of a reflector, which allows a greater percentage of the light to be harvested by the reflector. This principle once again demonstrates the importance of developing **point light sources** for more efficient luminaire designs.

SPHERICAL REFLECTOR A spherical reflector reflects light that would otherwise exit through the back of a lighting instrument back through the same focal point from which the light originated onward towards the front of the luminaire. In this manner, light that would normally be wasted can be redirected through the front of the fixture. Spherical reflectors are usually created with polished, mirrored surfaces that help to maximize their light in a frontal direction.

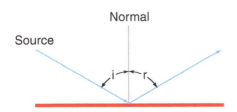

Figure 6.1a The Law of Reflection and Three Variations on Reflection. a. Law of Reflection where the angle of incidence ($\angle i$) is equal to the angle of reflection ($\angle r$). Light is reflected from a surface at an angle to the normal (perpendicular) that is the same as the light that strikes the surface.

Figure 6.1b Specular Reflection

Figure 6.1c Spread Reflection

Figure 6.1d Diffuse Reflection

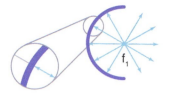

Figure 6.2a Four Popular Optical Reflectors. Each reflector illustrates the path of light waves associated with placing the source at the primary focal point (f₁). a. Spherical Reflector: Light is reflected back through the focal point (f₁) at the same angle as it strikes the surface.

Figure 6.2b Parabolic Reflector: Light is reflected into parallel rays.

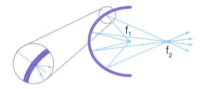

Figure 6.2c Ellipsoidal Reflector: Light is reflected back through a second or conjugate focal point (f2)

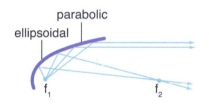

Figure 6.2d Compound or Asymmetrical Reflector: Illustrated is a combination of parabolic and ellipsoidal reflector shapes.

PARABOLIC REFLECTOR A parabolic reflector is similar to a spherical reflector with the exception that it is flattened to some degree. Because of its flattened (or parabolic) shape, any light that strikes it after leaving a source at its focal point is reflected in parallel rays.

ELLIPSOIDAL REFLECTOR An ellipsoidal reflector differs from other reflectors in that its shape is based on an ellipse and its unique characteristic of having two focal points. The focal point closest to the reflector is called the **primary focal point** and is where we locate the light source. The second focal point is the **secondary** or **conjugate focal point** and is the location to which all of the reflected light will be directed.

A unique property of this reflector is that any light or images that pass beyond the conjugate focal point are reversed. An ellipsoidal reflector is one of the most efficient means of concentrating light at a given location and is the basis of many spotlight designs.

COMPOUND/ASYMMETRICAL REFLECTORS A compound reflector is shaped with more than one principal shape along its surface. In this manner they more efficiently direct light in a given direction. Variations of such a reflector shape are common for many lighting fixtures that use tubular lamps to wash a large area. The quartz floodlamps that are common in security or cyclorama (cyc) lighting often make use of this type of reflector.

All reflectors work best when matched to a proper light source. In many luminaire designs it is important that the lamp be oriented so that its light is directed primarily to either the front of the fixture or to the reflector at the back of the instrument. If the filament of the lamp is not oriented with the focal point of a reflector, the light will not be reflected in an optimal manner. In this case, much of the light will become scattered and will be converted to heat within the body of the fixture. An electrician should always confirm that the proper lamp is selected for a luminaire and that it is properly mounted for maximum efficiency with the reflector. Properties such as a lamp's **light center length** (**LCL**) should form part of this consideration. There are a number of lamps with bases that are designed to assure this proper orientation. Most luminaires are also equipped with controls that allow technicians to adjust the relationship between the reflector and lamp for maximum light output. This is referred to as lamp **alignment.** If the filament and focal point of the reflector are not oriented properly, the light output of the fixture will be diminished.

Finally, since the focal point of a reflector is an infinitely small point, it is impossible to have a lamp with a filament small enough to follow the ideal light-ray patterns of any of the reflectors discussed earlier. We can only approach these as technology improves and light sources become smaller. In the meantime, many manufacturers have developed a variation of mirrored reflectors that feature a series of prismatic faces over the entire surface of a reflector. This creates a limited amount of scattering but more importantly produces an effect that results in more light behaving in a way that would be dictated by the shape of a given reflector. These are called **flatted reflectors** and are quite common in a number of luminaires that use ellipsoidal reflectors. In an even more recent innovation, manufacturers have created reflectors that permit heat and other forms of electromagnetic radiation to pass through the back of the reflector while visible light is reflected in a normal manner. These are **dichroic** or **cold mirror reflectors,** which create nice, crisp beams of light that produce a cooler operating temperature for luminaires and reduce heat damage to gel, gobos, shutters, and other devices that may be placed in a fixture.

Transmission

Transmission refers to the principle by which light moves through materials. While most theatrical designers prefer to use light in its purest form, there are occasions when a lighting designer may want to soften a light source. Just as with reflection, there are different forms of transmission (direct, spread, and diffuse). In many luminaires a piece of glass, plastic, or other material called a **diffuser** is placed over its front to scatter or soften the light while preventing a direct view of the light source. The prismatic lenses of fluorescent ceiling fixtures are examples of common diffuser panels. Other examples include frosted glass and opal ceiling panels—skylights are also often made of diffuser material. In entertainment lighting (especially in the film industry) we use a variety of diffusion materials that range from gel-like media to silk fabrics that are commonly called **frost** or **diffusion media.** They are made by many of the gel manufacturers.

Refraction and Lenses

One of the most important principles of optics that affects the design and function of luminaires is associated with the effects of refraction. **Refraction** simply refers to light being bent as it moves through materials of different densities. Earlier I stated that light has a specific speed (186,000 miles/sec). This speed is only true of light moving in a vacuum; in reality, light travels through different materials at different speeds and with varying degrees of success. This effect is called the **optical density** of a material. Through measurements, scientists have been able to express the relative speed of light moving through **translucent** materials as a proportional ratio compared to the speed of light in a vacuum. This is called a material's **index of refraction** and all materials that transmit light have one. Air, water, oils, plastics, and different types of glass all have different indexes of refraction.

More importantly, refraction (or bending) of the light occurs at the surfaces where light passes from one material into another. As the light enters a new material it will be slowed down or sped up depending on whether the material that it is passing into is more or less dense than the material that it is traveling from. The degree of bending is dependent on the relative densities and thickness of the different materials. A common effect of refraction is the apparent offsetting that can be observed in objects such as a stick being placed in a pool or a straw in a glass of water. The effect of this physical principle is governed by **Snell's Law,** which has commonly

been simplified into a basic principle known as the **Law of Refraction** (Figure 6.3). The law of refraction simply states that as light passes into a more dense material, at the surface boundary between the two materials the light will be bent towards a normal angle with the surface, while light passing from a more dense material into one of less density will be bent away from the normal angle with the surface. Refraction separates natural light into its various component colors or wavelengths. Phenomena displaying this behavior include the formation of rainbows, prismatic effects within the spray of a water hose, and the use of prisms. The effect is due to the slightly varying speeds of the different colored wavelengths along with the differences between the optical densities of various materials. At times, this can produce an unwanted side effect in luminaires, such as a rainbow effect produced along the edge of a beam of light. The effect (**chromatic aberration**) is more typical of luminaires containing inferior lenses and we refer to the resulting prismatic effects as **color fringes.**

Refraction is a major consideration in optics due to the fact that it determines one of the primary means by which we control light within a luminaire. We do this by making use of the principles of refraction to create **lenses.** The curvature of a lens can be thought of as a plane of "infinite prisms" where varying degrees of refraction occur along the curvature of the lens's surface. Varying the thickness and shape of the front and back

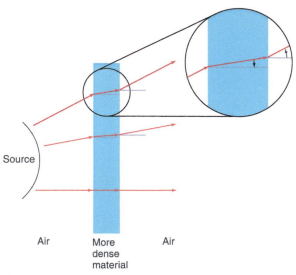

The amount of refraction is dependent on the index of refraction and the thickness of the materials.

Figure 6.3 Law of Refraction: If the light is moving from a less dense to a more dense material it is bent toward the normal angle with the surface. If the light is moving into a less dense material it is bent away from the normal angle. The effect results in the light and objects appearing parallel and offset with the degree of offset being determined by the thickness of the material (thicker materials will produce a greater offset).

surfaces of a lens can redirect any light passing through the lens. Lenses are named by the shape of their front and back surfaces. A **plano** surface is flat like a plane, while **concave lenses** dip inward and **convex lenses** flex outward. Like reflectors, a distinguishing characteristic of all lenses is their **focal length.** This is a measurement taken from a given point of a lens (its optical center) to its **focal point.** The focal point is the point at which parallel light rays entering the lens will converge or be focused upon. As a rule, thick lenses provide more refractive power and have relatively short focal lengths while thin lenses provide less refraction and have longer focal lengths. Larger diameter lenses also capture more light (making them more efficient) and tend to have longer focal lengths.

The most popular lenses used in the lighting industry are variations of a **plano-convex lens** design. These lenses have one flat side while the other is convex. In principle, if a light source or lamp is located at the focal point of a lens, the resultant light should form into essentially parallel rays. If the light source is placed between the lens and focal point, the resulting light will undergo **divergence** and spread outward. If the light source is moved outside of the focal point, the lens will produce **converging rays** that will cross over one another. Figure 6.4 illustrates these three conditions. Lenses are not typically identified in any way that reflects their focal lengths. While they may appear to be the same, they can actually be quite different from one another. One way of differentiating between lenses lies in a measurement of their diameter, while a second refers to estimating their focal length. While the diameter is easily measured, lenses can appear to be the same while having very different focal lengths. To identify the focal length, we can hold a lens above a surface upon which we focus an image of a distant light source. This is the same principle as using a magnifying glass to scorch a piece of paper with the sun. By moving the lens back and forth until the image comes into sharp focus you identify the point where the distance between the surface and the lens is equal to the focal length of the lens. While there is only one point or plane (the focal point) where a lens will form a perfect image of an object or truly parallel rays, there is actually a range of distances on either side of the focal point where objects will remain in relatively good focus. This is commonly called **depth of field** and will vary according to the construction of a luminaire and its lenses. In lenses designed for cameras, this range is affected by the f-stop setting, which regulates how much light enters a lens. Smaller f-stop settings (with higher numbers) allow for a larger depth of field, while larger f-stop settings (with smaller numbers) provide a relatively narrow depth of field.

Thick lenses are prone to crack and shatter from heat buildup because they are traditionally made of glass, which makes them heavy while also having

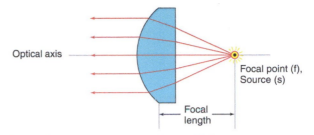

Figure 6.4a A plano-convex lens with its optical relationships and the effects of light-source placement. a. Parallel rays of light are created by placing a light source at the focal point of the lens

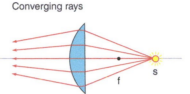

Figure 6.4b Converging rays of light are created by placing a light source beyond the focal point

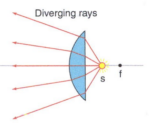

Figure 6.4c Diverging rays of light are created by placing a light source between the lens and the focal point

poor coefficients of expansion (when placed under the extreme heat of stage lamps). Due to this, several variations of plano-convex lenses have been developed that approach the optical qualities of a single plano-convex lens without the shortcomings of the traditionally thick lenses. In the first variation, two separate plano-convex lenses are placed in line with one another (plano sides facing outward) as a means of replacing a single, thicker lens. This was a common arrangement for many spotlight designs that are still in use today. In other designs, high-quality plastics are used rather than glass. Other variations include removal of some of the glass from either side of a lens, which reduces the thickness of a lens while still approximating the overall shape and properties of the lens. The **Fresnel lens** (easily spotted by its concentric rings and dimpled or frosted back surface) is a variation of the plano-convex lens that has portions of the convex surface removed. The dimpled texture adds a diffusing effect that softens any images that the rings on the other surface might cause. A less popular version that removes elements of the plano surface while leaving

Figure 6.5a Popular spotlight lenses. a. Plano-convex lens

Figure 6.5b Fresnel lens

Figure 6.5c Step lens

the convex surface intact is the **step lens**. The step lens was popular in the 1950s and '60s but produced a series of concentric rings in the beams of many spotlights that used them. Figure 6.5 illustrates each of these different lenses.

An Essential Luminaire

In order to create a luminaire a designer needs to produce a given combination of light source, reflector, and lens along with an enclosure to mount the components in proper relationship with one another. Light created at the focal point of the reflector by the light source is gathered and redirected along the optical path in a way that provides a maximum concentration of light near the focal point of a lens (if the fixture has a lens). This light is then directed into essentially parallel rays that radiate away from the fixture. In reality, the production of perfectly parallel light rays is not possible and the light produced by most luminaires approaches a conical pattern. The enclosure of a lighting instrument forms the actual body of a luminaire and not only provides a method for mounting the reflector and other optical components but also provides a way to hang a fixture in the theatre along with any accessories that might be added to its design. This enclosure is often called the **body** or **hood** of the luminaire. The body also provides electrical connections for the light source. We broadly distinguish between **spotlights** and **floodlights** as the two primary groups of luminaire design. A floodlight tends to have a soft, diffuse light with undefined edges and usually washes a large area evenly. A spotlight is more focused and defined than a floodlight. It will have well-defined edges and a fairly tight distribution pattern. As a rule, spotlights contain lenses and floodlights do not. Because of their sharp beams, many spotlights also contain devices that enable a designer to actually shape the beam of light.

Photometrics

While most lenses may be identified through their diameter and focal length, this information is not all that helpful to most lighting designers. What is more important for a lighting designer is the overall distribution pattern that a luminaire produces. Due to this, it has become common for lighting designers to identify lenses by their distribution angles rather than by focal length. In fact, even if we know the focal length of a lens, we must still translate this information into an angle or beam pattern when plotting a design. Every luminaire creates a specific pattern of light that radiates away from the instrument in a variety of intensities in different directions. Most luminaires cast light outwards in a conical shape, while others create more complex patterns like an elliptical beam. **Photometrics** is the study of light intensity and distribution. We use photometrics for making fixture selections as well as for plotting the coverage of the lighting instruments. When determining distribution patterns, light is measured around the principal optical path or axis of the fixture as it radiates away from the luminaire. Presently, most manufacturers of entertainment luminaires present their photometric data based on the distribution patterns of beam and field angles, while architectural manufacturers use a more comprehensive study of **candlepower distribution curves**. The architectural method provides much more information and is determined from actual intensity measurements at various angles around a luminaire. The **Illuminating Engineering Society of North America (IESNA)** has created a standard by which manufacturers report this data. The result has been the representation of this data in a format that allows easy comparisons to be made between luminaires. Through the efforts of the **Entertainment Services and Technology Association (ESTA)** and **Professional Light and Sound Association (PLASA)** (international trade organizations of entertainment equipment manufacturers and distributors), the entertainment industry is moving towards adopting the IESNA standards for reporting photometric data for entertainment luminaires as well.

Sidebar 6.1 LUMINAIRE MAINTENANCE

In order to maintain maximum light output from a luminaire, several maintenance procedures should be performed on a regular basis. Dust and grime accumulate on the lens and reflector of luminaires and can have a significant effect on the light output of a unit within a very short period of time. Many theatrical companies clean and perform routine maintenance on their lighting instruments annually. Other organizations modify their maintenance schedules based on how dusty an environment that the units must perform within, degree of use, etc. Unfortunately, there are a number of lighting installations, especially in the architectural arena, where luminaire maintenance is ignored—resulting in energy efficiency losses as well as compromised lighting levels.

Basic luminaire maintenance is quite simple and involves not much more than cleaning the optical components and making adjustments in a luminaire's alignment. The body of a lighting instrument can be cleared of dust by blowing compressed air into the fixture. To clean reflectors, most manufacturers recommend that a soft cloth be used to wipe the reflector(s) clean. A mild solution of vinegar and water may also be used. Lenses can be cleaned with a mild solution of soap and water or a high-quality glass cleaner. Care must be taken to thoroughly rinse the lenses to avoid any streaking and soap film or buildup. Newer lenses and reflectors are often restricted to cleaning with soft cloths and solutions of distilled water and isopropyl alcohol; ammonia-based glass cleaners should be avoided. An electrician should also check all the electrical and mechanical components of the luminaire for both safety and ease of operation. Any questionable connections, knobs, and bolts, or other features should be repaired or replaced at this time. Once all of this has been done, the unit is aligned in order to produce the best beam of light possible. To prevent damage to lighting instruments between productions, the units should be hung from their C-clamps in a face-down position on a free batten or on storage racks that are outfitted with 1 1/2–inch pipe. A rolling version of these racks (**meat racks**) are often used in facilities where the lights are moved between several different stages or theatres. Units with shutters should have all their shutters fully inserted while in storage but should have them pulled all the way out as soon the unit is hung for a show. Proper storage will insure that lighting instruments and their lamps are not damaged between productions.

Beam Angle and Field Angle

The most common way of expressing distribution patterns for theatrical lighting fixtures refers to the concept of beam and field angles. This is due to the fact that most distribution patterns for theatrical luminaires are quite directional, with light radiating away from a lighting instrument as a cone. By contrast, many architectural luminaires distribute light as a wash over a wide area in many directions. If light is projected onto a flat surface from straight on, most theatrical luminaires produce a circle. Beam angle and field angle are simply measurements of the relative intensity of the light as you move toward the outer regions of its pool and away from its optical axis. In older luminaire designs the highest intensity concentrations were typically found at the center of this pool and there was a significant drop in intensity as one measured the brightness from the center of the pool toward its edges. By definition, **beam angle** refers to the angle that represents that area of the beam where the intensity has fallen off to 50% of the initial intensity. The **field angle** represents a larger portion of the pool and represents an angle where the intensity drops off to 10% of the initial intensity. The beam angle is contained within the larger field angle of a luminaire. Both beam and field angles are illustrated in Figure 6.6.

Most lighting fixtures contain mechanisms that allow designers and electricians to manipulate the light beam in ways that adjust the evenness of the distribution pattern while also maximizing the amount of light that leaves a luminaire. These adjustments in a beam are called **alignment** and may be set through the manipulation of several screws (traditional) or a knob or joystick-like device on the back of more recently designed fixtures. They may be used to create a concentrated hotspot near the center of a beam (**peaked field**) or to create an even coverage over the entire beam of light (**flat field**) where for all practical purposes the field and beam angles become nearly the same. Many of the newer enhanced spotlights that have come into popular use since the early 1990s have relatively flat fields when compared to earlier luminaires and are often called **flat-field luminaires.**

Throw Distances

Lighting designers refer to throw distances when making determinations of what lighting instrument is

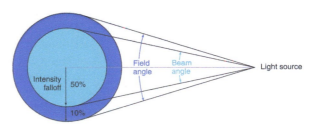

Figure 6.6 Beam and field angles: The beam angle represents the most intense portion of the light—where intensity falloff drops to 50% while the field angle is inclusive of the beam angle and is defined by an intensity of at least 10% of initial light output

appropriate for a given application. **Throw distance** is nothing more than the distance between a lighting instrument and its target, or the distance that the light actually travels before striking an object. Throw distances are important for two reasons. First, as light moves away from its source it spreads away from its optical center and covers a greater area. Second, due to the Inverse Square Law, the light's intensity also drops off dramatically at greater distances. This is due to the same amount of light being spread over a larger area. We use throw distances to determine just how much beam spread and intensity dropoff will occur at particular distances from the luminaire. Architectural lighting designers use a similar manner of determining throw distances but usually refer instead to **mounting heights,** which can be a bit misleading because the mounting height is where the fixture is physically mounted (based on a measurement to the floor) in a straight-down orientation. The throw distance is also usually measured to the working plane, which is where the lighting task is actually located (typically measured to a desktop or work surface rather than the floor).

Photometric Data and Cut Sheets

Numerous luminaire designs have been developed throughout the years. Each one creates a unique pattern and quality of light as a result of a specific combination of individual components used in a fixture's physical construction. While luminaire designs may vary considerably from one field of lighting to another, there are a limited number of luminaire styles found in each area of lighting design. Each of these groups include luminaires that can vary considerably in beam pattern, size, and power. Furthermore, the actual light output will commonly be different between manufacturers of similarly named fixtures due to the use of superior components, slightly varying optical controls, or better efficiency in one design over another. It therefore becomes important for a lighting designer to not only understand the difference between different types of fixtures but to also be able to make comparisons between fixtures of essentially the same design. Because of this, luminaires should be matched (if at all possible) by both type and manufacturer when completing similar tasks in a particular lighting application—otherwise, variations might be observed in the light output from one luminaire to another. The best way that we have of understanding the specific optics and light output of a fixture is through the use of comparative graphs that report specific photometric data that is related to each luminaire. Manufacturers will make this information available in product literature called **cut sheets.** Though the actual display of information will often vary from one company to another, these sheets typically provide a photograph or sketch of the luminaire, physical data like the weight and dimensions of the luminaire, lamp information, and (most importantly) photometric data relating to the instrument's specific beam pattern and distribution levels. Fixtures that have an adjustable beam angle (spot/flood settings or zoom features) often have additional photometric graphs that represent the extreme ranges of the fixture.

IESNA has developed a standard means of representing photometric data for display and architectural luminaires so that comparisons can be easily made between luminaires. Nearly every architectural manufacturing firm has adopted this format for representing photometric data in the cut sheets of their luminaire products. The most common element of these tables is a graphical representation of the light output (intensity) of the luminaire at various angles to either side of a fixture's centerline. This graph is called a **candlepower** or **candela distribution curve** (Figure 6.7). Zero degrees represents a point directly below the luminaire, while 90° represents points on the horizon directly to either side of the fixture. The plotted lines represent the intensity (distribution pattern) of the luminaire's light in each direction between these extremes. In some cases, light may be measured above the horizontal position, which is indicated by distribution curves that continue above the 90° position. Other important data such as spacing considerations, overall efficiency, physical dimensions, lamp and ballast data, and other forms of photometric data are also found on a typical cut sheet.

Candlepower Distribution

Test No. H22250
HD6-6700C
Lamp=150W A19
Inside
Frosted
Lumens=2850

Spacing Criteria=1.0
Efficiency=63.7%

Figure 6.7 An architectural photometric (candela distribution) chart showing luminaire data for Eaton's Portfolio recessed downlight fixture (model HD6–6700). Note the pattern of intensity over various distribution angles.

Credit: photometric diagram from an Eaton cutsheet

While the entertainment industry has not yet adopted the IESNA standard for reporting photometric data (there is a movement to follow this standard for entertainment luminaires), the information is still readily available, and a fairly common method of representing the data has been in use for many years (although often changing slightly between manufacturers). Figure 6.8 illustrates a common manner of displaying photometric data.

Even though terminology may vary, the basic principles of measurement are essentially the same between architectural and entertainment lighting systems. In theatrical-based graphics, the throw distance is plotted along the central axis of the fixture, while the beam angle and field angle bisect this axis and extend outward from the luminaire toward its target. Most importantly, a series of numbers are displayed along the axis of theatrical photometric charts that indicate both the size of the light pool as well as the intensity of the light at corresponding distances from the light source. The intensity is usually expressed in either candelas or footcandles. Some manufacturers provide additional information such as multiplying factors that allow a designer to determine a pool size for a luminaire at any distance

Source Four 19

Throw Distance (d)	25' 7.6m	40' 12.2m	55' 16.7m	70' 21.3m
Field Diameter	8' 2.4m	13' 3.9m	18' 5.4m	22' 6.8m
Illuminance (fc)	392	153	81	50
Illuminance (lux)	4,217	1,648	872	538

To determine center beam illumination in footcandles at any throw distance, divide candela by the throw distance squared.

For Field diameter at any throw distance, multiply the throw distance by .32

For Beam diameter at any throw distance, multiply the throw distance by .26

Source Four 26

Throw Distance (d)	15' 4.6m	30' 9.1m	45' 13.7m	60' 18.1m
Field Diameter	6.7' 2.0m	13.4' 4.1m	20.1' 6.1m	26.8' 8.2m
Illuminance (fc)	783	196	87	49
Illuminance (lux)	8,432	2,108	937	527

To determine center beam illumination in footcandles at any throw distance, divide candela by the throw distance squared.

For Field diameter at any throw distance, multiply the throw distance by .45

For Beam diameter at any throw distance, multiply the throw distance by .32

Source Four 36

Throw Distance (d)	15' 4.6m	25' 7.6m	35' 10.7m	45' 13.7m
Field Diameter	9.2' 2.8m	15.3' 4.7m	21.4' 6.5m	27.6' 8.4m
Illuminance (fc)	404	145	74	45
Illuminance (lux)	4,348	1,565	799	483

To determine center beam illumination in footcandles at any throw distance, divide candela by the throw distance squared.

For Field diameter at any distance, multiply distance by .61

For Beam diameter at any distance, multiply distance by .47

Source Four 50

Throw Distance (d)	10' 3m	15' 4.6	25' 7.6m	30' 9.1m
Field Diameter	9.3' 2.8m	14' 4.3m	23.3' 7.1m	27.9' 8.5m
Illuminance (fc)	457	203	73	51
Illuminance (lux)	4,914	2,184	786	546

To determine center beam illumination in footcandles at any throw distance, divide candela by the throw distance squared.

For Field diameter at any distance, multiply distance by .93

For Beam diameter at any distance, multiply distance by .65

Figure 6.8 Comparison of Source Four® photometric data in typical entertainment format

Credit: photometric displays by Electronic Theatre Controls (ETC)

by simply multiplying a throw distance by the multiplying factor. Since individual cut sheets and photometric tables may vary considerably from one theatrical manufacturer to another Robert C. Mumm has compiled a reference called the *Photometrics Handbook* that presents luminaire data in a standard format for nearly every theatrical luminaire that has ever been manufactured. This reference is an essential tool for anyone working in the entertainment lighting industry. Figure 6.9 illustrates a theatrical luminaire's photometric data in Mumm's standardized format. The same information is also available through software packages like John McKernon's Beamwright, which not only provides the photometric data but also allows you to determine the effect on pool size and intensity falloff while manipulating the hanging position of the unit. Beamwright can even recommend a list of luminaires for an application by allowing you to establish a set of parameters like pool size and hanging position (trim and distance from target) prior to making a fixture selection. A screenshot of the distribution patterns of a theatrical unit in Beamwright is shown in Figure 6.10.

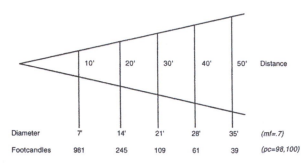

| Diameter | 7' | 14' | 21' | 28' | 35' | (mf=.7) |
| Footcandles | 981 | 245 | 109 | 61 | 39 | (pc=98,100) |

Figure 6.9 A photometric diagram by Robert Mumm for an Altman Shakespeare S6–40 luminaire as published in *Photometrics Handbook*, second edition, Louisville, KY: Broadway Press, 1997

Credit: distribution chart by Robert Mumm

Figure 6.10 A screenshot of a photometric display for an ETC 19° Source Four in John McKernon's Beamwright software.

Sidebar 6.2 TWO METHODS FOR DETERMINATION OF BEAM SPREAD

Method 1: Multiplying Factor

You want to determine the approximate diameter of the pool of light created by a given lighting instrument at a distance of 30 feet from where the instrument is hung. The luminaire's cut/data sheet lists a multiplying factor (mf) of 0.55.
Solution:

30 feet × 0.55 = 16.5 diameter for the light pool

Method 2: Photometric Graph

Using the photometric diagram in Figure 6.11 for an Altman PHX 26 HPL Ellipsoidal Reflector Spotlight, determine the diameter of a pool of light and its associated level of footcandles at a distance of 25 feet from the luminaire.
Solution:

❝Locate 25 feet along the distance axis of the diagram (you'll have to estimate its position) and then glance directly above this to find the associated beam diameter and footcandle level. In this case, the pool would be around 12 feet wide and have an intensity of approximately 75 footcandles.❞

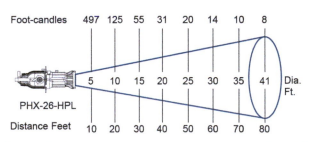

Figure 6.11 Photometric diagram for an Altman PHX 26 HPL ERS

Credit: photometric diagram provided by Altman Stage Lighting

CHOOSING LUMINAIRES

Selecting luminaires is one of the most critical tasks that a lighting designer must accomplish when specifying the lighting for any production or environment. A lighting designer learns how to match the quality and distribution of the desired light with the specific characteristics of a given luminaire. Once the quality of light and style of fixture have been determined, the designer considers more specific variations of that fixture based on issues, such as desired intensity levels, distribution patterns, and the throw distances required for an application. While there are luminaires—like moving lights or units with zoom features—that allow some modification in the light qualities associated with a particular fixture, most lighting instruments can produce only a single quality of light with only minor adjustments in the beam. Therefore, luminaires are chosen for the unique contributions that they make to a design.

Several considerations that designers face when making specific luminaire choices include the desired quality of light (harsh/diffuse, even/uneven distribution, textured, edge definition, etc.), the type of light source (source characteristics, intensity, and color temperature), control desired within the fixture (beam shaping and focus modification), throw distances, and finally any physical restrictions that may affect how and where a luminaire may be mounted. While entertainment luminaires are typically mounted with ease from a pipe with clamp devices, architectural fixtures are more commonly mounted in ceilings and walls where ceiling clearance (both within and outside of the ceiling) and other mounting obstructions such as duct work and conduit runs may exist. Additionally, designers must also avoid obstructions in the path of the light that moves away from a luminaire. Typical obstructions that entertainment designers must be on the lookout for include scenic elements and maskings like borders and legs. Theatrical designers must also deal with a series of pre-existing conditions that require them to be adaptive throughout their design. Luminaire selections must take into consideration the mounting or hanging positions that exist in a theatre as well as the inventory of luminaires that are available for a design. When luminaires are rented from a production house, transportation costs and rental budgets place further controls on a designer's choice and placement of luminaires. Even on Broadway productions, considerations like these can have a large impact on a design.

CONVENTIONAL LUMINAIRES FOR THE STAGE (TRADITIONAL AND ENHANCED)

Unlike architectural luminaires that are mounted permanently, entertainment luminaires are mounted on a temporary basis (one production to another)—in many cases being hung and struck in a period of only a few days or weeks. In touring, the luminaires may be hung for only a few hours. Entertainment luminaires therefore contain a number of mounting features and readily accessible controls that allow fixtures to be easily manipulated from one project to another. Many controls are easily changed through a couple of hand or wrench adjustments. They are also simply clamped to pipes or

battens that are hung throughout a venue. The most popular clamp is the **C-clamp,** which not only secures the fixture to a pipe but also allows the unit's orientation to be easily pivoted from side to side **(pan).** The C-clamp is typically attached to a U-shaped piece of metal called a **yoke** that holds the body of the luminaire. By loosening or tightening the bolts or handles that mount the luminaire to the yoke, the fixture may also be adjusted upward or downward **(tilt).** To make hanging and focusing the units easier, a C-clamp should be mounted as close to a straight-down orientation as possible or in another position that places it perpendicular to this orientation. Two variations on mounting a fixture include **yoking out,** or spinning the C-clamp around the pipe so that it is mounted somewhere between straight down and 90°, and a **rooster** or **overhung mount,** in which the unit is spun up so that it is mounted directly above the pipe. The former is used to shoot around obstructions such as neighboring luminaires, while the latter is used to stretch some additional height out of a mounting position. In entertainment venues a lighting instrument should always have a **safety cable** mounted to the body of the luminaire so that it can be further secured to the position from which it is hung.

Spotlights

As discussed earlier, spotlights produce more controllable light than other luminaires. The overall quality of light produced by spotlights is relatively intense and even throughout their beams. This is due to the inclusion of a lens in most spotlights. Spotlights usually have well-defined beam edges and often contain optical devices that allow the light to be shaped or altered in some way. Because of this, they are the most common luminaires used in entertainment lighting.

Fresnel Spotlights

The **Fresnel spotlight** (Figure 6.12) is named for the inventor of its lens, Augustine-Jean Fresnel. The essential elements of this spotlight include a lamp, spherical reflector, and Fresnel lens. The light from Fresnel spotlights is moderately harsh and even throughout the beam that they produce. While you can determine roughly where the pool of light from a Fresnel begins and ends, its actual edges aren't clearly defined. Several Fresnels are often used together to create washes that cover adjoining areas of a stage since their beam edges can be easily blended between different spotlights.

For the most part, a Fresnel spotlight is simply pointed in the direction in which a designer wishes the light to be focused. While there isn't much optical control, these luminaires do contain an assembly that allows the reflector and lamp to move together along the optic axis of the fixture. This allows the light to be modified

1. Color-frame holder
2. Housing/lens set screw
3. Ventilation holes
4. Light baffle
5. Fresnel lens
6. Lamp (filament aligned with reflector focal point)
7. Socket
8. Spherical reflector
9. Lead wire with pin connector
10. Spot/flood adjusting knob

Figure 6.12 The Fresnel spotlight

through its relationship to the focal point of the stationary Fresnel lens. If the lamp is moved closer to the lens, the light undergoes divergence and spreads out—what we call a **flood focus**—while if the assembly is moved toward the back of the fixture (beyond the focal point of the lens) the light converges through a central point, the **spot focus.** Some Fresnels use a simple wingnut or knob on the bottom of the unit to make this adjustment while others may use a crank device on the front or back of the unit to change this setting. Still others may have some variation of knob device that is mounted on the side of the fixture that is used to control the spot/flood setting.

Fresnels come in a variety of wattages and sizes. The manner in which we identify these variations is based primarily on the diameter of a unit's lens. As the diameter of the lens increases, Fresnels have progressively smaller beamspreads and are therefore used for increasingly longer throw distances. The 6-inch and 8-inch variations form the most common fixtures found in many theatrical applications, while 12-inch versions may be used on large stages. Six-inch Fresnels are common in small venues like community theatres and black box facilities where there are relatively low hanging positions and small throw distances. Fresnel spotlights used for distant throws in the film industry may have lenses as large as 36 inches or more. If you enjoy going to the beach, you may be familiar with a variation of the Fresnel spotlight that is used in many lighthouse designs. As a rule, the wattage of the fixtures increase with larger diameter lenses. The smallest version of the Fresnel is the 3-inch **inky** that can be mounted in confined spaces like a cove or balcony trim. While most Fresnels use incandescent TH light sources, many of the larger versions

used in video and film applications have arc sources. In the video and film industry it is also common to refer to Fresnels by their wattage (1K, 2K, 5K, 10K, etc.).

Plano-Convex Spotlights

The **plano-convex (P-C) spotlight** is quite similar to a Fresnel spotlight in the way in which its optics are created. This luminaire represents one of the earliest forms of theatrical spotlights; it consists of nothing more than a spherical reflector, light source, and single plano-convex lens. These spotlights have sometimes been called **box-spots,** since many of the units were housed in a box-shaped enclosure. They could also be outfitted with a Fresnel lens. Although variations of this spotlight are still in common use throughout Europe and other parts of the world, it has been virtually replaced in North America by the **ellipsoidal reflector spotlight (ERS).** The P-C spot can be adjusted in much the same manner as a Fresnel to produce pools of light with a variety of different sizes. The range of field angles that a P-C spotlight will be able to achieve is fairly extensive, with typical ranges on the order of 10°–60°. Like the ellipsoidal reflector spotlight, this luminaire produces a crisp beam of well-defined light.

Ellipsoidal Reflector Spotlights (ERS)

The **ERS** is the most extensively used spotlight in the world today. The optics of this luminaire are superior to most other spotlights and produce a crisp, evenly distributed pool of light. Most noteworthy is its ability to create a very sharp, well-defined beam edge, along with its capacity to actually shape the light. Beam shaping is accomplished through the use of various accessories that are placed in the optic path of the luminaire. This is done at a location close to the focal point of the unit, which is called the **gate.** While a crisp edge may be given to the pool of an ERS, it can also be softened or fuzzed so that the light from two or more of the fixtures can easily blend from one unit into another. Since they produce little **spill,** they are often used in hanging positions such as the **front of house (FOH)** where control of the light is particularly important. When these luminaires were first introduced to the theatrical community, many companies produced their own version of the luminaire and marketed their fixtures by unique brand names like Klieglight (Kliegel Brothers) or Lekolight (Strand-Century), which was simply shortened to **Leko.** The Leko (named for its developers, Joseph Levy and Edward Kook) became such a popular fixture that many people began to refer to all ERSes as Lekos.

There are essentially three variations to the basic design of an ellipsoidal reflector spotlight. The earliest version, the **radial ERS,** made use of lamps that burned in a base-up configuration that resulted in the lamp housings being located on the top of the unit. A later version, the **axial ERS,** placed the lamp directly on the back of the instrument, where the lamp was inserted into the very center of the reflector. These fixtures produce a much more efficient light. Axial fixtures appeared in the mid-1970s when TH lamps became popular; both types of ERS can be found in many theatre inventories even today. Century Strand Lighting manufactured a very popular model of radial ERS in the 1960s and '70s that was known for its characteristic blue-gray body, while Altman Stage Lighting produced an axial ERS (the 360Q) that continues to be a staple of many theatres and rental houses. Figure 6.13 illustrates these two variations in ERS design. Newer models may vary the lens configuration from the traditional method of placing

1. Gel-frame holder
2. Focus setting knob
3. Lens barrel
4. Plano-convex lens
5. Shutter
6. Gate
7. Ellipsoidal reflector
8. Lamp (filament at f_1)
9. Socket
10. Lamp housing (cap)
11. Lead wires and pin connector

Figure 6.13a Cross-sections of ellipsoidal reflector spotlights. a. Radial ellipsoidal reflector spotlight

1. Gel-frame holder
2. Focus setting knob
3. Lens barrel
4. Plano-convex lens
5. Shutter
6. Gate
7. Ellipsoidal reflector
8. Lamp (filament at f_1)
9. Socket
10. Lamp housing (cap)
11. Lead wires and pin connector

Figure 6.13b Axial ellipsoidal reflector spotlight

two plano-convex lenses in a back-to-back orientation. The third version of the ellipsoidal reflector spotlight was introduced as the Source Four® Spotlight by Electronic Theatre Controls (ETC) in the early 1990s. This style has come to be known as the **enhanced ERS** design. The enhanced ERS uses a newer lamp design that produces far superior light when compared to traditional designs and has become the luminaire of choice for most designers. These are discussed in detail later in this chapter. Another variation of the ellipsoidal reflector spotlights is the **profile spotlight,** which is popular throughout Europe and other parts of the world.

The primary optical components of an ERS include the lamp, a single or double set of plano-convex lenses, and the ellipsoidal reflector for which the luminaire is named. In ERSes the lamp and reflector are mounted in a fairly permanent manner, while the lens or lenses (mounted in the **lens barrel**) move back and forth to control the focus of the light. The lamp housing holds the electrical connections along with a socket that keeps the fixture's lamp in proper orientation with the reflector. A set of four screws or a joystick-like device on the top or back of the lamp housing allows electricians to position the lamp within the reflector (**lamp alignment**). Figure 6.13 provides cross-sectional views of the optical components of two of the popular ERS designs. Light that leaves the lamp (located at the primary focal point of the reflector) is reflected by the reflector and passes through a secondary (**conjugate**) focal point that is located near the center of the fixture. This area, known as the **gate**, is the place where the light is most concentrated. A number of optical controls are introduced to the luminaire at the gate for shaping the emerging light.

The most important controls in ERSes are four **shutters** (top, bottom, left, and right) which are metal plates that can be inserted into the path of the light to flatten or shape an edge of a spotlight's pool. Shutters may also be rotated so that diagonal cuts can be made across the light. Since the conjugate focal point is actually located a bit closer to the lens than the gate, light actually crosses over or is inverted as it passes through the lens system and continues on to its target. This results in all optical devices, such as the shutters, working in a manner that is opposite of the light observed on the stage. To shutter in the top of a light, an electrician would use the bottom shutter while they would have to use the right shutter to close in the left side of the light. While this may sound confusing, electricians quickly become skilled in manipulating the shutters as required by a designer. Most ERSes also have a secondary slot at the gate that allow patterned images created from slides fashioned from thin plates of metal or glass called **gobos** or **templates** (Figure 6.14) and other optical accessories to be inserted into a spotlight. While a designer may choose to design their own gobos, hundreds of designs

Figure 6.14 Sample gobo patterns, from left to right: Rosco Lattice, Great American Bare Trees, Apollo Stars, and Rosco Medium Leaf Breakup Pattern. Pattern holders are shown in the front row.

are commercially available through a number of different manufacturers. In addition to shutters and gobos, a designer may also place an **iris** within the gate of an ERS. An iris allows the light to be shuttered in a circular manner that permits an operator to change the diameter of the pool of light. Followspots typically have an iris. Additional accessories like gobo rotators may also be inserted into the gate to add movement to the patterned light.

ERSes come in a wide variety of styles and sizes. As a general rule, the beam angle decreases as focal length increases. Most ERSes have fixed focal lengths, while others have zoom capabilities where the beam and field angles can be varied. These zoom or variable-focus spotlights have an extra lens. There is a slight tradeoff in comparing the light produced from a zoom fixture with the more efficient light of a comparable unit that is equipped with a fixed lens system. For this reason, the most common ERS designs in use today are still of a fixed focal length. As a compromise, some companies developed ERSes with lenses that could be swapped out and positioned in different orders to produce different beam spreads for a luminaire. Unfortunately, changing

the lenses was time consuming, and in theatres where there were inexperienced electricians, the units were frequently assembled incorrectly, negatively affecting the unit's light output.

There are two popular manners of distinguishing between ellipsoidal reflector spotlights of various sizes and focal lengths. Ultimately, each can be associated with different beamspreads. Most traditional ERSes are distinguished from one another by using a nomenclature that refers to both the lens diameter and focal length. The first number states the diameter of the lens, while the second refers to the focal length (e.g., 6 × 9). Both are measured in inches. In this example, the luminaire has a 6-inch lens diameter and a focal length of 9 inches. Several of the more popular units include the 4 1/2 × 6 1/2, 6 × 9, 6 × 12, and 6 × 16 ERS designs. However, this method of specification doesn't provide any information regarding beam size; designers have to commit luminaire field and beam angles to memory or look them up in sources like cut sheets. Due to this, some manufacturers created lines of ellipsoidal reflector spotlights that are specified according to their field angles (e.g., 20°, 30°, and 40°). A special group of ERSes are based on a 3 1/2–inch diameter lens (3 1/2 × 6, 3 1/2 × 8, and 3 1/2 × 10), which many designers fondly nicknamed **pinspots** (though not technically correct). Earlier versions of ERSes made heavy use of larger-diameter lenses (8-inch, 10-inch, and even 12-inch fixtures) that produced narrower beam angles as the fixture and lens sizes got bigger. To allow more fixtures to be placed along a hanging position, designers now frequently choose to use 6-inch diameter luminaires with ever-increasing focal lengths (e.g., the 6 × 16 and 6 × 22) for longer throws instead of the units with larger lens diameters. As with Fresnels, the larger ERS units typically have lamps of higher wattages.

Matching a luminaire with an associated throw distance and beam diameter is a critical aspect of any lighting design. Luminaires with narrow beam angles are usually better for longer throws, while wide-angled luminaires are better for small venues and shorter throws. Although a fixture with a large field angle will quickly open up and spread across a larger portion of a stage, its intensity also drops significantly due to the Inverse Square Law. This can be compared to adding a packet of KoolAid™ to the recommended amount of water. Yes, you can add more water to produce twice as much drink, but it will be diluted and not be as satisfying. Also, if significant shuttering needs to be applied to a fixture, it is better to select a different luminaire with a smaller field angle so that more light can be directed to the target rather than being blocked by the shutters and converted into heat. Due to the need for traveling longer distances, it is also common for narrower beamed spotlights to be equipped with lamps of higher wattages.

Finally, a number of companies have introduced ellipsoidal reflector spotlight designs with variable beam and field angles or a zoom capability (Figure 6.15). These designs allow the pool of light to be easily changed within a range of beam and field angles. In most cases,

this is done through the movement of an additional lens that is housed in the luminaire. A typical range of field angles associated with zoom spotlights is 25–50°, although it is common to have zoom spotlights with ranges that are narrower (15–30°) or (30–50°). One popular version of these spotlights has a box-shaped silhouette called a **shoebox design.**

Enhanced ERS

In 1992 ETC introduced a new variety of ellipsoidal reflector spotlight that has revolutionized luminaire designs in the theatrical community. This new ERS, based on a new lamp design, was called the **Source Four Spotlight** and produced a far superior light when compared to traditional ERSes. Other manufacturers have developed their own versions of this design, and we collectively refer to all of these units as **enhanced ellipsoidal reflector spotlights** (Figure 6.16). In addition to ETC's Source Four, Strand Lighting offers the SL Coolbeam Spotlights, while Altman provides the Shakespeare series of luminaires. One of the most significant improvements involved the newly conceived energy-efficient 575-watt HPL lamp, which with its filament design and enhanced optics can produce about the same amount of footcandles as a traditional 1,000-watt ERS. Other significant improvements include a dichroic reflector that allows heat to escape through the rear of the fixture, which reduces the temperature at the

Figure 6.16 Enhanced ERS design: Source Four (fixed focal length)

Credit: photo courtesy ETC.

1. Alignment joystick	7. Gate
2. Lead wires and pin connector	8. Baffles
3. Lamp housing	9. Focusing lens (adjustable)
4. Socket	10. Beam spread lens (adjustable)
5. Lamp	11. Gel-frame holder
6. Modified reflector	12. Shutter

Figure 6.15 Sectional view of a zoom ellipsoidal reflector spotlight (ERS)

gate and prevents heat damage/warping of the shutters (it also adds to gobo and gel life); improved shutters that produce sharper edges; and a body that allows the shutter plane to be rotated for better control of the shutters. The units also have enlarged gobo slots that allow for the insertion of modular accessories at the gate (e.g., multiple or composite gobos and effects equipment like gobo rotators). These fixtures are especially good at producing sharp shutter cuts and crisp gobo patterns. The luminaires have a slightly smaller profile than traditional fixtures and also have slightly smaller lens diameters. Many enhanced ERS luminaires can be upgraded to a 750-watt lamp for even more punch.

Enhanced ERS luminaires produce a crisp, intense beam that can be focused to an extremely sharp edge. They are essentially flat-field fixtures with smooth and even light across an entire beam. These qualities may at times make softening their edges a bit more difficult during focusing. In fact, a number of designers add diffusion media or frost to nearly every enhanced ERS in their designs to further soften the edges of a unit's beam. On the whole, they mix fairly well with traditional fixtures although their increased intensity and slightly cooler color temperature can cause them to punch through the light of traditional fixtures. Like traditional ERS luminaires, the enhanced ERS comes in a variety of sizes and beam spreads. These, too, may have fixed focal length or zoom lenses. Common sizes include 50°, 36°, 26°, and 19° varieties. Larger versions include 5°, 10°, and 14° units. The enhanced ERS designs have become widely accepted for not only their superior lighting capabilities but also their efficient use of energy. In fact, many of these enhanced fixtures have been embraced as a luminaire for some architectural applications. Over time, ETC has developed even better optics for these fixtures and now offers an optional lens tube called the **Enhanced Definition Lens Tube (EDLT)** that produces even sharper beam edges and gobo images.

One final form of ERS that has been gaining popularity in recent years is the Selecon Pacific line of enhanced luminaires (Figure 6.17). These luminaires have unique designs when compared to other enhanced ERS fixtures. They, too, cut down significantly on heat buildup but are designed around the principle of placing the lamp in an orientation that inserts the lamp through the base of the instrument (like the radial designs but with the lamp on the bottom). These also come in a variety of beam spreads and zoom designs.

Beam Projectors

Beam projectors produce a very intense and harsh beam of nearly parallel rays of light. This is due to the parabolic reflector that is used in their design. The beam projector is unique in that it is the only spotlight that does not contain a lens. In this luminaire (Figure 6.18),

Figure 6.17 Inverted Philips Selecon Pacific 14°–36° Zoomspot ERS design

Credit: photo courtesy Philips Lighting

1. Gel-frame holder
2. Baffle
3. Spherical reflector
4. Baffle
5. Parabolic reflector
6. Lamp
7. Socket
8. Focus assembly
9. Lead wire with pin connector

Figure 6.18 The beam projector

a small spherical reflector is placed directly in front of the lamp as a means of maximizing the parallel rays coming from the unit. Light that would normally scatter from the front of the fixture strikes this reflector and is redirected back to the parabolic reflector, where it is redirected again toward the front of the unit as parallel rays of light. An undesirable effect of this reflector is a noticeable shadow at the center of the luminaire's beam. Because of their strong directionality, we typically use beam projectors where strong light sources are needed. Backlighting doors and windows, indications of sunlight, and specials like "God lights," or even short-throw followspots are effectively created by beam projectors. At one time, it was common to use banks of beam projectors in backlighting for dance productions.

Beam projectors come in a variety of sizes based on the diameter of the fixture. The 10-inch and 12-inch varieties are the most popular ones associated with theatrical applications. Fourteen and 18-inch versions are also available, and the film industry may make use of beam projectors with even larger diameters. Some beam projectors use an arc or DC lamp to reduce the filament size and produce a smaller point light source to create an even more powerful luminaire. Despite their unique quality, beam projectors are not as popular as they once were due to the invention of parabolic aluminized reflector (PAR) lamps, which produce nearly identical light without the central shadow.

Parabolic Aluminized Reflector (PAR) Luminaires

The **PAR lamp** represents a critical development in that a relatively cheap fixture was designed to be durable, easily hung, and designed specifically for the quick turnarounds required of concert lighting. The light produced by a PAR is harsh and crisp with essentially parallel rays and relatively soft edges that allow adjoining units to be easily blended from one light to another. Since the beam quality is essentially the same as a beam projector, the PAR luminaire has pretty much replaced beam projectors for producing this particular quality of light. The central element of the PAR fixture is its lamp, which contains a parabolic reflector, a filament/light source, and a lens that focuses the light to a given beam pattern—forming a self-contained luminaire within the actual lamp. The fixture is no more than a cylindrical housing with a socket for the electrical connections and a spring ring for securing the lamp and a series of troughs or clips for securing gel to the front of the unit. Due to their simplicity many designers refer to these luminaires as **PAR cans** (Figure 6.19). PAR cans are unique in that they have no provision for altering the light and are simply pointed to where the light needs to be focused. As a means of controlling distribution, a designer specifies a lamp with a specific beam pattern. Lamp options are named according to the amount of spread that the lamp will produce and include the following: Very Narrow Spot (VNSP), Narrow Spot (NSP), Medium Flood (MFL), and Wide Flood (WFL). While some lamps produce a circular beam, most PAR lamps create an elongated or elliptical pattern. Electricians are often asked to turn or twist the

1. Lead wires with pin connector
2. Socket
3. PAR lamp
4. Light baffle
5. Gel-frame holder

Figure 6.19 Sectional view of a PAR can fixture

lamp within the fixture to orient the axis of the lamp's filament (**spinning the bottle**) to control the direction of this elliptical pattern.

PAR units come in a variety of sizes, each based on the lamp used in a specific luminaire. Popular sizes include PAR-38, PAR-56, and PAR-64. PAR-64s often use 500-watt and 1,000-watt lamps. PAR-38s and 56s have lower wattages. Smaller versions like the MR-16 are often called **birdies** and are used in applications where there is limited space. Low-voltage versions of the MR-11 and MR-16 units are often found in landscape and display applications. The PAR-64, through developers like Chip Munk and Bill McManus, has become the most popular unit associated with the concert industry (though this is now being challenged by moving lights). Assemblages of PAR-64 fixtures are often rigged (along with their circuiting) into modules of six fixtures which are hung together on short pipes called **PAR-bars** that are mounted in larger metal frames that can stretch across an entire stage (**trusses**). Each is easily assembled and struck with no need to hang, circuit, or color the individual units from one show to another. Many trusses simply bolt together after rolling off the trucks and upon being flown will have the PAR-bars simply dropped out of their traveling positions into their show positions. The **aircraft landing light (ACL)** is another version of PAR that runs on a 24-volt DC current and produces an extremely narrow beam of light. These units were adapted from actual landing lights and are also popular in the concert industry.

ETC also designed an improved version of the PAR fixture around the same lamp that it used in its Source Four ERS design. This was called the **Source Four PAR** and opened the way for the production of **enhanced PAR** fixtures. This luminaire also produces a superior light when compared to traditional PAR-64 fixtures. A special feature of the Source Four PAR is its four interchangeable lenses, which are used to change the beam

1. Ballast/power supply	10. Damper (chopper)
2. Power leads	11. Iris
3. Lamp hour display	12. Lens 1
4. Power switch	13. Color boom (6 colors)
5. Arc strike switch	14. Lens 2
6. Short-arc lamp	15. Tilt lock
7. Reflector	16. Handle
8. Modified Reflector/baffle assembly	17. Leveling screw
9. Dowser	

Figure 6.20 A short-arc followspot and its components

spread without having to change a fixture's lamp. Each lens produces a pattern that is roughly equivalent to the traditional PAR lamps. Also, in order to "spin the bottle," an electrician only has to turn a ring located at the front of the unit. Other manufacturers have developed their own versions of enhanced PAR fixtures. Finally, ETC has developed yet another luminaire that combines the light output of a PAR with the adjustable beam of a Fresnel. This luminaire, appropriately named a **PAR-Nel**® is also designed around the 575-watt HPL lamp, but an electrician can vary its beam spread from a spot to flood setting through twisting a knob at the front of the unit. Unlike Source Four PAR's elliptical beams, the PARNel has a circular-shaped beam.

Followspots

Followspots are special variations of ellipsoidal reflector spotlights. The optics are essentially the same as the zoom spotlights with the exception that followspots are larger, have additional controls for manipulating the light, and use more powerful light sources. Followspots (Figure 6.20) are used to punch through the light of conventional fixtures to establish focus on whatever lies in their beam. Anyone who has seen a concert, ice show, or musical has seen these luminaires used to follow the performers around the stage.

A followspot gets its intense brightness from a high-wattage lamp or other light source like an arc or short-arc. When followspots use an incandescent lamp they may be assigned to a dimmer, but a separate non-dim circuit must be provided for the unit's fan or damage could occur to the unit's lamp, gel, or lenses. With arc sources, the light must be dimmed by a mechanical dimmer called a **douser.** If a followspot uses an arc source, it will also require a ballast or transformer for striking and regulating the lamp's voltage. While many followspots used to be powered by carbon-arc sources, these have for all practical purposes been replaced with newer short-arc lamps like xenon, HMI (hydrargyrum medium-arc iodide or halogen metal iodide) and HTI (tubular metal halide) lamps. A primary consideration of these short-arcs is the initial warm-up time that it takes for them to come up to full power—often nearly five minutes! One of the principal controls of a followspot is an **iris** that allows the light's operator to easily modify the diameter of the beam. Another control, the **damper,** provides a set of shutters that allow the operator to quickly cut the light across its top and bottom edges. Other controls found in most followspots include easily adjustable pan and tilt controls, a **boomerang** or **color boom** to quickly change the spotlight's color, and a zoom and focus assembly (called a **trombone**) that allows the unit's beam angle and focus to be modified easily. A typical color boom provides up to six different frames of color for the spotlight.

Short-Throw

Short-throw followspots have beam angles that are sized for small venues. The throw distances that these followspots are optimally designed for are usually in the range of 25 to 50 feet. These units are miniature versions of their full-size cousins (long-throw followspots); they can be as small as 30 inches in length and often weigh in at less than 100 pounds. Short-throw followspots and their operators can even be mounted in the overhead trusses of concerts. They are often used in hotel lounges, churches, and many night- and dance-club venues. Designers may even use ERSes with iris kits as alternatives for these followspots.

Long-Throw

Long-throw followspots are used in venues like large auditoriums, arenas, and sports stadiums. They have narrower beam angles, contain more powerful light sources, and are usually much larger than the short-throw spotlights. Many of these followspots are around 6 feet long and can weigh several hundred pounds. Today, nearly all these spots use short-arc sources that require a ballast. The ballasts are a separate box-shaped unit that is placed on the ground near the followspot. Power is fed to the ballast, where it is converted and then directed to the lamp via a second cable. Long-throw followspots are designed for distances of up to 500 feet. The long-throw followspot is an essential element of many large-scale events and spectacle productions. Strong International produces several long-throw followspot models in the Trouper and Super Trouper lines that have been very popular in concert and arena productions.

Floodlights

While spotlights contain lenses, are controllable, and produce well-defined intense sources of light, floodlights are designed to cover a broad area evenly, don't have lenses, and have soft edges that allow them to be easily blended with other units. This makes them popular choices for **wash** luminaires. There are essentially two types of floodlights in popular use. The first makes use of a single lamp and reflector, while the second uses multiple lamps or chambers and gels. This second type allows a luminaire to mix colors through circuits that are controlled and colored independently from one another.

Ellipsoidal Reflector Floodlight (Scoop)

The **ellipsoidal reflector floodlight (ERF)**, or **scoop** (Figure 6.21) as it is more commonly known, is the simplest floodlight in common use today. These fixtures create

1. Ellipsoidal reflector (matte finish)
2. Gel-frame holder
3. Lamp
4. Socket
5. Lead wire with pin connector

Figure 6.21 Sectional view of a scoop or ellipsoidal reflector floodlight (ERF) a wide distribution pattern that spreads soft, diffuse light evenly over a large area. The edges are very soft so that they can be blended with other fixtures quite easily. The reflector is of the ellipsoidal reflector style, but the soft diffuse quality comes from a matte, rather than polished, reflector surface. In some cases the reflector is made of untreated spun metal, while in others it is painted with a flat white paint. Scoops are relatively large, and many theatres stock sizes that are 10, 14, 16, or even 18 inches in diameter. Lamp wattages can be as small as 250 watts for the 10-inch variety to up to 1.5–2kW for the larger 18-inch versions. The 14-inch scoop is fairly standard and is typically lamped to 750 or 1,000 watts. While most scoops are nothing more than a lamp placed in an ellipsoidal reflector with a mechanism for holding gel, there are also several focusable versions that will allow the scoop to be altered between a spot and flood focus.

Due to their wide beam distribution and uniform coverage, scoops are often used to light large expanses of scenery like drops and cycs. A bank of scoops is hung downstage of the scenic element with a spacing interval that allows the units to blend with one another while evenly washing the associated scenery. Additional circuits of scoops can be placed between the first set of scoops for each additional color that the designer wants to use in a design. A popular version of this wash lighting has been used for lighting cycs and includes alternating three different circuits of scoops in each of the primary colors (red, blue, and green). By using various combinations of these three colors a designer can theoretically create any color on the cyc's neutral surface. Scoops are also often specified as worklights for stages.

Striplights

Striplights are a unique luminaire in that they are one of the few fixtures that make use of multiple lamps. These units get their name from their elongated trough of individual lamps that are arranged in a side-by-side fashion that forms a strip of lights. Each lamp is set apart from its adjoining lamps by a baffle that allows its chamber to be colored and wired separately from the others. A typical striplight contains three or four circuits with every third or fourth lamp wired to a common circuit (Figure 6.22). These luminaires produce an even wash of light along a linear axis that is parallel to the length of the unit.

Striplights are often used for washing scenic elements like drops and cycs as well as for toning a stage from overhead. It is common to run a series of striplights in an end-to-end configuration that is parallel to the scenery that they are lighting. Most striplights are wired with a set of male connectors for each circuit on one end and a set of female connectors on the opposite end that facilitate this end-to-end configuration when circuiting a show. When placed the correct distance from the scenery, lamps sharing a common circuit or color will blend evenly from one lamp to another. If placed too close, scallops appear between each of the individual lamps. Due to the close proximity that these fixtures might share with scenic elements a designer often adds **frost** to the luminaires to keep these scallops from appearing. While each lamp may be gelled with any color, several especially popular colors are created through using glass filters called **roundels.** These are offered in only four or five colors (the primaries, a canary yellow, and white), and in situations where color is not often changed, the more expensive roundels are a popular alternative to using gel.

Striplights come in a variety of sizes and shapes. One of the most popular versions is a 6-foot unit containing 12 lamps and three circuits. Another popular variety is the 8-foot/16-lamp version, which has four circuits. Lamps may vary in size from the small low-voltage MR-16 lamps (Figure 6.23) to units containing banks of PAR-64 lamps. Many other luminaires use R and PAR lamps or double-ended tube lamps in their designs. A fairly recent innovation even makes use of the Source Four PAR design (Source Four MultiPAR). Unfortunately, the R-40 striplights that were at one point arguably the most popular striplight design have fallen by the wayside due to the unavailability of R-40 lamps. These lamps have fallen prey to the "ban the bulb" movement. Striplights are often hung above the stage along battens with specialized hardware called **hanging irons**—one on each end of every fixture. They may also be mounted on the stage floor using **trunions,** which allow the luminaires to sit on the floor and point upward to wash a drop from below. We refer to this as a **ground row** lighting system. Some stages even have a trough in an upstage position so that a lighting ground row can be hidden from an audience's view. Other stages will have a trough along the front of the stage to create a footlight system that may make use of these units. If a trough isn't present, striplights may also be hung directly across the front of the stage using trunions that are mounted to the front of the stage to create this footlight lighting.

| Cir. 1 | Cir. 2 | Cir. 3 | Cir. 1 | Cir. 2 | Cir. 3 | Cir. 1 | Cir. 2 | Cir. 3 | Cir. 1 | Cir. 2 | Cir. 3 |

Figure 6.22 Typical circuiting of a three-circuit striplight

Figure 6.23 Low-Voltage MR-16 Mini-Striplight (Altman 3 Circuit/30 Lamp Econo Strip)

Before spotlights became the dominant luminaire for creating general illumination, stages were often equipped with several overhead banks of permanently wired striplights that stretched across the entire width of the stage. These banks were called **borderlights** because they typically ran along the upstage side of the border maskings. Most general-purpose auditoriums and high school stages built in the 1950s–'70s had borderlights specified as part of their basic lighting package. Regardless of whether a designer uses borderlights or individual striplights, each can be used to provide general illumination and color toning of the entire stage. Dance companies have even used striplights as a source of sidelight by simply mounting the units vertically on booms. Some refer to these as **Vertical Toning Strips (VTS)**. In the mid-1980s, manufacturers introduced a **mini-striplight** that was based on a low-voltage MR-16 lamp design. The low voltage (typically 12 volts) allowed for a more efficient lamp that took up much less space. Each fixture has a transformer associated with the three circuits and the lamps are often wired in pairs where every two adjoining lamps operate together as a single unit. The new striplights are only about half the width and height of traditional striplights, which allows them to be placed much closer to their targets while avoiding the unwanted scallops. Just as with PAR lamps, the distribution patterns of many of these units are altered through the selection of different lamps.

Cyc Luminaires

Lighting manufacturers have developed another style of luminaire as an alternative to using scoops and striplights for lighting cycs and backdrops. While there are brands associated with these fixtures, most of us have come to know them as **cyc lights** or **far cycs** (Figure 6.24). These units are usually developed around double-ended TH lamps that are placed within a specially designed asymmetrical reflector. The lamps are generally rated at 500 or 1,000 watts, with each lamp/reflector unit forming an independent circuit (1,500- and 2,000-watt versions also exist). The reflector typically has a pebble finish that creates a spread reflection and a shape that wraps around the back of the lamp that is flattened out across the lower portions of the reflector. This produces an intense wash of light that is dispersed over a wide area. Due to the uneven shape of the reflector, the luminaire produces a sharper upper edge and a smooth graded wash over the lower part of its coverage. A single unit can cover the entire height of many cycs or drops. In addition to this large vertical coverage, these units also have a wide horizontal coverage that will often allow as few as four to six units to cover the entire width of many stages.

Just as with striplights, far cycs are also used as multi-colored wash luminaires. This is done by combining several individual lamp/reflector assemblies into a larger fixture—each individual assembly being referred

1. Yoke
2. 2-cell unit
3. Compound reflector
4. Lamp
5. Gel-frame holder (slot in curved edge)
6. Lead wires and pin connector (one per cell)

Figure 6.24 A cyc luminaire (far cyc): A four-cell unit

to as a **cell.** Cells, even though wired independently from one another, are typically bolted together and hung from a common yoke/C-clamp assembly. Most far cycs contain three or four cells that are usually gelled in different colors. The actual arrangement of cells can vary from a series of side-by-side cells to an orientation where four cells are mounted in a two-over-two arrangement. Because of their greater intensities and smooth coverage, far cycs are now the preferred luminaire for lighting large flat pieces of scenery. However, their large physical size and need of being mounted farther away from their target can make them hard to use in some situations. For instance, striplights are more commonly used in ground-row positions.

ACCESSORIES FOR CONVENTIONAL LUMINAIRES

Optical Accessories

These devices allow additional manipulation or control of the light coming from a luminaire. I've already mentioned a number of internal accessories when I discussed ellipsoidal reflector spotlights. Iris kits and gobos form the most common accessories used with ERS and enhanced ERS luminaires. Images can even be printed on high-temperature acetate that is then inserted into the gate of an ERS (in enhanced ERS designs). A **gobo rotator** allows gobos to be spun in a circular motion. Some hold two gobos that can be spun both in different directions and speeds to form composite images and effects.

External accessories (Figure 6.25) are placed in front of a luminaire to modify the fixture's light as it leaves the lighting instrument. In most cases, these accessories simply slip into the gel-frame holder of a luminaire. The first device is a **gel frame** or **color frame.** It is nothing more than a thin square of sheet metal that has a large hole in its center that is sized proportionally to the diameter of the luminaire. Gel is cut and inserted into the color frame, which is then held in place by slots located at the front of a fixture. Gel frames come in a number of sizes that are based on the size and shape of their associated fixtures. Another accessory that is commonly slipped into a gel-frame holder is a **doughnut.** This is a thin sheet of metal or foil that is similar to a color frame, except that the hole in the center is relatively small in comparison to a luminaire's lens diameter. Doughnuts are used to sharpen gobo patterns that are difficult to focus by using the luminaire's focus adjustments alone. This effect is known as **halation.** The simplest accessory is a black foil that is simply bent around the face of a luminaire to control **spill** (e.g., GAM's Blackwrap™).

Two of the most popular accessories for theatrical luminaires are **barn doors** and **top hats.** Barn doors provide folding panels that can be tilted to block unwanted light that may be coming from a fixture. They are also used to reduce glare from luminaires that are hung in positions where audience members might glance into a light. These accessories slip into the gel frame holder of a luminaire and can usually be rotated to orient the panels as needed. There are **four-way** (top, bottom, and two sides) and **two-way** (two opposite sides) barn doors. Barn doors are commonly used with Fresnels and PAR

luminaires. Top hats, in contrast, provide no means for modifying a light and are simply tubes that are soldered to a gel frame to prevent the light from opening up or spreading too quickly. Like barn doors, top hats are used to control spill, glare, and ambient light that may be coming from a fixture. They are frequently used to eliminate glare from backlights or in arena setups where the lens of a fixture is within view of an audience. A variation of top hat design that provides only half a cylinder is called a **half hat** or **eyelash** and is used to control spill in only one direction. An accessory that is very similar to a top hat is the **color extender,** which simply is a top hat with additional slots for placing gel frames and gel farther along the tube and away from the light source. This extends the life of the gel. As a way of preventing glare, particularly with Source Four PARS, **egg crate** accessories are also used to help shield viewers from the direct glare of a fixture's lamp. These are especially helpful in small theatres. Another accessory that may be used with large capacity Fresnels or other luminaires that make use of arc sources is a **douser.** This is a mechanical device that uses a set of panels or blinds to produce a mechanical dimming effect on a luminaire.

Hanging Accessories

In addition to the luminaires themselves, there are a number of accessories that might be used to hang the lighting instruments. Some of these provide additional methods for mounting fixtures while others are safety devices that can protect the crew, performers, and audience. Most entertainment professionals tend to collectively call all of this hardware **irons.** The most popular mounting device for entertainment luminaires is the **C-clamp** (of which there are several models). Some irons combine a C-clamp with other hardware to produce alternate ways of hanging theatrical luminaires.

At times luminaires must be mounted on pipes that are oriented vertically. These vertical positions are called **booms,** although some refer to these pipes as **trees.** Booms are secured to the floor by a flange or through a heavy metal base called a **boom base.** Booms frequently become top heavy and are often tied off to the grid from above. A **ring top** is a piece of hardware consisting of a metal loop that is screwed to the top of a boom pipe to create a method for attaching a rope that is then tied off to the grid. If an electrician uses a traditional C-clamp to hang a luminaire on a boom it is much more difficult to adjust the pan and tilt of the unit during focus. An iron called a **sidearm** provides a way of hanging lights so that the pan and tilt adjustments can be oriented normally. A typical sidearm consists of a pipe about 3/4 inch in diameter that is mounted to a C-clamp. The C-clamp secures the sidearm to the boom pipe, while a second piece of hardware called a "T" slides over the smaller pipe and secures the yoke bolt of the luminaire. The T

Figure 6.25 Popular luminaire accessories. Front row (left to right): a template or gobo holder and a gel frame. Back row (left to right): a top hat, an eyelash or half hat, an egg crate or baffle, and a four-way barn door.

has set-bolts that allow its position to be locked anywhere along the length of the pipe. Typical sidearm sizes include 1-foot, 18-inch, 2-foot, and 3-foot lengths (but can be as long as 6 feet or more). While many sidearms only have one T, a designer may specify two or even three luminaires and associated Ts for a sidearm. While not required, it is preferable to use sidearms to hang luminaires in vertical positions.

Every luminaire and associated piece of hardware that is hung from above should be secured with a **safety cable** for protection against falling equipment. The only exception should be in those areas where a protective mesh or other device is provided for catching falling objects. C-clamps fail and handles that lock the tilt of a unit can slip, causing a light to dump its contents (like a barn door) to the ground below. While most safety cables simply slip around the yoke of a luminaire and are then clipped around the pipe that forms the hanging position, the best precaution requires that the safety cable be secured to the body of the luminaire. Heavy accessories like color scrollers and barn doors should be made safe by fastening a safety cable to the accessory and securing the additional safety cable to a luminaire's yoke.

AUTOMATED ACCESSORIES FOR CONVENTIONAL LUMINAIRES

The largest drawback of traditional luminaires lies in the fact that a fixture can be dedicated to only one set of functions at a time. This cannot be altered without climbing a ladder and changing something at the lighting instrument. As the control problems associated with using more luminaires were overcome, light plots grew exponentially with more and more units being used in productions (i.e., lighting an area of the stage with two different colors from the same position would require **double-hanging** two units—each gelled in a different color). Eventually, a point was reached where it was physically impossible to squeeze all the lights into a given location and innovators looked into ways of modifying a luminaire's functions remotely and on demand throughout a performance.

Most advanced gear was initially developed to produce some form of special effect. Some of this equipment isn't that sophisticated and includes devices like **color wheels, flicker devices,** and **animation disks** that produce a shadow or color effect that is simply loaded into the color frame holder of an instrument. Many were nothing more than a disk with patterned holes that was rotated in front of a fixture's beam by a low-speed motor. Many of these devices are still in use today. There are also special effects projectors like GAM's **scene machines** that produce similar, but more advanced, moving effects. For the most part, all these effects had a single AC motor that was simply plugged into a non-dim circuit. The effect would be turned on just prior to

its use, allowing the motion to already be established as the fixture's lamp was dimmed up. In an attempt to control the effect's speed, many of these effects have a potentiometer that provides a way of presetting the speed of the rotation. Unfortunately, the speed is usually changed only by going to the instrument and changing the potentiometer's setting. Because of this, many designers plugged these motors into a dimmer so that the speed could be varied. This wasn't the best practice, and designers had to take care that this didn't damage the motor or dimmer. Many of these effects, like fog/hazing machines and strobes, also had controllers that were operated independently of the lighting system.

Scrollers

The first devices that enabled true changes to conventional lighting instruments usually allowed a designer to change the color of a light. The earliest devices were effects related and included **color wheels** that placed a revolving disk of several colors in front of a light. Fire effects were often created with these mechanisms. Later devices, known as **color scrollers** because of their manner of operation, have a series of gels (a **gelstring**) taped together into a scroll that is loaded onto two rollers. A color is selected by moving the gelstring to different positions along the scroll. A designer specifies the gels and order in which they should be placed when ordering a gelstring. Most scrollers require a power supply that provides both the power and control data for the devices. Each scroller can be assigned to its own DMX address (see the Attributes and Addressing section later in this chapter) or may be operated in tandem with other scrollers that have a shared address. Each color or position is associated with a specific intensity level for the assigned channel. The simplest scrollers provide 12 to 16 colors while more sophisticated models can mix color by combining two overlapping gelstrings that are independently controlled from one another. Dual gelstring units can typically create more than 400 different colors.

For many years, more expensive automated lights have mixed a seemingly infinite number of colors through a color mixing technology called **CYM mixing** (also known as **CMY mixing**). CYM mixing allows a designer to manipulate three dichroic disks or leaves of varying color densities (cyan, yellow, and magenta) through individual channels that can mix the light to virtually any desired color. In reality, each of the filters produces a new color through being inserted to varying degrees into the optical path of the light. Some designers take issue with this method of producing color because it can be difficult to project the same color uniformly throughout the entire light beam. Also, because the resultant color is a product of mixing, the colors aren't usually as intense or saturated as those produced with filters. On the other hand, in addition to providing so many colors, you can also cross-fade directly between colors, which can't be done with scrollers. A second innovation in color accessories involves placing a CYM mixing module in the body of an ETC Source Four fixture. This accessory, called the SeaChanger Color Engine, is produced by Ocean Optics and brings full CYM mixing to any Source Four. The basic operation is much like any other CYM mixing technology with the exception that a fourth disk (green) is often added to the cyan, yellow, and magenta plates. This provides more variety and stronger saturation in some of the colors that it produces. Figure 6.26 provides photographs of a scroller and SeaChanger accessories.

Figure 6.26a Color-changing accessories. a. Wybron CXI IT, a scroller with two gelstrings that are used in combination to mix up to 432 different colors

Credit: photo courtesy Wybron, Inc.

Figure 6.26b Ocean Optic's Seachanger Color Engine

Credit: photo courtesy PIXELTEQ Inc.

Moving Yokes

Probably the most desired option that lighting designers want from their luminaires is the ability to redirect a light's focus. In the past, this required designers to commit to automated lights that were often too expensive for many theatrical productions. The units were also quite large and could generate an incredible amount of fan noise that made them less desirable for theatrical applications. This led to manufacturers experimenting with the idea of creating an accessory that allowed conventional fixtures to be mounted in a specialized yoke that could be repositioned by remote control. The result was the creation of a relatively inexpensive **moving yoke** accessory that allows a luminaire's focus to be adjusted on command. The movements are completed through DMX instructions and a series of servo motors that adjust the tilt and pan settings for the fixture. Moving yokes have become a popular accessory and have seen widespread use in Broadway and regional theatres as well as in spectacle productions like Las Vegas revues and nightclubs. City Theatrical's AutoYoke® (Figure 6.27) is one of the most popular moving yoke accessories that are available to a designer.

Figure 6.27 Source Four mounted with an AutoYoke® accessory

Credit: photo courtesy City Theatrical, Inc.

Moving Mirror Accessories

Moving an entire luminaire through a device like an AutoYoke can create torque, resulting in a lot of stress on the moving parts of a unit as well as creating a swinging movement in hanging positions like battens that are not rigidly mounted. The forces have also caused problems in returning to a specific focus point on a repeated basis. An alternative to moving the entire fixture is found in placing a movable mirror at the front of a luminaire. By moving the mirror, the focus can be redirected in much the same way as moving the entire fixture while avoiding the problems associated with actually moving the lights. These devices are placed in a unit's gel frame holder and are called **moving mirror accessories.** While moving mirrors provide less torque and stress to a lighting system, the fixture and accessory must be mounted in a position that results in the range of movement being more limited than with moving yoke accessories. The Rosco I-Cue Intelligent Mirror™ (Figure 6.28) is an example of this type of accessory.

Gobo Rotators

Gobo rotators (or just **rotators**) (Figure 6.29) provide an effect where shadow gobo projections are animated to produce moving effects. Fire and water effects are commonly produced with gobo rotators. In the simplest rotators, a single motor with an independent speed control is plugged directly into a non-dim circuit while more complex units have additional controls that are powered by a special power supply and control signals from the light board. Each type of motion is usually controlled by a separate channel. Gobo rotators are

Figure 6.29 Two examples of gobo rotators. On the left is Rosco's Vortex Rotator®, which must have its settings preset at the device. On the right is Gam's Twin-Spin Rotator, which can have its controls adjusted through DMX commands at the lighting console. Both are examples of double rotators.

inserted into the gate of a fixture and some **(double rotators)** may enable composite effects to be created by making it possible to overlay two different gobos on top of one another. Motion can then be initiated to either or both gobos. Not only the speed, but also the direction of each pattern can be varied by making adjustments to the individual channel levels. Through **indexing rotators,** a gobo can even be instructed to stop at a specific point in its rotation, allowing gobos to be stopped in exact positions like an upright orientation.

AUTOMATED LIGHTING

One of the most important advances in the entertainment lighting industry has been the appearance of automated lighting. The ability to move beams of light freely throughout a venue while also providing numerous effects that couldn't be created with conventional lighting equipment is what drove the development of these luminaires. Due to the expense of developing these luminaires, early developments in creating the units was limited primarily to the concert industry where money was much more readily available. Rental fees for additional equipment, transportation costs, and setup time were additional factors that played a role in driving concert promoters towards developing automated lighting. In the early days, many crews referred to these units as **moving lights** or **wiggle lights,** while we now prefer to call them either **automated** or **intelligent lighting**. One of the first incentives to use automated lighting is its ability to replace a number of individual specials. A fixture focused on one person can be redirected to another position and focus later. The effect of moving the light

Figure 6.28 Rosco's I-Cue Intelligent Mirror® moving mirror accessory

Credit: photo courtesy Rosco Laboratories, Inc.

around a venue while producing color changes, beam zooming, and gobo-related effects soon led to automated lighting becoming an expected spectacle element of concert lighting. Put simply, these lights' movements were choreographed into many of the most popular artists' shows. On the other hand, one of the dangers of automated lighting is in letting the lights become a distraction and using them solely for effect.

Due to the spectacle associated with automated lighting, much of the initial development of these luminaires was directed towards producing effects. Features like number of gobos, whether they rotated, number and range of colors, and strobing capacities as well as movement became important options for making comparisons between different luminaires. These fixtures are usually lamped with short-arc sources that with their higher color temperature cut through the light of traditional luminaires, which allows them to easily establish focus when used with conventional fixtures. For a number of reasons (fan and servo-motor noise, arc source, expense, etc.), automated lighting wasn't practical for theatrical venues in its early years. These units are very expensive (many are $3,500 or more)—and the more features they provide, the pricier they become. Several models actually retail for over $10,000. Even lower-end automated lights cost just under $2,000, which puts them out of the price range for many organizations. Finally, the fixtures are fairly heavy (typically weighing in at 25–50 pounds, with some weighing more than 100 pounds), which can create a fair amount of swinging motion in the electrics even if they are used in a more subtle manner.

While they are still expensive when compared to conventional fixtures, the costs of automated units have dropped significantly over the years, making them affordable for many organizations and applications that wouldn't have used them even 10 years ago. Sophisticated features like programmable shutters, composite gobos, and a number of effects have also been introduced to the fixtures. More importantly, their once-questionable reliability has stabilized, and consistent performances can now be expected from show to show. Due to these factors variations of automated luminaires have become popular in virtually all areas of lighting design. Most concert plots now contain a substantial number of automated luminaires: in some cases, shows are lit entirely by automated lighting rigs. Industrial shows, awards shows, television programs, and even churches have come to rely on these fixtures. *The Tonight Show* uses them, large spectacle events like the opening and closing ceremonies of the Olympic Games use them, and sporting events like the half-time extravaganzas of bowl games rely heavily on automated lighting. In fact, I can't think of a recent television awards program that hasn't made extensive use of automated lighting. In architectural applications, automated fixtures and scrollers have even

been placed in protective housings so that they can be used to light building facades and other outdoor features and events. Use of these luminaires is growing and we can assume that we will see continued growth in their applications. Sidebar 6.4 lists several choreographed moves that are popular in automated lighting.

Sidebar 6.4 COMMON AUTOMATED LIGHTING EFFECT CUES

Ballyhoo	A manner of sweeping moving lights in a seemingly random pattern throughout a venue. A ballyhoo may be done over the stage or audience.
Strobe Sequences	Luminaires programmed to flash in rapid succession. Flashing may be within a single fixture or could flash between multiple fixtures.
Color Rolls	Luminaires moving through a series of color changes.
Chasing	A series of luminaires turned on and off in a sequence that forms a pattern.
Sweeps	Moving the light from one location to another while the lamp is lit.
Fans	A group of luminaires moving together either toward or away from a reference point—an example being lights pointed straight downward and then moving upward and outward away from the stage.
Kicks	A single unit sweeps from a downward position to an upward position where it is extinguished as another fixture repeats the motion, moving much like a dance kick line.

Attributes and Addressing

Every automated luminaire comes with a predetermined number of attributes or functions. Each attribute is controlled by a separate control channel on the lighting console. The actual number and type of attributes will vary from model to model and manufacturer to manufacturer, but several of the most common attributes associated with automated fixtures include shutter, color (one channel for dichroic filters, three for CYM color mixing), gobos (spot units only), intensity, pan, tilt, and speed. Additional attributes might include a second color or gobo wheel (with or without rotation), zoom, and focus. Some units will have both fine and coarse pan and tilt controls. Others can have 20–30 attributes or more. The intensity of the channel controls the movement of the attribute, with 0–100% covering the full range of the function's movement.

Addressing is the assignment of channels to attributes, which is how we control the functions of automated lighting gear. This includes many or the automated accessories for conventional lighting instruments as well as moving lights. While each attribute of this equipment is controlled by a separate control channel, the order in which the channels or attributes are controlled is dictated by the manufacturer. For instance, Channel 1 for a moving light might be assigned to a pan function while Channels 2, 3, 4 and 5 would be assigned to tilt, dimmer, color wheel and gobo selection functions respectively. The order of these functions cannot be changed unless it is reassigned at the control console. For a unit to be controlled properly, the first channel of the automated device is assigned to a given control channel on the console, which essentially tells the console that the first attribute is assigned to this channel and that the following channels will be sequentially assigned to the additional attributes in the same order as assigned by the equipment's manufacturer.

Moving Heads (Moving Yokes)

Moving heads form a specific group of automated lighting in which the actual luminaire or head moves. The earliest automated luminaires were primarily of the moving head variety. The units were large and heavy due to the number of mechanical devices and motors that were used to control the attributes of the fixtures. The company that led the early innovations of automated lighting was Vari*Lite, Inc. They introduced the first moving head fixtures with the 1981 "Abacab" tour of Genesis. The fixtures were so revolutionary that Vari*Lite went to unusual lengths to guard the trade secrets of its technology. For the first 10 or so years, the units could not be purchased and had to be rented directly from the company. In fact, only Vari*Lite employees were permitted to work on the luminaires, and they even provided the technicians who ran and maintained the equipment as part of the rental agreement. It took several years before the competition introduced automated fixtures that didn't infringe on the patent rights of Vari*Lite. However, a key philosophical difference was introduced when other manufacturers allowed their fixtures to be purchased rather than rented. Since then, companies like Clay Paky, Coemar, High End, Martin, Chauvet, and Robe—along with Vari*Lite and others—have developed numerous automated luminaires. During the early years, control of the automated lights was done through special dedicated consoles while all of the conventional fixtures were run through traditional lighting consoles. Over time, manufacturers shifted their control protocols so that the units could be controlled through conventional consoles. However, though the consoles could theoretically control all of the functions of automated lights, they lacked interfaces that suited these units and the control of these devices was quite cumbersome. Specialized consoles appeared that were more user-friendly towards automated lighting—and once again designers often chose to use separate consoles to control the conventional and moving lights of a rig. More recent lighting consoles address many of these issues and provide appropriate interfaces for operating both automated and conventional lights together, which has once again resulted in a single console being used to operate both types of gear for many productions.

We break the moving head luminaires into two additional groups. The first, **spot luminaires,** are used as spotlights and have beams that can be focused to a sharp edge. Many of these units contain effect devices and one or two gobo wheels that can hold up to five or more gobos each. This allows the gobos to be composited on top of one another or spun in the same way as a gobo rotator might be used. Many spot luminaires also have an attribute that allows the focus to be softened or sharpened on demand. In most cases, color is produced through CYM mixing, although a color wheel with dichroic filters may also be used. Some of the more advanced luminaires even have shutters that can be positioned using DMX control. The second type of luminaires are **wash luminaires.** Unlike spot luminaires, these have a soft edge so that a series of them can be blended together to produce washes. Another difference between these and the spot luminaires is the lack of features like gobo wheels and shutters. Examples of both styles of moving head luminaires are found in Figure 6.30.

Some of the accessories that are available for these fixtures incorporate features like laser pointers that allow easy focus spotting during programming and infrared systems that can track a performer's movements. Over time, manufacturers have worked to modify the fixtures for theatrical venues and there are now units that work reasonably well even for these more subtle applications. Improvements have included the following: arc sources have been replaced by incandescent lamps that blend nicely with conventional units; the units have become smaller and weigh less; fan noise has been reduced; and the costs (though still high) have dropped to within reach of more theatrical organizations. The Vari*Lite VL1000 is just one example of an automated luminaire that was specifically designed to blend in with conventional fixtures while bringing the benefits of automated lighting to theatrical applications. Another example of an automated luminaire that has been designed around the needs of theatrical designs is the ETC Source Four Revolution (Figure 6.31). This luminaire is based on a modular design that allows several components or modules to be added or removed from the unit as needed. The heart of this luminaire is based on the needs for silent operation and an incandescent light source. The basic unit also has a 24-color scroller assembly, a

Figure 6.30a Automated luminaires (moving head). a. Philips VL3000 by Vari*Lite (a spot luminaire)

Credit: photo courtesy Philips Lighting

Figure 6.30b Studio Color 575 by High End Systems (a wash luminaire)

Credit: photo courtesy High End Systems, a member of the Barco Group

Figure 6.31 ETC's Source Four Revolution

Credit: photo courtesy ETC

zooming feature, and an internal dimmer. Other accessories that are available for the Source Four Revolution include a remote-controlled iris and shutter accessories. In the last five to 10 years, due to improvements in their design and lowering costs, moving heads have become the automated lighting unit of choice for many lighting designers. LEDs are also having a significant impact on the automated lighting market. In addition to being a light source, many of the moving lights that incorporate LED arrays in their heads are also used for effects. Here, the individual LEDs are programmed into various patterns and/or chases that are often in full view of an audience.

Scanners (Moving Mirrors)

A **scanner,** or **moving mirror,** is another form of automated luminaire (Figure 6.32). Rather than moving an entire head, only a mirror located at the front of the unit is moved to adjust the pan and tilt of a moving mirror luminaire. The mirrors are relatively small and lightweight, resulting in a much more economical means of redirecting a light beam. The luminaires are also hung in a stationary position that results in much less stress to the unit's motors and movement being introduced to the trusses or battens from which they are hung. Scanners typically work better as spot luminaires because the

Figure 6.32 Martin MX-10 scanner

Credit: photo courtesy Martin Professional, Inc.

focus is usually set only at the fixture itself. Scanners come in a variety of sizes and have many of the same attributes that are found in moving head luminaires. Pan and tilt, color, dimming, and gobo patterns are frequently provided in these fixtures. The units also cost less than moving head fixtures, with the tradeoff being that the range of tilt and pan control is more limited. Despite their drawbacks, these luminaires are quite popular, and most designers have learned to work within their limitations. If more extreme angles are desired, a unit can be hung in a modified position that allows the light to hit those areas of a stage where required. Scanners have become very popular in bar and dance club venues due to their size and ease of maintenance. They've become so popular in nightclubs that many are of these lights are equipped with audio sensors that change the attributes to the beat of the music. On the other hand, in corporate, concert, and theatrical applications scanners are losing popularity due to the continuing technological advances and lowering costs of moving head luminaires.

LED LUMINAIRES

A more recent innovation that is taking the industry by storm is the continuing development of **LEDs** and luminaires that make use of LEDs as a light source. In

the past, LEDs did not produce enough light to warrant their use in applications much other than as indicators that we could observe directly (e.g., the power or signal strength indicators of electronic devices). Later developments led to increased intensities that allowed LEDs to be put to more common uses such as in traffic lights, signage, and large video screens like the ones found in Times Square. In applications where intensities don't have to be as high and throw distances not so great (e.g., museum, architectural, and display niches), these fixtures have been appearing in numerous applications for a number of years. To recap some of the advantages of LEDs from Chapter 5: LEDs have incredibly long life cycles (50,000 hours or more), produce little heat, and can provide full color mixing. At the same time, they are also rugged and can withstand many of the environments where traditional light sources don't fare so well (extreme cold, for example). They can also significantly cut the costs associated with the energy used and maintenance (no lamp replacement) of a lighting system.

Color Mixing With LEDs

The LEDs have continued to grow brighter and now produce enough light to be used as an actual source of illumination on stage. This has come about with the creation of **High-Power LEDs (HPLEDs)**. More importantly, by creating clusters of differently colored LEDs, additive or RGB color mixing can be used to produce a variety of colors in the light that emits from these units. Each color is controlled by a separate control channel. Typical colors for LEDs in these clusters include red, green, and blue (often called **tri-colored** units) but may contain up to seven different colors (adding colors like amber, cyan, and possibly white). Two issues that are often associated with fixtures that have fewer channels are the inferior color rendering and especially high color temperature of these units' unnatural white light. ETC's Selador™ units use the primaries plus amber, red-orange, cyan, and indigo as a means of providing better color response in the X7 LED units. Individual LEDs are mounted in clusters that are spaced regularly within the luminaires. The LEDs themselves do not produce much light, but an array of multiple LEDs creates light that is strong enough to warrant packaging the arrays into lighting fixtures. Tri-colored LED luminaires come in two varieties. Earlier versions used clusters of individual red, blue and green LEDs while later technology developed single LEDs that had elements within them that could produce the three individual colors. Both are often called tri-colored LED units.

Wash and Strip or Linear Luminaires

LEDs have been designed into a number of luminaires with successful applications to stage design. The area where we have seen the most success of LEDs in the past lies in applications where we are creating washes of light. Some of these fixtures produce a compact source similar to a floodlight or soft-edged spotlight like PAR luminaires, while others function as linear luminaires that are designed like traditional striplights. A typical control arrangement for these units uses a separate channel for each of the LED colors plus an additional channel for overall intensity of the unit and strobing functions. Tri-colored LED PAR units (Figure 6.33a) have become particularly popular in the lower-end market where throw distances are not that great. Dance clubs, small bands, theatre companies working in intimate spaces, and a number of contemporary churches have made

popular use of these luminaires. In some cases, the entire face of the unit is covered with lower-wattage LEDs of the various colors, while in others, a limited number of LED clusters of higher-wattage LEDs are mounted on the instrument's front surface.

There are also a variety of LED wash or floodlight luminaires that are more linear in their designs. These LED arrays are typically mounted in a rectangular cluster that is several inches wide by roughly 12–18 inches long (Figure 6.33b). These are often used to color limited areas or to create colored accents in the lighting. Fairly recent variations of this type of LED array include **block matrix lights** where multi-colored high-intensity LED sources are designed in a grid-like arrangement. Typical arrangements include 4 × 4 and 5 × 5 grids of these sources. These can be found in both stationary and moving heads. Most importantly, they form a series of bright light sources in which each individual source or chamber can be individually programmed through **pixel mapping**. Multiple units can even be combined to produce larger composite digital images. Striplight versions of LED units (Figure 6.33c) are used in the same manner as traditional striplights. An added feature of these units is that they often have separate channel controls

Figure 6.33a Examples of LED luminaires. a. Tri-colored American DJ 64B LED PRO RGB PAR-64

Credit: photo courtesy ADJ Products, LLC

Figure 6.33b Philips (Color Kinetics) ColorBlast® 12 Powercore, an LED wash luminaire

Credit: photo courtesy Philips Lighting

Figure 6.33c ETC Selador Vivid CE seven-color LED striplight

Credit: photo courtesy ETC

Figure 6.33d Altman Spectra-Cyc

Credit: photo courtesy Altman Lighting, Inc.

Figure 6.34a Additional variations in LED wash luminaires. a. Rosco LitePad® Vector

Credit: photo courtesy Rosco Laboratories, Inc.

Figure 6.34b Rosco Micro Cube®

Credit: photo courtesy Rosco Laboratories, Inc.

for each segmented array that is formed along a unit's length—allowing the units to also be used in complex chase effects. One final form of LED floodlight design is in versions of cyc lights that have been created to make use of LED light sources. In this case, the multi-colored LEDs are fashioned into a tubular enclosure that resembles the double-ended tube lamps used in many conventional cyc light designs. The units also make use of the same asymmetric reflector design as traditional cyc lights. The Spectra-Cyc by Altman Lighting (Figure 6.33d) is an example of this type of luminaire.

A special variation in white LED technology has been created by Rosco in the form of its LitePad products (Figure 6.34a). These illuminating panels come in a variety of sizes (3 × 3 inches to 12 × 12 inches) and are lit from one side by a row of white LEDs. As with side-emitting fiber optics, these panels transmit light along the flat surface of the panel, which makes them an extremely compact light source for situations where there is no room for conventional fixtures. The units operate on a 12-volt system that can be powered by transformers or batteries—and may even be plugged into a car's cigarette lighter. Similar LED technology is used to create a very compact light source in Rosco's family of Cube products (Figure 6.34b). On the larger scale, LED panel sources that are comparable to traditional soft-lights for video and film lighting have been created by a number of companies. These are becoming especially prominent in location shooting. Rosco's Silk series of LED luminaires is based on this type of design and application.

Ellipsoidal Reflector Spotlights

With all of the excitement of LED sources being incorporated into almost any imaginable lighting application it is only logical that in time the makers of entertainment luminaires would discover a way to work LEDs into ellipsoidal reflector spotlight designs. We are now at the point where LEDs are not only being used to produce white sources of light but also colored light within an ERS. In the past, technical issues like low lumen output, directionality of the source, color rendering shortcomings, and multiple images in shutter and gobo patterns prevented LEDs from being incorporated into ERS designs. Additionally, there was the increased expense of the units as well. In the last several years, the majority of these factors have been overcome and we are now seeing a variety of ERSes that are designed around LED light sources.

There are essentially three different styles of ellipsoidal reflector spotlights that make use of LED light sources. The first is quite simple and was introduced in Chapter 5 with the ETC Source 4WRD Retrofit lamp housing, which replaces a Source Four's HPL lamp with an LED light source. The second and third forms make use of spotlights that are designed around a LED light source. The first of these creates a white light source through using either a single or combination of white LEDs while the second makes use of multi-colored LEDs or miniature arrays in order to mix an infinite variety of colored light. The units that form white light can have several white LEDs of different color temperatures, which allows them to create various versions of white light, but they must use traditional gels or other color modifying practices to produce colored light. The multi-colored units will make use of no fewer than the three primary colored arrays of LEDs but are often supplemented with additional LEDs in colors such as amber or various whites. These lights can be used to

mix nearly any color and will most likely help push gel towards obsolescence. In both cases, each color of LEDs are controlled by a separate control channel. Figure 6.35 provides several examples of these newer LED ellipsoidal reflector spotlights.

LEDs in Scenery and Costumes

LEDs are being utilized in a seemingly infinite number of special applications for the stage. Single LEDs can

Figure 6.35b ETC Source Four LED–Series 2 with Lustr® array

Credit: photo courtesy ETC

Figure 6.35c Philips PLPROFILE4 MKII LED Luminaire (back panel)

Credit: photo courtesy Philips Lighting

Figure 6.35a LED-sourced ellipsoidal reflector spotlights. a. Altman PHX 150w Zoom ERS

Credit: photo courtesy Altman Lighting, Inc.

Figure 6.36 Multi-colored LED tape and multi-channel LED driver

Credit: photo courtesy City Theatrical

be incorporated into a variety of props, lamps, and fire sources such as candles and lanterns. Since they draw little power, they can be especially useful when a source must be battery powered, such as when a practical light must be moved around a stage. With the proper electronics, they can also be programed to flicker if needed. An especially interesting version of this technology comes in LED tapes (Figure 6.36) where individual LED sources are mounted approximately every inch along a special tape that contains all of the internal wiring. These tapes can be mounted to scenery and props in a way that allows the LEDs to produce light along the path of the tape. The tapes are very fragile, but can be purchased in a variety of different colors and are powered by a DC power supply. More sophisticated tapes contain multi-colored LEDs that not only allow the color of the light to be changed but also provide the additional possibilities of RGB mixing by various combinations of the different colored LEDs. These LEDs can be programmed like any other lighting fixture; effects like creating color chases of simulated neon or other types of edging effects are possible. I have personally used this tape to produce a number of colored chase effects for platform edges in musicals like *The Who's Tommy*. This LED technology is also used within costume designs to create a variety of mystical effects.

Companies that specialize in LED technology, such as Philip's Solid-State Lighting Solutions, Inc. (Color Kinetics) and ETC, have become instrumental in developing luminaires that provide color mixing as part of a designer's toolkit. Nowadays, most lighting manufacturers have started to incorporate at least some, if not a number, of LED sourced luminaires into their product lines. In situations where color rendering is not a primary concern, a number of quite affordable LED fixtures are already in common use. For instance, a medium-end tri-colored PAR-64 LED luminaire can often be purchased for under $200—I've seen low-end models for as low as $50. Color rendering is constantly improving as companies develop luminaires with stronger light outputs, add additional LED colors to fill in the gaps in the spectral response of the light, or shift to newer technologies that make use of white LEDs that have better Color Rendering Index (CRI) ratings and associated spectral responses. More importantly, even though the more sophisticated units are still priced beyond the financial limitations of many would-be users, the technology continues to improve while the costs of these units keeps coming down. The fact that these sources keep getting more powerful while at the same time becoming more energy efficient, combined with the lowering costs, makes it most likely only a matter of time before we see LEDs becoming the most dominant light source for the stage. Despite all of this, conventional luminaires are still going to be around (especially in the lower-end markets) for a number of years while the industry makes its transition to LED sources.

Allen Lee Hughes

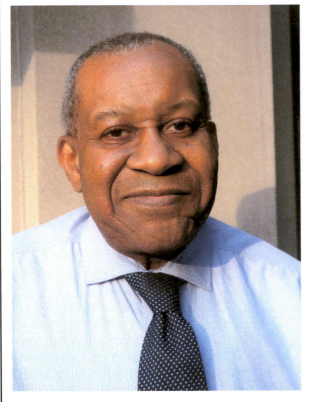

Credit: photo courtesy Janice Davis

Several of the more significant regional theatres that have seen Allen' designs include the McCarter Theatre, Seattle Rep, Goodman Theatre, Guthrie Theatre, and Mark Taper Forum. Additional New York credits include work at Roundabout Theatre Company, New York Theatre Workshop, Playwrights Horizons, New York Shakespeare Festival, and Lincoln Center Theater. His designs and career have earned him numerous awards, including three Tony nominations, Audelco and Ovation Award nominations, Outer Critics Circle Award, Joseph Maharam Award, USITT's Distinguished Achievement Award in Lighting, Merritt Award for Excellence in Design and Collaboration, two Helen Hayes awards, and eight other Helen Hayes nominations. The fellowship program at Arena Stage bears his name, and he was recently the recipient of the 2015 National Black Theatre Festival Outstanding Achievement in Lighting Design Award. Hughes also serves on the faculty of New York University's Tisch School of the Arts.

Allen started lighting plays as a young high school student, and continued to do so while in college. As an undergraduate student at Catholic University in Washington, DC, he received a liberal arts education. While there, he was inspired by observing lighting designer James Waring. He then spent four years working in the field before deciding to pursue a MFA at New York University.

He designed his first opera while he was still in college. It was also during this time that he became associated with the Arena Stage in Washington, DC which would become his artistic home and where he honed many of the design skills that he would use later in life. Said Allen, "My dance career was fostered by designing dance in graduate school and working with the renowned choreographer Dianne McIntyre. These experiences led to several years collaborating with Eliot Feld." Other dance companies that Allen has designed for include the American Ballet Theatre, Pilobolus, New York City Ballet, and San Francisco Ballet.

Allen credits a number of people with helping him to achieve the successes that he has had throughout his career:

> "I have had many mentors in my lifetime including the great lighting designer Arden Fingerhut, the wonderful Jennifer Tipton, Vincent Reed, Frank Birmingham and John Gleason. All have touched my life and made me a better designer. If I had to single out a single incident that really opened the door to my professional development, it would be when a famous designer turned down a regional show that became my first Broadway show."

Though he has lit many different types of projects, including small industrial and architectural projects, and even an inaugural anniversary celebration for a former president and elements of the National Zoo, he sees himself primarily as a designer in the more traditional areas of theatre and dance:

> "I now pretty much exclusively do theater design because that is what I am asked to do. However, I am an associate arts professor at NYU and we believe that if you can master the ability to come up with ideas and execute them for live performance, you can transfer that knowledge to most types of design. When I have ventured outside the area of live design, I just read the spec sheets for the equipment involved or observed the process done by others. Observation is a key component of lighting . . . in order to design lighting, one must be able to see light."

Allen also provides some additional advice for anyone who is considering the field of lighting design:

"In designing for live performance, I believe that the performer must remain the center of the work. It is not desirable for the set, sound, lighting, or clothes to be the center of attention unless specifically called upon to do so. I believe that this quality in my work has led to many successful productions and transfers to Broadway."

He also believes that;

"Coming up with the lighting idea for any project is not unique, but is one of the most challenging parts of designing. Collaborating with your production family is also a consideration that is as enjoyable as it is crucial in this field."

Like many other teachers of lighting, Allen states that his students help him to remain abreast of new developments in the field:

"My students tend to push me along, but I also remember reading a *Live Design* article by Zachary Borovay that said, "If you don't know how to design for the theatre, 100% of the technology of tomorrow will be useless to you." Pretty much every lighting book will put rule number one as selective visibility. This means putting the light where you want it and taking it away from where you don't want it according to Robert Edmond Jones and Max Reinhardt. There are, of course, many other elements that go into lighting design but we sometimes forget or ignore this rule in modern design."

Allen enjoys the magic of opening nights and typically will stay on location for them if at all possible: "If everyone has done their job well, we have an enjoyable and relevant evening in the theater." On the other hand, one of the things he likes least is the current trend of all the videotaping of audiences and theatre practitioners for every minute of the production process: "All artists need private time to ready their art for public viewing. Otherwise, it just becomes one shallow constant show."

Finally, artists of color are sorely underrepresented in not only lighting design but all areas of backstage activity and design. Allen Lee Hughes represents one of the few designers of color who have gone on to a very successful career in lighting design: "I would be remiss if I didn't mention that artists of color have extra challenges. People try and do manage to get away with things that they would ordinarily not do." Allen began his career with the Arena Stage in the late 1960s, and in 1990 it honored him by creating the Allen Lee Hughes Fellowship Program which was founded with the specific purpose of cultivating the next generation of theatre professionals of color, and increasing diversity within the field. This program was the first of its kind and to date has trained more than 700 young theatre professionals, the majority of whom have gone on to pursue careers in theatre. Seventy-nine percent of these young professionals now work in the theatre industry; of those not in theatre, 71% of the remaining individuals are still employed in the arts.

PRACTICALS AND LIGHTING EFFECTS

One last area of lighting relates to luminaires and accessories that could be used to produce a given visual effect. Though this last portion of Chapter 6 does not discuss luminaires in the sense of being theatrical lighting instruments, it covers a variety of lighting practices and effects that a lighting designer is often called on to produce. Only the general approaches and techniques for producing these effects are presented here. You should consult additional resources if you need more detailed instructions.

Practicals

A **practical** is nothing more than a lighting fixture that must actually appear to work on a stage or set. Popular examples include desk or table lamps, wall brackets, floor lamps, and ceiling lights such as chandeliers. Such fixtures do not give off enough light to actually light a scene and are typically supplemented by stage lights (accents) that give the illusion that the practicals are lighting a scene. Practical sources should be placed on a dimmer so that the console has control of the fixture and the relative brightness of the units can be kept in balance with the rest of the scene. These lights also tend to cause glare and usually need to be frosted and run at intensities of 25% or lower. If the lower intensity levels on a dimmer cause the lamps to flicker, a designer can replace the normal wattage lamps with lamps of a lower wattage. This will allow the same level of brightness to be established at a higher dimmer level and will most likely eliminate the flickering effect.

Flame and Fire Effects

Flame and fire effects are among some of the most common effects that a lighting designer will have to produce. Being able to produce these effects has become especially important now that "live flames" are banned from the majority of our stages. The type of flame or fire effect that a designer chooses is dictated by the size of the flame that is needed. In the case of candles or small lanterns, something as simple as a battery-powered LED or flicker light source may be sufficient. How successful these are is primarily dependent on if the effect is strong enough to read (be seen) on stage and what degree of control you need over the effect. In many cases, a performer can simply turn the effect on and off as needed. The believability of these effects is essentially dictated by the amount of money that you spend: on the cheap end you can find these devices at a dollar store, but you can also purchase candles specifically designed for the stage for $100 or more. If the candle effect can be permanently mounted in a prop or on the set—such as in a wall sconce or chandelier—a line-voltage lamp can be used so that the effect can be run through the normal dimming system. There are even flicker lamps designed to look like live flames that are quite believable for this type of application.

In bigger effects, such as a campfire or fireplace, larger lamps (such as three or four birdies) can be assigned to individual channels and colored in flame colors. These can then be programmed into a random chase effect on most consoles for a believable fire effect. For an even more convincing effect, add additional lights that illuminate not only the fire, but also add accents to the effect and shine light into the setting. If you can't spare the extra dimmers, another believable solution that takes a single dimmer involves wiring three or four conventional lamps (again appropriately colored or wrapped in gel) together in parallel but with each individual lamp also wired in series with a fluorescent starter. The entire assembly is then plugged into a dimmer. The dimmer can be used for overall intensity of the effect while the starters cause each of the individual lamps to flicker. If actual flames are required, either effect can be modified by introducing a fan and colored silks into the fire in addition to the effect's light sources. This solution can also be used for larger-scaled fires such as behind windows where a fairly large piece of lightweight fabric is loosely suspended and lit with flickering stage lights while also being blown upon by a fan.

For large-scale fires, a lighting designer is most likely going to have to rely on some sort of projection effect. Here, the effects are most successful if they are either more stylized or just offstage (projecting light onto the stage). In the simplest solution, washes or accents of flame-colored light from light sources like PAR units can be flashed or channeled into chase sequences that form a lighting accent to produce the fire effect. For larger effects gobo rotators that spin a flame-colored glass gobo in possible combination with a second gobo can be used to create a motioned effect. Still more believable fire effects can be produced with effects projectors like Rosco's X24 X-Effects projector and the right combination of effects wheels. For the largest effects, where actual

flames are required on stage, a pyro technician should be brought on board for the production. Here solutions might involve specially constructed devices that involve propane or gas systems, self-extinguishing mechanisms, and a range of safety precautions that must be adhered to by the crew and performers. Even with a specialist in pyro design, any solutions that the team comes up with must be done under consultation and approval of the local fire safety officer. In most states, the pyro specialist must be licensed and individual permits will most likely have to be issued by the local authorities in order to use these types of effects.

Water Reflections

Water effects are in many ways very similar to flame effects except for the colors in which the effects are produced. The traditional way of producing a water reflection is to shine a lighting instrument onto a mirror that has been submerged in glass casserole dish. The water needs to be agitated in some manner, usually by placing a fan somewhere near the setup. The distance from the plate will determine the strength of the waves that are generated. An alternative method that I have used to produce reflected water and ripple effects involves creating square panels (roughly 2 × 2 feet) of silver rain curtain that are hung out of sight from an electric or another location in the theatre. Each panel is then lit by a Fresnel gelled in several colors that are appropriate for the effect, from a distance of about 2 feet and in a placement that casts the light's reflection onto the desired location of stage. As a final touch, a small clip fan is mounted near each of the panels with its speed and distance from the panel determining the strength of the effect. Getting the effect to look just right will take some experimentation, but I have produced the effect over most of a stage with as few as two of these setups. Again, a final technique of producing these types of effects could be done through using gobo rotators or various effects projectors.

Fog, Smoke, and Haze

Though fog, smoke, and haze are not technically lighting effects, it is usually the lighting designer who is charged with the responsibility for providing these **atmospheric effects** (treatments of the air). They are very similar effects, both in the way that they appear as well as in the way that they are created. The primary differences lie in the specific manner in which each one appears. By definition, fog and smoke are pretty much the same. They are fairly heavy atmospheric treatments, with the difference being that fog remains low-lying while smoke rises. In reality, one of the biggest problems with most theatrical fog or smoke systems is in keeping the effects from rising and dissipating. Haze is a light charging of the air with particles and gives the appearance that dust is present in the atmosphere. This is especially popular in spectacle shows like concerts because it allows an audience to observe the beams of light as they radiate away from a luminaire.

Nowadays, the most common method of producing fog and smoke is using machines that superheat a special solution ("fog juice") that vaporizes and forms a cloud as it exits the machine. Settings on the machines can control both the volume and density of the discharge. The only real downside to many of these machines is the noisy hiss that they can generate. More complex machines can be run by remote control through either an independent controller or by DMX commands given through the lighting console that is used for a production. Hazing requires a different machine (a **hazer**) that provides a more subtle but constant manner of charging the air. Only approved fluid should be run through these machines; other substances can cause irritation to the lungs and throats of performers and audience members as well as possible damage to the machine itself. Another issue with many of these machines relates to the fact that they can be unpredictable from performance to performance since the fog or haze can be affected by temperature, humidity, and air currents that are generated by the heat and air-conditioning systems in a venue. On one night a fog effect may come off perfectly while the next night the entire effect blows completely into the wings or worse, right into the audience. For fog, one of the challenges is keeping the fog low-lying. Traditionally, the best method for producing fog has been using a home-made dry ice fog machine where dry ice is dropped into a drum of hot water. Even to this day this produces some of the best fog possible, which is characterized by the thick white clouds that stay low and seem to roll across the stage. Unfortunately, the effect produces carbon dioxide, which can be dangerous to anyone breathing it. In addition, it can be used only once due to having to reheat the water once the dry ice has been dropped. Finally, it cannot be stopped once it has been started, and only redirecting the fog to locations other than the stage can help dissipate it. Fog and smoke machines tend to produce fog that rises and quickly dissipates, which makes it difficult to achieve a thick low-lying fog with the machine alone. In this case, various ways of chilling or cooling the fog have been used to keep it on the ground for a longer period of time. The most common ways of doing this involve placing a dryer hose on the face of the fog machine, which is then attached to a container that is filled with ice or dry ice where it cools and then passes on to a second hose, where it is directed to the stage. Though there are commercial chillers available, you can create your own chiller units with something as simple as a Styrofoam ice chest. For the most extreme cases (theme parks and large spectacle productions), commercially available highly pressurized nitrogen and carbon-dioxide fog systems can be used.

A final problem with using these effects lies in that a number of fog and hazing machines can trigger the fire alarm systems that are found in many performance facilities. Test trials should be made to determine if this will be a problem and if so, a solution such as deactivating certain sensors must be found.

Lightning

There are two different types of lightning that a designer might have to produce. The first relates to creating images of actual bolts of lightning on stage while the second gives a simulated flash of nearby lightning. In the first situation, bolts of lightning can be created by simply focusing lighting gobos onto a scenic material like a cyc or skydrop. Each of the gobo manufacturers offer several different lightning gobos that can be easily purchased or a designer might also design and make their own lightning gobos. Ideally, several different patterns and colors should be used along with channeling each light separately so that the bolts can be flashed individually and manually by the board operator. For added punch, strobe units can be mounted in ellipsoidal projectors in which the gobos have been placed. The effect can also be increased by placing a black scrim in front of a cyc. This creates further depth and a second offset image of the lightning will appear as one image is projected onto the scrim while the second image appears on the cyc.

For more general lightning effects, flashes can be created by adding units like PARs that are gelled appropriately and flashed (manually or programmed) by the board operator. A more believable method involves the use of strobe lights where the unit can be set to fire single flashes or if programmable, the lightning can be programmed through the board to various intensities, durations, and frequencies for the flashes. I have also loaded these strobes onto submasters where a bump button could be used to manually flash the units to predetermined intensities and durations.

Sun, Moon, and Stars

Suns and moons have traditionally been produced in one of two manners. The first involves backlighting a cyc or drop with an ellipsoidal reflector spotlight that is equipped with an iris that allows a circle of light to be produced in the proper diameter of the sun or moon that is being created. The light is gelled in an appropriate color and should be hung from as much of a straight-on orientation as possible. For a variation of the effect, a translucent drop can be used with the translucent material forming the appropriate sun or moon shape. This is then backlit either directly by a lighting instrument or by using reflected light from a **bounce drop**.

A second popular manner of creating a sun or moon relates to creating what we call a **moon box** or **shadow** box. This is nothing more than a box that is created from panels of wood that are larger than the diameter of the sun or moon being created (the face must also be large enough to hide the light sources/lamps) and several inches deep. The front face of the box has a circle (or other moon/sun shape) cut into it and is then covered with a material to diffuse the light (diffusion media or muslin) and a gel in the desired color. The box is then lined with standard incandescent lamps around its perimeter (making sure that none of the lamps are visible within the cutout on the face of the box). Ropelights and other miniature lamps can also be used if the moon box cannot have much depth to it. To increase the intensity of the effect the inside of the box is painted white or may be lined with aluminum foil. If needed, a baffle may also sometimes be added to prevent hotspots from the lamps appearing in the image. Once assembled, the box is hung directly behind a scenic element, such as a cyc, where it is illuminated when needed. For added effect, these boxes can be rigged to move as a means of suggesting a rising or setting moon/sun. Shadowboxes can also be used to produce effects like neon signs, clock tower faces, windows in city skylines, or any other scenic elements that must appear to be lit or glow.

Stars can be created through a variety of different methods. In the simplest method, homemade or manufactured gobos with various sized pin pricks can be projected onto a cyc or other scenic material with ellipsoidal reflector spotlights. A more traditional manner involves placing random lengths of miniature Christmas lights (or even seed lamps) on the backside of a drop. The random lengths will cause the stars to appear to have different intensities—but care must be taken to not use too few lamps in any given run, which could increase the line-voltage and cause the lamps to be overloaded and blow out. Care must also be taken to keep the bulbs right up against the fabric or halos will appear around stars. If the star drop is placed against a black background and behind a scrim, the lights can simply be hung randomly from an open batten. To make the effect more credible, the individual lamps can be taped up or spray painted unevenly in order to create a more random appearance to the lights. Other, more expensive methods of creating a star drop involve punching holes in a drop and lighting the cyc or a bounce drop behind the initial drop, or either renting or purchasing a fiber-optic star drop. One final method of creating a star drop that I have found particularly effective is to simply hang chandelier crystals that are about the size of a dime at random heights from a batten in front of a cyc or black traveler using thin black thread. A black scrim is placed downstage of both battens and several ellipsoidal reflector spotlights with appropriate gels are hung at a variety of heights on booms directly offstage and to either side of the star drop. The ERS units are focused as a narrow strip of light onto the crystals and are then set at different intensities to create the starlit sky. The final effect of this setup is that the stars will appear to twinkle as air currents cause the crystals to rotate within the sidelight. Care must be taken not to run the levels of the sidelights or background too high or the threads that suspend the crystals may become visible.

Explosions and Pyro Devices

These effects generally relate to creating explosive bangs and various fireworks-like effects. There was a time when many of us were responsible for creating many of these effects and we all had our methods of combining gun powder, rocket igniters, homemade firing mechanisms and various other materials to produce the effects that were commonly found onstage. However, due to the many circumstances where fires, maiming accidents, and even deaths have occurred, these effects are now provided almost exclusively by specialists known as **pyro technicians** or **pyro techs**. Furthermore, these specialists must be certified and, in many cases, even licensed by each state in which they practice. Most municipalities also require that a firing permit be applied for and secured prior to the use of any pyro devices with an audience—often with a requirement that the promoter provides additional liability insurance coverage for the event. In fact, some local authorities even require a separate permit for every performance in which pyro will be used. As a further precaution, the days of creating your own explosive devices are long gone: most pyro effects now come in pre-packaged charges that ensure that the mixture has been combined properly and that the right proportion of explosives are present in each charge. An incredible range of pre-made effects in a variety of styles and colors are now available such as air bursts, gerbs, waterfalls, fireballs, mortars, and a variety of different types of flashes. However, it cannot be emphasized enough that this is an area of entertainment production that is best left to the experts. Not doing so can place you and others in danger as well as in a position of liability if something should go wrong.

For Further Reading

Mumm, Robert C. *Photometrics Handbook*. 2nd ed. Louisville, KY: Broadway Press, 1997.

Pilbrow, Richard. *Stage Lighting Design: The Art, the Craft, the Life*. New York: Design Press/Quite Specific Media Group, Ltd., 1997.

Rae, Mark. ed. *IESNA Lighting Handbook*. 9th ed. New York: Illuminating Engineering Society of North America, 2000.

CHAPTER 7

CONTROL FUNDAMENTALS

WHEN I DISCUSS lighting control, I am usually referring to manners of controlling the brightness or intensity of the luminaires. This often relates to two aspects of luminaire control. First, it determines which fixtures are wired together so that they function collectively as a unit; and second, it determines the actual intensity or brightness of a unit(s). This can be done by using different wattages/powers of lamps or by using devices that regulate the power, which are called **dimmers**. Efficiency and luminaire placement also play a role in luminaire control but will not be considered here. Lighting intensities can be modified in some cases with electrical hardware as simple as the dimmer used for a dining room chandelier. While this represents a very simple control system, entertainment lighting systems are usually quite complex and can contain hundreds if not thousands of dimmers and luminaires. In reality though, many of the principles of dimming remain the same no matter how complex a control system becomes. In recent years, control has expanded well beyond simple dimmer control into the control of a variety of lighting accessories, automated luminaires, and projection equipment as well.

In this chapter I present an overview of a number of principles relating to brightness or intensity control. The first segments of the chapter provide materials related to control through circuiting and dimmers. Principles of dimmer operation and several specific types of dimmers are introduced in these discussions. Following these discussions there are sections presenting information related to control protocols and addressing which are important for controlling luminaires with multiple functions like automated lights. Later portions of the chapter provide an introduction to both manual and memory-control systems, in which the dimmers are controlled through some form of light board or console along with an overview of some of the different types of lighting consoles that are available. The final portion of the chapter introduces several additional features that relate to developments in dimming technology.

ILLUMINANCE AND LUMINANCE—FIVE METRICS

In addition to examining the characteristic wavelength or color of a light and its distribution, we also attempt to describe light through its **intensity.** Intensity can generally be thought of as the strength or amplitude of the energy associated with light. More commonly we think of this as brightness. However, while at times one must consider the absolute intensity of the light or the actual amount of energy represented by it, we are more often concerned with the brightness perceived by a viewer. To quantify the manner in which we describe the intensity of light, the **Illuminating Engineering Society of North America (IESNA)** has established five metrics or measurements for describing intensity (Figure 7.1).

Luminous Flux

Luminous flux refers to a measure of the actual flow of energy from a light source, with the most common unit being the lumen. However, we do not generally observe light itself, but rather, we see the effect of light on other surfaces. Also, light moves away from its source in all directions, which means that in most cases much of the lumen output created by a

a. Luminous flux: (lumens) The flow of light

Lumens radiated
in all directions

Power (watts) is converted
to light (lumens)

Figure 7.1 Five Measurements for Describing the Intensity of Light General Note: Illuminance refers to intensity of light (luminous flux) being emitted or reflected from a source or surface—you cannot see illuminance. Luminance can be seen and is a product of light being conducted over a given surface area (source or surface).

b. Illuminance: (footcandle or lux)
The density of light striking a surface

← 1 ft. →

A density of lumens over a square area
• Lux = 1 lumen/meter²
• Footcandle = 1 lumen/foot²

c. Luminous Intensity: (candela or candlepower)
The intensity of light in a given direction

Intensity will vary at different positions around lamp
(i.e., stronger intensity at sides, less at top,
and virtually none below base)

d. Luminance: (candelas/foot² or candelas/meter²)
The intensity of a source or surface in a given
direction over the area of the source seen
by an observer

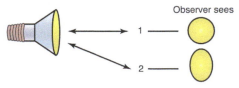

Observer sees

1
2

1. PAR lamp viewed straight on (higher luminance)
2. Same lamp viewed from off-center (lower luminance)

e. Luminous exitance: (lumens/foot² or lumens/meter²)
The intensity of a source or reflective surface
in all directions—the total luminous flux being
reflected or transmitted

light source is wasted. Think of the poor efficiency of a bare bulb that hangs in an attic or garage ceiling. What we, as designers, are more concerned about is how this light responds to being reflected off surfaces and how we can process this information into a significant image.

Illuminance

As light radiates away from its source with a given luminance flux, it can proceed only along a straight path until it comes into contact with an object. At that point it may either be **reflected** or **absorbed** to some degree by any object that lies in its path. In some cases, the light may also be **refracted** if it should pass through the material. Most objects have a surface area that is capable of reflecting or absorbing the light that strikes it. **Illuminance** is the second metric given by IESNA and refers to the density of the light that has the potential of striking an object's surface and being reflected back to an observer. It can be thought of as a measurement of concentration. Two typical measurements of illuminance include the lux (one lumen per square meter) or the footcandle (one lumen per square foot). A light meter will typically measure illuminance, and most specifications in architectural projects will be based on recommend levels of illuminance for a given task (job or visual activity) or environment. While the effect of illuminance can be seen, illuminance itself cannot be seen.

Luminous Intensity

Luminous intensity refers to the ability of a light source to produce intensity in a given direction and is generally measured in candelas. Simply put, no light source produces light of equal luminance flux or intensity in all directions. Luminous intensity is a manner of measuring this unequal distribution pattern around a light source. If we go back to our example of the bare bulb, it can be easily recognized that the area directly above or below the bulb (where the socket/base is located) will be deficient in the amount of light produced as compared with those areas located to the sides of the lamp.

Inverse Square Law

The importance of these three metrics comes about through their interrelationships. When brought together, they create a relationship that can be expressed through a formula known as the **Inverse Square Law:**

$$E = I\,/\,D^2$$

where
E = Illuminance   I = Luminous Intensity   D = Distance

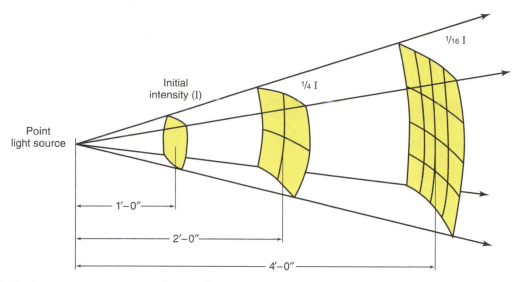

Figure 7.2 The Inverse Square Law. As distance from the light source increases, intensity drops off in a manner that is inversely proportional.

The law simply states that the illuminance of a light source is inversely proportional to the square of the distance from the source. Practically speaking, this means that the light's intensity drops off much more quickly per unit area as the distance from the light source is progressively increased. A quick examination of this principle can be demonstrated through playing a flashlight on a wall and noting the apparent brightness of the light while varying the distance that the light is held from the wall. Figure 7.2 illustrates the effect of distance on illuminance.

Luminance

There are two more metrics that allow engineers and designers to describe light. Unlike those already mentioned, the final two metrics can be directly observed by a viewer. The first, **luminance,** refers to the intensity divided by the surface area of the source as observed by the viewer. This is a directional function, and its value will be dependent on the viewing angle of the viewer to the source. The viewer would actually observe the light source but the source may or may not be in a direct path of observation from the viewer. An example of this impact can be seen when viewing a theatrical light source dead-on versus from a position somewhere to the side. In this case, the surface area of the source would appear as a circle from dead-on, while from the side, the same source would appear oblong and distorted while presenting a smaller surface area to the viewer. Therefore, even with no change in illumination there would still be a lower luminance associated with viewing the source from the side position.

Luminous Exitance

The final metric for quantifying light intensity is **luminous exitance.** This, too, refers to light reflecting or leaving a surface, but it is not direction-dependent like luminance. In this metric we relate the amount of luminous flux to a given reflectance or transmission value for the material of the source or object being considered. Hence, in a situation where two objects are exposed to the same luminous flux, with one colored black and the other white, the object with the white coloring would have a higher associated level of reflectance and therefore higher luminous exitance than the black object.

BRIGHTNESS CONTROL AND DIMMING

We most often refer to brightness or intensity control as **dimming.** While the name naturally implies dimming a lighting fixture to lower intensities, it may also mean that the brightness of the fixture might be raised as well. Dimming refers to any change in intensity (up or down), and we refer to either **dimming up** or **dimming down** based on whether the intensity is being raised or lowered. In most cases, dimming is achieved by introducing a specialized device called a **dimmer** to a circuit. As a general principle, dimmers are used to regulate the amount of electricity (voltage) that is available for any lamp(s) contained in the dimmed circuit. In this way, a lamp will glow to approximately half its potential intensity if only half of the required voltage is available for its use. If the dimmer provides full voltage, the lamp will glow to full brightness. The dimmer is placed in a circuit in the same manner as a switch and alters the voltage that is made available to all of the lamps that are wired in that circuit. While most dimmers vary the voltage, some dim the lighting through other methods, such as adding resistance to a circuit. Like fuses or switches, a dimmer should be placed on the hot wire and located at a point in the circuit that is ahead of the lamp(s) that it controls. There are a number of different principles upon which a dimmer may be constructed, but only those used in today's lighting systems are examined in this chapter.

Another means of controlling intensity is by varying the amount of light that is being produced in an environment. The simple choice of a particular luminaire or lamp can produce an incredible range of lighting intensities. Lamp wattage alone can make the difference in whether you can clearly see a stage or are forced to strain your eyes to decipher the scene in front of you. The distance that separates the light source from the task also plays a role in the intensity that is observed in an environment. Rooms with higher ceilings require higher wattage or more efficient luminaires than rooms with lower ceilings to produce the same amount of footcandles on a desktop. Another popular method of controlling intensity is by selectively turning on and off various elements of a lamp, luminaire, or circuit. In the simplest case, a lamp will be provided with two separate filaments of different capacities. In order to provide one level of brightness, power is provided to one of the filaments. To provide a second level of brightness, power is provided to the other filament, and for maximum brightness, power is provided to both filaments. This is the basic principle in which a three-way table lamp operates. On a larger scale this principle is applied to luminaires that contain multiple lamps in which one or more lamps may be powered at any given time. Bathroom vanities and makeup mirrors often contain lamps wired in several circuits that can provide a limited amount of intensity control. In office buildings, the familiar ceiling fixtures that contain four fluorescent lamps were frequently modified during the energy shortages of the 1980s and '90s so that two of

the lamps were used during normal conditions while the other two were placed on a separate switch and turned on only when needed. Finally, a room's lighting can be broken down into several different circuits as opposed to having all of the lights controlled by a single switch. In commercial buildings, this allows the occupants to turn on the lights only in those areas of the room that they are using—once again saving power and lamp life.

CIRCUITING

Circuiting forms the pathway by which electricity is distributed to the individual luminaires (see Figure 7.3). A circuit may provide power to a single fixture or to a number of lighting units. Regardless of the number of fixtures that are contained in a circuit, they all respond to any electrical change as a group. For more specific information regarding electrical distribution refer back to Chapter 4.

In the simplest form of electrical distribution, power is provided directly to the dimmers through a **distribution box** (or **company switch**) and **feeder cables**. The lights are wired directly from their hanging positions all the way back to the dimmers through a series of cables that are often called **jumpers**. This type of wiring is called **spidering** and is often used in road houses or rental facilities where maximum flexibility is required for the lighting installations. Some electricians may also refer to this as creating **home runs.** Most Broadway theatres are equipped in this manner. and all lighting equipment—luminaires, cables, and even the dimmers—are rented from a rental house or shop. In theatres like these, cable is run only where required, any batten can be converted to an electric, and producers need only rent the exact amount and type of gear that is required for a given production.

In cases where many circuits are run to a single position (like an electric) a number of individual cables are

Figure 7.3 Common theatrical electrical distribution. Circuits may be plugged directly into the dimmers (home runs) or may be part of a prewired installation that is hardwired permanently to specific dimmers in a dimmer/circuit system (DPC). The patchbay is optional and usually found only in older systems that have a limited number of dimmers.

simply tied together to form a single larger unit known as a **bundle.** Another version of cabling makes use of **multi-cables (multi)** in which a number of electrically insulated circuits are combined into a sheathing and run together as a single cable. These cables terminate in individual male and female connectors that are placed at the ends of each circuit. A multi may also have fittings that allow specialized adapters to be added where the wires are split into their individual circuits and connectors. The male end of the cable will often interface with a special connector in a circuit box, while a female fitting with the individual circuits and connectors is typically added to the other end of the cable, which is called a **break-out.** If the male end separates into individual circuit connectors, it is called a **break-in.** One popular style of multi-cable that is used quite extensively in entertainment applications is the **Socapex Cable** (a brand name that has become fairly universal), which carries six individual circuits in one of its most popular configurations. Multi-cables, despite being expensive, reduce the overall weight and volume of cable that is required for a hang. They also make for much more efficient cabling by the electricians. Bundles or multi-cables are often used for circuiting hanging positions like electrics or booms and are typically stored in hampers or cable boxes as they are transported from one theatre to another. In many touring operations, bundles and spidering are used for wiring the **overheads** (lights above the stage) while different provisions are made for circuiting locations like the **front of house (FOH)** positions. Most contemporary theatres provide a combination of pre-wired electrics along with other circuiting features that can facilitate cabling throughout a facility. Some venues even have **transfer circuits** or **panels** so that permanent circuits from locations like the front of house can be plugged directly into a touring company's dimmers and run by their console.

In permanently wired facilities, many circuits are pre-wired to popular hanging positions within the theatre. These circuits are often provided through permanently wired raceways, such as along an electric where individual circuits are located roughly every 12 to 18 inches apart. In some facilities the spacings are greater due to the costs involved in their installation. In most theatres it is common to have pre-wired circuits provided in the front of house catwalks, along several overhead battens at various depths throughout the stage, and in **floor** and **wall pockets** (circuit boxes containing four to six circuits each) located in the wings and upstage areas as well as along front of house positions like the **balcony rail** or **box booms.** Additional circuits are often provided through **drop boxes** that are lowered from the grid to locations such as booms and additional battens. Some theatres are equipped with just drop boxes for lighting from over the stage, but will have a significant number of them placed throughout the grid. Through

this, much of the cabling required for spidering is eliminated, and luminaires can often be plugged directly into a nearby circuit outlet without any additional cable. Some raceway circuits use **pigtails** (a 12–18-inch cable with a female connector), while others provide female outlets that are face-mounted directly to the raceway. Each circuit is usually labeled independently and is wired permanently to a central distribution center for the theatre.

Sidebar 7.1 DIMMER LOAD CALCULATIONS

Safe determination of dimmer loads is an important responsibility of an electrician or lighting designer. Here are two practical examples.

1. How many 575 watt Source Four® spotlights can you safely place on a 2,400 watt dimmer?
Solution: 2,400 watts/575 watts = 4.17. This must then be rounded down to four Source Four spotlights

2. What size dimmer will you need in order to carry the full load of seven spotlights? Each is lamped with a 750- watt lamp.
Solution: 750 watts × 7 lamps = 5,250 watts Dimmers are manufactured in variations of 1,200 watts (1.2 kw) with those sizes being 1200, 2400, 3600, 4800, and 6000. This load will then have to be assigned to the 6,000 watt dimmer.

In the last 20 years the costs of dimming equipment, like most electronic gear, has dropped significantly. It has now become popular to provide individual dimmers for every single circuit in a theatre, in a **dimmer-per-circuit (DPC)** system. However, there are a number of older theatres that predate DPC systems or where the costs of such a system is prohibitive. In these situations, each circuit is run to a panel called a **patch panel** that allows the circuits to be temporarily connected or assigned to a limited number of dimmers. While a theatre utilizing a DPC system often has **low-capacity dimmers** (dimmers with wattages of 1.2 or 2.4 kW), theatres with patch systems frequently make use of dimmers with a variety of load ratings—many being of higher capacities such as 3.6, 4.8, and 6.0 kW or even higher. The two most popular versions of patch panels are the **interconnection panel/patchbay** (Figure 7.4) and the **slide patch** system.

Figure 7.4 Interconnection patch panel

The interconnection panel system is very similar to the switchboard that operators used in the early days of telephone service. A single cable and plug is provided for each circuit, while each dimmer contains outlets for plugging four to six circuits into it. To make a **patch,** or dimmer assignment, the plug of a given circuit is simply inserted into an outlet of a specific dimmer. In contrast, the slide patch contains a small handle that is wired to a circuit and slid over a row of electrical contacts that are in turn wired to each dimmer. Sliding the handle over the desired dimmer's contact and pressing the handle downward into position creates a connection between that circuit and the assigned dimmer. Overload protection is also usually provided to each circuit through a circuit breaker that is located on the patch panel.

Mastering

Most early dimming systems mounted individual dimmers into metal assemblies or frames that held 6–12 individual dimmers. Even today, many systems are based on some combination of 6 or 12 dimmers. **Mastering** refers to the way that dimmers are operated or controlled together. In the early days, electricians could only run the systems manually with some clever manipulation of the handles that were assigned to each dimmer. As additional dimmers were added, more electricians were required and complex mechanisms were developed for mastering the dimmers. As control became even more complex, designers demanded larger systems that eventually grew to the point where they could no longer be controlled mechanically. Through **electronic control,** today's dimming systems can have hundreds of dimmers and control channels—all controlled by a single computer or operator.

Mechanical Mastering

Mechanical mastering is more of a control form of the past, although it can still be found in facilities where

the lighting installations date back to the 1950s–'70s. Older-style resistance and autotransformer light boards were mastered in this fashion. In **mechanical mastering** a physical device is used to link the control handles of the individual dimmers of a lighting system. In most early dimming systems the operator manipulated controls at the dimmer to raise and lower the intensities of the lights. Electricians pulled leavers up and down, rotated circular coils, or flipped switches on or off to control these lights. This was called **manual dimming.** By far the largest disadvantage of these types of systems was the fact that every cue had to be performed live. It wasn't possible to prepare cues ahead of an execution point and the complexity of the cues depended on the manual dexterity of the operators. It should come as no surprise that manual dimming was rapidly discarded as the industry developed the ability to preset cues once electronic dimming became readily available.

The most popular form of mechanical mastering is done by using **interlocking handles** and involves mounting the dimmers in banks that allow their control handles to be aligned in a row. Each individual handle has a twisting device that allows a spring-loaded pin to be inserted or withdrawn from a hole drilled into a shaft that is mounted to a larger submaster arm. For independent control, the handle is twisted so that the pin is withdrawn from the pipe; for mastering, the handle is twisted so that the pin is inserted into the hole. Any handle with its pin engaged in the shaft will be under the control of the larger-handled **submaster** and will operate in tandem with all the other handles that are locked into a given shaft. A submaster often controlled six individual dimmers. Submaster handles are also mounted to common shafts using interlocking technology that allows them to be placed under the control of an even larger single handle known as a **grand master.** By using this technique, a single operator had a reasonable chance of achieving full-stage blackouts and dim ups even when running 12–18 or more dimmers.

Electrical Mastering

In electrical mastering, as in mechanical mastering, individual dimmers are grouped into larger banks that are controlled by submasters, which in turn are controlled by a grand master. The difference with **electrical mastering** lies in the fact that rather than a mechanical connection being created between the different dimmers, the individual dimmers are wired together and assigned to dimmers of a larger capacity. For instance, six 1,000-watt dimmers could be assigned to a single 6,000-watt dimmer that would operate as a submaster. Additional submasters, each with six associated dimmers, would be wired to a single grand master that had a large enough capacity to hold the load of all the submasters together. In this example, two banks of six 1,000-watt dimmers would require two 6,000-watt submasters and a single 12,000-watt grand master. Many dimming systems that made use of **rotary dimmers** (dimmers operated by a knob) used this form of mastering. Most cueing performed by this type of dimming also had to be executed live, although there was some ability to preset the levels of the individual dimmers prior to powering up the grand master or a given submaster. Manual cues requiring the individual movement of more than two dimmers by a single operator was difficult, if not impossible, due to the rotary design.

Electronic Mastering

Electronic dimming and mastering has become the standard for control systems over the last 50 or so years. As electronics have become smaller, control boards have gotten more compact, become more sophisticated, and grown to incorporate the individual control of hundreds, if not thousands, of dimmers. **Electronic mastering** is a low-voltage variation of electrical mastering that became possible through the development of solid-state electronics. In essence, these variations contain two systems: a high-voltage segment where the actual dimmers and circuits are contained, and a low-voltage control segment that is located in a remote location away from the actual dimmers. In an electronic lighting system an electrician uses a control board such as a computer to operate the system, which in turn is connected to the high-voltage components via a **control cable.** A major improvement offered through electronic mastering is the ability to place the control board away from the actual dimmers, allowing board operators to be placed in the wings or rear of a theatre where they can see the effect that they are having on the lights that they are controlling.

The importance of electronic dimming lies primarily in the many ways in which the control voltages of individual dimmers can be manipulated to produce ever more sophisticated dimming operations. The low voltage provides a means of combining control signals from individual dimmers so that many dimmers might be controlled as a single unit with no consideration for the actual loads of the dimmers. The rated capacity of the dimmers must still not be overloaded: we are discussing only the signal and control voltages of the dimmers. Individual dimmers are frequently assigned to specific controllers known as **channels.** A channel is the actual identity of control that a console recognizes as the basic element for assigning control voltages to a particular dimmer(s). Channels are typically assigned an intensity level that falls between 0 and 10 or 0% and 100%. Today, even if a designer is only using a moderate number of dimmers, they often assign each dimmer to a control channel as a means of both arranging the console into a control system that is logical for that designer and providing a means of combining

dimmers that operate together under a single unit of control. The concept of assigning dimmers to channels is known as creating a **soft patch,** and one of the most common examples is in the control of cyclorama (cyc) lighting which requires several dimmers to power a single color wash over the entire length of a cyc. Since all of the assignments are done electronically, the actual loads of the dimmers do not factor into the mastering assignment at the control board, and all of the dimmers that are assigned to that color may be assigned or patched to a single channel. In fact, every dimmer in a facility could technically be assigned to a single control channel if that were the desired effect.

More importantly, an electronic control system provides a number of features that give designers a variety of tools for creating more complex cue operations. Probably the most important quality of an electronic control system lies in the ability of an operator to preset cues. While one cue is live on stage, future cues are set up on a second set of controls (**controllers**) prior to the execution of the cue. Both sets of controllers are duplicate copies of one another. When it comes time to execute a cue, the operator simply uses a lever or **fader** to shift between the two sets of controllers or presets. Consoles may contain only one or two presets (additional sets of controllers) or can have provisions for storing hundreds of cues (as with computer boards). The terms "controller," "fader," and "channel" are often used interchangeably, although there actually are subtle distinctions between each of them. While the channel forms the ultimate form of control assignment, a controller refers to a piece of hardware that in most cases comes in the form of a slide control that provides command of any lights, dimmers, or effects that are assigned to it. Controllers generally provide a range of intensity control (0–10 or 0–100%), while a fader is used for moving or fading from one assignable item to another. An example is in fading between two different cues on a console. The amount and types of special features on any board are directly proportional to the board's price tag. The more expensive the console, the more individual channels it can control and the more sophisticated effect and playback features it will have.

PRINCIPLES OF ELECTRONIC DIMMING

The event that provided the most significant impetus for our current dimming systems was the development of the **Silicon Controlled Rectifier (SCR).** In many ways this was directly attributed to the drive toward producing solid-state devices and the need to provide miniaturization of electronic components like tubes. Since the theatrical industry is relatively small, with little money for extensive product development or research, much of this technology came through borrowing or modifying equipment that had been developed by other industries.

Most electronic lighting systems place the control board in a booth at the rear of the house. The dimmers, on the other hand, are typically located backstage, which allows the high-voltage cables associated with the power that feeds the dimmers and stage circuits to be located close to the hanging positions—near the **company switch** and hopefully out of the way of the operator, crews, and performers. Traditionally, the **racks** or cabinets containing the dimmers are located in the wings, trap room, or along the upstage wall of a theatre. In many permanent installations, the racks are located in a room that may not even adjoin the stage but is only in the vicinity of the stage. In recent years, especially in road houses where spidering is commonly practiced, dimmers and their associated disconnects can be placed on a catwalk in the wings somewhere above the stage. This helps reduce the hazards of all the extra spidered cable that is typically piled on the floor in front of the dimmer racks. More importantly, it frees up space on the deck for scenery storage and movements of the cast and crew.

Gating

In electronic dimming a low-voltage control signal is created at the light board, which in turn is used to regulate the high-voltage power supply that provides power to any circuit and luminaires under control of a given dimmer. SCRs represent a specialized form of electronic hardware that function as a switch that can turn on and off very rapidly. This actually happens once every AC cycle (60 times every second for a 60-cycle service). To further complicate things, SCRs are similar to diodes in that they permit electricity to flow only in a single direction. This results in two SCRs being required for any AC-powered dimmer (one for each side of the AC curve). SCRs are silicon rectifiers under the control of a low-voltage signal and are in many ways quite similar to transistors. Applying a low-voltage signal to an SCR can instruct it when to turn on and off during an AC cycle. In turning on and off, they effectively sample the voltage at a given point in the AC cycle and then provide that portion of the AC voltage to the circuit from that initiation point onward through the remaining part of the cycle. It is said that the SCR **fires** when it is instructed to turn on or sample the voltage. Once the voltage is reduced to zero (as the wave passes through its zero point) and begins to shift direction, the SCR shuts off until it is instructed to come on again during the next cycle. If the SCR fires at any point after the voltage reaches its maximum potential (at half cycle where full voltage is supplied, e.g., 120 volts) the voltage provided to the circuit will be something less than 120 volts depending on the exact point at which the SCR was fired. This process of dimming through firing an SCR is called **gating.** Since a typical AC current goes through 60 cycles every second,

SCRs must be capable of switching on and off (firing) at this extreme rate of speed. Figure 7.5 illustrates several examples of how gating controls an SCR dimmer. Another electronic component, a **triac,** has also been used in electronic dimmer designs and functions in a way that is quite similar to a SCR.

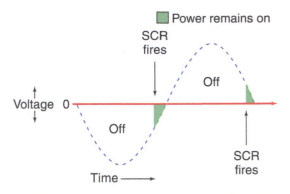

Figure 7.5a Electronic Dimmers and Gating Two SCRs fire (once each) during each half cycle (60 times/sec). a. Dimmer at 20%

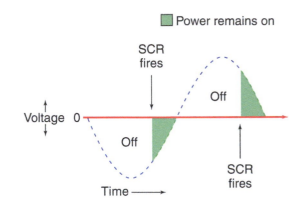

Figure 7.5b Dimmer at 50%

Figure 7.5c Dimmer at full

Due to the rapid on/off switching, many early electronic dimmers created various forms of noise in lighting systems, the most noticeable being a buzzing or "singing" quality (**filament sing** or **lamp sing**). This can be observed in lighting fixtures and is caused by a vibration of the lamps' filaments. Audio cables located in close proximity to lighting cables not only pick up this interference but also often amplify it into a noticeable hum in the sound system that might change pitch as lighting levels are adjusted. Even contemporary dimmers can create this problem if a dimmer gets out of adjustment or if sound technicians place their cables too close to any lighting cables. The fix for this generally comes through introducing large coils called **chokes** to the dimmers that filter the unwanted electronic noise.

Most dimmers are manufactured in a modular format that combines two dimmers and all their components into a single unit. A typical dimmer module is relatively small and contains the SCRs, chokes, circuit breaker, **heat sinks** (a metal fin-like assembly for mounting and cooling the SCRs), and an electronic interface that forms the link between the low and high-voltage portions of the dimmer. Most dimmer modules house

components for two separate dimmers. These modules are mounted in rack systems that allow the modules to be easily inserted and exchanged or replaced as needed. In today's applications, we often use **high-density racks** with numerous dimmers due to the negligible space required by today's modules. Where a rack once held 36 to 48 dimmers, a comparable amount of space using today's racks can hold close to 200 dimmers. Several of the more sophisticated racks and dimmers can monitor individual dimmer voltages and profiles, sense burnouts and overloads, store backup cue information, and can even monitor rack conditions like temperatures for overheating conditions. Figure 7.6 illustrates high-density touring and permanent installation racks.

Both triacs and SCRs are quite susceptible to damage and can blow before a circuit breaker reacts to a heavy overload or short-circuit condition. Also, while

Figure 7.6a Dimmer racks. a. 48-dimmer touring rack by Leprecon Lighting

Credit: photo courtesy Leprecon Lighting

Figure 7.6b 96-dimmer Sensor rack by Electronic Theatre Controls

Credit: photo courtesy Electronic Theatre Controls (ETC)

it's easy to understand that a blown SCR can result in no current being provided to a circuit, it's not as obvious that they can also blow in the closed position, which results in the circuit remaining at a constant full intensity (**continuous fire**). Another word of caution: even if a console has a channel turned off, there is still current in the circuit that could be potentially dangerous. This **warming current** is used to pre-heat the lamps so that a sudden surge of a dimmer coming to full intensity won't over-stress the filaments. While the amount of shock will most likely not be fatal, the surprise may be enough to cause an electrician to fall from a ladder. For this reason, care must be taken to unplug any items that are being worked on when dealing with a problem circuit.

Sidebar 7.2 DIMMER CURVES AND TRIMMING

One problem with electronic dimmers occurs when a dimmer does not react smoothly as the control voltage is regulated from its off through full up settings. The relationship between how smoothly a dimmer controls its load as it progresses from off to full up is often expressed as a **dimming curve**. A properly adjusted dimmer will be synchronized with the control voltage so that it not only goes fully up and down but also progresses smoothly and proportionally as the voltage is regulated across the full range of dimmer settings. A dimmer must be adjusted if it never quite goes out, appears not to move and then rapidly shifts to full intensity, or appears to stay full long after being lowered. We use the term **ghosting** to refer to a dimmer that does not go completely out. The process by which we make adjustments to the dimming curve is called **trimming** a dimmer. In most cases, a dimmer has two trim settings, one for low trim and one for high trim, with each typically being adjusted as simply as through an adjustment with a screwdriver. An electrician simply adjusts the trim screws so that the dimmer goes completely out while the controller is set in the off position and at full when the controller is brought to full.

Sine Wave Dimming

In the last several years leading lighting manufacturers have perfected a new type of electronic dimming that makes use of a variation of the SCR called an **Insulated Gate Bipolar Transistor (IGBT)** as one of the principle components of its design. This device has the capability to sample an AC current several hundred times throughout each half cycle of a dimming cycle, unlike the single sampling that occurs with traditional SCRs. The sheer frequency of the sampling allows the pattern of the sampled voltages to much more closely reflect the true pattern of a sine wave than the choppy samplings associated with traditional electronic dimmers (Figure 7.7). Along with this ability to more closely match the sine wave comes several other unique advantages for the newer IGBT, or **sine wave dimmer.** First, sine wave dimmers effectively eliminate the harmonic distortion that is often associated with electronic dimmers. This technology can dramatically reduce the hum or interference that lighting systems can introduce to audio, video, and other electronic systems. A second side effect of traditional electronic dimming that can be essentially eliminated is filament or lamp sing. Since this new technology virtually eliminates lamp sing, dimmers no longer need choke coils, which ultimately reduces both the cost and weight of the dimmer modules. Other important benefits of these dimmers include the ability to produce an effective dimming curve regardless of how small a load is assigned to a dimmer (which is good for low-wattage practicals and LED loads that create sensitivity problems for traditional dimmers) and the ability to place many types of non-traditional loads on the newer dimmers, including motors and ballasted units like HMI and fluorescent lamps. Two additional benefits relate to the fact that these dimmers use electrical power more efficiently and that they react to load changes so quickly that they can sense and react to overloads such as short-circuits more quickly than conventional dimmers. Three of the more popular concerns discussed regarding sine wave dimmers tend to revolve around the issues of higher initial costs (due to the more sophisticated components), the need for maintaining better cooling and air circulation at the racks (because of the increased amount of heat produced by these dimmers), and possible reliability issues (there are many more components and therefore more to go wrong with these dimmers). Despite these initial concerns, many believe that IGBT or sine wave dimming could represent the next major

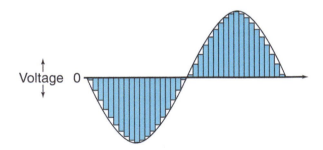

Figure 7.7 Sine wave dimming: note the increased sampling method (gating) that more closely follows the overall AC analog cycle

advance in dimming technology—though dimmers may possibly be discarded all together as LEDs and other solid-state light sources continue to be developed.

CONTROL PROTOCOLS

A control protocol is nothing more than the language that an electronic lighting controller uses to communicate with the dimmers. The light board is connected to the dimmers via a control cable that is constructed of a series of small-gauge wires that conduct the low-voltage signal between the console and dimmers. There are several different protocols, but in each case the voltage is relatively small. Also, most electronic dimmers have been designed around one of two basic control variations. The first, **analog control,** places a continuous signal voltage between the controller and the dimmers while the second, **digital control,** sends packets or bursts of information to the dimmers.

Analog Control

The only control format available for early electronic dimming systems was analog control. In these systems, the console or light board created a low-voltage signal that was proportional to the desired voltage that would be made available to the actual circuit and its associated luminaires. In most cases, this voltage was on the order of 0–12 volts, although some systems had control voltages of as high as 24 volts. The larger the control voltage, the higher the voltage at the dimmer. In analog dimming, an actual wire must be connected between each individual controller and dimmer throughout the entire system. In addition to a control wire for each dimmer there are additional wires that form common connections between the dimmers. Every control wire was quite small (approximately #22 gauge) and was contained in a control cable with a number of other control wires that ran the entire distance between the console and dimmers. The cables terminated with low-voltage connectors called **Cinch-Jones Connectors** that were designed to control from 6 to 36 dimmers at a time. Control cables could vary from five to hundreds of feet in length.

One of the largest problems of analog control relates to the need of an actual physical connection between the console and each of the dimmers. If a control cable became disconnected or the Cinch-Jones Connectors wiggled loose, luminaires would often flicker or go completely out as the control signal was interrupted and no longer available to the dimmers. In permanent installations, this wasn't so much of a problem, but in touring situations many of us cursed the connections between our control cables and dimmer packs. Maintaining good electrical connections was often difficult because the control cables had a tendency to become dislodged as the larger circuit cables were plugged into other outlets within the dimmers. In many dimmer packs the cables used to plug the circuits, feeders, and control cables all came together into a very tight space, which created a snake pit of cable that frequently caused a host of problems when trying to troubleshoot or make power connections to and from the dimmers. In addition, the control cables were very fragile, breaking when bent excessively, breaking solder joints at the connectors, or being crushed due to too much weight or pinching. Many control cables were destroyed by having a forklift or heavy road case roll over them. A final problem in analog dimming relates to the fact that many manufacturers used different control voltages in their dimmer and console designs. This meant that a console might be capable of communicating only with dimmers that had been designed by the manufacturer of the light board. While some dimmers and consoles were compatible between manufacturers, the majority of the companies had their own protocol, which prevented designers from matching their favorite console to a particular set of dimmers. More importantly, it also meant that in many renovation projects, both the dimmers and light board had to be replaced at the same time, using the same manufacturer's equipment.

Digital Control

As dimmers got smaller and electronic control became more sophisticated, designers began to specify more and more dimmers for their productions. This also meant that each dimmer required a physical connection to the console and more of the famed control cables that everyone was having so much trouble with. Much of the driving force behind the use of more dimmers was the acceptance of computer-based control systems that made it easy to control a countless number of dimmers. In the past, the number and talents of the lighting operators dictated how many dimmers were used for a production. Productions that were lit by 24 dimmers in 1970 are now frequently lit with 100 or more dimmers. It is rare for a Broadway production mounted today to use fewer than several hundred dimmers. With productions using an ever-increasing number of dimmers, it became apparent that there was a limit to the number of dimmers that could reasonably be controlled by the analog control systems.

In order to accommodate the needs of the increased number of dimmers, manufacturers developed a new control protocol that was based on sending bursts of information to the dimmers. This form of dimming is based on **digital control.** A digital console can control several hundred dimmers through a cable no thicker than a standard microphone cable containing only three to five conductors. Rather than requiring a constant control voltage, as with analog dimming, this protocol sends bursts of information to the dimmers only when a change is required in the levels, and the cable remains inactive except for when a lighting change actually occurs. A digital controller packages information regarding the location or dimmer number (**addressing**) and level setting for each dimmer under its control. One of the most significant advantages to this protocol is that many more dimmers can be controlled through a single control cable. Today a single control cable can provide instructions for up to 512 individual channels or dimmers. Also, if there is an interruption in control signal by an event, such as the control cable becoming disconnected or the console being shut off, the dimmers remain in the same state in which they were last addressed or instructed. In an analog system this would result in plunging the stage into darkness. Digital control also allows for more specific control of the electronic dimmers, causing the intensity scales to be shifted from 0–10 to 0–100% scales.

Just as with analog dimmers, each manufacturer initially created its own digital protocols. It was rare for a designer to get a console from one manufacturer to communicate with dimmers from another manufacturer. The situation became more complicated during many renovation projects in which facilities managers wanted to upgrade to a digital console while leaving the original analog dimmers in place. In these cases, where digital and analog systems were actually mixed, a **digital-to-analog converter** was required to act as an interface for translating the digital outputs of the control cable into analog signals that could be sent to the dimmers. Some refer to these converters as **multiplexers.** A **Jones Box** was often used as a means of connecting all the individual control cables of the analog dimmers to an interface with the converter. Several protocols that came out of these early digital systems included Strand Century's AMX (Analog Multiplex Data Transmission) control and Colortran's CMX control. AMX is more properly regarded as AMX192 because a single control cable could be used to communicate with 192 analog dimmers housed in two of Strand's dimmer racks (96 dimmers/rack). Other companies such as Lighting Methods, Inc. (LMI) used still other control protocols. It didn't take long for manufacturers to discover that they could significantly increase the sales of their new digital consoles by creating a universal control standard that allowed any manufacturer's console to communicate with any dimmers.

DMX512

The United States Institute for Theatre Technology (USITT) standards committee developed **DMX512 (Digital Data Transmission Standard for Dimmers and Controllers).** This digital control protocol was primarily developed in 1986 by industry leaders and manufacturers during a conference session. Simply put, a manufacturer who follows the DMX512 standard agrees to abide by a predetermined set of guidelines regarding the protocol that it uses in the manufacturing of its dimmers and control consoles. This includes technical specifications as to what type of information must be carried on each conductor of a control cable, how addressing and level information are packaged or sent, and specific wiring and connector specifications. The current DMX512 standard makes use of a five-conductor cable with five-pin XLR-style connectors. Although only three wires are critical for conducting control signals in the majority of today's dimming applications (Pins 1, 2 and 3), the other conductors are reserved for future uses. If a manufacturer is fully compliant, its consoles and dimmers should work perfectly well with any other DMX512-compliant device. With the creation of this universal protocol it is now possible for designers to mix and match consoles, dimmers, and any other DMX-controlled equipment in nearly any manner that they wish. The "512" notation refers to the fact that a single control cable has the capability of addressing 512 individual dimmers—what we call a **universe.** In some cases, manufacturers have opted to wire their gear using control cables with only three conductor plugs and cables. While this saves money and allows the gear to be controlled with readily available microphone cables, it departs from the five-pin standard for data-compliant cable and will most likely see some problems when later control standards requiring the use of all five conductors become popular.

At the time that the DMX512 protocol was developed, everyone agreed that 512 dimmers represented a more than adequate configuration for dimmer control. However, lighting designs expanded, and we began using DMX512 to control not only more dimmers but also all sorts of other equipment as well. Moving lights, pyro devices, foggers/hazers, scrollers, and strobes are several of the more common devices that can now be placed under DMX control. As equipment manufacturers developed more advanced gear, they also started to place more stringent demands and additional functions on top of the standard DMX512 control. In some cases, automated lighting companies even created variations of the DMX standard that actually placed voltages on the rarely used Pins 4 and 5 of the control cables, once again resulting in some manufacturers' equipment not being compatible with other gear. This practice even resulted in damage to unmatched equipment from different manufacturers. Since DMX512 became the standard for controlling equipment that wasn't even produced when it was first developed, the standard was once again updated and revised to accommodate the more stringent needs of the newer gear. This resulted in a new version of the standard known as **DMX512-A** that was formally accepted in 2004. We have also outgrown the 512 channel limitations and now provide duplicate control systems of two, three, or even more universes of DMX control in many lighting systems, each universe containing an additional 512 channels. As we continue to tax our systems, new standards are already under development so that the ever-growing amount of data can be communicated between each element of a lighting installation. More recent means of managing all of this control data have been developed through two new standards that are addressing the more demanding needs of our newer equipment. These are presented in more detail later in this chapter and include both the **ACN (Architecture for Control Networks or Advanced Control Network)** and **RDM (Remote Device Management)** standards.

Ethernet

A relatively new technology for control and dimming is borrowed from the world of computer communications. Nearly everyone should be familiar with Ethernet and the high-speed, fast-access communication that is commonly employed for computer networks that connects computers to one another and the Internet. Lighting manufacturers now use this technology to move control information throughout a facility. While many of the components still utilize standard DMX512 protocol, various elements of the control circuitry are replaced by high-speed computer networking cable and interfaces (**hubs**). This not only provides for faster communication between the console and the networked devices but also, and more importantly, allows signals from multiple universes and individual DMX control signals to be conducted over a single Ethernet cable. A number of termination points called **nodes** (Figure 7.8) are generally located throughout a facility; these become the points where the Ethernet signal is converted to individual DMX universes and a standard DMX512 connection. A lighting console might control both the stage and architectural dimming for a performance space or possibly the entire physical plant. Ethernet systems have become extremely popular in architectural applications, where they allow a number of rooms, wings, or even floors to be monitored or operated through some form of central lighting control. Another advantage of Ethernet networks is their ability to support two-way communication between the console and the dimmers or other equipment. Rack temperatures can be monitored, lamp burnouts can be detected, and modifications in dimming curves might be observed or controlled by these systems. These systems can even determine the particular model and attribute assignments of sophisticated gear like moving lights when a networked cable is plugged into a fixture. In each case, a window containing an alert is displayed on the monitor of the control console. Examples of this technology include Electronic

Figure 7.8 A network node (Net3 two-port node by ETC)

Credit: photo courtesy ETC

Theatre Controls' (ETC) ETCLink and Strand's ShowNet systems. As Ethernet networks become a more integral part of our lighting systems, the industry will once again be required to define more specific standards so that everyone's components will be compatible with one another. With the advancement of more sophisticated gear requiring two-way monitoring (e.g., moving lights), the need to link several consoles together for online backup systems, and the fact that many lighting consoles are now being used to control additional devices (such as video and MIDI), we will see even more extensive uses of networking in future lighting systems.

PRIMARY CONTROL OF ADVANCED LIGHTING GEAR

After the appearance of electricity, theatrical lighting quickly evolved and rapidly became exponentially more complex through the benefits of technology. When lighting manufacturers provided us with piano boards, we brought on more boards and operators; as they delivered presetting and electronic control, we discovered the need to use more dimmers and wanted a more rapid yet accurate means of setting cues; when the manufacturers gave us computer control, we wanted even more lighting fixtures and dimmers—and now additional luminaire functions and data-hungry equipment like moving lights and media servers have been added to our rigs. We've now come to a point where it's almost impossible to keep track of all the data associated with a lighting design. What may be even more amazing is that despite all the increased numbers in fixtures and data, we still set our cues in roughly the same amount of time that we have been using for the last 20 or 30 years, becoming more efficient in order to maintain the sophistication that a lighting design now requires. Creating multiple colors, textures, and positions for a light form just a few of these possibilities.

DMX Control

With the advent of digital control and the acceptance of DMX512 as a standard protocol it became evident that lighting consoles could be used to control many more elements of a show than just dimmers. As new equipment evolved, manufacturers capitalized on the DMX512 format. It wasn't long before lighting consoles were used to control virtually any type of stage equipment. Foggers and hazers can be instructed to begin and end on cue, while strobe lights can be triggered while making adjustments in their speed and intensity. Even complex pyro sequences are now being fired through DMX signals and lighting consoles.

In simple dimmer operations a designer assigns or **patches** a dimmer to a specific control channel that then becomes the ultimate form of control for that dimmer. The board operator then uses that channel whenever they wish to make modifications to the level of that dimmer. In the day of analog dimming this was always a **one-to-one** assignment (Dimmer 1 was assigned to Channel 1, Dimmer 2 to Channel 2, etc.) and a designer had to think about how they arranged their dimmers so that operators could run the board efficiently. Load or capacity of the dimmers also played a role in the assignments since dimmers of the same capacity were grouped together in the dimmer packs. If dimmer assignments weren't done properly, the operation of the board could become more complex, making the execution of some cues impossible. Designers also tried to make these assignments in a logical board layout that kept dimmers with similar functions near one another (i.e., grouping all of the dimmers controlling a given color or area). As the number of dimmers increased, a limit was reached in the number of faders that the electricians could control. Digital control brought about the concept of **soft-patching,** in which dimmers could be assigned to any controller or channel regardless of the load of the dimmers. This gave designers the ability to assign the dimmers based on the best organizational means of arranging a light board. While dimmers may still be assigned to a one-to-one patch, it is now far more common to use soft-patching to create a logical board arrangement for the dimmers. This is especially true where dimmer-per-circuit systems are in use.

Attributes and Addressing

In basic principle, a DMX channel produces a control signal that sends bursts or packets of digital information that identify both the particular channel and its intensity

to a DMX-controlled device. In DMX512, the system is capable of controlling up to 512 different channels. This is based on the principle of computers storing information in the form of **binary numbers,** which are the product of a base-two numbering system that is used to represent whether circuits are turned on or off. In DMX control, one binary number represents a specific channel, while a second number represents its intensity. While the control system is based on 512 channels, the actual levels are represented through a numbering range of 0–256. This is because 256 is the highest number that can be represented with eight digits of binary code. Why eight digits? Because most microprocessors at the time that the code was written used 8-bit processors. The levels are then equated to an intensity range of between 0 and 100% based on a binary number between 0 and 256. While this explains the individual levels, a console also needs to identify the particular dimmer with which the intensity level is associated. To do this, a designer must also assign each piece of gear like the individual dimmer packs or racks to a particular group of channels. This is usually done by turning a series of **addressing switches** on or off at the dimmers or other DMX-controlled device. The process of assigning the beginning channel to a DMX-controlled device is called **addressing.** The first channel of any multi-channeled device is the one that is actually assigned and is called the **starting address.** Virtually all DMX equipment has only one set of addressing switches and a single starting address regardless of the number of **attributes** that a unit may have.

While a dimmer has only one function (intensity), most specialty equipment has several control functions, each requiring a separate channel assignment—an example being strobe units that typically require three elements of control (intensity, duration, and speed). More advanced gear, like **media servers,** may require several hundred channels. When making addressing assignments, each dimmer in a dimmer pack is automatically assigned a progressively increasing channel number until all of the dimmers have been assigned a channel. At that point, a new starting address is assigned to the second and any additional packs that are included in the control system (for example, a six-pack would assign the next set of dimmers beginning with Channel 7, while a 48-dimmer rack would start the next set of dimmers at 49). This same process holds true of all other DMX-controlled equipment with multiple attributes. Although designers cannot rearrange the specific order of the attributes associated with a particular unit (unless reassigning them in the console), they do assign the beginning channel, which coincides with the first attribute associated with a device. By assigning the strobe unit mentioned earlier to Channel 30, what I have actually done is set its first attribute (intensity) to channel 30, while the duration and speed attributes are assigned to channels 31 and 32.

While soft-patch assignments are easily made at the console through a keyboard, the equipment addressing must also be assigned at the device and needs to be matched to the channel assignment. If either one is not set correctly the equipment will not communicate properly with the console. The actual addressing is done through one of several mechanisms that are located on the fixture. This might include an independent LED display and keypad, a set of three numbered wheels (one wheel representing each digit up to 999), or a series of dip switches (miniature slide switches) that are set in various combinations to represent the address.

All DMX addresses are in binary code and are simply coded into the system based on the on/off positions of a set of eight switches that represent the address in a binary format. Zero is represented by all of the switches being in the off position while 1 is indicated by the last switch being set to the on position. Each switch represents a digit of the binary code: from left to right, 128/64/32/16/8/4/2/1. As the numbers increase, each progressive number is represented by turning on the next available open switch and resetting any switches previously assigned to an on position back to 0 (off). In this way, there is a constant rollover of switches as higher numbers are assigned to progressively higher addresses. Continuing with the example, 2 is indicated by a rollover in which the second switch is turned on while the first resets to 0, 3 fills the first position and is represented by both switches being on, while 4 causes another rollover where the third switch is turned on and the two previous switches reset to 0. Each number can be represented by a combination of switches that are set to particular on/off positions. While the sensitivity for most level assignments are adequately represented through the standard range of 0–256 (with the exception of moving lights), even the early days of DMX control saw the need for addressing more than 256 channels, and provisions were made for adding one more switch and digit of addressing information. This led to the 512 (256 × 2) channels that have become the industry standard. While you can determine which switches to set on and off for a particular address using the rollover system as in the illustration or by using division techniques (Sidebar 7.3), most of us rely on tables or apps that cross-reference the DMX channels with settings that are appropriate to the addressing switches.

Most DMX devices not only provide switches for addressing a fixture but also a second set of switches for making alterations to a unit's personality. A **personality** simply sets specific qualities to a unit. Unlike addressing switches, these switch functions can vary considerably from one piece of equipment to another. Several features that are seen regularly in the personality settings include setting the fixture's lamp to a power-saving mode, reversing the normal direction of a unit's pan and tilt controls (used when a unit is mounted in a reversed condition), running a diagnostic/self-testing mode, setting attributes to high or low-resolution modes, and placing the unit in a stand-alone mode (i.e., rather than using DMX, the unit uses an audio sensor to trigger its responses). As lighting equipment has become more sophisticated, DMX512 has struggled to deal with the ever-increasing amount of data generated by this gear and as one set of 512 channels becomes completely assigned, additional groups or **universes** are added to the control system (each with another 512 channels). Many of today's consoles are manufactured with three or more universes and have the capacity to be expanded much further. A lot of the gear can even provide **bi-directional** data or feedback to the console and operator.

Sidebar 7.3 BINARY CODE AND ADDRESSING

Channel 46 = 32 + 0 + 8 + 4 + 2+ 0						Actual Numbers
32	16	8	4	2	1	Binary Digits Places
1	0	1	1	1	0	Binary Code (1 is on, 0 is off)

Sidebar 7.4 PRACTICAL TIPS FOR SETTING UP DMX NETWORKS

1. Split data runs into logical subsystems so that problems can be more clearly identified and troubleshot (e.g., data runs to specific locations like each truss/electric or type of equipment like scrollers, automated lighting, dimmers, etc.).
2. Try to keep similar equipment on the same data run.
3. Use data-compliant cable only.
4. Keep data cables away from sources of electrical interference like electric cables as much as possible.
5. Never split a data signal by splicing cables together.
6. For protection, use an opto-isolator between the console and any DMX cable run or gear using DMX signals.
7. Use terminators at the end of any data run.
8. Use distribution amplifiers in any data runs that exceed 1,500 feet—in some cases, even more frequent placements may be required.
9. If possible, don't mix different types of gear intermittently. If four scrollers are located along the length of a batten and a gobo

rotator is placed on the centerline, daisy-chain the scrollers first, then run the data/power cable back to the rotator so that it is the last device in the data run.

10. When patching DMX fixtures, first assign a one-to-one patch to any dimmers that share the same number as the channel that will be assigned to a fixture's attributes. Try to avoid assigning any attribute channels to a number associated with any existing dimmers in a system—the circuit/dimmer may already be assigned to another control channel, which can cause confusion in the control of the attribute channel (e.g., if a facility has 200 dimmers, have your attribute assignments for the advanced gear assigned to channels over 200).

11. As you set up your console and DMX equipment, take time to make use of the various pan/tilt invert assignments that will allow your encoders to function in a similar manner for all fixtures. Also, make full use of the setup features that a console can provide for patching, assigning fixture numbers to moving lights, their associated attributes, and how they are assigned to the board's channels and encoders. It's usually preferable to make these assignments at the board rather than at the actual luminaire.

Over the years designers have required more control of an increasing number of dimmers and DMX gear, and console manufacturers have developed a number of features that aid operators in effectively controlling the many attributes and their related channels. The most popular technique for doing this has been through creating ways to group a console's channels into common elements. There are several different levels of this type of control. The first technique is arranging the board into groups of channels where dimmers with common functions are assigned next to one another. A second technique involves assigning channels to **groups** that share similar qualities. For instance, all of the warm area light might be assigned to a single group or **submaster,** while all the cool area light would be assigned to another group. In more complex consoles that provide a **page** feature, many of the submasters and **encoders** may be reassigned by simply pushing a button. Another variation of this layering is found on the more advanced consoles (**palettes**) that are popular in the concert scene. Palettes are nothing more than a group of predetermined settings or presets that have been stored in a console. These can speed up the programming of a show considerably because a programmer only has to pull up a series of palettes to set the basic elements of a new cue instead of programming each

channel individually. Predetermined settings for color, focus and position assignments, moving effects, and gobo combinations form several of the more popular palette settings that many programmers create before writing the actual cues for a production. Most automated lighting consoles provide a means of creating and storing numerous palettes that are then used for writing the majority of the show. A fairly common example of when palettes can streamline the cueing process is when a designer wishes to shift all of the moving lights to a given performer. Such a moment exists just before each sequence of questions are asked in the television show, *Who Wants to Be a Millionaire*, when all of the moving lights sweep from the perimeter of the stage to the center podium where the host and contestant are seated. Two different position or focus palettes would be used to define the central and perimeter positions of each light, while color palettes would be used to assign different colors to not only the sweep itself but also for both before and after the effect.

Sidebar 7.5 PROGRAMMING TIPS FOR AUTOMATED LIGHTING GEAR

1. Take advantage of a console's tracking functions when programming automated lighting equipment. This conserves storage and memory demands on the console.

2. Use **block cues** or **hard blackouts** to record all channels to a level of zero at critical breaks in a program. This prevents tracking information from continuing past these points. For example, place these at the beginning and end of each song for a concert or at the end of a scene in a play or musical. By doing so, cues can be edited through tracking instructions that track through all the cues up to the block cue but not into future songs or scenes. In productions like concerts, where the order of the show may change from one performance to another, this becomes especially important since all of the attributes of a light must start with the same initial settings for the beginning of a musical number.

3. Create a number of palettes before you begin the actual cueing of a show. Many programmers have a library of palettes that they store on disks or flash drives and simply load them into a console as part of their initial setup process. Create **focus palettes** for principal performers and stage positions that are frequently used, **color palettes** that provide a variety of colors in a range of tints/saturations,

a selection of gobo/texture breakup palettes, and a selection of effects that are tailored to the types of productions that you work on. Develop a manner of organizing these palettes so that you can access them quickly.

4. Use focus palettes whenever possible for defining focus positions for moving lights. This is especially important for productions that tour and where focus positions will shift as the spacing of a stage or the height of the trusses or other hanging positions are adjusted from one venue to another. With focus palettes, an entire show can be quickly updated by simply redefining the focus points.

5. Use **mark** or **move cues** to preset scrollers, focus points, and other attributes ahead of the time when the effect is actually executed. This prevents the distraction of "live moves" where scrollers scroll through a series of colors or moving lights sweep to a new position as they come up. Many of us create specific numbering systems that clearly identify a mark cue. I use either a .2 or .7 assignment for many of my mark cues. You should also label the mark and block cues if the console has the ability to label cues on your display.

6. Don't use moving effects just because they are available. Carefully consider if the effect will add to the performance. If the answer is yes, then go about working the effect into the show. If not, it may be better not to use it. In theatre, subtle cueing is often more effective than pulling out the stops and creating a distraction. Designers and programmers often speak of **flash and trash**, which refers to using lighting predominantly for effect. The only problem with this is that after a while many of these designs seem to come down to just flashing and moving the lights around with no real connection to the event.

Lighting Networks, ACN, and RDM

As lighting has become more sophisticated, additional demands have been placed on consoles in terms of the number of channels and universes that they must support. By the year 2000, the DMX512 standard had been extended to the point that newer gear was taxing the efficiency of many control systems. In today's environment, control consoles not only are expected to control an increasing number of DMX devices but also are often linked to other controllers (rigging, special effects, midi devices, etc.). They may also tie a console to its backup and can synchronize other control systems that are operated in conjunction with the lighting system. Due to this, several new standards have been introduced to equip DMX512 for the future.

The first advancement was mentioned earlier and makes use of common computer networking conventions to convert DMX signals to standard Ethernet cables and routers. This allows for especially rapid transmission of data throughout a networked system. An Ethernet system is not only much faster than traditional DMX control, but also (and more importantly) can carry a much larger volume of data and universes than traditional DMX systems. In addition, there is no need to use a control cable for each universe. Most of the network hardware required for these systems is also readily available from computer or electronics stores. Primary components of these systems still communicate through DMX instructions, but the parts of the system that would be dedicated to long cable runs are replaced with Ethernet cables and hubs. The **node** is piece of network hardware where the connection/conversion between a network connection and a standard DMX interface takes place. The resulting network allows for rapid bi-directional communication between the console, dimmer racks, and any other equipment that is contained in the system. Several manufacturers have created their own versions of networking through systems like ETC's ETCLink and Strand Lighting's ShowNet systems. At present, most DMX-controlled equipment uses standard five-pin XLR cable, and a node converts the networked cable back to the standard XLR fittings. However, some equipment has started to appear with Ethernet ports that allow these units to be plugged directly into the network.

Another technique for addressing increased data demands was to build more in-depth protocols around the existing DMX512 standard. The first revision occurred around 1990, while the current version, known as DMX512-A, was officially accepted in November 2004. Two new variations in control protocol have more recently been introduced to the lighting community. Both are becoming the primary protocols of the future. The first, ACN, was adopted as a standard in late 2006 and consists of approximately three to five different control protocols that are specific to various types of equipment in a lighting network. These individual protocols are packaged and function together as a whole unit—what some are calling a **suite**. More importantly, ACN addresses the networking problems of interchangeability, as manufacturers have once again developed their own protocols while shifting to the Ethernet systems. It is thought that in the future ACN will not only become the primary control network for lighting but also for nearly any other type of entertainment control system as well. This might include hydraulics, lifts, rigging, and special-effects equipment. In fact, all of these systems could run under the umbrella of a single ACN control system. The system also looks to alternative techniques of transmitting control data by providing standards not only for wired networks but also for wireless control and future carriers such as fiber optics systems.

The second aspect of the new protocols, RDM, functions as a link between DMX512-A and a fully implemented ACN network. In reality, it is a protocol that builds on the standard five-pin DMX networking. RDM addresses some of the shortcomings of DMX512-A and then builds on it to provide a number of improvements in the way that data is used throughout a lighting system. Several of the immediate benefits of RDM include a designation of how bi-directional data is exchanged between a console and a device that is plugged into the control system. This communication takes place along the two wires that have not traditionally been used for data transmission and provides bi-directional capabilities for future equipment as well as backward compatibility for older equipment that can be supported by the new protocol. More importantly, RDM has been developed so that it can provide a "plug-and-play" feature that works like our personal computers (PCs). Electricians simply plug a luminaire into a network cable. When the console powers up, it identifies the equipment and then goes on to determine the number and type of attributes that should be associated with the unit. It can also automatically assign control channels to each of the unit's attributes—virtually eliminating many of the burdens associated with soft-patching, addressing, and setting up a console. Most importantly, it ensures that the console and lighting equipment are communicating properly. While this sounds wonderful, skeptics point to the early days of Microsoft Windows plug-and-play technology, when computers more times than not failed to correctly identify and install new pieces of peripheral equipment like printers. In reality, as with Windows, the worst that can happen is that we have to continue to upload fixture libraries and support files or use **firmware** for installing fixtures on our consoles. In time, the process will more than likely become relatively seamless. Also, the bi-directional communication makes it possible to incorporate more features into many control systems. Information like lamp hours, housing temperatures, and homing positions might all be monitored with this control system. While ACN deals primarily with those aspects of control associated with Ethernet networking, RDM addresses issues related more to the traditional (DMX-based) elements of the control network. Both are much more sophisticated than DMX512-A and are leading us into the next generation of communication between consoles and the equipment that they control.

LIGHTING CONTROL CONSOLES

Lighting control consoles, often called the **front end** of a dimming system, have become exceedingly complex over the last 50 years. In the early days, control changes could only be made live, and the operators had to physically move levers, dials, or switches to make changes in the levels of the dimmers. Due to the development of electronic dimming our consoles soon went through a host of changes that evolved into the complex consoles and control systems that we use today. This section provides overviews of several of the more important control systems that have been used since the appearance of electronic dimming.

Preset Control

Preset control provided the first truly practical manner in which designers could have one cue on stage while setting up future cues ahead of time on an additional set of controllers. These boards (Figure 7.9) provided a set of duplicate controllers (**a preset**) for each of the dimmers or controllers that were contained in the lighting system. Another portion of the board, often called the control section, provided master controls and some form of fader that would allow operators to shift (**crossfade**) between the presets. In this manner cue operation became much simpler since an operator could set a number of individual controllers to their pre-assigned levels ahead of time without the stress of trying to manipulate each controller to its proper level while the cue was actually being executed. The consoles were typically built to provide control in multiples of six channels or dimmers (popular varieties included 12, 18, 24, and 36 dimmers). Larger versions such as a 48-channel board were also available. As always, designers wanted more, and these boards soon grew in number of presets and control features. While the two-scene board was the simplest, many boards were designed around three, five, or even more presets. In these cases, an additional set of buttons allowed the fader to be reassigned to different presets between cues. Sidebar 7.6 provides explanations of several of the more common control features of many electronic consoles. These are general features, and individual names may vary from one console or manufacturer to another.

Preset boards were used quite heavily in the early days of rock and roll lighting. Many of these were equipped with special features that allowed a designer more control and even the ability to flash the lights in accompaniment to the music. While a number of these features developed out of the needs of the concert industry, many also found their way to consoles that were used for more traditional forms of theatrical entertainment as well. Sidebar 7.7 provides a summary of a number of these additional features.

Figure 7.9 A two-scene preset lighting board (Lite Control Console by Electronics Diversified, Inc.)

Credit: photo courtesy Eaton

Bump/Flash Buttons	Most controllers and submasters were provided with an additional momentary push-button switch that could instantly bump the level up to full regardless of the actual controller setting.
Applause Button	A button that is similar to a blackout button but which instead bumps the intensities of all the lights to full rather than out.
Pin Matrix	A pinned grid system for electronically assigning control channels to specific submasters that also usually featured a bump/flash button. The pinning system was quite similar to that found in the game of Battleship®.
Effects Module	A pre-programmed effect such as a chase sequence that could be assigned to specific control channels. Operators could usually vary the speed/tempo and intensity levels of these effects before engaging them.
Soft Patch	A means by which specific dimmers, accessories, and other lighting hardware are assigned to controllers on a lighting console. Individual dimmers that shared a common purpose could be assigned to the same controller using a board's soft-patching features.
Proportional Patch	Allows channels to be locked into a maximum setting that is lower than 100%. An example might be running work light dimmers at only 80%.

Memory Control

When I discuss **memory control** I am referring to lighting consoles that actually store cues in some type of memory. Computer consoles form the most notable example of memory control. The first memory boards were variations of the preset board that could store cues in a temporary memory. Some lighting designers refer to these boards as **smart preset boards.** Levels of the individual controllers were set on a given preset and then a record/store button was pushed to create a snapshot of the individual settings. These settings were then stored in the board's memory until the cue was actually executed. Once a cue had been stored the operator was free to move the preset's controllers to set up an additional cue. While this represented a huge improvement from the basic two-scene boards, these boards typically only held four cues at a time. As cues were executed they were dropped from the board's memory and new cues

would be entered into the preset memory in their place. Despite what now appears to be an awkward manner of recording cues, these boards allowed operators to work farther ahead and were a welcomed improvement at the time. These boards can still be encountered as backup boards in many theatre and studio operations.

At the same time that the first memory boards were being introduced, the world was being overrun by the computer revolution. With computers becoming more popular for every imaginable application, it didn't take lighting manufacturers long to see the potential for using modified computers for lighting control. Broadway lighting designer Tharon Musser is given credit for bringing the first computer lighting to Broadway and laying the groundwork for the acceptance of computer consoles for the entertainment industry. Through Musser's sensational lighting of *A Chorus Line*, Electronic Diversified's LS-8 computer was introduced to Broadway. Computer lighting happened so quickly that many manufacturers skipped the smart preset boards and instead opted to leap right into developing computer-controlled lighting consoles (full memory boards) that could store and replay the cues for an entire show at any time. However, in the early days, computer lighting experienced many problems, some from untrained operators, some from equipment that wasn't perfected, and many from the memory or storage devices themselves. In most cases, both the cues and level settings at that time were stored in a console's RAM memory and something as simple as a power failure (typically someone accidently disconnecting the console's power or tripping a breaker) could result in the loss of an entire show. For backup, the consoles used a variety of memory cards or floppy disks but if the show had not been recorded to these correctly, you could once again loose the entire show. As many of us have learned the hard way, productions need to be backed up frequently, and if you become careless you can lose your entire show and hours of work nearly instantly through a simple combination of incorrect keystrokes. With the initial lack of memory reliability, it was quite common to keep two, three, or even more backup copies of a show's cue data. Even now with consoles with reliable hard drives, backups should be a regular practice for anyone using a computer console.

One of the biggest problems that the first-generation computer consoles had was that when a computer crashed there was often little hope of returning a show to normal operation if the console went completely down. With the lighting systems that preceded computers, problems were usually confined to specific dimmers, one segment of a control board, or a given dimmer pack and the show could continue by using those dimmers that were still in operation. In cases where designers feared complete crashes of a lighting console a smart board was often specified as a backup. Today's computers are extremely reliable when it comes to both storing and backing up a production's cueing data; most problems tend to be associated with operator error. In extreme cases, when it is critical for the lighting to remain on track, two consoles with duplicate cue programming are run in tandem during a performance with one console acting as a slave/backup to the primary console. The precision of computer lighting not only provides an accurate means of replaying complex cues with vast amounts of control data, but also allows for smooth transitions by pre-programing the cue executions. As far as most designers are concerned, the increased number of channels that computer boards can support is secondary to the manipulation of the cue data. In reality, because of their ability to control transitions, it's actually fairly common to see computer systems controlling lighting systems with 24 or even fewer dimmers despite the fact that a preset system could still be used quite successfully in these situations.

Due to the level of complexity that we now associate with the programming of a production we rarely refer to these computers as light boards anymore. Most people in the industry prefer to call these specialized computers **lighting consoles** or **desks.** With the shift to computer desks and increased complexity of these systems it has also become appropriate to call individuals who run the lighting console **programmers** rather than light board operators.

A key distinction between lighting consoles is in whether they are **tracking** or **non-tracking.** Non-tracking consoles essentially record data in the form of a specific intensity level for every channel in each cue. This creates an immense amount of data. Tracking consoles, on the other hand, simply record any differences that are made between one cue and another. If a group of channels is never brought up in a series of cues, no data will be recorded for these channels. This manner of recording data makes more efficient use of a console's memory. Since tracking consoles record only the changes that occur from one cue to another they offer several particularly useful secondary benefits. Most importantly, if a series of cues must be modified, the designer need only make a change in the first cue of the sequence and all the subsequent cues are updated automatically. The modifications will continue to track to the point where the original channel levels change once again. This is particularly helpful for fixing an entire scene such as when an area of the stage is too dark, a special has been added, or a background color must be modified. On the downside, tracking can cause problems or unpredictable results when cues are not run in order or when a cue is inserted between cues where tracking information is contained. One of the most common mistakes is having a change track through large segments of a show unintentionally (i.e., changes tracking through several

scenes). This can become a particular nuisance when programming moving lights where additional parameters like pan and tilt positions can quickly become altered accidently by a programmer. Most tracking consoles offer the option of recording a lighting change in either a track or single cue (**cue-only**) mode, and designers will frequently alternate between both modes while programming a show.

Computer lighting (Figure 7.10) has created several changes in the way that designers refer to their consoles and cueing information. The most significant change probably lies in the manner in which we make reference to individual channels. A **channel** is now simply a reference of control. Where in the past a channel was always synonymous with a dimmer, today channels don't necessarily have to be assigned to a dimmer; they can be assigned to lighting accessories like scrollers and gobo rotators, or any number of **attributes** that are associated with an automated light. Other practical changes have resulted in the practice of channel levels being referenced with a percentage scale rather than the former scale of 0–10. Rather than using physical controllers, much of the level setting with a computer console is entered through a series of keyboard instructions that are displayed on a monitor. The consoles are also typically operated through recalling pre-recorded cues simply by the push of a "go" button. Even despite this automation, provisions are always made so that an operator can override the computer and take manual control of a cue or controller. While this is not necessary, computer consoles are also often equipped with additional controllers that may be used as submasters or individual channel controllers, and could even be used to store full presets. Through all of these features, cueing is not limited to pushing a "go" button and can also be improvised or done **on the fly.**

Figure 7.10 Philips Strand Light Palette (Classic Model), a later-generation console

Credit: photo courtesy Philips Lighting

Sidebar 7.8 ADDITIONAL CONTROLS IN COMPUTER CONSOLES

Live or Stage Mode	A console or monitor mode that illustrates the channels and their associated levels for the actual intensity settings that are "live" on stage.
Blind/ Preview	A console or monitor mode that illustrates channels and their associated levels for any previous or upcoming cues. This allows a designer to work on both past and upcoming cues while another cue is live on stage.
Tracking Mode	A mode by which level changes made in one cue are copied, or tracked, through future cues, at least until those channels undergo another level assignment. Tracking allows a designer to make a change such as adding a table lamp to an entire act without having to type the information into every cue.
Cue Only Mode	A mode by which any changes made in a cue are performed and recorded on that cue only and will not have any impact on any future cues.
Time/ Count	A pre-programmed timing element (in seconds) for a cue that aids in providing smooth transitions between sequential cues.
Rate	This refers to modifying timing sequences in a cue. While a cue is generally given a count (a predetermined transition speed) these may have to be slightly modified due to changes in a given performance. Rate settings allow operators to speed up or slow down a given cue sequence.
Wheel	A mechanical input device that allows an operator to manually adjust any channels or rates that are placed under its control. The wheel is often used to manually set channel levels by sight during a cue-writing session.
Autofader	When cues are played back they are assigned by the computer to a fader where they run automatically (operators still generally initiate the cue and can take control of it at any time). Most computers have several autofaders and can run up to eight or more cues simultaneously.
Effects	An elaborate set of menus that allow a designer to create sequencing effects through being able to fully program selected channels into a sequence, set up transition speeds between steps, and create lighting patterns such as having moving lights trace a predetermined pattern. A chase pattern is a common effect.
Pages	A utility that allows controllers to be assigned to several different functions. In this manner controllers may be reassigned to multiple tasks throughout a production. For instance, controllers might be assigned to a selection of dimmer channels for Page 1 and then in Page 2 could be reassigned to scroller control.

To this day, most computer lighting consoles are **dedicated controllers,** meaning that they are designed specifically for the operation of lighting gear, with no other function. Over the years, though, several control systems have appeared with specialized lighting software that can transform common PCs into practical lighting consoles. In the late 1970s and early '80s the Micro-Star (MAC) and ProStar (DOS) lighting systems were popular, while today we have systems like Sun Lite's Control System and Daslight's Daslight 4 software that work within a Windows or Mac environment. Rosco's Horizon software was another popular system that can still be found in some theatres. These and similar packages can even run on a laptop computer. When using this type of control system a hardware interface must be purchased that allows the computer to convert its output to DMX instructions. Many companies give the software away so that designers can use the full-blown program to pre-cue or edit their designs **off-line.** Manufacturers also offer hardware such as wing panels, which provide an interface of manual controllers for the computer system. Unfortunately, Rosco has discontinued the Horizon product line, although other DMX software packages like Chaovet's ShowXpress and Martin's LightJockey 2 continue to be popular alternatives to traditional lighting consoles. Rosco still supports Horizon, and you may still come upon it in smaller theatre companies and some architectural applications. ShowXpress provides a control interface not only for programming the lighting, but also controlling any DMX device—including multimedia applications. It also contains a three-dimensional visualization module that provides a computer simulation of a show's programming as well as tools that aid in the programming of moving lights.

Automated Control Consoles

In the early days of intelligent lighting a dedicated or specialized console was required to operate the automated luminaires and was used in addition to the standard console that controlled the traditional luminaires and dimmers—what we often call the **conventionals.** Concert tours that first used automated lighting saw companies develop specialized consoles like the Vari*Lite (which first introduced intelligent fixtures) Artisan Board, which was used for the control of just their own fixtures. Now, through the DMX512 standard, most automated fixtures can be operated with a traditional console even though these boards weren't designed to deal with the additional control elements that are demanded by these luminaires. Programming becomes tedious and the memories of the conventional consoles can become overtaxed with the increased amount of data generated by these automated fixtures. Automated lighting consoles form a group of more specialized consoles that have been designed to respond to the increased demands of automated lighting. They are also equipped with a number of special features that allow them to have more convenient control of the intelligent lights.

What sets automated control consoles (Figure 7.11) apart from other lighting consoles generally relates to the increased number of channels that such consoles can control, the variety of display and assignment modes that consoles can produce, and the presence of additional control devices that help create more designer-friendly operation of the automated fixtures and their attributes. The number of control channels that many of these consoles might be outfitted with is typically in the thousands. These consoles often include several specialty knobs or rotary devices called **encoders** that are particularly helpful for programming intelligent fixtures. Touch screens are another popular feature. Finally, control attributes may be assigned to encoders, groups, and submasters; these attributes can be reassigned through

multiple-page assignments that provide an easy way of giving operators access to all the data that they will need for programming a show. We often refer to these control assignments as **palettes,** and common manners of organizing them might be by colors, focus points, gobo assignments, and beam-shaping qualities. Two of the most popular automated lighting desks in current use include the Whole Hog (Figure 7.11a) console by High End Systems and the GrandMA by ACT Lighting, Inc. The introduction of consoles like the Eos by ETC (Figure 7.11b) moves in a slightly different direction through being designed to control both conventionals and automated lighting with equal ease.

Latest Generation Lighting Consoles

For a time, it was common to run two different lighting consoles for many large-scale productions that made use of both automated and conventional lights. With this, syncing the consoles so that it appeared as if all of the lights were under the control of a single operator could be challenging. One solution to this was programming each of the consoles separately and then slaving or transferring the cueing of the one console to the other so that all of the control was run under a single console. As another remedy, console manufacturers started to develop a new generation of consoles that combined those programming features and controls that worked best for the automated fixtures along with those that worked for the conventional fixtures. These have met great success in the business and are now used frequently to light shows that have a decent mixture of both types of fixtures. The EOS series of consoles from ETC and NEO consoles by Strand Lighting are popular consoles that combine both types of features.

The latest consoles are designed to make it possible to grab a lighting control by function rather than through the indirect means of accessing channel numbers. While addressing and channel assignments are still part of the process, they are hidden during the programming of a show; interfaces such as touch screens, color wheels or tiles/chips, and magic sheets give a designer immediate access to not only a fixture's intensity (conventional and automated), but also—and more importantly—to all of a light's individual attributes. This makes programming much simpler if the programmer has taken the time to properly set up the console since all attributes of a unit can be accessed by calling up a single channel that will automatically load additional features such as patterns, pan, tilt, color, etc. to encoders or other console features such as color pickers. Many consoles using RDM architecture can automatically recognize and propagate (assign) the fixtures and their associated attributes to their channel assignments. Other features of these consoles are tailored for the control of newer light sources like LEDs in addition to the easy manipulation of

Figure 7.11a Consoles designed for controlling conventional and automated lights. a. Hog 4 Console by High End Systems

Credit: photo courtesy of High End Systems

Figure 7.11b Eos is a later-generation console that is designed to work equally well with both automated and conventional lighting units

Credit: photo courtesy ETC

Figure 7.12a Latest-generation consoles. a. ETC ColorSource®

Credit: photo courtesy ETC\

Figure 7.12b ETC SmartFade ML

Credit: photo courtesy ETC

Figure 7.12c Philips Strand 250ML

Credit: photo courtesy Philips Lighting

Figure 7.12d Philips Strand NEO

Credit: photo courtesy Philips Lighting

automated fixtures' attributes. These consoles are not limited to high-end systems and large lighting rigs but are now being designed for small to moderate-sized rigs as well. Figure 7.12 provides several examples of these later generation boards that move toward providing control through elements that are more related to actual function rather than the traditional means of control channel.

OFF-LINE EDITORS

As I mentioned earlier, over the years there have been several attempts to use personal computers (PCs) and specialty software to convert computers into basic lighting consoles. In each case, specialty software was loaded onto a computer and an interface or black box was connected between the computer and the dimmers. This permitted designers to run the software on their PCs for precueing or blind editing a show without using an actual lighting console. Once programmed, the show file would be transferred to a computer at the theatre that was equipped with the DMX interface and the design would be ready to go. Manufacturers of traditional lighting consoles saw the potential in this process and started making versions of the software that powered their full-featured consoles available for free downloads to anyone's computer. These software packages that replicate a manufacture's console are known as **off-line editors.**

Off-line editing has become a very important tool that allows designers to download software that simulates a lighting console. In off-line editing, show files are created and edited without having to complete the work in the theatre with the actual lights and console. This software is useful in cases like touring, where a production has already been designed and a designer needs to modify a design for each venue. Off-line editing is particularly helpful when the designer is prevented from programming a show live in the actual performance space or when making adjustments in focus points and choreography for moving lights. Entire shows can be pre-written or roughed-in outside of the performance venue using this technology (writing a show **blind**). The pre-written cues are loaded into the console once the designer gets to the theatre and are then **tweaked** or edited once they are seen in rehearsals. Manufacturers of all the major lighting consoles provide off-line editors that are available as free downloads from their websites. There are even utilities that can translate data from one manufacturer's console to another. Manufacturers of more complex consoles that are heavily oriented towards the moving light industry supply off-line editors that provide excellent simulations of their consoles.

VISUALIZATION

Visualization is an even more sophisticated form of off-line editing and computer rendering. In visualization the entire rig of the setting, the props, and the lighting (including colors, levels, and movements) are all modeled within a computer simulation. In some cases, an image might be so accurately calculated that it depicts a photometrically correct image. This might be just what is needed in the case of making a presentation for a major architectural project, but such images take an immense amount of time and expense to create. In entertainment situations, this is rarely possible—plus, unlike architectural projects, stage images are dynamic and constantly changing. Even if there is time to do such visualizations they are often limited to either a single image per scene or a couple of important moments of a production. There is another type of visualization that generates images without using photorealism and that work in real time. With these, accuracy and detail are sacrificed so that a complete animation, including moving light choreography, can be made for a project. These visualizations are accurate enough to account for most design decisions that a designer would make in an actual theatre—even

illustrating the transitions between the cues. Entire virtual theatres can be created where model sets are lit with virtual luminaires hung in lighting positions that completely mimic the real plot that will someday be hung in the theatre. The luminaires replicate the photometrics of the actual fixtures and are virtually focused and gelled as they would be in the theatre. Hookups and channel assignments are created automatically and will match the actual plugging of the show in the theatre. Finally, cues are written using the virtual image just as if the production were being lit in the actual space. When the virtual programming is complete, the cues have been roughed-in and the show is ready to be loaded into the console after the rig is assembled in the theatre. This process saves immense amounts of time in the venue and has become so beneficial that virtual studios have started to pop up across the world where lighting designers can rent a computer and the software on an hourly or daily basis. The first popular theatrical visualizer was CAST Software's wysiwyg (Figure 7.13). Wysiwyg is a stand-alone program that contains its own computer-aided drafting (CAD) software. It not only creates design visualizations, but also aids designers in drafting the plot and section, keeps track of inventories, and generates all of the design's schedules and paperwork.

An even more powerful application of computer visualization connects the PC to the lighting console through some form of DMX/USB interface. This allows the virtual program to drive the console in the actual venue. When a change is made in the virtual world, the change is immediately reflected in the real rig. The communication between these systems is bi-directional, and changes made through the lighting console will also create changes in the virtual lighting. Over the years wysiwyg has evolved into this type of visualization tool and has been bundled into many of ETC's consoles as part of the Emphasis® product line. This type of visualization has also opened up to other manufacturers and an increasing number of consoles are now being shipped with some form of visualization software. A visualization package that is comparable to wysiwyg is LD Assistant by Design and Drafting (Figure 7.14). This software comes with a large symbol library (not only lighting instruments but also props and other stage equipment) and also produces all of the draftings, inventories, and other paperwork required for completing a lighting design. It, too, can be equipped with a DMX module that allows the PC to interface with a console. The primary difference between this product and wysiwyg is that LD Assistant is designed around AutoCAD and therefore has all the tools and sophistication of AutoCAD while wysiwyg uses its own CAD software.

Entertainment designers tend to reserve the term "visualization" for systems that display rendering results in real-time or a live time frame/mode. In reality, visualization can just as easily pertain to static images as well.

Figure 7.13 "Grease" Visualization done in wysiwyg

Credit: Courtesy of CAST Software

Figure 7.14a LD Assistant by Design and Drafting: software interface illustrated along with block navigator and wire-frame model of a nightclub design by R. Dunham

Figure 7.14b LD Assistant by Design and Drafting: a rendering of the nightclub design by R. Dunham

Visualization techniques tend to be used most often in situations like concert lighting or big spectacle events where complex demands are placed on automated luminaires and where there is a limited amount of time to work in the actual venue. A real advantage to using visualization software comes in its ability to deal with the movements of automated lights. In addition to creating the different cues, a bigger attraction is how easily this software can be used to redirect moving lights to new focus points or to work out the choreography of the moving light beams. Timing of these moves can be checked against a piece of music while the accuracy of the moves can be plotted from one stage to another without stepping foot in a venue. Software that is used to create architectural visualizations tends to be more sophisticated than in entertainment applications, but these images also tend to be extremely detailed (photorealism is the most popular style) and are based on true photometric calculations. One of the most popular architectural visualization and design analysis packages is Lighting Analysis's AGi32.

Show Control

Show control refers to linking two or more consoles or other remotely controlled devices together in a master/slave relationship. One console controls other consoles, which in turn execute their pre-programmed cues and associated effects. Through this, multiple effects can be coordinated so that they can be executed consistently from one show to another. Several applications where show control is commonly used include linking traditional and automated lighting consoles; triggering specialized equipment like video projectors, video walls, and fog machines from a lighting console; and coordinating the firing of pyro devices. In a number of entertainment events like musical reviews or theme-park rides the timing and soundtracks for an event and its associated cues remain the same for every performance. In these situations, the lighting console (as well as all the devices that it controls) might be triggered by instructions that are associated with specific cue placements in a soundtrack. This is commonly done with a **timecode** that places signals at specific points in a soundtrack that trigger the light cues or other effects at a specific time. When played back, a signal is sent to the console that triggers the cue, which in turn executes a previously programmed set of instructions. In effect, the instruction simply tells the console to execute a cue from a **cue stack** much like an operator would execute a cue by hitting the "go" button. Some of the more common programming codes used to control this type of automation include **MIDI Show Control (MSC), MIDI Time Control (MTC), and SMPTE (Society of Motion Picture and Television Engineers).** MIDI Show Control simply connects devices so that one can control another. The two timecode protocols are embedded in a soundtrack or run from a console's internal clock and are used to automate a console and its associated cues. The SMPTE code initially came from the film industry and was used to sync the sound and images of a movie. Just as with having to set addresses properly for DMX-controlled devices, these consoles must also be set up with addressing information so that the slave units can communicate with the master console or timecode signal.

STATE-OF-THE-ART CONTROL

Modern lighting control has gone through a number of changes since the appearance of electronic dimming. The availability of smaller, more efficient dimmers coupled with the means of controlling more and more data have resulted in the continual growth of contemporary lighting systems. In a way, we have created a cycle that encourages increasingly more complex systems each year. While most recent improvements in lighting control have evolved around providing better control of larger numbers of dimmers and attributes, there have also been several other innovations that allow us to bring additional control to our luminaires.

Dimmer-per-Circuit

With the drop in electronic component prices and the continued miniaturization of dimming modules, it has now become cost effective to simply provide every circuit of a lighting installation with its own dimmer. These are known as **dimmer-per-circuit (DPC)** systems. The practice has become especially popular in areas like educational facilities where the majority of the circuits are permanently run to different locations throughout a theatre. The need for long runs of cable is virtually eliminated, and luminaires can frequently be plugged into nearby circuits with no need for any additional cable. Issues of maintaining cables and connectors, failed connections, and messy installations are minimized by dimmer-per-circuit systems. A further benefit of these systems is that there is less need for ganging luminaires into common circuits, which results in less demand for high-capacity dimmers. Many dimmers in DPC systems are limited to capacities of 1.2 or 2.4 kW. It is common practice for dimmers and circuits in DPC systems to share the same numeral designation.

Sidebar 7.9 DESIGNER PROFILE: FRED FOSTER

Fred Foster

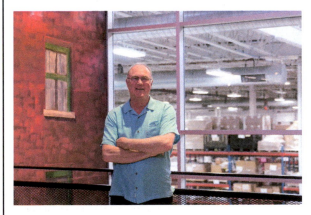

Credit: photo courtesy ETC

Fred Foster is the founder and CEO of Electronic Theatre Controls (ETC)—one of the most successful upstart manufacturers in the lighting industry. Though the company began in Fred's garage in the mid-1970s by making lighting consoles, over the years it has grown into a company of more than 1,000 employees that manufacturer dimmers, luminaires, and a variety of other lighting and rigging equipment for both entertainment and architectural

lighting systems. These are all in addition to manufacturing some of the industry's most popular lighting consoles. In addition to being the visionary that guides ETC, he has performed virtually every role that you can imagine in regard to operating a manufacturing firm, including inventor/engineer, industrial designer, product developer, tech support, salesman, and marketer, as well as administrative roles of president and CEO. Fred is also known for his faithful support of his employees, student mentoring and training activities, and his philanthropy both within and beyond the lighting industry.

Fred's entry into the world of lighting wasn't that much different from many others who pursue a career in lighting. His earliest exposure to lighting was when he started working backstage in eighth grade and continued with those activities throughout high school. In 1975 he began to study lighting at the University of Wisconsin under Gilbert Hemsley:

"While studying lighting design, it became clear to me that, while I could design and hang/focus a good light plot, I did not comprehend the artistic use of color. I can bore people to death with the science of color, but I cannot choose a shirt to match my trousers."

He discovered that "I didn't have the chops to become the lighting designer that I had hoped, but instead was drawn to the technical side of the business. I was also intrigued by lighting control and the technology." Because of this, he, his brother, and a couple of friends who were into computers experimented with the new technology and developed one of the first microprocessor lighting control consoles: "After two years of school, I dropped out and started ETC." Much of both Fred's and ETC's success can be traced back to several key factors that continue to drive his company. He explains:

"ETC started in this narrow field of lighting consoles, but as the business grew, we expanded into dimmers, spotlights and architectural control systems. This challenged me to learn about all of these aspects of lighting and understanding the needs of designers, as well as the processes that they apply to create their art. From community theatre to opera houses, theme parks to convention centers, we have had to develop products that meet the diverse requirements of these markets. I learned to design products by having to make them in the metal shop. I learned marketing by having to promote our products and I learned to listen to what the customers needed to make our products better."

As the company grew, he had to shift his focus as the company's administration took more of his time:

"Originally, I was most interested in the development of products, but as time has passed, I have realized that there are many people in ETC who are closer to the markets and have better insights into the needs of our customers. I am now more focused on creating an environment where people can explore their passions in ways that improve our products and company."

Fred's path to becoming a successful lighting manufacturer is still very much connected to his associations with other leaders in the lighting industry. After he stopped studying lighting design, he worked as an IA stagehand while he and his partners started the company, which helped to instill the "show must go on" ethic in him: "While not trained in computers or engineering, starting ETC from scratch has taught me many things, not the least of which is how important it is to surround yourself with brilliant people." Even after Fred

left college, Gilbert Hemsley still had a significant impact on him:

"I would have to say that Gilbert Hemsley was a critical factor in my ending up where I am. The opportunities that Gilbert offered to us, taking us with him when he worked professionally were unique. The two weeks I spent assisting him at the Metropolitan Opera (mainly getting sandwiches for the design table) introduced me to the workings of a grand opera house. This helped me to set a goal of providing a computerized lighting system to the Metropolitan Opera. It took 20 years, but we installed an Obsession system in 1976. We have since upgraded it several times with our newest technologies."

Fred states that being a manufacturer of lighting equipment is very different from designing lighting:

"In a sense, we make the paint brushes, but do not paint the pictures. It is critically important for ETC to understand the needs and processes that designers have and use. This is an exciting challenge, particularly as lighting technologies have developed so dramatically in the last 45 years. We have witnessed the introduction of computers into lighting control, the development of dimmer per circuit, automated lighting, the Source Four, and, now LED lighting. It is our job to bring these technologies to the market in ways that make them truly useful tools, and not simply clever widgets."

He goes on to explain that there are additional considerations that he must also take into account as a manufacturer:

"When we started ETC, we certainly didn't envision it becoming a company of more than a thousand people working in more than a dozen countries. We grew organically, entering new markets when we found ways that we could improve the tools that they used. We did this by finding and keeping the best people. We have great products because we have people who understand our markets and developers that love to design cool things. We have great customer service because we have people who revel in delighting our customers. And we have a company-wide ethos that truly understands that "the show must go on" and while we are not directly involved in the creative aspects of lighting, we treat our deadlines as opening nights."

In closing, Fred relates that "I miss the days when I could get my hands dirty and be more involved in product development. However, I find that I have to admit that there are people in ETC who are much better at this than I am." He remains abreast of new developments through ETC's employees: "There are many people at ETC and in the industry who are very close to new technologies and ideas. I try to understand what these developments are and look for connections between technologies and the markets' needs." As a final bit of advice, he states:

> **"**You can build a successful company by getting and keeping the best people, but to make this work, you need to provide continued opportunities for those people to grow and develop their interests. This also means that you have to be willing to let go of the things that they can do better. This is always a challenge to do, but is rewarding in the end.**"**

This is advice that clearly works, as evidenced by both Fred's and ETC's successes.

Multiplexing (Dimmer Doubling™)

As the need for more dimmers continues to be a concern for lighting designers, many facilities have reached a point where they are locked into their current dimmer configuration, which cannot be expanded any further. The costs of renovation, limited space for racks, or inadequate sources of power form some of the more common factors that might prevent a facility from upgrading their lighting system with additional dimmers. One development, called **multiplexing,** allows designers to add additional control to a lighting system through adding specialized hardware to an existing dimmer that supports multiplexing and effectively converts the original dimmer into two separate dimmers. ETC has developed a system called Dimmer Doubling in which a specialized two-fer is circuited in combination with an ETC Sensor® dimmer that allows the original dimmer to be split into two different outputs. These dimmers must be in a rack controlled by a special control module that essentially creates a Dimmer A and Dimmer B from a single dimmer. The multiplexing two-fer contains a mechanism for splitting the two signals and can be located at any point along the circuitry of the assigned dimmer. The basic concept of Dimmer Doubling comes from assigning each load to voltages on either side of the 120-volt output of the associated dimmer. One circuit's voltage is associated with one side of the dimmer's AC output, while the other's voltage comes from the opposite side of the power supply. This output is around 77 volts (due to phase control) for each side of the dimmer rather than

the 120 volts that is associated with a normal dimmer's output voltage.

There are two catches to using multiplexing. First is the need to use special lamps that are rated for 77 volts. The lamps are pinned in a unique manner that prevents them from being plugged into a socket rated for a standard 120-volt circuit. The luminaires and specialized two-fers are also equipped with special plugs/connectors and cabling that prevent accidental plugging of the wrong lamps into a circuit or dimmer. The second catch relates to the numbering and patching of the multiplexed channels. More sophisticated consoles that provide alphanumeric input can support the multiplexing by simply inputting the dimmer number and then an A or B for either side of the multiplexed signal, while boards that do not have this feature must assign the first dimmer by using the actual dimmer number and then adding 256 to this for the second dimmer: i.e., the dimmer numbers associated with a multiplexed Dimmer 5 would be designated by Dimmer 5 and 261 (5 + 256). This will work for up to 256 multiplexed dimmers, which will complete a single universe of 512 channels. After dimmer 256, the new multiplexed channels are assigned to a second universe. The 77-volt lamps provide full intensity for the multiplexed fixtures and blend seamlessly with lamps of normal voltages. Total lamp loads, however, cannot exceed the rating of a dimmer.

Distributed Dimming

Another innovation is **distributed dimming, which** makes use of solid-state electronics for shortening circuit runs by placing the dimmers in locations that are typically occupied by circuits. In this case, a circuit box or raceway is mounted in a position relatively close to where the luminaires are hung (much like any standard circuiting hardware). The housing not only contains the dimmer outlets but also the electronics of the dimmers themselves. A distributed dimming strip or box needs only a cable supplying power to the dimmers and a control cable in order to provide a complete dimming system contained within a single housing. Typical distributed dimming units are manufactured with four to six dimmers of 600- or 1,200-watt capacities. The only setting that many of these units require is a series of wheels or dip switches that allow the unit to be assigned to specific DMX addresses or channel numbers.

Distributed dimming has actually been around for quite a while, with the most popular application being in the portable lighting systems that many small bands or lounge acts carry with them. We've all seen them: two booms with four PAR heads each that are operated through a control system of two dimmer modules (one to each boom) and a simple controller. Smaller club setups can contain as few as four 600-watt dimmers per module and can be plugged directly into a standard 20-amp convenience outlet. One particularly popular distributed dimming module that is often used to supplement stage lighting is Lepricon Lighting's ULD-360-HP module (Figure 7.15). While there have been previous attempts at distributed dimming for larger stages, these dimmers have only recently received more thorough consideration for these larger applications. Popular systems that have made use of distributed dimming principles include the bar style SCRimmer Stik with four 600-watt dimmers by Electronics Diversified (no longer manufactured), modular hanging units that make use of the older SCR technology, Intelligent Power System (IPS) dimmers by Rosco Laboratories, and ES750 silent dimmers by ETC, which are designed for individual fixtures. The ES750 and IPS systems make use of a newer technique that combines microprocessors with the same IGBT technology associated with sine wave dimming. Since the noise of the dimmer and weight of the chokes are eliminated in these designs, these dimmers can be manufactured into smaller housings that allow them to be placed near the luminaires (the ES750 actually mounts on the fixture). Although a number of these systems were designed around a modular box design, many newer models have linear designs that resemble a traditional raceway containing multiple dimmers that are simply attached to a batten and are then supplied with a

Figure 7.15 Distributed Dimmer Module by Leprecon (Dimmer 6x600w ULD-360-HP)

Credit: photo courtesy Leprecon Lighting

control cable and power feed. These dimmers often have relatively low load capacities of 1.2 kW (as compared to traditional dimmers) but in some cases can be upgraded to 2.4 kW.

Wireless DMX and Wireless Dimming

A relatively new revolution in control technology is **Wireless DMX** and **Wireless Dimming,** of which there are two slightly different variations. Though wireless dimming has been around for a number of years, it has only fairly recently become popular in smaller theatrical applications. The first variation of wireless control (wireless DMX) transmits DMX data between two locations. Wireless DMX systems make use of special radio frequencies that transmit control data from the console to a receiver that is located at the dimmers or other DMX-controlled devices. This eliminates the control cables that are required to be run between devices. Rather than running separate receivers for every device, a transmitter located at the console typically sends signals to a receiver that is then connected to some form of splitter device where individual DMX runs are then split out and run to other locations or to specific lighting equipment. Outdoor concert venues frequently use this technology in order to transmit control signals between a console and the onstage control and data lines. Large exterior architectural installations can also use wireless control for the more distant luminaires of an installation. In reality, the wireless solution is much better than trying to create DMX cable runs between luminaires that are located in hard to reach places like adjoining rooftops such as in the case of many exterior installations. These devices can also be used to eliminate the more complicated cable runs that would be associated with theatrical applications like controlling color scrollers or automated fixtures that are mounted on the balcony rail or other FOH positions. A transmitter module is plugged into a DMX output at the console, and receiving modules (sometimes as small as a pocket flashlight) are plugged into the DMX input of any remote device that is to be included on the network. As an added feature, additional DMX units can be run down-line from the unit with the receiver by simply using the same input/output ports on the fixtures and continuing to hardwire the data links/cable runs between the devices. Figure 7.16 illustrates such a wireless dimming system.

One concern regarding wireless dimming relates to radio interference from neighboring networks in the 2.4GHz and 5.8GHz frequencies. Today's venues are often full of Wi-Fi access points and the chances of running into shared frequencies are much greater than in the past. The majority of these devices operate in the 2.4GHz band while others work in the 5.8GHz band. As an alternative, a couple of systems are now operating in the 900MHz band where few others operate. There

Figure 7.16 2017 RC4Magic-900 MHz Wireless DMX and Dimming system

Credit: photo courtesy Sean Dane, RC4Wireless

are advantages and disadvantages to each frequency that should be researched and an effort should be made to determine what other neighboring systems are in use. While interference might be an issue, it is important to know that wireless DMX systems are used reliably every day throughout Broadway, the West End, major concert tours, and other live events around the world. With proper setup, wireless DMX technology can be depended on for shows both large and small. In 2.4GHz systems you will find a typical operating range of 200 to 400 feet, even though the actual distances can vary considerably depending not only on what other wireless networks are in an area but also issues like the overall electrical and radioactivity of an area, the weather, and how much metal is in a venue. In 5.8GHz systems you should expect a range of 150–300 feet and in 900MHz could see distances of 1,000 feet or more. Each transmitter is usually capable of distributing data for 512 DMX channels or a single universe.

A second variation includes wireless DMX dimming. Several manufacturers (including City Theatrical and RC4) offer systems that can provide both power and control for several wireless dimmers at a time. Wireless dimmers provide untethered control of low-voltage (5–35 volts DC) lighting and motion effects that are powered by internal power supplies. Costumes, props, and even modular scenic devices may now contain an integrated wireless dimmer with effects engines, addressable pixel control, and more—all being controlled wirelessly by a lighting console. Unlike wireless microphones,

an unlimited number of receiving devices can listen to a single transmitter; some even have different paring methods. Most wireless dimmers have multiple outputs that can each be set to their own DMX address, thus allowing for RGB color mixing and individual control of incandescent lamps or motors. Some will even allow the output of the wireless dimmers to be combined as a means of providing more voltage to higher-powered loads.

Another variety of wireless control that is being experimented with in theatrical applications involves transmitting DMX data over the normal electrical lines that already exist in a facility. In this way, a DMX signal is carried by the same wires and circuits that provide power to each lighting device, effectively eliminating the need for control cables altogether. These carrier technologies have been used in architectural lighting control and data transmission systems on a regular basis in recent years. Problems that still need to be ironed out include dealing with the electrical noise or interference that is present on a normal electrical line (i.e., the large motors from equipment like air-conditioning systems), the effect of power surges, and any interference that the control signal might create with the other electrical systems of a building.

One final observation that I must make before concluding this chapter relates to the issue of the future of dimming within the entertainment industry. With the impact that LEDs are now having on the industry, we are going to have to rethink the manner in which power distribution is done in our theatres. LEDs are powered by line voltage and provide their dimming internally—which means that in time, there will no longer be a need for dimmers in theatrical installations. Instead, well-distributed sources of non-dim power will have to be made throughout our facilities along with a more comprehensive manner of providing data nodes for the data links that will have to be provided to all these fixtures. At present, there are new or newly renovated theatres that have been completely wired for this new technology, but the bigger issue is in how we will make the transition to these new light sources in theatres where our equipment will ultimately be a mixture of traditional sources and dimmers along with the new LED technology. In the meantime, manufacturers have developed LED retrofits that can work on traditional dimmers: for example, ETC has LED retrofits for its Source Four® luminaires. Specialty areas of lighting such as corporate theatre or concert design, where the entire rig is temporary or rented, will be able to make this transition much more readily than traditional venues like theatres in which there are permanent lighting installations. With that, for some time most of us are going to have to find some form of compromise in which both systems will have to be supported by our theatres.

FOR FURTHER READING

Bellman, Willard F. *Lighting the Stage: Art and Practice*. 3rd ed. Louisville, KY: Broadway Press, 2001.

Cadena, Richard. *Automated Lighting: The Art and Science of Moving Light in Theatre, Live Performance, Broadcast, and Entertainment*. 3rd ed. Oxford and New York: Taylor & Francis/Routledge, 2018.

DiLaura, David L., Kevin W. Houser, Richard G. Mistrick, and Gary R. Steffy. eds. *Illuminating Engineering Society–the Lighting Handbook Tenth Edition: Reference and Application*. New York: Illuminating Engineering Society, 2011.

Essig, Linda. *The Speed of Light*. Portsmouth, NH: Heinemann Press, 2002.

Huntington, John. *Control Systems for Live Entertainment*. 3rd ed. Amsterdam and Boston: Elsevier/Focal Press, 2007.

Mobsby, Nick. *Practical Dimming*. Cambridge, UK: Entertainment Technology Press, 2006.

Penzel, Frederick. *Theatre Lighting Before Electricity*. Middletown, CT: Wesleyan University Press, 1978.

Rae, Mark. ed. *IESNA Lighting Handbook*. 9th ed. New York: Illuminating Engineering Society of North America, 2000.

Sandström, Ulf. *Stage Lighting Controls*. Oxford and Boston: Focal Press, 1997.

Schiller, Brad. *The Automated Lighting Programmer's Handbook*. 3rd ed. Amsterdam and Boston: Elsevier/Focal Press, 2017.

Simpson, Robert S. *Lighting Control: Technology and Applications*. Oxford and Boston: Focal Press, 2003.

CHAPTER 8

PROJECTIONS AND LIGHTING

PROJECTIONS MAY BE as simple as shadow projection or as complex as a full-blown video that is delivered in real time. They may cover a limited portion of a stage or may surround the entire stage environment. Sometimes the image is formed from a single projector while at other times a number of projectors are used to form a complex composite image. Projections also don't necessarily have to be an image on a screen—any surface, even performers, can serve as a projection surface. While we may think of a number of projections requiring expensive or sophisticated equipment, many can be created quite simply. On a grand scale, projection technology seems to be growing in complexity on a daily basis and designers who choose to use this technology have a number of options available to them beyond the traditional slide and shadow projection techniques that have been around for many years. Video walls, digital lights, and laser or holographic images are just a few of the more advanced forms of projection that are now also available.

The question of who is responsible for the projections in a production has always formed a gray area in the entertainment industry. At times the scenic designer has been in charge of them while at other times the lighting designer has been responsible for providing the images. Some even draw a distinction between those responsible for the projection gear and those who are responsible for the **content** (the actual images, animations, or videos). If projections are a significant element of a production it is common to bring a specialist on board as another designer, with that individual being given a title such as **projections designer** or production designer. As projection has become more complex, these specialists and designs have emerged as a bona fide design area. What remains clear is that the field is still emerging and that we're still figuring out issues like specific duties/responsibilities and titles. Whether or not a specialist is part of a design team, a lighting designer must be very involved in any discussions regarding projections because of the profound effect that the lighting can have on the final images. Projection design is evolving at an incredibly fast rate. New equipment and technologies appear every year and the roles of lighting and projection designers keep overlapping more and more. In many cases, projections become a shared responsibility in which all of the designers need to be sensitive to each other's needs and collaboration must be especially high due to the impact that projections can have on other design and performance areas. No matter how insignificant the projections may appear, they can't help but to alter the audience's perception of the scenery, costumes, and other designs. The more dominant that they are in a production, the greater impact they will have and all more important that the discussions with other designers become. Projections can also easily steal the focus of a scene, becoming a distraction rather than component of a scene or production.

Over the last several years the roles of projection and lighting designers have become so nested within one another that many professionals discuss this overlap by means of a special term called **convergence**. Much of this is due to the fact that a significant amount of projection equipment is under DMX512 control which is ultimately programmed into the lighting console. The trend of using more projections will continue. Whether specialists are used or not, those lighting designers who embrace this technology will be at an advantage as they work to design the entire lit environment of a production.

In this chapter I cannot begin to provide a full treatment of projections since this is an area of design that is so quickly changing. The **digital lights** and **media servers** that are revolutionizing the way that we think about projection weren't even around much more than 15 years ago and **LEDs** are now having an amazing impact on the entire lighting industry. While I discuss projection equipment, the majority of this chapter focuses on how to use the technology rather than dwelling on the specific equipment. It is also important to note that **digital projection** has revolutionized the way that we are using projections. Though I have chosen to keep many of the older projection technologies in this second edition of the book, many are approaching the same fate as the dinosaurs.

A Brief History of Projection

Some forms of projection have been around since the beginning of time, and images of shadows from around a campfire or the Indonesian art of shadow puppetry have existed for hundreds if not thousands of years. However, much about projection remained mostly theory until the 1900s due to a lack of sophistication in optics and light sources. Although designers understood the potential for using light as a major element of a setting, they didn't have the means to produce it in a way that could be considered successful. Scenographers like Adolphe Appia, Edward Gorden Craig, and Robert Edmund Jones saw the potential for using light and projection as significant elements of their designs and rendered them into their sketches and renderings, but they had no way of producing the effects that they felt were so central to their designs.

The forerunner of traditional optical projectors was called the **magic lantern,** the development of which is generally credited to the Jesuit father Athanasius Kircher during the late 1600s. This projector is crude and produces a fairly weak image by today's standards but is important in that it provides the principle by which most traditional projectors are designed. In its original form magic lanterns were used in pairs of two so that a set of projectors produced overlapping images that could be cross-faded from one to another. Originally the projectors were set in the center of a theatre and were illuminated by oil lamps. Later versions used limelight as their light source and were moved to the back of the stage, where through rear projection much of the "magic" of the scenic effects could remain with the technicians. Variations in the use of magic lanterns became an essential element for many of the epic operas of Richard Wagner as projectors became stronger and motion was added to the projections. Moving clouds formed a principal application of these moving images.

Josef Svoboda was the scenographer often credited with first making use of modern projection technology and developing techniques that could produce the projections envisioned by the earlier scenographers. Svoboda spent much of his life developing projection equipment and techniques that have become the foundation for contemporary projection. He developed most of his theories during the mid–late 1900s while working on opera productions in Prague. Several areas in which he made significant contributions to the field of projection include his development of light curtains, use of low-voltage lamps, creation of large-scaled projections, and experimentation with techniques for charging an atmosphere with particles that reflect a projected beam of light—the foundation for the **hazers** and fog machines that are in common use today. As time has evolved, projectors have become more powerful and sophisticated. even though the basic techniques of projection have not changed. Traditional projection still requires the same elements that were used over the last century.

A recent development in projection technology over the last 15 years has been in the use of light and images that are produced through electronic or digital methods rather than optical methods. In this type of projection the slide is replaced with a digital image and projectors like those that might be used for Microsoft PowerPoint presentations in a classroom or conference hall are used. In the most extreme cases, we may even use automated luminaires (**digital lights)** to project the images. With this technology an image can be moved to a new location, refocused, sized, and even cropped as needed. Even basic distortion like **keystoning** can be corrected with these projectors. In some versions of digital projection, rather than projecting light onto a surface such as a screen, these new technologies allow audience members to view the sources that are creating the image. Popular versions of this innovation are the **video walls** and **LED scrims** that are used on many concert tours. A network of video monitors may also be assembled into a configuration where images can be sent to the individual screens or to the entire group as a composite image. Finally, LEDs can be assembled into clusters to form screens of almost any proportion. Individual LED intensities are controlled by software that allows a large-format image to be produced on the surface of a screen in the same way that a television or computer monitor produces an image. Displays like these are becoming more popular all the time and can be seen in places like concert backgrounds in arenas and stadiums, Times Square advertising, jumbotron scoreboards, and digital billboards. In large-scale celebrations and special events, both the screens/projection surfaces and projections can be large enough to fill an entire side of a building.

Projection Considerations

Whenever a design team considers using projections, every lighting designer should perk up—this is true whether they will ultimately be responsible for the projections or if a projection designer has been added to the design team. While there are many valid reasons for bringing projections to a production, they should not be thought of as a cheap alternative to scenery. In reality, they can be time consuming to create, can require turnaround times that may or may not be under the control of the designer, and often cost more than a typical scenic budget by the time you pay for the specialized equipment and image processing that they require. The projections must be thoroughly planned, and there may be many unknowns that don't appear until the production loads into the theatre, resulting in compromises where mistakes might have to be lived with. Many novices think that projections form a simple solution to a design problem when, in fact, they have no idea what they are getting themselves into. On the other hand, when the designers are thoroughly prepared and a producer is committed to making the expenditures that will allow the projections to be presented successfully, the images can add immensely to a production. Sidebar 8.1 provides some comparisons related to the good and bad of using projections in a production.

Sidebar 8.1 CONSIDERATIONS OF PROJECTION DESIGN

Advantages to Using Projections	Cautions for Using Projections
1. Ability to easily facilitate a change to a number of different locations or settings.	1. Maintaining proper contrast and balance between the intensity of projections and the rest of the stage.
2. Transitions between scenes can become quick and fluid using cross and split-fade techniques between scenes and other split-focus effects.	2. Cost and time issues related to the projection equipment and preparation of the slide materials.
3. Can initiate moving effects and scenic elements.	3. Loss of resolution or clarity when projecting to large full-sized images.
4. Can add texture and depth to a design.	4. Distortion (and its correction) in the form of depth-of-field, focus, and keystoning effects.
5. Transporting of equipment and slides for touring is more minimal and easily done than with comparable scenic elements.	

Advantages to Using Projections	Cautions for Using Projections
6. Can establish focus for an audience.	5. Determination of the proper density or translucency of the slides for optimal projection of rich colors without having the slides become opaque with an associated loss of transmittance.
7. Can create an effective presentation style for a production. Projections allow abstract style and color to be used as a primary design element while providing an ability to soften or modify the effect as needed.	6. Can distract or steal focus from the primary action of a scene or production.
8. Can provide economical design solutions once the initial equipment has been procured.	7. Loss of stage space due to creating proper throw/position distances and neutral zones where actors will not cast shadows onto the screens or within the optical paths of the projectors.
9. In digital design, images can be manipulated and edited much more easily and economically than actual scenery (at times, even on the fly).	8. Consideration of the reflective/transmission properties of the screen/projection surface.

ELEMENTS OF PROJECTION

Most projection involves projecting an image of an object such as a slide onto a screen or other material. Therefore, traditional projection usually involves three components: the **projector** (with the light source), the **slide** or original material, and the **screen** or projection surface. A projector will contain at a minimum a housing that is outfitted with a high-powered lamp and some means of attaching or holding a slide. A slide can be created from any translucent or transparent material like glass or plastic that allows light to pass through it with various degrees of **transmission.** An opaque object may be used in place of a slide to cast shadows, as in the famous shadow puppet theatres of southeastern Asia. The slides are typically (although not always) mounted near the front of the projector and parallel to the lamp or back of the housing. Most projectors make use of a set of **objective lenses** that are placed in front of the slide to help intensify and sharpen its image. Although most projectors hold a single slide, some models accommodate multiple slides added at various positions to form a composite image. Images produced in this manner create different degrees of focus for each layer, which helps to create the illusion of depth in the final image. It is important to note that images can be projected onto any surface and that screens form only one type of projection surface. Scenery and even actors can be viable projection surfaces if the team feels that it is appropriate. The relationships between the light source (projector), slide (size and position), and projection surface (distance and type of material) all play a significant role in the appearance of the final image that an audience will observe. These interdependencies hold true whether a designer is using front or rear projection. One final concept to consider in projection design relates to the fact that many projections work best in an abstract format and that these images frequently look better if their focus is softened slightly instead of being in sharp focus. On the other hand, this would be undesirable in a project that provides documentary images or film clips for a production. Here again, success is dependent on the context in which the effects are applied. **Depth of field** (the range of what is kept in focus) can be used effectively by allowing portions of an image to soften at various locations throughout a stage or screen.

FRONT OR REAR PROJECTION?

Should the images be projected from in front of or behind the screen or projection surface? This is one of the most important considerations that must be made at the very inception of a production using projections. The decision affects not only the projection designer but also the lighting and scenic designers as well—actually, even the blocking of the performers. Too many times projections come off as an added layer of an event rather than as an integral part of the overall production. This is frequently a result of other design areas (most commonly scenic) being designed well ahead of the projections and projection surfaces, without the input of the projection designer. In some cases, the scenic and costume designs may have been completely designed before the projection designer has even been hired. Thankfully, this situation is becoming a lot less common.

The consideration of **front projection** versus **rear projection** (Figure 8.1) is dependent on an individual production. At times the manner in which a director envisions the use of a stage will dictate one manner over another, while at other times the nature of the performance facility, the scenic design, or even the available equipment may determine which method

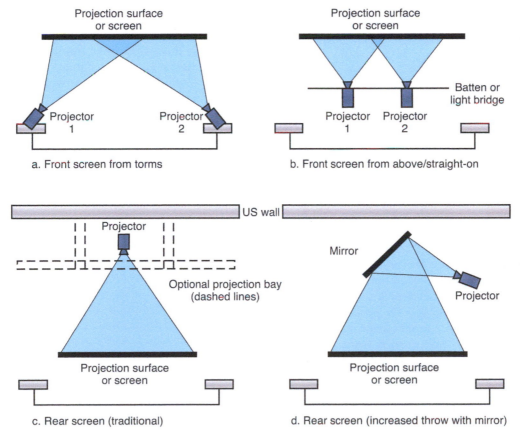

Figure 8.1 Projector/Screen Relationships—Projectors are typically elevated in each situation to avoid hitting scenery and performers (especially in front projection systems).

is most appropriate for a given situation. As a rule, we try to avoid conditions that cause performers to cast shadows onto a projection surface, thereby often favoring rear projections, but if a director or designer wishes textured projection patterns to fall on the actors or scenery, rear projection is out of the question. In the case of front projection, the projectors may be located either straight ahead of the screen or at an angle to either side or above the screen. On the other hand, when mounting a projector from any angle other than dead-on, distortion enters the situation through **keystoning** as well as through issues related to depth of field due to the image being cast to a variety of distances from the projector. On occasion these effects may be desirable, but in most cases some form of correction will have to be made to compensate for the distortions. One way to reduce effects like these is to mount the screens and projectors in such a way that both remain centered along the same optical axis and that the planes of the slide and image remain parallel to one another. Using front-projector locations has an advantage in that the image will appear approximately the same to all viewers across the entire width of an audience, but this also requires that precautions be taken to prevent performers from casting shadows in the projected images.

Throw distances form a consideration in that the size of any image is directly proportional to the lens combination and the projector's distance from a screen. For a number of reasons rear projection tends to be the favored solution because actors can pass close to the projection surfaces without casting shadows onto the images. Since the screens used in rear projections actually glow, rear projection also tends to produce more vibrant images than those created through front projection, unless the screen material used in front projection is treated with highly reflective materials like white paint or reflective glass beads. However, it is rare that a highly reflective screen would blend in aesthetically with the rest of the elements of a production. Common disadvantages of rear projection might include the presence of a **hotspot** at the center of an image that is related to the lens of the projector and the fact that images tend to drop off in intensity and clarity as a viewer moves toward the sides of an auditorium. Another consideration of rear projection lies in dedicating a sufficient amount of backstage space to a neutral zone to give the projectors sufficient throw distances for creating satisfactorily sized images. If the stage does not have enough depth, throw distances can be increased by using a mirror as indicated in Figure 8.1d. Because rear-screen projectors are out of view of the audience, they can be mounted in a way that eliminates problems like keystoning. Crews will also have relatively easy access to the projectors and might be able to troubleshoot them at any time (even during a show).

TRADITIONAL PROJECTION EQUIPMENT

As stated earlier, the basic elements of projection are the projector, slide/object, and projection surface. All three play a role in the success or failure of a projected image. In this portion of the chapter I am not concerned so much with specific equipment as with the general principles, physical properties, and optics that are used within each area of projection design. This first segment deals with more traditional equipment, while current trends like digital projection are discussed later in the chapter.

Lensless Projectors

Lensless projectors form the simplest example of projectors and in many cases can be compared to simple shadow projections. The earliest designs were based on variations of the magic lantern. An intense light source is placed at the rear of a housing and objects or a slide are placed in front of it. The smaller the filament and overall light source, the sharper the image that is created by the projector. Some projectors use the smaller filaments of low-voltage lamps to capitalize on this principle. Slides in these formats may be opaque and used for shadow projections but are more often colored with transparent dyes and high-temperature paints that allow light to pass through them to create a colored image. The less densely that a slide is painted, the brighter the associated image will appear, while the larger the slide, the more detail that can be rendered into both the slide and resulting image. The slides are created from large pieces of glass or plexiglass that are mounted near the front of a projector. The size of the image is directly proportional to not only the distance between the projector and screen, but also the distance between the slide and the light source. The closer that the slide is to the projection surface, the sharper it will appear, while the closer that it is to the lamp, the larger the image will appear. The best focus occurs when the distance between the screen and slide is kept approximately the same as that from the slide to the lamp. However, if a designer wishes to create an image of any significant size that is in relatively sharp focus, the slide must also be larger in order to create the intended image. Limitations such as these result in these projectors being used primarily for more abstract, suggestive projections. A series of composite slides might even be spaced at different depths within a projector to create a layered effect where each slide is progressively more focused than those that are closer to the lamp (Figure 8.2). This can add great depth to an image.

By far the most popular lensless projector is the **Linnebach Projector**, developed in the early 20th century by Adolph Linnebach, a stage engineer from Germany. Linnebach made modifications in the basic design of the lensless projector to create an effective scenic projector. His projector was capable of creating a much

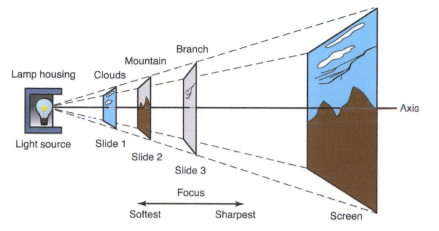

Figure 8.2 Lensless projector with multiple slides

larger-scaled image than the earlier projectors could make. One of the general design principles of these projectors is that the slide should be placed as far from the light source and as close to the screen as possible. One of the problems with this projector lies in the fact that even with a small lamp, different surfaces of the filament do not perform as true **point light sources**, which creates a **penumbra effect.** This causes a bit of fuzzing or blurred edges in any image created by the projector. Another issue results from the intensity of the image dropping off at the edges due to the increased distances that the light must travel from the source. Some general rules regarding these projectors relate to using the largest slides that you can, using the smallest light source or filament possible, and keeping the distance between the slide and screen to a minimum. The closer that the slide is placed to the light source, the larger the resulting image will be, with the tradeoff being that additional blurring will appear around the edges of the final image. While a Linnebach projector has a flat front face and makes use of flat slides, a variation with curved sides, the **Cinebach projector,** is designed to project onto the curved faces of a plaster or wrap-around cyclorama (cyc). Slides for these projectors are made of plexiglass, rather than glass, so that they can be bent into the curvature of the projector.

Lens Projectors

Lens projectors have a set of objective lenses placed in front of a slide that are used to concentrate and focus the image onto a projection surface. Much of this type of projection produces high-quality images that are sharp and well-illuminated. One requirement of most projectors with lenses is a light source capable of producing an intense beam of light. Projectors often have lamps with wattages of several thousand watts, while some can even make use of arc sources. In cases where a projector makes use of an arc, dimming can be accomplished only

through some form of dowser or mechanical dimmer. In the majority of projectors, an additional set of lenses (**condenser lenses**) need to be added between the light source and the slide to both protect the slide from the extreme heat of the light source while also providing maximum coverage and illumination of the slide.

The Ellipsoidal Reflector Spotlight (ERS)

Lighting designers are quite familiar with the simplest form of lensed projector, which is the **ellipsoidal reflector spotlight (ERS).** Shadow projections are made through simply inserting a **gobo** into the pattern slot or **gate** of the luminaire. While these are often used to create textured breakups where orientation and distortion are not an issue, there are other occasions—such as when a gobo depicting an architectural detail is projected onto a cyc—where the hanging position and effect of keystoning must be taken into consideration. The majority of the gobos that a designer will use are purchased from theatrical manufacturers who produce a vast collection of different patterns. Even colored gobos that are cast onto glass are available. Custom gobos may ordered from a manufacturer, while they can also be made by cutting pie plates or other thin-gauged metal into patterned templates, or by etching a design onto print plates using an acid. In the case of enhanced ERSes, designs can even be transferred to acetate sheets that are used directly as gobos. Full-colored gobos produced on glass or acetate can even carry photographic images or artwork containing company logos or other detailed images. All of these methods produce simple projections relatively cheaply. Gobos and their accessories were discussed in detail in earlier chapters.

The 35mm Projector

Another form of lensed projector that was used fairly frequently until recently is the 35mm **Ektagraphic Slide**

Projector by Kodak. This projector has a variety of lenses (including zoom lenses) that allow it to be modified to a number of different throw distances. More importantly, the projector was fairly easy to acquire and could be used to project full-color photography. There are also accessories that allow a designer to easily complete transitions or **dissolve effects** between two or more projectors. Designers have often modified these projectors by separating the fan and lamp circuits from one another so that the lamp can be assigned to a theatrical dimmer while the fan can run on a non-dim circuit for constant cooling. If this is done, precautions need to be taken to ensure that the lamp is not turned on without having the fan circuit already running. While a designer must take into account the lead time and costs associated with film processing, the slides are for the most part easy to create, and most medium-sized cities have photo labs that can develop slides in 24 hours or less—however, do not confuse this type of photo service with the one-hour processing that might be found at drug or discount stores. The finished slides are placed in a carousel and are advanced through a simple remote control. When using a number of projections, care should be taken to use the lower capacity (80- versus 140-slide) carousels to help eliminate jamming within the projectors. For those times when the projections need a bit more intensity, there are power modules available that contain a more powerful lamp and improved optics that slide into the modular design of the projectors and can increase the light output by another 20–30%. The largest issue with these projectors lies in the fact that with the age of digital photography both film itself and these processing labs are rapidly disappearing.

For larger applications the projector can be modified into a more powerful version such as the **Buhl projector.** Buhl projectors take an Ektagraphic projector and replace the standard lamp with one of a much higher wattage (from 300 to 1,200 watts), add a system of heat sinks along with a high-powered fan for extra cooling, and use a superior set of lenses for producing higher-quality images. These variations of the projector already have the lamp and fan circuits separated and crews must take extreme care to ensure that the lamp is never turned on without having the fans already running. The heat that can build up in these units is so intense that permanent damage can be inflicted quickly on the projector and slides if a problem develops in the cooling system. Because of the extreme heat of the powerful lamp, any slides placed in a Buhl projector should be protected by mounting the slide between a set of glass cover slides and changing the cardboard slide mounts to ones made of either plastic or metal. In reality, switching the mounts to plastic or metal is a good idea for any 35mm slides because they eliminate much of the friction and warping that are associated with cardboard mounts. Buhl Optical has been associated with superior

optics for many years and manufactures a variety of lenses for both the Buhl and Ektagraphic projectors. Designers simply have to match the proper lens to the throw distance and desired image size that they need for their project. The focal length of a lens is inversely proportional to the angle of projection or beam dispersion, and the shorter the focal length, the wider the projected image will be. The overall goal should be to select a lens that will create the intended image size while at the same time placing the projector as close to the screen as possible to create projections of maximum intensity.

Sidebar 8.2 CALCULATIONS REGARDING PROJECTORS AND LENSES

A. Relationship Between Size of Image and Focal Length of Lenses

F = Focal Length of Lens   D = Throw Distance
I = Image Size   S = SlideSize

$$F = \frac{D \times S}{I + S}$$

*All units must remain the same (e.g., mm).
*Image and slide measurements are taken along comparable sides of a slide and image.

To determine the focal length of a lens required to produce a 10-meter-wide image from a 35mm slide for a throw distance of 10 meters:

$$F = \frac{10,000mm \times 35mm}{10,000mm + 35mm}$$

$$= 34.88 \, (or \, a \, 35mm \, lens)$$

B. Relationship Between Throw Distance and Intensity of an Image

I = Illumination Intensity   O = Projector Output
D = Throw Distance

$$I = \frac{O}{D^2}$$

To determine the illumination intensity of an image created by a projector with an output of 2,000 lumens at a distance of 3 meters:

$$I = \frac{2,000 \, lumens}{3 \, meters^2}$$

$$= 222.22 \, lumens / meter^2$$

This same relationship can be used to make determinations of the maximum screen area that can be covered with a specified level of brightness from a projector with a given light output. As an example, if the targeted illumination intensity is 500 lumens/meter^2 and your projector is capable of producing 5,000 lumens:

$$D^2 = \frac{5{,}000 \text{ lumens}}{500 \text{ lumens} / \text{meters}^2}$$

$$= 10 \text{ meters}^2 \text{ or } 10 \text{ square meters}$$

the approximate equivalent of a 3.16 × 3.16 meter screen.

Scenic Projectors

Scenic projectors are designed to deliver high-quality projections to the stage; even the least expensive projectors can represent an investment of several thousand dollars. There are large-format projectors capable of filling an image over the entire side of a 10-story building that can exceed $55,000. Features that set these projectors apart from the smaller projectors include a more powerful light source (a minimum of 1,500–2,000 watt lamps for incandescent or arc sources), larger slide formats for adding clarity and detail to the images, and superior optics in the objective lens system. Some projectors also have animation accessories that add moving effects to the projected images. While these projectors may be used to produce less realistic effects, their improved optics and light sources make them ideal candidates when detail and more photographic-like effects are desired.

Perhaps the most common small-format scenic projector that has seen popular use is Gam's **Scene Machine** (which is no longer in production). The basic model provides a modular housing and lamp/reflector assembly equipped with a 1,500 or 2,000 watt lamp. The unit is also equipped with a powerful fan assembly. The Scene Machine is unique in its modular design. Effects like animation disks, slide carousels (4 × 5 inch format), and film loops form several of the popular accessories that can be snapped into place at the front of this projector. Many of the accessories can be stacked on top of one another to produce composite effects. The moving effects have speed, directional settings, and remote controls that allow crews to modify an effect as needed. Several of the more popular effects include film loops, fire and rain animation disks, and a large-format slide head. An objective lens selected from a variety of focal lengths is placed beyond the effects heads for optimal control of the image. Some of the lenses have extremely wide beamspreads that can be used to cover a large area

even at a relatively short throw distance, while others are fairly narrow and can be used at considerable distances from the stage. Rosco has also introduced a small-format projector, the X24 X-Effects Projector, that makes use of a high-intensity short-arc light source and two wheels that are oriented and rotated in a side-by-side relationship that overlap within the projector's optic path. Traditional, dichroic and textured glass gobos are placed into the wheels to produce a number of animated effects such as for flames/fire or water reflections. The speed and direction of the wheels can be controlled independently from one another.

Large-format projectors start to get very expensive very quickly and are often not feasible for many production companies. Not only are the projectors expensive, but also the production of the slides (almost exclusively in large-format glass) can add considerably to the costs of this type of projection. Projection at this scale needs the skills of a specialist who is dedicated to the preparation and execution of the projections and their associated equipment. Projectors of this caliber can deliver a bright image from a significant distance. If a wide-angled lens is used, much of the image can be dispersed over a large area. Often, only two of these projectors can cover an entire cyc (one left and one right). The use of large-format projectors is quite popular in opera houses throughout the world. For example, the Metropolitan Opera in New York has no fewer than 10–12 large-format projectors in its repertory plot.

Lamps used in large-format projectors are often rated in the 5,000-watt range, with several models even exceeding 10,000 watts. The brightness of even the smallest of these projectors is well over 100,000 lumens and some can exceed 800,000 lumens. In a number of projectors HMI (hydrargyrum medium-arc iodide or halogen metal iodide) and arc sources are used rather than incandescent lamps and a mechanical dimmer is incorporated into the projectors' designs. There's also an argument for equipping all scenic projectors with mechanical dimmers due to the negative impact that an incandescent lamp can have on an image's color when going through **red-shift** while being dimmed through an electrical dimmer.

Pani Projectors, from Austria, provides one of the most popular lines of large-format projectors used in the world today. Along with their superior light sources and optics these projectors can be used for both still and moving effects—even film projections. The projectors are large and bulky, often weighing in at well over 100 pounds and requiring several crew members to maneuver the units into their operating positions. Many of these projectors are large enough to come equipped with their own mounting frame and caster/dolly system, complete with leveling adjustments. The larger format of the slides (typically 4 × 5 inches and larger) causes the slides and their preparation to be expensive. One way to eliminate some of the costs is producing the original slides on acetate or film transparencies and then sandwiching them between two plates of cover glass. Several common slide formats for these projectors include 3 × 4 inches, 4 × 5 inches, 4 × 6 inches, 6 × 8 inches, and even 8 × 10 inches and 11 × 14 inches.

SLIDES AND SOURCE MATERIALS

The slide or source material is an extremely important element of any projection and in many cases determines the overall success of a resulting image. The quality of a projected image can never be better than that of the original slide—with the notable exception of abstract designs where blurring and less-defined resolution can actually work to the advantage of an image. The larger the slide, the more detail and resolution that a designer can build into the image. A variety of methods can be used to produce slides. In the simplest cases, as with gobos, the pattern of the image is simply cut away from an opaque material like a thin sheet of metal. Most slides, however, are designed to produce an image based on the use of some form of translucent or transparent materials. The slide is usually made of glass and is painted with high-temperature paints, markers, or by means of an etching process. Images may also be painted or drawn on films or acetate and treated as transparencies. Sometimes the images may come from film or other transparencies like photographic slides. Dr. Martin's paints, which have been treated with an additive, or special projection paints from companies like Rosco seem to provide the best results for adding color to these slides. If painting the slides, a designer must pay attention to the density of the painting so that the paint doesn't build any unintentional opaque areas into the slide—these will appear as shadows as opposed to the intended color.

PROJECTION SURFACES

Projection screens are more appropriately called "projection surfaces" because many projections are not necessarily directed onto a traditional screen. The cyc, scrims, scenery, and even the performers can be viable projection surfaces. In front projection, the surfaces need to exhibit enough reflectivity that the audience can see the images. In rear projection, the screens have to be translucent enough to allow the image to be seen on the projection surface. Additional conditions that can either aid or obscure projections include the contrast between the projections and the colors, textures, and overall values of the scenery. Rear projections often appear more vivid because you see the light on the screen's surface as opposed to a reflection of the image. The size and shape of the projection surfaces do not matter as long as they fit within the rest of the scheme and style of a production. Many of the considerations of front versus rear projections were discussed earlier; only the actual screens are examined here.

Front-Projection Screens

The traditional idea of a projection screen is what comes to mind when I mention front projection. The basic principle of casting an image on a highly reflective surface that reflects the image back to the viewer forms the basis of this screen. The more reflective the surface, the more successful the material will be as a screen. A bigger issue in front projection relates to disguising the screen on a stage. This is an especially important consideration when the screen is being viewed when there are no projections on it. Usual attempts to deal with this issue relate to filling the screen at all times with either projections or washes of colored or textured light. In this way the screen never appears untreated and becomes a part of the overall stage composition. All sorts of materials may be used for front projection systems. Hard-covered wood panels such as Masonite that have been painted white, muslin, scrim, and even bedsheets and shower curtains have been used successfully as screens in a pinch. Many screens are made specifically for projection and are crafted from especially reflective materials. Beyond the traditional idea of a projection screen almost anything can become a projection surface. This also holds true of the color of a projection surface: screens can be of any color but with the correlation that some colors are more reflective than others.

One way to characterize a screen's ability to reflect light refers to the **gain** of the screen. The higher the gain, the better the material will perform as a reflector, and the better projection surface that it will become. In some cases, such as in movie screens, the gain of a screen is increased significantly by adhering miniature glass beads to the projection surface. This increases the reflective capabilities of the screen and makes the images appear brighter, but with a negative effect in that the intensity of the image appears to drop off significantly as you move to either side of the screen. These screens work fine when an audience is not spread across any great width, but can present problems in wide auditoriums. This is one of the reasons why movie theatres are often built in a fairly narrow configuration. Matte screen surfaces, on the other hand, are less reflective but tend to have gains that are less affected by viewing angle and are best for working in auditoriums with fairly wide sightlines.

Rear-Projection Screens

There are a number of issues related to front projection that have caused projection designers to consider rear projection as a more successful alternative for projections. The most notable issues relate to avoiding the keystone distortion that is common in front projection by providing a straight-on relationship between the screen and projectors. This also helps prevent objects or performers from interfering with and casting shadows in the beams of the projectors. One of the most positive features of using a **rear-projection screen (RP screen)** is that performers can be blocked right up to the projection surface. The biggest negative consideration in rear projection is getting a sufficient backstage throw distance and lens combination for creating properly sized images. Venues in which there is a known need for using projections are often designed with a cubby-hole known as a **projector bay**, which is an inset that extends several feet into the upstage wall. Figure 8.3a illustrates an example of a rear projection screen (the window of

Figure 8.3a Projections in the University of Georgia production of *A Christmas Carol*. a. Rear-screen projection in shop/office window that combines green-screen technology with animation and composite video

Credit: photo courtesy University of Georgia, Department of Theatre and Film Studies

Figure 8.3b Front projection of Marley's Ghost onto a combination of mesh screen and fog

Credit: photo courtesy University of Georgia, Department of Theatre and Film Studies

Scrooge's office) being worked into the scenic design of a production. This allows projectors to be placed directly behind the stage at an additional distance from the cyc and projection surfaces. The Disney Cruise Line uses this technique in its shipboard theatres to gain additional throw distances for the scenic projectors.

Almost any material can be used as a projection surface. In rear projection, however, the designer must pay particular attention to the transmission ability of the material used for the projection surface. A rear-projection screen works on the basis of a certain amount of light being stopped or **diffused** on the projection surface upon which the image is observed. All rear-projection screens must display a certain degree of translucency. If the screen material is too opaque and has too low a **transmission rate,** no light will be observed on the front surface of the screen. If the transmission rate is too high, the light will pass completely through the material without having a chance to strike and scatter at the screen to form an image. This is one of the reasons that projecting onto fog or haze is not always successful—if the density of the haze drops below a critical level (e.g., the fog dissipates) the light simply passes into space without reflecting and forming an image. I produced an adaptation of *A Christmas Carol* several years ago where Marley's Ghost was projected onto a combination of fog and crumbled mesh-like material (Figure 8.3b). Initially, the idea was to use just the fog, but when we had problems during techs with keeping the fog from blowing away from the location where the projector was focused, we added additional material behind the fog as a means of safeguarding the projected effect. Nonetheless, fog and haze are often used very successfully as a projection surface, from as simple of an effect as making the light beams visible at rock concerts, to the rotational effects of spinning gobos in a haze to create textured patterns of revolving light, to full-blown slide projections that appear magically after being cast onto a screen of fog or even water. In Disney's Hollywood Studios Park closing show, *Fantasmic*, video sequences are projected onto a screen of water that is formed by a series of fountains that extend across the entire width of the show pavilion's lagoon.

Special materials have been created that work especially well for rear-projection screens, which are usually made of relatively thick yet pliable plastic that comes in black, neutral gray, and white colors. The most important aspect of these materials is that they have comparably high gains and can shield an audience from the hotspot of the lens that can be associated with rear projection. Gray and black materials are popular because they are easier to disguise or blend with a production's scenery. However, as the material gets darker, the images drop off in intensity and are not as visible to people who are to the sides and outside of a critical viewing angle. This lowered appearance property is known as **bend.** White screens can provide nearly 180° visibility for a projected image while this viewing angle can become quite narrow in dark materials; people to the extreme sides of an auditorium will not be able to see the projected images very well at all. In addition to actual RP screen, I have used muslin, bedsheets and even shower curtains for creating these screens.

Another consideration with rear projection is whether the projector lens becomes visible behind the screen. This is most commonly seen as a hotspot behind the screen's surface. The best way to avoid this is to use a screen or material with a transmission rate high enough that successful projections are created, yet low enough to hide the projector lens, which is most likely located directly behind the screen. Another method involves mounting the projector in a location that is out of view of the audience. This may be an easy solution for more abstract projections but will mean that the designer will have to consider distortion corrections in other types of images.

It is best to cover the entire surface of a screen with a single sheet of projection material and to avoid placing any seams across a projection surface if at all possible. Rear projection screens made of actual RP material can be custome made to almost any dimension but are considerably expensive (seamless screens) and beyond the budgets of many shows or organizations. A screen exceeding a dimension of more than about 55 inches will most likely have to be assembled from more than one width of material and can be created by joining strips of the material together with clear tape. Precautions must be taken to ensure that a perfect butt joint is created between each strip. If the strips overlap, a shadow will be created, and if the seams don't quite meet, glare and a direct view of the projector's lens will be visible.

Other Materials/Projection Surfaces

With a projector that has enough power, almost any material can be used as a projection surface. Various scenic materials both with and without texture as well as in nearly any color can be projected onto. The success of such projections is determined primarily by the reflectivity and degree of texture that is present in the materials. Materials with less texture are easier to focus on while those with higher degrees of reflectivity (or transmittance in the case of rear projection) will also meet with more success. Surfaces that are heavily textured tend to work best with abstract projections. Designers have even been able to successfully project onto the performers themselves and their costumes.

PRACTICAL ISSUES OF PROJECTION

When a design team first considers projections they should be aware that the amount of time and number of issues involved in making successful projections can often be underestimated. On first impression, projections can appear deceptively simple to produce, but in many ways they can add levels of complexity to a show that could have never been imagined on first appearances. While even professionals can be burned by adding projections into a production, novices should be especially cautious any time that a director casually mentions projections as part of a general production scheme. Issues such as playing space, lines of sight, expensive equipment rentals, projection surfaces, distortion, slide preparation, and turnaround time are all additional elements that must be factored into the production schedules and budget. On the other hand, projections can add another wonderful layer to a production. Projections can also become a more economical solution to production design with the ever-increasing costs of scenic materials and labor. The remaining parts of this section refer to several considerations that a lighting designer should examine when designing a production that uses projections.

Image Definition

One of the most important aspects in projection relates to making specific determinations of the properties that the final image will have. Issues like size of the final image, proportion of the images measurements, and amount of detail are just a few of these properties that need to be described. This will also determine the properties of the original material or content that the projection designer will have to work from.

Resolution

Resolution refers to the amount of detail in an image. The smallest element of detail that can be represented in an image defines the resolution of the image. In traditional photography and film projection this is seen in the graininess or density of the dots that are printed

Figure 8.4 Projection onto performers: *Clytemnestra* at SUNY-Stony Brook (Scenic and Projection Design by R. Finkelstein, Lighting by R. Dunham)

Credit: (Photo Courtesy of Richard Finkelstein)

on the film: the more grain or higher the density of dots, the more detail that the image will display. In digital images the smallest element of an image is a **pixel** (essentially a square in which a value is stored for color and intensity data). The more pixels that are recorded or displayed in a given dimension, the greater the sampling and the more detail that will be displayed within an image. The amount of detail required in an image will vary depending on factors including the amount of detail required in the final image, size of the final image, throw distance, and lens configuration of a projector. Most digital images contain thousands of pixels of information; the overall resolution of an image is defined as the number of pixels making up the width of the image multiplied by the number of pixels making up the height of the image. A number of standard display resolutions have been given specific names like VGA (640x480), SVGA (800x600), XGA (1024x768), SXGA (1380x1024), and UXGA (1600x1200). You may also hear resolution described by **pixel density**, which is nothing more than the number of pixels per unit measurement. A fairly common expression of this is in number of pixels per inch (PPI)—again with more detail and higher resolutions associated with higher pixel densities.

We may also describe an image by its **aspect ratio**. The aspect ratio of an image is the proportion of the width to the height of the image. Common aspect ratios for many images are based on the older television display mode of 4:3 or the newer high-definition video standard of 16:9.

The more that an image is scaled up, the bigger the issue of resolution becomes. In digital images and video you may also hear people discussing **refresh rate,** which is nothing more than the number of times per second that an image is regenerated. Refresh rates that are too slow will cause jumpiness in the final video image.

Contrast

Contrast in an image refers to the differences in intensity between the lightest and darkest parts of an image. Quite often this is expressed by a mathematical representation that we call the **contrast ratio**. If there is too great or small of a difference in the contrast ratio of an image the projection may be prone to being washed out or too dark for proper projection of the image.

Two Critical Considerations: Path and Balance

While there are a host of issues that will contribute to the success or failure of any projection, there are two essential areas of consideration that provide the most insurance for delivering successful projections for a specific project. Both hold true whether a production uses front or rear projection.

The first consideration relates to the **path** that the projection will follow: There must be an unobstructed path between the projectors and the projection surface. While a straight-on relationship produces the best results, this isn't always possible, especially in the case of front projection. Therefore, some form of correction must often be introduced to deal with the distortion caused by these offset positions.

The second primary consideration relates to maintaining a correct intensity or **balance** between the projected images and the stage illumination. At times, the levels of one or the other may be purposefully increased as a manner of drawing focus to a specific area or feature, but more importantly, both of these must perform together for the entire stage. If the intensities of the projections are too high, they steal focus, and if too low, they cannot be seen appropriately. One of the dangers of using projections relates to having to lower the intensities of the general lighting in order to maintain proper balance between the overall stage and weak projections. This most commonly occurs when the projectors aren't strong enough for a given situation. The overall effect can then cause visibility issues for the entire production while also creating a muddy grayed-out effect in the stage illumination due to red-shift issues.

Spill and Ambient Light

With one of the primary successes of projections being determined by the balance of intensities between the projections and the rest of the stage, it stands to reason that **spill** and **ambient light** need to be major considerations on the part of a lighting designer. Probably more so than anything else, a lighting designer needs to be sure that spill in no way falls onto a screen or projection surface. Several ways of accomplishing this include using tight shuttering and focus control; creating neutral zones that are 4–6 feet wide between an acting area and a projection screen; using steeper angles in lighting systems that are focused near the screens; and avoiding low, flat washes from the front of house (FOH) lighting positions. Other techniques that can help include emphasizing sidelighting in areas directly downstage of the screens, placing a scrim several feet in front of a screen (for rear projections only), and avoiding blocking the actors to positions directly in front of the screens. A lighting designer has to consider the effect of not only direct spill but also reflected light bouncing off the floor or other surfaces onto a projection surface. One way to control some of the reflected light coming from the floor is to locate the screens 4–5 feet off the floor (even higher if possible) so that the light from the floor is reflected into the scenery rather than the screen. Another technique places a scrim between the screen and downstage light sources. Careful consideration of the floor treatment and its finish can also prevent this from happening.

This is especially true when FOH lights reflect off of the stage floor up onto the screen.

Ambient light is harder to control because it doesn't necessarily strike the screen surfaces directly but instead gives an overall glow to a stage. Most of this is simply due to a general presence of reflected light. The best manner of controlling ambient light is to use only as much light across the stage as needed. Don't run excessively high-intensity levels on anything and try to avoid full-stage lighting as much as possible. Try to use the lighting to establish tight focuses and keep the light confined to those performers that form the primary elements of a given moment. You might also encourage the scenic designer to use black- and matte-finished materials in their masking and other scenic treatments in order to absorb as much of the stray light as possible. The more that you can control the spill and ambient light, the better chance you will have of maintaining a proper balance between the projections and the rest of the stage.

Image Size

Another area of concern relates to achieving the proper size for a projection. This is a function of several issues but is most dependent on the lens configuration and the throw distance between the screen and the projector. Different projector lenses are used to spread an image over larger or smaller areas for a given throw distance. The differences between lenses can be expressed in several manners, one being a focal length in millimeters (with lenses with larger focal lengths being used for greater distances and the image not opening up as quickly) and another as a throw ratio such as 1.5:1 or 2:1—which means that the throw distance must be 1.5 or 2 times away from the screen to project an image of a given size. For example, if your screen and final image is to be 20 feet wide and you are using a 1.5:1 lens, you would have to have a throw distance of at least 30 feet in order to completely fill the projection screen with your image. In contrast, if you are using the same projector and screen but are now going to rear-project the image, and you have a limited throw distance of only 20 feet, you would now need a lens with a 1:1 throw ratio. If you had to place the projector even closer to the screen you would need a lens such as a 0.8:1 or smaller (short or ultra-short throw). Many projector companies provide tables and/or apps on their websites to help determine the proper lens for various throw distances and screen size combinations.

While it may seem that all you need to do to get a larger image is to increase the throw distance or shift to a wider-angled lens, the increased size comes with sacrifices. The most notable is through the effect of the **Inverse Square Law,** where the same amount of projected light is spread over a greater surface area, resulting in a dimmer image. A way of compensating for this lowered intensity is by dividing the projection into smaller units that are each projected separately using additional projectors. This not only allows more complex images to be created through a composite effect but also (and more importantly) allows the projectors to be placed closer to the screen, with each one projecting a smaller portion of the image. The technique is known as **tiling** and automatically increases the intensity in the final image since there are more lumens of light striking the screen through the additional projectors; the effect of the shorter throw distances for the projectors also affects the intensity.

Distortion

The last area of concern relates to **distortion** and other factors that have an influence on how a projection appears to an audience. We tend to refer to distortion as any variation or shift in appearance between the original slide and the projected image. While some distortion may come into the system through any of the three primary components of a projection system, the majority of any image distortion usually comes about through issues related to either the actual slide, the manner in which the slide is projected, or how the image strikes a projection surface.

RESOLUTION In most cases, any slide used in a projection application will be magnified considerably. Therefore, any detail (or blemish) will also be magnified significantly in the final image. Because of this, projection designers should provide as much detail as possible in the slides that they create. They should also take special care to avoid careless imperfections as they make any of the projection slides. The amount of required detail in the slide will vary depending on factors like the detail needed in the final image, throw distance, and lens configuration of a projector. In computer-based images special attention should be paid to the resolution of an image so that problems with **pixelation** can be avoided. In photographic images, this is seen in the graininess of the film: the more grain or the lower the density of the film, the greater problem this will be for the projection. The more that an image is scaled up, the bigger the issue of resolution becomes. This is why large-scaled projections are created with larger-sized slides.

FOCUS Focus refers to the overall sharpness of an image. The original image in the slide should be sharp and in focus. The projector can always be used to soften the slide if necessary. If a slide is out of focus to begin with, its focus cannot be sharpened beyond that point. This principle holds especially true if you are using photographic images. You can never improve the sharpness of a slide through projection—you can only make it worse!

DEPTH OF FIELD Once an image is focused onto a screen, there is an area both in front of and behind the screen where sharp focus will be maintained (Figure 8.5). **Depth of field** refers to this range. When a screen and projector are kept in a flat-on relationship, depth of field isn't a major issue. However, if the screen is placed in a position that is oriented diagonally in relationship to the projector, depth of field can become an issue: the plane coinciding with a sharp focus only exists at one point throughout the depth of the screen, and some areas of the screen will be closer to the projector while others will be farther away. This results in portions of the image falling in and out of focus depending on which part of the screen the image is actually focused to. The way to correct this situation is to select a lens that has a large enough depth of field to keep the entire image focused throughout the depth of the screen. The larger the depth of field, the more of the screen that will remain in focus. Lenses with shorter focal lengths (wider angled) will have a larger depth of field. This works well for trying to keep throw distances short, but if using narrow lenses to project longer distances, the depth of field will be narrower and more

precisely defined. Longer throw lenses also tend to have an overall light output that is lower than shorter ones. Tilting a screen forward or backward so that more of its surface falls within the depth of field is another way of correcting this problem.

KEYSTONE EFFECT When a screen-to-projector relationship is anything but straight-on, a form of distortion takes place called **keystone effect** or **keystoning**. A prime example of this is seen when two sides of an image that would otherwise be parallel appear to tilt in or away from one another. The effect can happen within a single plane or in some cases a double plane resulting in all four sides of an image being distorted. This type of keystoning occurs when a projector is mounted either above or below and to one side of a screen. The best way to fix keystoning is to create slides that are themselves distorted in such a way that they counter the distortion that would be found in a projected image. The approach follows the idea of two wrongs making a right. The following methods are typical solutions for correcting keystoning in slides (also see Sidebars 8.3 and 8.4).

1. The simplest manner of correcting for keystone effect is as simple as tilting the screen so that it ends up being placed in a flat relationship with the projector lens. If a projector is mounted from an overhead position for a frontal projection, the screen's bottom would be tilted out. This practice of tilting the screen can be done in one or several planes, however, the angle that the screens make with an audience may become an issue. Often, this type of correction for a straight-on or straight-back situation isn't perceivable to an audience.

2. Photographic film in the form of slides is one of the most popular choices of slide material for many projection designers (withholding digital images). One of the most popular manners of correcting for keystone effect involves shooting a photograph of the original artwork from a perspective (position and angle) that corresponds with where the projector will be located in relationship to the screen. The first step in the process involves plotting the exact horizontal and vertical angles that a projector will make with the screen and then taking a photograph of the original artwork with a camera placement that simulates exactly the opposite of where a projector will be located. While this fixes the angle issues, the designer must also crop the photograph to adjust for the proper distance that the projector will be from the screen. If the projector were located 30° above a

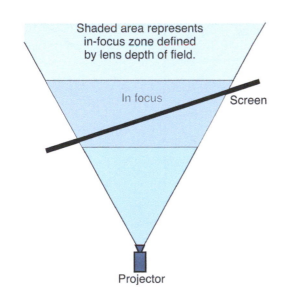

Figure 8.5 Depth of field with angled screens: position the plane of the screen within the depth of field of lens for good focus control

horizontal reference line to a screen, then the photograph for the slide should be taken 30° below this reference line. The resultant slide should fully correct for the given projector position. However, this is a one-time solution, and if the projector or screen are relocated in any way a new set of slides will have to be produced based on the new positions.

3. A mathematical construction may be used to plot out and calculate the keystone effect that will occur within any particular screen/projector relationship. Sidebar 8.4 illustrates this technique.

4. In a number of theatres that use projections on a regular basis, scenic projectors are often hung as part of a rep plot or from a series of standard locations. Many large-scale opera houses throughout the United States and Europe have projectors mounted throughout their theatres. Companies making use of this system have master slides already configured with keystone guidelines based on the screen positions that a particular projector is typically used for. These master slides contain a skewed grid that is oriented along the axis and planes of a given screen location in the same manner that the mathematical grid construction is done. The designer then uses the master slides as guides in producing the distorted production slides required for each projector/screen combination. Sidebar 8.4 illustrates a distortion grid that might be used for a master slide.

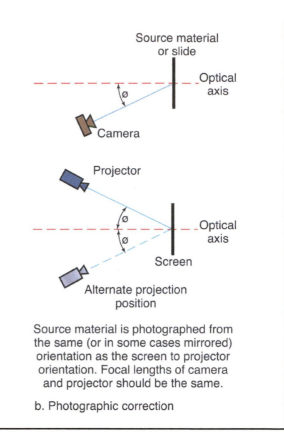

Source material is photographed from the same (or in some cases mirrored) orientation as the screen to projector orientation. Focal lengths of camera and projector should be the same.

b. Photographic correction

Sidebar 8.4 MATHEMATICAL GRID FOR KEYSTONE CORRECTION

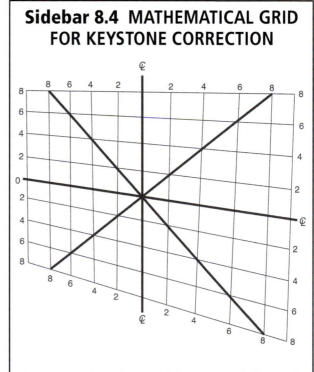

A master distortion grid is prepared for each screen-to-projector combination. The grid is then used as a master template for all slides that will be used for that projector/screen combination.

Sidebar 8.3 KEYSTONE CORRECTION

a. Tilting screen

Dashed lines represent screen in tilted position to correct keystoning.

Master grids are frequently made by hanging a gridded drop in the proposed screen location and taking a photograph of the drop and its markings from the proposed projector location.

5. For abstract projections a designer might paint a portion of a slide and periodically put it into the projector to view it on the actual screen that the image will be projected on. This is a trial-by-error technique that isn't often practical because most of the time the slides have to be completed prior to a show's load-in.

DIGITAL PROJECTION

Digital projection represents the future for the projection industry—actually, in many ways, digital projection and video have pretty much already replaced many traditional means of projection. The basis of digital projection is the replacement of the slide that serves as the source of an image with a digital source or computer file and the traditional optical projectors with digital or electronic ones. One of the great attractions of digital projectors is in their ability to display both video and computer images along with the ease with which the images can be modified. This allows immense potential for not only creating but also manipulating source material. Video sequences can be edited and input to a projector while still images may be created and modified with software packages like Adobe's Photoshop or Microsoft's PowerPoint then sent directly to a digital projector. The sources of these images are readily available through paint programs, image downloads, image scans, and digital cameras (both still and video). No matter how the artwork is created, it is sent by computer to a digital projector that is set up for either front or rear projection. Duplicate images using multiple projectors can be created through a process that is as simple as placing a signal splitter and extra set of cables for each of the projectors rather than having to have duplicate sets of slides prepared for each projector. Transitions between images can also be done as a simple cross-fade command within a single projector. Multiple projectors, just like their predecessors, can be tiled to produce larger composite images where the edges can be edge-blended into a seamless image.

A significant advantage to digital projection is in the ease with which the images can be modified, sometimes even on the fly. Today's software allows images to be edited with an everyday computer, often a laptop, while today's projectors can aid us even further with features that are used to correct issues like varied resolutions and aspect ratios, color correction, and a limited amount of keystoning. Most importantly, turnaround times requiring film processing and special labs are eliminated. Sources of media that can be very easily projected

through today's projectors include traditional video tape (though VHS cassettes are now pretty archaic), live video feeds, computer-designed graphics and animations, web content, and digital images (still and video) from memory chips/cards and hard drives, CD-ROMs, and DVDs. All of these sources have led to imaginative new uses of projections in the entertainment business. Many opera companies make use of digital video and still image projection to produce scenic backgrounds for their productions. Several years ago the University of Georgia produced a play (*The Living Newspaper*) featuring a live chatroom that allowed people online to simultaneously respond to segments of the production that were being presented as a live webcast. To make matters even more interesting, the chatroom conversations (though delayed for 10 seconds and edited if appropriate) were projected live on a screen that was worked into the scenic design of the production. The online audience thus became active participants in the performance event.

Media Servers

One of the most important elements of many digital projection systems lies in a piece of equipment called a **media server.** Media servers are specialized computers (some running the MacOS, others running Windows) that allow a designer to create and edit media content for any of the digital screens or projectors that will be discussed in the next several sections of this chapter. A media server can be as simple as a personal laptop, but for more advanced work a true media server that features all of the bells and whistles that you will need for storing and manipulating the content is often preferred. Once the content has been developed or stored in the media server, it is transferred to a digital projector or screen. The media content is sometimes run from the server directly and sometimes downloaded to the fixture and run independently of the server. These devices generally come pre-loaded with a diverse collection of video and animation files that can be used either directly or with modifications to produce a number of visual effects. Additional content can also be imported from existing collections found on CDs and DVDs, shared media libraries, and websites, or more importantly, unique content that is provided to the programmer by the designer or any other member of the production team. Several of the most popular media servers in use today are the Catalyst and Axon Media Servers by High End Systems (the Axon being a second-generation media server), the Hippotizer (Figure 8.6) by Green Hippo Ltd, and the Mbox Extreme by Production Resources Group (PRG). These servers are extremely complex and provide an incredible number of variables for creating and modifying media content and various effects.

Media servers can severely tax a lighting control system, but designers continue to use them because of the

Figure 8.6 Hippotizer V4 Media Server Pixelmapper Software interface

Credit: photo courtesy Green Hippo, Ltd.

potential that they bring to a production's media design. As lighting consoles get faster and less expensive, and as we become more comfortable with adding additional universes to our control systems, we will continue to find media servers becoming more popular in entertainment lighting. This area of technology is changing so rapidly that it is nearly impossible to stay on top of all the trends and equipment innovations that are related to digital design and projection. To offset this, many manufacturers keep up-to-date Web pages that are dedicated to their equipment as well as online forums where users can exchange information and share ideas.

As production costs continue to escalate, media servers along with digital projectors, video walls, digital lights, and LED scrims/screens are becoming viable alternatives (or an important supplement) to theatrical scenery. Recent Broadway hits like *Young Frankenstein* and *Ring of Fire: The Music of Johnny Cash* have used media servers to support the effects and scenic illusions demanded by these productions. Digital screens and media servers have become especially popular in concert productions, television shows such as *The Voice*, and large spectacle events like the Super Bowl halftime shows and the Olympic opening and closing ceremonies. In fact, the Olympic ceremonies in Beijing used 110 media servers to produce the images that appeared on surfaces like the deck of the stadium, the video on the upper level that surrounded the stadium, and scenic objects like the gigantic sphere that became an icon of the Beijing games. On the downside, a small media server and single associated luminaire may require 70 to 80 channels of independent control simply to achieve the basic motions and projection capabilities that may be required for a projection sequence. More extensive servers can demand more than 300 channels of control. This degree of sophistication makes this technology understandably expensive, and more importantly calls for an individual whose sole function is to deal with the projected images. Now that automated fixtures are capable of projecting digital images and video, the lighting industry is once again debating the nature of the relationships between the lighting, scenic, and video designers as these disciplines draw closer to one another—once again coming back to the issue of **convergence.**

Sidebar 8.5 DESIGNER PROFILE

Wendall K. Harrington

Credit: photo courtesy Paul Vershbow

Wendall K. Harrington is one of the most significant figures in contemporary projection design. Some even call her the "queen of projections." By her own admission, she happened to be at the right place at the right time when projection (as we have come to know it) was in its infancy, but her career blossomed and grew just as the field of projection design developed over the last 30 or so years. In addition to a continuing design career, she heads the projection design concentration at the Yale School of Drama and has been a sought-after lecturer on projected media and projection design since the 1990s. Just a few of her Broadway credits include *Annie, Driving Miss Daisy, Grey Gardens, The Heidi Chronicles, The Will Rogers Follies, Company, Ragtime*, and *The Who's Tommy*. Opera and dance collaborations have been with such prestigious directors and companies as the Sir Richard Eyre, Julie Taymor, Alexei Ratmansky, the Los Angeles Opera, the MET, Brooklyn Academy of Music, and the American Ballet Theatre, as well as designs for concert/pop artists like The Talking Heads, Pete Townshend, Chris Rock, and Simon and Garfunkel. Wendall is the recipient of the Drama Desk Award, the Outer Critics Circle Award, the American Theatre Wing Award, the TCI Award for Technical Achievement, the Michael Merritt Award for Excellence in Design and Collaboration, the Obie Award for Sustained Excellence of Projections, a USITT Education Award, and was named 2015 Players Club Person of the Year.

Harrington came to projection design by a non-traditional path:

"I had no formal training—there was none. Opera used large-format projectors and hand painted glass slides or 35mm film that for the most part were created by set designers like Ron Chase and Josef Svoboda. Broadway used very little projection design, as the available equipment in the 1960s was pretty arcane, expensive and unreliable. In college, I had studied Art History and Studio Art. Later, I worked in a film company and learned the elements of editing and production, then jobs at animation companies and later in advertising that enriched my skill set."

Her entry into theatrical projection design was completely by accident.

"I was making slide shows for business meetings using my film background to explore and push the storytelling potential. I learned the technique of making slides of clear gel colors. One of the people to whom I will always owe an enormous debt of gratitude, Bill Batchelder of Staging Techniques, told me that Tharon Musser wanted to experiment with slides and recommended me to her. I met Tharon, successfully executed her wishes, and the next thing I know I'm making the slides for *They're Playing Our Song*, for Douglas W. Schmidt."

At that time, the use of slides and media was such a complicated effort:

"We had the miracle of punched tape to run the computer that ran the projectors—it was like, putting squirrels in a cage, but it was reliable. *They're Playing our Song* opened on Broadway in 1979. The reviews said that this use of projection would change the look of Broadway but, it wasn't until *The Who's Tommy* in 1994 that I actually made my living working solely in theatre."

She took every theatrical gig she was offered—there was no one else to do them—while also training producers in the care and feeding of the art and equipment to make the projections reliable. "They trusted me," she says.

Currently, most of Wendall's design work is in dance because that's what she wants:

"Dance is abstract and can be supported by abstraction. I find theatre to be more interested in illustration and I've moved somewhat away from that. "The measure of theatrical space is the human body"—that's not my rule I think it's Adolf Appia. Live theatre needs to feel alive, projection is digital, mechanical, it doesn't breathe, so it is important that this "perfection" does not upstage the humans. The one thing that never belongs on stage is "look what I can do"—except for the actual performers."

She loves the collaboration that she shares with the rest of a design team and that "whatever I am doing is made more by the other collaborators. I can work with a lighting designer to make my work teeter on the edge of visibility or can even revoke the audience's trust of the space they are looking at." What she likes least about working in dance is that there are no previews:

"In ballet you never see it all together until you open, then all I can do is take notes and hope to fix things if it is remounted. Opera is the same way. Even an invited dress does not tell you what that first house does. It is an audience that completes any design with their consciousness."

Words of advice that Wendall provides include:

"I'm not particularly tech driven or even interested in it, I'm interested in telling the story. Once I know what I want it to look like, there is always someone who can tell me how—like Paul Vershbow (my programmer) or Lars at Worldstage, without people like them, it's all in my head."

She adds:

"I think that the most valuable skill for a designer is reading and being aware of visual iconography. It is important to research widely and have as many influences as possible. From the Renaissance masters to video games, they are all conversant. It takes your mind to pull the threads together. Step outside your area of interest as often as you can, read anthropology, economics, and literature—it makes you a better collaborator . . . gear second, or maybe even third."

Digital Projectors

Early video and digital projectors were large and bulky while also being marginal in terms of their lumen output. This frequently resulted in placing limitations on the size of a projection screen and lowering the overall stage lighting levels so that a proper balance in intensity could be maintained between the projections and the rest of the stage. The excitement in digital projection over the last 10 years relates to a series of innovations in projectors that have made them especially attractive to the entertainment industry. Among some of the most important changes are reduced physical size and weight, less fan noise, more complexity, the ability to deliver higher resolution images, reduced cost, and most importantly a much higher lumen output. While the lumen output of projectors several years ago was relatively low, there are now projectors that can be purchased through an office supply store (and are used in classrooms and business offices) that have strong enough lumen outputs to work in many small theatres. These projectors can produce outputs as high as 3,200 lumens. Bigger projectors that are more applicable to the entertainment industry and large-scaled applications have outputs that frequently fall in the range of 5,000–20,000 lumens, while some large-format projectors have outputs that can exceed 50,000 lumens. Figure 8.7 provides an example of a large format digital projector.

The first widely used digital projector was the **cathode ray tube (CRT) projector,** which projected three overlapping images of red, blue, and green light onto a screen—and was based on the same technology used in the first generation of widescreen TVs. This technique had a relatively low light output, but it was all that we had in the late 1970s to '80s. Many of these projectors were popular in bars and nightclubs, and they were used to project news and sports programs to a bar's customers. Newer versions, **LCD projectors,** break an image into its three primary color components (red, blue, and green) through the use of dichroic filters and mirrors, then combine the output of the three colors through three different LCD plates/panels whose density is affected by the amount of each component color of light that is present at each LCD panel. These outputs are then once again combined and transmitted through a single high-intensity light source that is usually produced through some form of short-arc xenon or metal halide lamp. The manner of image creation in a LCD projector is essentially the same as the **LCD screen,** with the exception being that the light source is located behind and projects through the LCD panel or display. These projectors are very common in classrooms and conference centers. Large-scale versions of these projectors have become a popular element of the concert industry, awards shows, industrial meetings, and trade shows, where close-ups of the performers or

Figure 8.7a Large-format projectors. a. UDX Series Laser Phosphor High-Brightness Projector by Barco

Credit: photo courtesy Barco

Figure 8.7b The Barco UDX Projector in action. The Legend of Egret; Xiamen Egret Island

Credit: photo courtesy of Barco Business Partner (Pandora Box advertisement company and New Vision New Lighting Company)

speakers are placed on screens located to either side or behind a stage (**I-MAG**). Many of the mega-churches that are popular today use these displays as a regular part of their worship experience. Two issues that a lighting designer must consider when lighting performers who are being videoed for projections during a live performance include maintaining a proper balance between the illumination of the stage and the screens while also achieving the required illumination levels required for both the audience and cameras to maintain visibility throughout a performance

A more recent innovation in projector design, the **Digital Light Projector** (**DLP**), makes use of digital micromirror devices (DMD) that split the image into its three dichroic color components and use a solid-state device with a surface comprised of thousands of miniature or micro-mirrors that are used to reflect the various components of light through the optical system. These mirrors represent a single pixel of the greater image and rotate to either reflect (on) or deflect (off) the light of a corresponding color to the lens and output of the projector. These rotations happen at a very fast speed, continually recycling or refreshing the image many times per second. The more micro-mirrors that a projector contains, the higher the resolution that it will deliver. These projectors tend to be much more expensive than LCD projectors but have better color reproduction (especially in the reds), can better support fast motion/animation effects, and most importantly don't appear to have the color-shifting problems and image spotting that can appear in the dichroic panels of a LCD projector due to aging. These projectors tend to be used in high-end applications where clients are especially critical of the images that are being created.

On a grand scale, large-format LCD and DMD projectors have been used to project video and other animated sequences onto the entire façades of buildings. These have typically been associated with spectacle events like the grand opening of a resort or specific celebrations, but they have also been used in a number of concerts and other large-scale performance events. For Queen Elizabeth's 75th coronation anniversary the entire front façade of Buckingham Palace was covered with video projections for a special performance. A similar use of the technology was used for the grand opening of the Atlantis Casino and Hotel in Dubai as well as for a number of sports events like the opening and closing Olympic ceremonies and Super Bowl halftime shows. In each of these examples, a number of projectors carrying a particular portion of the total image were focused onto different areas of the buildings' facades or playing fields. When synced together, the entire facades/fields were covered by what appeared to be single images (**video tiling**). Using digital control of projections or individual LEDs in larger LED arrays and screens or other display/projection devices to produce images (projection or video) onto two-dimensional surfaces is known as **pixel mapping** while **projection mapping** refers to mapping a projection over three-dimensional surfaces.

Digital Lights

Another form of projection is the use of **digital lights.** These are special variations of automated lighting fixtures that perform not only the standard operations of automated lights, but also many of the functions of a projector, including projection of both still and video images. Some of the earliest renditions of these units weren't much more than a LCD projector housed in a variation of moving yoke assembly. They were very similar to traditional moving heads with the exception that certain mechanical elements like their gobos and associated rotating wheels and shutters were replaced by digital versions of gobos that were produced by the projector element of the unit. In this way, entire gobo inventories/libraries along with image and video files could be stored

and instantly accessed and projected through commands that were sent to the unit via a lighting console.

With a digital light, projections can be moved at will to a new screen or surface, then resized and focused as needed. The images can even be corrected for the new position's keystoning and individual shuttering needs. These unique projection tools are especially complex and expensive, but with all the features that they bring to a production, more design teams are choosing to use them all the time. One of the most important aspects of these specialized projectors is their ability to be run from a DMX signal that allows them to be operated from a traditional lighting console along with all the other lights. While some digital lights have all the control software loaded into the lighting unit (which uses an onboard media server), most digital lights and displays require that their video content be developed and sent to the fixture through a media server (discussed earlier in this section). High End's DL.2 and DL.3 (Figure 8.8) even have cameras that can be used to capture video images or perform as infrared sensors for locating pickups and observing an otherwise dark stage. Control can be an issue with these units since all of the many functions and attributes require additional channels; for example, the DL.3 will use up to 170 channels of DMX control. As the projection, video, and lighting fields become more closely married, digital lights will perform more common tasks and will become an even more vital tool in the future.

Figure 8.8 Digital light: DL.3 by High End Systems (Barco)
Credit: photo courtesy Barco

LCD and LED Displays

In the last 15 years the electronics industry has perfected several techniques for generating screened images with LEDs that are produced through a composite effect. In these technologies a screen is made up of clusters of red, blue, and green light sources (typically LEDs) that glow at various intensities to create a full-color image. The final image is a combination of light outputs that work much like a color television on a grand scale—the process isn't that much different from that used in the pointillism painting technique. While these techniques don't represent a true form of projection since we actually observe the light sources by looking at the screens, they are becoming a popular means of adding video and other computer material (content) to a production. Each cluster of sources becomes a pixel of the larger image, and the smallness of each, along with how closely they are arranged with the neighboring clusters, determines the overall **resolution** of a screen. The screens may be a single entity or may be formed from a matrix of several smaller screens that produce a tiled effect, with each screen carrying a portion of a larger image. **Video walls** are a variation on this tiled treatment. One of the primary screen varieties that make use of this technology is the **LCD.** In this case, the output and associated colors of each small element of the screen (**Red, Green, and Blue**) are based on the individual transmission of each of these color elements as varied by a small control voltage. Large-screen versions of this type of media can be seen in advertising screens in major population centers—Times Square is filled with displays based on this technology. Even displaying live video on these screens is possible. Newer versions of this technology that have been introduced in the last 10 years use LEDs as light sources (Figure 8.9). In some cases, individual LEDs of each primary colors are mounted into a matrix that is then fed control voltages that vary the intensities of each LED in order to create an image. Newer technology makes use of tri-colored LEDs, which allow each of the individual LEDs to be mounted again in a common matrix, but with the additional feature that the color of each LED is modified by varying the voltage of each of the RGB (red, green, blue) emitters contained within the single LED lens/housing. This allows the LEDs to be assembled into a much tighter arrangement. Still newer technology makes use of four-colored LEDs. All of these innovations, even though not technically projections, are having an immense impact on the industry.

One issue that must be considered in working with screens that are based on LCD or LED technology relates to the **pitch** of a screen. Pitch is the size or spacing of the smallest element of a screen (the spacing between the clusters that make up a minimally sized area or pixel of a screen; i.e., each cluster of three different colored LEDs or spacing of the tri-colored LEDs). The pitch is a factor

Figure 8.9 LED screen: Hi-res Roll-up Video Screen by PixelFlex

Credit: photo courtesy PixelFLEX

because it determines not only the cost of the screen but more importantly the resolution and optimal viewing distance, or range, of a screen. While a higher-resolution or higher-definition screen is desired for relatively close distances, a lower-definition screen can be used at larger distances. If the lower-definition screen is viewed from too close, however, the image will be distorted because the individual imaging elements will be visible. Another property that affects the appearance of these screens relates to the **color depth** or number of colors that a screen can effectively create. The simplest screens display eight-bit data, which translates to 256 different levels for each of the three primary colors and a total of 16.7 million different colors. A 16-bit screen, however, can create 65,000 color levels in each of the primaries for a total of 275 billion colors. LEDs form a special point of interest in screen developments because of their capability to be formed into video walls. One early version of this type of system was installed in Radio City Music Hall and created a complete scenic background for its epic-sized stage. Similar walls have made appearances in Broadway productions such as the musical *Ring of Fire: The Music of Johnny Cash.* In other applications, LEDs are arranged in a 4 × 4-inch grid-like arrangement on a netting material that forms an LED scrim through which pixel mapping creates large-scale images of the given content. In a recent University of Georgia production of *Macbeth* (Figure 8.10) for much of the performance we used four such LED scrims to project both animation and video sequences that were created by our media department.

LASERS AND EFFECTS PROJECTION

There are a number of times when projections may be used to create a special effect. The simplest versions of these effects are produced by nothing more than a moving wheel, such as an **animation disk** that is placed in front of a traditional spotlight. These devices can be used quite successfully for creating effects like rippling

Figure 8.10a LED scrims in the University of Georgia production of *Macbeth*. a. A series of computer generated animations

Credit: photo courtesy University of Georgia, Department of Theatre and Film Studies

Figure 8.10b One of several video images created for the production

Credit: photo courtesy University of Georgia, Department of Theatre and Film Studies water, rain, or fire. I created a variation of this effect a number of years ago to suggest the moving windmill that Don Quixote/Cervantes attacks in a production of *Man of La Mancha*. Newer versions of animation disks can be found in devices like Rosco's Infinity accessory. The Scene Machine and other **effects projectors** mentioned earlier function in much the same manner to produce a variety of projection effects. Other projected effects involve using mirrors with transparent materials like glass or plexiglass and light to reflect images from one place to another. The famous effect known as **Pepper's Ghost** (Figure 8.11) that is used to create ghostly images is created in this fashion. If you've ever experienced the Haunted House ride at either Disneyland or Disney World you've witnessed a variation of this effect in the last few moments of the ride as ghosts appear to sit by you in your vehicle. Another variation of this effect with more recent technology was in the virtual return of Michael Jackson (who died in 2009) to the stage at the 2016 Billboard Music Awards, where he danced and sang among live performers.

Several unique forms of projection can be found in the use of **lasers** and **holograms.** Most of these effects are created through an intense directional beam of light. Some effects are nothing more than reflecting laser beams off a series of mirrors that have been precisely located and focused or aimed throughout a venue. Many concert tours place mirrors at various points throughout their trusses, and when the air is charged with haze, the laser paths become visible. A special version of laser, called a **scanner,** moves the laser very quickly along a path that traces a shape or outline of a figure or image. This movement is so fast that the eye cannot see the tracing action and instead sees the full path or image that the laser has scanned or traced. A hologram is an advanced effect produced through a combination of laser and film effects. The unique quality of a hologram is that it can be used to produce an illusion of a three-dimensional image.

Many of these effects use lasers that are powerful enough to cause damage to a person's eyes and therefore need to be regulated carefully. As a result, licensed operators and special permits are often required to use lasers in a performance. In order for the majority of these effects to work properly, they, too, need to be projected onto a surface—with haze or fog often used for this purpose. However, due to their power and concentrated beam, lasers can cover large distances. For this reason these effects are quite popular in large arena or stadium productions like rock concerts and outdoor events where they are used to produce a number of aerial effects and projections. In large aerial displays the projection surface may be clouds, or more commonly the smoke associated with fireworks that have also been worked into an event. Near Atlanta, a local event at Stone Mountain Park produces a lavish light and laser show that is accompanied by music and fireworks almost every night throughout the summer. It is thought to be the largest permanent exterior laser installation in the world. The evening fireworks and finale production (*IllumiNations*) at Disney World's Epcot Center is another example of laser projections. In this event, a series of lasers are beamed from the world pavilions, from building to building, across the large lagoon that forms the centerpiece of the park. In the grand finale, scanning lasers are projected onto the geosphere structure that houses the Spaceship Earth attraction, transforming the giant sphere into an image of a rotating earth.

CONVERGENCE

Convergence is a relatively new term to the lighting industry that we use to discuss the interrelationships that are emerging between the scenic, lighting, video, and projection disciplines. With the advent of digital projection all sorts of new potential has been introduced to the projection industry. It is becoming more difficult to separate where any projection issues may fall between each of these varied disciplines. Projection surfaces are often elements of the setting, video is becoming an ever more important element of content, and luminaires are now effectively being used as projectors. While each of these areas will most likely remain as separate disciplines and a "super" designer who designs all of these elements will probably never emerge, convergence does refer to the need for more collaboration and troubleshooting between the different design specialists. Why not a "super" designer? Each design expert came about as a result of increased sophistication and complexity in a given area of design. This trend continues at an

Figure 8.11 The Pepper's Ghost illusion

Credit: Le Monde Illustré, 1862

ever-increasing pace as a result of an industry that is becoming ever more specialized and technical. All these developments are driving the industry in much the same way that technology in the lighting industry eventually led to the acceptance of the lighting designer as a specialist in the 1950s–'60s and the programmer as a specialist around the turn of the new millennium. Projection has now evolved to a point where there's a projection design classification within the IATSE/United Scenic Artists (USA) and projection is recognized as a valid design discipline within the entertainment industry.

For lighting designers, convergence is extremely important for two reasons: first, just as in the past, we are the individuals most responsible for maintaining the balance and overall look of the entire stage composition; and second, our equipment is now being called upon to deliver more and more of the content used in contemporary productions (especially video). More importantly, the area between lighting and video is becoming more blurred all the time through the continued development of digital technologies. While many video or projection designers tend to concentrate on content that is specific to a given situation, there seems to be a tendency for designers coming from a lighting background to use this technology as a texturing tool, much like an advanced form of gobo or animated effect. Lighting designers and programmers are also finding themselves being regarded as the individuals who are responsible for specifying and maintaining this technology, even though the content may have been developed by another member of the production team. Finally, a single designer often sees things differently than if there were two separate designers representing their own areas. In the end, a single designer should be able to maintain balance between the different areas more effectively while creating a more cohesive final image than if a video and lighting designer focused on designing their own areas. In the

2005–'06 season alone digital technology played a significant role in more than a few new Broadway productions. A few of these included *The Woman in White* (a musical by Andrew Lloyd Webber), *Lestat* (a vampire musical), *Ring of Fire* (the Johnny Cash story) and *The Color Purple*, as well as the London revival of *Sinatra*, and a Toronto production of *The Lord of the Rings*. Several additional Broadway productions that have made successful use of digital projection and convergence in the last several years include *Wicked*, *Jane Eyre*, and the recent revival of *Into the Woods*. The productions by Blue Man Group make widespread use of both digital and conventional projection techniques, not to mention all of the digital imaging associated with the concert industry and spectacle productions such as the opening and closing ceremonies of the Beijing and Rio de Janeiro (Summer) and Vancouver and PyeongChang(Winter) Olympic Games. With all these successes, it can easily be concluded that digital projection and screen technologies will continue to play an ever-increasing role in future productions.

FOR FURTHER READING

Bellman, Willard F. *Lighting the Stage: Art and Practice*. 3rd ed. Louisville, KY: Broadway Press, 2001.

Claiborne, Vickie. *Media Servers for Lighting Programmers: A Comprehensive Guide to Working with Digital Lighting*. Oxford and Boston: Focal Press, 2014.

Gazillo, Eric. *Projection Design and Production for Live Entertainment*. New York: Focal Press, 2017.

Kook, Edward F. *Images in Light for the Living Theatre*. New York: Edward F. Kook, 1963.

Kramer, Wayne. *The Mind's Eye: Theatre and Media Design from the Inside Out*. Portsmouth, NH: Heinemann, 2004.

Saxby, Graham. *Manual of Practical Holography*. Oxford and Boston: Focal Press, 1991.

Walne, Graham. *Projection for the Performing Arts*. Oxford and Boston: Focal Press, 1995.

PART THREE

LIGHT: DESIGN FUNDAMENTALS

CHAPTER 9

ESSENTIALS OF LIGHTING DESIGN

GOOD LIGHTING DESIGN doesn't simply happen. It is the result of many hours of planning that leaves little room for chance or random occurrences. Every luminaire, its placement and focus, its color (by color temperature or filter selection), and its intensity are decisions that should be considered prior to moving into a venue. The process of lighting design entails a number of specific steps—many that are shaped specifically by the working methods of an individual designer. While we all go through roughly the same process, we each have our individual ways of approaching a design. Part One of this book examined the nature of light, and Part Two focused on the technology and tools of lighting. Part Three examines the process of lighting design. While this part of the book provides essential information relating to the design process, it also goes on to present a number of specific techniques that you might consider working into your own personal methods of designing. Some come from practices that have worked for me personally while others come from my observations of other designers. Feel free to use, adapt, or disregard any of these suggestions in your own personal practices. Even though all lighting designers go through similar stages in the evolution of a design, there is no single formula that will work for everyone. The process is personal and one that you will need to experiment with—adapting, revising, and refining it throughout your career. In fact, you will often modify your design process based on the specific needs of a given project.

This chapter begins with the process of lighting design and focuses on the task of establishing a vision or **lighting scheme/lighting concept** for a project. Some may even refer to this as a **vision of light.** Although entertainment designers and illuminating engineers may have different approaches to designing, both ask questions that will guide their decisions as they design a project. The task of establishing a vision or image of a project is an essential first step in the design process; all design decisions will ultimately refer back to this part of the process. These stages in the early development of a design are commonly called **analysis** and **conceptualization.** Several of the more popular names that may be given to the vision itself include **lighting scheme, lighting concept, image of light,** or **point of view.** In each case, these refer to nothing more than an image of the lighting that is envisioned for a given project.

SPECIAL CONSIDERATIONS IN LIGHTING DESIGN

One of the most difficult elements of lighting design lies in the fact that we don't get a chance to actually work with our medium (light) until very late in the design process. Everything that we produce—up to moving into a facility—can only indirectly represent a design. A **light plot** or **lighting plan** is just a tool for hanging the lights, while **storyboards** and photographs represent our intentions through another artistic media—but not in light itself. **Mock-ups** and **light labs** provide a limited representation of a design and computer **visualizations** simply represent the design in yet another indirect way. Despite all the technical knowledge that we must master, most of it allows us only to indirectly control or experience the medium of light. It isn't until we work in the venue with the actual luminaires that we begin to truly design with the real medium of light.

Time and budget form another set of conditions within which we must work. In the best situations, a lighting designer will be brought onto a project at an early stage and will have lots of time to be part of the team and to plan the project. However, lighting often isn't given serious consideration until much later than the other production elements. Other areas of a production can also fall behind schedule or could become more costly than initially planned, and the lighting department will often be asked to help make up for the shortages that these other areas have produced. I can't remember the number of times that my focus or cue-writing sessions have been cut short or even eliminated due to problems that occurred with the load-in of the scenic elements of a production. Despite these compromises, the lighting must still be created in a manner that does justice to a production. It does no good to whine about the problems. The first performance or opening must go on as scheduled, and the lighting designer needs to remain cool and collected during these stressful rehearsal times. Most importantly, we must remain flexible so that we can adjust to the bumps in the road that frequently occur throughout the production process. In reality, to a certain degree, many of us like the excitement of living on the edge that this produces.

The best remedy for coping with these unexpected occurrences lies in being completely familiar with your design and comfortable in your decisions throughout the design process. It is imperative that you have a well-developed plan so that you can react to changes as they develop. Much of this planning must happen well before moving into a facility. Time in the venue is at a premium and every decision that can be made outside of the theatre allows designers to concentrate more fully on the actual lights and levels that they are setting during the limited time that is assigned to lighting rehearsals. During these times, only decisions that require actual observation of the lighting should be dealt with; and anything that could have been set earlier, outside of the venue, should have already been worked out. This will maximize the amount of time that you can spend working in the theatre with the actual medium of light. I've frequently observed lighting designers at the design table suffering from the consequences of not making decisions like determining cue placements prior to their cue-writing sessions. Another consequence of this lack of preparation can occur when a designer creates cues alongside a director during a cue-writing session. In these cases, I've witnessed the director actually creating the cues while the designer becomes nothing more than a translator for converting the luminaires into control channels. So, in all fairness to yourself, you have to come to the design table as well-prepared as you possibly can.

DIRECTORS AND COLLABORATION

Unlike many fine artists, lighting designers do not operate in a vacuum. We are part of a team; we don't shut ourselves away in a studio as a fine artist would when creating a sculpture or painting. Our art is only one aspect of a much larger art form in which other individuals are also charged with particular aspects of a project. More importantly, as part of a design team, we must work together to create cohesive projects under the guidance of a leader who has a master vision for the final product. In entertainment projects, the director or producer fills this role. As lighting designers, we control only one aspect of a project and must work to help unify our work with all the other designers. In the entertainment world, in addition to a director this team often involves designers in the specialty areas of scenery and costumes as well as lighting. Other specialists who are also usually part of the team include sound designers, media and projection designers, property designers, and choreographers.

While each individual is charged with a given specialty, everyone works together to complete a design project. This type of teamwork is called **collaboration** and represents a very different process than that followed by many studio artists. Each member of the team responds to the ideas of the other team members and everyone works together to produce a superior product in which all of the individual elements are tied together. Through collaboration and the guidance of a director, the designers work through an approach to a project and make decisions that reinforce one another. Topics such as style, color palettes, themes, and historical detailing form just a few of the considerations that a design team will discuss in regard to a project. Team members also deal with practical concerns like budgeting, scheduling, and sharing resources such as rigging and cabling locations. In theatre, we often make reference to **unified productions,** in which all of the individual elements come together to form a single cohesive project.

Directors are charged with the most important responsibility as the team leader in these collaborative projects. While every member of the team is expected to make contributions and bring their personal ideas to a production, the directors are ultimately responsible for accepting or rejecting anything that each designer brings to a project. Directors must also be capable of motivating and inspiring their team in a way that produces the best solutions for a project. While directors want to encourage the full participation of their team, ultimately, if a director cannot be convinced to support an idea, the designer must defer to the director's judgment and should accept the director's decision to reject that idea. While directors often receive the most credit for successful productions, when a production fails, the director bears the largest amount of responsibility and bad press.

THE INFLUENCES OF LIGHT

Light influences all things. You might recall that at the beginning of the book I made a statement to the effect of, "nothing would be visible without light." In a designed environment everything that we see is due to the manner in which light is used to reveal that environment to us. The specific manner in which a subject or environment is lit can make a significant contribution to the way in which an observer perceives and responds to the environment and anything that is contained within it. In the performing arts, light is used to reveal and modify performers, their costumes, the scenery, and anything else that is associated with a production. Light might even become a design element in itself in some situations, such as when fog or haze are used in concerts or aerial productions. In fact, we rarely see the true physical qualities of many objects—only those qualities as influenced by a given set of lighting conditions. If the lighting changes, so will the appearance of these qualities and the associated objects. At this point, it is wise to review several of the basic influences of light.

Controllable Qualities of Light (Reviewed)

I noted in earlier discussions that all light can be described by means of four specific characteristics. The specific combination of these qualities makes any light unique. If any one of these are modified, the lighting itself will be changed, and the response that it creates in an observer will also be modified. Some of these variations can produce dramatic changes, while others may be quite subtle. These controllable qualities include **intensity** (brightness), **distribution** (angle and overall quality such as harshness or texture of the light), **color,** and **movement** (changes). In reality, the first three are used to describe the lighting of a given moment while movement addresses changes or transitions of the lighting from one moment to another. These qualities are used consistently as a means of describing the unique characteristics of any light throughout all areas of lighting design.

Each quality has an influence on how we perceive an object. Intensity can be used to make a subject more or less visible, direction can be used to create a more dramatic impact or to reveal textures in an object's surface, and color can be used to modify the perceived colors that are observed in an object. A lighting designer can manipulate all of the controllable qualities to create a desired response to a subject. It's important to fully understand how to manipulate these qualities since they ultimately become the lighting designer's equivalent to a fine artist's palette of paints and brushes.

Functions of Lighting (Reviewed)

Whether designing the lighting for a play, a client's garden, a house of worship, or the Radio City Music Hall's *Christmas Spectacular*, lighting is counted on to perform numerous functions within the scheme of a typical design project. Through manipulation of the controllable qualities and providing a variety of lighting functions, a designer can create a positive experience for anyone who witnesses a production. Unfortunately, just as there are good examples of lighting, there are also many examples of bad lighting where for one reason or another a designer missed the primary intent of a project and the controllable qualities were not utilized in a way that was particularly beneficial to the design. Again, to review, I want to briefly mention several significant functions of theatrical lighting. **Visibility** (or selective visibility), **establishing a scene** (setting a location or appropriate environment), **modeling** (sculpting/revealing form), **mood** (producing an emotional response), **focus** (bringing emphasis), **composition** (an arrangement of elements that may or may not unify an image), **style** (conforming to a specific visual representation), **staging the story** (facilitating the progression of events), and **rhythm** (patterns of design elements or transitions) are all specific functions that lighting can produce for a given project. A lighting designer uses the qualities of light in order to fulfill these functions. A lighting designer should always keep these functions and the controllable qualities of light in mind as they work through any design project. How can an image envisioned for a particular project be established through each of these functions and qualities? What type of mood must we create? What is the central focus of the image? How realistic does the image have to be? Is there a time frame to consider? All of these and many more questions should be considered as a designer works through the specifics of any design project.

ANALYSIS FOR LIGHTING

When I discuss analysis I am referring to defining the specific needs of a lighting project. In entertainment lighting this most commonly is associated with some form of **script analysis.** Some areas of entertainment such as opera or musical theatre may require a designer to read a score, libretto, or lyrics rather than a script (although all perform the same function). In entertainment areas that do not make use of a script, as in dance, a design is developed through observations of rehearsals and conversations with the rest of the team of associated artists. Even without a full script, some form of synopsis, project scheme, or storyboard will usually be available to aid a designer throughout the design process. While a script may play a significant role in the analysis of a dramatic production, additional elements of observation and discussion are also important to the development of a production, even more so if a script does not exist. A designer needs to become familiar with all of these techniques of analysis to ensure that the most effective design is developed for a project. Even architectural projects that at first glance appear to require little analysis benefit from a more careful examination of the design problem and a detailed analysis of the lighting needs of a specific project. Analysis is the first step in the development of a lighting scheme or concept for any project or production.

Script Analysis

Lighting analysis for most entertainment events involves a combination of several different processes. The script, if one exists, is the first place where a designer should begin their work toward developing a lighting scheme. Other elements such as attending rehearsals and production or design meetings will also help a designer grasp the approach that a director is taking for a specific production. Rehearsals allow a designer to observe blocking relationships, character associations, transitions, and specific interpretations that the director has brought to a production. This additional work is intermixed with further script analysis to determine the details that will emerge and shape the unique qualities of the show. If a script is not part of the design process a designer, must concentrate even more diligently on the information that they receive through observing rehearsals, listening to soundtracks, and having conversations with the rest of the design team. Even if a performance event does not make use of a script, a designer should still be able to analyze the piece since nearly all performance events follow some form of storyline or plot that can be analyzed in regard to themes, moods, characters, etc. Even modern dance pieces, which have a reputation for being abstract, have a conceptual framework and some sense of storyline that the choreographer is usually more than happy to share with their lighting designer. Since most productions begin with a script, the next several pages examine ways in which you can create a successful process for analyzing scripts.

Sidebar 9.1 DESIGNER PROFILE

Brian MacDevitt

Credit: photo courtesy Brian MacDevitt

Brian MacDevitt is an award-winning lighting designer who works primarily in Broadway and other commercial venues such as touring and regional theatres. With more than Broadway credits to his name, he continues to design regularly on Broadway—where his lighting designs have earned him five Tony Awards. He spent nearly 10 years designing in downtown Off- and Off-Off-Broadway theatres, where he honed his skills before landing his first shows on Broadway. While he predominantly lights dramas, he also lights musicals, dance, and other projects. He even worked on the film *The Cradle Will Rock* as Theatre Lighting Consultant. Several of his more significant Broadway and other New York credits include the 2012 revival of *Death of a Salesman* directed by Mike Nichols, *The Wedding Singer*, *A Fish in the Dark*, *A Raisin in the Sun* (with Denzel Washington), *The Color Purple*, *The Pillowman*, *Into the Woods* (2002 revival), *Urinetown: The Musical* and finally *The Book of Mormon*. New York theatre companies that he has designed for include Shakespeare in the Park, The Roundabout, Circle Repertory, Public Theatres, Playwrights Horizons, and the Manhattan Theatre Club. Several regional credits include the Mark Taper Forum, Kennedy Center for the Performing Arts, and the Yale Repertory Theatre. His lighting designs have won a number of awards, including multiple Drama Desk nominations and awards, an Obie, a Bessie Award, a number of Tony nominations, and five different Tony Awards for Best Lighting (*The Pillowman*, *Into the Woods*, a shared award for *The Coast of Utopia*, *Joe Turner's Come and Gone*, and *The Book of Mormon*). Brian also served on the faculty of SUNY Purchase and the Tisch School of Drama at New York University and is a frequent speaker at seminars like the Broadway Masters Classes. In the last 10 years he

---

has gone on to share his expertise as an Associate Professor of Theatre at the University of Maryland, where he juggles his academic duties and his design career. Often, he can be found on a train traveling between his projects in New York and his campus back in Maryland.

Brian's formal training came through pursuing a BFA in Lighting at Purchase College under the training of Bill Mintzer. Mintzer strove to prepare his students to enter the field after completing their BFA degree and felt that the MFA was unnecessary. Most of Brian's training came informally through on-the-job training by assisting Mintzer and other designers like Francis Aronson. However, he didn't want to get pigeonholed as an assistant and soon broke out to design lighting on his own. He started doing projects downtown (in lower Manhattan and in the village) and used Off and Off-Off Broadway as his training ground:

> "A major part of my training was the downtown theatre . . . Watching dance . . . understanding how to explore dream states . . . figuring out how the subconscious and unmotivated lighting could be explored through dance and other areas of lighting design."

It was over this time that Brian began to work with Tere O'Connor, who has been one of his closest collaborative partners over the last 30 years. When he finally got his opportunity to work on Broadway, he was ready for it: "It's the same thing I had been doing for 10 years . . . just a bigger audience and more production money at stake. On the other hand, Broadway gets all the resources . . . I feel spoiled now." To remain fresh he goes back to his roots and continues to light projects in small venues when he has an opportunity and where resources can be stretched, and he may even have to carry ladders around with the assistants.

Brian believes that it is important to get a good liberal arts background:

> "Art, music, and architecture are all important to lighting. Theatre makes use of my background in music and art history . . . they apply to every play that I do and I am thankful for my study in these other arts. However, there still has to be that association in how it fits with the theatre. While working on *American Buffalo* . . . I wanted to know about what was happening in Chicago at that time . . . the historical facts of that era. . . . I needed to understand what was meant by the term "American Buffalo.""

Brian also believes that much of a designer's work comes through the circle of associates that you keep company with:

> "My work comes mostly through being recommended by producers or other people that I have worked with. I want people to feel that I can light anything . . . to be comfortable in how I interpret the work and communicate it to the audience through light."

He adds, "It doesn't matter what you light . . . lighting a Bar Mitzvah should have challenges to it . . . find something out about the kid and the family . . . then channel that into the room or gallery." Location also has something to do with the type of work that a designer gets:

> "There's even something to your address. Many theatres want to see a New York address on a designer's resume—even those outside of New York. In fact, some may even want to see a Manhattan address. I actually weighed the issue when I was trying to decide between living in Manhattan or Brooklyn."

Brian considers light to be an amazing medium: "We bring and reflect energy across a stage . . . We are painters who illuminate and compose with light and bring shape and form to what already exists on a stage." He also likes the sense of control and adrenaline rush that accompanies his sitting at the design desk:

> "I love being in the hotseat and riding the edge . . . the burst of energy and ability to think clearly throughout a very stressful tech process. In many ways it's about being in the moment and trusting yourself. Light is an emotional medium and our profession is in many ways about instant gratification . . . something that is very different from most jobs in the real world."

Something that he worries about is that he feels that at times Broadway is becoming too homogenized:

> "Sometimes we try too hard to second guess the audiences . . . becoming too commercial . . . catering to the ticket-paying crowd. These days, it's easy to get locked into the commercial part of the business . . . especially anything based on music. The juke box musical now seems to be the most popular formula for gaining an audience."

In recent years, Brian has ventured into directing and producing as well as production design—not to mention his usual activities in the world of lighting design. He has now completed several projects at the Studio Theater in Washington, DC, and as of this writing was both producing and acting as production designer for a new New York City play called *Occupied Territories*. At this writing, he was also working on another revival of *Carousel*, which opened in the spring of 2018. One of the challenges that he has found is in maintaining a schedule as a full-time professor of theatre while still making himself available to take on the personal projects that he feels are essential to maintaining his career. On the other hand, he states that:

> "I've personally done pretty much everything and now feel that one of my personal thrills is seeing my former students succeed who are now themselves designing on Broadway—although it can be interesting when a former student and I have both been nominated in the same category for awards like the Tonys."

Some of those former students include lighting designers Ken Posner, Jason Lyons, and Jeff Croiter.

One of Brian's cardinal rules involves the issue of carefully paying attention to the play: "You've got to read the play. . . . It's all about the play or all about the score. There's a lot of work out there that has a different agenda than serving the piece." A pet peeve relates to his observation that it's not about the gear. He believes that moving lights are starting to dictate what is happening in color palettes on Broadway and other stages, and he wants designers to be able to tell manufacturers what gear they need for the theatre rather than having to use fixtures that have been developed for other markets like rock and roll:

> "The equipment is dictating our choices rather than the artist making a decision based on the required qualities of light. Time is also at a premium in commercial theatre. . . . You don't get invited back if you can't work within the constraints that are assigned to a show regarding crew calls and rehearsal schedules. There simply isn't time to experiment in these situations."

He recommends that if you are just getting started you should err on the efficient side:

> "Simplify and be prepared. . . . Get everything that you can in place before showing up

at the theatre. Good paperwork is essential and needs to be complete. . . . The electricians will see right through shoddy paperwork and plots."

Brian usually likes to light the scenery first, then adds in the actors and their lighting. When building cues he suggests approaching the design in the same way that a painter would work: "Start with the sky and then work forward to the performers and settings that lie in the mid-ground and then the foreground. Finally, add specials to pop out whatever has to be highlighted." He also takes pride in not stopping rehearsals very often to deal with lighting issues, fixing problems while the actors are working in the actual scene, especially when changing marks for moving light cues. All in all, he likes the speed and works best on the fly. In reality, many of the problems get ironed out during the previews. With the newer generation moving lights Brian finds that he frequently places a half-dozen of the incandescent movers on many of his shows. These are then used in a very subtle manner to move light to where it is needed on stage—in effect using them as re-focusable or momentary specials: "In many situations, the moving lights need to be used in a more subtle treatment . . . using them only to pop someone out as needed."

In closing, Brian shares his attitude toward work and the associates that he has come to work with over the years: "I have reaped the rewards of being surrounded by a number of good colleagues. When there is a problem in the lighting area, I'll take the blame, if it is warranted, because I lead the area." He also believes that you can still be a "good guy" in this business. To be trusted and honest is what's important:

> "Don't undermine other people. I probably could have been more demanding at times, but I'd rather be known as a good guy who can pull off a successful design while still making the experience worthwhile as opposed to being someone who uses confrontation to make their points and pull off their art. I think that you get better results and cooperation when you treat people decently. The work must be fun and people need to come into it with a positive attitude . . . it's infectious, and when someone comes in with a good positive attitude, the production itself will also often do better as a result of this positive interaction."

A script analysis is nothing more than a careful study of the script. A designer must evaluate many issues relating to how the script has been crafted. While a director interprets the script, it is the playwright who actually created the event. It should be obvious that the designer must find an understanding of the plot or storyline of the script, but in reality, the script analysis must go a considerable degree beyond this initial treatment. A designer must also understand the characters, their associations and motivations, the themes and stylistic intentions of the playwright, and many other qualities that may not necessarily be apparent to an audience member who will most likely only view the production once. In short, this detailed understanding of the script forms the parameters that will ultimately shape the decisions that drive the designing of the production.

Most script analysis begins with an initial reading. It is important to approach this first reading from the perspective of an audience member. This is the only time when you can approximate the reactions of an audience. Once you have read the script more than once, you begin to gain a familiarity with it that the majority of the audience members cannot have. You must try to create an experience during the first reading that bests creates the type of conditions that an audience member might experience for the play. Therefore, during the initial reading you should focus on reading the script for enjoyment. Do not be concerned with a formal script analysis or writing down any specific references to light. Try to imagine the action in a way that allows you to experience the play in a way that would be similar to how an audience might experience it. Most importantly, try to complete this initial reading in a single sitting and remove any distractions that could interrupt your reading of the play. The script isn't something to be read on a bus or subway during a daily commute or in half-hour intervals when you have a moment of spare time between other activities. Interruptions should be minimized because they prevent you from experiencing the pace and tensions that build in the script and its associated actions.

After the initial reading, designers will read and analyze a script several more times. With each reading, more specific details are discovered that will be used to refine the designer's response to the text. Significant elements affecting the lighting design will be discovered in initial readings. It may take three, four, or even more readings to establish some of the less apparent details of a script. A fairly typical process for many lighting designers calls for reading a script three or four times. However, the actual number of times that a designer reads a script can vary considerably from one project to another and can also change based on the type of project that is being designed. Regardless of the number of readings, each additional reading exposes more details that will lead to more effective decisions for creating a production's lighting.

Several tasks often associated with a second reading involve responding to specific images that you might imagine while reading the script and creating a **scenic breakdown** that lists the locations and time frames for each scene. Sidebar 9.2 provides an example of a scenic breakdown for Arthur Miller's *The Crucible*.

Sidebar 9.2 SCENIC BREAKDOWN OF ARTHUR MILLER'S *THE CRUCIBLE*

Scene #	Location/Time Reference	Light Reference
Act I, Scene 1	Bedroom in Parris's House Salem, Mass. Spring 1692	Dawn
Act I, Scene 2	Common Room of Proctor's House Eight Days Later	Dusk
Act II, Scene 1	The Wood Five Weeks Later	Night
Act II, Scene 2	Vestry of a Salem Meeting House Two Weeks Later	Middle of day
Act II, Scene 3	A Cell in a Salem Jail Three Months Later	Pre-Dawn

---

In subsequent readings the lighting designer should look at specific references to light. The designer should identify specific staging requirements such as motivational lighting needs, lighting effects, and character associations for more specific lighting demands. Places in a script that provide such information include scene synopses, stage directions or business, and any additional notes found throughout the script that document the original production. Line references (where characters make direct mention of lighting conditions) form one of the most important clues to the specific lighting needs of a production. Some of these references may be direct, such as when a character states, "Look at that burning building over there," or when they describe a specific quality of light, "Look at the golden glow of that sunset." Other references may be inferred, such as when a character speaks of a specific lighting condition ("It's now 7:00 p.m. and I don't know where John has gone.") or when a synopsis lists a scene taking place in a particular location or geographical region, a specific type of room, or if a particular weather condition is indicated. The designer should also be sensitive to the mood or emotional elements that are present throughout a script. All of these examples create conditions that provide clues to successfully lighting a play. The following paragraphs address several specific areas of script analysis that a lighting designer can use to get a better understanding of the lighting requirements of a given play.

GENRE Genre is perhaps the first place to get clues to the lighting style that might be appropriate for a given script. Genre can best be understood as a broad classification of dramatic style. The genres that most people are familiar with include comedy and tragedy (drama) and musicals. Several other genres that are less familiar to a typical audience member include melodrama, farce, and docudramas. Each genre reflects general stylistic elements or conventions that can be considered to be characteristic of that particular form of theatre. Through simple association with a given genre a specific production style may become an expectation of the final lighting design. A familiar association between lighting and genre that was followed for many years involved using brightly illuminated scenes and pink or other warmly colored gels for lighting comedies. More serious plays such as tragedies were typically associated with dark shadowy lighting and were characteristically lit with cool colors like blues, greens, and lavenders. Genres are very broad classifications of drama and lighting decisions should not be based solely on the specific genre of a production. To put things simply, be familiar with what these associations may mean for a lighting design and then go on to a more detailed analysis to further refine your design decisions.

THEMES One of the most important areas of script analysis lies in an examination of the themes that a playwright chooses to address. Most importantly, what is the author's meaning of the play? The playwright was most likely trying to convey a message to an audience. What are the major themes or messages of the play? Which themes are emphasized? Should one theme be played against another? Does a theme keep recurring throughout a script? These theme-related questions can have a significant impact on the lighting of a production. A director may choose to ignore an obvious theme of a script while choosing to focus on some of the more obscure themes that might also be present in a given piece. Symbolism may be used as a means of drawing attention to themes when elements of the play represent other larger concerns or problems. A designer should also look to see if any of the themes play to universal concerns. Plays often address issues such as aging, sacrifices of war, selfishness or greed, broken relationships, power and corruption, love interests, and abusive behaviors—all examples of universal themes. Are the themes of a play written or set in the 16th century pertinent to today's audiences? Themes form a manner in which a playwright presents a message to an audience and communicates to society. The entire design team should explore the themes as a means of aiding the playwright in delivering a message to an audience.

DRAMATIC FORM (STRUCTURE) Plays are generally crafted in a manner that provides a structure for the script. This structure creates a mechanism by which information is presented to the audience while also allowing for a logical progression of events that move the play toward its conclusion. One manner of examining a script's structure is through observing various informational events that typically occur at various points throughout the play. Most plays begin with an *exposition* in which the playwright introduces the audience to the themes, characters, and other essential information that they will need for viewing the play. The exposition often presents background information by having characters recall or talk about events that have occurred prior to the start of the play. The exposition forms a frame of reference for the play's action. Once the playwright has provided the necessary background information, they usually shift to providing the remaining information through using actual onstage action to present the event to an audience (what is frequently called the **point of attack**). We also examine a play based on its actions—both physical and emotional. The play must create some form of **conflict** in which a desire of a character may or may not be realized. We call these **objectives,** with the major dramatic conflict being the **super-objective.** What drives the action is the conflict that exists between achieving or not achieving this goal or task. Will Oedipus discover who is responsible for the plague in his kingdom? Does Godot in *Waiting for Godot* ever show up? Will a given social injustice be righted? Will the guy get the pretty girl? All of these situations form questions that can represent conflicts within a play. We may refer to these issues and actions as events that form the **dramatic spine** or **major dramatic question** of the play. Each conflict is used to draw upon an audience's inquisitiveness and to lure them into forming an interest in the play. A good play and production strives to have an audience interact with the play and have empathy for at least some of its characters. That point in the play where an audience is exposed to the major dramatic question or primary conflict is commonly called the **inciting incident.** It is at this point where the audience discovers what the play is truly about and what the major conflict of the play will become. Throughout the play, forces will work toward either achieving the primary objective/major dramatic question or preventing it from happening. The playwright then goes on to create a series of events or **actions** through which the emotional responses and tensions of an audience will vary based on how closely we come to achieving the major dramatic question. As the characters face a given conflict, the tension rises until the conflict is temporarily resolved. Then a new action and tension is introduced that will once again move toward creating further conflict within the play. We often refer to these variations in tension or emotional responses as **rising** and **falling action**. As a play progresses, the conflicts generally become more intense, while the overall level of tension steadily increases. At some point, the primary conflict of the play must be resolved and the characters either achieve or do not achieve their primary objectives and the dramatic question is answered. This point in the action is called the **climax** of the play. Once the play has reached its climax the tension will be lowered and the playwright will bring the play to a conclusion by wrapping up any remaining unfinished details or situations. This final portion of the play is typically known as the **resolution.** Figure 9.1 illustrates an example of the rising and falling action that might exist for a theoretical production of a script.

STYLE Style refers to the overall manner of presentation for a production. In reality, the style of a production comes about through the combination of a number of individual elements. The acting, directing, and visual styles are several of the primary elements that contribute to the overall sense of style for a production. It is also important for each of the individual styles to reinforce all the other elements of a production. One common method of examining style is based on the concept of realism, and we often use the degree of realism as a means of comparing one production to another. An extreme form of realism, **naturalism,** attempts to present an event in as realistic a manner as possible—down to the last detail in materials, speech patterns, acting styles, etc. As you move in the opposite direction from naturalism, style becomes more simplified and symbolic, becoming more **stylized** or abstract. In this manner, elements of a production are modified in ways that move away from a realistic mode of representation. In some cases, the images and overall style can become quite distorted. The artistic movements that were represented by schools such as impressionism,

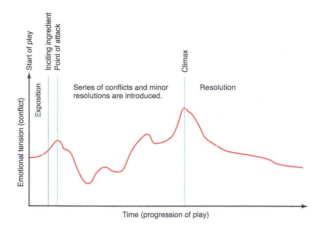

Figure 9.1 Rising and falling action. This graph plots the emotional tension (conflict) through a series of dramatic events. The actual conflicts are theoretical and only illustrate the overall relationship between conflict and a play's structure.

expressionism, and surrealism (along with many others) were nothing more than groups of artists who agreed to work within a given set of parameters of style. Because of this, their work shares a set of similarities or conventions. We may also look at **period style** as a manner of establishing or placing a production within a specific time frame. For instance, if we were to suggest that a production be set in the Renaissance, the director would look at Renaissance acting styles, while the designers would look at the clothing and architecture of that period for inspiration and historical research. A lighting designer would research light sources of that time and how productions would have been lit in that era. One of the primary tasks of a director is making sure that there is a consistent style being presented between each of the different elements of a production.

There are many places where a lighting designer can use the script as a resource for determining the overall style for a specific production. Scripts written in verse or rhyme suggest a different approach to presentation than those written in prose. Using a narrator requires a different approach than a script where all the information is presented through the characters. What is the progression from scene to scene? Do scenes progress in chronological order or are there flashback conventions used throughout the script? Are there ritualistic or symbolic elements within the text? How are these to be presented? All of these issues have an impact on the overall style that would be used to illustrate a script. While several broad elements of style may be determined through the general type or genre of script, most scripts can be produced through a variety of different styles, and the director has the responsibility for determining the overall style for a given production. With Shakespeare's plays, for example, many different stylistic approaches have been used successfully for productions of a given script. A designer should also look beyond the script to other productions of the play, as well as to other scripts that have been produced or written by the same playwright, since these plays are often written in similar styles. Style relates very closely to convention, the next form of analysis, because conventions form the rules by which a team agrees to present a production—with many of these rules ultimately determining the overall style of a production.

CONVENTIONS Every play comprises a series of experiences that expose an audience to events created by a playwright. As an audience views these experiences, they come to accept the various techniques and conventions used by the playwright and production team that make the "telling of the story" or presentation of the event possible. In short, **conventions** are methods that allow the team to present the story to an audience. Using a narrator to describe events that are not enacted for the audience, using simultaneous scenes on stage at the same time, or using blue lights for scene changes or to simulate night all form examples of common conventions that audiences are willing to accept as a normal part of a theatrical event. How might time progression be illustrated within the production? How does a team solve the logistical problem of creating all the scenes required for a production when time, space, and money are in short supply? Different styles of production are often associated with the use of specific conventions. For instance, most Shakespearean productions make use of **aside** techniques (where an actor comes to the edge of the stage and directly addresses the audience). A lighting designer will often place a special light on the actor during the time that an aside is delivered. Both conventions are widely accepted techniques for the production of these plays. Another popular lighting convention is to create a blackout between adjoining scenes. While there are a number of conventions that can be associated with the specific work of various playwrights or groups of productions, what is more important is that a production remain consistent in the conventions that are adopted throughout its presentation. The conventions form a set of ground rules or parameters within which both the creative team and audience agree to work. Making exceptions or not sticking to the conventions can confuse the audience.

CHARACTERS After the dramatic question, the characters are probably the next most important element of a play or performance event. Designers need to have a thorough understanding of every character and their motivations, and the relationships between characters. It's their struggles, conflicts, and relationships that the audience follows and it is the characters with whom the audience will develop a relationship of either empathy or hate. Is this character controlling another? What is the personal relationship between the two characters? Does this character belong to a larger group? Which character is most important at any given moment? Why does this character appear in a play? What is their dramatic function? What's this character's motivation? A designer should also develop an understanding of the personality traits of each character. Are they a slob? Are they a flirt? Are they the favorite or least favorite child of the parents? Are they soft-spoken? Should the audience like or dislike this character? Should they feel empathy for this character? If not, who should they feel empathy toward? Much of this information can be gathered through what is said in the dialogue of the play and the situations that the characters face. Even if unique character traits are not specifically expressed in the script, it is often helpful to create your own background information for the characters, as long as the information is consistent with the material already presented in the script. By creating a full history for the characters, designers can go on to use this information on **character development** as a means of approaching specific design decisions. One character may become associated with a softer or more romantic quality of lighting while another may be tied to a particular tint of color. Characters that bring conflict to a scene might be connected to a harsher, more intense form of lighting, while some roles might be identified with a particular group of characters and a specific color or mood that is shaped by the lighting. The character analysis provides a context for this design and decision-making process.

MOOD Plays often create a specific emotional response in an audience. While there may be an overall general mood or response to the play as a whole, it is also true that the mood of an audience will change throughout a play. The mood may even change several times in a single scene. There is often an association between the individual conflicts of a play and the moods that are created throughout the play. If a play is based in comedy, the mood will generally be light and airy. The lighting and other design areas will respond to this by creating designs that produce appropriate moods for specific times throughout the production. The dark, foreboding shadows that a lighting designer might produce for the final crypt scene of *Dracula* produces an appropriate atmosphere or mood for this particular scene—but those qualities would most likely be inappropriate for a comedy scene. A lighting designer must be able to identify the situations in the script that are associated with these emotional changes and needs to manipulate the lighting in a manner that reinforces these qualities. While some mood changes may be abrupt, many are subtle, and the designer must learn to modify the lighting in a manner that gently enhances these changes without necessarily calling attention to the fact that a change has been made in the lighting.

SPECIFIC REQUIREMENTS While I have chosen to leave specific requirements for last, they probably represent the easiest area of analysis for a lighting designer, and they are often the first area of script analysis that a lighting designer might complete. Specific requirements are nothing more than the lighting requirements that are actually specified by the script. These specific lighting needs may be represented through either a direct or inferred reference to the lighting. Much of this area of analysis is presented later in this chapter in the Style in Lighting discussion of **motivated** and **non-motivated lighting.** The most obvious examples are specific lighting needs that are named directly by the script. A synopsis or stage direction that describes the lighting or a specific reference to lighting in a line stated by a character is a most common example of these demands. When a character refers to the "golden color of the sun," or the "broken patterns of light cast by an overhead tree," the lighting must reflect these qualities. Action may also dictate specific lighting changes. When a character turns on a lamp or opens a window shade, the lighting needs to respond to these changes. Not quite as easy to spot, but just as important, are those lighting qualities that can be inferred from a script. The lighting of a scene that takes place in mid-July is quite different from the same scene taking place in November. Time of day and season play an enormous role in the lighting of a scene. Weather conditions provide an example of inferred lighting, and geographical location indicates yet another area of inference that plays a significant role in lighting a scene. Is the scene set in London or Los Angeles? What happens if we set the location in Panama? How might we differentiate between interior and exterior scenes? What are the light sources in the scene? Is there a characteristic image of light associated with the environment in which a scene takes place? How does the lighting for a hospital room, Gothic church, or manufacturing facility differ? All of these imply specific demands that a lighting designer must consider as they design a given project.

In summary, the script is the basic blueprint of the dramatic event and is the first place a lighting designer should explore in regard to identifying the lighting requirements of a production. While there may be direct references to lighting within a script, much of what a designer needs to know is not immediately obvious and must be gleaned through multiple readings and a detailed analysis of the script. Many times these less-obvious details don't come into focus until after further discussions with the director or direct observations of the actors in rehearsals. The principles of analysis discussed over the last several pages hold true not only for plays that make use of scripts, but also for any event that uses some form of written text; for example, the scores and librettos of musical theatre and operas are texts that can also be analyzed like a script. Even if no text or script exists, most performance events tell some form of story and can be analyzed in a manner that is similar to what has just been outlined. Ballet and even short modern dance pieces are good examples of visual forms of storytelling in which a designer's analysis will not be based on a written text. With experience, a designer can become familiar with how each of these events is analyzed, ultimately leading to more effective designs.

Analysis for Other Forms of Entertainment Design

When some form of written text does not exist, a lighting designer must find other ways to analyze a performance event. In much the same way as dance is analyzed, a designer can make observations of the piece or have extended conversations with the primary artist(s) and other collaborators to guide them in their lighting analysis. Some forms, like dance, will express their storylines through movement while others will use elements like music to tell their stories. Installation events or performance art might also be analyzed in this manner. A musician or band that performs concerts will typically create performances in which every song will have some form of storyline that is presented to an audience. In this case, the lyrics often provide the clues that a designer will need to analyze a piece. But, even without lyrics, the instrumentation, rhythms, and overall mood and transitions within the music will give a designer the information that they are seeking.

STYLE IN LIGHTING

Even though style is a specific function of lighting it is especially important to understand style as a guiding principle in determining the overall image for a project. Style on the whole refers to combining visual elements that produce a characteristic quality for the production or project. Style is something that is determined through discussions with the entire production team and not something that a lighting designer should develop on their own. We may also use style as a means of comparing and contrasting one project with another. The previous section spoke to a number of variants that are used to define the style of a production: degree of realism, themes, genre, structure of a play, etc. All of these have an impact on the overall style of the lighting as well as the other components of a performance event. Are we simplifying our image so that it contains only those elements that are absolutely essential to the action? Is historical accuracy important to the piece? Should there be a limited color palette? How are the traditional elements of design (line, form, texture, etc.) characterized? All of these questions form examples of issues that will help the lighting designer and other members of the design team define the style for a given project. Each of the designers and the director need to share a common definition of a show's production style in order to create a **unified production** that results in a successful project, with each element reinforcing all the other elements of a production.

In addition to the overall visual style, lighting can be broadly characterized by two specific types of lighting style. These can work within any other style that might be used for a particular project. The first, **motivational lighting,** seeks to anchor the lighting in a realistic element. As a rule, it has a naturalistic quality and attempts to approach the lighting from a perspective that represents how the light would appear if coming from a natural light source. Luminaires are linked to actual objects such as sunlight, an overhead chandelier, or a fire effect, and the resulting lighting is suggestive of how these sources are observed naturally. Colors, highlights, shadows, and any movement would be based on the natural occurrences of these light sources and the lighting should appear to be created or driven by these sources. A special form of this lighting is represented by those occasions when the light sources can actually be observed on stage. These are known as **motivating sources** or **motivating light**, and several common examples include placing candles or lanterns on stage, having actors use flashlights, locating a fire somewhere within a setting, and placing lighting fixtures such as wall sconces, table lamps, or chandeliers directly on a set. While these sources are in plain view, motivational lighting does not necessarily require an observer to actually see the light source. In these cases, the lighting may

simply give the appearance of coming from a particular source without actually revealing the source itself on stage. This is called **motivated lighting** and is represented by examples like sunlight streaming through a doorway or window, a room being lit from above despite the lack of an overhead fixture like a chandelier, or a field being lit by the sun that has been located somewhere behind the audience and from the rear of the auditorium.

Motivated lighting may be used to reinforce any motivating light sources that are present in a given setting. This is common since many motivating light sources are either too weak to produce a level of illumination required to light a theatrical scene on their own or produce too much glare as a concentrated light source when lit as part of a stage composition. I always take several precautions when I use **practicals** (working light sources) on stage. First, I assign the practical fixtures to a dimmer so that I can control the brightness and glare of the source. I also often replace the fixture's lamp(s) with one(s) of relatively small wattages as a further means of not only avoiding glare but also of providing a larger range of control through the dimmer (higher wattage lamps at very low intensity settings have a tendency to flicker at levels below 10–15%). The independent dimmer assignment also allows me to control the light through the console, making it less difficult to coordinate actions with any performers who are required to turn the associated lights on or off. If at all possible, it is always better to create a system where the performers simply mimic any changes to the practicals or light switches on a stage. This setup also prevents the problems associated with tracking whether a practical is on or off at any specific point in a performance and should eliminate the need for resetting switches between scenes or act breaks. Most importantly, I add stage luminaires as a form of **accent lighting** that supplement the practicals that are seen on the stage. These luminaires provide the light that is actually required for producing the effect of the practicals and are hung in a way that suggests that the light is actually coming from the practical light sources. Through these techniques, light can be made to appear as if it is coming from the practicals while at the same time avoiding the drawbacks of using the actual sources alone to create this illusion.

Finally, there may also be **non-motivated lighting** where the lighting is not tied to an apparent light source at all. In this case, the lighting is based on an emotional response, mood, or symbolic element of the play and the designer isn't overly concerned with producing a realistic response in the design. Instead, the lighting is approached more from a thematic or symbolic basis. The lighting observed during most pop concerts or frequently associated with events like Cirque du Soleil productions, in which the production is clearly presentational or contains a high degree of spectacle, form good examples of this non-motivated lighting style. In reality, just as there are degrees of realism, there are also extremes at which lighting may exist between motivated and non-motivated lighting styles. A designer may even begin a lighting scheme based on a motivated design approach that eventually becomes exaggerated and shifts to a more abstract non-motivated variation of the initial style. An example of this would be when a dream sequence is created within an otherwise realistically designed setting.

CONCEPTUALIZATION

Conceptualization refers to an approach to a design problem. Issues such as style, themes, and the overall framework of a production are determined through conceptualization. In the entertainment world, the person in charge of the project is typically a director who is responsible for guiding the team through the conceptualization process. Initially, the director presents a series of guidelines or personal interpretations of the script or event that are used to shape each of the other team members' contributions to the production. Often this is presented through a statement known as a **director's concept** in which issues such as themes and meaning, character analysis and associations, placement of the time and locale of the production, and a specific interpretation of the script are presented. The degree of realism or amount of stylization or abstraction and any symbolism within a production are also considered in most directors' concepts. Production teams may also make use of **metaphors** as a manner of representing specific meanings within a script—a metaphor being a figure of speech in which an object or series of words are used figuratively to represent or make comparisons or create meanings between various objects. One example of a metaphor would be equating Juliet in *Romeo and Juliet* with light.

The **concept** represents a series of parameters or conditions through which the team explores and answers specific production demands for a project. Simply put, the concept gives the context from which all other elements of the production are shaped and becomes an approach to a production. As an example of working with a concept, consider a director who might wish to equate the character of Juliet with an association of light as given in the metaphor that was just mentioned for a production of *Romeo and Juliet*. Light could be thought of as a metaphor for truth or knowledge or as a symbol of innocence and first love. Regardless of personal interpretation, each of the members of the design team would search for manners to associate Juliet with the element of light. A scenic designer might provide scenes in which she is featured with structures that reinforce natural lighting conditions, even to the point of working practical light sources such as torches, firelight, or lanterns into Juliet's scenes. The scenic designer might also introduce warm color tones into those scenes in which Juliet plays a significant role. A costume designer could clothe her in colors that are suggestive of flame or fire, while the lighting designer could tint all of her scenes with warm light. The lighting designer might go even further and place her in specials that are gelled in pink, orange, or yellow colored light. If the design team remains true to the director's approach or concept, each member represents an individual design concept that reinforces the director's concept, which in turn should produce a unified production. All design decisions made by each of the designers should then be examined and based upon information that supports the design concept for each area and overall concept for the entire production.

ADDITIONAL DESIGNER PREPARATION

While it is important to understand the script, score, or written text, and underlying needs and principles of a particular design, there are a number of additional areas that a designer should also explore as they create the lighting scheme or concept for a production. Even though the script forms the basis of the design, it by no means should be the only source of input for a design. Discussions with other members of the design team, rehearsals, and design research are additional areas of study where further analysis is required for completing a successful design.

Design Research

Research is an important element of the design process and is most commonly displayed through developing some form of visual research for a project. Visual research is nothing more than exploring visual examples or references for a design. Photographs, paintings, sketches, and actual objects such as artifacts or architectural elements like door or window treatments are all examples of visual research. In lighting, visual research might include the quality of light suggested by a Vermeer painting, a site visit to observe the light in a particular type of room or setting, or a photograph of a sunset in a particular distant location. Verbal descriptions or examples of lighting can be used but may cause confusion and can often be misunderstood. This can lead to unwanted surprises as it becomes apparent that the director and designer have had a different understanding of the lighting. The best way to get an accurate response and understanding between a designer and the rest of the production team is to expose everyone to a number of examples of visual research. By doing this, the designer will not only be able to identify their personal preferences for a design, but will also be able to narrow down specific choices with a director as comparisons are made between different images. Photographs or illustrations of similar productions, examples of art for visual inspiration, or even technical data are all areas of research that should be explored each time a designer approaches a new assignment. Visual research is especially important for providing examples of an intended lighting effect. Important information can also be learned through carefully listening to the responses that a director makes to a particular visual reference. The old saying, "A picture is worth a thousand words," is especially appropriate for lighting design since conversations often leave plenty of room for misinterpretation and we rarely have the means to illustrate or experiment with our choices in actual light. These visual illustrations form one concrete manner of communicating the designer's intentions to a director while also providing a sampling of analysis for a production.

VISUAL REFERENCES   Visual references form the most important type of research that a lighting designer can provide to a director or client. In an area where verbal communication can lead to bad communication, a photograph can provide a clear example of an intended lighting condition. While it is rare that a single visual source will reflect the exact qualities that a designer may want to bring to a specific project, a visual reference provides an opportunity for the director and designer to talk about the lighting in a more tangible manner than through using words to describe a mental image of light. More importantly, by viewing and comparing images, a director and designer can come to a common understanding of the specific look that the designer envisions for a particular scene or moment. Paintings, photographs, sketches, films, and videos all form examples of sources that a designer may explore for specific images of light. It is quite common for me to present a director with numerous images that we use as a means of sorting out what qualities of light would be most appropriate for a given moment, scene, or overall image for a play. Directors can contribute to the process by providing their own examples of visual research to a lighting designer. When I lit a recent Off-Broadway production of *The Maids*, the director asked me to become familiar with images of the film noir style. These were black-and-white films produced in the 1940s and '50s that had a rather harsh quality of lighting with strong contrasts, well-defined shadows, and up-light as common lighting qualities. The director asked me to watch *The Third Man*, *Double Indemnity*, and *The Big Sleep* prior to our first meeting. Many painters, such as the Dutch Masters, can also serve as great illustrations of

lighting within an image—though on occasion you might run into situations where the lighting that has been painted doesn't necessarily follow the laws of physics. However, these images can still be valuable for representing the general tone and feeling of the lighting. Visual references are good not only for communicating ideas to the rest of the design team but also for exposing a designer to a variety of images that can serve as inspiration. These images can then be used to help discover appropriate choices that might influence or be incorporated into the final lighting design.

PERIOD RESEARCH   Period research simply refers to examining a project within the context of the time period in which the event is to be set. If a play is to be set at night in a Depression-era farm house, the interior lighting would most likely reflect the qualities of kerosene lanterns. If the setting is changed to nighttime in ancient Greece, the lighting designer will need to become familiar with the torchlight that these plays would have been presented under. I once designed a production that was based on a historical presentation of the ancient Kuttiyattum rituals that are traditionally performed as temple dramas in South India. These productions are typically performed only in temples under a single light source in the form of an oil lamp that is placed on the floor at the extreme down center location of the stage. The lamp is lit and extinguished as part of the performance ritual. Therefore, the lighting for the production had to appear as if it was tied to this motivational light source. While the most common form of historical research relates to identifying how the light may have appeared or been created for a given time period, there are other aspects of period research that a lighting designer should consider when lighting a project. What were the performance conventions for a given time period? Were chandeliers hoisted into place at the beginning of a performance? What were the conventions for illustrating nighttime? Does the play fit within a period that dictates a given style of presentation (e.g., the demands of an expressionistic play versus a realistic play)? How does this play relate to other plays that were written by a given playwright or others of a particular era? All of these form examples of questions that relate to how period research should play a significant role in the design process.

TECHNICAL RESEARCH Most designers conduct technical research as a way of facilitating the practical decisions of translating a lighting concept into actual choices of luminaires and other equipment that will be used to create a design. The most common form of technical research is going to the product literature while making selections of the actual luminaires that will be used throughout a design. **Cut sheets** are used to identify specific lighting instruments with optical qualities that will match the requirements of a particular concept. These materials allow designers to easily compare characteristics such as quality of light, beam distribution, luminaire output, and throw distances. If a designer does not have a particular binder containing the specific cut sheets for the fixtures that are under consideration for an application, the information can still be obtained in a variety of other ways. Single cut sheets can be obtained by request through a lighting distributor or manufacturer and are also usually available directly from a manufacturer's website. There are also specialized resources such as Robert Mumm's *Photometrics Handbook* or John McKernon's Beamwright software that provide comparative data for luminaires. Both references present data in a common format that allows for making easy comparisons between luminaires of different styles as well as from a variety of different manufacturers. Reference literature and materials are not limited to the luminaires themselves—information is also available for dimmer specifications, lighting consoles and control equipment, gel, and even wire and other electrical hardware. In addition to specification literature, a designer can access application guidelines, product/instructional manuals, testimonials, blogs, safety information, data studies, and a host of other reference materials to support the design process.

In addition to researching specific lighting equipment, a designer must also conduct research in regard to the physical characteristics of the production venue. Most facilities that are a home to a production organization or function as a road or touring house have a standard informational packet that provides floorplans, sections, and other critical information that a designer will need to know in regard to designing in that venue. Today, many organizations have this information posted on their facility's website. In addition to the master plans, these packets typically contain information regarding hanging positions, number and location of in-house circuits, lineset schedules, and the dimming/control equipment that is available—all form several of the more obvious areas in which a lighting designer needs to gain important information about a particular facility. Just a few of the additional technical areas that should be examined by the designer include the power and company switches available, any in-house lighting inventory, arbor capacities (the maximum load/weight that a batton can carry—which ultimately determines how many lighting instruments can be hung on it), crewing requirements, budget, and loading access to the venue.

Design and Production Meetings

Design meetings and **production meetings** present some of the most important opportunities for a lighting designer to gather information that will shape the design of a project. These meetings are attended by all of the principal individuals who are involved in a project. Design meetings occur fairly early in the process and provide an opportunity for the entire design team to share and discuss a project. While a director is generally responsible for facilitating the meeting, each individual designer is expected to bring something to the table. A lighting designer is often reactive during these presentations since other parts of a production must generally be agreed on prior to determining how to light the project. Other designers will present renderings, sketches, plans, or even models to communicate their design intentions to the rest of the production team. However, the lighting designer should respond to these designs and must feel free to become an active participant in these discussions. The lighting designer should add to the collaborative effort by expressing their ideas and concerns while providing insight into how the lighting might impact the other designs. Once further along, these meetings offer opportunities for a lighting designer to share their ideas for lighting a project by making presentations that illustrate their personal research and design intentions. These meetings are critical for developing an understanding of the visual representation of a project. The overall concept, along with the individual design concepts for each area, comprise the primary area of discussion during these meetings. More importantly, issues related to unity and how the individual design components fit together as a whole are major objectives of these meetings. Although design and production meetings bring all of the individual collaborators together, these meetings cannot replace additional one-on-one discussions between the director and other designers. While these meetings are typically conducted with everyone in physical attendance, when designers are brought in from out of town, a producer will often not want to pay the additional travel and hotel costs of bringing everyone to a common site for these meetings. In these cases, we use technologies such as conference calls and Skype to bring members of the team who can't travel to a meeting; in addition, we use e-mail attachments and electronic drop boxes to share files of our research and other materials with members of the production team.

Production meetings follow design meetings but are typically more concerned with the practical elements of mounting a production. While topics related to artistic concerns may come into these discussions, the majority of these meetings are concerned with the logistics of getting a project up and running. Scheduling, practical issues related to working out details between production areas, and progress reports form typical concerns that are addressed during these meetings. Production meetings occur much closer to the completion of a project and are frequently scheduled on a weekly basis. Design meetings are scheduled on a more irregular basis much earlier in the production process. Often, several weeks are also allowed between design meetings to give designers time to work on designing their specific elements of the project. In most cases, design meetings are completed and the designs are finalized before a project moves into actual production. After that, the team shifts to conducting regular production meetings.

Rehearsals

Rehearsals provide another important opportunity for a lighting designer to gain a more in-depth understanding of a play. It is through rehearsals that a designer can directly observe actor movements and blocking, methods of line delivery, and specific staging that a director has chosen for a play. Rehearsals also allow a designer to gain an understanding of the moods, focus, pace, and transitions that a director is developing for a piece. On the whole, the more rehearsals that a lighting designer can observe, the more prepared that they will be for lighting a production. However, some rehearsals are much more productive for a lighting designer to observe than others. As a rule, **working rehearsals** are not productive for a designer and should generally be avoided. It does a designer no good to spend an entire rehearsal watching a director work and rework the same three pages of a script over and over. It's not only a waste of a designer's time, but also can lead to confusion in how the final version of the staging was actually set or locked in. Instead, a lighting designer is much better served by attending **run-through rehearsals** in which a segment of the play is run from beginning to end without interruption. A run-through doesn't necessarily require that the entire play be run; it might involve the rehearsal of an entire act, several adjoining scenes, or even a single scene. Designers should understand that it is a luxury to observe actors working on the actual set or within the theatre where a production will be mounted. While many universities can provide this experience, most professional situations operate using the more economical practice of minimizing the time in which the actual theatre is made available to a new production. This is due to the simple fact that every day of renting a theatre without a paying audience means lost income to a production organization. In most cases, rehearsals are conducted in rehearsal halls and studios where rental fees are substantially lower than those of a theatre. The traditional practice is to not move into the theatre until just before the first technical rehearsal.

While university theatres typically have an open rehearsal policy where a designer may come and go as often as desired, this frequently isn't the case in commercial theatre operations. Even though directors are happy to have a designer at as many rehearsals as possible, economics generally prevents this from happening. This is especially true when a designer is being brought in from out of town. There just isn't money to pay for the transportation and other related costs of putting up a designer for many days outside of the time that they are actually required to be in residence for the technical and dress rehearsals as well as any preview performances. Due to this, a lighting designer must develop a method of recording the rehearsal information that they will later need for creating the light plot and other materials related to a lighting design. This must also be done as quickly and efficiently as possible. Directors will not stop a rehearsal to repeat a segment of action or to respond to a question posed by a designer. I am often brought in to observe only one or two run-throughs prior to moving the lights into a theatre. In fact, in the professional arena I have frequently had to develop the light plot without seeing a run-through at all. In this case, I rely very heavily on my personal script analysis, research, and the conversations that I have had with the director and other members of the production team.

I have used a number of different manners of documenting rehearsals over the years, but I have found that the two most effective techniques are relatively simple. Both provide me with the information that I will later need to reconstruct the events or actions of the production as I work through the design somewhere away from the rehearsal hall or theatre. The first technique I use is to obtain video recordings. Video often provides one of the easiest means of recording the movements of the performers and documenting these rehearsals. When I have designed for dance while being located away from rehearsals I have often been mailed a video copy of the ballet or other pieces to be performed for a given production. This allows me to get the information that I require even though I could not be brought in to observe the actual rehearsals. This also provides a complete record of the event and can be very useful not only for keeping track of the movement patterns but also the transitions and mood changes that exist throughout a piece. The biggest disadvantage with using recordings is that it may be difficult to locate specific moments in a piece, which means that the information isn't immediately accessible. You must also have the video gear around to gain access to this information.

A second technique that I use is based on a variation of dance or blocking **notation**. As I observe a

Figure 9.2a Blocking notation for lighting design. a. A page of notation from a production of *Titus Andronicus*.

rehearsal, I produce floorplan sketches of a scene that form a record of the movement patterns of the performers. This isn't much different from the way in which the blocking might be recorded in a prompt script by a stage manager. A method that works particularly well for me involves dividing a page in half vertically (to form two columns) and creating six to eight floorplan sketches of a scene on each page. Room is left between each sketch for written notations that will also be made in regard to the blocking. All major actor movements are sketched on the floorplans using lines and arrows that document

the blocking while also giving me an understanding of the physical location of each of the principal characters for every moment of the play. Principal characters are generally indicated in their location by a letter within a circle that indicates the initial of the character's name. Secondary characters or extras are simply marked with an "x" as a means of documenting the stage picture. If a sequence of movement patterns occur within a single image, numbers will be added to indicate the progression of events. The page number(s) of the script that correspond to each major composition are recorded

Figure 9.2b A page of notation from a production of King Lear. This is a more formal style of photocopying miniature floorplans onto a series of master sheets to which you only have to track the blocking.

to the left of each image and additional details may be noted just below each diagram. Figure 9.2 illustrates this notation. While this doesn't provide the complete record of a rehearsal that a video can produce, it is an excellent method of documenting the primary compositional moments of the play. When I am working through the notation at a later time to write a cue synopsis or when working on the actual cues in the theatre, this method allows me to quickly identify specific moments of the play. It also provides a direct reference to the corresponding script. The system is especially useful for productions such as musicals where the stage composition undergoes frequent changes. In most cases, I can get a solid record of most, if not all, of the performer movements during a single run-through of even complex dance or musical pieces. This technique takes practice, but with time most designers become proficient at recording the movements of the performers. While Figure 9.2b displays fairly formal, well-drafted floorplans, quick sketches are just as adequate for recording the blocking information. Figure 9.2a illustrates a page of notation using this more informal style.

Developing Lighting Schemes and Concepts

A **lighting scheme** or **lighting concept** is nothing more than a specific approach to a lighting project or problem. Lighting schemes tend to be associated with architectural projects, while lighting concepts tend to be connected to performance or entertainment-related events. Once an overall concept has been developed for a project, the lighting designer will go on to develop the specific lighting concept for their design. This is accomplished through a more detailed analysis of the play, observing rehearsals, and having in-depth discussions with the director and other team members. The lighting concept should be based on the overall production concept while also outlining the particular manner in which the transitions and individual scenes will be lit by the designer. A general discussion of the qualities of light for the major moments or scenes should form the most significant portion of a lighting concept. What is the overall lighting style? What's the mood? Is it realistic? Where are we geographically? What time of day is it? What season is it? What's the weather like? If the lighting is motivational, what are the light sources? If not, what is driving the lighting? Are there symbolic connections to be expressed through the lighting? How are transitions managed? What lighting conventions will be established for this production? These are all specific considerations that a lighting concept should address. At this point in the process, individual lighting qualities should be described visually rather than becoming overly technical. This is not the place to discuss whether a luminaire is gelled with an R-83 or L-120 or whether a particular channel will be used. Instead, references should be on the order of specifying a deep blue color for the light. The lighting concept represents an approach for lighting a project; once completed, it will be used as a point of reference for the designer to work from while actually designing the lighting and making specific selections of fixtures, colors, and hanging positions. Every lighting project, whether for an entertainment event or permanent installation, should make use of a lighting concept for providing guiding principles for the realization of the design. Projects that have weak concepts are frequently not as successful as those projects for which a carefully considered scheme or concept has been developed.

Lighting Keys

One of the first concrete decisions that a lighting designer often makes in regard to a lighting design usually involves creating some form of **lighting key.** A lighting key is a visual representation of the primary lighting angles and colors to be used as an overall scheme for lighting a scene or project. A typical lighting key presents a plan view from directly above a central point that represents a performer or subject. This reference point is generally indicated with a hatch mark. Directional arrows are then drawn around this point to indicate the directions from which light will be focused onto the subject. A lighting designer will also make an indication of the colors of the lights that will be coming from each of these angles. This color may be expressed in terms of a general hue or color description but is more commonly indicated by a specific color of gel (by gel number). In some cases, designers may go further and might also indicate an approximate intensity level (by percent) for the light coming from each direction. Figure 9.3 illustrates two different lighting keys. These keys are representative of the basic **washes** that strike a subject and should not be thought of as an indication of individual luminaires (they are a representation of the lighting that essentially covers the entire stage). The choices of angle and color that are used in a lighting key should be directly related to the

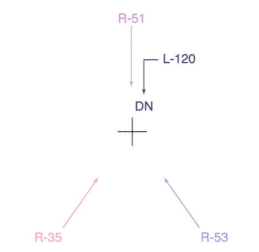

Figure 9.3a Color keys for a production of *Noises Off*. a. Interior box setting (Act I and III)

Figure 9.3b Backstage (Act II)

lighting concept that was developed earlier. While the most common view associated with lighting keys is from above, I have found that the technique may be expanded to include two sectional views that provide additional views of the subject from the front and side. In a situation where there is a single overall lighting scheme, such as what might occur in a single setting where there are no significant lighting changes, the lighting key is illustrated through a single diagram. On the other hand, in a production with multiple scenes and several lighting schemes, a different lighting key may be developed for each scene or significant **moment** of the show. A moment represents a single point in time where all of the elements of a stage image are frozen or recorded—much like taking a snapshot of the stage composition. Another common technique involves providing a general or overall composite lighting key for an entire production rather than creating lighting keys for each scene or crucial moment. It is not necessary to create a lighting key for every moment; the gaps and transitions between these moments are dealt with at a much later time.

The lighting keys become important elements for guiding the designer through the process of creating the light plot, which is the next step in the design process. Everything related to the lighting and its design ultimately should begin with this vision of light. Even if a lighting key is not formally represented on a piece of paper, the lighting designer should have thought through the process of creating the lighting key. This approach to lighting design is significantly different from

earlier approaches, when basic illumination was developed through a couple of set formulas or techniques and then modified for the needs of an individual production. What is important at this stage is that the designer has a strong image for guiding the rest of the design process.

Sidebar 9.3 DEVELOPMENT OF A LIGHTING KEY

1. Identify the wash lighting systems that will be used to light the majority (if not all) of the areas across the stage. These washes should reference both color and distribution angles.
2. Place a hatch mark at the center of the color key that will represent a top view from directly above a performers head.
3. Place arrows with color or gel labels around the hatch mark to indicate the approximate floorplan angles from which the color washes are focused onto the performer.

COMMUNICATING DESIGN IDEAS

The majority of this chapter has focused on a number of ways in which a lighting designer analyzes a design problem and works through the process of determining a specific image of light for a project. The resulting design may remain static but more often is dynamic, changing many times over a given period of time. Regardless of whether a project is dynamic or static, each image relates to a specific combination of lighting qualities that the designer believes best represents or enhances the needs of a production at any given time. Even with the best analysis and concept, a design may still fail due to the designer either not being able to realize or produce the intended image(s) or not successfully communicating the proposed lighting to their collaborators. Although the following methods are best known for communicating a lighting designer's intentions to the rest of the design team, they can also be used by lighting designers themselves as a tool for discovering and defining the qualities of light associated with particular moments of a play. Again, it must be emphasized that communicating lighting intentions through any other means than actual light increases the chances for miscommunication of the design idea.

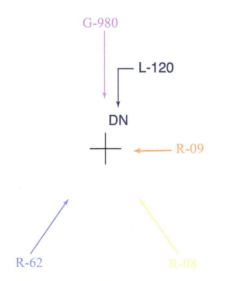

Figure 9.4 In this example: The R-08 (SL) color wash and R-62 (SR) color wash are striking the performer at opposing 45° angles while there is a R-09 sidelight wash coming from SL and a G-980 being used as a backlight. There also is a L-120 downlight wash. The assumption is that a performer will be able to be lit with each of these washes from anywhere on stage.

Image Research

Much of this has already been addressed earlier in reference to the personal research that a lighting designer may undertake while preparing for a production's design and conceptual meetings. Photographs, original artwork such as paintings and sketches, and media images from video and film programs can all be used for communicating design intentions to a director and other collaborators. On occasion, this communication may even include the viewing of other productions and performance events that are similar to the project that is being designed. The important issue is to show examples of the ideas to be conveyed to the director and other members of the design team.

Storyboards

Storyboards are pictorial representations of all the stage components, including the lighting, for specific moments of a production. These images are based on a perspective sketch of the stage and often take on qualities that are similar to a miniature rendering. A typical format for a storyboard is between 4 × 6 inches to 8 1/2 × 11 inches in size. The images may be produced in full color but can also be represented by simple black-and-white value studies. In the latter case, white represents light as illuminated by the light sources while black and grays represent shadow areas and textures. Common media for creating storyboards include pastels and colored pencils. Markers may also be used for producing storyboards. Light can be quickly rendered without much need for elaborate proficiency with the medium. While some designers may use white paper as a base for their storyboards many lighting designers prefer to use black paper or illustration board because of the increased theatricality represented by the negative space. In this case, each line or shaded area can be equated to an illustration of actual light as it strikes and reveals an object (Figure 9.5).

The lighting key is used as a resource for determining the specific lighting qualities that are reflected in a storyboard. It is fairly common for lighting designers to produce a collection of storyboards for several of the most significant moments of a production. Figure 9.6 illustrates two black-and-white storyboards that were done for two different scenes for a production of *Cabaret*. Figure 9.7 provides several color storyboards for a production of *Henry IV (Part I)*.

While creating storyboards requires a lighting designer to be proficient at drawing and rendering, there are alternate ways of communicating design intentions for those who are not confident in their traditional artistic skills. For these designers, one method of working around this is to spend time developing a single good line drawing of the image, which is then photocopied onto a number of individual pages (including black construction paper). These are then used as a base drawing upon which the lighting is added (Figure 9.5). With this technique, much of the time (and angst) involved in drawing and redrawing the scene are eliminated, and the lighting designer can churn out a number of storyboards, saving the storyboards that are appropriate and discarding those that aren't as successful. Variations of this technique make use of computer software like Adobe Photoshop to create storyboards (Figure 9.8). In this case, digital photographs are taken of the scenic model (or the renderings are scanned/photographed) and then manipulated to produce electronic storyboards that can be printed or e-mailed to members of the production team.

Lighting Scores

As an alternative to storyboards, **lighting scores** may provide an avenue by which a lighting designer can communicate the specific lighting qualities found on stage at specific moments of a production while avoiding the need to become proficient in the use of art media.

Figure 9.5 A storyboard using colored pastels and pencils on black construction paper

Credit: Storyboard by R. Dunham based off of a sketch provided by Thomas Schraider.

Figure 9.6a Lighting storyboards for Music Theatre North's production of *Cabaret*. Storyboards by R. Dunham and scenic design by Michael E. Daughtry. a. Cliff's Apartment

Figure 9.6b Finale

A lighting score (Figure 9.9) is best represented in a table format. It lists specific moments or scenes along one axis while associated lighting functions and properties are identified and characterized along the opposing axis. Several functions that are commonly found in a lighting score include time of day, physical setting, sources, intensity, focus, primary light source or key, and mood. Many of these qualities, such as intensity or key, may be represented with a simple visual representation or diagram.

Figure 9.7a Lighting storyboards for a production of *King Henry IV (Part I)*. Storyboards by R. Dunham and scenic design by Russell Hastings. a. Tavern Scene

Figure 9.7b King's Encampment

Figure 9.7c Henry versus Hotspur Final, Battle

Light Labs

Light labs can be created for either full or miniature representations of the lighting for a stage. Most university theatres have some form of light lab where luminaires can be hung and gelled with the actual colors that would be used for a design project. These labs also usually provide a way to dim the luminaires so that a designer can play with color mixing, contrast ratios between different light sources, and the red-shift effect of using lamps at lower intensities. Since the lab actually works with light, it represents a much more accurate means of displaying the intent of a lighting designer. More importantly, light labs allow a designer

Figure 9.8 A digital storyboard of *Lend Me a Tenor* created with Photoshop.

Production OTHELLO Act V-2	(DESDEMONA BED CHAMBERS) SCENE OPENS	W/ OTHELLO ENT	W/ OTHELLO X TO LET EMILIA INTO ROOM
Blocking (D) = DESDEMONA (O) = OTHELLO (E) = EMILIA	HALL / TABLE / MOONLIGHT / (D) ASLEEP IN BED	(O) ENTER W/CANDLE AND PLACES IT ON TABLE	AFTER (O) CLOSES DRAPES
Time/Location	MIDDLE OF NIGHT DESDEMONA'S BED CHAMBER	⟶	
Tension and Pace	CONFLICT IS HIGH (NEAR CLIMAX)	BUILDS W/ CONFLICT AS (O) CONFRONTS (D)	SOME RESOLUTION BUT NEW CONFLICT DEVELOPS W/ (E) ENT.
Key	MOONLIGHT ENTERING ROOM THROUGH WIND. HIGH WIND	ADD CANDLE + WARM ACCENT FOR MOTIVATED SOURCE LOW	BUILD ROOM BLUES (BOTH SIDES A TOUCH) FOR VISIBILITY — KEEP SHADOWY BUILD ACCENT A TOUCH
Intensity	② LOW / DEEP SHADOWS W/ EXCEPTION OF MOONLIGHT THROUGH WIN.	BUILD (3.5-4") ADD ACCENT TO BED AREA	BUILD OVERALL LEVELS A TOUCH (4-4.5)
Color	DEEP BLUE BASE W/ LIGHT RAW MOONLIGHT ACCENT	ADD GOLDEN ACCENT FOR CANDLE LIGHT	KEEP ROOM COOL AND SHADOWY EXCEPT CANDLE ACCENT
Mood	- FOREBODING - DARK / MYSTERIOUS - SINISTER	INTENSIFY ⟶	
Focus	(D) LYING ASLEEP IN BED	PULL FOCUS TO BED AREA (W/ CANDLE ACCENT)	OPEN UP TO MORE OF ROOM
Practicals	N/A	CANDLE W/ OTHELLO	KEEP CANDLE AND ACCENT US
Effects	N/A	N/A	N/A

Figure 9.9 A lighting score: This score plots the first few moments of Act V, Scene 2 of *Othello*, in which Othello murders Desdemona. Each column represents a new moment, while the rows provide specific information regarding each moment and their associated qualities of light.

to experiment and to make comparisons between different design solutions while also studying the true effect of the lights on other design elements like costumes and scenic materials. The size of the lab is irrelevant. While many light labs make use of regular theatrical luminaires, the actual space can vary considerably. What's important is having the option to work with light, regardless of size.

In addition to the luminaires, a light lab usually provides a control system of 6–12 theatrical dimmers set within a space that has an easily accessible grid (approximately 8 feet in height). In more limited situations, I have created labs using birdies or inkies in a space as small as a stairwell, with dimmers that were bought off the shelf from a hardware store. In these cases, materials are simply placed on a table top while the dimmers are powered from a common wall outlet.

Model Theatres

Model light labs have also been created with figures or even scaled models of a production's sets that are lit using a variety of luminaires. In the simplest cases, birdies, inkies, or other small display luminaires are hung in various locations around the set or subject. These units' colors can then be altered with gel. The intensities can usually be modified with some elementary dimming system—often, as simply as the basic radial dimmers that can be purchased at any hardware store. Yeagerlabs has created a special 1:6 scale lab theatre (Figure 9.10) that makes use of specially crafted framing and lighting packages that light subjects or model sets in a very successful imitation of how the lighting would appear if actually mounted onstage. The model lab can be purchased with several different equipment options that even have scaled draperies, different lighting packages (some even with miniature moving lights) and a full

dimming system. Another relatively new model theatre, the LightBox, makes use of specialized heads that are outfitted with fiber-optic cables (see Figure 9.11). This lab also works on a miniature scale, and it is used in conjunction with the models that scenic designers build. It, too, can have the luminaires colored and run through a dimming system. In addition to being used as a production resource, model theatres are also used as teaching tools.

Architectural practices also use light labs and **mockups** to experiment with fixture designs, wattage, color temperature specifications, and mounting positions that are being considered for a given design application. In a mockup, the actual luminaires that are being considered for an application will be used in a simulated or temporary onsite installation that replicates how the units might be used in the final installation. In residential landscape lighting it is a common practice to take several luminaires to a client's home to demonstrate the effect of different fixtures and mounting positions on the building and associated landscape before specifying and installing a lighting system.

Computer Design Analysis

Software that is created predominantly for design analysis helps a designer to see and understand light in a given application. While this software may be used as part of the design analysis for a specific situation, these products are also excellent learning tools for designers who are just beginning to work with photometrics and color theory. Although some of these packages are designed

Figure 9.11 LightBox by Thematics. A miniature fiber-optic model theatre using the LightBox Model Lighting System for Syracuse University. Scenic models are placed within the structure and are lit by miniature fiber-optic heads that are scaled optically to actual stage luminaires. The system can be colored and is controlled by a standard console that allows the actual cues to be pre-programmed and simulated.

Credit: photo courtesy Syracuse University

Figure 9.10 Yeagerlabs 1:6 Scale Model Lab Theatre

Credit: photo courtesy Yeagerlabs

around a particular company's product line (especially in the case of architectural applications), there are others that are representative of the entire industry. Many of these packages even include lighting equipment that can still be found in some theatres even though the manufacturer is no longer in business.

The first type of examination in which designers use design analysis software concentrates on the effects of distribution, throw distance, and the photometrics of a design. A luminaire is selected and placed at a given trim and distance from a target, while a cone of light resembling the beam is drawn in a particular view (usually sectional). The program plots the beam pattern and uses photometric data to calculate the intensity (footcandles) that would be present at the target. By examining the distribution patterns and intensity levels, a designer can make an appropriate selection of both luminaire and hanging position for a given situation. Additional details like lamp combinations, hanging weight, and accessories are also provided along with the photometric data. McKernon's Beamwright (Figure 9.12) and Crecit's Light Shop are examples of this type of software.

One of the most difficult tasks for beginning designers is making appropriate color choices for a production. Not only are the individual selections important, but also—and more importantly—we are interested in how the light from different gels and angles will react and mix with one another and the other colors that will be found on a stage. Two popular programs that simulate the effects of color mixing and angle distribution are Virtual Light Lab and Light Grid. Both allow a designer to place lights on a grid that is designed to simulate a number of the fundamental lighting angles. Each light is then assigned a gel from any of the major filter suppliers. The designer can then study the effects

of the color mixing of the gels. In addition, the intensity of each light can be varied in the simulation. In some cases, gobo breakups and scenic backgrounds can be entered into the program and evaluated as well. Virtual Light Lab (Figure 9.13) allows a designer to paste images such as a scanned paint elevation or digital photo of a scenic model into the background of its simulations. By experimenting with different filters, hanging positions, and intensities, a designer should be able to get a pretty good indication of how a particular combination of these variables will affect the appearance of the subject.

Digital Renderings

Creating simulations or **renderings** will provide images of how an object or environment might look when

Figure 9.13a Virtual Light Lab. a. A screenshot of an image/model within lighting lab view ("Don't Tell Mamma," *Cabaret*)

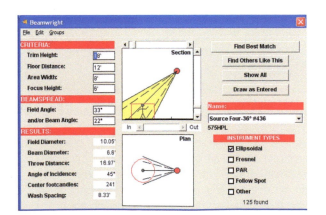

Figure 9.12 Screenshot of a luminaire analysis in McKernon's Beamwright software

Figure 9.13b A screenshot of the scene window and rendering of the same moment ("Don't Tell Mamma," *Cabaret*)

placed under a given set of lighting conditions. Originally, renderings were nothing more than elaborate storyboards based on what the designer hoped the final designs might look like. Paint and illustration programs like Adobe Photoshop or Corel Painter were among the first software programs that were used to suggest what designers hoped to achieve in their lighting. These renderings are not linked to actual photometric data and can therefore be misleading. Despite this, even today we continue to use these products for storyboarding. In contrast, computer-aided drafting (CAD) programs have grown into three-dimensional modeling packages that can create virtual images with quite accurate renderings of both the materials and the lighting of a subject. Both AutoCAD and Vectorworks have lighting and materials modules in their basic programs, while products like 3ds Max (formerly 3D Studio or 3D Studio Max/Viz) and Lightwave are more complex programs for modeling and rendering light—but once again, the image isn't necessarily linked to photometric data. These images are called **computer renderings** (Figure 9.14). The advantage to programs like 3ds Max is not only in their modeling ability, but also in their capacity to create animation. This includes their ability to create a **flyby** or **walk-through** in which an observer either is directed through a view down a previously determined path or may freely navigate through a virtual environment in any direction that they wish—often in real time.

Visualization

Computer visualization is a sophisticated form of computer rendering. In some cases, an image might be so accurately calculated that it depicts a photometrically correct image. This might be just what is needed in the case of making a presentational rendering for a major architectural project, but creating such images involves an immense amount of time and expense. The files that they create are extraordinarily large and it can take many hours of calculation to produce a final photorealistic rendering. In entertainment situations, this is rarely possible—plus, unlike architectural projects, stage images are dynamic and constantly changing. Even if there is time to do such visualizations they are often limited to either a single image per scene or a couple of important moments of a production.

Computer visualization works from the principle of creating a three-dimensional model of an environment within a virtual or simulated space. This may take the form of a three-dimensional composition of a single room, exterior facade of a building, or fully developed

Figure 9.14 A Vectorworks rendering: design and visualization of *The Foreigner* at Snow College Department of Theater (scenic design by Michael Helms)

Credit: Scene design by Michael Helms

scenic design for a production. After the model is completed, the lighting designer goes on to assign textures and materials, and add lighting fixtures and accessories to the virtual environment. The luminaires in a computer model can be modified or manipulated in much the same way as the luminaires would be used in the real world. Images can then be created that indicate what the final design might look like (based on the calculation power of the computer). While initial versions of visualization software were relatively crude, newer editions have become so accurate that the final image can approach the quality of a photograph. Some software packages are even capable of creating cueing sequences that can produce a sequence of virtual events that can be pre-programmed and imported directly into a lighting console. Electronic Theatre Control's (ETC) Emphasis system, CAST Software's wysiwyg (Figure 9.15a), and Design and Drafting's LD Assistant (Figure 9.15b) are three examples of visualization software that are in popular use due to their abilities to interface with lighting consoles.

There is also a variation of computer visualization that generates images without using photorealism. More importantly, this software works within the framework of real time. With these programs, accuracy and detail are sacrificed so that an animation that will run in "real"

or actual time can be made for a project. The entertainment industry has arrived at a point where these visualizations can account for most design decisions that a designer would use in an actual theatre—even illustrating the transitions between cues. Entire virtual theatres can be created with model sets that are lit with virtual luminaires hung in lighting positions that accurately mimic the real plot that will someday be hung in the theatre. The luminaires replicate the photometrics of the actual fixtures and are virtually focused and gelled as they would be in the theatre. **Hookups** and channel

Figure 9.15b LD Assistant (design by G. B. Stephens)

Credit: Design and Drafting

Figure 9.15a Lighting visualization. a. wysiwyg rendering and screen interface

Credit: CAST Software

assignments are created automatically and will match the actual plugging of the show in the theatre. Finally, cues are written using the virtual image just as if the production were being lit in the actual space. When the virtual programming is complete, cues have been roughed in and the show is ready to be loaded into the console after the rig is assembled in the theatre. This process saves immense amounts of time in the venue and has become so beneficial that virtual studios now exist where lighting designers and producers can rent the computer and software on an hourly or daily basis. The first popular theatrical visualizer was CAST Software's wysiwyg. Wysiwyg is a stand-alone program that contains its own CAD, paperwork, and visualization modules. This software not only generates design visualizations, but also aids designers in drafting the plot and section, keeps track of inventories, and generates all of the design's schedules and paperwork. Most importantly, wysiwyg's animation features allow designers to plot cues and transitions in real time—which is especially important to lighting designers who are precueing automated lighting moves and choreography outside of the venue, without the use of the actual lights.

An even more powerful application of computer visualization connects the PC to the lighting console through some form of DMX/USB interface. This allows a PC to drive the console in the actual venue. When a change is made in the virtual world, the change is immediately reflected in the actual lighting rig. As a further form of sophistication, communication is bi-directional, and changes made through the lighting console will also create changes in the virtual lighting. Over the years wysiwyg has evolved into the powerful visualization tool it is today; it was even bundled into many of ETC's consoles as part of the Emphasis® product line. Today it interfaces with most current lighting control systems. This type of visualization has become possible for other manufacturers and an increasing number of consoles are now being shipped with their own proprietary forms of visualization software. LD Assistant by Design and Drafting is another popular visualization package and is comparable to wysiwyg. This software comes with a large symbol library—which includes not only lighting instruments but also props and other stage equipment that are popular within the corporate/industrial and concert areas of the industry—and, like wysiwyg, produces the draftings, inventories, and other paperwork associated with completing a lighting design. It, too, can be equipped with a DMX module that connects the PC to a lighting console. The primary difference between this product and wysiwyg is that LD Assistant is designed around AutoCAD and it's menu/tool structure (it is offered both as a stand-alone program or as an add-on to AutoCAD) and therefore has all the tools and sophistication of AutoCAD while wysiwyg uses its own CAD program.

Entertainment designers tend to reserve the term "visualization" for systems that render results in a real- or live-time frame/mode; however, visualization can just as easily pertain to static images as well. Visualization techniques tend to be used most often in situations such as for concert lighting or big spectacle events like the opening and closing ceremonies of the Olympic Games where complex demands are placed on automated luminaires and there is a limited amount of time to work in the actual venue. A real advantage to using visualization software lies in its ability to deal with automated lights. In addition to creating the different cues, a bigger attraction is how easily the software can be used to redirect moving lights to new focus points or to work out the sophisticated choreography of the moving light beams. Timing of these moves can be checked against a track of music, and the accuracy of the moves can be plotted from one stage to another without stepping foot in a venue.

Software that is used to create architectural visualizations tends to be more sophisticated than that used in entertainment applications due to the fact that the images that are desired in this field tend to be extremely detailed (photorealism being the most popular style) and based on true photometric calculations. The most popular architectural visualization and design analysis packages include Lighting Technologies' Lumen Designer and Lumen Micro, as well as Lighting Analysis' AGi32. Though some of these are no longer commercially available (Lumen Micro) all three are still used in the industry.

While this last section on computer rendering and visualization has moved well beyond simply communicating a lighting design, visualization at its very core strives to produce the primary elements of a lighting design in such a way that much of the design is communicated to a production team well before moving into the venue and working with the actual lights and programming. With the rising costs of rehearsal time and ever-growing number of parameters that must be programmed into a production there is an increased desire to use pre-visualization software throughout many areas of the lighting industry. Visualization studios are popping up in major cities all over the world and allow programmers to develop virtual creations for upcoming tours and productions in a studio without the immediate pressures of designing in the actual arena or theatre where a production is set to open within hours. With the increased use of intelligent lighting and their ever-increasing number of attributes, visualization has become not only an option but in some cases a necessary part of the design process. Once on site, the finished program is simply loaded into the console and the designer performs a series of final tweaks to fine-tune the settings for the venue and actual lights.

For Further Reading

Ball, David. *Backwards and Forwards: A Technical Manual for Reading Plays*. Carbondale and Edwardsville: Southern Illinois Press, 1983.

Essig, Linda. *Lighting and the Design Idea*. Fort Worth, TX: Harcourt Brace College Publishers, 1997.

Ingham, Rosemary. *From Page to Stage*. Portsmouth, NH: Heinemann, 1998.

McCandless, Stanley. *A Method for Lighting the Stage*. 4th ed. New York: Theatre Arts Books, 1958.

Mumm, Robert C. *Photometrics Handbook*. 2nd ed. Louisville, KY: Broadway Press, 1997.

Palmer, Richard H. *The Lighting Art: The Aesthetics of Stage Lighting Design*. 2nd ed. Englewood Cliffs, NJ: Prentice Hall, 1994.

Rosenthal, Jean and Lael Wertenbaker. *The Magic of Light*. New York: Theatre Arts Books/Little, Brown and Company, 1974.

Tharp, Twyla. *The Creative Habit: Learn It and Use It for Life*. New York: Simon & Schuster, 2003.

Thomas, James. *Script Analysis for Actors, Directors, and Designers*. 4th ed. Oxford and Boston: Focal Press, 2009.

CHAPTER 10

BASICS OF GENERAL ILLUMINATION

ONE OF THE most important functions of lighting is to provide illumination or visibility to a subject or space. Not that long ago, most lighting designers were concerned solely with this function and strove to bring ever-increasing intensities to a stage or environment. As lighting design has evolved, designers have gone on to consider many more criteria than just brightness for creating quality lighting. In fact, it is often desirable to illuminate only what has to be seen—and only to the degree that a viewer gains an understanding of a subject or environment (**selective visibility**). A scene where Frankenstein's monster is pursuing several teenagers wouldn't be as successful if lit with day-like lighting as when lit with the low intensities and shadows of a night scene. However, even though we now consider a number of additional factors for creating quality lighting, visibility is still one of the most important functions that a designer must fulfill. This basic provision of visibility is frequently created by **general lighting**, and the principle holds true for both entertainment and architectural applications.

In this chapter I provide some guidelines for developing lighting systems that create the basic illumination or visibility for an environment. One of the most important aspects of these systems is that rarely will a single light source be sufficient for lighting an entire environment. In practice, the light from most luminaires is directional enough that they can only light a limited amount of space. As one moves throughout the space, the angle of the light appears to change because not enough distance exists between the source and the subject to create parallel light throughout the space. We therefore use additional luminaires as a way of duplicating the light of a selected source, creating the appearance that the environment is lit by a single source. Even though much of this chapter is devoted to theatrical practices, the principles can be adapted and modified for many other areas of lighting design as well. In this chapter, I present several methods for developing general illumination and discuss working with resources like sections and floorplans.

LIGHTING THE SUBJECT

The **subject** represents the object that must be lit. In theatrical applications this is usually the performer, while actors in the video and film business are called the **talent**. In architectural applications we make reference to the type of work or **task** that must be accomplished in an environment. On stage, a certain level of visibility must be achieved so that the audience can gain an understanding of the play. Older people require higher levels of illumination for visibility than younger people. It has been a long-understood principle that people who can't see a stage's action also have difficulty hearing the performers. Sometimes we make a distinction between **general lighting**, which typically washes the entire stage, and **area lighting,** which is broken down into more specific areas that combine together to produce general illumination. When we provide general illumination, we provide a base level of light so that visibility is accomplished.

When we examine illumination, we realize that what we actually see is affected by a number of factors that relate to the light that is used to illuminate an environment. One of the most important elements relates to the sheer **intensity**, or brightness, of the light. In reality, the range of intensities that we observe on stage is immense compared with what can be conveniently recorded by film or video. More importantly, since what we see is based on perception, stage designers light for what they see, not necessarily a recommended level of footcandles. The problem with this is that people have varying degrees of light sensitivity—while a 20 year old may be quite comfortable with a dimly lit scene, a 50 or 70 year old may struggle to see the same scene. While there are no hard and set rules for illuminating a stage, cameras usually require that a given intensity level be maintained. Cameras also have a much narrower range of **contrast ratios** that they can process. Fortunately, both restrictions have greatly improved with each generation of film and video cameras. Even though illumination levels may vary significantly in live entertainment, the *IESNA Lighting Handbook* still offers several guidelines related to footcandle levels that are considered characteristic of stage applications. On stage, a basic level of 50–100 footcandles is considered adequate for many performances, while 185–200 footcandles or higher is often required to bring significant focus to a subject or performer. In reality, these levels can vary considerably based on the size of a venue and the physical proximity of an audience to a stage—not counting design issues like trying to establish specific moods or settings.

The **Inverse Square Law** plays a significant role in the illumination of an environment: The farther away a light source is placed from a subject, the weaker it becomes. In fact, the rate of intensity drop is exponentially related to the distance between the source and the subject. In most performance facilities, the locations used for hanging luminaires are set at specific distances from the stage. A mismatched lighting unit can result not only in a luminaire's light being spilled uncontrollably over a larger area, but also in a loss of base-level illumination (footcandles) since the same amount of light is spread over a larger area. If we are using a luminaire equipped with shutters, we could shutter the light to the desired size, but this does not change the reduced intensity of the beam nor the fact that a greater portion of the light now becomes trapped in the luminaire and is converted into heat.

A designer may light a subject from almost any direction, with each angle creating a characteristic effect on the subject (**distribution**). Backlight produces a different image than sidelight, while an up light creates a different mood than light coming from a steep overhead angle. A designer learns how to associate these angles with viewer perception and creates different moods and effects through using various combinations of angle and other lighting properties in a design. Distribution not only plays a role in the shadow and highlight patterns that are found on a subject, but also in revealing which surfaces are illuminated as well as the amount of color mixing and revelation of texture that occurs on a particular surface. Distribution plays a significant role in how a subject is perceived by an audience.

Once a designer develops an understanding of what they wish the lighting to accomplish, they go on to analyze the specific combination of angles, colors, and intensities that will produce the desired effect. In reality, this is accomplished by working with the **lighting concept** and developing a **lighting scheme** or **lighting key** for a production. In a very real sense, this is how the subject will actually be lit. Using this information, a designer goes on to develop the general lighting for a project.

TYPICAL THEATRICAL LIGHTING POSITIONS

Luminaires need to be mounted from solid structures so that they will remain in their focused positions. In most theatrical facilities, these structures or **hanging positions** are found as a series of horizontal and vertical pipes that are mounted throughout a theatre. Some are welded in permanent locations, such as in the ceiling above the audience, while others are characterized by moveable positions like **battens** (pipes located above the stage). Some theatres may even have hanging positions mounted to winched catwalks (**light bridges**) that hang over a stage. Some battens have permanently wired circuits attached to them, but most do not. To supplement the electrics, many theatres have provisions like **drop boxes** for adding circuits to these positions. In some cases, there are no raceways and all of the circuiting is provided by drop boxes. It is also possible to have battens that are not moveable and are simply hung at a given height above the stage (**dead hung**). In arenas, convention centers, and gymnasiums, temporary frames constructed of tubular metal called **trusses** are often hauled into place above a temporary stage and are used to create hanging positions for a show's lighting equipment. Trade shows and the concert industry make extensive use of trusses.

Proscenium Theatre

For many years the proscenium theatre has been considered the most popular form of performance facility. We divide the hanging positions of a proscenium theatre into two broad categories: the **front of house (FOH)**, which is located in the audience or auditorium areas, and the **onstage** positions, which are located upstage of the proscenium wall. The onstage positions may be further broken down into **overheads**, **booms** or **torms**, **set mounts** and **floor mounts**. The overheads are located on battens above the stage while the booms or torms are vertical pipes that are typically located to the sides of the stage in the wings. Set mounts are physically mounted to a set while floor mounts are placed on the floor or deck. The names of the hanging positions (Figure 10.1) may change in different regions of the world.

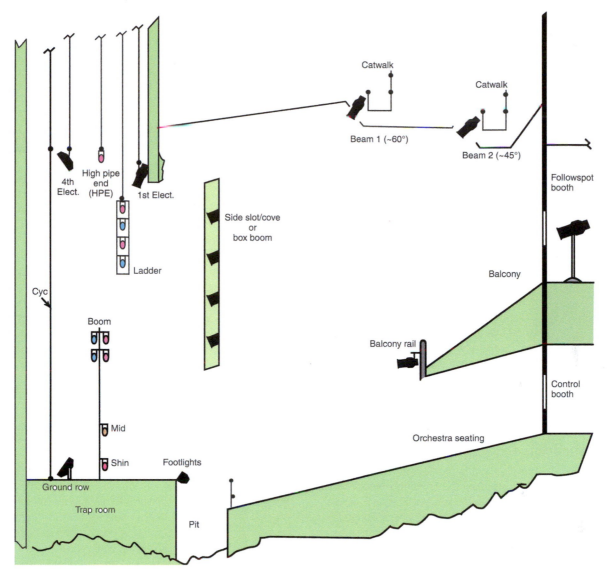

Figure 10.1 Proscenium lighting positions

Sidebar 10.1 Proscenium Hanging Positions and Lighting Distribution

Projection Booth (Spotlight Booth)
These positions are typically located at the back of the house at the uppermost level of a theatre. They may also be found on the orchestra level at the rear of the house. They are often used for followspots (offering relatively flat angles) and also frequently house sound gear and the lighting console.

Balcony Rail
This position is common in many older theatres and is nothing more than a pipe that extends along the front of a balcony. Additional balcony rails may be present in theatres with several balconies. The traditional balcony rail provides a very flat lighting angle. While the angle can produce extreme shadows behind a subject, it is good for creating relatively distortion-free projections and for washing the entire stage with just a few fixtures.

Beam or Port
Beam positions are horizontally mounted pipes that run across the width of an auditorium in the ceiling above an audience. Catwalks are often located behind the beams to help facilitate the hanging and focusing of the instruments. Sometimes, rather than a full beam, ports

housing four to six instruments each are found in these positions. Beams are among the most important positions for creating general illumination for a stage. The most common beam positions create roughly a 45° vertical angle with the front of the stage. Another popular position creates a steeper 60° angle and is found closer to the stage. Many theatres have at least two beam positions and the positions are assigned numbers that progressively increase as one moves farther away from the stage. These positions may also be called galleries, FOH positions, or a unique name that is given by the local crew.

Truss | A framed metal structure that is either ground supported or flown from a theatre's superstructure to form a temporary hanging position. Trusses are often used to create additional FOH lighting positions when beams are now available.

Footlights | The footlights are located across the very front edge of the stage at stage level. The position is historical and associated with the way in which stages were lit in the days of candles and oil lamps. Footlights create an unnatural uplight that can be good for washing the stage, filling in shadows from the overhead lighting, or bringing a unique effect to the stage. Musicals often use this angle by placing striplights along this position. In order to mask these units from sight, a trough is sometimes built into the lip of the stage.

Box Boom, Slot, or Cove | These are vertical lighting positions consisting of a boom that is traditionally mounted in the box seats of an auditorium. **Box booms** create front diagonal lighting for a stage. In some theatres, there may be two or three box boom positions on each side of the auditorium. In older theatres that do not have beam positions, the box booms and balcony rail form the only sources of front light for a stage. In this case, these positions can become quite complex and may contain pipe arrangements that allow 20 or more luminaires to be hung in a single position. Many theatres built after 1960 do not have box seats at all: front diagonal lighting is provided through vertical coves or slots that are cut into the walls of the auditorium. Like beam positions, box boom numbers get larger as they move farther away from the stage (while also noting the side of the stage that they are located on—e.g., SL Box Boom#1 or SR Box Boom#2).

Light Bridge | A light bridge is a variation of catwalk that contains several different pipes for hanging luminaires and runs parallel to the proscenium. Light bridges are typically winched and located throughout the depth of a stage at popular locations where electrics would be located (i.e., a bridge might replace the first electric).

Electric | An electric is a hanging position directly above the stage that consists of a pipe or batten running horizontally across the stage. Most stages have several electrics flown from different linesets at various depths throughout a stage. Their **trims** are usually adjusted from the fly rail. The battens are lowered to 3 or 4 feet above the deck for hanging, gelling, and circuiting and are then flown to their normal or **working trims** once everything is working properly. Permanent raceways contain pre-wired circuits every foot or so along the length of a batten, while temporary electrics have their circuiting supplied by **drop boxes** or circuits that have been cabled between electrics **(married)**. In some cases, circuits may run directly from the unit all the way back to the dimmers **(home run).** Downstage electrics generally provide frontal lighting for the mid- and up-stage portions of the stage while, upstage electrics are usually used for backlight. Mid-stage electrics can be used for either backlight or frontlight depending on what portion of the stage they are focused to, while virtually any electric can be used for downlight. The extreme ends of electrics may be used for high sidelight—what we call **high-pipe-ends (HPE).** Electrics are numbered progressively upward from the electric closest to the plasterline toward the upstage wall.

Booms or Ladders | These hanging positions allow luminaires to be hung in vertical positions that are usually located to the sides of the stage, in the wings. The positions provide a variety of sidelight angles. A **boom** usually consists of a single pipe mounted in a vertical position from the stage floor, while a **ladder** (similar to an extension ladder) performs the same function but is hung from the end of a batten or the grid, allowing a sidelight to be created without getting in the way of the deck traffic patterns that a boom might create. Another variation, the **dance tower,** uses a truss-like structure to support the sidelights. Booms and ladders are identified by their side of the stage and relative positions from the plasterline, once again numbering progressively higher as they move toward the upstage wall. In many theatres a special boom is found just upstage of the proscenium opening. These are commonly called **torms** (SL Torm and SR Torm), which is short for "tormentor." We characterize sidelight by height, with the highest angles coming from the HPEs and tops of the booms (12 to 16 feet or higher off the deck), standard sidelight is roughly in the 8- to 12-foot range, head height (about 6 feet), often called **mids,** and low sidelight from below 2 feet (**shins,** short for **shin busters** or **shin kickers**).

Ground Row This series of luminaires are mounted on the floor and run parallel to a cyclorama (cyc) or backdrop. Striplights and cyc lights are frequently used in ground rows to wash scenic backgrounds from below. In some stages, a trough may be built into the upstage deck to mask these units from sight.

Black Box Theatre

Black box theatres allow the performance and audience spaces to be modified from one production to another. This flexibility requires that the lighting also be set up in a flexible manner. Most luminaires in black box theatres are hung from a network of intersecting pipes called a **grid** that is usually permanent and extends over the entire theatre. The pipes are generally spaced about 4 to 6 feet apart. In especially friendly theatres, a **suspension** or **tension grid** consisting of a mesh of woven aircraft cable is provided that allows electricians to walk almost anywhere above the theatre, giving them easy access to the luminaires.

Other Variations

In some cases, performance facilities may make use of a combination of flexible positions and a permanent grid. The most obvious example is thrust theatres, where a grid is provided over the thrust portion of the stage while a fly loft with battens and moveable electrics are provided in the upstage areas. Catwalks with more traditional hanging positions are often placed over the audience and are typically oriented so that they are parallel to the edges of the stage.

FLOORPLANS AND SECTIONS

As designers create a lighting design they need to be able to make calculations in regard to throw distances, beam spreads, and distribution angles (e.g., determining hanging positions) associated with the luminaires that will light a space. **Beam spread** refers to the angle at which light spreads away from a lighting instrument. Through using floorplans and sections along with information regarding the physical properties of a luminaire, the light that it produces can be translated into graphical data that illustrates the light's behavior in a specific situation. The **floorplan (groundplan)** provides a scaled top view of an environment that can be compared to a map of a room or theatre with its roof removed. The **section** provides a drafting of a space from a side view that is typically drawn along the centerline of a stage. Floorplans aid lighting designers in determining beam spreads and throw distances throughout the width and depth of a stage, while sections are used to determine the vertical angles, heights, and beam spreads based on the **trim** positions of the luminaires. Sections are also used to determine the **masking** positions for a production. The **light plot** or **lighting layout** will be based on a detailed study of the floorplan and section—especially in the planning of the general lighting systems. In this chapter I focus only on how these plans are used in developing the general stage illumination for a production.

BASICS OF GENERAL ILLUMINATION OR AREA LIGHTING

The majority of lighting designers would agree that the most essential task of any lighting design is to provide general visibility for an environment. **General illumination** was developed to bring this visibility about. In most cases, this means providing a system of luminaires that creates a consistent even coverage of light across the entire stage. While we tend to refer to general lighting as being characteristic of washes that light an entire stage, area lighting tends to be more specific in that in addition to providing basic illumination, it also provides an opportunity to control specific areas of the stage separately. For a proscenium stage, area lighting generally refers to a series of instruments that light the stage from above the audience in a frontal direction. For other facilities, the issue of area lighting becomes more complex. If we consider a distant light source like the sun, the distance that the light travels is so great that the light appears as parallel rays when viewing objects that are in close proximity to one another. Any objects viewed under such a source share similar qualities in terms of highlights and shadows, shading, and the shadows that they cast. If the objects are separated over great distances, changes may be noted in their appearances, but for the most part the differences are insignificant when they are a great distance from the light source. Designers try to re-create this condition in most general or area lighting systems and use multiple lights to create the illusion that the area is being lit by a single distant source.

In one form of general illumination, often called the **single source system,** a single light source is used to illuminate an entire scene. This can be highly dramatic, but it is often not the best solution for creating general visibility on a stage. It can cause shadows and other lighting characteristics to change as a performer moves through a space and is usually considered undesirable because it can cause distractions. The effect is even more critical (and unwanted) in architectural lighting. For this reason, lighting designers usually work to provide a lighting system that creates the illusion of light coming from a single distant source rather than actually using a single source lighting system. In order to accomplish this, designers divide the stage into a series of smaller spaces **(lighting areas)** that are all illuminated with as much duplication as possible. Each area is then lit by the same type of luminaire, shares a common light source, and is colored by the same color media. Just as importantly, each luminaire is placed so that its distribution patterns (beam spreads) and lighting angle are consistent with all the other luminaires that are lighting similar areas of the stage. The net effect produces a well-lit stage that gives the illusion of being lit by a single distant light source. This combination of luminaires that produce similar qualities and functions of light in adjoining areas form what is called a **wash,** while the overall combination of luminaires that are used to create the unified appearance throughout the environment (i.e., the whole stage) is a **lighting system.** Most general illumination is based on a variation of these approaches.

In order to develop an area lighting system, designers need to examine several issues related to a space and how they will light it. Factors like type and number of luminaires in the inventory, hanging positions, required illumination levels, and desired amount of control form several of the more important considerations for determining how a stage is divided up into smaller areas. When we talk about **area control** we are making a determination of how many areas a designer divides a stage into. After a designer observes a production's blocking, they will decide whether they will need to pull into very specific areas of the stage (requiring more acting areas) or if they can make do with fewer, but larger, acting areas. While a luminaire or two may in theory cover an entire stage, the resulting intensity will most likely not be high enough to provide a sufficient level of illumination. An example of this is seen in playing a flashlight on a wall and observing how the light spreads out over a greater area while also becoming dimmer as the light is moved farther away from the wall. In a similar way, if a designer chooses luminaires that have beam spreads

that are too large, the units will spread their light over a much greater area with a resultant loss in intensity.

An acceptable acting area size is based on a diameter of 6–10 feet. The center of these circles becomes the focus point, while adjoining circles should just touch edges with one another. The diameter of an acting area is not set in stone; it should be emphasized that the sizes can vary considerably from one design or even lighting system to another. It is also common for the diameters of these pools to vary even within a given lighting system. A large stage requires more acting areas while a small stage may require as few as six or nine areas. Designers usually attempt to establish acting areas in some version of a grid system that produces planes set at even spacings throughout a stage's depth. In an open stage, such as for dance production, area lighting is often indicated by a rectangular array of lighting areas; in contrast, a production containing scenery requires that the layout be modified so that it is consistent with the scenic elements of a production. Two methods of naming these areas include assigning a letter or number to each area or identifying the areas based on stage positions (Figure 10.2).

The designer creates general lighting by combining the lighting key with the area lighting breakdown for a stage. Each area is lit with a combination of units that are based on the directional and other visual requirements of the lighting key. Once the focus point of a lighting area has been identified, the designer needs only to use the master floorplan to plot a line from the focus point to a lighting position along an angle that is consistent with the angle found in the lighting key. At this point, a luminaire with an appropriate beam spread is matched to the diameter of the acting area and **throw distance** associated with the given lighting position. Designers can use an acetate or vellum template (Figure 10.3) to

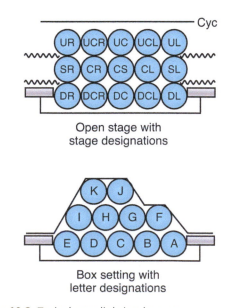

Open stage with
stage designations

Box setting with
letter designations

Figure 10.2 Typical area lighting layouts

Figure 10.3a Determining the relationship between throw distance and acting area size. Area coverage based on beam spread and angles using a homemade acetate template. a. The template being used to determine coverage in plan view.

Figure 10.3b The template being used to determine coverage in sectional view.

make a determination of which beam angle (and associated luminaire) best matches the diameter of an acting pool from a given position. This technique is easily adapted to computer-aided drafting where the angle templates can be inserted temporarily into a drawing to make decisions regarding hanging positions and instrument choices. Lighting designers consider beam angles rather than field angles in these determinations so that the most intense light is concentrated on the acting areas. As a result, the added coverage provided by the larger field angle allows the dead zones between the acting areas to be lit adequately. The combination of these effects should produce an even coverage of light across an entire stage. The diameter of a light pool can also be determined by looking at a fixture's **multiplying factor** (found in product literature and references like Mumm's *Photometrics Handbook*) and multiplying this number by the throw distance. However, the most accurate determination can be calculated by using the following formula:

$$\text{Beam Diameter} = \text{tangent} \times (\text{Field Angle}/2) \\ \times \text{Throw Distance}$$

Once a luminaire and hanging position have been identified, they are plotted and the process is repeated for the other acting areas. A variation of this approach is used by some designers when using **flat field luminaires** like the Source Four®. The layouts are determined as described earlier, but diffusion or frost is added to the units once they have been focused. This fills in the shadows between the adjoining areas. Another method of creating area coverage is based on overlapping only the areas of an instrument's beam associated with the field angles of adjoining instruments. This, too, provides overlapping coverage between neighboring fixtures. Figure 10.4 illustrates each of these area lighting options. It is important to note that the plane in which the lighting is planned is usually 5 to 6 feet above the deck (at the actors' faces), not on the stage floor.

When a designer is developing a lighting system where both the acting areas and hanging positions share similar locations, the choice of luminaire is usually the same for all the areas. The designer, therefore, places identical units at locations along the hanging position that are consistent with the angle indicated by the lighting key. The lines representing the throw distances should be parallel with one another. While a protractor or adjustable triangle might be used to plot the intersection of these angles with the hanging positions, another technique allows the designer to locate the fixtures by simply placing them at the same spacing interval as the distance between the areas. If the distance between the centers of each acting area is 10 feet, the placement of the luminaires along the hanging position should also be 10 feet. The result is a combination of luminaires

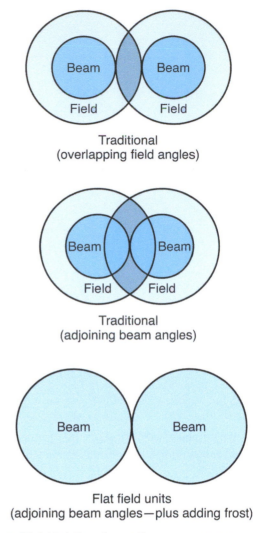

Traditional
(overlapping field angles)

Traditional
(adjoining beam angles)

Flat field units
(adjoining beam angles—plus adding frost)

Figure 10.4 Variations in creating area coverage

covering the stage in light beams that are essentially parallel with one another, creating the illusion of a single distant light source. While luminaires used for general illumination are typically identical across a given hanging position, angles and distribution patterns often change as different planes and hanging positions are used throughout a design. Angles must also often be cheated when approaching the extreme sides of a hanging position. To ensure proper vertical coverage, the same principles are applied to the sectional drawing to check the vertical angles and beam coverage of the luminaires. It is important to exam the beam spreads in both floorplan and sectional views because the true throw distance may not be apparent if using only one of these views alone. This entire process is then repeated for each lighting angle of the lighting key. In cases where beam spread is critical, a designer can calculate the throw distance based on the Pythagorean theorem (Figure 10.5).

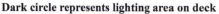

a = **Floorplan distance between unit and target**

b = **Trim Height (less head height distance)**

c = **Throw Distance**

$$a^2 + b^2 = c^2$$

$$\sqrt{plan^2 + (trim - height)^2} = \text{Throw Distance}$$

Shaded area represents lighting plane at head height

Dark circle represents lighting area on deck

Figure 10.5 Determining throw distance in three-dimensional space

PRIMARY FORMULA APPROACHES FOR AREA LIGHTING

Using the basics of general illumination, several formulaic methods have been developed to aid lighting designers in achieving good area coverage for a stage. While most lighting designers now relate many of their choices of area coverage back to a lighting key that is created for a specific scene or production, these formula approaches can be used to help beginning designers as they create general illumination for a production. A lighting designer may also develop modified versions of these systems to suit their needs.

Single Source System

Single source lighting, which was introduced earlier, gives the appearance of light emitting from a single light source. It is one of the most desirable illusions that we create as lighting designers—an example being the light that comes from the sun. However, the problem often is that the source cannot be placed far enough away for the light to take on the parallel qualities that allow the objects to share common features like shadow and highlight definitions. Instead, the highlights and shadows change as you move the subject around the stage. At times, this type of illumination may be desired, and a single source is used to provide a very directional distribution for the stage. This form of illumination is especially useful for establishing a specific light source for a scene and is often associated with lighting styles that are anchored in **motivational lighting.**

A designer generally arrives at a design solution through one of two approaches when attempting to create lighting that is suggestive of a single source. In the first situation, a designer simply uses an actual light source that is positioned on or off stage in a location that creates the desired shadows and coverage. A particularly successful use of this technique can be observed when designers place sources like a streetlamp, fireplace, table lamp, or chandelier on stage (Figure 10.6). These units may become the only source of illumination for a scene, and the light spreads out away from them in a naturalistic manner. More distant single sources are less common but may include the suggestion of a street light or some other light source somewhere out of view of an audience. Despite the fact that the actual source is not seen, the light still goes on to illuminate the stage as if the source were visible to an audience.

Figure 10.6 Effect of a single light source across a stage: note how both direction and length of shadows change with stage position.

Often these sources may not be strong enough to actually light the scene or could cause excessive glare (if the source is actually seen on the stage). In order to support the single source illusion, a second approach adds stage luminaires to accent these light sources. This can be done by hanging a cluster of lighting fixtures around the apparent center of a desired light source. The multiple instruments allow the designer to achieve the additional lighting angles that would be suggestive of the single light source. An example where multiple instruments can be used effectively involves the depiction of light coming from a chandelier mounted at center stage. Here, multiple luminaires are hung around the intended chandelier (imaginary or actual) to suggest that light is radiating away from the chandelier in all directions (Figure 10.7). A second example involves hanging a cluster of instruments with a coverage that fans outward and away from a light source. This might be used to create the effect of an onstage streetlamp. An offstage streetlamp could be indicated by placing an ellipsoidal or other stage light at the extreme end of a batten (**high-pipe-end,** or **HPE**) or at a relatively high height on a boom.

Wash System

The **wash system** (Figure 10.8) is actually the system that I have already described as the basis for creating much of the general illumination for a stage. The stage is divided into areas that are each lit in a duplicate manner. Each group of luminaires that share common qualities is known as a **wash.** Washes typically share basic beam distribution patterns, lighting angles, and colors. In many

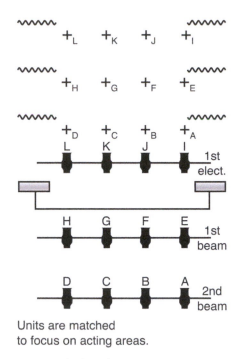

Units are matched to focus on acting areas.

Figure 10.8 A typical wash system

earlier approaches to lighting design, washes were developed to provide full coverage of the stage from essentially four primary angles (straight front, back, and each side). Multiple colored washes were often provided from each of the angles. Early concert lighting made heavy use of color wash systems, and dance lighting to this day is solidly based on providing warm and cool colored washes from many of these directions. These washes may or may not be oriented in the principal 90° orientations of traditional theatrical wash lighting. In fact, a wash can be provided from almost any angle that a designer desires.

The McCandless System

One of the earliest problems that theatrical lighting designers struggled with related to creating lighting that had a naturalistic effect on the performers. Prior to the advent of electricity, stage personnel were more concerned with achieving visibility than they were with the aesthetics of a lighting design. When electricity became the basic means of control, it didn't take long for pioneers to develop several formulaic design approaches for creating basic visibility for a stage. One such pioneer, Professor Stanley McCandless of the Yale School of Drama, developed a system for producing area lighting that would have a profound impact on the lighting industry. His formula was introduced as "A Method for Lighting the Stage" in his publication of *A Syllabus for Lighting the Stage*, and became so influential that people have referred to it as "**The Method.**" Simply put, the

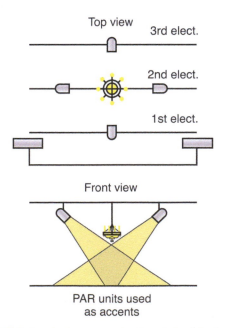

Figure 10.7 Luminaires around a chandelier (single source)

McCandless System is a method for creating a realistic image in the general illumination of a stage. The historical significance of this approach is that it came at a time when spotlights were first capable of achieving the longer throws associated with placing luminaires in an auditorium and as hanging positions above the audience first started to be incorporated into theatre designs. The McCandless System became so successful that entire auditoriums and circuiting systems were built on his concept.

One of the compositional problems of theatrical lighting is that it is often difficult to distinguish the mass or depth of objects and performers while they are on stage. As lighting positions began to shift to the FOH, McCandless noted that light coming from straight front washed out the dimensional features of a performer and determined that to create a more naturalistic lighting quality a subject needed to be lit by two separate sources from opposing directions. He stressed that the opposing sources should reveal more of the sides and dimensional qualities of a subject and that color could also be used to emphasize dimensionality in the lighting. As you may recall, most lighting environments include a combination of the actual source or **key light** and varying degrees of ambient or **fill light.** In a theatre, where most surfaces are painted black (and purposefully kept black so that they absorb light), there is often little, if any, ambient light on a stage and a designer must often use additional light sources to create this ambient lighting. By providing light from both directions, a designer has a much better ability to reveal form while also providing clues to the directionality of the implied light source.

McCandless recognized that most naturalistic lighting involves light sources that are located above as well as to either side of a subject. He went on to incorporate this into his two-instrument method of lighting as well: one instrument would represent the key (source) light while the other would be associated with the fill for the scene. In his method, McCandless broadly characterized these light sources as coming from a location at about 45° from above and 45° to each side of a subject. In addition, he realized that he could enhance this effect by creating some color contrast by gelling each light differently. By using complementary tints, he could produce a naturalistic quality in which each side of a subject was influenced more directly by one of the two sources while the subject's front was lit through additive mixing of both sources, which essentially produced some variation of white light. This basic system of two light sources with complementary tints located at 45° from above and to each side of an acting area has become the general formula for the McCandless method (Figure 10.9) and the basic distribution pattern is repeated throughout as many lighting areas as required by a design. The system had many ramifications throughout the lighting industry and was the standard approach to lighting for much

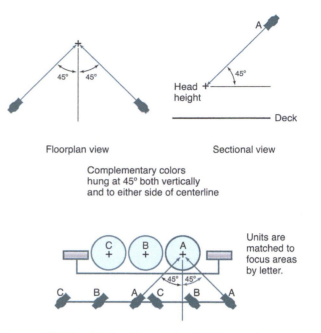

Figure 10.9 The McCandless method lighting system

of the 1900s. Even today, it is still used or slightly modified as a basis for general illumination in many lighting designs.

Double or Triple Hanging

While double or triple hanging do not truly relate to formula based lighting systems, they do reflect an approach to lighting design. Due to the limitations in numbers of dimmers and lighting instruments, it used to be common for lighting designers to create only a minimal lighting scheme for a production. This often provided only a single wash or basic McCandless hang for each area of the stage and placed large restrictions on the number of choices that a designer might have for lighting a production. As a way of providing more variety, a lighting system or collection of instruments representing a given wash might be duplicated **(double-hung)** while modifying one or more of the specific qualities of the wash. The most common example of this involves providing a second system of luminaires that duplicate every element of a lighting system except color (Figure 10.10). Matching instruments are hung next to one another and colored and controlled as two separate systems. Each light of the second system is focused to the same focus points as the original units. Double-hanging is most commonly used to provide a warm and cool color option from the same lighting angle. If this is used in a McCandless hang, where a neutral color is hung from the opposite direction, it provides an opportunity not only for alternating the warm/cool relationships between either side of a subject but also for achieving a

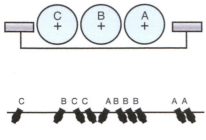

Units are matched to
focus areas by letter.

Figure 10.10 Double and triple hanging areas: A, B, and C essentially follow a McCandless hang with one unit each coming from SR and areas A and C being double-hung from SL while area B is triple-hung from SL. Each additional unit could provide an additional color, angle, or focus to an area.

full range of color mixing. In addition, it achieves higher intensities through the combined output of lamps coming from the same direction. For example, if one wash is colored pink while the other is blue, not only can a designer provide pink and blue colors from an angle, but also a diverse range of lavenders by mixing various proportions of the two colors. Before the advent of LEDs it was (and still can be) a fairly common practice to specify double-hanging throughout a number of lighting systems in a lighting design. While most double-hanging is associated with providing additional colors, other possibilities include changing the angle of the light (e.g., steeper angles or wider-set angles) and creating more tightly or narrowly defined focus areas. A **triple-hang** provides a third alternative for a wash. However, **color scrollers** have become an especially helpful accessory for eliminating double or triple hanging and luminaires while colored LEDS will ultimately replace the majority of the needs for double and triple hanging.

Area versus Color Control

In an ideal world a designer would have enough circuits and dimmers to provide independent control for every luminaire and every area contained in a lighting design. This is rarely possible, and fixtures with common functions are often assigned to the same circuits and dimmers so that fewer dimmers are required for a design. The designer must evaluate whether it is preferable to have independent control of a smaller area of the stage or to have more control of the individual colors of a design (**area versus color control**). There was a time when both cross-lights (with different colors) in a McCandless hang were ganged together to a single dimmer because designers wanted control of each area. A shortcoming to this is that the intensity proportions of the paired lights

cannot be varied: the color mixing will always have the same proportional values, often muddying the colors at medium to low dimmer levels. Today it is more popular to gang a single color from several adjoining areas as a means of lowering the number of required dimmers because designers tend to prefer color over area control in many of their lighting systems. In reality, the decision greatly depends on the given situation. I frequently design shows where I create some systems with more stringent controls based on color, while other systems are designed with a stronger concern toward area control. Personally, I usually prefer to keep color and distribution angles together; I will almost always choose to combine adjoining areas into larger portions of the stage as opposed to combining lights of different colors or angles.

ALTERNATIVE SYSTEMS FOR AREA LIGHTING

Over the years, a number of formulas for creating general illumination for theatrical productions have been put forward. Most have been developed for the proscenium stage. While many of today's lighting designers follow a general approach to developing area lighting systems, most don't adhere to a strict formulaic approach to their lighting anymore. Instead, design decisions are based primarily on the specific image that a designer envisions for a scene or production. By referring back to the lighting concept and lighting key, many designers develop very specific distribution patterns for the general lighting of a production. Despite the current trend to avoid design formulas, you should still be familiar with the more popular approaches because they are techniques for lighting a stage that have proven themselves over time.

Key and Fill

Key and fill lighting had its beginnings in the film and television industries but is now often used as a design formula and general reference throughout the entire lighting industry. In its inception **key light** was associated with the primary or most intense light source and was often equated with the motivating light source for a scene while the **fill light** was associated with the ambient or reflected/scattered light in a scene. In the early days of video and film lighting, cameras and film had very low light sensitivities—and if intensities fell too low, areas of the image would appear dark and unlit. The lights had to be capable of creating a high enough threshold of illumination simply to allow the subject to be seen by the cameras. In studio lighting (just as on a stage), there is little or no ambient light and cameras had problems of not being able to see into the shadow areas. To compensate for the relatively low or nonexistent light in the shadow areas, additional luminaires (**fill lights**) were added to fill in the shadows and provide a base level of illumination so that these areas wouldn't be completely dark. Once a relationship is established between the distribution angles of the key and fill light, the system is repeated throughout a series of adjoining areas—just as is done in area lighting. Today, most general lighting makes some use of the key/fill principle with light coming from at least two different directions. Each pair of luminaires work together to create a key/fill relationship that provides an indication of the light source in one direction and enough shadow illumination to sustain visibility in the other. In reality, the McCandless Method is a variation of a key/fill application.

The Washed Stage

The **washed stage** formula dates back to before the days of electricity and to lighting fixtures that were primarily of a wash/flood variety. Spotlights did not exist yet, and lighting sources were typically candle or lantern flames. The method was based on horizontal rows of luminaires that were hung above and across the stage or along the front edge of the **apron** in the form of footlights. Additional luminaires were mounted on stands in the wings and provided sidelight across the stage. The washed stage was often lit primarily for the benefit of revealing the scenery—even though the illumination levels were often so low that much of the lighting was actually painted into the scenery. In later years, performers might have been highlighted by a spotlight like a limelight, but for the most part the stage was illuminated in a soft low-intensity manner. Because much of the lighting came from above, it was common to have unnatural shadows on the performers' faces. This was compensated for by placing a strong emphasis on light from the footlights, which filled out and softened the harsh shadows of the overhead lighting. The lighting style had the tendency to make the actors appear flat and two-dimensional while also making it difficult to separate the performers from the scenery. The balance of intensity between the overhead washes and footlights was critical because exaggerated shadows could be cast onto the scenery if the intensity of the footlights got too high.

Zone Lighting

Zone lighting represents a special variation of the washed stage and is used in designs where a layered effect is created in the scenery. Productions making use of drops and wing/border settings such as those found in musical theatre or ballet are often associated with this type of lighting. Zone lighting makes use of wash luminaires that light the scenery from above and are then supplemented by other sources of light. To emphasize the sculptural quality of the performers, high-angled sidelight (usually HPEs) is used to light across the stage.

The sidelight is usually the dominant source in a zonal system and is often hung in a minimum of two colors (warm and cool) on each side of the stage, which adds variety to the colors from a particular angle. Backlights are often added to push the performers forward and to help separate them from the background. In a zonal system, most units are focused into the planes that are created by the drops/legs or depth of the stage. The final element of zone lighting includes a wash of light (typically from straight front) that is used to soften the shadows created by the sidelight while adding some front fill to provide visibility for the performers' faces. Dance companies frequently use zone lighting because so many choreographic patterns fall within the planes that are created between the leg sets that are placed throughout a stage. Recent variations of zone lighting, particularly those found in modern dance and musical theatre, have shifted much of the sidelight from the high angles associated with the HPEs to lower angles that are created through using booms that are set within the wings of the stage. These booms are usually placed just upstage of each set of legs. Figure 10.11 provides an illustration of a basic zone lighting system layout.

Jewel Lighting

Jewel lighting is a more recent version of zone lighting in which the emphasis is placed on the higher intensity levels of more recently developed lighting equipment. The most important revision from traditional zone lighting is that the primary source of the lighting shifts to relatively low-angled sidelight that is hung mostly from booms positioned along the sides of the stage. In addition to the basic washes, jewel lighting adds accents and specials to bring more interest to a design. It gets its name primarily from the fact that a variety of angles and colors are used to light a subject—the effect being compared to light being reflected and refracted by the many facets of a jewel. Tom Skelton was one of the earliest advocates for this type of lighting. A significant change from other approaches lies in its dominant use of front diagonal lighting as more units started to be placed in the front of house positions. In addition to traditional booms, the front-diagonal angle is achieved through placing booms in the box seats of many theatres. This allows additional instruments to be brought to the FOH (now capable of side lighting the apron) to support the strong sidelight systems of the onstage booms (Figure 10.12). In many theatres dating before the 1950s, box booms form the only frontal lighting positions outside of the balcony rail. Contemporary theatres generally provide vertical slots in the auditorium walls for the front diagonal angle while overhead catwalks or beams are used for the more frontal lighting positions. Jewel lighting has become a characteristic quality of Broadway musicals. Designers in Broadway theatres must often create these frontal

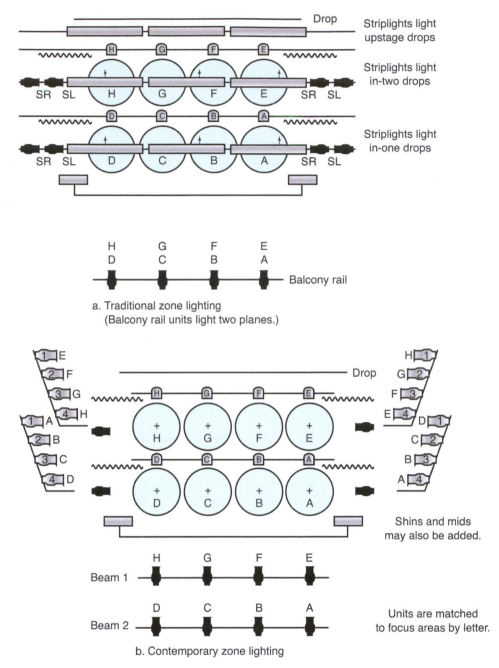

Figure 10.11 Zone lighting

positions by rigging a temporary FOH **truss** that is hung for a specific production and adding booms or other structures to the theatre's box seating areas.

BUILDING ON GENERAL LIGHTING

Even though area lighting provides the basic source of illumination through most of a stage, there are also specialized needs that must go beyond the provisions of general lighting. Some of these needs are satisfied through additional washes while others have very

specific functions in a lighting design. The categories discussed in this section represent several special areas of lighting that are used to supplement the general lighting systems. The majority of these are created by washes that come from different locations throughout a theatre. The most significant washes are associated with the primary directions of a stage and include straight front, front-diagonal, a variety of sidelight angles, downlight, and backlight. The number of luminaires required to complete a wash is a function of the size of the stage, the angle that the wash strikes the stage, and the beam

Figure 10.12 Jewel lighting

spreads and throw distances of the associated units. In most cases, the stage is divided into zones or areas such as planes where a single wash will require anywhere from one to five or more units per plane. As few as one or two lights are all that most sidelight systems require. Near-throw units usually have the widest beamspreads, while the units that are focused to the center or far side of the stage have more narrow beamspreads. The diagrams illustrated in Sidebar 10.2 represent a relatively small stage where only two lamps are required to cover many of these washes. For larger venues, a third lamp with an intermediate beam spread is inserted midway between the existing lamps while the focuses are spread out evenly across the stage.

Special Areas

While the majority of a stage is lit with area lighting, there are often locations where it is impossible to achieve basic visibility using the area systems alone. These are called **special areas**. One of the biggest distractions that can occur in stage lighting comes as a result of having a performer's appearance (in terms of lighting composition) change as they move throughout a space. As an actor moves up a stairway, the lighting should appear consistent even if the area lighting at this point is no longer based on the main level of the stage. Nooks, balconies, hallways, and locations where walls come together in a way that obstructs the area lighting are examples of

these types of problems. Even though these special areas cannot be lighted by the general systems, they must still appear to be lit by the same sources as the rest of the room. Designers accomplish this by making minor modifications in hanging positions and instrument choices to produce a best attempt at continuing the general lighting systems. In many cases, some compromise must be made when laying out these systems and a designer can only provide their "best attempts" at keeping all of the lighting angles consistent. The overall goal is to produce the appearance that the special areas are part of the same lighting environment as the rest of the surroundings.

Sculpting and Modeling Accents

With general systems lighting the stage from mostly frontal angles, there is significant potential for creating a flat, two-dimensional quality to anything that is lit in this fashion. The effect becomes more pronounced as the area lighting becomes flatter. To enhance depth perception, we add side and back lighting not only to supplement the area lighting but to also emphasize the sides and backs of the subjects. These systems are commonly called **modeling/sculpting systems** and are characterized by washes that come from the back and sides of the stage. These washes bring a three-dimensional quality to a subject and help push them forward while separating them from the background. Sidelight may come from a variety of angles, while back light tends to be

Sidebar 10.2 FOCUS PATTERNS FOR COMMON WASH SYSTEMS

a. Front light

b. Front diagonal (two-lamp)

c. High-pipe-end (two-lamp)

d. Sidelight (two-lamp)

e. Mids

f. Shins (shin buster/kicker)

g. Downlight

h. Backlight

relatively steep angled due to having to be set at trims high enough to prevent the lights from either blinding or being seen by an audience. Many designers refer to the light that etches or rims a subject from these angles, particularly the backlight, as **rim lighting** because of the effect that they can give to a subject.

Blending and Toning Accents

At times it may be desirable to provide a wash over the entire stage to accomplish a specific design function. Examples of this might include **toning** or coloring a stage in a full color wash or using an overhead wash to fill in or soften (**blending**) any shadows in the general lighting system. Blending and toning accents can be particularly effective when there are limited resources or where the area lighting isn't as well-developed as one might desire. Blending and toning accents typically use wash luminaires like striplights or scoops that cover a wide area. Two scoops might be all that are required to effectively cover a moderately sized stage. A common application of toning can be found in many high school auditoriums where a series of striplights are hung directly above the stage with the primary purpose of coloring the stage in a variety of colors. While the colors may sometimes be quite extreme—such as when using just the blue circuits for a night scene—it is more common to use a combination of colors to supplement the area lighting while creating subtle variations in the overall color of a scene. These accents may come from any direction but are most commonly located directly above the stage or from the front of house. Even though **wash/floodlight luminaires** have been described primarily for this function, it doesn't prevent a designer from creating a blending or toning system using **spotlights** whose sole purpose is to create a wash. Many of the washes from the balcony rail form examples where spotlights are used to fill in the performers' faces or to tone a stage.

Motivational Accents

There are times when a lighting designer may wish to provide lighting that clearly indicates a specific light source on a stage—what we call **motivational lighting**. One of the problems associated with area lighting is that it commonly becomes a generic design solution. Although it accomplishes the task of providing visibility, it doesn't necessarily make a significant statement or contribution to the specific needs of a production. If a designer uses area or visibility lighting only, they will struggle to achieve a unique image for a given situation—and one design might not change that much from any other design. Therefore, it is important to carefully examine how a general lighting system might be modified so that it can make a unique contribution to a particular moment on the stage. While an indication of a specific light source might be accounted for within the general lighting systems, this in itself might not be enough to produce the desired effect. In order to support the motivational light source, a designer should attempt to add additional luminaires and washes that enhance or provide a clear indication of the given source. These accents are known as **motivational accents** and may be as simple as a single instrument (e.g., light coming from an imaginary streetlamp or a full-stage wash representing light coming from a distant setting sun). Many of the special lighting requirements discussed earlier relating to motivated lighting (e.g., the chandelier) can be created by using motivational accents. Motivational

accents are a key ingredient to adding variety to lighting and should be used fairly liberally throughout a design.

ADDITIONAL LIGHTING DEMANDS

All of the lighting solutions discussed to this point share a common quality in that they provide illumination that covers a significant portion, if not entire stage. This last group of tasks relates to a number of specialized needs that a designer may have to address while lighting a production. Although many of these solutions can be quite specific, making them a unique element of a design, many can appear in virtually any show that a designer works on. These demands are usually solved through a more limited application than creating widespread systems like full-stage washes, and often just one or two luminaires can fulfill the needs of a particular design problem. We refer to a lighting instrument that is used for a specific need or design function as a **special.**

Special Visibility

Special visibility refers to providing luminaires for a specific function of illumination. This may be necessary when the area lighting does not provide adequate coverage of a given feature, or there is a special quality of illumination that cannot be provided by the general or accent lighting systems.

Performer/actor specials are luminaires that are dedicated to revealing performers in a special manner. The obvious use of this technique is when a lighting designer provides a single light for a performer during a specific moment of a performance. General lights may fade away, leaving a performer in a single spotlight, a performer may be revealed from the blackness as a single light is brought up, or a performer may walk into an isolated area of light at a particular moment of a play. These techniques are often used when a performer addresses an audience directly (an aside or narrative moment) or when a designer is creating a more dramatic image for the stage. Specials do not have to bring full visibility to a performer; they might be even more effective if they provide only partial visibility to a subject (e.g., an actor in a backlight for a final tableau). Actor specials can also be used in a subtle manner to punch up or add focus to an area of the stage where special visibility is required. Two examples of this include placing specials on doors to draw focus to entrances and adding lighting instruments to cover seating clusters where actors may gather for an extended time.

Scenic specials come in a variety of shapes and sizes. In some cases, a single fixture fulfills a lighting need, while in others an entire wash or accent system might illuminate a particular scenic element. The most common examples place specials on statuary or paintings to bring a highlight or focus to special features of a set. Others are used to make symbolic statements. Scenic specials may also include adding sidelight to emphasize the three-dimensional elements of a set piece or grazing lights to enhance the texture of a scenic surface. Another use of scenic specials is on signage.

Lighting for Costumes

A lighting designer's decisions can have an immense impact on how costumes are revealed to an audience. While we may worry about the performers' skin complexions and how they might be modified by lighting and makeup, much of how a performer is revealed relates specifically to how the costumes are illuminated by the general lighting systems. For this reason, it is rare that a lighting designer has to create any specialty lighting based solely on the costumes of a production. Instead, designers address the majority of the costume needs as they set up the general lighting and accent systems for a lighting design. The most essential rule relates to the fact that a lighting designer should be making choices that have a complementary effect on the costumes. Colors should in general appear rich, not dull or grayed, and there shouldn't be significant distortion in the perceived color of any costumes (unless there is a logical reason for allowing the shift to occur on stage). If a costume designer uses a wide color palette, the lighting designer will on the whole have to use more tints to avoid graying down some of the colors. On the other hand, an intense color choice on the part of the lighting designer may cause some costume colors to "scream" and become almost neon-like, while others might actually appear to be black. Finally, a designer may want to tone down the color of given fabrics or paints and could purposely choose colors that would prevent particular colors from appearing too vibrant. Lighting can also be used to reveal textures both within the fabrics themselves as well as through the manner in which they are draped or swagged. If a heavily swagged costume is lit with a deep blue downlight from above and also accented with a more natural pink light from the side, from front, the deeper portion of the folds will most likely be lit by the downlight, while the raised surfaces will be highlighted by the pink sidelight.

It is imperative that a lighting designer become familiar with the fabrics that the costume designer has chosen for a production. At the very least, the costume samples or swatches should be examined under gel swatches of the colors that a lighting designer anticipates using on a project. If possible, they should be viewed under lights containing the actual gels that are being considered for a production. One of the benefits of viewing costume swatches under gel and actual light is discovered when hidden dyes cause a fabric to behave differently than anticipated. This often occurs when dark brown or black fabrics are viewed under saturated blue light: the blue filters often allow a high transmission of not only blue, but also red-colored light. The dyes used to create these dark

fabric colors often contain a high concentration of red pigment. While the fabric may appear black under normal lighting, under blue light the red dye is enhanced, causing the "black" fabric to appear reddish-brown or even maroon. These principles hold true for scenic design as well. Similar effects can be observed in patterned or plaid fabrics where the patterns will actually appear to change or even disappear as a result of being exposed to different colors of light. Regardless of the design area, the effects of various color combinations can be significant, and it is important that the lighting designer and other designers be in agreement as to how much distortion is acceptable for a given design.

Lighting for Scenery

In many cases, the general lighting systems are often sufficient for lighting a production's scenery, and there are frequently few, if any, additional demands for lighting the scenic elements of a show. In other cases, entire systems must be devised for lighting the scenery.

Architectural Features

Often, the ambient light created by the area lighting is sufficient for lighting many architectural features and no further instrumentation is required. However, elements of the set may need to be emphasized, colors might have to be modified, and specific textures/patterns may need to be highlighted or toned down. One example of this being used in a practical manner is in disguising wallpaper patterns in the painting of the walls of a set. Here, one wallpaper pattern is revealed under one set of lighting conditions (say under blue light) while a second wallpaper pattern is revealed under other lighting conditions (under gold light). As a rule, the primary focus of a setting should be kept in the lower 8–10 feet of a set (where the performers are). There is seldom a reason to light the walls completely evenly: if walls are lit too evenly, the lighting can diminish the perception of the corners and jogs that are contained in the set. It is also preferable to let the light progressively fade into shadow toward the top of a set. A cornice being lit as well as a door entrance can steal focus, while features like a picture rail can be used as a place to cleverly shutter light that falls onto a wall.

Special types of architectural features are found where entrances appear to lead from the main setting to other rooms or areas of a stage (**maskings**). In these situations the scenic designer is often trying to create the illusion of an adjoining room, and a lighting designer must reinforce the illusion by lighting these areas so that performers don't appear to be coming from or going into a dark void. This is called **lighting the maskings,** and we hang luminaires to specifically light these walls and the performers that use these areas. The lighting instruments may be hung from overhead electrics but are frequently mounted on the offstage faces of the walls of the principal setting. While maskings may be lit using any type of instrument, many designers prefer the soft, even distribution of flood luminaires like scoops for completing this task.

Cycloramas (Cycs) And Drops

Cycs form a special type of lighting concern. Most cover a significant area of the stage opening and form a neutral backdrop that is found in an upstage position. Cycs are used in combination with lighting to create an illusion of a panoramic background for a stage. A true cyclorama—rarely found today—is a plastered wall that curves around the upstage corners of the stage and is painted white. Cycs are now more commonly formed of fabric that is stretched across the width of a stage and may, or may not, curve or wrap around the upstage corners. Due to their neutral color (an off-white), lights can be played upon them to create scenic backgrounds that are easily modified through lighting changes. Dance productions make significant use of cycs to produce a variety of backgrounds for their dancers. Cycs or drops may also be used to reflect or bounce light downstage to light other drops from behind. In this case, you may hear stagehands referring to a **bounce drop** rather than a cyc. A special variety of cyc is the **skydrop**, which for all practical purposes functions the same as a cyc, with the exception that it is colored light blue.

The most common application of cyc lighting involves placing a series of wash luminaires (striplights or cyc lights) across the length of a cyc so that the units hang parallel to the fabric with their beams overlapping and mixing evenly between adjoining units. In most cases, three or four different circuits/colors are provided across the width of the cyc, each being colored in one of the primary lighting colors (red, blue, and green). A designer may choose to use any colors they wish based on the specific needs of a production. Cyc lighting is usually done from an overhead batten that is just downstage of the cyc, focusing the units so that the light washes down the cyc toward the floor. In some cases—such as when a designer wants additional flexibility, or the cyc is large enough so that the light does not carry all the way to the deck—the cyc is divided into zones. A top zone and bottom zone are the most common arrangements, with the top zone being lit from the traditional top angle while the bottom is lit by a second set of fixtures that are set on the floor (**ground row**). Sunset images are produced in this manner. If it is impossible to place a ground row in front of a cyc, the additional instruments lighting the lower portion are hung above the stage and are focused to the lower portions of the cyc (Figure 10.13). In extremely large cycs a third (middle) zone may even be required.

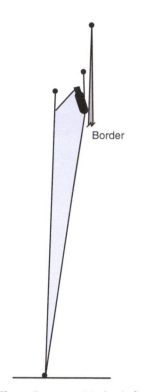

Figure 10.13a Three Common Methods for Lighting Cycs and Drops. Cyc lights or striplights are hung along an electric that runs parallel to the cyc/drop. Distance from the drop will vary with specific units but is typically between 1 and 3 or 4 feet. a. Lit from above.

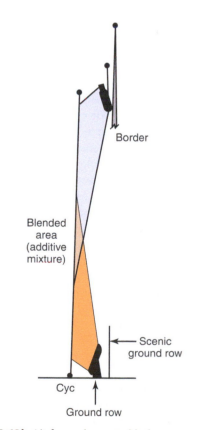

Figure 10.13b Lit from above and below.

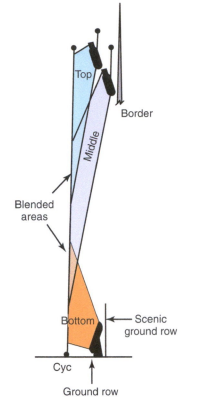

Figure 10.13c A large cyc/drop with three zones.

Although most cyc lighting is done through creating washes over most, if not all, of the surface, not all cyc lighting needs to be of a wash nature. A cyc can also become an effective area for projecting simple scenic images such as gobo clouds or sophisticated projections containing slide or video images. I've played beams of light across different parts of cycs to create geometric patterns, pulled lenses from Fresnels and focused the light to create setting suns, produced luminescent moons by backlighting cycs with spotlights or **moonboxes** and **shadowboxes**, and have even used a cyc in combination with projectors and gobos to create star fields of distant stars and galaxies. One of the challenges in lighting these scenic elements is in preventing performers from casting shadows on a drop or cyc. Techniques that help to avoid this include creating a neutral lighting zone several feet in front of a cyc/drop, taking care to avoid general lighting angles that are so flat that the light spills directly onto these scenic elements, and being mindful of any light that could reflect off of a floor back onto a drop or cyc. These side effects might be softened or eliminated by placing a scrim downstage of a cyc or drop.

Scenic drops are often lit in the same way as a cyc but typically have a couple of restrictions that must be addressed. First, since a drop contains some form of scenic art, the lighting designer must pay attention to the colors that are found in a drop and should strive to

enhance, not distort, them. Second, while a drop may be hung at the rear of a stage like a cyc, many drops are placed in clusters throughout the depth of a stage. Because of this, lighting designers typically opt to light drops from above and place striplights just downstage of the first drop in a given cluster. There are times when this too, cannot be accomplished and a designer will have to use alternate methods of washing a drop by focusing a series of wash luminaires like scoops or even spotlights with soft focuses to different parts of a drop. Finally, specific parts or features of a drop may be accented with scenic specials.

Translucent Drops

Translucent drops form a special classification of scenic materials. These allow light to pass through them while not allowing the audience to see through the scenic material itself. A number of translucent materials may be used on a stage—frosted plexi-glass, treated plastics, rear-projection screens, and even muslin can be used to create translucent drops. Using a bounce drop or placing lighting fixtures upstage of these drops and shining them directly onto a drop's back surface will cause the translucent material to glow and project light (Figure 10.14). Although a translucent drop may cover an entire stage, it is more common to cut out portions of a traditional drop and replace the missing areas with a translucent material. An alternate technique involves

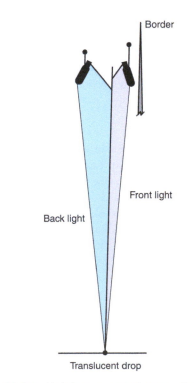

Figure 10.14a Lighting a translucent drop a. Direct backlighting

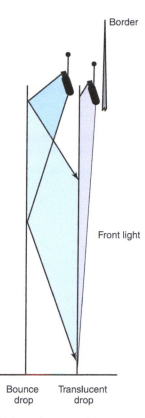

Figure 10.14b Using a bounce drop

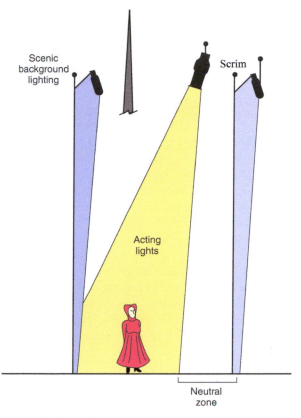

Figure 10.15 Lighting a scrim: high-angled cyc lights or striplights wash the scrim from the front, while lights upstage of the scrim are used to produce the reveal effect

back-painting or masking out those areas of a drop that need to be opaque. The artwork in the translucent areas is then painted with either scenic dyes or light washes (glazes) of paint that allow the light to be projected through them. Stained-glass windows, moonlit rivers, and nighttime city skylines form just a few examples of how this technique can be particularly effective.

Scrims

Scrims have an open mesh-like fabric that allows them to take on either an opaque or transparent quality. Because of this, we use them to "magically" reveal objects. They are frequently hung across the entire width of the stage and are often colored white or black. As a general principle, scrims appear opaque if lit from the front and there is no light present behind them. As light is added behind the scrim, we see through the mesh holes and anything located behind the scrim is revealed. Figure 10.15 illustrates the relative placement of the luminaires in regard to lighting a scrim. Scrims work best if the light in front of them is relatively steep so that the light striking the individual thread elements is reflected upward rather than passing through the material and lighting the objects that the scrim is hiding. Lighting designers frequently shutter lights off of scrims and try to avoid using any lights that will strike a scrim while it is in use.

In most situations, designers attempt to create a neutral lighting zone directly in front of a scrim while trying to avoid hitting the scrim with any light at all. However, there are times when scrims are treated with scenic painting that must be lit. In these circumstances a lighting designer must take care to ensure that any front light for the scrim comes from a fairly steep angle. If the angle is too flat, light passes through the mesh and continues upstage to strike whatever needs to remain hidden. Even when precautions have been taken, spill can still occur upstage of a scrim, and it might become necessary to create a neutral zone behind the scrim where performers and scenic elements shouldn't be placed. In extreme cases, a **blackout drape** or **curtain** may even have to be placed upstage of a scrim until just before the effect is initiated. Finally, anything viewed through a scrim tends to have a soft, hazy quality, which makes scrims particularly effective for fantasy sequences like the dream ballets in musicals like *Oklahoma*.

A white scrim may be painted with dyes so that the pores of the fabric are not filled even though extensive scenic images may still be created on a scrim's surface. When lit from the front, the scene on the scrim appears opaque, while it dissolves on cue as light comes up behind the scrim and reveals the upstage setting. This is called a

scrim-through. Designers also reverse the process with a **scrim-back** where the upstage areas fade as the scene that is painted on the scrim's surface is restored. This effect is used quite effectively in musicals where a show drop is painted onto a scrim and a scrim-through is used to transition into the opening scene during the overture. Although it is common for scrims to cover the entire stage, they may also be used in smaller applications like in a flat or photograph. I once did a production of *Dracula* where a piece of scrim was placed in a wall section that was painted to look the same as the rest of the walls. The wall appeared solid under normal lighting but revealed Dracula standing behind the wall when light was added behind the section of the wall containing the scrim.

A black scrim is often hung several feet in front of a cyc to stop bounce light from the front light spilling up onto a cyc or to create a completely black surround for a stage. This is especially common for dance productions. With this technique, a cyc can have the appearance of going black while still being lit with a variety of colors. When a scrim is used in connection with a cyc (or drop), the luminaires used to light the cyc must be located between the cyc and scrim.

Implied Scenery

There are times when for one reason or another lighting may be used to suggest scenery; in some situations, it

is impossible or undesirable to use a physical structure. More importantly, there are times when the style of a production might be better served by providing suggestive rather than realistic scenic elements. In these stylized modes, it is quite possible for lighting to be responsible for establishing a scene. One of the simplest examples of using luminaires as implied scenery include shuttering a spotlight's beam into a rectangle that suggests that light is coming through a doorway or window. Some of the most popular sources of implied scenery are achieved by using **gobos.**

Effects Lighting

Effects lighting can meet a host of different needs for a lighting designer. A special concern regarding this type of lighting is that while effects can add to the theatricality of a production, they can also become a distraction and should be considered very carefully in a lighting design. If an effect must remain visible throughout a scene, the designer has the added problem of determining how prominent it must be. Often an effect will be quite strong when it is first introduced and can then fade into a less prominent focus once it has been established. This usually helps to prevent it from becoming a distraction to a scene. Many effects, like fire, can be made by using several low-wattage lamps and programming a random chase effect into a lighting console.

Sidebar 10.3 DESIGNER PROFILE

Jeff Davis has worked very successfully in several disciplines of lighting design over the years. His career has gone through phases when he has been associated primarily with a given area of lighting, even though he has actually designed for a variety of lighting disciplines throughout most of his career. His early career was characterized by theatrical productions through designing a number of Broadway shows (*Play On!*, *Born Yesterday*, *The Man Who Came to Dinner*, *The Musical Comedy Murders of 1940*, and others), Off-Broadway designs, national tours and pre-Broadway trials, and a number of regional credits. The second phase of his career shifted to a strong association with television lighting, where his credits are found on many of the major networks (ABC, CBS, NBC, FOX, and PBS, as well as specialty networks such as TBS, ESPN, and CNN). Many of these credits were for special events like the 2016 Republican Convention for Fox News, numerous figure skating specials such as Brian Boitano's *Canvas of*

Ice, and *Skates of Gold* for ABC, while others were for network daytime productions including *One Life to Live*, *All My Children*, *As the World Turns*, and the syndicated *The Maury Show* and the *Sally Jesse Raphael Show*. Several of these designs earned him Emmy nominations. His television experience opened the door for his third career phase, which is predominantly in opera design and began with his becoming resident lighting designer for the New York City Opera. His television experience payed off with the company's need to adapt its productions' lighting for the popular *Live at the Lincoln Center* series. Jeff designed 25 new productions for the company and many were adapted for live television broadcast. Davis soon gained a reputation that led to designing for opera companies throughout the country (Washington National Opera, Pittsburgh Opera, Opera Company of Philadelphia, Indianapolis Opera, and more) and internationally. He continues to design in these areas while also lighting a

---

Jeff Davis

Credit: photo courtesy Jeff Davis

number of industrial or corporate productions for clients such as Coke, Honda, Minolta, Johnson & Johnson, and Wendy's. He has also lit unique projects such as the productions on the cruise ship *Disney Magic* (Disney Cruise Lines).

Jeff lights within a variety of disciplines but currently lights primarily plays and operas with an occasional return to television. He graduated from Northwestern University with a degree in Speech (the theatre department was within the School of Speech). His informal training came from working as an assistant to Tharon Musser and later as an associate designer to Jo Mielziner. "Tharon gave me my start and introduced me to the particular workings of Broadway production," he says. "More importantly, she taught me how to be a proficient and effective collaborator." Jeff goes on to offer several tips for preparing for a career in lighting design:

"The study of painting and art history has truly helped me to understand foreground, middle ground, and background as well as composition. Learning photography was also helpful in developing a sense of visual composition . . . and I learned how to read music, which is essential to designing opera. I cannot play music, but I can read it."

When asked how he came to work primarily in opera he shares that he more or less fell into it:

"I have enjoyed opera since I was introduced to it as a teenager by my grandmother, attending performances at the Santa Fe Opera. I mostly designed plays and occasional musicals for Broadway and regional theatre until I was hired as the resident lighting designer at New York City Opera in 1991. I feel that there were other designers who applied for the position who had more opera experience than I, but believe that I was selected because of my television experience."

At the time, New York City Opera productions were being televised for the PBS programs *Live From Lincoln Center* and *Great Performances*. Jeff shares an interesting story about being "typed" as a designer. "After NY City Opera, it took seven years before someone hired me to design a production where people only spoke. Producers did not realize or remember that until 1991, I had almost exclusively designed plays." Currently, his work is three-quarters in opera design, but this depends on the year and how the individual projects line up.

Jeff sees one of the fundamental differences between working in opera and other entertainment genres being related to the scale of productions:

"Opera, by its nature, is larger than life, even though the human emotions are the same as in a play. They are simply expressed in a larger emotional way. . . . Singing and orchestration makes it larger. . . . The scenery also follows the bigger-than-life emotion. Thus, the lighting follows. Opera is driven totally by music and the way that light moves is totally aligned with the music."

Despite the issues of scale, time is also a unique consideration in opera design: "Opera is large in every way, and time in the theatre is very expensive." Most opera companies operate in unionized houses—add stagehands, musicians, and singers, and an average opera can employ 70 to 80 people who will be directly involved with the production in the theatre. "Time is the enemy (financially)," Jeff says. The companies are very tightly budgeted and have a finite amount of time (and money) for rehearsals in the theatre: "The production must be completed in the allotted amount of time." A typical schedule in regional opera has the production loading-in on a Sunday or Monday and opening the next Friday:

> "As a lighting designer, I must know how much equipment I can hang and focus in the amount of time that is scheduled. More importantly, I must have a very clear idea of the lighting and visual look of the production because my time for lighting is very limited. More often than not, I am lighting over staging rehearsals and have no other time than these rehearsals to create light cues."

A typical situation involves cueing a production over two three-hour staging rehearsals and a four-hour session without the cast: "You do not have the time to discover the concept and look of the production with the director in the theatre. This speed of production is not for everyone." While time constraints are a challenge, what he likes about working in opera is that "Producers pay me to listen to pretty music. I also feel that there is more respect

in the opera community for the contribution of the lighting designer than in other disciplines." When pressed to comment on what he considers an essential rule for working in opera, he states:

> "For me, it is the same as in any theatrical venture . . . We must tell the story and support the emotion of the piece at every moment. Lighting tells the audience how to see and where to look. Lighting is cinematography for the theatre."

To remain current, Jeff continues to work in opera, theatre, and television so that he knows the trends, current tastes, and artistic vision of the various companies that he designs for. He also tries to keep up with the equipment by reading trade magazines, visiting manufacturers and lighting shops, and trying to see as much theatre as he possibly can. He offers the following as a final bit of advice: "Go to the theatre. Go to museums. Light anything, within reason!"

Other lighting effects include automated lighting moves and visual chase sequences or other patterns of illumination that aren't necessarily created by a specific set of specials but by cueing luminaires that are already a part of a lighting design. A cyc sequencing through various color combinations in a dance recital is an example of this type of effect. Lighting effects also do not necessarily have to involve motion; a scene may shift into green light for a specific reason (a symbolic connection to greed), a designer may want to create a visual connection or reaction to a character (the symbolic lights used when Salieri talks to God in *Amadeus*), or a series of specials may be used to create specific points of focus (specials for asides). Finally, projections also form a special area of lighting effects. The projected images may be either realistic or stylized.

FOR FURTHER READING

McCandless, Stanley. *A Method for Lighting the Stage*. 4th ed. New York: Theatre Arts Books, 1958.

McCandless, Stanley. *A Syllabus of Stage Lighting*. 5th ed. New Haven, CT: Yale University Press, 1941.

Mumm, Robert C. *Photometrics Handbook*. 2nd ed. Louisville, KY: Broadway Press, 1997.

Palmer, Richard H. *The Lighting Art: The Aesthetics of Stage Lighting Design*. 2nd ed. Englewood Cliffs, NJ: Prentice Hall, 1994.

Pilbrow, Richard. *Stage Lighting Design: The Art, the Craft, the Life*. New York: Design Press/Quite Specific Media Group, Ltd., 1997.

Shelley, Steven Louis. *A Practical Guide to Stage Lighting*. 3rd ed. Oxford and Boston: Focal Press, 2014.

Warfel, William B. *The New Handbook of Stage Lighting Graphics*. New York: Drama Book Publishers, 1990.

CHAPTER 11

PLOTTING THE DESIGN

THE **LIGHT PLOT** or **lighting layout** is a scaled drafting of a stage/auditorium or environment (top view) that illustrates critical information related to a lighting design. Light plots are used in entertainment lighting, while lighting layouts are used in permanent installations like themed and exhibit designs as well as architectural projects. The light plot and lighting layout can be compared to a road map where every luminaire is placed in a location directly related to where it will be hung in the installation. In addition to identifying the type and location of each instrument, the light plot also provides essential information relating to the wiring and accessories that are associated with each fixture. Some of the more essential information contained in most light plots includes gel colors, instrument numbers, and control channels. Additional information might include dimmer and/or circuit numbers, focus notations, lamp size and type, and manufacturer designations.

Everything discussed to this point in the design process has been purely theoretical. When we arrive at this stage; a designer should have completed the majority of their research, developed their lighting concept, drawn lighting keys, and explored a number of potential options regarding a lighting design. It is when the designer gets to this point, when they begin to create the light plot, that they start to commit to specific choices that will eventually dictate the outcome of a final design. Light plots and layouts fulfill two very important functions. First, in rough form, they are used as a worksheet for lighting designers to develop their ideas and translate their images into specific design decisions. Designers explore which hanging positions are best suited for a given angle of light, examine how much coverage a given luminaire and throw distance might provide, and explore issues related to the relationship between the luminaires and the settings or performers. Second, and more importantly, the light plot will ultimately become the principle form of communication between the designer and the electricians who will hang and wire the lights for a production.

Every light plot should be drawn from the perspective that the plot will be hung without the designer being present at the **load-in.** In fact, it is quite common to send a plot ahead of a designer with the intention that the hang will be completed and ready for focusing once the designer comes to town. Neat drafting skills are essential to completing this aspect of a lighting design. On the other hand, the plot is a tool for producing the design and should not be thought of as the final product in itself. While good drafting practices are important, they alone will not produce a successful light plot or final lighting design. I have seen many well-drafted plots with critical problems relating to issues like luminaire selection and placement, angle distributions, and color selection despite having an attractive drafting style. This can be especially misleading in computer-aided drafting (CAD) plots. The light plot is an extremely important step in the overall process of a lighting design. If a designer makes a major mistake when they create the plot, there may not be much that can be done to fix the problem once the load-in at the theatre has been accomplished. If all the angles of a wash system are too severe, the only practical way of solving the problem will most likely require moving the units to new hanging positions, which may or may not be possible once a show is hung in the theatre. It's an even bigger issue in architectural applications where fixture openings in walls and ceilings, mounting hardware and conduits are involved. One final area of concern lies in that the plot is still only one aspect of designing a show. Even with the best plot, lighting designs have failed miserably due to the designer not being able to produce appropriate cues and/or transitions for a show.

This chapter and the light plot form an essential step in the design because it starts the process of converting the vision of the designer into physical decisions that will ultimately determine the outcomes of a lighting design. The process of creating a light plot is a very personal one that many designers tailor to their individual ways of working. Factors such as time allotment, type and scale of project, collaborators, facility, and the number of tech and dress rehearsals all play a role in the way in which I approach a design. Throughout this chapter I discuss a general process and several specific techniques that I use to translate the mental images of a concept into the physical demands of a light plot. This information should provide beginning designers with a starting point and overall methodology for approaching a light plot and design. While the techniques presented here will work for many individuals, you should feel free to adopt and revise them in ways that align with the specific manners in which you work as a designer.

Translating Concepts and Lighting Keys Into Practical Design Choices

One of the most important functions of a light plot is to aid a designer in turning their images into actual choices that control the properties of light. We have spent the last several chapters developing an image for a production. What should the lighting look like? Are there motivational lighting elements? Are there practical sources on the stage? Where is the light coming from? What is the quality, color, texture, and intensity of the light? Lighting functions should also be considered as part of this process. Is a particular environment or atmosphere called for? How much visibility is required? What direction is a motivational light coming from? How strong must a focus be and where should it be established? What is the mood? These and questions like them should be addressed in the **lighting concept.** When we get to the light plot, the job of the lighting designer is to convert these conceptual images into practical design choices like luminaire selection, hanging positions, focus points, and color choices. No matter how a designer solves these issues, the answers to all of the questions should be determined in a manner that supports or is founded in the concept—it is the basis for all your decisions.

Many designers create visual methods for representing specific moments or images of a production. In Chapter 9, I introduced **storyboards** and **lighting scores** as two methods of communicating this information to other members of the production team. We might even create computer renderings of these moments. In addition to supporting the concept through storyboards or lighting scores, many designers choose to illustrate the lighting compositions through **lighting keys**. A lighting key may be developed for any moment of a production but is used most often to illustrate the full wash systems that cover the majority of a stage. More importantly, they provide a tool for matching the specific intentions of a concept to practical choices of luminaire, hanging positions, and color associations for a plot. It is common to have separate lighting keys for different scenes or acts of a production. Often, the lighting keys become the foundation for the layout of the general illumination or area lighting systems for a show.

Working With Floorplans and Sections

As we move toward creating a lighting design we need to make calculations in regard to throw distances, beam spreads, and distribution angles that are associated with the luminaires that will light a scene. By using scaled plans, the unique physical properties of light emitting from a particular luminaire can be translated into graphical data that represents how that light should perform in a given situation. Lighting designers have come to rely on two key draftings for working through this part of a design project. The first, a **floorplan** or **groundplan,** provides a scaled top view of an environment, while the second, the **section** or **sectional view,** provides a variation of side view for a facility.

Floorplans or Groundplans

Floorplans (also called groundplans) are usually considered the most important drafting for many design applications. In lighting design, the floorplan is frequently used as a template for the **light plot,** which represents the single most important design document that a lighting designer produces. With these plots, we do not typically illustrate the entire auditorium, only the stage and adjoining spaces. Many floorplans and light plots also indicate a portion of the house or audience areas and **front of house (FOH)** lighting positions as well. Several features found on virtually all master floorplans include the proscenium or stage opening; the edge of the stage; all architectural walls, columns, and doorways; an indication of any permanent lighting positions like torms, box boom positions, beams, and the prewired electrics; and a lineset schedule that provides the location and identification of all the flown equipment (scenic, lighting, and maskings) and their associated **linesets.** Common reference lines like the **centerline** and **plasterline** are also indicated. Other information that is often found on a floorplan includes references to a facility's sightlines, inclusion of scaled rules that allow for the measurements from either side of a centerline or stage depths from the plaster line, and labels or notes that clarify information relating to any unique features of a space. When a designer is first contracted to design in a facility they should obtain a packet of information that includes a set of master drawings containing the floorplan and section of the performance space as well as any special information regarding lighting within that facility (e.g., circuit layouts, number and capacity of dimmers, lighting inventory, etc.). A special variation of master plan that is especially helpful is the **circuit layout.** This drafting includes all the information found in a floorplan plus an indication of all the circuit locations throughout a facility. Most theatres have this information readily available and many actually post it on their websites.

For a floorplan to be truly beneficial to a lighting designer it should make a clear indication of every permanent hanging position throughout a theatre. In a theatre equipped with a fly house, all of the linesets should be indicated and labeled with whatever is to be hung on them for the given show (electric, scenery, maskings, and even empty). This is a **hanging section,** and each of these linesets should be placed in their actual positions throughout the depth of the stage. In those theatres that have a substantially large auditorium, it is common to compress or shorten the distance between the FOH positions and the stage to produce more economically sized draftings. Floorplans may be created using conventional pencil and paper drafting techniques or computer drafting and CAD (Computer-Aided Design or Drafting). Lighting designers, in particular, have embraced CAD due to the repetitive nature of many of the tasks associated with drafting a light plot.

The scale of these drawings may vary due to a variety of issues like the amount of detail required, facility size, and complexity of a design. The issue of scale usually balances between being large and detailed enough so that the electricians can easily read all the specification information while at the same time being small enough that the plot doesn't become awkward to carry around and use throughout the design process. Popular scales in hand-drafting include 1/4 inch and 1/2-inch (to the foot) scales. The 1/2-inch scale provides good clear information but can produce a plate or drawing that is too large to handle easily. On the other hand, a 1/4-inch scaled drawing reduces the details to such a small size that vital information might be missed. A common compromise is to break the space down into smaller areas using separate plates with larger scales like 1/2 inch = 1 foot for areas like the **overheads** (area directly over the stage) and the FOH hanging positions. Another scale that has gained popularity is the 3/8-inch scale which is midway between the other two scales. With CAD software, scale has become less of an issue since it is so easy to change the scale of the finished print of a drawing.

Floorplans are an essential tool for helping lighting designers determine the **throw distances** and **beam spreads** of luminaires. The throw distance represents the line of sight distance between the luminaire and its target. Beam spreads are an important element in a lighting design because they effectively determine how much coverage is created by a luminaire. If a lighting instrument is chosen with a particular beam spread, a variety of different sized light pools are produced as the instrument is moved between different hanging positions. As the unit is moved farther away from the stage, its throw distance is increased and the resultant beam gets larger. However, even though the light covers a larger portion of the stage, it is also weakened by being spread out over a greater area. Through using a manufacturer's **cut sheet** and other photometric data regarding a specific luminaire, a lighting designer can determine both the pool size and resultant intensity of a lighting instrument at different distances between the stage and various hanging positions. A designer can also make an approximate determination of throw distance simply by drawing a line between the location of where the lighting instrument will be mounted to the location that corresponds to the point where the light will be focused. The resultant line represents an approximate throw distance (in scale) between the two points. The throw distance can then be referenced to a manufacturer's cut sheet to determine the photometric output (in footcandles) and size of its associated pool at that distance. If a designer wants to increase or decrease the brightness of the light, they must either move the luminaire to a different mounting position (closer or farther away) or should select a luminaire with a different output (more or less footcandles for a given distance). For more accurate determinations, a geometric construction can be made that illustrates the throw distance as the hypotenuse of a right triangle. The height of the luminaire (**trim**) is plotted along the vertical axis of the triangle, while the floor distance between the luminaire and target is plotted as the horizontal axis. This allows the true throw distance to be determined using the Pythagorean Theorem ($A^2 + B^2 = C^2$). As a rule, the base of the triangle should be placed at about 5 to 6 feet above the stage floor so that the focus point is at the approximate head height of the performers (See Figure 10.5 in the last chapter).

As discussed in Chapter 10, an important first step in many lighting designs after completing the conceptual framework of a production is breaking the stage into specific areas that will each be lit by individual luminaires. A practical size for these lighting areas ranges from 8 to 12 feet in diameter, with many designers using 10 feet as an average-sized area. By creating a simple template, lines can be constructed that represent the beam spread(s) of a given luminaire(s). These angles are split symmetrically across a central line representing the axis of the luminaire and shortest path or **throw distance** between the luminaire and target. The template is laid over the floorplan with the originating point being placed over the location of the luminaire and the line representing the throw distance oriented so that it passes directly over the target or focus point of an acting area. A second line is then drawn perpendicular to the line representing the throw distance so that it intersects both the focus point and lines that define the beam spread of a given instrument. The length (in scale) of this resultant line represents the diameter of the light pool at that distance from the light source. Pool size is a function of the throw distance, mounting position, and the beam spreads of the luminaires. On the other hand, if a circle representing the diameter of a lighting area is drawn around the focus point, the template can also be used to determine which beam spread and associated luminaire will best match the size of a lighting area from a given hanging position (i.e, which beam spreads on the template come closest to intersecting the full diameter of the area circles). If the luminaire is moved to a closer position, the resultant beam diameter will be smaller, while it will increase if the luminaire is moved farther away from the target. By working with various combinations of hanging positions and beam spreads a designer can determine the most effective luminaires and hanging positions for producing light pools of a given size. While a template can be made as simply as through placing lines representing the throw distance and beam angles on vellum or acetate, commercial templates are also available. You can refer back to Figure 10.3 for more information regarding the use of these templates. Particularly helpful software packages like John McKernon's Beamwright®allow a lighting designer to examine pool diameters, lengths of shadows, beam spreads, intensity measurements, and other photometric data. The information is modified based on the data of a specific luminaire and various mounting parameters (trim and floor distances) that are associated with its location. Beamwright® contains data for most luminaires associated with the entertainment industry and allows a variety of instruments reflecting different model types and manufacturers to be compared with one another.

Regardless of the way in which a designer prefers to work with a floorplan, what is most important is that the designer uses this material to identify the most effective positions and luminaire choices for a given application. These distances, even as approximations, are usually accurate enough for making comparisons between most luminaires and mounting positions. However, two important exceptions exist where the scale of the drafting can be compromised through issues like using conventions such as compressing the FOH hanging positions. In the first case, one must remember to adjust the location of the luminaire origination points in a FOH position to reflect the true distance of the hanging positions from the stage. The second case comes when a unit is used in a relatively steep angle like

downlight, when the floorplan distance is much shorter than the actual throw distance.

Sections

There are two especially important reasons why a section is vital to a lighting designer. First, sections provide the same information in a vertical orientation that a floorplan displays in the horizontal or plan view. Beam spreads, vertical angles, and length of shadows can all be determined from this drafting. Second, the section provides a means by which a lighting designer can determine the **trims** or heights of the electrics while also studying the **maskings** that will be hung from above a stage. A properly masked show will usually block an audience's view of the electrics while still allowing clear shots from the luminaires to their targets. Some lighting designers skip this step in the process—and get burned. I have witnessed issues like electrics being placed at trims that, once masked, caused backlight to point directly into the back of borders as well as upstage platforms that could not be hit due to the trim of a border falling lower than anticipated by a designer. A lighting designer should always take time to complete a section for a lighting design. The more levels that appear on stage, the more important the section becomes. Even if not doing a formal drafting, a rough section that is done in scale will eliminate many of the issues that might come up if no sectional study had been done at all.

Sections are typically drawn with the centerline being the cutting plane through which the view of the theatre is taken. In most cases, it extends from the back wall of the stage to a location somewhere in the house. All vertical elements of a stage are indicated in this drawing. While a master section only illustrates the physical theatre, it is just as important for scenic designers to provide a lighting designer with a section of the scene design for a production. If the scenery warrants it, the cutting plane and associated view may be taken from almost anywhere across the width of the stage. Study of lighting angles, beam spreads, and photometric data are done in the same manner as for floorplans with the exception that the analysis is now done in a different plane—where height becomes a critical determinant in the analysis of the luminaires and hanging positions. Again, most target points are placed at a height 5 to 6 feet above the floor, which aligns the hot spots with the performers' faces rather than their feet. More importantly, by using the same template of beam/field angles, a designer can get a clear indication of the coverage of a lighting instrument in sectional view. This time, the origin of the template is located at a position corresponding with the hanging position, while the line representing the throw distance is oriented directly over the corresponding focus point (at head height). Figure 11.1 illustrates the use of a section for determining lighting

Figure 11.1 Vertical determinations of position and beam spread with a section

angles and beam spreads for the principle hanging positions used in a production of *Measure for Measure*.

Just as important as determining mounting positions and beam patterns are decisions related to masking a show. This ensures that the trims of the electrics and borders are set so that audience views of the electrics are blocked while also ensuring that the luminaires can hit their targets. To establish proper maskings for a show, an extreme sightline is indicated on the section that is based on the head height of an audience member seated in the first row of the audience. This point is used as an origin point for sightlines that extend from it to the bottom edge of any maskings that are hung from above the stage (e.g., borders). These sightlines are extended beyond the borders so that the electrics can be placed above the sightlines and out of view while also being low enough that the units can hit the parts of the stage where they will be focused. Figure 11.2 illustrates the use of the same section to set the border and electric trims for *Measure for Measure*.

Just as a scenic designer provides the lighting designer with a scenic floorplan, a section should also be included in the scenic design packet. This section should include the placement of each border and any other maskings that are hung from above the stage. Other scenic elements like platforms, wall and scenic unit heights, and flown elements with both high and low trim markings should be indicated in these plans. Specific hanging positions and trim heights are often discussed between scenic and lighting designers, and there

have actually been a number of times where I, as the lighting designer, was allowed to mask and set the trims for a show. If a scenic designer does relinquish control of the trims and maskings to a lighting designer, it is important for everyone to understand that it may not be possible to go back and change the masking and trim placements once a show has begun its load-in and focus. There are also times when it may be desirable to place electrics in full view of an audience. On these occasions, the section helps a designer to once again determine the best positions for these trims. I designed a production of *Noises Off* in which the electrics were fully masked in Acts I and III, where the setting took place from a traditional audience perspective, while for Act II several of the electrics and borders changed trim to bring the electrics into view to suggest that the audience's perspective had been switched to backstage. I have used a similar technique in the productions of *The Who's Tommy* that I have designed in order to expose many of the electrics for creating a concert-like experience. Even though experienced designers may have lit many productions in a given facility and have a good understanding of which luminaires work best from different house positions, it is still important to study the floorplan and section due to the unique requirements of a particular scenic design. The section becomes especially important the first time that a designer works in a space. It also helps, if possible, to arrange a **site survey** where personal observations and measurements can be made of a stage prior to developing a light plot.

Figure 11.2 Setting borders and trim heights with a section

AN APPROACH TO PLOTTING A DESIGN

Throughout this discussion I use a production of Moliere's *The Miser* as an example of how to apply a design process to creating a light plot. This production was designed as part of the Jean Cocteau Repertory Theatre season at the Bouwerie Lane Theatre in New York City. This production was of a limited scale, which should make it easier to analyze throughout the process. While I may modify this process based on individual projects, there are several essential steps that are taken for nearly every design that I complete—whether with some formal methodology as presented here or only intuitively as part of the design process. For designers with relatively little or no experience, these steps should provide a more practical way of approaching a design, while those who are more experienced may use these suggestions to review their personal design process. I will continue to use this production as an example in Chapter 12 as we move the production into the theatre.

Preliminary Tasks/Preparation

When I discuss preliminary tasks, I am referring to the acquisition of background materials that will be needed to execute the planning stages of a lighting design. This information should be gathered and fully understood prior to making any specific decisions regarding the light plot. In reality, some of this information will be available, while some will remain unknown due to tight rehearsal schedules and the fact that it is common for a light plot to be completed before a company moves into a venue. The designs that I have completed for the Atlanta Lyric Theatre have always required that the plot be mailed ahead of my seeing a single run-through of a production. In cases like this, a lighting designer must rely heavily on the conversations that they have with the director and other members of the artistic team.

A key step at this point in the process involves determining the lighting scheme and concept, and creating the storyboards and lighting key(s) for a project. These were discussed extensively in previous chapters and form the basis for most of the decisions that a designer will make in regard to a light plot.

Advancing a Venue

When we **advance** a venue, we gather as much information about the performance venue as possible. Sometimes this is done indirectly through gathering materials such as design packages for a theatre while at other times this may actually mean traveling to the facility, taking measurements, comparing design documents to what actually exists in the theatre, taking digital photographs of the space and equipment, and talking to the local house representatives to ask about unique issues related to both the space and operating within the space. Some designers may even perform an actual **site survey**.

Essential information to be assembled at this stage of the project and before attempting to work on the light plot include copies of the master floorplan and section of the facility, a copy of the scenic floorplan(s) and section for the production, color indications (swatches, photographs or copies of paint elevations, models, renderings, etc.) from the costume and scenic designers, and a lighting specifications package for the facility. Lighting equipment inventories are an important item on this list. Although most productions must work within set inventory limitations, there are occasions when an inventory might be supplemented or even fully supplied by gear that is provided by a rental house or by combining equipment from other resources. Frequently, equipment provided by a facility is fairly limited, and it is the production's responsibility to provide most of the lighting equipment. Even the dimmers and console are included in many of these rental packages. Most Broadway and touring houses operate in this fashion.

Rehearsals

Rehearsals give a lighting designer the opportunity to view an event prior to moving into the performance venue. While it is common in educational theatres for rehearsals to take place in the actual space where the performances will take place, this is more often the exception with productions outside of an academic setting. Most rehearsals are conducted in rehearsal halls or studios so that the time used in mounting a production in the actual theatre is kept to a minimum. Even if an organization owns its own facility, it is common to rehearse outside of the theatre so that other shows can complete longer runs. Additional issues, such as how long a producer can afford to have a lighting designer in residence, will also determine how many rehearsals a lighting designer gets to see. Usually, a lighting designer is brought in only for the last week or so of the production process. This eliminates per-diem expenses, hotel or room costs, and additional transportation required when a designer is in residence. In many cases, light plots have to be completed even before designers see their first rehearsal. This type of scheduling requires a heavy reliance on developing good communication skills with the director.

Observing rehearsals is important because it allows the designer to become familiar with a production. A designer makes important discoveries regarding the performers' and director's interpretation of a script when attending rehearsals. However, what is most important is understanding the movement patterns of the performers. In addition to studying the physical relationships between the actors, the designer should also evaluate the scenes for focus as well as for pace, mood, and transitions. **Run-throughs** are much more beneficial to see than working rehearsals for making these observations.

Even if a lighting designer can see only several scenes, they will still gain an understanding of the actions, the way in which the director uses a space, and a feeling for the moods and transitions of the associated scenes. At these rehearsals I take care to make accurate records of the **blocking notation** (Chapter 9).

For *The Miser*, my preliminary design discussions were conducted with the director through e-mail and telephone conversations before I left town for New York. The lighting inventory, plans, and technical specifications for the theatre were also sent to me earlier. In reality, I already had many of the materials since I had lit a production of *The Maids* in the same theatre a year earlier. Even though I had this information, it was important to determine what had changed from the last time that I had worked in the space. In this case, the Cocteau had upgraded to a new lighting system of 60 high-density dimmers. The inventory was also revised to include a number of new luminaires that were purchased as part of the same grant that the organization had received to upgrade its lighting equipment.

The Wish List

Once I have completed my analysis and research for a design, developed the lighting concept, had discussions with the director and other artistic staff, and hopefully attended a run-through or two, I am at a point where I can begin to develop the actual plot. While there are many different ways of working, I have found that developing a **wish list** for a production is an excellent way to identify those elements of a design that I believe are most essential. It also allows me to prioritize all of the lighting needs and translate them into specific choices that will ultimately be drafted into the final plot. By the time that I finish working with the wish list, a number of the major decisions regarding the design will have been committed to and the design will be ready to enter into a preliminary or rough light plot. Later, this plot will be converted into the final drafting. Throughout the entire process, the lighting concept and visual references like the storyboards or lighting scores and lighting keys are used as a basis for evaluating each task within the wish list.

In creating a wish list, a designer simply makes determinations of those lighting features that they would like to provide for a production. Issues such as the number of color washes from various locations, amount of coverage or area breakdown required, director-requested specials and images, lighting of scenic elements, effects considerations, accents, and other personal design choices all form part of these considerations. The lighting key plays a significant role in identifying the components of the general or area lighting that will appear in the wish list. The actual list is simply jotted down on a notepad and framed in such a way that the item or "wish" can ultimately be translated into specific choices of luminaire, color, and control (channel and dimmer). Area lighting and other wash systems are further broken down into the number of area components or zones that the designer will ultimately hope to use for each lighting system. If a designer wishes to use a system with a breakdown of five areas across and three deep, this is indicated in the wish list. If there is even a hint of a desire for a particular special or specific lighting feature I include it somewhere on this list. As I create the list, I try to group each demand into areas of the list that match related lighting needs (i.e., groupings like area lighting, accent washes, specials, cyclorama [cyc] lighting, etc.). Those elements of the design that I consider most important are placed further up the list while those with less-demanding needs are entered further down the list. In many cases, my wish list may contain five or six pages (often more) of specific demands that I hope to incorporate into a lighting design. Basic components of the design in terms of color and angle distributions, area/zone breakdowns, and specific needs like accents and specials form important elements of the wish list. Figure 11.3 provides a partial listing of the wish list for the Cocteau's production of *The Miser*.

A designer must be realistic about the demands that they place in a wish list. Availability can be restricted due to the actual inventory, the rental budget, and/or the amount of time and number of electricians available to hang and focus a show. Most design decisions come about through restrictions in the number of dimmers or luminaires that are available for a design. One question that a lighting designer needs to address early in this process is which of these limitations is ultimately going to be the primary restriction on a design. In a theatre where there are many instruments and relatively few dimmers, the number of dimmers will ultimately shape a design. This was the manner in which most of us had to design prior to dimmer-per-circuit lighting systems. Today, since we commonly have theatres with hundreds of circuits and dimmers, it is more common to have design restrictions based on not having enough inventory to fulfill all the wishes of a lighting design. Even with dimmer-per-circuit dimming, it is still possible to run out of dimmers in a complex design.

Making a Design Practical

Once all of the demands of a design have been placed on the wish list, the next step in the process is assessing the practical limitations of the inventory. I already made reference to the fact that most of today's designs are limited more by luminaire rather than dimmer limitations. Therefore, the inventory is used in combination with the wish list to establish practical solutions for each demand of the list. By working through this process, most (if not all) of the demands will be addressed and hopefully worked into the final design.

Figure 11.3 *The Miser* wish list (partial)

Table 11.1 A sample lighting inventory/use table

Unit Type	Wattage	Number in Inventory	Specific Use:	Lighting Used	Inventory Remaining
6" Fresnel	500 w				
PAR64	1000 w				
S4-36	575 w				
S4-26	575 w				
S4-19	750 w				
Far Cyc	500/cell				

The first step is establishing a complete inventory of each lighting instrument that is available for a production. To work through this, I have developed a table that indicates several key sources of information relating to the luminaire inventory. The first column lists the type of luminaire while the second lists the wattage of the units. The next column provides the total number of units of a particular instrument type that are available for a production. The form also makes a distinction between luminaires of the same type but of varying wattages or from different manufacturers. The next area of the table lists the specific uses of each light that is used from the inventory. Finally, the last two columns indicate the number of each luminaire type actually used and the remaining units still available.

The next step is crucial: it involves matching the lighting needs of the production outlined in the wish list with the luminaires that are available in the inventory list. Washes are established with common luminaires, throw distances and beam spreads are matched to hanging positions, and specific specials are matched to instruments that best emulate the characteristics desired in that special. A designer begins by assigning luminaires to the most important tasks first and then moves through the wish list matching luminaires to specific purposes on a priority basis. A general listing of priorities that extend from most to least important would normally include area or general lighting systems, accents and other wash systems, critical specials, motivational units, scenic specials, and finally additional accents and subtle specials. When making luminaire assignments, a floorplan containing the lighting positions and set design is used along with a section to help match the specific needs of beam spread and throw distances to particular lighting fixtures. As a lighting instrument is assigned to a specific function, a tick mark is placed in the "Used" column, while the actual function and number of units assigned to that function are listed in the "Specific Use" column of the inventory worksheet. Additionally, the type and number of luminaires is also listed next to the need/function in the wish list to cross-reference the information between the two forms. Once a function has been assigned to specific luminaires, a check mark is placed on the wish list to indicate that the particular need has been addressed. More complex systems such as area lighting arrangements may use graphical illustrations to indicate the specific instrument layouts.

As a designer works through the lists, the decisions become more difficult—and as instruments of a specific type become depleted, the designer has to make sacrifices in order to achieve as many of the needs as they can for the design. Instruments may be substituted with luminaires that aren't as good of a match with the initial intentions of the designer, two or more specials might be combined by dedicating both functions to a single instrument, an insufficient number of dimmers might require that specials be **re-patched** through common dimmers, individual area control may be sacrificed by ganging several luminaires from different areas to a single dimmer, or in the worst case scenario, specific wishes are simply cut. The process is simple at first but becomes more challenging as fewer instruments remain and more compromises must be made to complete a design. On the other hand, the advantage to this process is that it provides a means for accomplishing many of the wish list demands that could have been too easily dismissed otherwise. When the wish list and inventory have been matched as closely as possible, the design has been brought within the practical limitations of a production.

If the number of dimmers is of concern, these can also be matched to specific items on the wish list. By doing this, it is possible to identify those functions where higher capacity dimmers must be specified. Together, through using the wish list for assigning specific luminaires to specific functions and evaluating dimming needs, items on the wish list will be translated into specific choices of luminaire and dimmer control while at the same time bringing the design into the practical limitations of a given situation. Finally, if this has not already been established in the lighting key or other color assignments, assign each lighting function a specific gel color based on the research and lighting keys. The choice of gel, too, is indicated somewhere on the wish list. By following this process most of the decisions affecting the design will be addressed and many of the wishes of a designer will be fulfilled as originally intended. Later, the design information is used to create a tentative or rough light plot for the design.

The Tentative Hookup

The next step in the process comes in developing a **tentative hookup** for the production. The **hookup** is a listing (in a table format) of all the luminaire and control information of a design. This information is organized by control data, which more specifically is identified by either the channel, control number, or dimmer assigned to a particular function or purpose of light. The hookup begins with Channel 1 or Dimmer 1 and then moves sequentially through each of the channels or dimmers that will be used throughout a show. If a hookup is organized by channel number it is called a **channel schedule** and if done by dimmer, a **dimmer schedule.** It is the designer's preference as to which format is used, although dimmer schedules tend to be preferred in cases where dimmers are the limiting factor in a design. Today, with many theatres using dimmer-per-circuit lighting systems, the channel schedule has become the most popular format. Designers often don't have to worry about individual dimmer or circuit assignments, preferring to let the electricians make the assignments as they hang a show. The exception comes when a lighting system contains dimmers with multiple capacities and where the designer has to keep track of how many dimmers are used in each of the different capacities or when a designer is concerned about the number of dimmers/circuits that exist in particular hanging positions.

Most designers use **soft-patching,** which allows them to organize their console and hookups based on the function of the lights. Channels can be assigned with no regard to dimmer loads. This allows luminaires with similar functions and their channels to be organized into patterns that make sense to the designer. For example, all of the pink area lights associated with a 12-lamp system in a design could be assigned to Channels 1–12. The designer can also leave channels unassigned to provide more logic to their assignments—going on to assign cool blue area lights to Channels 21–32. for example. The ones digit essentially corresponds to a location of the stage for both lighting systems, while the tens digit designates different color systems. Downleft would be lit by Channel 1 in pink and Channel 21 in blue, while down right might be lit with Channel 4 for pink and Channel 24 for blue. Continuing with the *Miser* example, the pink (R-02) area lights are assigned to Channels 1–8 while the blue (R-362) area lights that are associated with the same focus points are assigned to Channels 21–28. One of the benefits of carefully assigning the channels is that this makes the operation of the lighting console easier and more efficient, eliminating keystrokes when inputting data. In this example, rather than having to call out and input each of the individual channels, a board operator could simply make use of the "thru" command (Channels 1 thru 8 would be entered to bring up the entire pink system).

A tentative hookup is a series of worksheets that list the control channel in the first column and then all the other pertinent data regarding the luminaires and their functions/qualities in subsequent columns. Other data typically displayed in a tentative hookup include instrument types and wattage (to determine dimmer loads), purpose/function or focus of the light(s), and color. If dimmer or circuit information is critical to the assignments, this information may also be added to the tentative hookup. Actual placement and unit numbers are not entered at this point in the process, even though the wish list should have already established which luminaires and hanging position will be assigned to a particular function. In working through the tentative hookup, the designer simply assigns each of the functions and associated luminaires to a particular control channel. The most important needs are usually assigned to the lowest channel numbers, while luminaires with more limited functions are given higher channel assignments. Most designers tend to assign their area systems to the lowest numbers. If any special area lighting is called for it is often assigned along with the generals. After all the area systems have been accounted for, designers usually go on to make control assignments for the other washes and accent systems (sidelight, front-diagonal, back, etc.), often working progressively from the front toward the back and downlight angles. Multiple colors or washes of similar lighting systems are traditionally grouped together, like the pink and blue area lighting examples presented earlier. Once the washes have been allocated, assignments of specific specials and finally any large scenic washes such as cyc lighting are worked into the hookup. As a function is assigned to the hookup it is once again checked off of the wish list. Once completing the tentative hookup, the only step that remains is determining the locations of where the luminaires will actually be mounted in the theatre.

The Rough Light Plot

Although I know lighting designers who don't create rough light plots, I have found that it is usually more beneficial to do a rough plot—this lets you work out a design without worrying about creating a beautifully drafted plot. You should feel free to make changes, correct mistakes, and try various options while you plot a design. There was even a product at one time (Marcplot, distributed by GAM) that included colored magnets with symbols of lighting instruments and a board on which the lighting designer could draw a floorplan and hanging positions with erasable markers. With this system designers could easily move luminaires around as a lighting plot evolved in much the same way that a child's magnetic board is used as a spelling primer.

Once all of the positioning decisions have been worked out on the rough plot, the luminaires are assigned their unit numbers and the designer moves on to drafting a final plot, with virtually no subsequent need for making corrections or changes. This philosophy has changed somewhat as designers have shifted to using CAD software, which allows luminaires to be moved easily and edited as the design evolves. Even with this software, however, issues like juggling instrument locations around due to space limitations and having to renumber them frequently occur. CAD programs can renumber the units of a lighting position through a simple command, while in conventional drafting it is best not to number the units until all of them have been placed.

While napkin sketches can play a role in some design development, the rough light plot should be an actual drafting that is done to scale. This drawing should show all the critical elements of the theatre in the same fashion that you would illustrate them in the final plot. Once a batten has been identified as an electric, it should be drawn as a single line on the plot just as any other permanent lighting position. Many designers will add small hatch marks along the battens at 18-inch intervals from either side of the centerline to mark positions where the luminaires might be located. The 18-inch spacing allows most neighboring instruments to have full pan control without bumping lens barrels. While the scale does not have to be the same as the final plot, scale is an important element of the rough plot: luminaires are drawn to scale so that the designer can determine whether there is enough space to hang all of the units that they want in a given location. I often find that a 1/4 inch (to the foot) scale works fine for the rough plot and will then shift to a 3/8 inch or 1/2 inch scale for the final plot. Many designers like to add an indication of the major scenic elements on a rough plot as well. This is done by lightly tracing the outline of the scenic components onto the plot or transferring the scenic design to the plot with colored pencils. Designers may also choose to place a copy of the scenic floorplan under the plot or use clear acetate to lay over the rough plot. In CAD, the process is as simple as importing the scenic floorplan into the light plot file and placing it on a layer of its own—making sure that it is placed correctly in relationship to reference lines like the centerline and plaster line. The final step in preparing the rough plot before adding the actual instruments is identifying those primary focus points associated with the area lighting systems. Most designers indicate the focus points with a simple hatch mark. These are further identified by placing a letter, Roman numeral, or stage designation next to them (e.g., A, B, C; I, II, III; or DC, CL, etc.).

The process of creating the rough plot is actually quite simple. The designer simply goes through the tentative hookup one channel at a time and places the associated fixtures on the rough plot. Those channels associated with luminaires that have more critical placements are transferred to the plot first, while those with less particular placements are added later. To ensure that the luminaires are created at the right size, a designer will use a specialized stencil called a **lighting template** (Figure 11.4) to draw scaled representations of the instruments on the plot. A lighting template contains a basic silhouette of the sizes and shapes of the primary lighting units. The drafting/symbol standards in the entertainment industry were established through a special review process by the United States Institute for Theatre Technology (USITT). In addition to the symbols, USITT has also indicated a manner (notation) in which information like unit number, channel identification, color, and focus are to be noted on a light plot. Figure 11.5 illustrates several common luminaire symbols/representations of the USITT standard (Recommended Practice), while Appendix D provides the full USITT RP-2 Lighting Graphics standard.

As a lighting designer examines the tentative hookup, they should be able to identify and prioritize those luminaires that require a more critical placement. Lighting design is not an exact science, and specific hanging positions may have to be altered slightly from the lighting key due to issues like the hanging positions being too close to or far from a subject, obstructions or sightline issues created by scenery or theatre architecture, and even other luminaires that may already occupy a space. The designer should approximate these positions and should not be overly concerned if a luminaire has to shift even as much as several feet either side of its intended position. This frequently occurs for area lighting positions at the extreme left and right sides of a stage—where the luminaires would actually fall outside the walls of the theatre if they were plotted according to the angle designated by the lighting key. There are other circumstances in which a luminaire, if it remains on its central axis, can actually shift forward or backward 6–10 feet to completely different hanging positions with little noticeable effect on the stage. On the other hand, there are times when only a few inches might determine whether an instrument can hit its target. Once a unit's position has been identified, its associated symbol is added to the plot, and other data such as its channel, color, and focus or purpose are noted by the luminaire. After all the channels and associated luminaires are entered on the rough plot, the unit numbers are added as the last element of the plot. This ensures that the units are listed in an accurate order without needing to be renumbered several times throughout the design process. This also encourages a designer to approach the drafting based on the needs of the hookup, since any changes that may be needed are easily made by shifting luminaires around as problems like space limitations become an issue. Once the rough plot is completed, virtually all of the design decisions have been made. The

Figure 11.4 Lighting templates

Ellipsoidals	PARs	Misc.
36° Source four	Source four PAR (WFL)	6" Fresnel
26° Source four	Source four PAR (MFL)	8" Fresnel
19° Source four	Source four PAR (VNSP)	14" Scoop
6 × 9 Axial ERS	PAR 64 (WFL)	
6 × 12 Axial ERS	PAR 64 (MFL)	
6 × 16 Axial ERS	PAR 64 (NSP)	Striplight

Notation

Gate accessory
Color Focus
Unit #
Circuit/Dimmer #
Channel #

Figure 11.5 Common USITT luminaire symbols and notation

information is then transferred to the final plot, resulting in a neat and accurate final plot.

DRAFTING AND THE LIGHTING DESIGN

The light plot and section serve important roles in communicating the intentions of a lighting designer to the electricians. In many cases the light plot, section, and associated paperwork will be sent ahead of the designer and need to be detailed enough that the hang can progress without their presence. This scenario of the plot and paperwork being used by the crews prior to the arrival of the lighting designer should provide a guiding principle in that a designer should indicate as much information on a plot as the electricians will need to complete the hang in their absence. At the same time, the light plot needs to be clear and concise. In addition to the plot and paperwork for *The Miser* (Figures 11.9–11.12), in Figure 11.6 I have provided a more extensive plot for a production of *Urinetown: The Musical* as an example of a more traditional proscenium plot (this is also be referenced throughout the following sections).

Figure 11.6 Overhead plot from University of Georgia production of *Urinetown: The Musical*

Drafting Light Plots

If the rough plot has been done properly, all that needs to happen to create the final plot is to simply transfer the information to a new drafting while using the industry's symbols and conventions. Care must be taken to display the information so that the lighting data is easily accessible and important details aren't lost in the sheer volume of information that is represented in a final plot. While USITT makes provisions for indicating virtually any property that you may want to provide for a luminaire, most designers provide only the most important elements on a light plot. These decisions usually depend on how much information the designer feels that the electricians need to accurately hang the production. Regardless of what may be indicated on the plot, all essential information for each unit will be provided and cross-listed in the **design paperwork**. The three current schools of thought on what information should be indicated on a plot for each luminaire include the following:

1. Nothing more than unit number, instrument type, and associated accessories
2. The items listed in 1 plus anything that the electricians need to know to hang/circuit the plot (unit type, number, color, and channel indication).
3. An academic approach in which everything in 1 and 2 are listed along with dimmer, circuit, and focus notations for each luminaire.

Additional information such as manufacturer designations, lamp types, and wattage can be indicated on the plot as well. Designers have their personal reasons for using any of these or other variations of these standards. I personally prefer the second method since it provides the electricians with all the information that they will need to hang my show without getting too detailed.

Everything on the light plot should be in scale. This gives an accurate depiction of how all of the elements, including the luminaires, fit into a facility and their associated hanging positions. Without using scale, a designer might find that they have squeezed too many luminaires into a given position, making it impossible for the electricians to hang that aspect of the show. The next several sections of this chapter take the designer through a typical process of developing the final light plot. The order of these steps is not critical and designers should work in any way that works best for them. What's important is that the information presented in the next several pages makes its way into the final light plot. The methods do not change significantly from drawing by hand to using CAD software, although there are many shortcuts that make the drafting of a CAD light plot much less time consuming and tedious. Using CAD for drafting will be discussed in more detail near the end of this chapter. Regardless of how a plot is created, the designer should never give away the original drafting and should only send copies (bluelines, large-format photocopies, or prints from CAD software) to a venue.

The Basics

The first step in creating the final light plot involves picking a scale that presents the information in a clear way without becoming so large that it is unmanageable. The more information that you choose to indicate about each unit, the larger the associated scale that you should draft in. On the other hand, if you are designing for a large facility, a large scale could make the plot awkward to both draft and carry around during a light hang. As an alternative, designers may choose to use a large scale but may opt to create several smaller plots for a design—each illustrating a different part of the theatre. I often create two plots (an **overhead** and **front-of-house**) for several of the larger facilities that I design in. On occasions, such as in the production of *The Who's Tommy* that is illustrated later in the chapter, I have created a third plot that was used solely for the ladders and booms or side-light. Additional plates can be generated for items such as scenic practicals. The most common scales that most designers draft in are 1/4 inch (to the foot) for small and 1/2 inch or 3/8 inch for large scales. In some limited setups, especially in location shooting for film or video designs, 1/8 inch scale may also be used. Once the scale of the plot has been determined, the designer chooses a sheet of velum or drafting paper that is of an appropriate size to not only illustrate the architectural features of the stage or facility but also leave ample room for additional features like the **title block, key,** and other information.

Primary Information

This gives the electricians the essential information they will need for interpreting the material that is presented in the light plot. It also gives them a frame of reference by identifying specific information relating to the facility. Some of the information that is first included in a light plot is of the same nature as in any other drafting. A borderline is drawn around the perimeter of the page and a title block is created that clearly indicates key information about the production. The title block is typically located in the lower right-hand corner and includes information like the title of the production, producing organization, name of the theatre where the production is being mounted, title of the drawing (e.g., Light Plot), month and year, the designer's name, and the scale of the drawing. Additional material that could also be included in the title block might include the name of the director, name of the master electrician or assistant designer, the initials of the draftsperson, and contact information such as a cell phone number or e-mail address for the designer. If a designer is union, there will also be union stamp somewhere around or within the title block.

One of the most important elements to include in the light plot is the floorplan of the theatre. This is marked in relatively heavy lines and includes the walls of the theatre, the edge of the stage, the pit (if one exists), smoke pockets, and any physical obstructions within the stage areas. Added to this is the hanging or lineset schedule, which is drawn to coincide with any battens that are hung in the facility. Most designers both identify the line number and list what is actually hung on a particular lineset in the hanging section. Both loaded and empty linesets are included since batten assignments might have to be changed at some point in a load-in. If possible, this schedule should be located in the wings, preferably in the same location as the fly rail, but it might even be placed outside of the theatre if the wings are filled with other equipment like booms or ladders. Regardless of the placement of the hanging section, the location of each lineset should be accurately depicted throughout the depth of the stage. Other general information that is drawn into the plot at this time are reference lines like the centerline and plasterline and scaled reference lines (scales or rules) that extend across both the width and depth of the stage. The horizontal rule crosses the centerline and is marked with hatch marks or ticks on 12- or 18-inch spacings (moving outward in each direction from the centerline) and allows electricians a quick way to identify the placement of luminaires along the electrics without having to use a scaled rule. A similar scale is also constructed through the depth of the stage with the plasterline forming the beginning point. A lighting designer may also include lightweight reference lines that trace the outlines of the primary scenic elements of the production. These scenic lines are often added once the plot is nearly finished because they are frequently broken as they cross any information related to the electrics.

Key and Notation

The **key** can be compared to one used on a road map and simply matches the drafted symbols with the actual lighting equipment. It is an area of the plot that lists all of the symbols that the designer has used throughout the drafting. The USITT *RP-2 Recommended Practice for Lighting Graphics* presents the standard symbol guidelines within the entertainment industry, while IESNA has established a common set of symbols for the architectural community. Regardless of how a designer illustrates the symbols, they should be clearly labeled as to the type of luminaire that they represent in the key. Wattage is indicated through the symbol's label and variations in the basic symbols may be made to designate different manufacturers or wattages of a given type of luminaire. Additional items that may appear in the key include lighting hardware and accessories like barn doors, scrollers, and templates. While the key provides identification of the various luminaires, the **notation** provides an explanation of the information that is related to a lighting instrument.

The notation may be labeled as "typical" by some designers. Information that is usually indicated in the notation includes unit number, channel and dimmer number, and color. Some designers show more information (e.g., dimmer or focus/purpose)—but regardless of what is shown, the notation explains each piece of information associated with a luminaire's symbol.

Luminaires

Each instrument from the rough plot is neatly transferred to the final plot using a template and the scaled symbols previously identified by the key. Additional information regarding color, hookup information, and accessories are also added to the luminaires as indicated by the notation. Each hanging position is marked where it is actually located in the theatre—with the exception of FOH positions like beam positions, which typically have the distance between them compressed as a way of saving space. If this is done, a note calling attention to the compression is placed somewhere near the FOH positions. Each lighting position is laid out lightly with a barely perceivable guideline that is then used to help place the luminaires (after the luminaires are placed, the line segments between the units are darkened to a normal medium/heavy weight line—this prevents having to delicately erase lines that fall within the bodies of the luminaires). There are two schools of thought in regard to orienting the luminaires on the plot. The first orients the units in the actual lines of focus, while the second places the units in the four primary directions only (straight front or back and to either side). Advantages of the first system are that it is easier to spot where a unit is focused as well as whether the barrels of neighboring units will interfere with one another. The major shortcoming of this system is in the more chaotic arrangement of the notations associated with each unit. Two ways of reducing this confusion involve using a standard spacing interval such as placing the instruments on 18-inch centers and using the 90° orientations. The lighting symbols are drawn in medium- to dark-weight lines since they are the most important elements of the light plot. Additional data such as channel and color information can be added at this time and are typically drawn using lightweight lines. Gel numbers are placed at the front of each symbol, while control channels are typically placed

Figure 11.7 Sample electric layout and notation: The unit with the missing channel is actually a spare (1st Electric #4). Many designers include spares in their plots that are hung and circuited so that if a future need develops, the unit is already in place and only has to be gelled, focused and channeled in order to be added to a show.

in a circle located at the back of the symbol. Once all of the units have been placed along the hanging position, the lines between the units that represent the batten can be darkened to the same line-weight as the luminaires. Each lighting position is then labeled and is also noted with its trim height (if applicable). Often, a listing of all the luminaires used in a position is added near this label. This aids the electricians in pulling the inventory for a hanging position. On occasion, designers may also list the minimum number of circuits that will be required for the given hanging position. The luminaires are then numbered so that every instrument has a unique number that makes it clearly identifiable from any other unit on the plot. Most instruments are assigned a number based on their hanging position. Sidebar 11.1 provides information relating to the most common numbering practices for both the hanging positions and the individual luminaires. If a luminaire is added at some point after the plot has been numbered (such as at tech/dress rehearsals or later stops in a tour) the unit is simply drawn in the location where it is to be hung and assigned the same number as the lowest unit number next to it plus an added letter component. If more than one instrument is added between existing units, additional letters will be assigned to the instruments (Unit 23, 23A, 23B, etc.). Booms and other vertical hanging positions are plotted in two orientations: the first is a bird's-eye view that is used for placing the boom (often illustrating only the top row of luminaires) and is hatched or shaded, while the second is an elevation view that provides information regarding the mounting heights of the units (a dimension or elevation marker that is taken from the deck to either the center of the luminaire or to its associated sidearm). Additional features such as floor mounts, set mounts, and practicals will be added to the plot as it nears completion. These

Figure 11.8 Sample boom and ladder layout and notation

may be indicated with a symbol placed at the location of a unit, or they could be listed in a table that is located somewhere else on the plot. At the designer's discretion, additional elements like scenic components, focus areas, maskings, and other information can be added to the plot. Figure 11.7 illustrates a detailed area of a light plot that depicts conventions that are typical for drafting the electrics, while Figure 11.8 illustrates conventions that

are typical for displaying **booms** and **ladders** (*The Who's Tommy* plot details). Figure 11.9 provides the final light plot for the production of *The Miser* that has been used as an example throughout this chapter. It also provides an example of a plot that follows a slightly different format than the more traditional plots that have been illustrated through the *Urinetown: The Musical* and *The Who's Tommy* light plots.

Figure 11.9 CAD design of the final light plot for *The Miser*

design without drafting a section, the results can just as easily be disastrous. It could lead to problems like creating hanging positions and trims that can't possibly hit their targets, luminaires that are impossible to mask, and lighting angles that become deceptively steep or shallow from what may be expected. For all of these reasons the section is an important document that shouldn't be skipped.

While the section doesn't necessarily have to be drawn to the same scale as the light plot, references and comparisons are more easily made if a common scale is shared between them. Once again, 1/4-inch, 3/8-inch, or 1/2-inch (to the foot) scales are the most popular scales for drafting sections. The drafting of a section involves many of the same practices followed while drafting a light plot. Borderlines and title blocks are indicated, but there is no key or notation for a lighting section. The section typically follows a cutting plane along the centerline of the theatre and illustrates information that would be needed regarding the vertical elements of the design. Scales are provided along the depth of the stage (both forward and backstage of the plasterline and along the height of the stage). Heights of any scenic elements and the trim positions of the electrics and borders are also drawn. Vertical maskings are checked through drawing partial sightlines from the critical seat (critical sightline) across the bottom edges of the borders to illustrate what may or may not be seen by an audience member from that location. Lighting angles and distributions are checked and illustrated by placing focus points at head height within each plane of the acting areas, then drawing lines representing the throw distances between these points and the hanging positions from which that area will be lit. Lines representing the beam spread of the fixtures are then drawn along the lines representing the throw distances to indicate how much coverage each luminaire will provide for the associated focus points. Some designers will choose to show the throw distance in their final sectional drafting while others show only the beam patterns of the luminaires. This process is repeated for each plane of focus as well as for each angle (e.g., front and backlight), and unique areas of a design (e.g., elevated areas like balconies or towers). Figures 11.1 and 11.2 illustrate these principles of determining trims, hanging positions, and beamspreads/angles.

Drafting the Section

Drafting the section isn't that much different from drafting the light plot, with the exception that the section is more concerned with positioning the trims of the hanging positions and maskings as opposed to providing specific information about each of the luminaires. While designers can pull off an acceptable or even good

LIGHTING SCHEDULES AND DESIGN PAPERWORK

Light plots tend to be large and bulky, making them hard to carry around and work with. While it is important to use them throughout the initial hang, most designers and electricians find it more helpful to have the information repeated in various table formats that are smaller and more easily carried around. These tables (**schedules** or **paperwork**) list all the same information as the light plot but organize the data on standard-sized pages that can fit on a clipboard. Each type of schedule organizes the data in a different manner and is beneficial to the designer or electricians at different stages of the design. About the only information that a plot can provide that the schedules won't is the actual physical location of the luminaires. Often, the paperwork is the only complete record of much of a design: many designers prefer to place only a limited amount of information on the actual plot while the schedules go on to list all of the data specified for the luminaires. Typical data provided throughout the paperwork include instrument number and location (hanging position), luminaire type and wattage, wiring data (circuit, dimmer, and channel numbers), focus/purpose information, color, and accessories (barn doors, templates, etc.). Lighting schedules often grow to many pages for each of the different tables.

With lighting designs growing from 50 to hundreds of luminaires, the creation of the paperwork for a production became a monumental task, often requiring an assistant who was charged with monitoring and revising the paperwork throughout the production process.

With the advent of affordable personal computers (PCs), it didn't take lighting designers long to figure out that all of the repetitive data in these schedules could be entered into spreadsheet programs like Microsoft Works or Excel. To organize a production's lighting data, many contemporary lighting designers use either programs like these or a specialized spreadsheet application created by John McKernon called Lightwright, which was designed around the special needs of lighting designers. Over the years this program has evolved; it now not only creates paperwork but can also track problems such as overloaded dimmers or circuits, make determinations of phase loads, keep records of focus/shutter patterns, check for errors like using bad dimmers or assigning circuits/dimmers to two channels at a time, track inventory lists and how many units of a particular type are used and yet available for a design, and even determine cut lists (with or without an existing inventory of gel). Other software packages also exist, and some even produce the paperwork as modular elements of comprehensive CAD packages. Vectorworks Spotlight®, LD Assistant, and MacLux can all produce not only a light plot but also all of its associated paperwork in a seamless manner that inserts the data directly into the appropriate schedules.

Sidebar 11.2 DESIGNER PROFILE

Steve Shelley

Credit: photo courtesy Steven Louis Shelley

Steven Louis Shelley has worked in theatre for more than 50 years as a lighting designer, production manager, and stage manager in New York City, throughout the United States, and on four continents. He is a member of United Scenic Artists, Local 829, and though he lights nearly anything related to the performing arts, dance lighting is a central core for many of his lighting credits. His designs are included in the repertories of many dance companies, including the Martha Graham Dance Company, the Joffrey Ballet of Chicago, Boston Ballet, and American Ballet Theatre. He has designed lighting on Broadway and Off-Broadway, as well as concerts, television presentations, regional theatre, and regional opera. Steve is the inventor and patent holder of the award-winning Field Template™ stencils, the designer of SoftSymbols™ (Vectorworks symbol libraries), and author of the popular lighting textbook, *A Practical Guide to Stage Lighting* (currently in its third edition— Focal Press, 2014).

Steve's initial studies in lighting started at the University of Nebraska at Lincoln, but he transferred to North Carolina School of the Arts. After graduating with a BFA, emphasis in Lighting, his learning continued through extensive domestic and international touring experiences, and assisting designers such as Jennifer Tipton and Tom Skelton. He says:

"I was naturally attracted to the form and structure of dance lighting, and got to learn from the best. As I grew as a lighting designer, I realized that dance lighting allows you to broadly interpret and visually reinforce what's psychologically taking place "under the surface"—as the lighting designer, you can accentuate that energy with color and angle—and no matter how visually extreme that might become, the form of dance allows it to be much more visually acceptable to an audience. When I grasped that concept, and as I learned how to accentuate form and create plasticity, I was sold. Once I understood those lessons, applying that understanding to other forms of presentation was a natural progression."

Steve acknowledges others who provided opportunities that advanced his career:

"My friend Todd Randall got me hired as the lighting designer for Ballet Trockadero; Jennifer Tipton allowed me to oversee the lighting for Twyla Tharp; David Eliott hired me to oversee and design lighting for American Ballet Theatre; Tom Skelton allowed me to assist him on some wild rides; and finally, John Paull hired me to be the Lighting Coordinator for the Spoleto Festival USA."

Steve has been attracted to several properties unique to dance lighting:

"In an ethereal sense, I've always felt that dance lighting allows you to be anywhere, anytime—and I've always felt much more of an active participant in the process of creating a dance. I've always felt that I'm more intimately involved in the practical creation of the environment. Privately, I often find that dance lighting lets you "get away" with a lot more; there's a lot less scenery in the way, and you can create a system of light in many different ways. Dance also guides the sequence in which I create and execute a plot. In straight plays, for example, one of the primary considerations is making certain the face is seen, so that the performer can be heard.—with dance, in comparison, I find that creating frontlight systems or adding frontlight to a cue is often one of the last steps that I take."

Steve also believes that there are several conditions, unique to dance lighting, that a designer must be prepared for—much of it based on his wealth of touring:

"Touring is often a significant environment of dance lighting. The speed of creating and executing dance lighting under those conditions, in my experience, can't be matched by any other discipline. In order to make all of the decisions to properly create the lighting for any dance you've got to be razor sharp, have a spatial grasp of everything surrounding the space, and an ethereal understanding of how all the elements of that specific dance fit into the choreographer's mind and heart—you become an extension of his or her eyes. You also have to be detail-oriented. The color of the floor; the cleanliness of the floor; the upkeep and appearance of scenic elements such as scrims, translucencies, legs and borders and finally the upkeep of the paperwork—making certain that the archival process is accurate and complete so that the dance will always be presented as the choreographer approved it. Oh! You also have to have a good color sense and a good eye. Sometimes you need to reduce intensity to get the right contrast, rather than increase candlepower."

The need for speed is one of the things that keeps Steve attracted to dance; he finds it hard to become bored in a typical dance production:

"You must be moving at 100 miles an hour mentally and be alert to everything and anything around you. The choreographer, the music, the dancers, the scenic elements, the costumes. Your challenge is to integrate them all and to strive to provide the visual bonding agent, unifying the choreographer's intent—all in one, maybe two tech rehearsals. You must also be able to listen, communicate, make snap decisions and believe that you're right. High speed dance ain't for delicate flowers."

What he likes least in the business are people who don't know what they're getting into, or aren't committed to the final product:

"What drives me crazy are jobs where they (the company or producers) pretend they're better prepared than they really are—you specify a color or equipment, and at the last minute, they can't provide it because they don't have the budget. Heck, had you known, you would have bought and brought the color with you."

Steve believes that dance is special, and gets frustrated with technicians who don't appreciate the opportunity to see and be part of something unique.

As far as dance design goes, Steve shares some random tips. For plotting:

"I always seem to construct the backlight systems first, followed by sidelight and then the rest of them." When constructing color systems: "I always start with skin tones, and then fill in saturation where there's otherwise shadow." For the tech table: "I always try to arrange my tech table before I start a focus call. I can't count the number of times I've finished touching the last lamp, and had to sprint to the table to start making light cues." Steve tries to remain abreast of new lighting developments by seeing and appreciating other dance productions. "I used to try to see every dance production that I could, but got burned out. Now I try to appreciate what dance lighting I see, rather than trying to analyze every possible performance."

On a final note, Steve shares:

"The great thing about dance lighting is that you get to see and create beautiful work, you get to work with incredible people, and you have the opportunity to work in great theatres in many different countries around the world. The bad news is that if you work for a dance company, and you're the lighting guy, you spend most of your time out front; either at the production table during techs, or in the viewing booth during performances. As such, you don't get to hang out backstage and form the same friendships as other technicians with the show. Bottom line: It can get pretty lonely. You need to deal with that, and fill your offstage life in other ways."

Hookup

The **hookup** is probably the second most important document that a designer produces after the light plot. The hookup takes all the information related to the luminaires and presents it in a table using control information as the primary form of organization. The first column in a hookup relates to the control element used to operate the associated instrument(s). The two most common forms of hookup organize the data by either channel (**channel schedule**) or dimmer number (**dimmer schedule**). While the channel or dimmer number must be placed in the first column, the rest of the data can be organized in any fashion that the designer thinks

is most appropriate. This additional information usually includes hanging position, unit number, unit type, wattage, color, accessories, and its focus or purpose. Designers may wish to include more classifications or could drop some based on the particular needs of a production. Hookups are helpful for troubleshooting wiring problems, dealing with lamps that don't come up, and completing **dimmer checks** prior to a rehearsal or performance. Figure 11.10 shows the first page of the hookup (the channel schedule) for the Cocteau production of *The Miser*.

Instrument Schedule

Instrument schedules follow the same format as hookups but are organized according to hanging positions and unit numbers. This piece of paperwork becomes especially helpful when an electrician is working on a particular hanging position. They can walk along a position (such as an electric) to check circuit assignments or can pre-stack the gel for easy insertion along an entire batten. In addition to the information presented in the hookup, many designers also like to list a gang column in instrument schedules. This allows electricians to quickly identify those instruments that are two-fered together and helps them to use fewer circuits. For a designer, the instrument schedule is extremely beneficial during a show's focus. The designer can move quickly down a pipe, focusing each unit in order, with easy access to the channel and focus needs of each instrument while avoiding the time losses associated with shifting a lift or ladder more often than absolutely necessary. Instrument schedules are often organized with each hanging position on its own page. This allows several people (e.g., designers and their assistants) to focus on different areas of the plot at the same time or for electricians to take those pages relating to the hanging positions that they are working on at a given time. Figure 11.11 provides a partial instrument schedule for *The Miser*.

Magic Sheets

Magic sheets are a special form of paperwork that designers use when they set levels or program a show. There are a number of formats for creating magic sheets, and each designer has a favorite. The format is not important. What is important is that the information is organized in such a way that the designer can quickly identify control information and thus easily modify cues throughout the rehearsal process. Magic sheets do not contain all of the information that the other schedules provide—they are abbreviated and contain only what a designer actually needs to set levels or cues. The only data typically presented in many magic sheets are just the control channel, color, and purpose/focus of the luminaires. At this point, the designer doesn't need to worry about

The Jean Cocteau Repertory Theatre
The Bouwerie Lane Theatre
R. Dunham, Designer

Channel	Dim	Position	Unit#	Type	Wattage	Color & Template	Purpose
(1)	4	PIPE 2	4	S4 -50	750w	R-02	SIDE -DL
	"	PIPE 4	"	"	"	"	"
(2)	11	PIPE 2	6	S4 -50	750w	R-02	SIDE -DC1
	"	"	7	"	"	"	"
(3)	13	PIPE 4	6	S4 -50	750w	R-02	SIDE -DC2
	"	"	7	"	"	"	"
(4)	12	PIPE 2	8	S4 -50	750w	R-02	SIDE -DR
	"	PIPE 4	"	"	"	"	"
(5)	57	PIPE 7	8	S4 -50	750w	R-02	SIDE -CS
	"	"	10	"	"	"	"
(6)	38	PIPE 7	5	S4 -50	750w	R-02	SIDE -SL AND SR
	"	"	11	"	"	"	"
(7)	49	PIPE 9	6	S4 -50	750w	R-02	SIDE -UC
	"	"	7	"	"	"	"
(8)	43	PIPE 9	4	S4 -50	750w	R-02	SIDE -UL AND UR
	"	"	8	"	"	"	"
(11)	5	PIPE 1	3	4.5x6	575w	R-51	F. WASH -DL
	"	PIPE 3	"	"	"	"	"
(12)	21	PIPE 1	6	4.5x6	575w	R-51	F. WASH -DC1
	"	"	8	"	"	"	"
(13)	17	PIPE 3	7	4.5x6	575w	R-51	F. WASH -DC2
	"	"	9	"	"	"	"
(14)	24	PIPE 1	11	4.5x6	575w	R-51	F. WASH -DR
	18	PIPE 3	12	"	"	"	"
(15)	37	PIPE 6	6	4.5x6	575w	R-51	F. WASH -UC
	"	"	8	"	"	"	"
(16)	53	PIPE 6	3	4.5x6	575w	R-51	F. WASH -UL AND UR
	"	"	11	"	"	"	"
(21)	1	PIPE 2	1	S4 -50	750w	R-362	SIDE -DL
	"	PIPE 4	"	"	"	"	"
(22)	2	PIPE 2	2	S4 -50	750w	R-362	SIDE -DC1
	"	"	3	"	"	"	"
(23)	34	PIPE 4	2	S4 -50	750w	R-362	SIDE -DC2
	"	"	3	"	"	"	"

Richard Dunham/Lightwright 4 (1) thru (23)

Figure 11.10 A partial channel hookup for *The Miser*

the actual instruments creating an effect or the manner in which they have been wired—only the effect and its control channel. The magic sheet reduces volumes of paperwork down to as little as a single page of key data that the designer will need for setting cues. While some designers prefer a table-like format (Figure 11.12a), many feel that this too closely approximates a hookup: if anything more than 50 or so channels are involved in a design, the format becomes inefficient and you might as well just use the hookup. Instead, a graphical format (Figure 11.12.b) that traces the directional or focus patterns of the lights onto a schematic representation of the set or stage is frequently used. The control channels are illustrated in a manner that links them to a functional pattern or description of the light. Magic sheets are also used for dimmer checks, with the understanding that if

PIPE F

U	Purpose	Type/Acc	W	Color	Template	Di	Ch
1	HIGH SIDE -DS1	PARNEL	575w	R-357		14	(30)
2	DOWNLIGHT	PARNEL	575w	L-119		36	(35)
3	GOBO LEAVES -SCRIM 2	S4 -50	575w	R-13, R-88, R-356	G-294	35	(51)
4	HIGH SIDE -DS2	PARNEL	575w	R-357		20	(31)
5	HIGH SIDE -MIDSTAGE	PARNEL	575w	R-357		39	(32)
6	DOWNLIGHT	PARNEL	575w	L-119		44	(37)

PIPE 6

U	Purpose	Type/Acc	W	Color	Template	Di	Ch
1	GOBO LINES -SCRIM 3	S4 -50	575w	R-55	G-673	56	(58)
2	DOWNLIGHT	PARNEL	575w	L-119		48	(36)
3	F. WASH -UL AND UR	4.5x6	575w	R-51		53	(16)
4	GOBO LEAVES -SCRIM 3	S4 -50	575w	R-13, R-88, R-356	G-294	54	(52)
5	DOWNLIGHT	PARNEL	575w	L-119		48	(36)
6	GOBO LEAVES -SCRIM 3	S4 -50	575w	R-13, R-88, R-356	G-294	54	(52)
6	F. WASH -UC	4.5x6	575w	R-51		37	(15)
7	CS SP	6" FRES	500w	G-440		52	(49)
8	F. WASH -UC	4.5x6	575w	R-51		37	(15)
9	DOWNLIGHT	PARNEL	575w	L-119		48	(36)
10	GOBO LEAVES -PERFORMERS	S4 -50	575w	R-54, R-87	G-218	59	(54)
11	F. WASH -UL AND UR	4.5x6	575w	R-51		53	(16)
12	DOWNLIGHT	PARNEL	575w	L-119		48	(36)
13	GOBO LEAVES -PERFORMERS	S4 -50	575w	R-54, R-87	G-218	59	(54)

PIPE I

U	Purpose	Type/Acc	W	Color	Template	Di	Ch
1	HIGH SIDE -DS1	PARNEL	575w	R-357		14	(30)
2	HIGH SIDE -DS2	PARNEL	575w	R-357		20	(31)
3	HIGH SIDE -MIDSTAGE	PARNEL	575w	R-357		39	(32)
4	GOBO LEAVES -PERFORMERS	S4 -50	575w	R-54, R-87	G-218	50	(55)
5	HIGH SIDE -UPSTAGE	PARNEL	575w	R-357		46	(33)

PIPE G

U	Purpose	Type/Acc	W	Color	Template	Di	Ch
1	HIGH SIDE -DS1	PARNEL	575w	R-357		14	(30)
2	DOWNLIGHT	PARNEL	575w	L-119		36	(35)
3	DC WIDE-2 SP	6" FRES	500w	G-440		31	(45)
4	HIGH SIDE -DS2	PARNEL	575w	R-357		20	(31)
5	DOWNLIGHT	PARNEL	575w	L-119		44	(37)
6	GOBO LEAVES -PERFORMERS	S4 -50	575w	R-54, R-87	G-218	50	(55)
7	HIGH SIDE -UPSTAGE	PARNEL	575w	R-357		46	(33)

Richard Dunham/Lightwright 4 PIPE D thru PIPE 6

Figure 11.11 A partial instrument schedule for *The Miser*

a problem is found, the electricians can go back to the instrument schedule or hookup to find the additional information they need to troubleshoot a problem.

Yet another version of providing control information is with a cheat sheet. A **cheat sheet** (Figure 11.13) also follows a table format. It lists all of the control channels in sequential order along with additional information relating to the purpose and color associated with a cue and each channel. A cheat sheet, however, is more like a track sheet (Figure 12.4) because it is based on indicating approximate channel levels for a given cue rather than as a general indication of control. Figure 11.14 illustrates pages from several different styles of magic sheets while Figure 11.15 provides examples of additional magic sheets that are tailored for shows that make use of automated lighting. In these, additional information relating to the individual attributes of the luminaires are also provided.

The Miser—The Cocteau Rep.   Page: __1__ of __2__

		DL	DC1	DC2	DR	MID-ON	MID-OFF	US-ON	US-OFF
Area	R-02	1	2	3	4	5	6	7	8
	R-51	11	12	13	14	15	16		
	R-362	21	22	23	24	25	24	27	28
HPE-SR	R-357		30	31		32		33	
DOWN	L-119		35	36		37		38	
GOBOS -SR	Mixed		50			51		52	
GOBOS -SL	Mixed		56			57		58	
Specials	DC tight	45							
	Bench	46							
	Inquisit.	47							

Figure 11.12a Magic sheets for *The Miser* a. Magic sheet in table format

Figure 11.12b Magic sheet in visual/graphic format

Production: The Miser   Company: Cocteau Rep
Cue #: 6   Count: 4/8   Preset: B
R. Dunham, Design

Chan	1	2	3	4	5	6	7	8	9	10	11	12
Purpose	AREA R02	AREA R02	AREA R02	AREA R02	AREA R02	AREA R02	AREA R02	AREA R02	X	X	AREA R51	AREA R51
Level	7	8	8	7	7	6	6	6	X	X	5	6

Chan	13	14	15	16	17	18	19	20	21	22	23	24
Purpose	AREA R-51	AREA R-51	AREA R-51	AREA R-51	X	X	X	X	AREA R-362	AREA R-362	AREA R-362	AREA R-362
Level	6	5	6	5	X	X	X	X	4	5	5	4

Chan	25	26	27	28	29	30	31	32	33	34	35	36
Purpose	AREA R-362	AREA R-362	AREA R-362	AREA R-362	X	HPE ① R-357	HPE ② R-357	HPE ③ R-357	HPE ④ R-357	X	Down L-119 ①	Down L-119 ②
Level	3.5	3.5	3.5	3.5	X					X	4	4

Chan	37	38	39	40	41	42	43	44	45	46	47	48
Purpose	Down L-119 ③	Down L-119 ④	X	Aisle Sp ①	Aisle Sp ②	Aisle Sp ③	DC(Test) Sp	DC(u) Sp	OS(u) Sp	Bench	Inqus.	UR Chairs
Level	4	4								6		5.5

Figure 11.13 A designer's cheat sheet: note the similarities between this form of paperwork and the tracking sheet discussed in Chapter 12

In addition to the more traditional magic or cheat sheets illustrated and discussed so far, designers or their assistants may also prepare variations of the forms to display frame/color designations of color scrollers, illustrations of gobo/pattern and color wheel assignments in automated fixtures, and magic sheets that indicate group or submaster assignments. In the end, there is a huge amount of variation in individual styles. Some magic sheets are very simple line drawings while others are elaborate, full-color creations that make heavy use of a variety of illustration techniques. However, the single most important demand that all must follow is that the control information be clear and easy to access while lighting a show. So, whatever works best for a designer in regard to their personal preferences and representing the material within the time constraints of the production schedule is what will determine the format of the magic and cheat sheets.

Shop Orders

Shop orders are inventories of all the materials and equipment that will be required to complete a lighting design. Often a designer will not have to complete a shop order because they are working in a facility where the console, dimmers, circuits, and even luminaires are permanent elements of a space. Here, the designer needs only to make sure that the design falls within the listed inventories and that they have ordered the **perishables** (expendables) for a production. Perishables include items like gel, templates, tie-line, and gaffers tape, which are either disposable or cannot be returned once they have been used.

When designing for a touring production or rental facility that is completely stripped, the lighting designer is responsible for specifying each piece of equipment that will form the lighting rig. This includes the dimmers and console, luminaires, cabling (circuits are not typically installed in these facilities), and hardware/accessories, along with the perishables. It is important to be completely accurate in this document because failing to include a single piece of key equipment could result in the entire rig not working. The shop order is the primary document that is sent to rental houses when a show is put out for bids.

The first page of a shop order usually lists specific information relating to the production. Items like the show title and name and address of the theatre or where the equipment will be delivered are important elements of the first page. Key individuals for the production

Figure 11.14a Additional examples of magic sheets. a. Hand drawn. *The Glass Menagerie.*

and their contact information are also provided on the title page. The producer or production organization, lighting designer, and master electrician are often identified here. One last bit of information usually included here is the rental period for which the equipment is required. This is specified with a load-in date on which the equipment will be picked up or delivered to the theatre and a second date for the strike and return of the equipment. Most rental houses bill their rentals on a weekly basis using a Monday-to-Monday schedule. The highest fees are charged during the first week, but are then reduced over additional weeks depending on how long the equipment is rented. If a designer is doing a single weekend gig, they can usually expect to pay the full weekly fee if they tie up a company's inventory for more than three or four days. On the contrary, if the

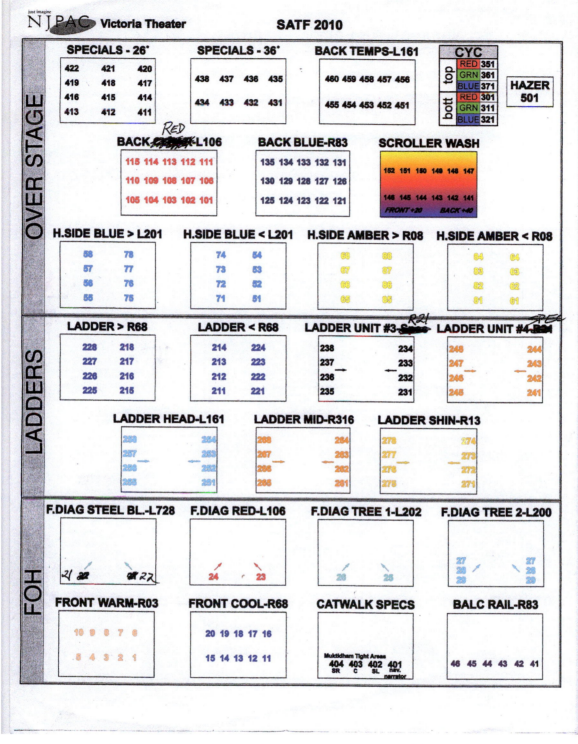

Figure 11.14b Drafting format. *The Clay Cart*, as part of the 2010 South Asian Theatre Festival. R. Dunham, Designer, using NJPAC SATF magic sheet and repertory plot by Jorge Arroyo

designer is a regular client or putting together a package that will be used for an extended period of time, many rental houses will cut you a break where they can. Also, representatives for most rental companies are extremely knowledgeable in how their equipment functions and are glad to help you with technical support both as you place your order as well as throughout the rental period.

The shop order is traditionally broken down into several key areas that list specific components of the lighting package. The first area, the **instruments**, contains a complete listing of all the luminaires that are required

Figure 11.14c Photoshop format. *In the Name of Our Father*.

for the production. Instrument types, lamp wattage, and general luminaire specifications are included here. The overall specifications are often given as a general note that includes a statement identifying how each of the fixtures should be equipped (e.g., each unit must be equipped with a color frame, safety cable, and C-clamp). An especially important specification is the connector type for the units. Once all the luminaires have been specified, a second area (**control**) is completed. This part of the order simply lists the console and associated hardware and cables (e.g., number of monitors, etc.), the number of dimmers and their capacities, and the number of feet of control and feeder cable that a rig requires. The third area, the **irons**, lists all the pipe, hardware, and accessories that are required for the production. Side-arms, boom bases, top hats, and hanging irons are some of the gear that is ordered in this portion of the shop order. Pipe lengths for each individual boom or other

Putnum County Spelling Bee

UGA Fine Arts Theatre

R. Dunham, Designer

Automated Lighting Magic Sheet

| Pro Scan | Track Spot | Studio Color | Track Spot | Pro Scan |

Start Address:

| 251 | 271 | 301 | 281 | 261 |

Attributes: First two digits of fixture + Single Unit Digit for Attribute (+10s for Studio Color)

`	ProScan			Track Spot			Studio Color (1)			Studio Color (2)
1	Pan		1	Pan		1	Pam (Course)	9		Yellow
2	Tilt		2	Tilt		2	Pan (Fine)	10		Lens Effect
3	Gobo Wheel		3	Color Wheel		3	Tilt (Course)	11		Frost Effect
4	Color Wheel		4	Gobo Wheel		4	Tilt (Fine)	12		Shutter
5	Shutter		5	Shutter		5	Color Function	13		Dimmer
6	Gobo Rotate		6	Dimmer		6	Color Wheel	14		M-Speed
			7	M-Speed		7	Cyan	15		Control
						8	Magenta	16		Check-Sum

Figure 11.15a Additional examples of magic sheets (automated lighting) a. Older format with individual attributes indicated. *Putnam County Spelling Bee.*

Chicago

UGA Fine Arts Theatre

R. Dunham, Designer

Automated Lighting Magic Sheet

Fixture Start Channels

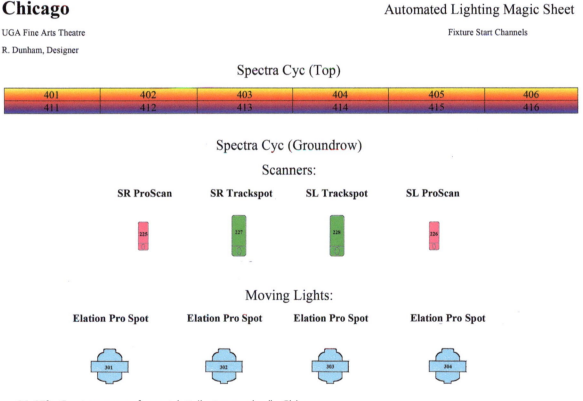

Spectra Cyc (Top)

| 401 | 402 | 403 | 404 | 405 | 406 |
| 411 | 412 | 413 | 414 | 415 | 416 |

Spectra Cyc (Groundrow)

Scanners:

SR ProScan   SR Trackspot   SL Trackspot   SL ProScan

225   227   228   226

Moving Lights:

Elation Pro Spot   Elation Pro Spot   Elation Pro Spot   Elation Pro Spot

301   302   303   304

Figure 11.15b Contemporary format (attributes masked). *Chicago.*

hanging positions are specified in the irons section, but battens or other permanent hanging positions are not included. Trussing may also be included in this section.

A fourth area of the shop order lists all of the **cables** and **two-fers** required for the production. There are numerous ways that an electrician or designer may determine the lengths of these cables, but two important points to keep in mind while specifying these cable runs include remembering to include the trim heights in the measurement of the cable runs and that most rental houses only provide cables in increments of 5 or 10 feet. It is also good to add a 10% safety factor to ensure that the estimates do not fall short. The shop order then includes the number of pieces of each length of cable and number of two-fers, three-fers, and other specialized cables that are required for the hang. The final part of the order relates to the **expendables** or **perishables.** These materials cannot be rented and must be purchased. Gel will be broken down into a **cut list,** which specifies the number of cuts and frame sizes that are required in each color as well as the number of sheets of each color. Other items that are often included in this section include items that help facilitate a hang. Extra connectors for practicals, tie-line for securing and dressing cables, china markers for labeling gels, paint or Sharpy Markers and white gaffers tape for labeling connectors and dimmers, and black gaffers tape for securing cables to the deck along with spike tape as just a sampling of these materials. One last task that should not be overlooked is to specify spare lamps for the production. Most designers will request that a spare lamp inventory of between 10 and 20% be made available for a production. When lamps burn out in rental fixtures, especially in the case of a long-running show, it is the responsibility of the renter, not the rental house, to replace the lamps. Each lamp type that appears in the design (even if there is only one unit making use of a particular lamp) should be covered by a minimum of at least one or two spare lamps. Often, different luminaires are lamped with the same model of lamp. If there are scenic practicals such as lamps that are part of a marquee, wall sconces, or strings of LED or holiday lights, these too must be specified and listed here.

CAD AND COMPUTERS IN LIGHTING DESIGN

Lighting designers quickly discovered the advantages of using computers: lighting design became the first theatre design discipline to use them as a regular part of the design process. Lighting, more so than any other area of design, deals with a huge amount of information or data that must be organized into a variety of repetitive yet different formats—a task particularly well-suited to computers. Computers are having an ever-increasing impact on all other areas of design as well, and designers are using them for more complex applications all the time. Not only do we use computers for a variety of design tasks, but variations of them have been incorporated into the very DNA of our lighting consoles and control systems. The only innovation that may arguably be as significant to the lighting industry as the desktop computer is the laptop computer. Laptops have made computers readily accessible to designers, who can now take their work directly to the theatres and hotels that they travel to for completing much of the design process. I carry a laptop almost everywhere that I travel to. They have had such an impact on our profession that it isn't at all unusual to see several of them on the design tables scattered throughout a theatre. Other innovations that are also having an impact on how we design are the computer tablets and phone apps. that are now being used for various aspects of the design process.

While there is still some debate on **Mac** versus **Windows**, both platforms are used extensively throughout the industry; much of the determination as to which platform a designer uses is simply personal. One major consideration that every designer must examine when determining which type of computer to purchase is the software that they will be using. Some applications run seamlessly on both Mac and Windows systems, some will require some form of file translation (with varying degrees of success), and others may be available for only one of the two platforms. A thorough examination of the operating requirements for the software that a designer will be using should have the greatest impact on which system they ultimately purchase. Some designers own and use computers that run on both platforms. As a rule, the computers that work best for lighting applications are equipped with the fastest processor, most amount of memory, and largest hard drive that you can afford. A good optical mouse is also helpful for data input (especially for working in CAD software).

While this last section of the chapter focuses primarily on how computers are used as an aid to generating light plots, it is also appropriate at this time to discuss several of the other areas where specialized software is being used in lighting design. These are organized primarily by type of application, with the major classifications being CAD, design paperwork, control and off-line editing, communication, and design analysis and visualization. In some cases, several applications work together as part of a suite that performs tasks in several different categories. Some of these programs were introduced in Chapter 9 because they are used as part of the design analysis and communication process. In these cases, I will simply mention the applications and refer back to the previous discussions.

CAD and Drafting Applications

In all fairness, one can say that the computer has revolutionized the drafting of light plots. Next to using the computer for design paperwork, using specialized **CAD** software is one of the earliest uses of computers in the lighting industry. CAD is especially useful to lighting designers because of the number of repetitive activities associated with creating a light plot. Light plots tend to be very mechanical and precise, making use of a number of straight lines, lots of lettering, and precise spacings. All of these are managed quite easily in CAD software. Mistakes are completely erased; a **plot** will always appear clean and unmarred as a perfect print of the final light plot despite the complexity of a design or drafting. More importantly, CAD packages have tools like copy/paste and **block** commands that allow the repetitive tasks of drafting a light plot to be reduced extensively. There are also more sophisticated versions of CAD programs that work in three dimensions and are known as **modeling programs.** Full three-dimensional models with realistic materials lit by real-world photometrics are now possible in CAD design. It is even possible to create images with a photographic quality where the CAD image itself becomes the final design—a **virtual design**. Film sequences may also make use of mattes or models that have been created through computer modeling or animation. Films like those in the *Harry Potter* series regularly combine animated elements with actual props, scenery, and actors. There are even feature-length films created entirely by computers (the *Toy Story* and *Shrek* film series, *Frozen*, *Tangled*, and *Zootopia*). The two most popular CAD programs currently used in the lighting business are AutoCAD and Vectorworks Spotlight, and the majority of the plots illustrated throughout this book were created with CAD software (most often AutoCAD).

One of the most popular features of CAD is its ability to copy elements of a drafting. This could mean copying an element as small as a single line, but it more often means that complex objects like lighting fixtures, scenic floorplans, master theatre plans, or even entire drawings can be used as a reference and copied. More importantly, objects can be copied between different draftings—and once an object has been drawn, it never has to be re-created because it is simply copied and modified as needed. Lighting symbols are easily copied and pasted into new locations throughout a plot while primary features of a facility can be made into a master drawing known as a **prototype** or **template.** In a real time-saving method, entire draftings can be made into these prototypes and used as base drawings for draftings that will become the light plots for specific shows. The tasks of redrawing the theatre, title block, key, and notation can be forgotten because a prototype containing all of this information is simply copied and used as a base to which specific details and luminaires for a particular project are added. Prototypes also permit drawing features like the borderlines, hanging schedules, and reference lines to be stored in a file that is opened each time that a designer wants to draft in a particular venue. Probably the most important single attraction of CAD software for lighting designers lies in its ability to store a host of pre-designed symbols. These symbols contain outline drawings of luminaires as well as a host of other information

regarding particular lighting instruments. We call these symbols **blocks.** What makes them so attractive for lighting designers is that they offer the ability to insert a symbol for a given instrument (**attributed block**) into a drawing and to then add (through prompts or dialogue boxes) specific data (**attributes** such as color, channel, focus, etc.) that are unique to the particular unit. This information is automatically posted with the associated symbol—and it includes the proper fonts, colors and positions as defined by the plate's notation.

Despite all of their advantages, CAD plots are stored in electronic files that can be lost if backup precautions are not taken: it is important to frequently store, update, and back up these files. Another issue that must be dealt with when using CAD is how to create a physical copy of the light plot. To **plot** (print) a large-scale image of a light plot in the traditional 1/2 inch = 1 foot or other acceptable scale requires a large-format printer or **plotter** (often as wide as 36–42 inches). Most designers do not own a plotter and must use a service to produce finished copies of the light plot. The costs and availability of these services must be considered, and even though times are changing, these services are rarely available 24 hours a day or on weekends—in smaller communities they may not even be available at all. In a pinch, smaller portions of plots can be output as a PDF file and printed on a personal printer, or larger portions can be output and printed as tiled images that are then taped together. An advantage to digital or electronic design lies in the fact that the draftings can be transmitted to other members of the design team by simply attaching the drawing files to an e-mail message or posting them on a common website or dropbox.

For the two most popular CAD programs used in the entertainment business—AutoCAD and Vectorworks—there are strong devotees in both camps. Each program has advantages and disadvantages that make it more or less attractive to an individual user or type of application. For Vectorworks, it should be noted that lighting designers use the lighting package (Vectorworks Spotlight) because this contains lighting tools and applications. AutoCAD does not offer such a package; if not creating one's symbol libraries themselves, add-on third-party programs like LD Assistant are necessary to provide the necessary lighting applications and symbols within an AutoCAD environment. AutoCAD has focused on the larger design market while Vectorworks has chosen to cater to the entertainment industry. The company has done this by keeping the price of the Vectorworks software lower and more affordable for entertainment designers, while also developing tools and applications that are specifically designed to aid lighting designers and other entertainment professionals. It should also be noted that there are other CAD packages that are available to lighting designers: these aren't the only CAD systems used in lighting design.

Sidebar 11.3 AUTOCAD VERSUS VECTORWORKS SPOTLIGHT

AutoCAD Advantages:

- Recognized as the CAD standard
- More complex drafting tools and functions
- Universal file format (.dwg or. dxf)
- Used beyond the entertainment industry by other design and engineering practices (if a lighting designer is working in themed or architectural lighting, architects and contractors use AutoCAD rather than Vectorworks)
- Sophisticated three-dimensional modeling and rendering support

AutoCAD Disadvantages:

- Expensive
- Lighting-specific applications such as lighting symbol libraries are not part of the software package and must be either developed by oneself or purchased from another vendor
- Very steep learning curve due to the complexity of the program

Vectorworks Spotlight Advantages:

- Much less expensive than AutoCAD
- Includes large symbol libraries and a number of application features that specifically address lighting and other entertainment design applications

- Interfaces with other lighting design software (i.e., Lightwright) for seamless data exchange
- Widespread acceptance by designers in the entertainment industry
- Provides tools that help to streamline the process of creating additional design documentation beyond the plot: magic sheets, beam spread/ focus indicators, and auto unit renumbering, etc.

Vectorworks Spotlight Disadvantages:

- Not recognized as a CAD standard in areas outside of traditional entertainment (i.e., themed, architectural, and a number of corporate producers)
- Translation of show files to. dwg format frequently isn't seamless and changes can often occur to data such as layer and block structures and definitions.
- Initially the drawing tools weren't as defined or user-friendly when creating more complex organic shapes and surfaces (this has improved significantly but some still consider it to be a challenge to create irregular shapes and lines)

Note: AutoCAD and Vectorworks Spotlight tend to be the most popular CAD programs used in entertainment applications. However, it should be understood that there are also a number of additional CAD choices available to a lighting designer as well. This is particularly true with visualization packages, which typically include their own propriety CAD programs.

Design Paperwork

Design paperwork is the area where lighting designers first discovered the power of the PC. Before then, all schedules had to be completed by hand. In the 1970s and early '80s the total number of units in a lighting design wasn't that significant—in many theatres less than 100. As the size of the rigs grew, the task of assembling all of the associated paperwork became more difficult and the potential for mistakes grew, while the penmanship of the designer or assistant usually got worse. Even to this day, on many shows an assistant designer is employed simply to keep track of all of the paperwork for a production. Since most paperwork is in tabular format, it didn't take long for designers to discover that computers could generate the majority of their schedules and paperwork quite easily; they simply needed to enter the information into their favorite spreadsheet applications. The real advantage to these applications comes in that all of the lighting data is entered into the computer only one time. Once entered, the software can manipulate the data to

generate the instrument schedules, hookups, and inventory lists that a designer needs for displaying the lighting data. Also, if the paperwork needs to be changed, the data is easily edited and a new set of accurate forms can be generated by simply reprinting the forms.

There are a number of lighting designers who use applications like Microsoft Excel or Works for producing their paperwork. There are also applications that have been specifically written to meet the needs of lighting professionals. Unique tools found in these programs include menus and questioning formats or input dialogue boxes that relate specifically to entering lighting data, ways of duplicating the input of repeating data, and lighting specialty tools like determining the total sheets of color or making power/load calculations. The standard for this software has been set by John McKernon's Lightwright software, which works on both Mac and Windows computers. In addition to creating standardized forms for paperwork like hookups and instrument schedules, the program has additional features such as lists for work notes, inventories, error checking for issues like irregular numbering and overloads, and comprehensive focus charts that can be stored in the computer. The sample pages from *The Miser* channel hookup and instrument schedule that were illustrated earlier in this chapter were created using Lightwright software. Other companies like Rosco and Stage Research, Inc. (formerly Cresit) also offer paperwork software.

Another type of lighting software comes in the form of a virtual magic sheet. This software, called Virtual Magic Sheet™ by Goddard Design/West Side Systems (Figure 11.16), contains a series of tools such as ovals, squares, and circles that can be laid out, colored, scaled, and arranged in much the same way as a traditional **magic sheet.** Along with the basic shapes, the designer also assigns a label or function (downlight, area light, John special, scroller, etc.) and associated channel to each shape. The magic of the software comes in when the computer containing the virtual magic sheet is interfaced with a lighting console using a DMX input. This produces an interactive display in which the magic sheet and its associated intensity levels for each channel are shown within the shapes and functions that have been previously defined by the designer. This gives the designer access to the control channels by function while also providing immediate feedback regarding the levels of the functions that are displayed by the magic sheet. This software is designed for both Mac and Windows

platforms. Some of the newer lighting consoles, such as those running the ETC Eos software, can also create virtual magic sheets that can even be activated through a touch screen interface.

Control and Off-Line Editing

Over the years, there have been several attempts to use specialty software to convert computers into basic lighting consoles. In each case, specialty software was loaded onto the computer and an interface or black box was connected between the computer and the dimmers. On occasion, an accessory containing a limited number of manual faders (a **wing panel**) could be added to bring some form of manual control to the console. Both Rosco's Horizon and Sunlite's lighting control system combine many of the features of more expensive consoles into a user-friendly interface that operates under the Windows environment. While there are still a number of Horizon installations, Rosco no longer distributes these products. More importantly, Rosco distributed the software for free through a CD-ROM or download that was readily available from the company's website. This permitted designers to run the software on their PCs for precueing or blind editing without the actual lighting console. Once programmed, the show file could be transferred to a computer at the theatre that was equipped with the DMX interface and the design

Figure 11.16 Virtual Magic Sheet by West Side Systems: Lighting systems are organized by color and function. Channel numbers are indicated in the center of each shape with levels indicated both graphically and by percent. Design by R. Dunham.

would be ready to go. There are a number of similar systems currently out there that offer software that is loaded to your computer (often a laptop), which then through a special dongle or interface converts the data to a DMX signal that is connected to the actual dimmers and other lighting equipment. Many VJ (video jockey) setups make use of these types of control systems—a number of these systems are even designed to handle more sophisticated lighting gear such as LED fixtures and automated instrumentation.

Off-line editing has become a very important tool that enables designers to download software that simulates a lighting console which in turn allows them to pre-program or edit the cueing of a production. In off-line editing, show files are created and edited without designers having to complete the cueing in the theatre with the actual lights and console. This software is useful in cases like touring, when a production has already been designed and a designer needs to modify or tweak a design for each venue. Off-line editing is particularly helpful when the designer is prevented from programming a show live in the actual performance space. Entire shows can be pre-written or roughed-in outside of the venue using this technology (writing a show **blind**). The pre-written cues are loaded into the console once the designer gets to the theatre and are then **tweaked** or edited once they are seen in rehearsals. Manufacturers of all the major lighting consoles provide free off-line editors that are downloaded from their websites. There are even utilities that can translate data from one manufacturer's console to another. Manufacturers of more complex consoles that are heavily oriented towards the moving light industry supply off-line editors that provide excellent simulations of their consoles and may even provide visualizations of the associated designs. Off-line editors also provide a great training mechanism for learning a new console.

Communication and Training

The ways that design teams communicate with one another have changed drastically in the last 15 or so years. In the past, most meetings took place in a face-to-face setting or plans and other documents had to be sent by express mail services that took several days to get from one city to another. Now, one of the primary means of transferring information from one person to another is through computers. Messages between members of the design team are often done by **e-mail** (even to our phones) while draftings and other visual images are frequently sent back and forth by attaching files (**attachments**) to e-mail messages. Design documents are also often uploaded to sites like Dropbox™ that the entire design team has access to. In the case of design meetings, it is often possible to use modern conveniences like the speakerphone on a cell phone or Skype for bringing a designer into a design

meeting when they cannot physically attend the meeting. Master plans of a stage or performance facility can also often be downloaded from the websites of many venues or performance facilities. In some cases, master drawings, research images and photographs, and sketches can be posted to dedicated websites (using Google Groups, Facebook, and Picasa). At the University of Georgia, we use Dropbox and Google Groups to link all of the members of a production team to the research that our designers are producing for our productions.

Another area in which the industry has changed significantly relates to the manner in which manufacturers and distributors make product literature available to lighting professionals. Several shelves of my office bookcase are lined with product binders and CD/DVD catalogs containing cut sheets for virtually any theatrical lighting product available. At my home office I have a whole bookcase devoted to product binders for just a few of the many architectural luminaire and lighting control manufacturers—which is small in comparison to most architectural lighting firms, which have a whole room dedicated to storing product binders. This method of distributing literature is rapidly going the way of the dinosaur as companies shift to distributing their catalogs and other product related literature to web-based **online catalogs.** In addition to cut sheets, these websites also provide aids to using the products, designer testimonials, price lists, and other resources related to a company's products. In the case of architectural luminaires, many companies provide tools that help a designer determine which products are best suited for a given situation and can even create the actual specification documents for a project. More importantly, these sites can be updated at any time and are available whenever needed. In addition to catalogs, many companies also provide technical support, product manuals in downloadable PDF formats, and learning tools for their equipment. I have found these sites to be particularly valuable for getting operating information for shows that I have done in theatres that use automated lights—often with any literature for these units being lost by that theatre long ago. On these websites I can quickly find critical information like a listing and order of a unit's attributes, setup requirements, and the striking (startup) and shutdown sequences needed for getting the fixtures up and running. I typically download each of the manuals for every type of automated fixture and specialized equipment that I will encounter or use on a project to my laptop as I begin to work on a design. I especially make sure that I have these on my laptop prior to traveling to an out-of-town gig where I might need immediate access to them at any time.

Design Analysis and Visualization

This type of software is created and used predominantly to help a designer and other production personnel to

Figure 11.17a LD Assistant by Design and Drafting a. Software interface illustrated along with block navigator and wire-frame model of a nightclub design by R. Dunham

Figure 11.17b Rendering of the nightclub design by R. Dunham

see and understand light within a given application. Some programs provide fairly simple tools to help analyze issues like lighting angles, falloff, and color mixing. Others are quite sophisticated and can go to the extent of producing complete virtual environments that are lit with virtual lighting equipment that replicates the same rig that will be created within the actual venue (visualization). Many of these visualizations can extend to the point of simulating actual cues that can then be imported to a lighting console and the actual rig. The simpler versions create computer renderings of given moments in a design while higher-end visualizers will be capable of even producing choreographed moving lights that simulate the actual moves of the lights in real time.

A number of these lighting analysis (i.e., Beamwright, and Virtual Light Lab) and rendering/visualization software packages (i.e., LD Assistant and wysiwyg) were discussed in more detail in Chapter 9. Figure 11.17 illustrates images of the software interface and final image of a project created with LD Assistant visualization software. What is most important to understand is that designers now have the capability to produce fairly accurate simulations (based on actual photometric data) of the entire lighting setup for a production well ahead of actually moving into a venue. Just as importantly (and why they are included here), at the same time that we are creating these simulations, we are also creating the light plot, paperwork, cues, and all other pertinent information that is related to producing the lighting design—even to the point of writing the cues and being able to pre-load them into the actual lighting console.

FOR FURTHER READING

Allen, Kevin Lee. Vectorworks *for Entertainment Design: Using* Vectorworks *to Design and Document Scenery, Lighting, and Sound.* Burlington, MA: Focal Press, 2015.

McMills, Anne E. *The Assistant Lighting Designer's Toolkit.* Oxford and Boston: Focal Press, 2014.

Mumm, Robert C. *Photometrics Handbook.* 2nd ed. Louisville, KY: Broadway Press, 1997.

Shelley, Steven Louis. *A Practical Guide to Stage Lighting.* 3rd ed. Oxford and Boston: Focal Press, 2014.

Warfel, William B. *The New Handbook of Stage Lighting Graphics.* New York: Drama Book Publishers, 1990.

CHAPTER 12

LOAD-IN THROUGH OPENING

ALL OF MY discussions regarding lighting design to this point have been primarily about preparation. In fact, it is quite possible to get this far into the design process without having touched a single lighting instrument. Much of this chapter, like the two previous chapters, is also concerned with preparation. However, a designer should feel some sense of accomplishment because they are now finally ready to move into the facility and will soon be working with the actual medium of light. Having said that, there are still several critical steps in the design process that must be diligently completed before moving on to actually designing with the lights in the theatre. At this time, luminaires are hung and circuited, colored, focused, and assigned or patched to channels/controllers associated with the lighting console(s). While this is happening, scenery, maskings, props, and costumes are also being assembled in the theatre as the final steps of preparing a production come together. It is at this point, as a show moves into a theatre, that a designer is finally free to begin the most important step in lighting a project. It is here that light and its controllable qualities are used to produce a variety of functions and effects. The true artistry of a lighting designer comes into play as they make design choices that are appropriate for every single moment of an event. The lighting designer is not only responsible for providing an appropriate combination of design choices for a given moment or **cue,** but also for the transitions that are made between each of the cues. All the work to this point has been related to preparation and creating the palette that the lighting designer will ultimately use to design from. Some lighting designers have even come to refer to this part of the process as **painting with light.**

This chapter provides information related to the tasks of a lighting designer and lighting crews as they move a production into the facility in which a show will be mounted. While the entire process plays a role in the final outcome of a design, the majority of the tasks associated with moving into a facility are once again technical and in themselves not the final design. It is only once all of these tasks have been completed and the designer is sitting at the design desk ready to **set levels** that the real process of lighting a show actually begins. Now, as light is created for each cue, the designer manipulates the intensities, colors, and instrument selections in order to produce the effects required by the concept. As lighting is added to the other production elements the lighting designer helps create the appropriate atmosphere, mood, and focus suggested by the performers, script, and other design areas. If done correctly, the preliminary work should pay off and the designer will find themselves with the proper tools to create what is required for the project. On the other hand, a designer can only do so much with a plot: if the tools aren't in the plot, an effect may not possible. Even a perfect plot (if there is such a thing) doesn't guarantee a successful design and might very well be used ineffectively when setting the levels for a production. This aspect of relativeness is especially important in lighting because what works well in one design or even moment may be completely inappropriate for another moment or design.

This chapter will take you through the process of getting the lights into the air, focused, and finally cued in combinations that are appropriate for any given moment of a production. Since lighting does not exist alone, at this point in the process we combine it with the other elements of a production to complete a full composition as we create the world of the performance event. This is done through a series of specialty rehearsals that are discussed toward the end of this chapter. By the conclusion of this chapter we will have designed the lighting and linked it in an appropriate manner to the script, concept, the performers, and the other design elements that are associated with a project. Due to space limitations, this book cannot begin to address all of the details associated with moving into a venue and will instead provide just an overview of the process. For a more thorough explanation of the load-in process you should refer to Stephen Shelley's book, *A Practical Guide to Stage Lighting*, which is a wonderful source of tips, procedures, paperwork, and common practices that can be used in bringing a lighting design to the stage.

FINAL PREPARATIONS FOR THE LOAD-IN

Many of the final steps in preparing for a **load-in** are completed as the lighting designer produces their **design packet** for a project. This packet includes all the information that the designer needs to communicate to the electricians who will actually hang the show. The design packet most importantly contains the light plot, other draftings related to the electric's department (e.g., the lighting section and plates containing signage or other scenic pieces containing practicals), the lighting schedules, and inventory lists and shop orders. This informational packet is often created as close to the load-in as possible so that the plot can address the latest needs of a production. If a show is to be sent out for bids, this material may have to be produced well ahead of the actual load-in date. Regardless of the individual conditions that a designer is working under, it is important that the material be assembled in a timely manner so that the load-in can proceed on schedule. When a designer is working locally it is common for the packet to be hand-delivered to the master electrician or shop so that it can be reviewed and prepped prior to the day of the actual load-in. It is also common, especially in the case of touring productions, for the design packet to be mailed to the performance venue using carriers like FedEx. Today, it is quite common to send these materials by electronic methods like e-mail attachments or to upload the files to an online dropbox. Regardless of how the materials are delivered, most electrical departments and master electricians need to have the design packet at least several days before the actual load-in.

Although much of the final preparations of a lighting designer are related to creating the lighting packet and getting the technical information together for the electrical crews, another area that should not be neglected is observing any rehearsals that are conducted in the final days before a load-in. This allows a designer to become more familiar with the blocking, moods, and transitions. These rehearsals are great sources for noting the specific placement of actor specials, getting a sense of pacing, and noting various transitional timings. More

importantly, these rehearsals will help the designer document much of the information that they will later need for creating appropriate cues for the production. The more familiar that a designer becomes with the production, the easier and more successful the later cue-writing sessions will become. Visits to the scenic and costume studios at this time will allow the lighting designer to check the final color and texture treatments of these elements of the production. These visits will also provide an opportunity to observe any unique conditions that may not be readily apparent from the plans and renderings that the other designers may have provided to the lighting designer at an earlier time.

Time is a luxury in the entertainment industry: producers cannot afford to spend any more time than absolutely necessary on the load-in process. One of the most important elements regarding final preparations for a load-in is in making as many decisions outside of the theatre as possible. This is particularly true in lighting, where we can't tell exactly what our final design is going to be until all the other elements of a production have come into place. Opening night is rarely delayed and all too often time is lost during a load-in due to a scenic or other production element taking more time to install or work into a performance than originally anticipated. Unfortunately, problems like these generally result in the lighting department having to pay the price in terms of lost time. A lighting designer should always strive to have the most amount of time possible for sitting at the design desk actually creating the cues. They should come into the cue-writing session with as many decisions already committed to as possible—prior to the load-in if they can, so that when they begin writing cues they will have the maximum opportunity to actually work and design with the medium of light. Decisions such as cue placement should be committed to well before the cue-writing session so that the designer can concentrate not on where the cues go, but on the actual look of the cues. Transitions and cue counts should also be completed prior to the cue-writing session as yet another way of making the cue-writing process more productive. By following these guidelines the lighting designer will maximize the amount of time and opportunities that they have for working with the actual lights in the venue.

THE CUE SYNOPSIS

The **cue synopsis** (Figure 12.1) is another piece of paperwork that is created by a lighting designer, but unlike other schedules and paperwork, it functions as a guideline for the actual creation of a production's cues. It does not contain the technical information that other forms of paperwork provide, but instead assigns a cue number to every cue or look in the production, and then provides specific information related to each

	Cue Synopsis			Urinetown: The Musical	
	R. Dunham, Designer			University of Georgia Fine Arts Theatre	
					10/15/2007
CUE#	Count	Page#	Execution Point	Description	Notes
0.5	5		Prior to house opening	Preset—Glow of scaffolds w/sidelight. Dark blue skyline. Blue Downs. Low overall levels. . . . more sculptural in overall quality.	
HS	**5**		**When Set**	**House to Half**	
1	5		With appearance of musical director	Build musical director special and pit band.	
			Overture begin		
2	10		About 30 seconds into overture	X-fade to deep blue shadowy quality over entire stage. Add some cool accents here and there. Slight build of area around Amenity 9— especially gobos. X-light cool scaffolds. Scrollers in lavender.	
HS	5		w/ LQ-2		
3	10	1			1–1 Amenity #9
			With music change to lead-in to Urinetown	Pull to deeper cool blue plus boost lavender backlight. Pre-dawn	
4	4		Following LQ-3 Just before Narrative		
	FS1 FS2	1		**Lockstock (L) -body**	**Frame 5**
5	6	1	. . . hear people referring to a lot ↓ through the show.	Slight build light around Amenity and where Penny (P) is setting up shop. Chorus is on all levels—even the top.	
				Spots should include Little Sally (LS) with L when needed	
6	30	2	What's that Little Sally.↓ w/people coming to life.	Suble build of Amenity areas as sunrise approaches	
7	10	2	. . . central conceit of the show!	Build all more for vocal w/ L. Warm it some . . . shift more lavander.	
8	3	3	. . . never bother with ↓ jail.	All build, keep cool . . . add front diags. And cool footlights	
9	4	3	You won't need bail.	Restore LQ-6 but not quite a full pull-down to LQ-6 levels.	
	FS1↓		w/ LQ-9		
10	4	3	**Visual** w/ Hope enters (Aren't we all)		
	FS1↑	3		**Add FS1 to Hope**	**Frame 4**
11	2			Add UGC tower special.	
		4	The gleaming tower ↓ on the hill?		
12	4	4	. . . directions and such. Bye	Tower drop to medium glow.	
	FS1↓		w/ LQ-12		
13	6	4	. . . to Urinetown (the musical)!	Restore LQ-8 Plus slight build.	
14	4	5	Often is a line.	Build backs and cools.	

Figure 12.1 A cue synopsis: Page 1 from *Urinetown: The Musical*

cue. A typical cue synopsis contains a cue number that allows easy identification of each cue (progressively numbering the cues in order), **counts** (transition times between cues), the execution point (specific action or line at which the cue is taken), and visual descriptions of each cue.

A cue synopsis forces a lighting designer to consider each of the images or looks of a production from curtain up to curtain down. To support the lighting concept, many designers think about specific moments of the play and then go on to answer questions that refer to the controllable qualities of light at those points in the action. Lighting functions are also considered as part of this process. What color should the light be? Is the entire stage washed in this color? Is there a specific direction or source suggested by the lighting at this moment in the script? What is the overall quality or mood? How much visibility does the scene require? Where should a cue's focus be established? How strong must the focus be? In many cases, lighting designers produce visual references such as color keys, storyboards, lighting scores, and even virtual images to assist in their creation of the cue synopsis. The blocking notation is another important aid to the designer at this time. The designer must consider the lighting image for each moment of the production. Cue placements can be tried and retried, transition times can be imagined and revised, but most importantly, a visual description must be created for each cue of the production. As a rule, cues should be described using visual language and the controllable qualities of light, with the discussion of the individual channels being kept to a minimum. This is done for two reasons: first, it eliminates the need to translate specific light sources into channel numbers (saving time), and second, designers often discover that the image that they are ultimately happy with may or may not be created with the same channels that they initially thought would produce the required look. If the cues are always written as descriptions, these revisions will not cause the cue synopsis to become irrelevant even through changes have been made in the channels used in the actual construction of the cues. This allows the cue synopsis to continue to be used successfully throughout the design process despite any changes that may develop in actually producing the desired effects.

One of the key advantages to completing a thorough cue synopsis is that it requires the lighting designer to make design decisions regarding the specific treatments of the lighting outside of the theatre. Cue sequences can be imagined and rehearsed in your mind where they can be worked out successfully without the pressure of keeping up with a rehearsal. With a good cue synopsis many decisions involving the design become nothing more than punching instructional sequences into the console at the actual cue-writing session—avoiding the need to make decisions regarding much of the more mundane information required throughout the cue-writing process. A cue synopsis is particularly helpful for entering repeating cues (**restore cues**) and counts into a lighting console. Productions with complicated cue sequences, such as musicals or dance performances, benefit greatly from a well-thought-out cue synopsis. In the case of musicals or operas, a copy of the soundtrack can prove especially beneficial, as sequences can be played as many times as needed to time cues to the music and to work cue transitions out well ahead of time. More importantly, once in the theatre, the designer can focus on those aspects of the cue-writing session that deal with the actual use of lights and their associated intensity levels. The more time that the designer can actually work and observe the lights, the better chance that they have of creating a successful lighting design. Probably the most common cardinal sin of beginning lighting designers is in coming to a cue-writing session without a solid cue synopsis. Time is wasted making decisions that could have easily been made outside of the theatre when the designer wasn't under the pressures of the time constraints and fatigue that are associated with the cue-writing process. There is nothing more counterproductive than watching a lighting designer and director sitting in a dark theatre struggling to decide on the placement of a given cue. More importantly, without this preparation the designer may find that they have designed themselves into a dead-end alley, which could result in having to go back to previous cues to make corrections or even having to discard cues and entire sequences that were created while going down the wrong path (and losing the time invested in creating those bad cues—even if it's hours). A complete cue synopsis also allows the lighting designer to maintain control of the lighting session by providing a detailed plan for lighting the production. If the synopsis is given to the director ahead of time, the director will be able to understand if the designer is on the right path and can discuss any issues ahead of the actual cue-writing process. The cue synopsis also provides a tool that the designer can use to pace themselves during the cue-writing session. If you're four hours into a six-hour cue-writing session and you're on cue 90 of a 200-cue show it becomes quite apparent that you'll have to pick up your pace or find some manner of simplifying your show. It is easy to spot designs where the team ran out of time as evidenced by comparing the number of cues that exist between the beginning and end of a piece. Finally, the cue synopsis can also be given to the stage manager so that the cues can be entered into the prompt script prior to the cue-writing session. Doing this saves valuable time in the cue-writing session because cue placements do not need to be transferred to the prompt script. Simply put, the cue-writing session should be a time where the lighting designer can focus on looking at the cues and transitions, not on making decisions about the general description or placement of the cues.

The cue synopsis can be created at any point in the process but is best done at a point where the designer believes that the blocking of the play is set and when there probably won't be any significant changes in the overall actions of the play. You don't want to do this too early because significant changes in the blocking could trigger changes in how you might light a given scene. However, you can also use any later rehearsals to check the cue synopsis along with the placement and counts of the cues that you are creating for a production. Cue descriptions can also be checked at this time. Through checking and rechecking the cue synopsis the cues can be refined even before the show moves into the venue. In some cases, due to limited rehearsal time, the cue synopsis may not be able to be completed until after the show has been loaded into the venue. When this happens, the designer will benefit from seeing the blocking as actually spaced in the theatre, but will also find themselves in a more extreme time crunch. As an alternative, there are some lighting designers who complete the cue synopsis even before they create the plot and paperwork for the production that they are lighting. Regardless of when the synopsis is created, it is important that it be checked, if at all possible, against at least one run-through prior to writing the actual cues.

Sidebar 12.1 CUE TERMINOLOGY

All Fade	A cue in which all of the lights are dimmed out, typically to a count that is greater than one second.
Base Cue	A cue that has the predominant elements of the lighting for a given scene or setting established. This is often returned to and then recalled and modified as needed for additional cues.
Blackout	An all-fade cue that takes place over a zero count.
Bow Cue	A cue used for curtain calls. This is usually fairly bright in intensity and covers most if not all of the stage.
Count	The time element of a cue transition. A count is associated with one-second intervals. Therefore, a cue with a five count would take place over five seconds.
Crossfade	An even transition between cues where the lights that are being added or are coming up in a cue are doing so at the same speed or count as though that are coming out or dropping intensity.
Curtain Warmer	A lighting cue typically done when the main or show drop is in for presets, intermissions, or scene changes where the drop or curtain is glowed with a wash of low-intensity frontlight. At times, the lights that form this wash may called **curtain warmers**.
Delay/ Wait	A manner of placing a hold on part of a segment of a cue's transition times. The actual nature of each is dependent on the specific console.
Follow Cue	A cue that is launched automatically without a "go" instruction by a preceding cue. For instance, Cue 12 brings up a special on a performer and is then automatically followed by Cue 13, which is a 300-count sunset fade that is launched with a pre-programmed time after Cue 12 has been initiated.
Pile-on	To add lights to an existing cue that is onstage.
Preset	A specific "look" for the lighting that can be called up on a repeated basis. In cue terminology, it refers to a lighting cue that is used prior to the start of a show or act and is present for when the audience is gathering.
Restore Cue	A cue that is a return to a previous cue or one that is duplicated at various times throughout a performance (i.e., Restore LQ-15).
Scrim-Through	A lighting effect done in conjunction with a scrim where the scrim changes from an opaque to transparent quality by adding light to the areas or subjects behind the scrim.
Splitfade	A cue in which the lights coming up in a cue will do so at one speed while the lights coming down or out will do so at another speed.

THE LOAD-IN

When I discuss a **load-in** I am referring to the time period in which all the scenery, costumes, and lighting equipment arrive and are installed or setup at the venue. The time that a load-in may require can vary considerably. In summer stock, where a new production must be performed for an audience in a day or two after closing the previous production, the load-in will typically be completed in less than 48 hours. In touring productions the load-in is often shaved down to 6–10 hours. On the other hand, in situations where elaborate production needs may be required, the load-in can extend to a week or two, if not more. No matter how long a load-in is scheduled, it is important for the lighting designer and their team to be productive and well-organized throughout the entire process. The lighting team must remain on schedule and cannot delay other aspects of the load-in. They must also remain flexible due to unforseen issues that may develop as the show comes together. For the lighting team, the process of loading in a show involves moving the lighting gear into the theatre, setting up and completing the power distribution and tie-ins to the dimmers and control systems, hanging and circuiting all of the luminaires, loading the color, and focusing the production. Many refer to the whole process of arriving at the venue and preparing the production as the load-in. Others think of the load-in as being only the physical setup of the equipment and will recognize additional calls like hang and circuiting calls, focus calls, and cue-in or cue-writing calls or sessions.

Proper scheduling during the load-in is extremely important to the overall success of this part of the process, and even more time must be allowed for the load-ins of productions that are being mounted for the very first time. This additional time is used for working out any kinks that may be discovered as the production is assembled for the first time. In touring productions, the load-in time will be trimmed down significantly due to everyone being both familiar with the exact tasks that have to be performed during the load-in as well as the creation of a number of specialized tools that will be used to streamline the load-in process. A production such as a touring dance company that has been on the road for a while can accomplish a fairly sophisticated lighting setup within the space of four hours or less. Some of the techniques for trimming down the repetitive tasks of loading-in productions such as these are discussed in more detail later in Chapter 13. The pool of labor must also be examined as part of this process. Are there enough electricians to get the production hung and focused in the time allotted by the producer? How many electricians does the house require for a focus call? Are the electricians union? A common guideline that many designers use for estimating crew calls and numbers involves using an estimate of three minutes for the hang and focus of each luminaire in the plot. Some units will take longer, some shorter, but this estimate accounts for all the tasks related to loading-in the lights for a given production. Are there student or union electricians involved in the load-in? If using students, the time estimate should be extended. Finally, other departments must also be considered in terms of load-in estimates. Where is the electrical gear in the trucks? What part of the stage will the carpenters use at any given time during a work call? Are there any in-house luminaires that can be set up prior to the load-in? Whose job is it to load-in and set the trims of the borders and other maskings? All of these questions are related to issues that will have an impact on the load-in process.

It is rare for electrics, or any other department, to have the entire stage to themselves for any extended amount of time. For the most part, all departments need to share the stage, and efforts must be made to coordinate the needs of each of the departments throughout the load-in process. The production manager and technical director (in consultation with the master carpenter, rigger, and master electrician) are most commonly placed in charge of this process and related scheduling. The number of crew members assigned to any department will also vary throughout a typical load-in. The largest number of stagehands and electricians will be employed for the initial load-in and setup, while the crews are made smaller for completing later portions of a load-in. I designed regularly for the Atlanta Lyric Theatre and my call for electricians during the initial load-in typically consisted of a minimum of 8–12 electricians. The initial lighting call must also include a flyman or two so that the battens can be operated and weighted throughout the load-in process. For the Lyric's focus calls the number of electricians was reduced to 4–6, and by the time I started my cue-writing sessions the crews were once again reduced to only those electricians who were running the production (the console and followspot operators). If the production didn't use followspots, even those electricians were pulled. The role of a lighting designer can vary significantly during a load-in. In some cases, the designer may have to function as their own master electrician or may be expected to coordinate the electric's crews during the load-in, possibly even taking on large elements of the physical hang and focus personally. In other situations (most significantly facilities under union control) the designer may not be involved with the physical load-in at all. Even if the designer is not permitted to participate physically in the load-in, if possible, they or an assistant should still be in attendance and readily accessible for answering questions and resolving unforeseen issues that come up during the load-in.

The first items of business for the lighting designer to complete at a load-in should be a quick survey of the theatre and a discussion with the house representatives, master electrician, master carpenter, and technical director of the production. Any surprises resulting from undocumented plans (which are more common than you might expect), issues related to the plot, production changes, and other items affecting the load-in are discussed at this time. The 15 minutes spent here are time well spent. Crew members can simply enjoy their morning coffee and donuts while this discussion is taking place. Everyone should review the hanging schedule or lineset assignments to make sure that the lines are positioned as everyone had thought and that any changes in assignments can be made prior to beginning the actual load-in. There is nothing more frustrating than having to move equipment from one batten to another because something had to change in the hanging assignments. If possible, many designers will even do a site visit to the venue ahead of the load-in in order to familiarize themselves with the facility and to meet key crew members as well as to discover any issues that might affect the load-in.

As a rule, electrics take the stage first. This is done so that the overhead electrics can be brought down to 3–4 feet above the deck, where they can be easily loaded, colored, and circuited from the ground. The electricians should also test and troubleshoot the electrics at this time since any problems will be much easier to trace and fix while the batten is near the ground. Beginning with the overhead electrics on the deck saves valuable time because lifts or ladders will not be needed—any work done from a ladder multiplies the time for completing a task by several factors. While I know designers who prefer to load the color during the show's focus, I think that it is far more beneficial to have the color placed in the fixtures during the initial hang. Problems such as sorting through a stack of color frames and looking for a particular gel in the dark, juggling color frames or running them up a ladder to the electrician, media falling out of its frames, and bumping units out of focus while dropping color are all eliminated. Most pastel to medium saturated colors can be easily focused with the gel in place, while any deeply saturated colors that make it difficult to see a unit's beam or fixtures that demand an especially critical focus can have the gel pulled and then dropped back in after the unit has been focused. Those designers who think that it is easier to focus lights without the gel can pull the color from the lamps on an individual basis or organize the gel into stacks that are given to the focusing electrician who will place them in the units once a particular light has been focused.

Once the electrics have been loaded and flown to trim or out of the way, the carpenters start assembling the scenic elements. The first scenic elements to be put in should always be the maskings and any soft goods like drops and scrims. This is often done when the electricians are working on the overheads because the stage is as open and as clear as possible. As the carpenters take over the stage, the electrics crew will shift to hanging and circuiting the front of house (FOH) and any positions such as booms or ladders that would be located in the wings. Much of the load-in must be carefully coordinated between both departments so that maximum efficiency is accomplished for the entire load-in. Another common arrangement involves having the carpenters work upstage while the electricians work downstage or vise versa. Through a coordinated effort both departments will share the stage and complete the load-in process faster. Any permanent scenic elements are assembled last, after the overhead electrics have been completed and flown out of the way. In a typical schedule for the Atlanta Lyric Theatre, the first call begins at 8:00 a.m. on Sunday mornings and consists of electricians only until noon; they use that time to hang and circuit the overhead electrics. When the electricians break for lunch at noon, the carpenters are first called and the trucks with the scenery

are scheduled to arrive at the theatre. The carpenters will have the stage for the rest of the day. The electricians come back from lunch at 1:00 p.m. and work until 5:00 p.m. completing the FOH, pit areas, sidelight, and any practicals associated with the production. By the end of the day the electrics will be completely functional and ready for focusing on the next day.

The schedule presented in Sidebar 12.2 is quite typical of an academic production while Sidebar 12.3 is more in line with what to expect for a commercial production—in reality, though, schedules can vary considerably from one situation to another. While Sidebar 12.3 is a common schedule for the Atlanta Lyric Theatre, other organizations have the luxury of additional technical rehearsals such as a **dry tech rehearsal**, a **tech with actors**, and as many as three or four dress rehearsals. In other cases, technical rehearsals may be nonexistent and there may only be a single dress rehearsal for a lighting designer to light a show. When I designed for the Brunswick Music Theatre (Maine State Music Theatre now) we would strike one production following a Sunday matinee, do a complete **changeover** throughout the next 24 hours, and have a single run-through of Act I from 7:00 to 11:00 p.m. on Monday night and Act II on Tuesday afternoon from 12:00 to 4:00 p.m. An audience would show up for the first performance later on Tuesday evening. I would cue the productions in the middle of the night with full work lights and house lights at about 50% as the carpenters worked on the settings, which were typically from completely different scenes than the ones that I was trying to light. More importantly, these two limited rehearsals afforded the closest thing that we could ever get to a dress rehearsal for observing what I had created with the performers. This represents the most compact of load-in schedules.

Sidebar 12.2 A TYPICAL ACADEMIC LOAD-IN SCHEDULE

3 Weeks Before Opening	Light plot due Begin load-in/light hang
2nd **Sat. Before Opening**	Focus day
2nd **Sun. to 2**nd **Wed. Before Opening**	Cue writing
Thurs. Before Opening	Crew watch
Fri. Before Opening	Dry tech
Sat. Before Opening	Full tech (10 out of 12)
Sun. Before Opening	First dress
Mon. Before Opening	TBD
Tue. Before Opening	Second dress
Wed. Before Opening	Final dress
Thurs.	Opening night

Even though schedules will vary, a lighting designer must be extremely efficient throughout this stage of the production process. Organization and preparedness are essential to running a successful load-in. Decisions should be made before entering the venue if at all possible, and the designer must remain flexible while retaining the ability to make snap decisions based on any issues that may come up during the load-in process. Those who can remain calm and make quick rational decisions, despite all the other tensions that typically arise at this point in the process, will do well in the business. A critical skill for a lighting designer to learn is determining where compromises must be made and when it is appropriate to move on. On the other hand, they must also be able to identify those times when it is necessary to take additional time to work out a problem and to hold on to a specific element of a design. In some ways, inaction can actually be worse than making a wrong decision. Making decisions is an important part of the process, and you learn from your mistakes.

Sidebar 12.3 A Typical Commercial Production Load-in Schedule

SUNDAY

8:00 a.m.	Electrics load-in overheads
	Carpenters hang masking/flying scenery
12:00 p.m.	Lunch
1:00 p.m.	Electrics hang FOH and booms/wing units
	Carpenters assemble platforming and main stage scenic units
5:00 p.m.	Crews released for Day 1

MONDAY

9:00 a.m.	Electrics focus call, wire additional practicals, and troubleshooting
	Carpenters as needed
12:00 p.m.	Lunch
1:00 p.m.	Continue focus
5:00 p.m.	Crews released for Day 2

TUESDAY

9:00 a.m.	Electrics cue-writing session
	Carpenters as Needed
12:00 p.m.	Lunch
1:00 p.m.	Cue-writing continued
6:00 p.m.	Dinner
7:00 p.m.	Tech/run with performers and lights
11:00 p.m.	All released for Day 3

WEDNESDAY

6:00 p.m.	Touchup call and notes
7:00 p.m.	Dress rehearsal

THURSDAY

6:00 p.m.	Touchup call and notes
8:00 p.m.	Performance

*Thursday Schedule Continues Through Performance Run (being adjusted for matinees)

THE FOCUS CALL

Once all of the lighting equipment has been installed and tested, the lighting team moves on to focusing the luminaires. When I discuss **focusing** I am referring to pointing the luminaires to the exact locations that the designer has planned. Electricians also adjust any other optical controls that may be provided by a lighting unit at this time. Pan and tilt, soft or hard edges, focus of any gobos, spot/flood settings, and shutter cuts form typical adjustments that are performed on luminaires at this time. It's also a time when a lighting designer checks for consistency between units that form washes and works with the electricians to even out any shadows that fall between individual lighting areas. Frost or diffusion media may also be added to help even out washes and to soften any units that have hot spots or hard edges. The time scheduled for focusing is commonly named a **focus call.** In most cases, the gear is installed on one day with focus calls being scheduled for the following day. However, in the case of one-day events or touring productions the focus will often be done immediately after the units are hung and circuited, since a performance will be scheduled for later that evening. If the hang and circuiting of a production take longer than anticipated, it is quite common for a portion of the crew to go ahead and start focusing while the remaining electricians concentrate on finishing up the circuiting and troubleshooting of the equipment.

The lighting designer plays a vital role in the focus of a production. Only the lighting designer can truly determine if a luminaire is achieving exactly what had been envisioned. Often, compromises will have to be made, and only the designer is in position to decide whether a given adjustment will be acceptable. There are times when parts of the plot or even the whole focus may be entrusted to an assistant or associate lighting designer. This is the exception in original productions but is quite common once a show has already been produced and is being remounted. This is especially true for touring and repertory productions. The assistant or associate designer will coordinate the day-to-day operation of the production and will make any decisions regarding compromises that must be made in regard to the different venues that the production will be staged in. A good assistant or associate will do this in a way that is consistent with the original production.

The number of individuals involved with a focus call may vary considerably from one production to another. A fairly typical arrangement involves the lighting designer, a board operator, the electrician who will actually focus the luminaires, and two additional electricians assigned to moving the ladder or lift that supports the focusing electrician. In fact, there are times when several teams of electricians may be organized for a single focus call. This will allow the designer to work several areas of the theatre at a time. I commonly use two focus teams and will alternate between them so that one team is focusing while the other is moving their ladder or lift to another position. I can also move on to focusing with the second team when the first team encounters a problem with a fixture. The Metropolitan Opera in New York City's Lincoln Center completely mounts and focuses a minimum of two different operas nearly every day (one in rehearsal or matinee and another for the evening performance). The overheads are frequently focused while the audience is gathering in the house and a number of the operas even require some focusing during intermissions. What is important during a focus call is that a logical order be established so that efficiency is stressed throughout the call. Designers must learn to make judgment calls in regard to what portions of the stage need to be focused first, how to move through the order of the focus, what elements of a luminaire's beam quality are critical and worth spending time on, and when to move on when an electrician struggles with an uncooperative unit.

There are several items from a designer's perspective that can be done to move through a focus in an efficient or productive manner. Probably the most important time-management rule for coordinating a successful focus involves focusing in such a way that creates minimal moves of any ladders or lifts. You don't want to be constantly moving the ladder from one side of the stage to another—you would spend valuable time shifting the ladder around instead of focusing the lights. Most designers try to focus all the lights from a single hanging position at a time as a manner of building efficiency into their ladder moves. Quite often the first light to be focused from an electric will be at its extreme end. The position will then be focused progressively from one end to another. The instrument schedule is a critical source of information for the lighting designer during a focus call because it arranges the luminaire's technical information by hanging order (unit number) and position. While I usually begin the focus at one end of an electric, there are times (such as when focusing critical washes) that I may begin to focus a position from the center,

such as a FOH catwalk, rather than from the ends. This helps ensure that I can create good coverage through the central part of the stage. If the coverage is spread a little thin it allows the light to be tapered off at the offstage edges as opposed to causing dips or shadows in the central portions of the wash or coming up short on the far side of the stage. Booms and other vertical positions can usually be focused more efficiently if focused from the top downward.

The most common method of focusing is having the designer stand at the exact point where a luminaire will be focused. Experienced electricians will have already prepped the unit to make sure that the shutters have been pulled and that the pan and focus bolts aren't excessively loose. Once the designer is in position the electrician should point the center of the pool of light or **hotspot** onto the designer's face or head. The designer then provides fine-tuning instructions to the electrician to ensure that the hotspot falls in the exact location that is desired. How designers observe the hotspot varies from designer to designer. Many of us vary our technique depending on how bright the light source is, how many hours we've been focusing, or how fatigued we are. One common practice is to stare into the lens of the fixture and to look for the dot of the lamp's filament. If the dot is centered in the lens, it can be assumed that the hotspot of the luminaire is focused on your face. Variations of this technique involve wearing sunglasses or facing away from the unit and observing your shadow within the beam of light. Facing away from the lamp and observing your shadow is the safest manner of focusing a unit. Staring directly into a lamp can create temporary blindness that can cause accidents like tripping or falling into the pit and may also have long-term effects like producing cataracts. There are some designers who stand or sit in the audience while observing the effect of the light on an assistant or electrician who has been placed at the focus point. For those of us who are of average height there is no need to compensate for height differences, but if you are taller or shorter than most performers you will need to adjust your focus position by moving several steps closer to the fixture (taller) or away from the unit (shorter) as a means of compensating for your height difference.

Hand signals are often used for communication between the designer and focusing electricians because of all the noise that is associated with a load-in. I personally use thumb signals for fine-tuning the focus—a thumb-up means to bump the focus up slightly while a thumb-down or to one side means to drop the unit or to inch it over to one side or another. It is important for electricians to understand that movements of the unit of only fractions of an inch can translate into movements measured in feet on the actual stage. Once the designer is happy with the focus, the electrician is instructed to **lock the unit down.** Upon this instruction the electrician tightens the pan and tilt adjustments while taking care that the focus doesn't drift or drop. These units don't have to be tightened down so securely that they'll remain in place for the next 50 years, but they do have to be snug enough that gravity or vibrations from air-conditioning or heating systems won't cause them to drop focus. There is no excuse for having to go back to fixtures to focus them a second time because an electrician didn't lock them down properly at the original call. After the luminaire is locked down and the designer is happy with the position of the hotspot, they will have the electrician set the actual focus of the unit. We often set ellipsoidal reflector spotlights with their barrels all the way out or forward (**running the barrel**), which usually produces the softest edge and focus to the pool of light. This is done to blend the edges of the beams from different luminaires. On occasions, such as with gobo patterns, a designer will want a sharper edge or focus for a unit. In these cases, the point at which the edge or pattern is sharpest will usually be found somewhere between the extreme points of the unit's focus adjustment. It is also at this time that many designers adjust any zoom or spot/flood controls that a luminaire may be equipped with. After the unit has been focused, the final adjustment is in making shutter cuts (if the unit has shutters) and shaping the beam as well as shuttering any unwanted light off of objects. It is important to remember that shutter cuts are made by manipulating the opposite shutter from what is observed on the stage. I use open hand and arm motions for communicating shutter cuts and their orientation to the electricians. The arms create the angle that the desired shutter should be adjusted to (think children and imaginary planes) while the hands coach the in and out placement of the shutter. Figures 12.2a and 12.2b illustrate a student designer using hand signals during a focus call. In lieu of hand signals many facilities now give the designer and electricians wireless intercoms to use throughout a focus call. This is particularly helpful for focusing FOH positions that are far away from the designer and where heat or air-conditioning equipment can cause communication problems.

While the designer is observing the actual focus and overall shutter cuts of the luminaire, the electrician should watch for any unwanted spill onto objects like borders or the edge of the proscenium. These problems are often hard to see from the designer's perspective. Once a unit is focused the designer will refer back to the instrument schedule to mark it off and to bring up the channel of the next luminaire that is hung in the position. At the same time that the designer asks for the next luminaire, the unit that was just completed will be shutdown or **saved.** With luck, the ladder will not have to be moved, but if it is necessary, the move is usually only several feet along the path of the electric to the next cluster of luminaires. Occasionally the

Figure 12.2a Focus call. a. Designer using hand gestures to fine-tune the focus of a luminaire

Figure 12.2b Designer using arm motions to have the electrician adjust a shutter cut on a luminaire

board operator or an assistant may monitor the focus with the plot or paperwork and call out the channel for the next unit to be focused. We often call this **riding the plot.** After a unit or two that share a common purpose have been focused (i.e., a common wash), electricians will often add additional steps to their prep by roughing in settings such as the spot/flood position or running the barrel prior to focusing the actual instrument. Even though these simple operations take only a few seconds the cumulative effect can shave a significant amount of time off the focus call. In a successful focus session a rhythm will develop between the electricians and the designer as the team steadily moves through the theatre until every instrument has been focused. The last items that are generally dealt with in a focus session are any set mounts and practicals that need to be made operational prior to the cue-writing session. When the focus session is complete, the designer should have a good idea of exactly what each luminaire is accomplishing within their design. It is at this point, after we have moved beyond the theoretical qualities of the plot and paperwork, that the first significant step is completed in the physical realization of the design.

THE LEVEL-SETTING OR CUE-WRITING SESSION

Everything that a lighting designer has done up to now has been in preparation for arriving at this point in the design process. The **level-setting** or **cue-writing session** is a time in which the lighting designer actually creates the images or cues for the production. In addition to creating the cues the designer also determines the transitional times and related effects that are used to go from one cue to another. We may also refer to this process as **setting levels** or the **cue-in.** The cue-writing session is the phase of the design process where the lighting designer truly becomes a full-blown member of the creative team. It is here, in the dark theatre, where the lighting designer uses all the tools that they have assembled through the plot and focus to actually light the production or to "paint with light," as many of us would say. The design may be created with just a few lamps or hundreds of luminaires but in the end the lighting designer is revealing, modifying, modeling, directing focus, and creating the composition and mood of the stage for every moment of the event. How bright a stage must be is dependent on a number of factors. A level of between 100 and 150 footcandles is often considered enough to provide adequate illumination for many stage situations. However, depending on mood, size of facility, and other factors like material reflectance, it is quite permissible to have illumination levels that fall both well above and below this range. In reality, theatrical designers design for perception and by what they see.

Preparation is key to a designer's success at this stage of the process. As stated earlier, a complete and thorough cue synopsis will make this part of the design much easier for a designer. If this has been done properly, the designer will not need to consider many of the more mundane tasks of the cue-writing session. This is also a time when many designers start to grow fatigued after having endured several hours or days of long hours from the load-in and focus sessions. The two most important documents that are required for the level-setting sessions are the cue synopsis and magic sheets. Once I get to the cue-writing session, I can often light an entire show using just these two documents. This doesn't mean that I don't keep a copy of the plot, paperwork, and script near me as I work through the cue-in process—they are still kept as references but in many cases simply aren't needed.

Several additional forms of paperwork may also be introduced at the level setting session (various types of cue, repatching and track sheets form several examples of these forms). If they are not introduced here, they will become part of the production process at some point in the rehearsals that follow the cue-writing session. In many cases, these too, are completed by the designer prior to the cue-writing session, often as the cue synopsis is completed. The first are **cue sheets** for any followspots that are associated with a production. These provide essential cueing information such as who to pick up, the color frame assignment, size of the spot, and any other information that the operator might need to know. We often tie the spot cues to the lighting cue numbers so that the information is more easily communicated to the spot and board operators by the stage manager. An example of a followspot cue sheet is presented in Figure 12.3. In another example of a form that might be created by a lighting designer, a facility may not have a sufficient number of dimmers for a production, which results in the need for reassigning dimmers throughout a performance. Here, a dimmer will be assigned to an initial circuit but will at some point have another circuit patched and reassigned to it (often following the completion of a certain cue). This is called **repatching** and these reassignments may be done several times throughout a performance. We often assign specials to repatching as long as they aren't used at the same time as any other luminaries that may be assigned to a given dimmer. There must also be sufficient time to make the actual wiring change before the new special is illuminated. Obviously, the designer must track each of the specials that are assigned to a repatching dimmer in order to ensure that the repatching occurs while the dimmer is off. Repatching may occur at the patchbay, the actual circuit outlet, or at the end of a given cable run. While the electricians must ultimately keep track of the actual circuit numbers many times we simply assign letters or colors to the circuits to make the repatching easier for the running crews. An example would be in

CUE#	In/Out	Count	Frame #	Pickup	Notes:	
	Follow Spot Cues				Urinetown: The Musical	
	R. Dunham	Designer			University of Georgia Fine Arts Theatre	
		Followspot # 1				10/15/2007
4	In	4	5	Lockstock (L) -Body	Just before narrative.	
					Spots should include Little Sally (LS) with L when needed	
9	Out	4				
10	In	4	4	Hope (H)—Body	w/her entrance	
12	Out	4				
20.5	In	6	6	Penny (P)—Body		
25	Out	4				
33	In	5	1	Cladwell (C)—Body		
47	Out	4				
51	In	2	4	Lockstock (L)—Body		
60	Out	6				
65	In	4	1	Hope (H)—Body		
73	Out	10				
80	In	8	4	Penny (P)—Body		
87	Out	0				
91	In	7	4	Cladwell (C)—Body		
100	Out	4				
106	In	4	3	Bobby (B)—Body		
127		5			Random searching sequence	
128		1	3	Lockstock (L)—Body	Lands on Lockstock at end of search	
129	Out	0				
				INTERMISSION		
137	In	2 + 4	3	Hot Blades (HB)—Body		
138	Out	2+3				
140	In	2 + 6	4	Lockstock (L)—Body		
142	Out	2				
146	In	4	2	Josephine (J)—Body		
150	Out	3 + 6				
152	In	3	4	Lockstock (L)—Body		
155	Out	3 + 6				
157	In	2	4	Hot Blades (HB)—Body		
160	Out	2				
170	In	6	5	Bobby (B)—Body		
180	Out	3 + 6				
189	In	1	3	Cladwell (C)—Headshot		
190	Out	1				
194	In	2 + 4	4	F'PP (F)		
195	Out	4				
209	In	4 + 10	5	Little Sally (LS)—Waist	She's sitting on deck.	
211	Out	4				

Figure 12.3 Followspot cue sheet: a partial cue sheet for Followspot 1 for a production of *Urinetown: The Musical*

labeling a circuit and its repatches as Red 1, 2, and 3 or A 1, 2, and 3. The practice of repatching can go a long way toward helping a designer bring additional lighting elements to a production, provided that there is time for the electricians to swap the circuits around.

Level-setting relates to the times in which the actual cues are programmed into the lighting console or developed in a manual lighting system. This typically occurs just before tech rehearsals begin for a production. Ideally, a designer will have a day or so to program a show while in some theatres, this actually occurs during the technical rehearsals. In especially tight schedules, this may only happen during dress/spacing rehearsals and the lighting designer must work without any rehearsals that are geared toward lighting the show. One of the more important goals of the level-writing session involves creating the cue sheets for the light board and its operators. This has actually been pretty well eliminated in many theatres since most cue information is now stored electronically in the memory of computer consoles. While there was a time when none of us trusted the computer and we were paranoid about losing a show, technology has advanced to the point that we now have confidence in these consoles. In those earlier days, we typically made a handwritten copy of all of the cue information. The backups that we now make as we go through the cue-writing process are now done digitally (with hardrives, disks and/or flashdrives) and we frequently don't make written backup copies of the cues anymore. However, the only certain manner of safeguarding your cues and the time that it took to program a show is by creating a printed copy of the cues. In fact, most of today's consoles can print a copy of the cues onto paper using a conventional printer and a simple print command. This is what we call **tracking** a show. The essential information that is provided on these printouts includes the timing of the cues along with the intensity levels for every channel/dimmer for each cue of the show. At one time, an assistant was assigned to write down the levels and other settings for each cue. Figure 12.4 illustrates a typical track sheet. In situations where a designer is using a manual board, which is still fairly common for specific types of productions, the level-writing session also becomes the time in which the cue sheets are written for the operators. Sometimes the designer or their assistant will create the cue sheets, while at other times the operators are expected to write their own cue sheets. In the case of manual boards, like the older piano boards, it was common for the

operators to simply write down the actual action and levels that took place during a cue. In preset systems, master cue sheets (Figure 12.5) are frequently created that display rows of the dimmers in a series of presets that allow the levels to be written in a box just below each dimmer number. The levels portion of the cue listing is then supplemented with another section that documents the actions to be taken during particular cues. Such actions would include the cue number and count (transition time), which preset was becoming active, the cross-fade assignment required to complete the cue, and any special instructions such as manual or independent assignments.

Figure 12.4 A track sheet from a ballet of *The Orphan Train*: individual levels are recorded in the space below the channel numbers along with the cue number and execution times or counts

Figure 12.5 A preset cue sheet

The amount of time allowed for a designer to write or program the light board can vary considerably from one situation to another. Sometimes the designer has the freedom to create the lighting with the help of only the board operator, while at other times the director may sit by the designer throughout the entire process. Sometimes cues are set with the proper scenery on stage and at other times this is not possible. In the most extreme cases the cue-in will take place with the actors in attendance and posing in their blocked positions. Obviously, the more elements that a lighting designer has in place the more accurate the initial cueing will be. However, due to costs, this is seldom done outside of those situations where money is not a factor or where the producer is willing to pay for making sure that things are done properly the first time (as with some academic programs and on Broadway). Unfortunately, lighting designers must often come up with the best lighting that they can under significant time limitations and less-than-ideal working conditions. Sometimes cue-writing sessions are set outside of the traditional rehearsal schedule, while other times they are worked into the schedule through a series of special rehearsals called **technical rehearsals.** A technical rehearsal is a rehearsal in the performance venue with its focus on the technical elements of a production and issues like scene changes, light cues, sound cues, and their transitions. Performers are often not called to all the technical rehearsals. Time to cue in the actual theatre is scarce and a designer must find ways to be both quick and efficient. In some cases, the designer may choose to write the cues **blind,** or program the console prior to entering the theatre and without the use of the actual lights. This saves time because the cues will be roughed in prior to seeing them on the stage and you won't be starting your cue-in from scratch. This means that the cues only have to be tweaked or edited in the theatre—but you can also find yourself out in left field when writing a show blind. In reality, the more experience that you have, the more confidence you will gain and the better that you will become at using precueing for a show. Today's visualizers can also make the process of precueing a show much more accurate and faster.

By the time that a lighting designer completes the level-setting process they have cleared a second hurdle of realizing their design. Even though this is perhaps the most stressful part of the design process it is also the most fun and rewarding aspect of the experience for most designers. It is at this point that the designer turns all the tools (plot, focus, etc.) into an actual design in light. A common mistake made by beginning lighting designers is to not get enough cueing information into a console prior to a tech or dress rehearsal in which the performers are present. The objective of a cue-writing session should be to get something programmed into the console for every major moment of the production. If there isn't sufficient time to program all the cues, the major images should be programmed so that you can get a sense of how successful the base cues will be when the lights are first viewed with the performers. The skipped cues can be programmed into the board at a later time. Following these guidelines allows a designer to evaluate the cues during a rehearsal within the context of the moment—with the performers in their proper positions, compositional elements in place, and moods easily identified. Transitions should also be evaluated through this process. More importantly, if a designer has followed this technique they will not only be able to evaluate the success or failure of a cue based on the context of the moment, they will also be able to tweak or refine it based on observations that they can make in rehearsal. Issues like whether focus is properly established, if the color is too saturated, if there is enough visibility, or whether the proper mood is created are easily evaluated and fixed if there is something in the board to evaluate. Another mistake commonly made by beginning designers occurs when they run out of time when setting levels. In this case, the designer will not have anything to evaluate or react to beyond a given point in the rehearsal. When some plotting has been done beforehand, even if the recorded levels are completely wrong, you at least have something to evaluate and can make some concrete decisions in regard to how to fix the remaining cues. What's important is getting something to look at. Any absence of cues or information will always be wrong, but any information—even if bad—gives you an opportunity to see what is wrong with a cue and to start making corrections. In some cases, true inspiration comes from cues that were simply plugged into the console for the sake of just getting something to look at for that first rehearsal with the performers.

With the advent of automated lighting, the number of additional variables that a lighting designer must consider when cueing a show has grown astronomically. When programming a show with automated lighting, it becomes even more important for a lighting designer to be efficient through the cue writing session. In addition to the intensity of a particular lamp, they must also be concerned with factors like where it is pointed (pan and tilt), color assignment, gobos, shutters, beam spread, etc. All of this additional control data must be quickly accessible through the designer's magic sheets as they program all of this information into the console. Because of this, it is common for shows making use of automated lighting to require more tech time for setting up a console and programming a show. In fact, a specialized technician (**programmer**) has appeared whose primary function is setting up and programming all of the intelligent lighting. At the other extreme, even when using automated lighting and all of the additional programming, designers are often faced with situations where a theatre still only allots the same amount of time for programming a show with moving lights as they have when only convential lights have been used in their productions. Fortunately, consoles have evolved in a number of ways to make the tasks of programming automated lights much faster and efficient.

CUEING AIDS FOR MEMORY CONSOLES

While it is still possible to run across preset boards and other variations of manual lighting consoles in today's world of lighting design, most designers use some form of memory or computer console to program their lighting. Despite the variations between specific boards and manufacturers there are still a number of programming features that manufacturers provide in their consoles along with programming techniques that designers and operators may use to help make cueing a show easier and more efficient. Even though the specific manners of achieving these programming features may vary from console to console, a designer ought to be aware of how they can streamline the cueing process. In most situations, the board operator or programmer will be a stagehand (local) who frequently works in a particular theatre and operates/programs the console in that space on a regular basis. A designer should trust the local board operator for the specific techniques in which a particular console may operate because these programmers use the consoles day in and day out and are the people who will be most familiar with their board. They also have

most likely already been asked to create some unique effect or to use some buried feature of a console that was needed by another designer who passed through at an earlier time. In other settings, a designer may often have a favorite programmer that they will have hired as part of the production staff for a given gig. Use your console operators and trust them; they're a terrific resource for getting through the cueing process—most will take pride in figuring out how to program a unique effect or sequence of cues for you. The following pages will not give you time-saving keyboard shortcuts, but instead will discuss several essential cueing practices that will help minimize the number of keystrokes that it takes to achieve a cueing sequence.

Many consoles are equipped with features that enable the operator to be more productive in their cueing. Many of these were discussed previously in Chapter 7. **Tracking** or **cue only** modes, the **wheel, blind mode, submasters, groups, independent masters,** and **blackout buttons** are just a few console features that are used to help reduce keystrokes during the cueing process. Even individual keys such as the thru, and, plus and minus, full and out, and next and last keys can help to eliminate a number of basic keystrokes when programming a console. In the case of automated lighting, we also have specialized software to aid in both the cue writing and documentation of the moves and attributes of this gear. One software package uses a specialized

Auto	Trig	Cue	Name	Fade	Outfade	Delay	Link	I.Delay	I.Fade	
	GO	0.5	Preset	2s						Preset a
	GO	1	HL to Half	5s						
	GO	2	HL Out	3s						
	2s	2.1	Stage DBO	2s						
	FOLLOW	2.9	ML RESET	1s						
	GO	3	Lights up Bakery	0s						SONG -
	FOLLOW	3.5	Add FOH	7s						
	GO	4	Fill to DS	5s	15s					
	GO	5	Man At Door	2s						
	GO	6	Lose DS	2s						
	GO	7	Intro Starts	7s						
	GO	8	Every1 Loves Cake	0s						
	GO	9	lst Chorus	1s						
	GO	10	Pull Down Verse	3s						
	GO	11	2nd Chorus	1s						
	GO	12	Pull Down	3s						
	GO	13	Dance Break	0s						
	GO	14	Restore	0s						
	1s	14.09	ML RESET	2s						
	GO	14.5	Cake	0s						
	0.30	14.6	Cake	0s						
	0.30	14.7	Cake	0s						
	GO	15	Button	0s						
	GO	16	Playoff	5s	7s					
	FOLLOW	16.9	ML RESET	2s						
	GO	17	Button to Park	0s						
	GO	18	Lose US	7s						
	GO	19	BO	5s						
	FOLLOW	19.9	ML Resets	2s						
	GO	20	Mr Puffs Night	2s						

Figure 12.6 A screenshot of cue list documentation from Moving Light Assistant software that documents the setup and programming of moving lights

Credit: Courtesy of Andrew Voller Lighting Design Limited

spreadsheet to track the focus points that are assigned to automated lights. This software, Moving Light Assistant, allows every attribute of the automated fixtures and their focus points to be documented and tracked throughout a design. It also has an interface that allows the program to both trigger and respond to changes between the software and the console.

As discussed in Chapter 7, the designer also can play a role in eliminating keystrokes by paying careful attention to the manner in which they lay out the hookup or channel assignments of the production. Even beyond this organization and the specific console features, there are additional techniques that will lead to further efficiency in writing cues. Sidebar 12.4 provides a listing and explanation of a few of these aids to cueing. As lighting design has gotten more complex and we have incorporated more sophisticated gear into our plots the consoles have also evolved and now include many specialty features that are specifically designed to aid in the programming of these new technologies. Examples of this include the manner in which we program automated lighting, the methods that we can assign color to units in which color can be programmed, the ability to set the attributes for almost any multi-channeled device to readily recognizable console functions, the option to create macros for frequently repeated programming sequences, and many pre-programmed effects and other user functions.

Sidebar 12.4 Cueing Aids for Memory Consoles

Block Cues — Sometimes called **hard blackouts** and are cues placed throughout a program that have every channel recorded at a level of zero. They are often placed at the end of a scene where an actual blackout is required. Block cues prevent tracking channels from continuing to make changes past a given point.

Check Cues — Cues created to check or verify particular actions. They are commonly created before the preset cue for the beginning of an act or during an intermission sequence. An example is a cue that brings up all the repatch channels to a glow to verify that the circuits have actually been replugged at intermission. A **blackout check** plunges the theatre into complete darkness to check that all grid, fly, and worklights are out for the top of a show.

Cue Blocks — Cue blocks establish and number sequences of cues together as a group. The most common forms create blocks of cues where each act of a production begins a new numbering sequence (i.e., Act 1 begins with Cue 101 while Act 2 begins with Cue 201). Cue blocks are often used for dance concerts where each dance is assigned a block of 10–20 cues. Dance 1 begins with Cue 11, while Dance 2 begins with Cue 21, and Dance 6 begins with Cue 61, etc. The base cues (in this case 10, 20, or 60) form preset cues for each dance. Cue blocks allow dances to be cued in any order and are also used for when dances are shifted around into any performance order in a repertory situation. B e sure to stay in cue-only mode when programming these cues or set block cues when you do this or you could have unwanted tracking when programming lower-numbered cues that affect previously recorded higher-numbered cues.

Fixture Keys — Specialty keys on consoles that are user-friendly for automated lighting and provide easy access to an automated luminaire's multiple attributes through previously addressed assignments to a console's encoders and submaster pages.

Fixture Library — Store all attribute and profile/setup information that is unique to a given piece of equipment (automated luminaires, assignable color attributes for scrollers or Seachangers, hazers, projectors, etc.). They prevent having to address each individual function by channel. Consoles simply reference the library and all the control information for that unit is automatically loaded to the appropriate control interfaces. Fixture libraries are stored in the console and do not have to be reprogrammed for individual shows/productions.

Focus Points — A variation of a palette assignment that provides pre-assigned channel settings for pan and tilt attributes of automated fixtures that correspond to specific locations on a stage. Individual cues are referenced to these points so that if a point is relocated all the cues can be instantly updated through redefinition of the focus point.

Library Cues — Designers may find that they may want to go in a different direction for a cue or cue sequence but may feel unsure that the new cues will be any better than the first version.

	Rather than recording the new cues over the old cues, the old cues are moved to an unused area of the console and assigned new cue numbers. Old Cue 135 could be stored as Cue 535 (well after the last planned cue number) and a new Cue 135 is created. If the replacement cue isn't effective, the old cue (Cue 535) is used to overwrite Cue 135. Library cues can also be used for cues that will be copied frequently (i.e., a base cue for scene changes which is slightly modified each time that it is inserted into a show or when different specials are laid over a cue each time that it is used).
Move Cues	Also called mark cues. Cues created immediately before or after a cue utilizing a unit with moving attributes such as scrollers or automated lights. Move cues preset any attributes that must be assigned before the unit is illuminated. They prevent an audience from seeing lights slide into position or color scrolling through a series of colors as a gelstring shifts to a new color. Newer consoles may actually create mark cues automatically if instructed to do so.
Palettes/ Pages	A means of making attribute and channel functions more easily accessible. Common attribute assignments are pre-programmed into a console in predetermined combinations of channel assignments for each of the units. Faders or encoders can then take on multiple assignments or functions that can be changed through a simple page command. Color assignments, gobo combinations, or zoom settings all form fairly common palettes. Palettes are extremely popular with programmers who work with automated lighting—many carry their own personal disks/flash drives with predefined palettes that they use on a regular basis. The most common palettes are the focus palettes, which preprogram pan/tilt instructions or combinations to specific points on a stage and color palettes which store the individual combinations of color settings that create a programmer's favorite colors. Focus palettes are extremely helpful on touring productions where the size, trims, and other physical arrangements of a stage may change from one location to another. When changes in focus must be made, a programmer simply redefines the focus points to the new locations and the entire show will be automatically updated to the new focus points without having to redefine the positions in every cue.

REHEARSALS IN THE VENUE

Once a production has been focused, a series of special rehearsals are scheduled in the theatre or venue in which a show will be performed. This usually entails a series of **technical rehearsals** where the technical elements of a production are developed (including the lights) that may or may not include the performers and a series of **dress rehearsals** that emphasize getting the show into its final form and ready for an audience. The amount of time allotted for these rehearsals can vary significantly from one organization to another (e.g., touring productions have no need or time for any of these rehearsals) while additional specialty rehearsals may also be added (e.g., preview performances) for other productions. This section addresses rehearsals that would be typical for most productions. The specific number and lengths of each type of rehearsal may vary considerably between different organizations.

Technical Rehearsals

Technical rehearsals are dedicated to working out the technical elements of a production. Scenic changes, flying sequences, special effects, and the cueing of the lights and sound are all dealt with in these rehearsals. Different organizations have different manners of coordinating technical rehearsals. In most situations productions receive a minimum of two technical rehearsals. The first, typically called **first tech** or **dry tech,** may be the cue-writing session for some organizations. However, it is more common for the cues to be written ahead of time and to have the lighting designer simply present the cues (without performers) to the director and other members of the production team at a dry tech rehearsal. It's a time when reactions to the cues are discussed and revisions will be made based on comments from the director and other team members. Questions regarding the placement of the cues can also be addressed, and more elaborate sequences might be practiced and revised. Board operators will also experiment with the manner in which they must operate a console to properly execute a cue sequence. In especially sophisticated productions the team may schedule an additional meeting called a **paper tech** where cue placement and sequences are discussed outside of the theatre, some time prior to going into a full-blown technical rehearsal.

In many organizations, a second technical rehearsal is scheduled in which the performers are added into the mix and the cues are refined based on how the lighting interacts with them. This is called a **tech with actors** or in some cases a **wet tech.** The emphasis of this rehearsal should not be on performance issues but rather on how well the cues work with the actors. This rehearsal is typically long and tedious and is often scheduled as a 10 out of 12 day (working 10 hours over a 12-hour period).

If time is spent properly at these rehearsals to iron out any technical issues, the director's focus can shift back to the acting and overall appearance of the production at the later dress rehearsals. These rehearsals should not be rushed, or pushed through simply for the sake of getting through them, because valuable time will be taken away from later rehearsals as the same mistakes continue to reappear from one rehearsal to another. Issues such as determining whether there is enough base level illumination, if an appropriate mood is achieved, if a particular actor has a strong enough focus, or if a crowd is lit consistently enough are just a few of the issues that are examined during technical rehearsals. Once again, lighting levels are refined to accommodate the needs of the production, and transitions from one cue to another are examined and modified so that the cues flow with the action and pace of the performance.

In the best of all possible worlds a lighting designer would be provided with an opportunity for at least one tech with the actors. However, in many situations this is not possible and the first time that the lighting designer sees their lights with the performers will be at a first dress rehearsal. With the ease with which computer consoles record cue changes, most designers prefer to **edit** their cues or make most of their revisions live while a cue is in the context of the moment. During a dress rehearsal actors are in their staged positions, moods can be set appropriately, and focus assessments can be easily compared from one part of the stage to another. It is especially important for a lighting designer to maintain a calm, efficient manner of editing the cues and to make quick changes **on the fly** while the action continues uninterrupted. This is not a job for people who get flustered easily or who do not respond well to being under pressure. Any changes that cannot be made while the action is running must be carefully noted and fixed at some time when the performers are not rehearsing— what we call taking a **note.** Most designers will maintain at least two sets of notes. The first list (**work notes** or **technical notes**) refers to technical issues that will require an electrics crew and deals with problems such as refocusing, bad color assignments, or non-functional instruments. The second (**board notes**) refers to cue issues and includes notes that require some form of cue editing that could not be completed while the rehearsal was running, notes for the stage manager that refer to cue placement and calling the show, and finally notes that refer to director input or questions. I personally like to keep a notepad for each area of specific notes. I know designers who like to place their notes on 3 × 5 cards, which they then sort and distribute to each of the related areas. An honest effort should always be made to address all of your board notes before the next rehearsal. I have found that the best time for doing this is immediately after a rehearsal as the actors are getting out of costume. At that time not only will the director still

be available to answer any questions, but more importantly, any problems that I have experienced during the rehearsal are still fresh in my mind. I can also respond to any of the director's questions at that time. By fixing your cueing problems between rehearsals you can avoid repeating the same mistake at consecutive rehearsals. At the very least, even though the cue may not yet be right, you will have ruled out several potential solutions for a particular problematic cue or sequence. In most cases, you will find that the new cue, even if not perfect, moves you closer to a solution for the given situation. Technical notes will often have to wait until the next time that there is an electrics call. It's a fairly common practice to collect the technical notes over several days without bringing a crew in until later so that a number of notes can be completed at the same time and excessive labor costs in the way of minimum calls can be avoided. In situations that are not bound by minimum calls, the notes should be done at the earliest convenience so that you don't have to continue to see the same old problems.

Dress Rehearsals, Previews, and Openings

Dress Rehearsals

In dress rehearsals, all the final elements of a production come together to create the performance that the audience will come to experience. As much as possible, the team works together to produce rehearsals that approach performance conditions. Additional elements that have not yet been introduced to a production will be added during the dress rehearsals. Most commonly, costumes are introduced at the first dress rehearsal, while makeup will often be added on the second or third dress. As a team progresses through subsequent dress rehearsals the production is continually refined until it is ready for an audience.

From a lighting designer's perspective dress rehearsals are extremely important for fine-tuning a production. Performers often have weeks to develop and refine their actions and delivery of a given set of lines or scene, while lighting designers are not afforded this luxury. It is important for a lighting designer to achieve a final tweaking of a production's cues during these rehearsals. Just as important is the task of ensuring that the transitions between cues are accomplished in a way that appears to flow with the action of the show. As a rule, most production teams like to concentrate on running the production during dress rehearsals. Stopping a rehearsal is avoided except in those circumstances in which there are severe problems or a condition is created that could be potentially dangerous for the performers or backstage personnel. As with anything else, each dress rehearsal proceeds to get better than the last, and notes become more minimal and more specific as the team goes through the process. Most organizations have two to three dress rehearsals plus an additional **final dress** rehearsal. The final dress rehearsal is conducted so that the production is presented as if it were under performance conditions—with the exception of an audience.

Just as with technical rehearsals, board notes should be completed live within the context of the moment if at all possible during a dress rehearsal. This requires good organization skills and an ability to act quickly since each moment is quickly lost. By focusing on the largest problems first, a steady improvement will be observed from one dress rehearsal to the next. Magic sheets with clearly identified systems or channels and a good cue synopsis are critical to a lighting designer's success during dress rehearsals. The most successful designers use dress rehearsals to modify and refine the cues to the best point possible. Speed and the ability to not get frazzled are essential skills required at this point in the process. As a designer works to modify cues during dress rehearsals they should not cause any major distractions for the director or performers and must take care not to create any unsafe conditions such as an unexpected blackout while the performers are working on the stage. If one cue cannot be fixed before another cue is advanced or played back, the designer should make a note of the problem so that they can go back and edit the cue(s) at a time that will not interfere with the rehearsal. When making changes it is extremely important that any cue revisions are recorded prior to hitting the "go" button for an upcoming cue. Not observing this practice will result in losing any changes that you may have made—or even worse, having the board record a cue that reflects some sort of transitional state between the two cues that you were working on. To avoid this I always try to have the cue recorded when I hear the stage manager call the standby for an upcoming cue. As a rule, the initial dress rehearsals tend to focus on level-setting problems, while the later ones tend to be more involved with the transition and execution of the cues. These changes should be programmed by the actual console operator (if at all possible) so that the designer is free to concentrate on their paperwork and the stage. In most cases, an assistant lighting designer (if there is one for the show) is responsible for keeping the lists of notes so that the designer is free to watch the stage and make corrections during a rehearsal. An assistant (or on large shows yet an additional assistant) may also be assigned to tasks like coordinating the followspots or repatches—though the ultimate responsibility for all these tasks still lies with the lighting designer. Frequently, the design staff meets with the director immediately after these rehearsals to discuss notes and any problems that may have been observed during the rehearsal. The final dress rehearsal tries to replicate an actual performance condition, and in most cases lighting designers are discouraged from making changes while this rehearsal is in progress. In fact, the design table and intercoms that are assigned to the lighting designer and their staff will often be struck for the final dress rehearsal. Notes from this rehearsal will be collected and then addressed sometime following the rehearsal.

Previews

Previews are a special type of dress rehearsal in which a paying audience is in attendance. This allows the performers and production staff to get a sense of how an audience will react to a show while also providing further opportunities for the team to refine the production. Even though the company may reserve the right to change or even stop a performance during previews, most teams tend to treat previews as an actual performance, and the audience usually gets the chance to see the production in much the same form as the audience who will attend the opening performance. The number of previews associated with a production can vary considerably from one organization to another. Some theatres may choose not to offer any previews at all, while others like many Broadway productions offer two or more weeks of preview performances. The companies that I have designed for in Atlanta typically offer one or two preview performances, while the Off-Broadway theatres I have worked for often have one week of previews. In some situations, the entire production is treated as a preview where the production is tried out in a smaller, lower-cost market such as Off-Broadway houses or out-of-town theatres. These early productions are called **out-of town tryouts** or **pre-Broadway runs,** and cities like Baltimore, Boston, Philadelphia, Chicago, Cleveland, and Washington, DC, have often served as a testing ground for new productions. Currently, regional theatres are producing many new works that will eventually be transferred to Broadway. The recent Broadway production of *The Color Purple* was first produced at the Alliance Theatre in Atlanta. Other regional theatres like the La Jolla Playhouse (San Diego), the Guthrie (Minneapolis), the Long Warf Theatre (New Haven), and the Arena Theatre (Washington, DC) have also become regular contributors to the Broadway stage.

Openings

Opening nights are a magical moment in a production's history. With the opening night comes the celebration of all the work and preparation of the performers and production team. If there have been no previews, it is the first time that the show is presented to a live audience and it marks a pivotal point in determining whether the team has a hit or flop on its hands. It is also the first time the production will be reviewed by critics, and with that, the artistic and financial success or failure of a project will be established. For the lighting designer, it should be a time to observe and enjoy the production along with the rest of the team. A few notes might be completed following this performance but as a rule the night is reserved for supporting the show and celebrating its opening. Do not commit the cardinal sin of missing the opening of a show that you have designed. Yes, you might be exhausted, but you insult your fellow team members by choosing not to support your own production. While your teammates will understand if you have another out-of-town commitment, simply not attending your opening is one of the surest ways to get yourself removed from the network of artists that you have just collaborated with. Once a production has officially opened and gone into its performance **run,** the lighting designer's role is over. The master electrician will work to maintain the show, keeping track of lamp and gel burnouts, touch-up focuses, and any other problems that may develop, while the stage manager will maintain the execution of the show. When you arrive at opening night your contract ends and you are free to move on to the next project. In the case of a long-running production, the designer may be brought back occasionally to ensure that the production has remained consistent with how it was left on opening night. If it runs beyond a predetermined number of weeks, the designer may even be entitled to further compensation through **residuals.** These are nothing more than a weekly fee based on a percentage of the box office receipts that was agreed upon as a part of the initial contract.

RUNNING AND MAINTAINING THE PRODUCTION

When I discuss the run of the production I am simply referring to the production entering a period of regular performances. There are many different formats that a run may follow; each will have an impact on the type of crew required and the role that a lighting designer may play in the performance run. In most cases, the crew takes on all the responsibilities of the lighting once a production has opened. The most popular performance runs involve a straight run, in which the production is contracted for a predetermined number of weeks and performances. Typical runs extend from three to eight weeks with regular performances (five to eight) throughout each week. When the run ends, the production will be **struck** and a new production will open in its place. This format is used at most regional production companies. Runs are often shortened to as little as a week or two in the case of academic or summer stock theatres. The run of a production may also be extended by adding performances or weeks of performances if the production has met with success. Any run lasting longer than initially scheduled or more than six to eight weeks is often called an **extended run.** There are several exceptions to the lighting designer being finished once

a production enters its run. The most notable is in the areas of touring, when a production must maintain a consistent look from one venue to another even though the performance facilities might vary significantly from one another. In these situations the lighting designer may be retained to ensure that the plot, focus, and levels are modified so that the lighting will be consistent from one venue to another. When a lighting designer is not available, or is unwilling to travel, an **assistant** or **associate lighting designer** or a **lighting director** is often hired to take the designer's place. This individual has the responsibility of not only making the design functional in a variety of performance spaces but also for faithfully reproducing the design as closely as possible to the original designer's intent.

Regardless of the type of situation that may exist when a production enters into a run, there are several issues that must be addressed in order to maintain the show and keep it consistent from one performance to another. Those audiences who see the show in Week 4 or 8 are entitled to the same experience as those who were lucky enough to attend the performance on opening night. This principle should hold true even when a show goes into an extended run of months or years. While the designer is seldom involved in the actual run of the show, other members of the electrics team take on a variety of responsibilities to ensure that every audience receives a similar experience. The most important person in maintaining the electrics in most organizations is the master electrician. They ensure that there are no lamp or gel burnouts, circuit problems, or lights with bumped/dropped focuses between performances. This person also often operates the lighting console during the run and, along with the stage manager, is responsible for ensuring that the cues are executed properly from one performance to another.

Sidebar 12.5 DESIGNER PROFILE

Beverly Emmons is a renowned lighting designer who fits into the third generation of lighting designers, having assisted both Tom Skelton and Jules Fisher. She has a solid reputation in dance, drama, and opera lighting design. She has also lit a number of avant-garde productions and projects. Her credits include a varied collection of collaborations with many of the most influential companies and performing artists of the last 30 years. She has lit for Broadway and prominent regional theatres, a number of the most significant dance companies in the world, as well as both national and international opera companies. A brief sampling of directors and choreographers that she has collaborated

Beverly Emmons

Credit: photo courtesy Blanche Mackey

with include Robert Wilson, Merce Cunningham, Martha Graham, Bill T. Jones, Trisha Brown, and Joseph Chaikin. Her opera lighting has been seen at La Scala and the Welsh National Opera. She is the recipient of numerous lighting awards, including seven Tony nominations (*Jekyll and Hyde*, *Passion*, *Les Liaisons Dangereuses*, *A Day in Hollywood/A Night in the Ukraine*, and *The Elephant Man* among others). She has also been honored as a USITT Distinguished Lighting Designer, and has won an Obie, a Lumen Award (*Einstein on the Beach*), and two Bessies for her dance lighting. She has served on the graduate faculty of Columbia and Yale, is a regular panelist of the Broadway Lighting Master Classes, and frequently speaks and designs as a guest artist throughout the country. Even with such an active professional life she has raised a family and also shepherded a series of important projects by serving as the artistic director for Lincoln Center Institute and creating the website LightingDB.nypl.org for the New York Public Library for the Performing Arts as well as TheLightingArchive.org.

Beverly received a combination of both formal and informal education. Her formal training came through studying dance composition with Bessie Schonberg at Sarah Lawrence College. She also studied lighting at the Lester Polakov Studio. Informally, she assisted Tom Skelton and Jules Fisher in the early part of her career. She has not been pigeonholed as a lighting designer associated with a particular area of lighting, preferring instead to light a variety of projects, which allows the types of lighting designs that she creates to vary significantly in any given year. Beverly shares that, "An important interest of mine is not to be typed into any particular area of the profession. To be moving from one area to another keeps life lively." Originally, Beverly was a dancer who got involved in the backstage through her associations with Tom Watson and Tom Skelton at the American Dance Festival:

> **"**I was interested in the process of how dances were created in the quiet concentration of a studio . . . and then how to make the transition to performance on a stage. I was interested in minimizing the chaos of that process by having the stage preparation properly planned so that the lights were hung and focused and the floor washed in the scheduled time so the dancers could begin in a calm concentrated way.**"**

While working at summer dance festivals Beverly had the opportunity to observe some of the best dancers and choreographers in the world. She eventually became more interested in the technical areas and stage management than in performing. So, like many other lighting designers, she began her shift to lighting through becoming a stage manager. Dealing with the technical elements of the lighting, as well as calling other people's cues, were part of the job. Her early design experience came from re-creating her own lighting on the road, where she had to problem solve and think on her feet to re-create the lighting for a variety of spaces that were often quite different from the original facilities and equipment. Her first lighting design position came when she was hired by Merce Cunningham:

> **"**My work with Merce Cunningham "vetted" me for a wide range of "avant-garde" artists like Robert Wilson, Meridith Monk, and Joseph Chaiken. Many of these artists were moving off in a different direction from the more saturated lighting and color treatments that were fairly common at that time . . . rebelling from the style of the day and shifting to a cleaner, less intense association with color—insisting upon a white-light, no-color treatment of their work.**"**

Beverly speaks fairly specifically about some of the differences between designing in different areas of the profession:

> **"**It is part of a designer's job to understand the aesthetic needs of each art form. The economic

and structural differences between the genres are also very important. . . . Dance has to be quick. . . . Opera also has little time but adds advantages as well as additional restrictions. Dance usually has to work with a rep plot and you can't change much, while opera has rolling rep which can be confining with only hours to refocus and recolor the plot day after day. You have to understand the realities of each situation . . . especially the economic implications of time with crews and money. Commercial theatre is more flexible in that you can put equipment any place it needs to be. . . . Rent and use any lights available in the shops, and once the show opens the lights are maintained exactly as you left them. In terms of the design, you do the plot before the rehearsals start and you have to be flexible because at that point you don't know what you're lighting and you need to have many options. Most importantly you learn to trust and listen to other people."

Beverly adds that each genre has different cueing needs:

"Opera cueing relates to the music . . . dance is all about movement. A Broadway musical has so many cues: sound and scenic moves as well as lights, requiring that some of the standbys and cues are called with light switches."

Beverly, like others, sees both good and bad in working on a variety of different projects. While working in different areas of lighting keeps things fresh and exciting, it also means that there is much more material in which she must stay up-to-date. She believes that one of the best ways to remain current is by "seeing productions and observing what other designers are doing." She advises students to "look at light . . . look at how it behaves . . . look at it striking objects . . . observe the sky." She also advises:

"You have to decide what you want. There's good lucrative work for both designers and electricians, but you have to decide what you want to be. If you are a technician, learn how to program and fix moving lights. There is well-paid work in these areas . . . but you have to be good at it. If you want to be a designer . . . be an assistant. Assisting is a wonderful way to learn. You have to figure out where you want to get your experience . . . and then when you're designing be brilliant . . . be organized . . . do more than required. Get the other artists and the organization to think they could never do another show without you. Being present in the moment is what we do. Every project is important and one must always do one's best. Pay attention to beauty . . . pay attention to the art part of what you do . . . the problems will always be there and the way that you become successful is by recognizing the problems in advance and defusing or dealing with them . . . know that they never go away."

The most important task for maintaining a design is completing a **dimmer** or **channel check** immediately before every performance. To complete a dimmer check the board operator steps through each dimmer or channel, one at a time, bringing each channel up to a level of full. While the channel is up, the electricians check to make sure that all of the instruments assigned to that channel are operational, that each unit has maintained its proper focus, and that the gel has not burned out. If any problems are discovered, they are noted before moving on to the next channel. After going through the entire hookup, the notes are addressed/fixed to ensure that the plot is restored to its original condition. Dimmer checks should be completed when the crew is first called so that there is time to troubleshoot and fix any problems prior to opening the house to an audience. The channel check also allows the crew to check items like repatches to ensure that all of the patches have been restored for the top of the show. Many beginning electricians get sloppy during dimmer checks and tend to only check that a light is coming up. In reality a dropped focus or burnout of a deep blue gel can cause even bigger disruptions to a performance than a lamp that doesn't come up. I've witnessed performances where FOH luminaires that had dropped focus continued to come up in scenes only to light audience members who were seated directly below them. If this should happen during a show the board operator must find a way to prevent the light from coming up again by either soft-patching the channel out or parking the dimmer that is assigned to the offending light.

Another important task that should be completed prior to opening the house for any performance involves creating a blackout cue so that the theatre can be checked for complete darkness (**blackout check**). This ensures that light sources like worklights, gridlights, and lights from other adjoining spaces like catwalks are not accidently left on. Additional preset cues can be programmed that will allow the crew to check items like the **focus points** of automated lighting gear. If a problem should occur during a performance, it is the master electrician (along with the stage manager) who will have to determine how to make the correction and continue with the show. Some burnouts that occur during a performance will not cause significant problems and can be replaced at the next dimmer check, while the loss of a critical special might require the board operator to find a way of sneaking an alternate light into a scene that would have been lit by the failed lamp. All problems that develop during a performance require a solution that comes from sound judgment and quick actions on the part of the team. Occasionally, larger problems such as a console losing its memory or **dumping a show** can happen, but with today's consoles these are infrequent occurrences and the data can usually be restored both simply and quickly by reloading the show from a backup file. A full backup system, even to the point of running two consoles in tandem or in a slave/master mode, will exist in those situations where a failure cannot be tolerated.

Once a show has progressed through its run and to its final performance, the show is dismantled and the theatre is restored to its original pristine condition. This is known as the **strike** for the show. At this time, additional electricians are brought back to the theatre and all of the lighting equipment is taken down and returned to storage areas in the theatre or to the rental houses. In some cases, this may involve either restoring the lighting to an existing house plot (a rep plot) or possibly moving right into the load-in of the next show.

FOR FURTHER READING

Bellman, Willard F. *Lighting the Stage: Art and Practice*. 3rd ed. Louisville, KY: Broadway Press, 2001.

Pilbrow, Richard. *Stage Lighting Design: The Art, the Craft, the Life*. New York: Design Press/Quite Specific Media Group, Ltd., 1997.

Shelley, Steven Louis. *A Practical Guide to Stage Lighting*. 3rd ed. Oxford and Boston: Focal Press, 2014.

Watson, Lee. *Lighting Design Handbook*. New York: McGraw-Hill, 1990.

CHAPTER 13

VARIATIONS ON ESSENTIAL THEATRICAL DESIGN

IN THIS CHAPTER I build on the general principles of entertainment lighting presented throughout the last several chapters. While the earlier chapters primarily addressed the design process and the proscenium stage, this chapter expands to include considerations for other performance spaces, the nature of an event, and the role of genre and presentation style on a lighting design. These discussions focus on performance events like drama, although the concepts can be expanded to include opera, dance, and musical theatre.

The lighting designer must consider the specific nature of the event. Is the production to be mounted only once? Is the production touring? Will it be one of several productions in repertory? The role of genre and the specific nature of the performance event will also shape the way in which a production is lit. Each art form has an associated design aesthetic: for example, dramas are lit in a way that is different from the way that operas or dances are lit. Some of these qualities relate to style, while others are associated with the conventions that are characteristic of a particular type of event. Design choices that might be considered typical for a dance production will often be out of character for an event like a play. Regardless of the nature of a performance event, each can be designed through modifications in the techniques that have been discussed up to this point.

DESIGNING FOR SPECIFIC GENRE

One area of consideration for an overall design scheme relates to approaching a project based on the **genre** of the performance event. Genre refers to the specific type of event. The most obvious form of genre is drama, which consists of traditional plays. We may be even more specific and refer to several types of drama: comedy, tragedy, melodrama, etc. What is important to each genre is that specific performance conventions, including lighting expectations, are often associated with the particular type of event. For example, a farce would never be played or designed in the same manner as a Shakespearean tragedy. A melodrama is significantly different from a docu-drama. Manners of characterization, visual style, degree of realism, and acting style all share a common range of qualities that can be characterized as belonging to a given genre. Genre is perhaps the most important overall design consideration to examine because it sets general parameters for a production. Audiences and artistic team members will have certain expectations about the overall approach and conventions that the lighting, or any other design area, should follow when an event is associated with a given genre. Opera is performed in a very different manner from dance, and dance is different from farce—the lighting designer will typically light each type of event quite differently. Likewise, comedy has lighting qualities that most likely wouldn't be found in a tragedy. Once a designer understands the genre that a project belongs to they can work within the conventions of that genre to produce a unique design for a given project. The majority of these genre and specific lighting needs and techniques are discussed in detail in Chapter 14.

VARIATIONS IN THE AUDIENCE/ PERFORMANCE SPACE

All of the processes discussed in the previous chapters can be applied to lighting designs across a variety of specialties and types of performance spaces. The techniques are adjusted so that they apply to the needs of a particular project. We generally categorize these adaptations as belonging to one or more of several groups. These groups include: type of performance space, outdoor and festival events, transfer productions, touring productions, and repertory productions. The first relates to the type of space that an event is being produced in. The role of space relates primarily to the relationship that is created between the performers and the audience. While the scale of a venue has an impact on the design, the real consideration lies in the orientation that an audience has with the stage or performers. The most obvious examples of how a lighting approach must change comes when producing an event in a venue that has a different physical form than a proscenium theatre. Rather than having an audience facing the stage from a single direction, the stage may be surrounded by an audience on three (**thrust theatre**) or four sides (**arena theatre**). An arena theatre may also be called **theatre-in-the-round,** while a thrust theatre may be called **3/4-staging.** In the most extreme cases, the audience and performers may even be intermixed (**environmental theatre**). Each of these theatre arrangements requires a different approach to lighting. There are also **black box theatres**, which are nothing more than large rooms that are painted completely black and equipped with an overhead lighting grid. Sometimes we call these **flexible spaces** since they can be reconfigured in any manner that's appropriate for a production. A consideration for designing in black box theatres is that a designer must frequently specify the house lights (often theatrical luminaires like Fresnels) due to the flexibility of the spaces and the fact that the audience locations frequently shift around in the space.

Due to the variety of audience perspectives, sightlines become important issues for a scenic designer and director as they work in these performance spaces. The more that a stage is surrounded by an audience, the more critical the effect of sightline considerations becomes. Additionally, thrust and arena theatres aren't usually equipped with mechanisms for shifting scenery. These two effects tend to force scenic elements to become more minimal as productions move progressively towards arena orientations. Because of this, lighting is often used to compensate for these scenic compromises and plays a larger role in establishing the setting of a scene as the role of the scenery shifts to becoming more of a neutral background.

Most plays can be performed in a variety of audience relationships. Some are very formal and distant (such as proscenium productions), while others explore a more intimate relationship between the performers and audience (as in arena and environmental theatre). There are essentially two effects that must be considered when lighting productions in which the performers are surrounded on more than one side by an audience: the first relates to the varying perspectives of the seating areas, while the second relates to the proximity of the audience to the performer(s). Both reinforce the role of the performer as the major element of the stage composition and de-emphasize production elements like the scenery.

Audience perspective should play a critical role in how a lighting designer lights a production. The lighting is relative and must be considered differently for each of the audience perspectives. In a thrust stage, a single front special that creates a wonderful face light for a monolog will be seen as a sidelight by audience members seated on either side of the stage. In an arena production, the audience on the opposite side of the stage will actually see the performer in silhouette. In some situations this may be acceptable, while in others it would become a distraction that could take away from an audience's experience. A lighting designer must consider the relative views of each seating location while also ensuring that each area is well-lit throughout the entire production. A designer should understand that each perspective will be unique and should not attempt to duplicate the lighting from one perspective to another. It's actually quite amazing how different a design can appear through the different perspectives. Accept the fact that each will be different and simply work on achieving an acceptable solution to lighting each of the audience areas. It is imperative that a design be fully examined from each audience perspective for the entire show. I achieve this by moving the design table to different seating areas for different rehearsals. This practice allows me to check each cue within the context of the play while also providing me with an opportunity to fix any problems that might not have been apparent when I lit the piece from the initial perspective. My assistants also often view a show from different perspectives for me. Because these productions are viewed from multiple directions, the number of luminaires and dimmers required to provide the general lighting is also normally quite a bit higher than those required for proscenium productions. Other issues that relate to audience perspective include the fact that luminaires are typically hung in full view of an audience, with little attempt to mask them. We can also look beyond the stage to see other audience members who are directly within our view. Therefore, the audience becomes a part of the visual composition of the stage. All of these effects require a lighting designer to pay particular attention to issues like **glare** and **spill,** which normally have a much smaller impact on proscenium productions.

Proximity of an audience also plays an important role in how a lighting design is conceived for a thrust or arena production. With audience members on three sides, these theatres typically have steeply raked seating areas that allow the patrons in the nearest rows to be as close as close as 3 to 4 feet from the stage. Even the most distant viewers are often only as far as 50 to 60 feet away from the stage. In arena productions, the theatre seats patrons on four sides. These seating areas may be as small as being only three or four rows deep—some are even smaller. Theatres like this form intimate events where the audience and performers can clearly see and react to one another. This intimacy requires a lighting designer to be sensitive to issues that could distort the performers. Several differences can be observed in the way in which a designer must light thrust or arena productions from that of proscenium productions. Strong color saturations and extreme angles (both steep and flat) have to be used with care in arena and thrust spaces so that any distortion of the performers is based solely on the needs of the script and not by the general lighting. On the whole, subtle choices are better for thrust and arena designs, and strong choices such as steep angled specials, dominant downlighting, or deep color saturations are better left for those occasions when a specific effect is called for. A more intimate environment also typically requires smaller area lighting pools than those associated with proscenium stages. This allows the general lighting to be more controllable. Shorter throw distances are fairly common in thrust and arena theatres, which results in the use of luminaires that tend to have wider beamspreads than those used in proscenium productions. Because of the need for more area control and a desire to avoid audience spill, steeper angles also tend to be more common to thrust and arena productions. Other tendencies relate to spill forming a significant issue in thrust and arena designs where light continues past its target and spills into audience areas or is reflected off the stage floor. Glare from luminaires that light the stage from the opposite direction also becomes a consideration, and a designer should avoid situations that force audiences to look directly into lighting instruments that are focused towards them from across the stage. All of these effects are even more critical in environmental designs where performers are intermixed with an audience. In these cases, a certain amount of spill is usually unavoidable and a designer must simply work to make it acceptable. Each of these conditions usually result in more top hats and barn doors being used in thrust and arena lighting.

When designing the area coverage in thrust or arena productions, a designer should work to establish a minimum of two face lights coming from two different directions for each of the audience perspectives. By using two or more luminaires from different angles, both color and intensity can be better used to manipulate the sculptural qualities of the performers. Since color is seen as a relative lighting quality, coloring each lighting instrument differently creates a warm/cool relationship that will enhance the modeling effect of the two lights. While I know designers who focus a single light from each audience area to each acting area from straight-on, the approach tends to produce less shadow definition and can create a flat, uninspired form of illumination for a production. Instead, by following the practice of establishing a good key/fill relationship between the two face lights, a solid sculptural effect is created on the performers. Color choices for the area lighting are generally less saturated than those associated with proscenium productions; it is common for **pastel tints** to be used in the majority of area lighting systems that are created for thrust and arena designs.

Once the general illumination has been planned, there are additional demands that the lighting designer must meet layered on top of the general illumination scheme for thrust and arena productions. Unlike proscenium facilities, thrust and arena stages have aisles called **vomitories** or **voms** between audience areas that allow performers to pass through the audience as they enter and exit the stage. These aisles have to be dealt with specially so that the entrances and exits are lit and spill does not strike the neighboring seats. Instruments that are used to light these entrances are often hung along the axis of the aisle so that their light can be directed along the path both toward and away from the stage. Also, low lighting angles such as sidelight are hard to create in a thrust or arena environment, and it is within the voms that this low-angled lighting is typically arranged. This also helps to prevent audience members from having to look into the fixtures that are used to create these low lighting angles. If a designer wishes to use booms and low-mounted positions like shin-kickers they are almost always located within the voms or across the upstage area (thrust theatres). An important issue to keep in mind when comparing specials used in proscenium theatres with those used for thrust or arena designs relates to the fact that while a single luminaire can be used as an effective special in a proscenium design, this may not be the case in a thrust or arena designs. In thrust and arena design such an effect commonly requires two or three specials to achieve the same result due to the varied audience perspectives and the fact that a single special could be viewed as a front light for some audience members while for others the same special could appear as a side or backlight.

The following sections provide several specific techniques for creating workable lighting designs for thrust or arena productions. These techniques represent several standard approaches that have been proven over time. While these will satisfy the needs of producing a general illumination scheme for a production, designers should not think of these approaches as the only means for lighting thrust or arena events. Environmental productions generally follow design principles based on those used for arena productions with additional concern placed on the issue of audience spill. As a designer gains confidence, they will learn to modify these methods in ways that will create unique responses for a given production. There are few set rules to lighting any production—only that the design be appropriate for the given moment and event.

Thrust Productions

Thrust productions are unique in that the audience is situated around the stage on three distinct sides. The fourth side, often complete with a proscenium, generally becomes a scenic background for the performers. In many cases this upstage area will have a small staging area, wings, and possibly a full fly house and rigging system. In addition to the three different audience perspectives these venues tend to have steeply raked seating areas that allow the audience to look down on the stage while having a more intimate or closer proximity to the stage and performers. The floor often becomes a major scenic component in thrust theatres. Thrust theatres may also have balconies that are oriented along the three different perspectives of the stage. Aisles or voms are located between each of the seating areas, and performers often enter and exit the stage from these positions. More importantly, these locations often become transition areas as different scenes unfold for an audience. In some cases the voms are built under the second tier of seating so that audience members may sit directly over the voms.

Hanging Positions

Thrust theatres (Figure 14.1) may be constructed as permanent facilities or as temporary structures in a flexible space like a blackbox theatre. In the simplest arrangements, pipes are simply hung over the stage and used to hang both the luminaires and any scenic elements that need to be supported from above. In most cases, the scenery does not raise or lower and is **dead hung.** In more elaborate systems, a grid is hung from above the theatre. A grid consists of two perpendicular sets of pipes that are mounted on even spacings that typically

Figure 13.1 Common hanging positions in a thrust theatre: Catwalks may be masked by clouds or valences that are hung on the offstage side of the catwalks. Stagehouse hanging positions can include electrics, torms, booms, and ground rows.

range from 3 to 5 or 6 feet. In a permanent thrust theatre a grid is often located directly above the stage, while traditional battens are located in the upstage area of the fly house. Additionally, thrust theatres frequently have a series of catwalks that contain mounting pipes and circuiting that run parallel to the edges of the stage and seating areas. These catwalks are the primary hanging positions for much of the area lighting for a thrust theatre and often contain some form of cloud or baffle mechanisms that help mask or conceal the instruments from the audience. If a thrust theatre has a balcony there are often additional mounting positions across the front of the balconies in the form of **balcony rails.**

Low angles can be a challenge in thrust or arena stages. One obvious limitation relates to the fixed trim height of a grid. In cases where luminaires must be hung from a lower height, designers will mount additional pipes that hang below the grid—a practice that is called **tailing down** (Figure 13.2). As stated earlier, voms are usually lit through positions that are mounted along their axis from above or from booms placed just offstage of their entrance area which allows light to be shot along the path of the entrance. Other hanging positions in a thrust theatre include torm positions that are mounted just upstage of the proscenium and additional wall-mounted vertical pipes or booms that might be located around the perimeter of the theatre.

Figure 13.2b Horizontal underhanging from a batton

General Lighting Techniques for Thrust Design

I've already discussed the importance of providing two face lights for each of the audience perspectives. This becomes critical in thrust design because it helps model the performers as highlight and shadow are used to create depth and visual interest. In addition to the benefits of increased modeling, hanging positions based on variations of a 45° orientation with the seating and oriented more or less with the voms help to reduce glare and bounce of unwanted light into the audience and upstage areas. With spill being a major consideration in thrust design, the designer should choose mounting positions that are steep enough to avoid spilling light into adjoining audience locations. A common solution to this problem is to slowly increase the steepness of the mounting angles as one moves across the stage towards a given audience area (Figure 13.3). Audience members in the first rows should also be protected from looking directly into lights from across the stage. The steeper angles (especially if supplemented with barn doors or top hats) will help avoid this source of glare.

Audience members seated within the first several rows of most thrust or arena theatres will often be lit to some degree simply due to ambient light. When an audience area is particularly close to the stage care must be taken to shutter the top of the light so that the performers' heads will remain fully lit when standing at the edge of the stage while at the same time avoiding spill on the adjoining audience areas. I often try to shutter the light so that it is cut off the seats from about waist level for anyone seated in the first row—lower if possible. Barn doors and top hats are also frequently used to control spill and glare in audience areas. While all of this advice provides some general principles for developing the lighting for a thrust production, the following paragraphs provide several standard approaches that can be used or modified to fit the needs of a specific project.

Figure 13.2a Taildown lighting positions. a. Vertical underhanging from a batton

40° 50° 60°

Will have to shutter off seating but direct glare is avoided

Stage

Figure 13.3 Using progressively elevated angles to avoid spill and glare: While elevating angles helps to avoid spill and glare, it also creates a side effect of highlighting the forehead and browline and can cause eye sockets to go into shadow. The secret is in finding an appropriate balance between these two extremes.

One of the most popular techniques for lighting thrust productions makes use of three area lights for each acting area. Initially, the stage is divided into acting areas in much the same manner as one would for a production in a proscenium theatre. The lights can be mounted at almost any vertical angle, although 45°–60° is the most common range of angles. The three luminaires are arranged around the area or focus points approximately 120° from one another. The most common orientation places one of the luminaires as a direct backlight for the center or primary seating area. In this way, the flatness associated with hitting a subject from straight on is avoided since no audience members are located in this position. This approach is often called the **three-point system** or **three-point lighting.** In more complex variations, the orientation of the three luminaires might be rotated in relationship to the audience, or the angles between the luminaires could vary to include both more acute and obtuse angle variations in order to suggest a particular lighting scenario. The vertical angles may also be varied from one unit to another. Another variation is the more complex **four-point lighting** system, which requires an additional instrument for each lighting area. This system is discussed in the section on arena productions since it is the most common system for lighting arena productions. In the four-point system for thrust stages, the lights are generally oriented with the voms of the theatre with each of the units being placed 90° from one another.

There is a common practice for assigning color in the three-point lighting system based on the principle of color perception (Figure 13.4). This technique establishes some form of warm/cool or key/fill relationship between the three luminaires that light each acting area and makes use of different colors for each of the lighting instruments. Two units are assigned colors that provide a

Upstage

Neutral

120° 120°

120°

Warm Cool

Primary seating area

Figure 13.4 Three-point lighting with color associations: placing the neutral color in the upstage position is fairly common, but it can be assigned to any of the 120° angle orientations if required by the design.

distinct warm/cool relationship with one another, while the third color is a neutral color that appears cool when compared with the warm colored lamp and warm when compared with the cool colored lamp. With this technique, the relative sense of color can be used to create a suggestion of highlight and shadow from every audience perspective. The warm color is commonly associated with the key light for a scene and its color is often chosen to reinforce the primary light source for a scene. In many cases, the neutral color is placed in the luminaire associated with light coming from the upstage direction. A common example of this color scheme might involve using a pastel pink for the warm color, a pale blue for the cool, and some variation of lavender tint for the neutral colored gel.

Ideally each area and luminaire of a wash or area system would be controlled separately from one another. In reality, this is usually not practical, and a lighting designer must consider the most effective way of ganging instruments together in order to consolidate circuits and dimmers. Just as in working with proscenium systems, we refer to **area control versus color control,** and how a designer chooses to combine luminaires is very much dependent upon the specific needs of a production. In some washes, luminaires from adjoining areas can be two-fered together, while in others independent control may have to be maintained. The one condition that a designer should try to avoid if at all possible is ganging luminaires of different colors. Even though this may appear to be an attractive means of providing area control, the loss of the ability to control the key/fill ratio and color proportions isn't usually worth the sacrifice.

Arena Productions

Arena productions become even tricker for the design team because the designers and director have to consider audience perspectives that completely encircle the stage and performers. The issues and considerations are quite similar to those of designing for thrust productions but become more delicate since arena theatres offer an even more intimate environment for the performers and an audience. In addition to the fourth audience perspective, the closeness of seating areas becomes an even more critical issue in regard to spill and glare. Arena staging is often done in a black box theatre consisting of a central performance area with seating in the four surrounding areas and voms at each of the four corners.

Hanging Positions

As in thrust theatres, the grid represents the most common method for mounting luminaires in an arena format. Many arena stages are located in black box theatres with a grid that covers the entire theatre. While the simplest grids are nothing more than a network of perpendicular pipes spaced between 3- to 6-foot intervals that may or may not have an associated catwalk system (to facilitate the hanging and circuiting of the luminaires), there are two additional grid systems that a designer may encounter when lighting in a black box theatre. The first is a **tension** or **suspension grid,** which consists of a series of tensioned aircraft cables stretched across the entire theatre in two perpendicular directions at roughly 2-inch intervals. This allows electricians to walk directly on the grid and greatly facilitates the hanging and focusing of the luminaires. The instruments are either mounted directly to the grid with special hardware or more commonly are hung from horizontal pipes that are temporarily mounted above the grid across vertical uprights. The instruments hang just above the

mesh grid and are easily focused and maintained by the crew. Due to the closeness of the lens barrel to the grid, light from these luminaires passes directly through the grid and the audience does not see this mesh pattern. However, if a lamp is mounted too far above the grid, the shadows of the individual cables can become visible and will produce a gobo-like effect across the stage. Also, when audience members look up, not only will they see the circle of light associated with the lens of a lighting instrument but also a distracting secondary ring of light is cast onto the surface of the grid that is shaped according to the angle at which the light strikes the grid. Electricians must also take special care not to bump previously focused units and shutters when climbing around the grid as they work. This can become a real challenge when crawling under or trying to step over pipes that contain a number of luminaires and their associated wiring.

The second form of grid is an **egg-crate grid,** which consists of a series of portholes in the ceiling that are on a regular grid pattern directly above a stage. These grids look like an egg crate and generally cover the entire ceiling of a theatre. The portholes, which are actually fashioned into the ceiling design, are typically 2 to 3 feet square and contain a pipe or other hardware that allow several luminaires to be mounted in each opening. A particular issue associated with many of these grids is in the depth of the ceiling and size of the ports, which can result in luminaires not having as much clearance with the sides of an opening as a designer may wish. This can limit the angles in which the luminaires can be mounted.

General Lighting Techniques for Arena Design

Once again a designer should strive to provide two face lights for each audience area. Proximity and spill become even more important elements to consider throughout these designs, while distortion of any type must almost always be kept to a minimum. Though the three-point lighting system can be used when there is a limited inventory of luminaires or control, most designers prefer to use some variation of a **four-point lighting** technique for lighting arena stages. In a textbook example, four luminaires are arranged at 90° intervals from one another with their principal orientation being 45° from the central axis of any seating area (Figure 13.5). In this way, the luminaires are essentially oriented with the voms of the performance venue. The essential angles and overall orientation may once again be modified according to the needs of the project.

Just as with the three-point system, color is designed based on its association with perception and the relative sense of color. There are essentially two models that can serve as guides for color selection in a four-point lighting system. The first places a set of the same colored warm

Figure 13.5a Four-point lighting with color and control options. a. Units are ganged (two-fered) with warms together and cools together

Figure 13.5b Units are typically under individual control. If the neutrals are the same color they are often ganged together.

and cool gels across from one another on opposing diagonals that together create a warm/cool contrast and key/fill relationship for each of the audience perspectives (although warm and cool relationships will be inverted from one audience perspective to another). This works particularly well if there are a limited number of dimmers or circuits because matching colors can be ganged together for each area, providing a constant mechanism for controlling the key/fill ratio. A second model, which is generally more effective, requires a larger number of dimmers. It places a warm color directly across from a cool colored luminaire while the two remaining lights on the opposing diagonal are gelled with a common neutral colored gel. This provides a true warm/cool relationship throughout the entire design and best replicates a situation where a directional or strongly motivated light source might be desired. The color of the key light is based on the primary light source that the designer wants to create for the scene. In terms of control, it would be best if each light as well as each area were placed under individual control, but this is rarely possible. A common compromise involves ganging the neutral colored lights together while providing separate control for the warm and cool luminaires. This again provides good control of the key/fill relationships. A possible color layout that follows this approach might involve using a gold for the warm color (linked to a motivation source like the sun), a light blue for the cool or shadow color, and two light lavenders for the neutral tints that are used to tone the

performers from the other two directions. Like the other approaches that I have outlined, it is generally preferable to gang similar colors from adjoining areas rather than to gang different colors from the same area together. The four-point lighting system is also commonly practiced in thrust lighting designs where there are ample luminaires and control possibilities.

A final variation of general lighting used in many thrust and arena situations involves the addition of a downlight for each of the lighting areas. This may be referred to as a **five-point system.** The downlights can provide a strong sense of isolation for each area but can also cause severe shadowing. They are more commonly used to add strong color toning to the stage. The deep blue downlight washes that are often used to create night scenes are frequently produced in this manner. Gobo breakup washes can also be effective from this angle. Finally, several different downlight colors may be included in the basic illumination of an acting area to create additional flexibility through additive color mixing. Any one or all of these systems can be modified by angle, orientation, color, and control to make an appropriate statement for a design. A designer should not feel that they have to adhere rigidly to any of these approaches. With experience, most designers go on to create their own variations based on the specific needs of a production.

Environmental Productions

In environmental productions the issues that are found in lighting arena and thrust productions can be compounded even further. In this case, performers may even be intermixed with the audience and separation of the lighting between these two groups may be impossible. Often, staging areas in environmental productions are created within a room or blackbox theatre in what may appear as a rather random arrangement. Sometimes audience members may be encouraged to move throughout a space, viewing different performance areas from different perspectives as an event unfolds. In environmental productions it is best to light the performers as well as possible, using any techniques that a designer feels appropriate at a given time while at the same time avoiding as much spill and direct glare on audience members as possible. Often, despite the somewhat random arrangement of audience and performance spaces, staging areas can still be lit appropriately while also keeping these areas separate from seating areas for the audience. On the other hand, many of these performances are based on creating an intimacy with the audience, even letting them become active participants in the performance event. In these cases, spill and glare aren't as much of an issue and audience members may be lit along with the performers as part of the design.

Outdoor Dramas and Festival Productions

One of the largest outdoor productions in the United States is *The Great Passion Play* in Eureka Springs, Arkansas (Figure 13.6). Outdoor festivals have several unique qualities and conditions. First, in most cases there is no cover over the stage. While this is great in terms of providing a natural background or landscape for the productions, it also eliminates any overhead lighting that a designer would have access to through traditional hanging positions. Backlight and downlight are virtually impossible to create in many outdoor venues. The emphasis then shifts to front lighting, which may be done in one of several different ways. In the most desirable situations, lighting towers or some other form of front hanging positions will be located somewhere behind the audience. At one outdoor theatre where I have designed, the front of house (FOH)

Figure 13.6c View from stage of FOH lighting positions

Figure 13.6a The Great Passion Play (Eureka Springs, Arkansas). a. The outdoor amphitheater (village portion)

Figure 13.6b The outdoor amphitheater (hillside portion, upstage/behind village)

facilities were located in a barn behind the audience and the FOH units were hung on pipes that were set into the windows of the barn that faced the stage. Other outdoor theatres and amphitheaters make use of towers that are mounted at several different locations behind the audience as a means of providing front light to the venue. Whether using a structure or towers, these luminaires must usually be equipped with narrow beam angles and high-powered lamps because of the long throws that they have to the stage. Unfortunately, these angles often tend to be a bit flat—an effect that can become even more of an issue since backlighting is often not available. So, when possible, sidelight should be used to help sculpt or model the performers. Sidelight is located where it can be positioned on booms or towers to the sides of the stage—but it, too, is often difficult to provide in many outdoor venues. In a number of outdoor theatres towers are erected to either side of the stage near the front of the audience area. These are comparable to the box boom positions found in traditional proscenium theatres; in some outdoor venues, these side towers are the only FOH hanging positions. If this is the case, the general lighting is approached in the same manner as a proscenium theatre that has box booms as its only front lighting positions. If a designer is fortunate enough to have front lighting positions in addition to these towers, they can go on to treat these positions more as sidelight positions through using more saturated colors in these towers/booms. The front towers would then be gelled in less-saturated tints for the general lighting. The basic technique approaches that of the jewel formula that was discussed in Chapter 10.

In addition to the hanging positions, a designer should also be aware of still other concerns in regard to lighting in an outdoor venue. The most obvious ones relating to weather and waterproofing. Outdoor festivals can age equipment especially fast if no precautions are taken to protect it from the elements. C-clamps and shutter plates rust, connectors become stressed, and corrosion can develop in much of your gear. As many of the electrical components as possible should be placed indoors or in some sort of sheltered location. Control consoles and dimmers are the most obvious examples of equipment that should be located indoors. In festivals where there is no permanent shelter, measures should be made to create a temporary shelter for as much of this equipment as possible. A tent cover, tarp, or even a portable stage will help protect the equipment in times of inclement weather. If you don't have cover, be able to seek temporary cover easily—storms can blow up in almost no time. Understand that producers must often take a chance regarding the weather and will often decide not to let an event go on or continue only if the situation actually becomes dangerous. Outdoor events have a tendency to continue when under threat of a storm with the hope of getting the show in before the sky opens up. I can't count the number of times I've had to continue a show in a drizzle or even steady rain. In the case of an actual storm, you must be prepared to shut down and get any vital gear out of the elements as soon as possible. Lightning should be one of your biggest fears; and any close hits should be an immediate signal to start the shutdown process. It is also quite common to pick up a performance from where the show was stopped or to have a rain delay that could push back the performance by an hour or so. Special precautions regarding weather include proper insulation and weatherproofing of all your electrical connections, building shelters to protect the luminaires on the towers or other mounting positions, and adding brass fasteners to all the gel frames to prevent the wind from blowing the gel out of the lights. If your luminaires do get wet, proper care must be taken to ensure that lenses and lamps do not shatter as a result of cold rainwater hitting the hot glass. Once instruments are wet, precautions should be taken to ensure that they are dried properly before continuing with the show. Make sure that any standing water trapped in the luminaires is removed and slowly burn off the remaining moisture by heating the lamps. This is done by powering them up in increments of approximately 10–15% over a half hour in a procedure that many of us call **burning-off** the moisture. This allows the moisture to evaporate with little chance of cracking a lens or shattering a lamp.

Other unique elements of outdoor festivals involve the mist that often forms during summer evenings. This can produce the same effect as a hazer as small particles of water vapor reflect in the beams of light that come from the luminaires. The effect is quite dramatic and can add an element of spectacle to a performance. If a designer is aware that such a condition is likely to exist, they can make use of the natural haze to produce lighting effects that add to the production. Another unique quality of outdoor lighting relates to the fact that warm colors appear to be richer and more vibrant in an outdoor venue than they would in an interior setting. Finally, consideration must be made regarding the location of the sun and the time of day at which the performance is presented. Most outdoor programs begin around dusk, and the overall intensities of the lights have to be pumped up to be seen against the effects of the dwindling daylight. As evening progresses, more of the lighting becomes dominated by the theatrical luminaires and the intensities of these lights will not have to be as high to give a sense of a particular intensity level. Also, the length of daylight progressively changes from day to day and must be a consideration for outdoor productions that run for an extended period of time. For example, when designing for a history drama that runs for the entire summer, a designer must consider how much daylight is present at a given time in June versus July or August. A lighting effect that was successful at an early point in the summer might become completely washed out by natural daylight two weeks later.

TRANSFER PRODUCTIONS

When I discuss transferring a production, I am referring to moving it from one theatre to another. Most productions are mounted once and enjoy a **limited run** of performances that continue for a set period of time. A common run in many regional theatres extends somewhere between six and eight weeks, while the runs of other venues such as summer stock productions last on the order of only 7–15 days. If the theatre is free, a successful production may be **extended** beyond its initial run. These extensions may range from adding a single performance to months or even years as in the case of a successful Broadway show. Many productions are first mounted in one theatre where costs are minimal and then upon becoming successful transfer to a larger, more prestigious theatre. Years ago, many of the productions that ultimately landed on Broadway were first produced in cities such as Boston, Philadelphia, or Baltimore, where the costs of producing the shows weren't as high as in New York. Today, untried productions are often mounted by Off-Broadway, Off-Off-Broadway, or regional theatres. If these become successful, they are transferred to more prestigious venues like Broadway. The Broadway hit of *Spring Awakening* (with eight Tony Awards) was first produced at the Off-Broadway Atlantic Theatre Company while *Hamilton* (and its numerous awards—including eleven Tonys and seven Drama Desk Awards) was first fully produced at the Public Theatre. Other companies such as the Alliance Theatre in Atlanta, the Goodman Theatre in Chicago, the Arena Stage in Washington, DC, the Mark Taper Forum in Los Angeles, and Actors Theatre of Louisville have become regular proving grounds for new Broadway successes. Other organizations make a regular practice of transferring productions between several theatres. When I designed for the Broadhollow Theatres on Long Island in New York, nearly every mainstage production was transferred between two of the company's three or four theatres as a means of allowing the company to reach different audiences throughout Long Island. Other companies may pool their resources and mount the same production on each company's stage, using the same scenery, costumes, and even actors for their productions (although the lighting has to be modified for the different theatres and lighting inventories). In these situations, a lighting designer will receive additional compensation for lighting a production in the second space. The Gateway Playhouse on Long Island commonly shared productions with the Candlewood Playhouse in Danbury, Connecticut. Touring productions represent an extreme form of remounting where shows can be reproduced within as little as six to eight hours as productions typically play different theatres every single night. On the other hand, a major repertory company such as the Metropolitan Opera might retire an opera for 10 or 15 years before bringing it back for a public performance. In this case, the records from 10 years ago become an essential element in re-creating the lighting for the production. Whether transferring a show or prepping it for a tour, the record keeping is essentially the same. The more that a team can document of a design, the better the second and subsequent load-ins will be.

When a producer makes the decision to transfer a production, the design team may or may not have much advance warning. In the best situations, the team will be aware of the transfer well before the first production has been mounted. Whether the lighting designer is aware of an upcoming transfer or not shouldn't have an overwhelming impact on the manner in which a production is first designed. However, if there is even a hint of a transfer, the designer should take extra care to maintain good paperwork and to fully document their design. In order to make a transfer as easy as possible, every element of the lighting must be thoroughly documented. This includes producing a fully revised plot with all the changes noted from the original production, updated paperwork, track sheets and other cue-related documentation, as well as a set of **focus charts** that provides a record of the focus and shutter cuts for every single luminaire in the design. Making sure that the plot and paperwork are kept up-to-date allows a detailed set of plans to be created that will form a sound basis for the remount and any subsequent designs based on the original production. In contrast, sloppy paperwork and undocumented changes will make a production more difficult to remount—and some of the mistakes that were corrected in the first production might even be repeated. Further complicating the process of transferring a production are producers who do not want to take the same amount of time to load-in and tech/dress

the remount as they did in the original venue. In reality, the tech/dress time can be shortened significantly for a remounted production, but it's not realistic to expect a designer to load-in and relight a show in too short a period of time either.

There are several practices that a lighting designer can use to help a transfer occur more smoothly. Most importantly, the designer must document as much of the original design as possible. This means making sure that the plot reflects all of the revisions, the paperwork is clean and up-to-date, and that the cues and cue synopsis are tracked and completely accurate. If the designer is not aware that a transfer is going to take place until sometime during the run of the original production, they should revisit the production and complete any documentation and record keeping that isn't up to snuff as well as add any additional information that will be needed for remounting the production. While there is often no time to completely document all shows in every manner possible, if you know that the show will be transferring, additional time should be taken to complete focus charts and track sheets as part of the original design process. These tasks are frequently skipped when a production is not being considered for a transfer because they usually require that an additional assistant be hired. If the designer is aware of the possibility of a transfer, most will go ahead and complete the additional documentation as part of the original design process. Focus charts are completed during the focus sessions and track sheets are produced once the show has finished its dress rehearsals and been completely cued. With today's consoles, track sheets can easily be sent directly to a printer to create a hard copy of the cues. In addition to the track sheets the designer should also retain at least one or two copies of the show files and disks or flash drives that they are stored on. If a designer is lucky enough to be using the same type of console for the second production, they can cue the show through simply loading the show disk and associated file into the console and can then fine-tune the cues as needed.

In the best situations a designer will be moving the production to a facility that shares a nearly identical footprint as the original theatre, the hanging positions will be similar, and the console and luminaires will be the same. In some cases, the lighting package will be rented and can simply be moved between the different theatres. However, while having theatres that are essentially the same is ideal, this is generally not the case, and facilities and hanging positions like the FOH often differ from one venue to another. In addition, power supplies may vary, equipment may not be the same, and there might be conditions in the new space that will require significant modifications to the original design which will result in having to create new plots, paperwork, shop orders, etc.

When a designer is revising a plot for new venues, they don't worry as much about creating an exact duplication of the original plot as trying to re-create the same lighting systems and specials that are required by the original design. Therefore, function or purpose becomes a driving force in making these design decisions. It doesn't matter so much that Source Four 19° units are used over Source Four 26° units for front light as it does that you have the same number of acting areas, basic angles, and colors as those in the original design. It also doesn't matter so much that any front washes shift from one beam position to another or even to the box booms (if there are no beam positions in a given facility). It is more important to provide the systems and as much of the function of the original design than to slavishly try to produce an exact copy of the original plot. Channel assignments are the one element of the design that the designer should make all efforts to not readdress if at all possible. This is because all of the channel assignments are linked to the cues, and if these remain the same, the designer will be able to get the base cues loaded into the lighting console by simply loading the

original show file into the new console. With the softpatch feature, the new circuits and luminaires are easily assigned to their original channels—and the cue list that was loaded with the show file is finished, complete with cue numbers and counts or transition times. The production is now ready for fine-tuning with much of the preliminary effort of cueing already completed. Even if you are using a console that isn't compatible with the first production, it is easier to transfer the cueing information from the track sheets to the new console than to completely relight the show. By using techniques like those outlined here, a designer should find that productions can be transferred from one venue to another with relatively few hassles.

In order to document the focus of a production, lighting designers produce a set of forms called **focus charts** (Figure 13.7). These forms are often completed by an assistant lighting designer as the focus is being conducted for the original production. Information that is typically recorded in these documents includes each

Figure 13.7 Focus charts and documentation of lighting instruments' beam qualities: this is a page from a focus chart generated by Lightwright luminaire's focus position (hotspot placement based on distances from centerline and plasterline), beam characteristics (spot/flood settings, harshness/softness of edge/focus, etc.), and the lighting instrument's shutter positions. The form is usually based in some form of graphical record and often includes several different diagrams for recording a fixture's data. As a reference, the stage is broken down into even measurements (often 2-foot increments) that extend from the plasterline upstage and outward from the centerline in each direction. When the designer moves to the location of the stage where they wish the light to be focused, the assistant records the position on the form (e.g., 8 feet SL, 4 feet US). Once the position has been documented, the assistant goes on to complete the remaining areas of the form as the focus is completed. Degree of focus, spot/flood settings, and even a diagram of the individual shutter cuts are provided for each luminaire. Lightwright™ provides very workable focus forms that can be completed within a computer (including shutter cuts). In fact, the latest versions of Lightwright™ even allow designers to import digital photographs of a luminaire's focus, which is then used as a further reference for documenting the design. In today's production environments, much of this record keeping is done on a personal laptop by one of the lighting assistants.

While show data files can often be transferred between different console models made by the same manufacturer, they rarely transfer between consoles of different manufacturers. Unfortunately, the only way to make this happen usually involves typing the data for each cue into the new console by hand. Although it's unfortunate that the data will have to be re-entered, a hard copy of the original cues or **track sheets** is quite beneficial for turning this data transfer into an exercise of simply re-entering the data from the previous design. In addition to the channel levels, each cue's individual execution information is also fully documented in the track sheets and includes up and down fade times, delays or waits, auto-follow or cue-linking information, and any effects that are related to the show. Not long ago, when we were under the constant threat of dumping shows (when a lighting console crashed and all cue data was lost), we used to track all of this information by hand. In fact, it was generally one of the lighting designer's assistants who tracked or wrote down every setting for each cue of the production. Today most consoles can be connected to a printer to generate a full set of tracking documents. In recent years, our consoles have become quite stable and many designers now forgo hard copies of the track sheets, opting instead to keep digital files of the show on disks or flash drives that at stored in a safe place as well as on their PCs. These files can also be edited through console simulation software that replicates the console on a designer's PC. This type of software is known as an **off-line editor** (Figure 13.8). While digital files should be kept, no backup is safer than having an actual printout of a show's data. Floppy disks and flash drives are known to go bad over time or can be lost or damaged. Many designers are discovering that shows for which they had multiple backup copies are lost because they didn't get a printout of the track sheets for a show and the disk format is no longer compatible with the newer consoles.

Figure 13.8 A screenshot of a cue and related information from an off-line editor (ETC EOS series)

TOURING PRODUCTIONS

Touring productions do not vary that much in their approach and execution from transferring a production between theatres. Touring deals with transferring productions on a regular basis—sometimes weekly, sometimes nightly, and the time between stops can vary significantly. What remains constant is the need for moving in and out of the theatres in a timely manner. As when transferring a production, organization and detailed record keeping are key elements for success. In the best touring situations, the production will carry a lighting package that is easily adapted to each theatre but that remains in nearly the exact configuration for every single show.

When a lighting designer sets up a design for a touring production they should attempt to create a lighting package that for the most part remains the same for every stop along the tour. As a rule, the designer designs for the smallest theatre on the tour, while larger stages on the itinerary will **tab-in,** or move the torms toward the centerline and lower the grande teaser to create a proscenium opening of a consistent size. This results in the tour always playing within a standard-sized opening—a practice commonly known as **closing-in** a stage and which dictates the locations of the legs and borders along with the trims of both the borders and electrics. The plot and production are then designed around this opening. In most tours, the lighting designer sends a copy of the touring plot to the local electricians several weeks before the tour is scheduled to perform in a facility. The local electricians review the plot and work with the designer to satisfy as many conditions of the plot as possible. This may result in the substitution of luminaires based on the local venue's inventory, revised FOH decisions based on the hanging positions that are present in a facility, and modifications based on the power and circuiting options that are available in a particular theatre. In most touring arrangements the tour will provide the lighting equipment used on and above the stage while the local theatre provides the FOH equipment. Occasionally local crews will completely hang and circuit a show using a facility's inventory and the designer will be able to walk into the venue and go right into the focus. In those cases where the local facility cannot provide the equipment required for a design, the local producer is usually expected to rent the additional gear from a rental shop.

Finally, electricians have developed measures that provide a significant time-savings for remounting touring productions. Dance and concert tours form the most common examples of productions that make use of these techniques. In each case, steps are taken to package the lighting equipment so that much of the work becomes a matter of assembling modular units rather than individual components of luminaires and cables. This practice eliminates the redundancy of many of the load-in activities and reduces the time consumed in dealing with all the smaller elements. Concert lighting has set the standard for creating structures like **trusses** and **PAR-bars** that eliminate the need for hanging individual luminaires each time that a rig is assembled. These and other elements of concert design are discussed in detail in *Stage Lighting: Design Applications and More.* More traditional touring productions that use standard batten layouts (such as dance companies) can also make use of several time-saving measures to help the crews become more efficient as they move a show between facilities.

Several of the most common techniques that touring electricians use to shorten load-ins include packaging their luminaires in road boxes that are organized by hanging position (so that they can be rolled off the truck and taken directly to their assigned positions) as well as packaging the dimmers in rolling racks that are easily tied into a theatre's company switch. One significant time-saving measure involves the creation of **batten tapes** for a production. A batten tape is nothing more than a piece of scenic webbing that is secured to a batten and marked with a centerline along with an additional mark and label for every luminaire that is to be hung on the associated pipe. Some electricians prefer to use different colors of spike tape to signify various fixture types, while others prefer to write the unit type directly onto the webbing with a black marker. On tour, the batten tape is the first element to be secured to a batten and is referenced so that its centerline corresponds to the centerline of the batten and theatre. Using batten tapes eliminates the time-consuming task of measuring each luminaire's distance from centerline. If using colored spike tape, many electricians mark the yokes of each type of luminaire with the corresponding colors so that the house electricians only have to match the colors of the tape to ensure that the proper type of luminaire is placed correctly. In addition to the fixture type, some electricians also provide information such as circuit numbers (for a bundle), unit number, and gel labels on the batten tape as well. As a further means of speeding up a touring load-in, gel is secured to its color frames with brass fasteners and each frame is then marked with not only the color (R-57, G-870, L-120, etc.) but also with the electric and unit number that the frame should be inserted into (i.e., 1st Elect.-1, 1st Elect.-2, Boom 1L-1, etc.). This allows the colors to be easily sorted and stored in stacks that are organized by hanging position. Electricians can easily transfer these stacks to the instruments by simply walking down a pipe and dropping the colors into the appropriate lights. In some cases, such as in many rock-and-roll touring productions, the luminaires are shipped fully mounted, gelled, and already wired within manufactured truss structures that are simply assembled at the venue.

One of the problems with many light hangs arises when eight electricians gather around a single plot waiting to get information relating to the individual position that they have been assigned to work on. One way that much of this wasted time can be regained involves the creation of **hanging cards** that break each of the plot's hanging positions out into individual cards. Each card is a partial copy of the plot that contains all the information that an electrician will need to hang that position. In this way, an electrician working on the third electric would be given the hanging card for that position while those working on the first electric or a stageleft boom would be given those cards. Some electricians may laminate the cards or place them on cardboard backings so that they can stand up to the abuses of touring.

One last area where electricians have greatly improved the efficiency of a load-in involves creating pre-assembled **bundles** for cabling each of the primary hanging positions. These bundles begin at the dimmer racks: individual cables or circuits are plugged directly into the dimmers and terminate along a hanging position that the dimmers are powering. The entire bundle is tied directly to the electric after the luminaires have been hung and the individual circuits drop out of the bundle directly above the unit that they are powering. This allows the luminaires to be plugged to their associated circuits with no further cabling. Both ends of each circuit are clearly labeled so that it is easy to identify each of the individual circuits. All of the two-fers and individual cables are included the bundle in such a way that the bundle becomes a single entity that is tied to the batten. This greatly reduces the time that would be required for running individual cables to each unit.

Up to this point I have discussed techniques in prep work that can eliminate some of the hassles of touring a design. There are also a number of practices that can help the design to be mounted more efficiently even after the trucks arrive at the loading dock of a new venue. Speed is of the essence in the world of touring—not haphazardly fast, but simply efficient and methodical. Excess speed can be especially bad in touring situations when crew members get overly zealous running road boxes that weigh several hundred pounds each in and out of the trucks. Speed in touring refers to how quickly and efficiently a designer or touring electrician can conduct a load-in as well as being able to quickly size up a situation and make decisions regarding the lighting and local facility. Can the first electric be hung on line six or eight? Should I leave the fourth electric out in the truck because there isn't enough power? Do I use the house dimmers or the touring dimmers for the FOH? Is this shutter cut close enough or do I have to keep fussing with it? You have to learn how to be flexible when you're on the road. Understand what elements of the design are absolutely essential and where compromises can be made that will not have a huge impact on the design. Know where you have to be insistent with a local crew and

when you can back off and go with the flow. Pick your battles and know how to both motivate and work with strangers. Finally, you have to be able to remain calm and cool under stress. The show needs to go up at 8:00 p.m. even though the trucks got lost and you're running 2 hours behind in your load-in. The locals want your production to be just as successful as you do; understand that you and they are on the same team and that they are there to help you. Locals are extremely good resources to a touring designer because they know the town and their facility. Local crew members can recommend everything from a local gel distributor to the best burger and bar within walking distance of the theatre—even a local dentist (I've actually received tips on all of these from local crews). Use them, respect them, and have fun with them!

REPERTORY PRODUCTIONS

Repertory production is a unique area of lighting where a single plot must satisfy the needs of several different productions. There are a variety of formats in which repertory theatres may operate, but most follow some variation of scheduling overlapping performances of two to five productions. A common approach to many repertory operations is to introduce new productions to the performance schedule on a regular basis (e.g., every week or so). At some point the organization will have a set number of productions performing in repertory and shows will start to be rotated out of the schedule as new productions are added. While most repertory organizations confine their productions to a single season, others like the Metropolitan Opera in New York will store productions as part of their repertory for many years. In the case of the Metropolitan Opera (and many significant dance companies), a production may be brought back 20 years or more after the original production was mounted. The American Ballet Theatre still makes use of designs within its repertoire that were created or inspired by Tom Skeleton a number of years ago. Most dance companies use repertory light plots due to the number of individual dances that each production must support.

In approaching a repertory design, a lighting designer will face some added quirks in the process. First, you have to understand that your design is only one of several that must be supported by the rep plot. The more productions contained in the repertory, the less individual flexibility you have for the design of a given production. This can be further complicated by the fact that different designers will frequently be lighting the productions in a repertory. Many opera companies use repertory plots in which several different designers have designed the individual productions. On the other hand, there are a number of techniques used in repertory designing that add flexibility to a plot so that a unique quality can still be created for each production.

As a rule, repertory plots tend to grow in sophistication and number of luminaires and dimmers as additional lighting systems are added to these plots to provide more options for the individual designs. The repertory plot for the Metropolitan Opera (Figure 13.9) is extremely complex and contains several hundred luminaires and projectors. A designer is free to select, refocus, and repatch virtually any unit in the plot. The Metropolitan Opera also provides a stock inventory of hundreds of additional units for supplementing the rep plot with more electrics, booms/ladders, and specials that can also be added to a specific design. While the

Figure 13.9 The New York Metropolitan Opera's rep plot

Credit: courtesy of Wayne Chouinard, resident lighting designer

Metropolitan Opera supports so many designs primarily through the sheer size of its rep plot, most repertory situations do not have this option available to them. The following paragraphs provide several techniques that can be used to add more flexibility to designs that must be lit in a repertory situation.

Maintaining flexibility is the key to repertory design. While adding more luminaires and lighting systems may work in some cases, it is more common for designers to create flexibility in rep plots through using other techniques. This is due to expenses, changeover schedules, personnel, or any number of other factors that may preclude the addition of more luminaires. If you cannot hang a plot that incorporates all of the needs of each of the individual shows, you will have to find a means of combining the requirements of each production into some common denominators. As a first step, lighting systems that can be used for several if not all of the productions should be developed. In many cases, general washes such as those used in downlights and area lighting can be used by all of the productions. These washes may be double-hung or regelled as a means of adding flexibility to the designs. Multiple lighting systems provide increased variety for the individual designs—and the more of these that a designer can include in a rep plot, the more potential that the plot has for creating unique images for each of the productions. Dance lighting is often built on many basic lighting systems and a variation of repertory design. Many designers use technologies like color scrollers, moving mirror accessories, luminaires with color-changing LEDs, and automated luminaires to bring further flexibility to their rep plots. Once the area lighting and general washes have been developed, any accents and specials required for the individual designs are added and layered on top of the general layouts. Most rep plots are designed with a given number of specials that are dedicated to each of the individual productions.

Assuming that there are a limited number of luminaires available for a rep plot, additional flexibility can be built into a plot by having a lighting crew make limited modifications in the plot for each of the productions. This is called a **changeover** and can result in crews refocusing, regelling, or repatching portions of the plot between performances of each production. The amount of changeover that can occur between two productions is dependent on both the number of crew members and amount of time that is allocated to a changeover. The Metropolitan Opera has enough crew members that the plot can be completely changed from one production to another twice a day (two shifts of 20 or more electricians each). However, many repertory theatres need to be able to complete a changeover in less than an hour or two with only one to three crew members. This then dictates what is reasonable for a crew to accomplish during a changeover. The easiest changes to complete during a

changeover involve repatching the luminaires, which is particularly effective for specials in that lamps that are unique to each show can be assigned to common dimmers or channels for the different productions. This may be done by swapping the circuiting at the patchbay or switching some of the cabling at some other location within the theatre. If possible, the designer should try to avoid any re-circuiting that would require an electrician to use a ladder. If the specials are fortunate enough to be circuited to their own dimmer, the repatching can be as simple as changing the soft-patch when the new show is loaded into the console. If the changeover time is not as big a consideration, the designer may consider additional options like regelling several of the common systems or refocusing different luminaires within the plot. Often a series of specials are designated within a rep plot with the intention that each can be regelled and refocused for each production. If possible, it is best to keep any re-coloring and re-focusing to easily accessible areas like catwalks or electrics that can be flown in to the deck.

Sidebar 13.1 DESIGNER PROFILE

F. Mitchell "Mitch" Dana has an extensive background in repertory lighting and has lit almost 600 professional productions in addition to working as a technical director, head prop man on Broadway and on tour, stage manager on Broadway and Off-Broadway, and production manager. He was head of lighting design at Mason Gross School of the Arts at Rutgers University. Dana received his MFA from the Yale School of Drama, and his many Broadway credits include *The Suicide, Freedom of the City, Mass Appeal, Monday After the Miracle, Once in a Lifetime, Man and Superman, The Inspector General*, and *Oh Coward*. His opera credits include *La Rondine* for the New York City Opera, *Turandot* for the Royal Opera at Covent Garden, *The Magic Flute* and *The Merry Widow* for the Cleveland Symphony, *Carmen* (which opened Expo'92), seven operas for the Los Angeles Opera Company, and 10 seasons with the Opera Festival of New Jersey. He is vice president of United Scenic Artists, USA 829.

Mitch lit his first production, *Riders to the Sea*, for the Catholic Youth Organization in the gymnasium of a Catholic Church with RBG strips, six Fresnels hung from a basketball hoop support, six dimmers, and three on/off switches. He went on to light everything that came his way until he was about 22. His formal training began at Utah State University, where he initially was a Forestry major.

Mitch Dana

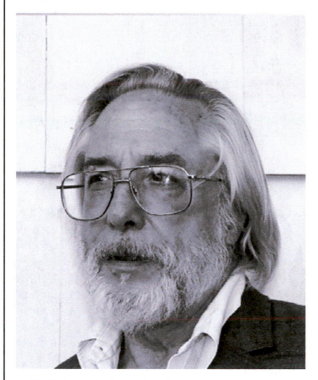

Credit: photo courtesy Tanya Dana

Grades in Organic Chemistry and spending too much time doing shows for the theatre department convinced him to change majors. His mentor, Ferd Manning, advised him to stay at Utah State University to study theatre since it was a small department with good people and he would be the only one doing lighting. In hindsight, he sees this as excellent advice. For three years he acted, built, stage managed, performed, and lit an average of three shows a week, ranging from Peter, Paul, and Mary with two followspots to piano thesis performances, and even the Mormon Tabernacle Choir. Then it was on to the Yale Drama School to study with Harvey K. Smith, Eddie Kook, Donald Oenslager, Ed Cole, and Charles Elson.

When asked how he broke into repertory design, Mitch, relates the following story. The American Conservatory Theatre (ACT) in San Francisco had its set and lighting designer hired on a Broadway show. The designer left ACT precipitously, and the theater called several lighting designers to fill the job. All were unavailable, which led to one of Mitch's former students (who had become a producer) suggesting him for the job. At the time, he was on tour filling a number of roles (including lighting designer) for a production of *A Doll's House* with Claire Bloom. The tour was in Philadelphia when he got the call, on a Friday, with ACT going into tech rehearsals for

Anthony and Cleopatra and *Caesar and Cleopatra* in rotating repertory on Monday. He was already scheduled to load the tour into the Kennedy Center on Sunday with an opening at the Eisenhower Theatre—with President Richard Nixon in attendance on Tuesday. After checking with his producer and Bloom, he told ACT that he could be there Wednesday morning. ACT had no other choice, and he was hired, lighting both shows in 10 days. He established a good relationship with ACT and the result was 54 productions with ACT in San Francisco, Hawaii, and the Soviet Union—and a reputation for rep that led to lighting seven seasons at the Pittsburgh Civic Light Opera, 36 productions in rep for the Opera Festival of New Jersey, two rep seasons for the Los Angeles Opera, seven seasons at the Muny in St. Louis, and six shows at the Mark Taper Forum.

Mitch relates that lighting design for repertory theatre differs from other forms of lighting, in that the design becomes part of a larger system of crew, maintenance, finances, scheduling, and a multi-year plan. With a single show you can focus on the design alone; it has no larger systemic concerns. In repertory light planning, one considers several shows over a longer period of time, potentially over several years: "At ACT, the one area that I had to consider more than others was the life of my crew—it meant time for their family and a better chance that a wife would put up with the crazy hours that repertory required." With an hour and a half changeover for all design elements, they could not do frilly things, so he learned how to pare down to the essentials of a production. Complicated things that might be less reliably re-created each time that a show was mounted were also dropped—if they failed, the audience might be cheated. "We learned to throw out good ideas that were only 90% reliable because only the artistic team missed them and the audience never knew what they were missing. . . . We focused on 'less is more.'" He also refers to the KISS acronym ("keep it simple stupid") for repertory design as well as the 7P rule ("Proper Prior Planning Prevents Piss Poor Performance"). But the fundamental principle is KISS. Another consideration of repertory design relates to the issue of the equipment being in the air most of the time: How can it be maintained? Producers do not allow time to do maintenance, so the owned equipment deteriorates, and the tax laws do not allow a not-for-profit to rent an entire rig each year. So roughly every 10 years the lights are replaced by a grant from some contributor, with the resulting problem that for at least five of those years most of the equipment is not efficient, or even desirable.

Mitch likes the brain exercise required in thinking about the many scenarios that he may run into when designing a series of repertory shows and how to accommodate them all:

"It is a great four-dimensional chess game: all physical dimensions and time. How can I make more possible? Is it the equipment, location, or control? How do I accommodate the more modern musical styles of shows like *Aida* and *Miss Saigon* as well as the older styles that are required for shows like *My Fair Lady* and *South Pacific?*"

He likes the speed required for lighting a production: "Let's get on with it and not spend forever discussing things. I am action oriented and this career appeals to me. My wife said I'm an adrenaline junkie and she wasn't entirely wrong." Ironically, what he likes least is the lack of time. There is little time to explore a production. "You have to hone in on the core issue, and go directly at it, which is both good and bad." He also feels that sometimes designing has become more of a job and less fun:

"There's no time for taking the loving care that we would like to have at the MUNY and I dislike the fact that it is so fast that it dilutes my contact with other theatre professionals, such as actors. I like and respect many actors and miss the sense of community that I had while in residence at ACT. That is why I will work for directors and producers that I like, even for less money than I am worth. It is less of a job and more fun. Most of us theatre folks are "people folks" at heart, and communication is our meat and drink.

The goals of good theatre have not, and probably will not change—only the techniques. Without clear goals there can be no well-directed, efficient, and effective result. Today's technology puts a premium on training, and an intelligent crew is necessary for the execution and reliable recreation of a design. In reality, the technology allows a lot of things to happen that often should not. Choice is still the major tool of the designer. We research, select elements, and then arrange those elements to tell a story that shines a light on a specific human condition so that an audience might be able to understand it. Even with all the technology available, the artist is still the one who must make the choices that clearly communicate an essential truth."

Since the genre and type of performance event plays such an important role in the overall approach to lighting a project, in the final section of this book I address the practical aspects of lighting design. The first chapter (Chapter 14) provides an introduction to the various practitioners, unions, and professional organizations that are connected to lighting design. Chapters 15 and 16 then go on to introduce a variety of specialized areas of lighting design. These introductions will provide several key concepts and design principles that relate to designing within a number of different specialty areas of lighting design. Chapter 15 refers to what I classify as traditional areas of lighting design (drama, dance, opera, and musical theatre) while Chapter 16 moves into non-traditional areas of lighting design that have become viable areas of employment: the music scene, spectacle performances, trade shows, film and video, retail and museum lighting, architectural lighting, landscape lighting, themed design, and virtual lighting. While these chapters provide an introduction to each of these areas; *Stage Lighting: Design Applications and More* goes into much more detail and provides a full chapter on each of these topics and other lighting specialties. Information such as essential differences in working in specific parts of the industry, basic equipment, and crucial design concepts and practices are discussed within each of these chapters. Many of the areas discussed within Chapter 16 and in *Stage Lighting: Design Applications and More* have only recently come into widespread acceptance as lighting specialties where entertainment designers are welcomed and represent fertile new ground and markets for lighting designers who can apply their skills to these emerging disciplines. At the same time, they can also provide very lucrative financial rewards and a relatively secure profession for those lighting professionals who venture into these other markets.

FOR FURTHER READING

Bellman, Willard F. *Lighting the Stage: Art and Practice.* 3rd ed. Louisville, KY: Broadway Press, 2001.

McCandless, Stanley. *A Method for Lighting the Stage.* 4th ed. New York: Theatre Arts Books, 1958.

Palmer, Richard H. *The Lighting Art: The Aesthetics of Stage Lighting Design.* 2nd ed. Englewood Cliffs, NJ: Prentice Hall, 1994.

Shelley, Steven Louis. *A Practical Guide to Stage Lighting.* 3rd ed. Oxford and Boston: Focal Press, 2014.

Watson, Lee. *Lighting Design Handbook.* New York: McGraw-Hill, 1990.

PART FOUR

LIGHT: DESIGN APPLICATIONS

CHAPTER 14

THE PRACTITIONERS

LIGHTING DESIGN IS rarely completed by a single individual. In reality, a number of team members and different specialists are connected to a lighting department and a project. In a typical entertainment situation, a director will be in charge of the overall vision of a production while specialists are secured to design the specialty areas of scenic, costume, sound, and lighting design. A **lighting designer** designs the lighting. In the construction industry, a project is usually under the control of an architect or client, and specialists are brought in to design or specify each of a building's systems (such as heat, ventilation, and air conditioning, or HVAC) in addition to bringing in mechanical engineers for materials and structural specifications, interior designers for finishes and furniture consultation, and **illuminating engineers** for the lighting.

There is also a distinction between the individuals who are charged with the design responsibilities or the artistic considerations of a project and those who actually execute the designs. Each professional can be identified through a prevalent set of job responsibilities along with, in many cases, membership in specific unions or trade guilds that collectively represent a particular position. While I may refer to general responsibilities that fall under the jurisdiction of a given job title, it needs to be understood that there are gray areas between the responsibilities of many of these positions. Frequently, a single individual may be charged with the responsibilities of two or more of these jobs in an organization. This is particularly true of small theatre companies and independent production agencies. The actual determination of an individual's duties lies within that person's job description for a particular organization. Responsibilities also often vary from one venue to another. Tasks that a person may not have been responsible for at one firm could fall within their responsibilities for another organization—even though both positions may share the same job title. In most moderate to large-scale operations, the unions are more involved and have worked to create consistency from venue to venue for individuals sharing a particular job classification.

This chapter examines the responsibilities typically associated with a variety of lighting professionals and how these positions fit into the overall chain of authority for an organization. The positions are organized primarily by the lighting industries with which they are associated (live performance, film/video, and architectural) and by whether the position is primarily artistic or trade oriented in its duties. At the end of the chapter I also provide a brief introduction to several of the professional societies, certifications, and unions that represent different areas of the lighting profession.

THEATRICAL AND LIVE PERFORMANCE PRODUCTION

Many careers in the entertainment industry are based on positions that were originally associated with the theatre. This is due to the fact that theatrical production dates back further than other forms of entertainment lighting. In general, the theatre also tends to be more specific in delegating which duties belong to a given position. The crew that is responsible for all the electrical requirements for a production is called the **electrics crew**. This crew traditionally covers the lighting and sound departments while also providing power to effects, lifts, hydraulic pumps, winches, and any other equipment that might be powered by electricity. Many projection responsibilities will also typically fall to the lighting designer and electrics crew. Even though we use electricians on stage, these individuals are not licensed in the same manner that an electrician working on your home would be. In fact, other than experience, there is currently no regulatory action controlling the qualifications of stage employees. In 2006, a voluntary certification program, the **Entertainment Technician Certification Program (ETCP)**, which qualifies stage electricians through an independent test became available. This is now being accepted as a significant program within the entertainment industry. Many producing organizations, production houses, venues, and the unions are now using the certification to identify potential employees. As of 2017 there were around 600 individuals who had passed the ETCP electrician test and were holding active certifications. The strong unions that controlled theatrical production in large East Coast cities like Philadelphia, Baltimore, Boston, and especially New York have probably played the most significant role in defining the responsibilities of each theatrical employee's position. On a practical side, this has preserved job security, benefits, and wages for the unions' memberships. As the entertainment business grew, these positions and their associated duties were widely accepted across the entire industry. We now use these classifications whether a production is associated with a union or not. There is also a distinction between those professionals who are associated with the crafts (execution) and those who are charged with the design or artistic aspects of a production. Both are represented by different unions, and it is considered improper for a member to perform any tasks that fall under the jurisdiction of another union. Lighting designers are members of the same union that other designers belong to, while the crews belong to unions that represent the craftspeople of the various theatrical trades. The designers' union is the **United Scenic Artists (USA),** which represents both designers and scenic painters, while the crews are unionized under the **International Alliance of Theatrical Stage Employees (IATSE).** It is often common to hear professionals referring to these unions as USA, USAA (the designer union), IATSE, the IA, or even the local (the crews). A couple of years ago, as a manner of being more aligned with the entertainment industry and increasing its member benefits, USA shifted its association with its parent organization so that it is also now affiliated with IATSE. These unions will be discussed in more detail later in the chapter.

Design Professionals

Lighting Designer (LD)

The most significant member of the design team is the lighting designer. This individual is charged with the overall artistic contribution of the lighting for a production. A lighting designer works with the director and other designers to produce an artistic vision for the production. The typical tasks of a lighting designer can be broken down into two specific time frames: pre-production and production. Pre-production involves tasks that are done prior to the **load-in** of the show, while production generally refers to the time in which the show is being developed in the theatre. Pre-production responsibilities for a lighting designer often include generating a script analysis, attending rehearsals and design/production meetings, developing a conceptual framework for the production's lighting, and producing the lighting plans and specifications for a production. The production phase occurs once the show moves into the theatre (**load-in**) and includes **hanging** and **circuiting** or positioning and wiring the lighting equipment, **focusing** (pointing and adjusting each light for optimum performance), **cueing** (establishing the looks and recording them so that they can be duplicated from performance to performance), and tweaking or refining the lighting throughout the final rehearsals and preview performances. Once the lighting designer and director are satisfied with the lighting (generally upon opening night) the lighting designer is typically released and moves on to the next production.

Anything related to lighting a show is under the jurisdiction of a production's lighting designer. While an extremely small theatre may require a lighting designer to execute their own design, this is usually the exception, and a designer more often delegates the execution of the lighting to other professionals. This makes for a more efficient design process since most productions are on schedules that require many people to realize a design in a very limited amount of time. This also supports the union's need to provide jobs for its members. The truth of the matter is that even simple productions have become so complex that a designer has enough to worry about just dealing with design-related issues. Because of this, it is best to have other lighting professionals working by a designer's side to help make the lighting the best that it can be.

In addition to making design decisions, the lighting designer must also communicate the design to other members of the production team. This relates first to communicating artistic information to the rest of the design staff; once an artistic vision for a production has been agreed upon, the designer turns to making the design a reality by selecting lighting equipment and accessories, color, hanging positions, and wiring specifications that are then communicated to the people who will physically prep and install the lighting. All of this information is communicated to the lighting crews through the scaled drafting of the **light plot.** The light plot communicates the information that a crew will require to execute a design prior to the designer actually coming to the theatre. Typical information presented in a light plot includes the choice of type and number of lighting fixtures, hanging locations, color assignments, and control or wiring information. Many light plots develop into drafted plates that can be 36 inches wide or even larger. This can make the plots difficult to store or use when consulting them during a load-in. In order to make the information more accessible, lighting designers also prepare forms that provide the same information in a table or schedule format. We refer to these schedules as the **paperwork** for a project. Often, the paperwork contains even more information about the design than the plot itself. Chapter 11 presents a full discussion of the light plot and the many types of paperwork that are generated for a design project.

In large productions, a lighting designer may feel that a project is large enough that they cannot manage all of the design responsibilities on their own. Schedules may also be an issue because there could be very little time to actually mount the design in the theatre. Here, two or more individuals working on various aspects of a design could enable a designer to produce a better design. This divide-and-conquer approach allows a designer to be more productive. Most lighting designers will also have a number of projects at various stages of completion at any given time—often scattered across the country. As a result, the designer may not be available to attend every meeting or discussion regarding a specific project. In these cases, a lighting designer often brings additional individuals to the project who are assigned specific responsibilities that the lighting designer delegates to them. The most common partner is the **assistant lighting designer** although an **associate lighting designer** may also be used on a project.

Associate Lighting Designer

An associate lighting designer operates at a level of authority just below the lighting designer. The responsibilities of an associate designer can vary considerably but are along the lines of providing artistic input and decisions for the lighting designer and production. The primary duty of an associate designer is being a second set of eyes for the designer. Other duties might include supervising elements of the design during a designer's absence and being a general source of input and feedback for the designer. An associate designer may occasionally be placed in charge of specific parts of a lighting design. Because of the importance of all these duties, this position is often assigned to an individual with whom the lighting designer is comfortable, trusts, and with whom the designer has had a long-standing professional relationship. Most associate designers have worked for a designer as an assistant on a number of projects that have spanned many years. These relationships often resemble some form of partnership that can range from an associate being assigned to a series of specific tasks or responsibilities to having a true design

partnership where both designers function together in most if not all of the artistic decision-making. One of the more famous Broadway lighting teams is that of Jules Fisher and Peggy Eisenhauer. This team has created some of the most successful musical theatre hits of all time. Eisenhauer began her association with Fisher as an assistant and through the years became entrusted with more and more design responsibilities. In a number of productions, while Fisher maintained the overall artistic vision, Eisenhauer frequently supervised much of the automated lighting of Fisher's designs. Over time, Fisher moved her into the role of an associate designer. In recent years it is difficult, if not impossible, to find a major musical credit that Fisher has designed in which Eisenhauer has had little or no involvement. They even shared the 1996 Tony and Drama Desk Awards for *Bring in 'da Noise, Bring in 'da Funk*. A production doesn't have to have an associate lighting designer, since many of the tasks that they might complete can be completed by the designer or by an assistant lighting designer. As a rule, only the largest productions have an associate lighting designer, and they typically are brought in at the specific request and negotiations of the lead designer. An associate lighting designer may also be responsible for supervising any remounts or tours of a production that a designer has created. Dawn Chiang (Sidebar 14.1) has been a longtime associate designer to Richard Pilbrow and spent a number of years traveling around the world ensuring that Richard's designs for various productions were staying consistent and being maintained properly.

Sidebar 14.1 DESIGNER PROFILE

Dawn Chiang is a successful lighting designer and consultant who began her career as an assistant lighting designer on the West Coast. After several years of working for a variety of theatres around Los Angeles, both as a designer or assistant designer, she moved to New York City, where she assisted many of the most prominent lighting designers of that time. The lighting designers whom she has assisted reads like a Who's Who of lighting, including Tharon Musser, Jennifer Tipton, Richard Pilbrow, Jules Fisher, and John Gleason. Eventually her assisting led to more opportunities to design her own lighting and she soon gained a reputation as a lighting designer herself.

Dawn has designed for a number of League of Resident Theatres regional theatres, and supervised the national and international tours of Broadway productions. She was resident lighting designer for New York City Opera, and designed a number of productions Off-Broadway. Additionally, she has

Dawn Chiang

Credit: photo courtesy Lora Karam

worked as the lighting director for tours for vocal artists such as The Carpenters and Paul Anka, and has been a senior consultant with Theatre Projects for a number of years. Another unique contribution that Dawn has made to the industry was authoring the operating manual for the first major computer lighting console, the Strand Light Palette 1 (writing it while on tour as lighting director for Paul Anka).

Dawn's foundation in the performing arts was set at a young age. She studied classical piano for 16 years and classical ballet for eight years. She completed a double major in theatre and psychology at Oberlin College and started working on plays, operas, and musicals while in school there. "Upon completing my undergraduate degree," she says, "I assisted a number of different set and lighting designers in Los Angeles, primarily at the Mark Taper Forum and the Ahmanson Theatre, which are part of Center Theater Group." One of her earliest mentors was H. R. Poindexter, a former assistant to Jean Rosenthal, who was a set and lighting designer, and technical director for the Center Theater Group. Dawn worked in Los Angeles for five years, both assisting and designing her own productions. When she lit the original production of *Zoot Suit* at the Mark Taper Forum, it went on to a successful one-year run in Los Angeles and then on to New York as her Broadway debut. A year later, she moved to New York:

❝Theater artists often speak about the joy and richness of having an "artistic home," where you can grow as an artist while not having to worry as much about where the next job may come from. My first artistic home was South Coast Repertory Theatre in Costa Mesa, California, where I designed 10 productions in three seasons. It was my first major opportunity to develop my craft and abilities as a lighting designer.❞

Several of the prominent lighting designers that Dawn assisted acted as mentors to her in her early years in the business. She credits Poindexter with helping her with her first big break into the professional world of lighting design, and introducing her to the many key creative and technical skills that allowed her to grow and flourish in the industry. Some of the most important lessons that she learned from assisting included the politics of getting a production from an initial design to opening night, the finer points of making major productions come together, and how to get a show through a rental shop—all learned from Poindexter, who also introduced her to important people. Tharon Musser coached her through her first Broadway show and showed her how to do the director's notes first each day. John Gleason gave her one-on-one lessons on color while waiting for tech to begin; he also taught her the importance of choosing lighting instruments with proper focal lengths in order to avoid excessive shutter cuts and doing a channel check near the end of a focus call to confirm that everything is focused and that there are no missing gels—but to also discover "happy accidents" like specials in one scene creating an unexpected result in another scene. Jennifer Tipton taught her the value of well-considered thought and preparation in advance of tech rehearsals, the importance of working quickly and accurately during techs, and the effectiveness of using split times as a method to smooth crossfading between cues. Finally, she had the privilege of being lighting supervisor for Harold Prince's production of *Show Boat,* which Richard Pilbrow designed:

❝The producer wanted me to fly to each city of the five companies of *Show Boat* to supervise the lighting on each jump. Over five and a half years I traveled to 33 cities on three continents to clean up the light cues—often in a single pass during the afternoon run-through before opening in a new town that evening. What a fantastic way to hone my skills in assessing what was happening onstage in terms of lighting, identifying how to fix it, and getting it done before moving on to the next cue in real time—in 33 different cities, each with different FOH particulars!❞

According to Dawn:

"As a freelance designer, you have to like to travel and work with different people, venues, and circumstances on an ongoing basis. I value the incredible talent, creativity, and mastery of the many people with whom I get to work. I love it all. You must also be able to work quickly, efficiently, and thoughtfully while approaching each production with a fresh perspective. All of this allows you to continue to grow as a designer and collaborator. I also love the teamwork, collaboration, and communication that is central to bringing these productions to life—on a deadline and on a budget. It is a joy to work in a field where telling the story and connecting with the audience is the focus of our work."

She remains abreast of developments in the industry by going to major trade shows, looking at new products and attending lighting demos by major manufacturers, reading the industry trade magazines and watching some of the related online videos, and talking regularly with colleagues.

Several key principles of advice that Dawn provides for anyone entering the profession include:

"It is up to you to take the initiative—to continue to meet people in the industry, keep abreast with what is going on, see shows, develop ideas, and hone your skills. As Richard Pilbrow has said, "Never ask, never get"—if you do not ask (i.e., for a meeting with a designer, a backstage tour, negotiating a design fee), it does not have a chance of happening. You have got to be hungry to succeed—your motivation, commitment, and ability to listen and process what you are receiving are what will help make things happen."

And finally, "Never stop learning, never stop growing—we never know everything and the performing arts are about continually leaning into that growth and discovery."

Assistant Lighting Designer (ALD)

The last member of the lighting design staff is the **assistant lighting designer** (ALD). Like an associate lighting designer, this individual serves as an assistant to the lighting designer. However, while an assistant's duties may vary considerably from one situation to another, their primary task is the organization and documentation of a design. They should have a background in design and are frequently charged with specific duties that come under the jurisdiction of the lighting designer. Assistants are hired to take care of the mundane yet important tasks that can take a designer's focus away from the actual lights and design that they are creating. Tasks such as drafting the light plot and generating all of the paperwork are often assigned to an assistant lighting designer. Once a production moves into the theatre, an assistant is often in charge of making sure that the paperwork is kept up-to-date, recording the focus of the show, keeping work notes, and tracking (maintaining a record of all the levels and cue settings) for a production. In large productions, assistants may be asked to help coordinate the designer's efforts related to specific tasks like cueing, integration of moving lights, or coordination of the followspots. In many ways, the assistant becomes a second set of hands and can be asked to help a designer in almost any particular need—even to the point of making coffee runs, keeping the design table clear of trash, and providing moral support to the designer. I know several assistants who were placed in charge of the candy and ashtrays (no longer permitted) that were kept at the design table. Assistant designers must be liked by the lead designer: you spend too many hours a day cooped up in a dark theatre for this relationship to be anything but friendly and encouraging. A good assistant will know not to offer any opinions unless asked and should be thoughtful, tactful, and supportive when responding to any questions. Large productions may have several assistant lighting designers on staff. In these cases, each assistant will be charged with specific duties and will be identified as the 1st Assistant, 2nd Assistant, 3rd Assistant or even given a title such as Assistant to Mr. Smith. The order of the ranking typically refers to either the importance of the tasks that are assigned to the assistant or the time that they have been associated with the primary designer. In small venues—especially in those that don't typically use assistants—a designer will have a lot more say in the hiring of a specific individual as their assistant. However, in situations where a designer can't convince a producer to hire an assistant, the designer themselves may actually employ the assistant—including being responsible for covering the assistant's pay and expenses! However, if a designer works on more demanding productions (especially shows under union jurisdiction), a producer usually hires—and is often even required to provide—assistants to the designer. In these situations a designer may or may not have negotiating power in the hiring of their assistants. If the show is under a union contract, the designer can be assured that the assistants will also be union members.

A second opportunity for assistant designers occurs when a production is operating under a condition in which the show will have to be remounted or toured. It is rare that a designer will commit to, or be available for, the daily or weekly needs of moving a design around the country for an extended period of time. When this occurs, an assistant or associate designer is hired with the understanding that they will learn the design well enough that they can maintain it and keep the personal aesthetic of the show as it plays different venues throughout the tour. Associate and assistant designers may also be affiliated with productions that are moved between different cities as part of the regional theatre movement.

A final situation where assistant lighting designers might be utilized is in resident companies that have a practice of jobbing in guest designers on a per-show basis. In this situation, an assistant lighting designer is a permanent member of the company's staff and functions as the lighting coordinator for guest designers (usually high-profile designers). The assistant acts as a liaison between the guest designer and the theatre organization. Typical duties of a resident lighting assistant may include coordinating the schedule for the guest designer's residency; making sure that the designer is supplied with the proper plans, inventory, and lighting suppliers; handling budget issues; and communicating any unique issues related to the company and its facilities to guest designers. Lighting assistants also often act as coordinators between several different designers who may bookend a project so that there are no complications in moving from one production to another. In repertory companies the assistant lighting designer is commonly the individual who is responsible for bringing the production out of storage and remounting it. Again, the assistant is also primarily responsible for documenting the show so that it can be remounted easily the next time that it is produced. Some of the operas contained in the repertory of the Metropolitan Opera in New York City were originally produced 40 or more years ago; yet, a detailed record has been created for each production so that the productions can be brought out of storage and included in future seasons with the lighting appearing to be faithful to the original production.

Theatrical Crews

Designers may occasionally be required to participate in or complete the actual hang and focus of a production, but this is usually delegated to other professionals. As productions get larger, crew positions become more clearly defined and designers are typically not permitted to help with responsibilities that are charged to the crews. This separation of duties first developed as a means of protecting crew employment, and it has created an added benefit by guaranteeing that crews have the necessary skills to competently complete their duties, which in turn allows a designer to concentrate on designing a show rather than with the details related to executing a design. Even with the separation of duties, a designer must be familiar with the mechanics of mounting a production so that they are knowledgeable and sensitive to the needs of the crews who are executing their designs. On one hand, while a designer can't usually physically participate in the crew activities, if possible they, an assistant, or another representative of the designer should be on hand at every work call to deal with any issues or questions that a crew needs to have answered. On the other hand, with the increased costs of production, it is fairly common for a designer to send the plot and associated paperwork to the venue before they are in residence. In these situations, the plot is typically hung and circuited without the designer's presence—with the designer's first day at the venue being focus day. If this is the case, the plot and paperwork must be especially thorough. In addition, a means of contacting the designer (cell phone or e-mail) should be made readily available so that any questions can be dealt with quickly and efficiently. I often include my cell phone number in the title block of the light plot for this purpose.

Master Electrician (ME)

The technician who plays the most important supervisory role in the lighting department is the **master electrician (ME).** Even though the specific duties of a master electrician may vary from production to production, this individual is charged with the overall task of making sure that the lighting is installed and operated in a safe, efficient manner. Depending on the type of production, the master electrician may be a permanent member of a facilities staff or a temporary employee who is contracted for the length of a production. A master electrician may also be associated with touring productions. Several tasks that typically fall within the responsibilities of a master electrician include being the mediator between the designer and the electrics crew, ensuring that the proper lighting gear is acquired (purchasing, renting, or pulling it from an inventory and prepping it for a production), determining wiring configurations that meet the designer's specifications (circuit layouts and planning), supervising the electrics crew and personnel, ensuring that the equipment is installed and wired according to safety practices, and supervising the electrical department (board operators, deck electricians, and followspot operators) during the run of the show.

In large operations a master electrician may delegate aspects of their responsibilities to other members of the electrics department; in a small venue the master electrician may take on additional tasks such as being the board operator. Master electricians should be familiar with those parts of the *National Electrical Code (NEC)* that are applicable to stage electrics and other safety practices to ensure that the lighting can be installed and operated in a way that is safe for the crews, performers, and audience members. A master electrician needs to be one of the more experienced crew members associated with a production and often trains less experienced members of a crew. In a union situation, the master electrician will often be the union steward for the theatre or touring personnel. A variation of the master electrician position is the **house electrician,** who typically has the same duties as a master electrician but is assigned to a specific theatre or performance space. Professionals who have this title are often both members of a union facility and representatives of **road houses,** or theatres that cater to touring productions. These individuals provide key links between the master electrician for a touring production and the management of a touring facility. This person is also responsible for the maintenance of a facility's lighting equipment, hiring local crew members on an **overhire** (per-show) basis, and will usually do the **tie-in** of the touring company's equipment. Both a master electrician and house electrician may have an assistant to help them perform their duties. A master electrician's second in command is the **assistant master electrician (AME),** while a house electrician's assistant holds the title of **assistant house electrician.**

Electrician

The majority of the technicians working in the electrical department are called **electricians.** Although they may be assigned to any duties that have a connection to electricity, the majority of them are associated with the preparation and execution of the lighting for a production. Some will have duties within special areas like projection, followspot operation, special effects, and sound. Typical duties that are assigned to electricians working in lighting include hanging and circuiting lighting fixtures, cutting and placing the specified gel into the fixtures, and focusing the lights. Additional duties may include wiring lamps and other prop/scenic practical units and running the light board or followspots for a production. A production will typically require a number of electricians to help with the initial put-in or installation of a show but will release many of them once the show moves into its performance run. This is simply due to the fact that most productions don't require many individuals to operate the lighting during the run of a show. At the end of the final performance, once again a number of electricians will be brought in to **strike** all the lighting gear. Once a production moves into technical/dress rehearsals and its performance run, the electricians that continue to work are usually identified by the specific function and equipment that they operate. A **board operator** works with the designer to program the light board; this person executes the cues as ordered by the stage manager during the performances. A **followspot operator** is assigned to run a followspot, and a **deck electrician** works backstage to help connect and disconnect temporary circuits, shift electrical equipment, and make new circuit assignments throughout a performance. While the design staff's jobs are finished when the show opens, the electricians who complete tasks like these continue to be employed for as long as a show is running. They are also charged with maintaining a production throughout its run. Common tasks that they complete in addition to running the shows include fixing burned-out lamps, replacing faded gels, and touching up the focus of lights that have slipped or **dropped focus**—whether the performances extend for a single week or a number of years. In long-running shows, electricians often rotate on and off productions as they deal with other projects and commitments.

Programmer

There is one more crew member that has been added to the list of electrical specialists over the last 15 or so years. This person, the **programmer** or **moving light operator,** is responsible for the programming and operation of a specialized console that controls moving lights. This individual is also often responsible for the maintenance of any moving lights that are part of a show. Changes in color, beam quality, gobo pattern, and most importantly movement of automated lights were at one time all controlled by a specialized console. Though this has changed with the latest generation of lighting desks, and while a traditional console may be capable of controlling moving lights, when more than a couple of moving lights were used in the past, it was often easier to use a specialized console that was designed to control all of the parameters associated with automated lighting. Even today, it is fairly common for large-scale productions with automated lights to use two different lighting consoles—one for the "conventionals" and one for the "movers." This gives a designer the added advantage of having two crew members programming their show, each dealing with a different set of issues. In recent productions, while both consoles may be used to program a show, when running the show one desk is often slaved to the other or the data of both consoles may be merged together and run from a single desk. Newer generation consoles can be used to program all aspects of a production, including conventionals, automated gear, media servers, and projection mapping as well as additional gear such as hazers, automation, etc. There are numerous people working throughout the lighting industry who are making a lucrative living solely as moving light operators or programmers. Due to the sophistication of operating many of today's lighting consoles, it has now become common to refer to any light board operator using these consoles as a programmer.

Sidebar 14.2 DESIGNER PROFILE

Brad Schiller

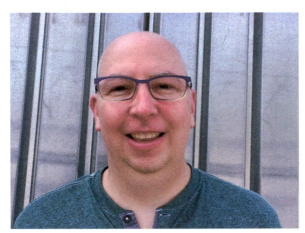

Credit: photo courtesy Robin Joy Schiller

Brad Schiller, one of the leading programmers in the world, has been associated with automated lighting/programming pretty much since the appearance of moving lights. Though he has also worked as a lighting designer and video content creator, he is known as one of the automated lighting industry's authorities and has programmed for productions that include everything from concerts, corporate events, architectural structures, and television award programs to spectacle events like the opening and closing ceremonies of the Olympic Games. Many of his favorite credits include the 1996 Academy Awards, the capitol of Puerto Rico, the Opening and Closing Ceremonies of the Sydney 2000 Olympic Games, and musical groups such as The Crystal Method and Metallica. He has also been employed by several of the leading automated lighting companies in various roles ranging from being a business development manager to positions leading product support and development. Always one to share, he is the author of the popular book, *The Automated Lighting Programmer's Handbook* (Elsevier/Focal Press, 2017) and continues to write a featured column (Feeding the Machines) for *Projection Lights and Staging News*. Brad was the recipient of the 2005 LDI Technician of the Year Award and has been described as "the programmer's programmer."

Brad is unique in that he joined the programming segment of the lighting industry on the ground floor. His formal lighting training was through his activities in high school and some college, but he learned automated lighting in the real world: "I was introduced to automated lighting programming at the very start of this portion of our industry and pretty much 'grew up' along with automated lighting." A lot of his initial success he attributes to simply being at the right place at the right time. His professional journey began while working in a local theatre in Irving, Texas, as a technician while simultaneously freelancing around Dallas. In the mid-1980s, he began programming various types of early automated lighting gear for an assortment of shows and events around Dallas that rapidly led to him developing special skills and a specialty as a programmer: "I learned the processes and gained skills with different consoles and fixtures and even established relationships with manufacturers by providing input and feedback on the products." His big break came when he was hired by High End Systems in the mid-1990s. At that time, there were very few automated lighting programmers and High End (as well as other manufacturers) each had their own team of elite programmers that could be hired for productions:

> "This was the only way to work as a professional "full time" programmer at that time. As a member of the High End Systems Programming Department, I was offered many programming opportunities for major productions. The position also established me as a leader in the fast-growing automated lighting industry, and in addition to programming shows, we would conduct product demonstrations, teach programming seminars, assist in product development, and much more."

Along with his freelance work, Brad has been employed by several manufacturers in some very interesting roles. As a product manager at both High End Systems and Philips Vari-Lite, he provided input into the development of consoles and fixtures that are widely used in our industry: "Working alongside engineers to create new products was an unexpected segment of lighting for me when I was starting out." Most recently, Martin by Harman employed him as a Business Development Manager, where he manages relationships with lighting designers and programmers.

Brad believes that the position of being a programmer is very interesting, as it requires many different lighting skills. First, the programmer must understand the syntax and procedures for getting data into a desk. Second, the programmer needs to bring actual lighting skills to the show. Third, the programmer must be creative and able to provide input and originality when needed. Lastly, a programmer should be organized both in thought processes and actual data management. Brad goes on to say:

> "A big part of working as an automated lighting programmer is being a good team player. As the person sitting at the console, the programmer must have a good working relationship with the lighting designer as well as many others involved with the production. Furthermore, a friendly personality mixed with a good sense of humor is generally required."

He adds:

> "Sitting at a console programming a production filled with technology is an incredible feeling. I enjoy being part of the creative process that adds to the performance without having to deal with the politics that often face the lighting designer. I also love the fact that I can apply my programming skills to a variety of entertainment genres and am not limited to only theatre or touring. I have been fortunate to program a bit of everything and travel the world while doing so."

Several of the things he likes least about being a programmer include the fact that lighting is often pushed off to the overnight shift and it seems that pre-production time keeps getting shorter:

> "As I get older, I find that working late hours and frequently shifting work schedules to be far more exhausting than when I was younger. The reduction of pre-production time has led to rushed workflows and less detailed lighting programming. It is also unfortunate that programmers are expected to work with more fixtures in less time."

Another shortcoming of the industry is in keeping fixture libraries current:

> "One of the key frustrations for programmers is the lack of updated fixture libraries within consoles. A good programmer will take the time to confirm that the libraries in a show file allow access to all the features of each light. Our industry has failed at providing quality libraries and it is the programmer that must pickup the pieces and make corrections."

Automated lighting programmers must stay up-to-date with the lighting technology as well as with the software and libraries. As an author of a regular column, Brad has a unique problem in that he needs to remain abreast of a rapidly changing industry while most programmers turn to him to get the latest news on the technology:

> "I enjoy reading user manuals and always read release notes for new console software as well as watch videos produced by the manufacturers that explain new features. Then, I practice the latest functions in a non-show environment to ensure that I have a full understanding of the capabilities."

He adds:

> "Any time I am presented with a new fixture that I have never programmed I will read the DMX protocol to gain an understanding of the abilities of the light and then ensure that my console library is up-to-date to access all those functions. In addition, I continually discuss programming with my peers so that I understand the trends both in programming and in lighting design."

Brad offers some practical advice:

> "Rule #1 is to remember that it is all about what is happening on stage. No matter how the show is programmed, what macros are created, or how the console screens are laid out, the only thing that matters is the lighting for the performance. Too often I see programmers that forget that the core job is lighting and they tend to focus too much on the minutia of the consoles and data. Rule #2 is to save the show file often!"

In closing, he says

> "I find the position of an automated lighting programmer to be very exhilarating and my passion for programming exceeds beyond the console. I love to share my knowledge and experience with anyone that is interested and hope that our industry continues to grow with expanded training and educational opportunities for all that are concerned. In doing so, all productions will improve with refined processes and procedures for programming that will inspire future generations to create exciting lighting designs and products."

FILM AND VIDEO

There are a number of similarities between the professionals who work in the film and video industries. Many people who work in these areas float back and forth equally well between both specialties of lighting. Additionally, these industries hire professionals who have production responsibilities that are quite similar to those who work in the theatrical industry. The two industries even have many of the same union affiliations. Designers are usually members of USA, while the crews are covered by IATSE. Though many of the responsibilities and departments are quite similar, there are different titles associated with many of these production personnel. Due to their similarities, I am keeping my discussion of the professionals in the film and video industries more abbreviated. In many cases, even though the titles may be different, the positions are quite similar to those already discussed in theatrical applications. There are also several significant differences between theatrical and film productions, including the live versus recorded nature of the final product, the direct exposure to the eye in live entertainment versus the indirect means of transferring images through a camera and film or monitor, and the viewer being exposed to an entire environment or scene (with distractions) versus the confined and very selective focus of a camera. While an entire stage or performance venue must be dealt with for a live event, a film or video shoot requires only a designed environment within the frame of the camera.

Design Professionals

Cinematographer/Director of Photography (DP)

The most visible designer in video or film production is the **cinematographer,** or **director of photography (DP)**. This person works extensively with the director and is responsible for creating the entire visual environment for a production. Cinematographers are affiliated with the film industry while directors of photography are more often associated with the video industry (but can be associated with either industries). Although these design professionals have overall responsibility for the lighting of a production, this is typically only one of the areas in which they may have responsibilities. The director of photography is also responsible for choosing the location of a setting, determining the camera angles and range of an individual shot, and selecting the camera lenses and film speeds for a take. Having said this, storyboarding and lighting probably form two of this individual's most significant contributions to a film or video. **Storyboards** are simple drawings that give an indication of the view and individual composition of each camera shot. This allows them to discuss each shot with a director prior to working with the cast and crews. While storyboards tend to be underutilized in theatrical production, they are a major form of communication in the film and video communities. Often a director of photography/cinematographer will have other design professionals or assistants working under them. These lighting professionals may be certified members of a professional society called the **American Society of Cinematographers (ASC)** and are identified by the ASC abbreviation following their names in a production's credits.

Lighting Director (LD)

Due to the size of many film and video projects it is common for a director of photography to bring another individual on board to supervise the lighting of a project. This lighting specialist is the **lighting director** and will have overall charge of the lighting for a film or video. This position is more commonly affiliated with video than film production. The video industry will almost always employ a lighting director, while cinematographers are more characteristic of the film industry. Just as in theatrical production, each of these professionals may have associates or assistants working under them. Several duties of a lighting director include analyzing and researching the script, working with the director or director of photography to develop a lighting concept for a project, researching light sources and creating the plot (if needed), producing the associated paperwork for the shoot, and designing the specific cues/looks for each segment of the project. You may also see lighting directors associated with live or taped performances such as concerts or spectacle events when there is an element of video (**I-MAG**, broadcast, or taped) or when the lighting designer is not physically present on a tour or event and their work is being re-created.

One special problem in video and film production relates to **continuity**—paying attention to details to ensure that everything remains consistent in terms of prop placement, scenic details, and costume treatments. For a lighting director, this means that each camera angle and **take** of a scene must be lit in exactly the same manner. If a scene is lit predominantly by sidelight, when camera angles shift, the light must still appear to be coming from this angle in relationship to the subject. Since film and video productions are usually shot out of sequence, special care must be taken to make sure that these details are dealt with consistently in each of the takes that are recorded for a given scene.

Sidebar 14.3 DESIGNER PROFILE

Patrick Cady

Credit: photo courtesy Patrick Cady

Patrick Cady, ASC, has been involved in the film/ video industry since the late 1980s. He first learned filmmaking while studying for a BFA at Ithaca College and then went on to earn a MFA at New York University's Tisch School of the Arts. During his time there he served as a camera intern for Roger Deakins on the John Sayles film *Passion Fish* and 10 years later was director of photography on Sayles' *Sunshine State*. He spent a large portion of those 10 years working first as an electrician and then as a gaffer (aka chief lighting technician) before getting noticed for his work on the Sundance winner *Girlfight*. In the years since, he has worked behind the camera on features like *The Stepfather* and *Lottery Ticket*, as well as TV series such as *Bosch*, *Insecure*, *Cold Case*, *In Treatment*, and *Body of Proof*.

Patrick's path to filmmaking and cinematography was fairly conventional through his studies at Ithaca and New York University; it was his experience on *Passion Fish* and working with Roger Deakins that really started his love of what lighting could do for a project and the odd mix of science and art that all good lighting requires. He shares:

❝While still taking classes and making shorts at NYU I worked as an electrician in NYC . . . mostly for a wonderful gaffer (now DP) Eric Schmidt. We worked on music videos, commercials and a couple independent features (including *Little Odessa*). When Eric started shooting himself, he made me his gaffer and my lighting jobs grew out of working for him.❞

In the mid to late 1990s Patrick had the great luck of lighting music videos, with a variety of cinematographers, for artists such as David Bowie, The Beastie Boys, The Dave Matthews Band, and Shawn Colvin—to name just a few:

❝Lighting all those different and stylized jobs while shooting student films really helped make me flexible about how to make the lighting match the particular story we were telling. When I made the move to being a cinematographer in 1999, I ended up shooting a few independent features. The first one that got released was *Girlfight* which was a huge stroke of luck as it won awards at Sundance while its photography was also written up in *American Cinematographer* and *Variety* magazines. At that point, my career shifted from the world of commercials and videos into the world of narrative filmmaking— features and television.

As the cinematographer, I'm in charge of the entire approach to the shooting of a project, the camera work, the lighting and the shaping of that lighting. camera, grip and electric . . . all working in unison to tell a story. That is what I would call my specialty, trying to tell the story the best way possible, in the time allowed, with the gear each project can afford. I owe most of my good fortune to Eric Schmidt, who took me on as an inexperienced electrician and eventually made me his gaffer and John Sayles, who let me be a camera intern on *Passion Fish*. Sayles also financed *Girlfight* (released in 2000) which I shot and then he hired me to shoot *Sunshine State* which came out in 2002. If there were a single event that I attribute to my success, I guess it would be either the success of *Girlfight* at Sundance, or Eric asking me to cover him for an episode of *Cold Case* during its first season. That led to me shooting the show when he left, and from then on I was easily approved by studios to shoot television shows.❞

Patrick believes that narrative filmmaking is all about drawing an audience into a story and that oftentimes this may mean making things seem "real" but still controlling the lighting in such a way as to create an emotion: "That's tricky—you want to influence people on an emotional level without calling too much attention to what you're doing." He and his gaffers often consider what exists in the real world and then find ways to blend that with their lighting. Lately, this has meant using industrial fixtures in conjunction with new LED technology and old school tungsten lights—all on a very tight schedule: "The mix of what works best, what we can afford, and what is fastest are constantly under consideration and often, managing the flow of activity on a set is just as critical as managing what the equipment is." When he was a gaffer he remained abreast of industry developments by subscribing to magazines in film and other disciplines, theatrical design, etc.: "Now I work with very skilled gaffers who bring the technology to me. Sometimes an idea will come before I even know what equipment can pull it off, and then I start researching on line and asking colleagues for advice."

What Patrick likes most about working as a cinematographer relates to how the team can create a setup where the final product looks like "they just got lucky.":

"Imagine a world where all the time the light was just right for what was happening to you and somehow beautiful. I love that I am surrounded by a few key people who also adore the way light works, how it can be shaped, and the way that it is a physical thing that we can make work for us. Every now and then in a 12-hour workday we will finish a lighting setup and it all just clicks. All of the people in charge had interesting ideas, they worked in conjunction with one another, and when you finish watching a take being filmed you notice that the smiles on everyone's faces are just like the one on yours. I love getting to work with other professionals that are still invested and interested in what they do. I am *very* lucky that I have a crew that won't give up and where we happen to agree many more times than not on when something looks right."

On the other hand, one of the drawbacks can be that time restraints are tough to work within:

"You know how much work needs to be done in one day and you look at your watch and realize you need to shoot when it is good enough instead of great—that is the hardest part of the job. The funny thing though, is that sometimes those restraints force you into crazy ideas that pay off."

In offering some closing advice, Patrick shares that in order to do this successfully you must be a storyteller:

"If I know what the story is or which story we are telling, then I know what the lighting needs to do . . . story, story, story . . . We are all telling tales. Knowing the story makes all the other creative ideas easier to come by." He also emphasizes the need to learn the basics. "When I was learning about the Inverse Square Law in school I had no idea it would be such a constant companion. I think that with new equipment (cameras in my line of work) it is easy to think you don't need a thorough understanding of the basics. . . . I'm here to tell anyone still reading that those basics are the solid foundation you need to be truly creative."

Production Crews

Gaffer/Chief Lighting Technician

Production crews in the film and video industries have similar responsibilities to their counterparts in the theatrical world. In many cases, despite their titles, the duties are the same—although there are additional professionals in film and video production that aren't typically found in most theatrical applications. The **gaffer,** or **chief lighting technician,** is the individual who is the most similar to a master electrician in theatrical production. There is a unique twist, however, in that the chief lighting technician actually translates the image of a director of photography into the instrument choices and placements of the lights and other related equipment for a shoot. This person works directly with the lighting director or director of photography to provide the specified lighting equipment, filters, reflectors or diffusers, and power for each shoot. They are also responsible for the direct supervision of the lighting staff for a project. If a gaffer has an assistant, this person is called the **best boy.** In recent years, it has become preferable to call the person in charge of this aspect of the lighting the chief lighting technician rather than the gaffer.

Sidebar 14.4 DESIGNER PROFILE

Derrick Kolus

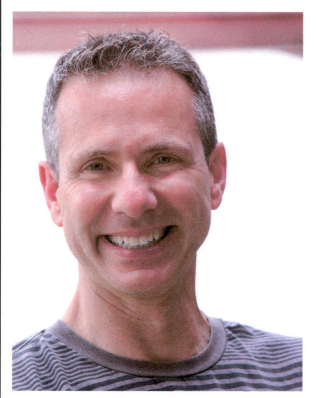

Credit: photo courtesy Karen Kolus

Derrick Kolus has worked as a gaffer in the film and video industry since 1989. He earned his BA degree from Pennsylvania State University, where he studied Film Production. Derrick has worked in both film and television, with the majority of his projects being in television. Several of his more recognized credits include *Bosch, Perception, Body of Proof, Heroes, Providence*, and *Without a Trace*.

After graduating from Pennsylvania State, Derrick moved to Los Angeles and spent a year as a Cinematography Fellow at the American Film Institute before going to work in the industry:

"At the undergraduate level, I don't think any of us really understood film lighting much beyond key light, fill light, and back light. While the AFI had no formal lighting classes, they did have a steady stream of working cinematographers giving seminars and workshops, which was a great way to learn. After AFI, I began working in the film industry as a camera assistant, the traditional first step on the road to becoming a cinematographer. But, I found myself watching the lighting crew during setups and thought what they were doing looked more interesting than what I was doing! Approaching cinematography from a lighting background actually made more sense to me, so I began working as an electrician and it didn't take long before I was gaffing. Over time, I became more and more fascinated by lighting and eventually decided to make it a career."

Derrick believes that film lighting is best learned by doing:

"We have so many lighting technologies and fixtures to choose from. I can make sunlight with a leko, a PAR-Can, a xenon, an HMI PAR, an 18K Fresnel . . . endless possibilities! Warm sun, cool sun, narrow sun, broad sun, distant sun, close sun—all are possible, depending on the story we're trying to tell and the physical challenges we're facing on set at the time. It's my job to know what each light can do, and I think that the only way to learn this is by turning lights on and looking at what comes out. We're always trying new things. Sometimes they work, sometimes they don't. Patrick Cady, one of my favorite cinematographers, likes to start our conversations with, "I have this crazy idea" . . . and it always makes me smile. But even when we're taking a chance with something new, we're drawing on our collective experiences to give ourselves the best chance of succeeding."

He goes on to say:

"A number of years ago, I was asked to light *The Scorpion King* movie, which remains the largest production I've ever worked on. I remember feeling very intimidated by the sheer scale of the thing. I was attending an awards dinner and got seated next to Dave Devlin, who had gaffed several of Steven Speilberg's films. He told me, "The big movies are exactly like the small movies, they just have more stuff." And he was right."

Derrick notes that there are differences between film and stage lighting:

"The dynamic on a film set is much different than stage—it's kind of like a rehearsal that never ends. Work on a scene usually begins with an actors' rehearsal with the director. Next, department heads assemble for a marking rehearsal, where we all see the scene for the first time. Then everything happens in rapid succession: the set is given over to the crew, the cameraman sets the shots, and the lighting and grip crews go to work. When everyone is ready, we shoot. This process is repeated for each scene. I work mostly in television, and we operate under severe time constraints. The minutes after a rehearsal are precious and decisions have to be made quickly about which lighting approach will work best for the story, the blocking, the position of the cameras, and the amount of time we have to get it all done. Each cinematographer is unique, and they all have different approaches to working with a gaffer. Some will describe what they want in broad terms and expect me to come up with the details. Others will be very specific. As the lighting setup progresses, I'm looking at the lens each camera is using and how each sees the light. Are there separation issues between actors and backgrounds? Are we seeing depth? Do we need fill? Is the light quality right for the scene? Do we need to cue? Once everything is roughed in, the cameraman and I sit down at the monitors, fine-tune the levels and solve any remaining problems. Then the cameras roll.

In film, we are most often striving for some degree of realism in our lighting, which dictates the kinds of fixtures we use and where we position them. We often shoot on location, and we use a wide variety of sources: incandescent, HMI, fluorescent, xenon, sodium and mercury vapor, halide and a huge assortment of LED fixtures. Most scenes begin with a wide shot, and the lights are positioned farther away or rigged above set to keep them clear of the shot. But lights that look great in a wide master may be problematic for closer coverage, so as the camera positions change, the lighting positions change as well, often moving lower and closer to the set. The changes can be quite drastic, but if we do our jobs well, no one notices as they watch the show. There are compromises. The best lighting for A camera may not be good for B camera. The best lighting position for the scene may not be available because one of the cameras sees it in the shot. There's always a balance between the cameras and the lighting, and it's up to the cinematographer to decide when one takes precedence over the other.

A shot begins with an actress looking out a window at a child playing in the yard, then follows her as she walks down a long, dark hallway. Because film involves technical elements like exposure and color temperature, we may choose to light the scene using large, 5600K sources to balance the interior levels and color temp with the exterior view thru the window. Or we may decide it's more efficient to gel the window to make the exterior view darker, warmer or both, thus allowing us to light the interiors with smaller, 3200K fixtures. Or we may change the camera's color temp, or shift the exposure during the shot, negating the need to balance interior with exterior at all. These are all possibilities.

Shooting for a typical feature film usually lasts from one to four months, and often has substantial prep time before shooting begins. The gaffer and cinematographer often scout all the locations in advance and develop detailed lighting approaches. In television, we shoot a one-hour show in 7–10 days and a full season may number 10–24 shows. We have minimal prep and I'm often receiving blueprints for next week's set design on my phone while we're shooting this week's locations. We sometimes shoot as many as four or five locations in one day and we have separate crews that rig ahead of us and wrap up behind us as we go."

Derrick acknowledges there are things that he both likes and dislikes about working in film: "It's an exciting time for lighting. LED technology is revolutionizing how we light—we can move faster and do things we simply couldn't do before." And there's the camaraderie:

"We'll all be huddled together around the monitors watching the same rehearsal, but we all see something different. I see a moment where the actor needs a little more light in his eyes. Our cameraman sees a dolly move that was too fast. Our makeup artist sees a little too much shine on a cheek. Our costumer sees a shirt that is rumpled in the back. Each one of us contributes something unique to each image—together, we all tell the story."

On the other hand, "We work very, very long hours. Your work becomes your life, so it's important that you love it." He stays abreast of new developments by reading trade magazines, watching movies ("Big budget movies will often showcase new technologies before they filter down to smaller budget shows,") attending theatre and dance performances, and talking to crew members who have worked on other shows. "Rule #1," Derrick explains:

> "There are no rules. There is no right or wrong way to light something. The second Rule #1 is to always remember the story that you're trying to tell and to make sure that the lighting choices you make are telling it."

Grips

The crew members for film and video are most often called **grips.** These people are responsible for the movement and setup of any equipment required for a shoot. This position is equivalent to the stagehand in theatrical production. Typical duties include the setup and strike of all scenic or prop elements, lighting equipment, and any reflective or diffusion devices. Grips are also responsible for the installation and operation of camera gear such as dollies and cranes—although a **camera operator** is responsible for the operation of the camera itself. Some organizations like to make a distinction between those grips who are assigned to lighting responsibilities and the rest of the crew: those with a lighting specialty are referred to as **gaffers.** In this case, rather than having the chief lighting technician credited as gaffer, this person will usually be given the title of **head gaffer.** With all of this confusion in titles, it can be seen why the title of chief lighting technician has become so popular. The head gaffer generally supervises the entire lighting department for a television or film production. As in theatrical production, light board operators and moving light operators/programmers may also be used.

Two additional lighting specialists are often added to a film or video team when there is a location shoot. When shooting on location, there is seldom enough power for the needs of the cameras, lighting equipment, and other gear that a shoot will require. Therefore, the production team needs to provide its own power by bringing a **generator** to a production site. These units may be as small as a portable unit that can be carried by a single crew member or as large as trailer-mounted units that are mounted on a semi-trailer. In major televised events like the broadcasting of network football games, producers often have several trailers of mobile production gear and semi-sized generators positioned just outside of an arena. The individual who operates and monitors these generators is the **generator (genny) operator.** A second specialist associated with film and video production, the **set wireman**, is an electrician who is responsible for the wiring and maintenance of all of the practical lighting fixtures—a **practical** being a lighting fixture such as a table lamp or wall sconce that is mounted on a set and seen by an audience.

ARCHITECTURAL LIGHTING

The specialized field of lighting that relates to architectural installations is called **illumination engineering.** Projects that commonly fall under this umbrella include lighting for building interiors and exteriors, display lighting like that found in museum and retail exhibits, roadway and bridge lighting, lighting for installations such as monuments, themed designs such as those found in amusement parks and attractions, and garden or landscape lighting. Architectural lighting includes a number of different applications, but all share a common trait in that the installations are permanent. Unlike entertainment lighting, where a production may go up in a few hours and then be struck immediately following a performance, or where long runs are measured in weeks or months, architectural practices demand that an installation be operational for years if not decades. The concept of permanent versus temporary dictates a very different approach to lighting these projects. Mistakes can be expensive, and design solutions need to be accurate the first time. A mistake in fixture type or placement in an architectural application could become an ongoing problem or safety concern. Due to the issue of permanence, architectural lighting requires a more rigorous regulation of designers and installers to ensure that a project is designed and installed safely. While mood and style play a role in architectural lighting, the emphasis of these designs is usually on the functionality of a lighting application. The activities that are planned for an environment determine the minimum amount of light to be specified for an area so that the activity or **task** can be completed in an efficient, safe manner. The more critical the task, the higher the illumination level that is specified.

Lighting design professionals who work in architectural lighting generally have two different backgrounds. The first, **illuminating engineers,** are the more traditional of the two professionals. Many individuals who design the lighting for architectural projects come from the electrical engineering discipline and are identified as illuminating engineers. These professionals are often part of a design team of an architectural or engineering firm that designs large projects like office buildings, hotels, shopping malls, etc. In the past, it was common for these professionals to be part of a department of electrical engineers that specified all of the electrical systems for a project. Building systems that these engineers are responsible for include outlet specifications, communication systems, elevator control, and the power for heat and ventilation equipment as well as the lighting design. Interior designers are another group of professionals who might design the lighting for a project as an additional element of their design services. The second type of professional, the **Lighting Designer**, has come about more recently. In the last 30 or so years, architects and their clients have gravitated toward a more artistic rather than solely functional approach to lighting buildings. With this new interest, many architects turned to entertainment lighting designers who work alongside the illuminating engineers to produce more innovative lighting projects. The title of lighting designer came with this crossover. Initially, it was reserved for designers who were providing a more aesthetic contribution to a design than simple illumination. Today, it has become a fairly common practice for even individuals with electrical engineering backgrounds to refer to themselves as lighting designers if they are charged with the responsibility of lighting architectural projects. Just as in entertainment lighting, an architectural lighting designer is responsible for the choice and location of luminaires, filters, control assignments, and wiring specifications. They are also responsible for the focusing or **aiming** of the fixtures and cueing any dynamic elements of a design.

An architectural lighting designer should also have a keen awareness of additional design parameters that entertainment designers rarely have to consider. Several of these include an understanding of both the *NEC* and any building or other electric codes that are specific to a given municipality, a knowledge of construction documents, familiarity with illumination engineering practices and calculation techniques, and an understanding of lighting economics and **green power.** Green power refers to using conservation practices to lower the energy demands of a project. There is a vast amount of regulation in architectural lighting—and virtually none in the entertainment industry. In addition to safety codes, many municipalities have codes that regulate the amount of power that a building consumes over a given area (**power densities**), which is based on the particular functions or tasks that a space may provide. Not specifying enough footcandles of illumination for a stairwell or creating a design that consumes too much power could result in civil lawsuits or regulatory charges. If a lighting designer has not been trained as an electrical or illuminating engineer, the detailed specifications for items like conduit sizes, wire gauges, number of wires in a conduit, and power specifications are handed off to an electrical engineer.

There are a host of professionals who are charged with the installation of architectural lighting systems; it is beyond the scope of this book to provide a full discussion of all of their duties. However, several different specialists who execute these designs include **project managers, electrical contractors,** and **electricians.** A significant difference between these and entertainment lighting professionals is that nearly all of them must be licensed by a local or state authority. Project managers frequently come from an electrical engineering background. They are responsible for supervising a design project and frequently deal with issues like matching specifications, keeping a project on schedule, code compliance, and installation procedures. An electrical contractor is a subcontractor of a general contracting firm and is hired (typically through a bidding process) to procure the electrical materials/equipment (including lighting as a portion of all the electrical systems) and the proper installation of the equipment. Electricians do the physical work of the wiring and installations.

UNIONS AND CERTIFICATIONS

Nearly every one of the professionals discussed earlier are represented by one of several unions. Whether an individual becomes a member of a union usually depends on whether membership is a requirement for obtaining gainful employment in a profession. Even if is not, however, union membership is often seen as a professional credential—although it needs to be emphasized that there are both good and bad union and non-union professionals working in any profession. Often, an individual cannot be employed in certain markets (theatres or studios), without becoming a union member first. However, this is typical of only the largest, most prestigious markets. Broadway theatres, feature films, significant touring productions, television studios in major markets (cities), and many regional theatres are venues where an individual will most likely have to become a union member before being employed.

Several of the reasons that unions became established relate primarily to providing crews with access to employee benefits. Health and pension plans are major benefits available to union members that aren't often provided to non-union employees. There are also provisions for regulating wage and working conditions in studios and theatres that are under union contracts. Even with so many areas covered by union jurisdiction, the majority of the professionals working in the industry are most likely not affiliated with a union.

Finally, it can usually be assumed that individuals with a union affiliation have demonstrated a minimal standard of proficiency, experience, and professionalism. The majority of the union members whom I have worked with over the years reflect a great sense of professionalism and competence in the business and take personal pride in getting my shows up and running.

A certification is very different from a union membership and has nothing to do with providing any tangible benefits like pay scales, pensions, or health plans. Instead, a certification provides recognition that the bearer has demonstrated a particular degree of competence in a discipline. Certifications are awarded by independent agencies or professional organizations in a chosen field and are commonly signified with a series of initials that are placed behind an individual's name. Just recently the theatrical community began certification programs for stage electricians and riggers. The program for electricians (Entertainment Electrician) is coordinated by the **Entertainment Technician Certification Program (ETCP).** The certification is based on the satisfactory completion of a standardized test that can be taken after documenting a certain degree of experience as a stage electrician. Those who complete their certification must be recertified every five years by either participating in a series of educational activities or retaking the test. The certification practice is beginning to have a significant impact on providing qualified personnel to those parts of the industry that represent the largest venues and entertainment markets.

In the area of film, certification is earned through the **American Society of Cinematographers (ASC).** This is conferred upon directors of photography who are members of the organization. A member is identified by the ASC that is seen after the name of the director of photography on most feature films. Most lighting certifications are found in architectural practices and are either earned through an exam or are conferred by professional societies. The **Lighting Certified (LC)** certification by the **National Council on Qualifications for the Lighting Profession (NCQLP)** and the more recent **Certified Lighting Designer (CLD)** are certifications that apply primarily to lighting designers. The LC certification is earned by exam and like the ETCP certification must be renewed on a regular basis (in this case, every three years by exam or by participating in a given number of educational activities). The LC certification is primarily a national certification in the United States (though there are many international members) while the CLD is an international certification program that first appeared in late 2015. As of spring 2017 there were only a few lighting designers holding the CLD certification and it is yet to be determined if this additional certification program will catch on.

Most entertainment design professionals, lighting designers included, are covered by USA. This union has three primary offices located in different regions of the country. New York is the primary office (Local 829) and represents the East Coast, while the Midwest is under the jurisdiction of the Chicago office and the West Coast is overseen by the Los Angeles office. Other offices are appearing in other cities that have significant film/video production industries. While USA remains an independent identity, the union has formed a partnership with the stagehands' union (IATSE) to form a more solid future for its membership in regard to healthcare plans and pensions. Membership is earned primarily through exam or by professional experience. There is also an apprenticeship program. While the majority of members are involved in theatrical designing, the union also covers a significant number of individuals, studios, and projects in the video and film industries as well. The West Coast office is quite heavily affiliated with these industries.

IATSE is the stagehands' union and has a much larger membership than does the design union. This union covers professionals who work in all forms of entertainment technology. Members may build, install, or form the run crew in scenery or electrics in a variety of different venues. Prop, wardrobe, and other crew areas are also covered by this union. Examples where IATSE is well represented include employment in theatres, touring productions, film and television studios, nightclubs and variety shows, arenas and convention centers, concert productions, and trade or industrial productions. Rather than regional offices, most medium to large cities have a local organization associated with the union that we commonly call a **local.** Membership requirements can vary considerably between different locals and can range from being a member of the right family to gaining experience through an overhire program or becoming involved in a full apprenticeship or initiation program. Many locals are using the ETCP certification programs as at least a partial path to union membership.

Sidebar 14.5 DESIGNER PROFILE

Gary Fails is most widely known as the founder and president of City Theatrical, Inc. (CTI). However, Gary began his career in lighting from the ground up—much of his career working as a Local 1 IATSE electrician on Broadway productions in New York City and on national tours. Gary founded CTI in a South Bronx garage in 1986 as a specialty lighting shop that manufactures unique lighting accessories that are developed to meet the specific needs of Broadway productions. Over the 30 years that the company has been in existence it has grown into a corporation with a catalog of lighting products and accessories, over 35 product and business awards, a 40,000 square foot production facility/home office in New Jersey, and a sales office in London. While most of CTI's initial product developments were in lighting accessories, the company has gone on to develop products in electronics, dimming, wireless control, and LED technologies—earning several patents along the way. As an accessories manufacturer, it has gone on to produce products for live theatre, television, motion pictures, and architectural lighting. Several of CTI's products have been awarded prestigious Product of the Year awards by both the LDI and PLASA lighting shows.

Gary's initial path into a career in lighting was a bit indirect, but it laid the foundation for what

Gary Fails

Credit: photo courtesy Jennifer Gennaro

would later give him special insights into the needs of Broadway designers and how he could use that to build a successful business:

> ❝I have no formal lighting training and never studied or worked in lighting before my first lighting job, which was driving a truck for a dance company [Dance Theatre of Harlem]. They asked me to cut gel, then to help hang the show. A few weeks later I was on a three-month European tour with them and quickly became their stage manager and lighting designer.❞

This led to a solid five years of touring with Dance Theatre of Harlem, including many cross-country US tours and 10 European tours, which was followed by another five years of touring as a production electrician with national tours of Broadway shows. "I learned my craft by hanging and lighting shows in hundreds of venues all around the world," Gary says

His experience in touring eventually led to his joining the New York City stagehand's union (International Alliance of Theatrical Stage Employees—IATSE Local One):

> ❝During my touring years, I took the Local One stagehands apprentice test and was put on

the list. When they called, I went back to New York and became the Local One apprentice at Four Star Lighting in the South Bronx—which in its day was the heart of the New York lighting world.❞

While Gary was at Four Star Lighting he became a certified welder and skilled sheet metal worker. More importantly, it gave him the opportunity to meet and get to know many of the Broadway electricians and designers:

> ❝After I got my Local One card I continued working at Four Star during the day and was a production electrician and house electrician on Broadway shows at night. Through working with designers and electricians each day, I realized that there were products which were needed that were not being manufactured. As a result, I founded City Theatrical to meet those needs. All of our products are tuned for the specific needs of the 'mission critical' high stakes world of professional lighting. Our wireless DMX products are trusted by technicians in a world where any problem could be a show stopper.
>
> It's pretty safe to say that if I had not worked at Four Star Lighting my lighting career would have gone in some other direction and because of that I would credit the DeVerna family (the owners of Four Star Lighting) for having a significant influence on my success—they were even my first customer when I started City Theatrical.❞

Just a few of the many notable Broadway designers who became friends and supporters of CTI over the years include the likes of Jules Fisher, Peggy Eisenhauer, Don Holder, and Ken Posner. Additionally, CTI has built a long-standing relationship with ETC, which continues through today, that started when CTI built the first accessories for the Source Four. Even to this day, Gary likes to work on shows several times a year—using new technology, working with designers and electricians, and being part of the crew:

> ❝It has always been the best way I have found to understand the needs of lighting users and what products we should be developing to meet those needs. The most fun I have is being a trusted advisor to the design team and helping them achieve their artistic vision. I particularly enjoy when designers call me to brainstorm a problem they are facing and ask us to create a solution for them.❞

In closing, Gary shares that:

"While some specific technical skills are important, I am not an engineer and there are many better technicians around than me. However, over the years I have found that common sense, problem solving skills, mechanical aptitude, the ability to accept risk without worrying about it, and an optimistic attitude are the most important traits to have in business. You can have anything you want if you want it badly enough. Don't hold back. . . . Dive in with your full commitment. There are plenty of dabblers in the world. Find what you like to do and be the best at it. I've built my business by making unique and esoteric things that are only needed by a few people in the world. I can honestly say that I love the role that I have created for myself in the international lighting world and that there isn't really anything that I would change about it."

In the broadcast industry, many directors of photography and lighting directors, along with other television employees and engineers like cameramen and other technicians, belong to the **National Association of Broadcast Employees and Technicians (NABET)** union. While this union has members and locals scattered throughout the country, its primary membership is associated with major network studios like ABC, NBC, and CBS in large cities or television markets. This union is affiliated with a larger constituency representing the **Communications Workers of America (CWA)**.

PROFESSIONAL ORGANIZATIONS AND SOCIETIES

Professional societies and organizations provide a variety of resources for their members. In the lighting industry there are numerous professional societies with which an individual might become affiliated. Some organizations are national or international, while others operate at the regional and local levels. Some are rather generic, while others relate to very specific niches in the lighting industry. In addition to providing resources for their members, these organizations bring public awareness to that portion of the lighting industry. Member benefits may include training seminars, publications, networking with other professionals, exposure to potential clients, and introductions to new technologies and lighting applications. Most organizations also recognize exceptional projects and award individuals for various design achievements. The organizations also have

various membership classifications based on experience and recognition of an individual's skills and stature in the industry. (Fellows—lifetime recognition in the field, Member—a fully recognized individual, Associate / Affiliate, Student, etc.). Those in the more prestigious membership categories may display various designations behind their names (FIESNA, IALD, IESNA, etc.). An extremely important service that these organizations provide is coordinating industry standards and self-regulation from within the lighting profession. Most of these societies also produce or co-produce at least one major trade show or conference each year and publish regularly produced trade magazines and newsletters.

The most prevalent theatrical organization that is aimed towards technicians and designers is the **United States Institute for Theatre Technology (USITT)**. This organization represents designers and technicians from across all areas of stagecraft. While most of its members are based in theatrical production, many are involved in a variety of other entertainment areas as well. USITT produces publications, educational programs, and an annual trade show/conference for its members. It also provides peer recognition, grants, and awards to professionals and projects within the industry, as well as working groups that define standards and guidelines throughout the entertainment industry. While USITT caters to all theatre professionals, it includes discipline-related groups such as the Lighting Commission that deal with specific areas of design and technology. USITT also has a number of regional sections that provide members with a means of meeting for local programs on a more regular basis. For those who are interested in theatrical design and technology at the international level, there is an international association affiliated with USITT: **Organisation Internationale des Scénographes, Techniciens et Architectes de Théâtre (OISTAT)**.

One of the largest organizations for individuals connected with video lighting is the **National Association of Broadcasters (NAB)**. A specialty society that represents lighting directors and gaffers in the film and video industries is the **American Society of Lighting Designers (ASLD)**.

There are even more organizations that represent special interest groups in the lighting industry, catering to the specific needs of theatrical dealers, manufacturers, and even to the special needs of venues such as theme parks and nightclubs.

Architectural lighting is represented by several major professional organizations, the two most prominent being the **Illuminating Engineering Society of North America (IESNA or IES)** and the **International Association of Lighting Designers (IALD)**. The IES is particularly important because it represents all aspects of the lighting industry, including designers and specifiers, manufacturers, distributors, and even researchers. The IES is comprised of a number of working groups that make a major contribution to the industry through reviewing and maintaining the *Lighting Handbook* and *Recommended Practices* that the IES publishes. These publications form the industry's specification standards for virtually any conceivable lighting application. Just as with USITT, there are regional/local chapters of the IESNA that allow members to meet with other members of the organization on a fairly frequent basis (often monthly).

In conclusion, anyone considering work in the lighting business has a number of options available to them as they begin to work in this industry. Additional career paths such as those associated with consulting, sales, and technical services are even more options for someone who wants to work in the lighting business. While a number of individuals will be content to work in one specific area of the industry—such as in live entertainment or theatre for much of their careers, many more enjoy moving between a variety of specialties within the lighting profession. In most cases, those who become lighting designers begin their careers in the more technical roles of the profession and later grow into the role of lighting designer. This often follows a combination of education and apprentice-like experiences as one moves along the path to becoming a lighting designer. Though the majority of lighting professionals are employed in positions that provide support for lighting design, with experience, a good work ethic, and the right network of contacts there are ample opportunities for an individual to establish themselves as a lighting designer within any of the fields that have been previously discussed.

For Further Reading

Geraghty, Katie (Certification Director). *ETCP Candidate Handbook (Entertainment Electrician)*. New York: Entertainment Services and Technology Association, 2006.

Moody, James L. *The Business of Theatrical Design*. 2nd ed. New York: Allworth Press, 2013.

Watson, Lee. *Lighting Design Handbook*. New York: McGraw-Hill, 1990.

CHAPTER 15

TRADITIONAL AREAS OF THEATRICAL DESIGN (DRAMA, DANCE, OPERA, AND MUSICAL THEATRE)

LIGHTING DESIGN, LIKE any other design discipline, needs to be appropriate for a given situation. In theatre, we often make reference to **conventions,** or sets of rules or practices by which we create theatrical presentations. One example of a theatrical lighting convention that most people are familiar with is the use of blue light to indicate night or darkness. This effect is rarely seen in real situations outside of the theatre, but is a method in which an audience can see in the dark. Audiences are usually very accepting of most conventions that a production team might establish—they just need us to remain consistent once we establish a particular set of ground rules for a production. While there are occasions when a convention might be changed for dramatic effect, it is usually better to establish the conventions early in a performance and to use them consistently so that the audience can buy into them and become engaged in the show. The longer that we take to establish these rules, the longer an audience will be left to try to figure them out. In the meantime, they might miss other information that is essential to their understanding of the performance. Likewise, if we choose not to follow our conventions, audiences may struggle with how to process the information and can become confused. Once confused, they may get frustrated or lost, and might again break their engagement with the production. Often, good productions can be separated from mediocre or poor ones simply based on whether or not the conventions have been adhered to.

One of the most important issues that any designer needs to consider relates to the fact that every type of performance has a given set of qualities and conventions that are characteristic of that mode of performance. Some of the more common qualities that can be associated with a particular event refer to the type of action, visibility of the performer, presentation style, subtlety of cueing, transitional mechanisms, and overall performance mode that an audience expects from a given form of entertainment. These qualities are often related to the conventions that are expected from or associated with a particular type of event. In this chapter I present information related to lighting more traditional forms of entertainment. These performance events have pretty much been around since the inception of theatrical lighting—in most cases even before—and include drama, dance, opera, and musical theatre. Each of these specialties are discussed in the following pages with regard to conventions that make each area unique, special issues or considerations related to lighting each type of event, and several specific techniques for lighting these events.

While each of the upcoming sections presents a number of guidelines for lighting a given discipline, there is no such thing as a universal approach to lighting design that will work 100% of the time. There will always be exceptions to any common practice: what worked in one situation may not be at all appropriate for another. Lighting is relative, as is the overall style of a production, and every event needs to be lit based on the specific needs of a given show and concept. On the other hand, the overall approach to lighting any of these events will not vary that much from one specialty to another: the general design approach that was presented in Part Three can be used and modified for each of the disciplines that are featured in the rest of this book. While I know many lighting designers who work predominantly in a single discipline, most designers work within several, if not all, of these areas on a fairly regular basis. Each year I typically light several dramas, one or two dance productions, and a few more musicals or operas. It is rare for a lighting designer to work exclusively in a single discipline unless they are on a company's permanent staff and unable to complete projects outside of that organization. However, most of us do have one area that we tend to acquire a reputation in—for myself, this is in musical theatre and opera, where I do the majority of my freelance designs.

LIGHTING FOR DRAMA

Drama accounts for the majority of traditional entertainment and is most commonly associated with plays. Even within drama there are a variety of genres of playwriting and dramatic production. Each can be associated with specific production styles and conventions that are considered acceptable for that genre. The most common genres that most people are familiar with are **comedy** and **tragedy. Docu-drama**, **farce**, and **melodrama** are several other popular genres of plays, each with characteristics that are considered unique. I must emphasize that there is no single approach to lighting that will always be correct for every script or genre of production. In reality, there will be a variety of design solutions that will be completely acceptable for a production: some will be better than others, some may even be great, and others may be unacceptable and can actually fail. Most of the design approach presented in Part Three of this book was written from the perspective of designing primarily for dramatic productions; that information is not duplicated here. However, there are a number of ways in which this process can be refined so that it is more applicable to the production of plays (as opposed to musicals or other genre of dramatic productions), which focus on the performance of a script. The following sections address some unique considerations related to the production of plays and introduce several design solutions that are relatively good guidelines for lighting plays and other dramas.

Performance Considerations

There are several performance qualities that are unique to dramas. Most noteworthy is the fact that the predominant mode of presentation is through dialogue. The performers themselves are major elements of the presentation, and what they say is critical to an audience's understanding of a play. The audience must be able to hear the actors to follow the storyline, make observations about character relationships, and understand the themes, meanings, and motivations of a play. An audience tends to have a more difficult time hearing if they can't see a performer's face. This condition goes back to a basic psychological phenomena: involving a second sense (e.g., sight and sound) allows an individual to observe and understand more information. When this principle is applied to theatre, sight and sound are found to be directly connected to the understanding of an audience. A major requirement for lighting most plays therefore relates to establishing enough visibility that the audience can easily observe the performers' faces. In addition to reinforcing the verbal elements of the play, increased visibility allows nonverbal communication such as facial gesturing to become a more significant element of the communication between a performer and an audience. The less physical action demanded by a play and the more that it is based in dialogue, the greater the need for good visibility. On the other hand, just maintaining visibility can lead to a design that doesn't add anything to the theatrical experience. A design that simply provides general visibility is often perceived as being boring or uninspired and will often fail to make any real contribution to the overall production. On the other hand, lighting shouldn't bring unnecessary attention to itself either. Lighting cannot upstage the action of a play—if elements of the design take an audience out of the world of the play, that, too, is a disservice to the production. One school of designers even claims that the best lighting should go unnoticed by an audience. My personal feeling is that such lighting often fails to add anything to a production and that a designer should strive to use their lighting to enhance a production rather than to simply illuminate it. The secret to good lighting is in creating an appropriate environment for the production, which can at times become as important as simple visibility (if not more important). The argument of **selective visibility** (Chapters 1 and 10) should be a major consideration of any lighting design because it relates to the specific needs of a production.

Production style is also a major consideration in determining the overall success of a lighting design for a production. The most significant element of style is the degree of realism with which a play is presented. Chapter 9 presented a fair amount of material regarding production style, and you should recall that an overall principle guiding the definition of style relates to placing levels of realism along a scale. While **naturalism** is an extreme form of realism, **abstraction** or **stylization** are at the opposite end of the scale. In drama, the range of production styles can be extreme, and while some plays are better performed in a very realistic fashion, others are meant to be dramatic and heavily stylized. Much of the determination of an appropriate performance style for a given script is based on the genre that the play is associated with. Comedy is produced differently than tragedy. In addition, issues such as when a play was first written, the writing style of the playwright, and any traditional approaches of producing a play start to define the degree of realism with which a production will most likely be produced. The production team's definition of realism also defines many of the conventions and expectations that an audience will need to accept for a given production. These expectations—and whether a design team chooses to accept, ignore, or experiment with them—often determine the success or failure of a production right from the start of the design process. While taking chances on ideas that lie outside the normal conventions can lead to innovative productions, this more commonly results in audiences having problems understanding the reasoning behind the choices and intentions of a production team. As a result of that misunderstanding, the audience fails to connect with the play. Trying to present a naturalistic production of a Shakespearean play is probably not a good choice simply because of the unnatural speech patterns and stylization demanded by the Shakespearean dialogue. In addition to writing style, there are a number of other elements that help define a production: acting style, directing style, visual style, and period style all bring specific qualities and conventions to the overall style of a production. While general qualities and conventions can be associated with the major genres of theatrical production like comedy or tragedy, further expectations and conventions are typically associated with more specific artistic movements like farce, melodrama, impressionism, expressionism, absurdism, etc. In all cases, the lighting needs to take on specific qualities and conventions that reinforce the other elements of a production.

Design Techniques

Visibility is a major consideration in lighting a typical play. Through selective visibility, a lighting designer plays an essential role in allowing an audience to see what is needed for their understanding of a play. If a lighting designer fails to do this properly, issues such as fatigue, eyestrain, restlessness, and a lack of communication can affect how an audience is engaged in a play. The best chance for providing a successful lighting design relates to developing good overall area lighting systems that can deliver an acceptable amount of visibility for each member of an audience no matter where they are located in the theatre. Such systems must work for audience members located in the farthest balcony as well as for those located in the center section of the orchestra seating area. Likewise, in facilities like arena or thrust theatres, visibility must be accomplished for each of the different audience perspectives. Chapters 9 and 10 presented a number of techniques for producing lighting systems that could provide general illumination for a proscenium stage, and Chapter 13 expanded on this to include solutions for thrust and arena stages. While some of these techniques, like the **McCandless System,** are quite specific in approach, others are more flexible solutions for lighting an entire stage. These techniques for accomplishing general visibility are often modified by designers based on their creativity and the specific needs of a production.

It is critical for a lighting designer to learn what lighting conventions are associated with a given performance style and genre of drama. The presentational style required for an expressionistic play with saturated colors, shadows, and harsh angles will be completely out of place with a naturalistic play such as *The Miracle Worker*, which chronicles the life of Helen Keller. It can become challenging when a precise production style isn't defined by a director or production team and the lighting designer must venture into creating their own conventions based only on the needs of a particular script. However, in many ways, this is what good lighting design is all about—creating an appropriate response to a given script and concept. Once the general visibility systems have been laid into place, the designer can go on to refine a design based on the specific needs of a production. A relatively safe approach to lighting plays is developing the area systems first, lighting specialty areas and scenery second, then layering on top of these the accents and specials that are based on motivational elements like practical light sources or light entering from windows or doorways. Final touches include adding accents based on mood, specific actor specials, various specific effects, and any other needs of a play.

In general, the design choices for lighting of plays or dramas are more subtle than for other forms of entertainment. The good visibility required by the majority of these productions generally calls for moderate to bright intensity levels, less saturated colors, and an overall use of more conservative lighting angles. In terms of absolutes, lighting levels for a well-illuminated scene are frequently somewhere in the 100–150 footcandle range. In reality, we often use levels much lower than this: visibility is relative; it's more of a function of contrast between intensity levels for different areas of a stage. For the majority of the performing arts, perception of intensity is much more important than absolute intensity levels. Cueing for plays also tends to be less dramatic and often involves transitions that may be barely perceptible to an audience. Subtle shifts of focus and mood are popular in lighting this type of entertainment. These productions also tend to be lit from a more naturalistic perspective than other forms of entertainment lighting and are often grounded in the use of **motivational lighting** and **motivated** light sources. As a play becomes more stylized, the lighting elements become more stylized and take on qualities that are less subtle, more dramatic, and have fewer connections to motivational elements. In the end, it is the appropriateness of the design decisions and how they mesh with the other elements of a production and concept that will in many ways determine the overall success of a given lighting design.

DANCE LIGHTING

Dance is unique in that the entire body of the performer is used to communicate a message to an audience, and dialogue (if there is any) plays a minor role in a performance. The story is moved along by movement and music. Some dances are short and can be performed in a space of 3–10 minutes, while others may contain a number of movements and can take several hours to perform. In ballet, dances are often used to tell a complete story. Famous ballets like *Peter and the Wolf* and *The Nutcracker* are popular throughout much of the world, and most people over the age of 10 can probably recall the basic plot and outcome of the stories that these dances tell. Almost all dances and their related **choreography** tell some sort of story while creating a performance event for an audience. In dance forms like modern dance, the story may not be as well-defined as in ballet and may become more representational of particular feelings or expressions—but these, too, are often constructed in some storyline fashion.

Performance Considerations

Because the emphasis in dance is placed on the body and not on the voice, as in drama, communication of themes, character relationships, and plot are of a very different nature than when performing a play. The choreography becomes the manner by which the story is presented to the audience through gestures, positioning of a body, movements, and the relationships that are created between performers. This broader, more dramatic quality of performance requires that the lighting be modified to allow for good revelation of a body's form and that a more modeled/sculptural quality ultimately be present in dance lighting. Side and backlight are important to performing this function. This also leads to a less subtle performance event that by its very nature is more stylized. A lighting designer is often free to use a much wider variety of angles and colors as a way of creating flexibility in a dance design. Also, mood, emotional responses, and dramatic images are often major elements of these pieces. At the same time, lighting is often the only visual element (other than the performers and their costumes) that is designed for many dance events. Lights are usually cued to change both frequently and more dramatically as a means of enhancing a performance. In addition, a variety of spectacle elements

are often associated with this type of lighting. Use of lighting to change mood, create isolation, provide texture, and direct focus are just a few of the more important functions that lighting typically performs in dance designs.

Dance, like drama, also contains different forms or genres. Each can often be associated with a particular style of performance. The work of Mikhail Baryshnikov's classical ballet is very different from the work of Jerome Robbins (ballet and musical theatre) or Michael Bennett and Bob Fosse's styles of musical theatre. This holds true of not only the performers and choreography itself but also of the visual style in which a dance is presented. Lighting, as well as the other design areas, is shaped by the demands of a dance genre. Conventions that may be appropriate in one type of dance may be inappropriate for another type of dance. Several unique genres of dance include ballet, modern dance, ballroom dance, spectacle/entertainment dance (tap or jazz), and ethnic dance (based on customs or regional qualities). The flashy lighting of a Las Vegas revue or *Follies* production will be quite different than that of a ballet. Ethnic-based dances and companies like *Ballet Folklorico* will be different from ethnic-based dances of other nationalities or cultures (i.e., the Indian dances found in the Little Clay Cart production that is illustrated in Figure 15.1). Even within a given ethnic grouping, style can vary considerably—an example being the simplistic overall presentation of clogging versus the highly spectacle presentation of clogging that has become famous through the work of Michael Flatley and his *Lord of the Dance* and *Riverdance* programs.

Another unique consideration of dance performance relates to the manner in which a group of individual dance pieces are presented to the public. While there are productions such as ballets in which the entire event is based on a single story, the majority of dance

Figure 15.1 A traditional Indian dance in a production of *The Little Clay Cart*. Despite good overall visibility, there is a predominance of sidelight on the dancers and a brighter spotlight on the performer at center stage. At the same time, the musicians are kept in lower background lighting.

programs are presented as collections of different pieces that are performed together in a single event. A typical dance concert or recital often contains a half-dozen or more individual dance pieces in both halves of a two-hour program. There have been occasions where I have personally lit up to 30 different pieces for a single concert. A variety of dance styles are usually represented by these programs because it is typical for the majority of the pieces to be choreographed by different choreographers. Due to this, the lighting must have a large degree of flexibility so that a designer can develop a unique creation for each dance. The best way to achieve this flexibility—while keeping the changes between the dances manageable—is with the use of **repertory light plots.** The key to successful dance designing is in finding ways to use the same tools of the plot over and over again while adding some flexibility for initiating changes that will create unique images for each dance. This is particularly true in the rep plots used in festivals that present the work of numerous companies and performers over an extended period. Recoloring and refocusing form the two most common methods of adding flexibility to these plots. A more extensive discussion of repertory lighting was presented in Chapter 13.

One final consideration of dance lighting lies in the extensive touring that dance productions are associated with. While some dance companies may have their own resident theatre, most rent theatres for a limited time based on a week or two of performances several times a year. Even if a company is associated with a home theatre, most tour on a regular basis. This means that a lighting designer must design a plot that not only addresses the many needs of the dances contained in a company's repertory, but also is capable of touring and being set up and struck in a very limited amount of time. Dance companies are notorious for conducting tours that operate primarily on a **one-night-stand** basis, and the lighting designer associated with such a company must be especially adept at making changes and going with the flow. Working fast, making quick evaluations of a space, being flexible, and committing to decisions that allow a performance to go up in a safe, efficient manner, on time, are important traits of a lighting designer working in dance. They must also be able to do this without compromising the artistic quality of the event in any significant manner. A common schedule for many dance tours involves loading a show into a theatre between 8:00 and 9:00 a.m. (hang and focus), writing and tweaking the cues so that the stage is ready for a spacing rehearsal in the late afternoon, presenting a performance at around 8:00 p.m., and then striking the show and being on the road again by midnight. This is repeated several days a week and often contains back-to-back performances in different cities with several hundred miles between each venue. It is also very common for a lighting designer to function as the stage manager or even technical director

for these companies, most often **calling** their own cues or shows.

Design Techniques

Probably the most important element of dance lighting lies in revealing the form of the dancers. This leads to a strong emphasis on side and back lighting in light plots that have been developed primarily for dance production. Front light should still be worked into the plot because facial expression can remain an important element of some dances. However, in most cases, front washes tend to be used predominantly for softening some of the severe shadows created by the side lighting elements of the plot. Due to the emphasis on side and back lighting, many designers attempt to provide as much variety in these angles as possible. This happens by providing a number of both angle and color choices from these basic directions. In a typical dance plot, two or more full-stage color washes (preferably a warm and cool) are provided from each of the primary lighting angles. This typically includes the following: straight front, both front diagonals, both sides, downlight, and backlight. Since revelation of form is so critical, designers then go on to develop a variety of side lighting angles for the stage. These typically include washes from a high angle from the offstage ends of the electrics (**high-pipe-ends,** or **HPEs),** medium **sidelight** (from **booms** or **ladders** 8–16 feet off the deck), **mids** (about head height), and **shins** (within a foot or two of the deck). In touring situations, the booms may be replaced by **dance towers** (a variation of vertical trussing), which provide a relative permanent manner of mounting the sidelight that is easily transported from one venue to another. Figure 15.2 illustrates a simple repertory dance light plot. If possible, two color systems are used in each of the higher side-mounting positions, while flexibility is created in the mids and shins through regelling them between each piece in the program. A short break of several minutes is often given between each dance so that the dancers can change into new costumes as the electricians regel the shins and mids for the next piece. To make the process even simpler, lighting designers are now often placing **scrollers** or luminaires with other color-changing capabilities in the shin and mid positions. Regardless of how or where the sidelights are mounted, it is important that the light spreads evenly across the stage and that there are no holes or shadow zones between each of the leg sets. It is just as important that no hot spots are cast on the performers as they enter the stage. These conditions can usually be avoided by making sure that the booms are positioned far enough offstage that the light can open up and fully illuminate the dances as they enter the stage. Making sure that the beamspreads of the luminaires are large enough to cover the area between the legs is a second consideration that will help a designer avoid

Figure 15.2 A basic light plot for dance

holes and hot spots in the sidelight. A final issue relates to the need to consider a higher overall focus for lighting dance. This is due to the **lifts** that take place throughout a performance. Sometimes lifts will be confined to specific locations and can be covered with specials, but if done throughout the whole space, it is better to cheat the focus of most of your instruments a bit higher than normal so that the dancers aren't lifted out of their light.

Lighting designers and technicians should also be aware of several unique precautions that are often taken to help guide performers and protect their safety. The first is marking and glow-taping each of the booms to protect dancers from running into these units as they exit the stage. Generally, a couple pieces of glow-tape placed on each edge of the gel frame clips/holder in the mids and shins will prevent performers and crew members from striking these instruments. If boom bases are used rather than flanges, it is also wise to tape out or mark these as well. Second, in ballet and several other areas of dance it is important for a dancer to be able to **spot** or determine very quickly which direction they are facing. This can be especially hard when performing the fast pivoting movements associated with many dance forms and being surrounded by a number of sidelights. To help orient the dancers, a small low-wattage lamp (usually red) is placed at the rear of the auditorium on the centerline of the theatre. This lamp, called a **spotting light,** is left on throughout the entire performance

and is used to help the dancers spot front and center when making many of their twirling moves.

Since dance is based on movement, cueing is also based on movement—a lighting designer must completely understand the choreography of any dance that they are lighting. Since there is no script, a designer must find a way to become familiar with the movements and stage positions of the dancers, and recording or tracking them. Most of us have developed variations of dance notation that allow us to draw schematic diagrams of the performers' movements. While some designers use classical dance notation and symbols that are fairly universal to choreographers, many of us with limited dance training have devised our own methods of documenting these movements. Several examples of blocking notation were introduced in Chapter 9. In the end, all that is really required is that you understand the system for yourself so that you can have a meaningful discussion with the choreographer and can place the cues properly. When the lighting designer must later perform the role of stage manager, this notation becomes an especially important tool for calling a show. In calling a dance, a designer must be extremely sensitive to the timing so that the transitions are perfectly synchronized with the performers.

Just as important as revealing form and providing a variety of color and angle choices is being able to isolate portions of a stage and to draw focus to different dancers at various points throughout a performance. To accomplish this, many of the wash systems discussed earlier are broken down into channel assignments that will allow a designer to isolate different areas of the stage. While in an ideal situation every luminaire in a system would be controlled by a separate dimmer, this is rarely possible due to the massive number of dimmers that would be required to light even a moderately sized stage. Instead, designers usually combine several luminaires of a wash system together onto the same dimmer to economize on the number of dimmers that are required for a production. These groupings allow a designer to isolate the stage into regions or areas that are based on the movements of the dancers. While some systems such as a front wash system may often retain individual control of each luminaire (in effect creating a special for every stage area), most lighting units are combined in a variety of ways that follow the movements of the dancers.

Several of the more important grouping patterns that are worked into virtually all dance plots include **planes, corridors,** and **diagonals.** Planes form pathways across the width of the stage and are located between each set of legs throughout the depth of the stage. This allows a designer to limit the lighting to a single row of dancers at a given stage depth or to light dancers differently when they are placed in different planes. Many designers also refer to planes as **zones** and reference each zone by its relative location in stage depth (**in-one** being the plane closest to the audience and farthest downstage, **in-two** being the next one upstage, then progressively up to **in-three, in-four,** etc.). Corridors follow movement patterns that form a narrow pathway extending from an extreme upstage position to an extreme downstage position. These allow a designer to isolate movement patterns across the width of the stage (i.e., dancers can be treated differently in stageleft, center, and stageright positions). The last of the major groupings, the diagonals, form diagonal pathways that extend from the extreme downstage corners to the opposite upstage corners of the stage. These groupings, along with a series of generic specials, often form the heart of a good light plot for dance. Figure 15.3 provides illustrations of these movement patterns. Several additional generic specials that are often included in a dance plot include both a wide and narrow downlight at center stage, downlight specials at the quarter or third lines and centerline along the downstage portion of the stage, and tight front specials in these same positions. Not all designs make use of all these specials or groupings, and in many cases additional systems can also be introduced to the plot based on the needs of the designer. For instance, I often like to include several full-stage gobo breakup washes within my dance plots. These add variety to a designer's toolbox for lighting dance pieces from a repertory plot. On top of all of this, individual specials are added based on the specific needs of the pieces that are being lit.

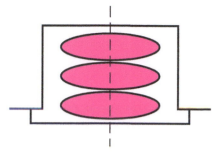

Figure 15.3a Dance control and grouping patterns. a. Planes

Figure 15.3b Corridors

Figure 15.3c Diagonals

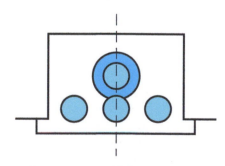

Figure 15.3d Center stage (tight and wide down specials) and other generic specials (down and front)

Because dance usually requires that the stage be kept as open as possible, scenery is often not incorporated into many of these productions. One common exception to this is ballet, where the scenery is still quite limited. When scenery is included, it is typically two-dimensional and comes as painted elements that are hung in the form of drops and wing and border sets. Any three-dimensional scenic elements required for these performances are almost solely confined to small units and props such as furniture pieces that are placed around the perimeter of a dance area. The majority of dance productions make use of no scenery at all and are designed against a neutral background. This background is typically either a set of black maskings and **traveler** drape or a **cyclorama (cyc)/skydrop**. The cyc provides a canvas for creating a variety of lighting effects through projections and color washes that function as key ingredients for creating unique images throughout a dance program. As a means of creating even more variety, many designers like to place a black **scrim** directly downstage of a cyc and any of its lighting (such as a ground row) so that the stage can be easily changed from a colorfully lit cyc into a more formal space with a black background. The scrim also helps prevent unwanted reflections from bouncing off the floor onto the cyc. Even recent Broadway hits like the revival of *Chicago* (Figure 15.4) employ these more simplistic staging conventions and make heavy use of a cyc.

Since dance lighting doesn't necessarily require strong visibility, a designer can often be more expressive and dramatic in the way in which they light a piece of choreography. Mood often plays a strong role in the design, and many times the music (if there is any) can be used as a clue for developing an overall emotional response to a dance. Be forewarned that the music may also be chosen to work in direct opposition to the movements of the dancers. Regardless of the role of the music, conversations with the choreographer and your observations of rehearsals will provide a means for correctly interpreting the meaning of a dance and what the lighting should contribute to it. As a further tool to understanding a dance, I am often provided a video of the dance(s) in rehearsal when I am not in residence

with a company. This, along with my conversations with the choreographer, helps me to develop an effective plot and cueing of the piece even before I am brought in to complete the final elements of the design in the theatre (focusing and actual cue writing).

The illumination of a performer's face often isn't as important in dance as it is in drama, and this can allow the lighting designer additional freedom. More contrast can be introduced into these designs, and gobo washes may be added to bring additional interest and texture to a lighting design. On many occasions the patterns are focused directly on the performers and include full-stage washes. In those cases where facial expression is important, additional light can be added to bring further illumination and focus to the featured dancers and their faces. Additional light can come from either picking up the levels of the general lighting systems or preferably through placing additional light onto just the featured performers by using specials or other techniques. In ballet this is often done through assigning followspots to the featured performers so that they are slightly highlighted while the modeling created by the sidelight isn't washed out by bringing up the front lighting systems. These followspots are often used in such a subtle manner that the audience may not even be aware that they are being used at all—what we call running **ballet dim.** While it is possible to create a design that is overly dramatic and intrusive to a dance performance, most lighting designers welcome an opportunity to work in dance because of the additional freedom and creativity that they can bring to a performance.

Figure 15.4 Drawing focus in dance lighting: Broadway revival of *Chicago* (lighting by Ken Billington)

Credit: photo courtesy Ken Billington

Sidebar 15.1 DESIGNER PROFILE

Jennifer Tipton is an internationally renowned lighting designer who designs primarily within the areas of drama, opera, and dance. She is probably best known for her lighting of dance and has lit many of the premier dance companies of North America. Just a few of her dance credits include the New York City Ballet, the American Ballet Theatre, Twyla Tharp Dance, The Paul Taylor Dance Company, and choreographers Mikhail Baryshnikov and Jerome Robbins. Her dance lighting has been further recognized with two Bessies and a Laurence Olivier Award. Her opera designs have also taken her throughout the world and include national credits with the New York Metropolitan Opera, Houston Grand Opera, and the Chicago Lyric Opera. She has lit numerous stage productions over the years and holds two Tony Awards for Best Lighting (*The Cherry Orchard* and *Jerome Robbins' Broadway*). She also is a recipient of

Jennifer Tipton

Credit: photo courtesy Lois Greenfield

the USITT Distinguished Lighting Designer Award. In addition to her busy freelance career, she is an Adjunct Professor of Lighting at the Yale University School of Drama, where several of her former students include lighting designers Don Holder, Christopher Akerlind, and M. L. Geiger. In 2008 she was further honored by being named one of the prestigious MacArthur Foundation Fellows as well as a US Artist Gracie Fellow.

Jennifer received a BA in English from Cornell University but had always been involved in dance. Upon graduation, she began a professional career as a dancer but ultimately transferred her knowledge of dance to lighting when she became a lighting designer. She shares that she actually had no formal training in lighting: "I learned my craft on tour with the Paul Taylor Dance Company from 1963 to 1970 and the craft of lighting ballet with the Joffrey Company as Production Supervisor from 1970 to 1972." Her most significant mentor in her early career was Tom Skelton: "He was terrific. He always pushed me but never farther than I could go without losing confidence." She lit *Celebration: The Art of the Pas de Deux* at the Spoleto Festival in Italy for Jerome Robbins in 1972. This resulted in numerous offers for lighting theatrical productions, some of which led to both Broadway and Off-Broadway. Once again, she learned through "simply doing it." After lighting

the Broadway production of *Le Bete* in 1990–'91 she was asked to light opera and began working in that area of the profession as well.

According to Jennifer:

"Lighting in any discipline asks the same questions and poses the same problems. The challenge is to answer in a way that is appropriate to the production at hand. I try to find a new vocabulary (light landscape) for each thing that I do."

She also feels very strongly that "Lighting onstage is the music of the eye and must follow the same rules of form and structure that music follows. If you establish a theme then it should be developed throughout a piece." What she likes most about lighting for dance is:

"Grappling with the questions that arise about the form and structure of each piece that I do. . . . It has kept me young of mind and very much in love with the art of light. What I like least is the focus . . . probably because it is so critical. It's the one chance you have to do it correctly; if you do it incorrectly there is often not enough time to go back to do it over again."

She considers the most important rule of lighting to be in providing "visibility to tell the story."

When asked to comment on how she remains current she provided the following insightful response:

"I have never worried about staying "current." I use the equipment that I have available to light the production that I am doing in that space. If rental is possible, it may give me more freedom in my choices, but so often the sky is not the limit."

On the other hand, "Of course I do what I can to stay knowledgeable about new equipment, and since I am a teacher, I also learn along with my students."

Finally, Jennifer speaks very candidly about how her attitude and passion have helped in providing such longevity in her career:

"When I first began as a designer I was always worried that my interest and passion would not last for my lifetime. I have discovered that by making each thing I do a new experience that I have no need to fear. I have had a long, productive, and rewarding life working with this mysterious stuff that is the measure of our universe. I feel very lucky."

OPERA AND OPERETTA LIGHTING

Opera is a variation of entertainment where the majority of the communication with an audience is through music and singing. With the exception of an occasional phrase or word, virtually all of an opera's dialogue is presented through song. Opera is almost always associated with a large scale of production. Tragic plots are also frequently found in this form of entertainment. The works of Richard Wagner are especially associated with this grand scheme of production, but other composers like Mozart, Puccini, and Verdi are noted for creating operas that are known for their epic qualities. In fact, many refer to this type of opera as **grand opera** simply based on the extreme scale that they represent. Much of the scale relates to the fact that these productions make use of a full orchestra (which can be more than 100 pieces) and the large number of chorus members (30–50 or more). Because of the sheer number of performers it takes a large venue to accommodate the needs of simply getting all the people on stage. Also, the nature of much of the material written by opera composers tends to call for a sense of epic scale and proportion. The sense of greatness, universal qualities, and conflicts of epic proportion are reflected in all areas of opera design. The costumes are massive, heavily adorned, and textured, and the scenery can be monumental, overpowering, and stylized. It is all "bigger than life," and opera usually equates with a form of entertainment that is created through spectacle. Just as with the other production areas, lighting takes on these qualities and can become a major element of opera productions. **Operettas** are a smaller version of operas that are often written from a comic perspective. They tend to have a shorter length, smaller orchestras and casts, and are generally of a much smaller scale than grand opera. Therefore, they also have fewer production requirements. Many of the works of Gilbert and Sullivan are examples of operettas that are produced on a regular basis.

Most opera production is extremely costly not only due to the massive demands of the visual elements of these productions but also due to the special needs of the performers. In addition to the large commitment of paying salaries for the large casts and orchestras to protect the voices of the star performers, an opera can only be performed every other day in order to give these voices a day's rest between performances. Unless there is double casting (which is rare since most audiences come to see a particular performer in a given role) an opera quite often must go **dark** or be without a performance every other night. Most companies avoid going dark by producing several operas at the same time and having the performances scheduled on some form of alternating or repertory performance schedule. Companies like the Metropolitan Opera in New York have operas that have been part of their repertory for 30 or more years.

Opera stars will usually be jobbed in by a company for performing a given role, the company chorus will perform the chorus and minor roles of each opera, and the scenery and costumes will be brought out of storage and once again assembled on the stage. The Metropolitan Opera can rehearse or perform two or three different operas in any given day during its repertory season. This is an extremely large company and there are several different shifts of electricians to complete the usual twice-daily changeovers.

Performance Considerations

Like dance, repertory design is often a large part of working for large opera companies. However, many smaller cities have companies that cannot afford to operate on a repertory basis. These companies typically engage in limited runs of an opera that often last only a week or two. The heart of the company is the chorus, which is typically made up of any number of local company members, while the principal or star roles are usually jobbed in and performed by singers who make an appearance during the last week of rehearsals. There are many opera singers who perform a limited number of roles and make a career of flying all over the country or the world performing these same roles over and over again. This can, and has, led to problems between local directors and those performing these star roles in regard to the interpretation and staging of these local productions. The orchestra is typically formed from local musicians.

While the majority of the performers may come from a local talent pool, the scenery and costumes used by many opera companies are often rented from other companies. This is predominantly due to the massive demands and scale of these designs, which ultimately equate to the exorbitant costs of producing these sets. Most opera companies own only a few set or costume collections that they produce and use for their own productions. Some companies use these to generate additional income by renting the set and costume pieces to other opera companies. While some companies may rent and store a number of their past productions, many find that it is more economical to keep and rent only a few of their best or most frequently used designs from past productions (storage fees are costly). When a company arranges to rent these settings they usually pay a weekly rental fee plus the trucking costs associated with transporting the scenery and costumes to and from the original company. When lighting a production that makes use of rented scenery, a lighting designer should pay particular attention to the floorplans and other documentation that are provided for these designs. A few words of caution: These designs often aren't documented properly, and there can be serious discrepancies between the plans and the actual finished setting. Unfortunately, you often don't find out about these problems until the scenery is loading into the theatre and your electrics have already been loaded and run to trim. In another worst-case scenario, artistic directors have been known to make decisions about renting a set based solely on production photographs that they have seen of the set as it stood in the original theatre, without any sense of scale. One opera company I know was involved in a production of *The Barber of Seville* in which the company rented a beautiful setting from the Houston Grand Opera. The major scenic element was a full-stage turntable with several stories of scenery on it. Unfortunately, the turntable was too big for the stage of the theatre that the company had rented and to accommodate this, platforms had to be added to the pit so that the last several feet of turntable could roll out over the musicians.

The essence of the opera experience is both in the visual and more importantly the musical elements of the performance. The most important element is the singing: this could be a solo as in the case of an **aria,** a **duet** between two lovers who are embracing, a duet or **trio** between different characters in two or more different worlds or time realms, or an entire chorus of more than 100 voices. In each case, the lighting designer has the important task of drawing an audience's focus to that one important voice that must be isolated from the masses. Creating layers of focus becomes an extremely important consideration of opera lighting design. As a general rule, the principals with the aria or duet will always require the primary focus, while the chorus takes on a secondary role and is often lit in a more sculptural and subtle manner—except when the chorus shifts roles and becomes the major vocal and visual element of the staging. On the whole, especially in the epic tragedies, the audience usually only needs to be aware of the presence of the chorus as opposed to being able to see each face clearly. Scenery, although often monumental in scale, needs to be treated as a background. While it should be lit in an interesting fashion, it cannot upstage the rest of the image—which is sometimes a difficult task, since these massive elements are often treated in decorative manners that demand attention. The sense of scale that is found in opera is demonstrated in Figure 15.5. Figure 15.6 provides a light plot from an operatta, *The Pirates of Penzance*.

Opera has traditionally not involved much physical action on the part of the performers. In fact, many traditional opera singers performed their roles by taking an extreme downstage position to simply sing the role (**plant and sing**), while the chorus and remaining characters became part of the background. This practice has changed over the last 20 years. Now many opera singers

Figure 15.5 Scale in opera design: *Don Giovanni* (lighting design by Jeff Davis)

Credit: photo courtesy Jeff Davis

Figure 15.6 A light plot: *The Pirates of Penzance* (Atlanta Lyric Theatre)

receive actor training and incorporate much more physical action into their performances. This trend will continue to produce a more natural performance style as singers who have received this training mature and become more popular in the larger roles.

Two other considerations that are often dealt with when producing opera relate to the use of projections and slides (scenic projections and supertitles). Many scenic designs in opera use large areas of the cyc as a means of creating huge expanses of background for the opera settings. In many cases, these expanses are created through projections. These projections form an important element of these operas, and the lighting designer needs to understand how to vary the stage composition so that the projections are presented in the most successful manner possible. Chapter 8 dealt extensively with projections, and specific information relating to them can be found there. A special type of projection that is frequently used in operatic design are **supertitles.** Most operas are performed in their native language of German, French, or Italian, and the majority of an English-speaking audience cannot understand the lyrics of many operas. Supertitles are nothing more than an abbreviated line-by-line translation of the text projected onto a screen that is located within easy view of the majority of the audience. These screens are typically hung directly above the proscenium opening or in some other prominent location in the house. Several newer solutions involve placing miniature LCD or LED

screens in the backs of auditorium seats, much like the screens that are popular on planes used for cross-country flights. This permits operas to be performed in their native language while also providing a way for an audience to understand the meaning of each of the musical phrases that are being sung at any given time. A lighting designer needs to know if a production will be using supertitles, as well as the location of any screens that will be used for displaying them, so that they can take steps to ensure that spill can be kept off of the screens' surfaces.

Design Techniques

Composers have traditionally not worried about the scenic shifting needs of a production and have consistently asked for large, epic settings that may change several times within a single opera's performance (usually at intermissions). With the need for additional sets comes the need to store them when they aren't on stage. While some stages have wonderful fly, trap, and wing systems, most theatres have much too little space to accommodate all of the storage required by these productions. I know of theatres that hoist scenery up into the wings to gain extra floorspace for storing additional scenery that is no longer required on the stage. Regardless of the size of a stage's wings, they are usually the most common location for storing scenery on stage, which makes the placement of booms and other mechanisms for creating sidelight a problem. To avoid hitting scenery or needing to move scenery around booms, many designers simply move the sidelight to higher elevations, making HPEs and ladders popular mounting positions in opera designs. While many designers like to **deadhang** ladders from the grid to save linesets, further flexibility can be created by hanging the ladders off battens so that they can be flown out of the way while a set is changed and then lowered back in to their working trims once the scenery has passed beneath them. When a company cannot use ladders, the lighting designer's primary source of sidelight may have to be several systems of HPEs. If a lower angle of sidelight is required, designers can often place one or two luminaires on a small boom that is equipped with dollies so that it can be rolled into place as needed (a **rover**).

I already spoke to some degree about creating levels of focus on an opera stage. This is accomplished primarily by setting appropriate lighting intensities to establish different levels of focus within the stage composition. What's brightest will usually receive the primary focus. Other levels of focus can be created by placing progressively lower intensities on less important subjects throughout the stage. Other techniques, such as using the relative sense of color or a variation in lighting angle can also be used for focus control. The huge scale of opera makes this especially important since an audience will often have problems trying to distinguish who is actually singing at any given moment on a 50-foot-wide stage with a cast of 60. Followspots are used quite often to establish the primary focus in an opera. How hard an edge that these are used with depends on how stylized the production may be. However, most followspots used in opera design are subtle, often just adding a bit of an extra glow to the principal singers. The chorus often takes on a secondary focus while the scenery is lit in a fashion that makes it unobtrusive. Use of textures and lighting of a sculptural nature, as in dance lighting, is often desirable for a number of opera designs. The rule, once again, lies in determining whether any specific design choice is consistent with the styles and conventions required by the given opera, the other design areas, and overlying concept for the production.

In situations where followspots are not used, lighting designers have to take precautions to make sure that they know the precise location of every aria and major piece of dialogue delivery. With this knowledge, cues are built where lights are brought up around the area where the performer will be located when delivering the given aria, duet, etc. Many times the general lighting systems are broken down into specific areas that are consistent with the manner in which much of opera has traditionally been staged. One consistent pattern involves placing solos directly at the down center position of the stage and placing duets in which performers do not share a common space or time in positions that would be equivalent to the down center-right and down center-left positions. This translates to an area breakdown that provides isolation at center stage and each of the quarter or third lines, which generally means creating an area layout that consists of an odd number of acting areas spread across the width of the stage. With large stages this would mean developing systems of five or seven areas across the width of the stage. While this can often be less intrusive than using followspots, it takes care in cueing and also leaves the lighting designer at the mercy of the performer, who may or may not choose to remain in their light. At one time opera performers were notorious for changing their blocking and going to areas of the stage that were outside of any light that had been added for a specific moment. To cover themselves, many lighting designers use followspots in a subtle manner so that the performers are covered whether they follow their blocking or not. For an even more subtle use of followspots, designers may place them upstage of the proscenium on a light bridge or other elevated position behind the performers. These positions create a nice rimming effect on the performers and can help separate them from the scenery and chorus. A fairly extensive use of specials is also often associated with opera designs. These, too, can be used to provide the proper degree of focus and illumination for a given area of the stage at a particular moment.

One final issue that a lighting designer must consider when lighting operas relates to the fact that the lighting cues are always set to the music and are therefore placed in and called from the **score**. The score differs from a **libretto** in that the score contains the actual music and orchestration while the libretto contains only the words to the songs or music. While I know designers who have designed in this area without being able to read music, it puts a designer at a real disadvantage if they cannot do so. The cues are set to the music (e.g., two beats after measure 46), the counts are tied to the music's tempo, and even the stops and starts during a rehearsal are communicated through the music (e.g., the second repeat after 97). Another popular manner of noting locations in the score is based off of a numbering system using three numbers. These are: page number, staff number, and measure number and as an example would be expressed as 35-3-4—meaning: page 35, staff 3, measure 4). This understanding of music not only helps a designer during rehearsals but is also extremely beneficial when following a recording of an opera that is in a different language while completing tasks like precueing a show on paper. At the very least, a designer should be able to follow the melody. If you can't follow music, you can find enough information in the libretto to light the majority of the piece, although you might still have some confusion in places of long orchestrations or transitions such as in overtures and large movement sections like **dance breaks** where there is no singing. It will also be more difficult to identify the exact point of musical entrances and cutoffs.

LIGHTING MUSICAL THEATRE

Musical theatre is the single largest contribution that the United States has made to the world theatre scene. It is the form of entertainment that has become most often associated with Broadway theatres in New York. Musicals are a mixture of narrative scenes like plays (**book scenes**) that are alternated with segments of song and dance. These musical elements can be small and intimate, such as in the case of a **ballad** or reflective song performed primarily as a solo or duet, or a large **production number** that brings the entire company together in a flashy, high-energy song and dance routine. The traditional form of musicals began in the first quarter of the 1900s but was perfected in the 1940s–'60s. Composers such as Cole Porter, Richard Rogers, Lerner and Loewe, Rogers and Heart, and Rogers and Hammerstein are credited with writing an incredible number of musicals that can all be associated with the American theatre scene. Hits like *My Fair Lady, Hello Dolly, Anything Goes, The Sound of Music, Camelot, Carousel,* and *Oklahoma* are just a few of the many musicals from this era that are produced on a regular basis even today.

In the 1970s, a newer variety of musicals appeared that were characterized by a strong blending of all three elements (dance, song, and scenes) into a powerful production that was tied together through a strong plot or storyline. These musicals had a very strong visual aesthetic and have become known as **concept musicals.** Musicals like *Cabaret, Jesus Christ Superstar, Evita, Gypsy,* and *Sweeney Todd* are some examples of these musicals. Later musicals of the 1980s and '90s continued to grow in scale, becoming known for their lavish production elements, and are typically associated with an immense amount of spectacle. Musicals such as *The Who's Tommy, Cats, Les Miserables, Phantom of the Opera, Miss Saigon,* and *The Lion King* are examples of these spectacle musicals. Multi-million dollar set and costume budgets, flashy song and dance numbers, and expressive lighting make up the important elements of these productions. Most new musicals appearing on Broadway are getting away from the strong reliance on concept and spectacle and are often remounts of older musicals (revivals) or are based on the songs of pop artists. In the latter case, songs that were written for the music industry are simply worked into a theatrical presentation that showcases a given band or pop artist's work. These songs are then linked together in some form of plot or storyline. Broadway hits like *Mamma Mia!, Movin' Out,* and *Jersey Boys* chronicle the songs of ABBA, Billy Joel, and the Four Seasons, respectively. Other musicals based on the songs of popular songwriters include the work of Johnny Cash, The Beach Boys, and Carole King. Current trends cover the gamut and are marked by a shift back to a more traditional format of presenting some form of story, though often with a heavy electronic sound. Several examples of these types of successful musicals include *Wicked, Billy Elliot, Spring Awakening, Disney's High School Musical, The Book of Mormon,* and *Hamilton.*

Performance Considerations

Musical theatre combines qualities from all three forms of entertainment that have been discussed throughout this chapter. During the book scenes, a production will take on a quality more in line with a play, while at other times the production will shift to a form of presentation that is more commonly associated with dance or opera productions. The lighting should also take on these qualities at various points throughout a performance. Spectacle, especially in the area of lighting, frequently plays a role in most musical theatre productions—especially in full company numbers like the opening and finale numbers of an act. The key to successful design in this mode of entertainment is in developing a plot that will allow the lighting to easily shift between these different presentational styles. Musical theatre tends to reflect an overall stylized approach because of its spectacle quality and more theatrical methods of presentation—we don't normally break into song upon losing or gaining a lover or when we discover that the bad guys aren't going to succeed in taking over the town. Scenery and costumes are often stylized, even to the point of sometimes having cartoon-like appearances, and the overall manner of presentation is seldom subtle. Lavish settings, bold use of color, flashy lighting sequences, presentational acting, and exaggerated costumes all make up production qualities that are typically associated with musical theatre. Performers can also step out of the reality of the production and interact with an audience directly. This form of entertainment is seldom created to generate any serious thought and is instead usually presented primarily for pure entertainment. Other elements of this presentational style include a strong association with moving lights and followspots, which may be used in a subtle manner but more commonly are used boldly with no attempt to hide the hard-edged beams that are formed around the featured performers.

Stage arrangement is a major element in the determination of how a given musical will be lit. Musicals are also notorious for the number of different settings that might be required for a production. *Gypsy* requires somewhere around a dozen settings for each of the two acts. There's one sequence where Gypsy Rose Lee enters a time progression in which the setting changes to three or four different stages/theatres in the space of a single production number while she's onstage, performing a striptease throughout the whole sequence! In many musicals, especially the traditional ones, the scenery is designed to work in a series of planes or zones just as in dance. Those scenes requiring the most scenery are designed as full-stage settings and use the depth of the stage, while those that can be designed in a more minimal fashion are staged against drops or backgrounds that correspond with various leg openings or depths of the stage. A setting like Henry Higgins' study in *My Fair Lady* will be created as a full-stage setting, while scenes like the streets of London or the Ascot scene have virtually no scenic requirements and can be set against a simple painted drop that is located near the front of the stage (traditionally in-one). These small scenes are often created to shorten the time required for scene shifts of more elaborate scenes that are set up behind the drop while these other scenes are being performed downstage. In the extreme form, **cross-over scenes,** the performers literally walk from one side of the stage to another, delivering a minimal number of lines or a single song while the scenery is changed upstage of the drop or curtain that is flown in behind the performers. If all goes well, the setting is changed by the time that the song has ended, and as the performers exit, the drop flies out to reveal a completely new scene. Because of these shifting demands, the lighting often plays a significant role in aiding these transitions from one scene to another.

Due to the sense of spectacle associated with musicals, cueing is a major element of the lighting design. Cues are almost always timed to the music and can become as complex as following the actual beats of an orchestration. Cues in musical theatre are rarely subtle and are often anchored in expressing moods and focus for a given stage moment. Rhythm and counts are extremely important to the cue structure of a musical; while a drama may require 80 to 100 cues, a musical will often have 100 to 200 cues at a minimum. I typically design musicals with well more than 100 cues in the first act alone. A production of *Hair* that I designed in the early 1990s had more than 600 cues—without even counting any of the chase/effects cues or the fact that moving lights were not part of this design! In designing dramas, there is often plenty of time to tweak a cue between the time that it and the next cue are executed, but this is seldom the case in musical theatre. When correcting a single cue in a musical you may find that several subsequent cues have passed you by. Because of issues like this, precueing and making efficient use of tech time are especially important elements of lighting musicals. In many ways it can get you through the cueing process successfully and with a minimal level of stress.

Design Techniques

Many of the principles for lighting a musical are based on the techniques used to light dance productions. This is predominantly due to two issues: first, the dance elements of a musical are best lit from the same perspective as a dance, and second, musical theatre staging is traditionally organized into a zone structure that is used to support the shifting scenic elements of a production. The multiple settings and relatively flat approach to scenic design with drops and cutout scenic pieces allows booms to be placed fairly easily between each of the leg sets, while isolation is created between the zones by the layered scenery that defines each plane. While some designers may add a layer or two of general lighting systems based on a variation of the **McCandless Method** to create a more naturalistic lighting for the book scenes, many designers prefer to place their emphasis on the development of a good **zone** or **jewel** approach for lighting musicals. These systems place an emphasis on sidelighting and on the modeling qualities that the dance sequences require. Good backlighting is also essential for separating the performers from their backgrounds. In addition to modeling, these methods allow for better control of spill and focus while also permitting an overall use of more saturated colors throughout the plot. Extra visibility is achieved where needed with followspots. This is particularly true of musical numbers and in the case of picking out the solos or featured performers. In all, this emphasis on sidelight aids in making the overall style of musicals more theatrical and interesting to an audience. The basics of all of these lighting systems were discussed both in Chapter 10 and in the dance lighting section of this chapter. Figure 15.7 illustrates two of the three light plots (the majority of the front of house, or FOH, units are on a third plot) for the 2001 University of Georgia production of *The Who's Tommy*. As an added element of spectacle, many lighting designers are also incorporating automated lighting into their musical theatre designs. At times, these are used in a subtle manner, but often they are being used in dramatic fashions and their movements are choreographed in much the same way that they might be in concert productions. Figure 15.8 illustrates my light plot for a 2016 production of *The Who's Tommy* at the Springer Opera House. Figure 15.9 provides several production shots from each production.

While dance is an important element of a musical, a designer cannot ignore the book scenes and songs that form the solos, duets, and ballads that are also a characteristic part of musical theatre performances. As a matter of overall approach, sidelighting does not work particularly well for these circumstances. Some form of front lighting must be used to bring a more natural quality to the book scenes. As already suggested, front lighting systems are frequently worked into a musical's plot to support the book scenes while followspots are often used to add visibility and focus to characters who are of significant importance at particular times throughout a production.

Because of their frequent use, followspots are an accepted convention of musical theatre and often play

Figure 15.7a Light plots for the University of Georgia production of *The Who's Tommy*. a. Overhead plot

Figure 15.7b Sidelight and set mounts

an important role in most of these productions. They are used not only to create the primary source of visibility on the principal performers, but also to allow the other theatrical elements of the lighting to be carried out more successfully in the background. Regardless of whether followspots are used with a hard or soft edge, or whether they are added to a scene in a subtle manner, they form a significant part of the musical theatre experience. In a full-stage production number where an entire company is singing and dancing, the lights are typically fairly bright over the entire stage, and a followspot may be the only thing bright enough to draw focus to the star at that given moment. I have witnessed shows where the followspots weren't powerful enough to cut through the rest of the lighting, causing the principals to be lost in the crowd that had been assembled on the stage. If a designer is faced with this situation and obtaining more powerful followspots isn't an option, the solution is getting the intensities of the rest of the stage low enough so that a proper balance can be maintained between the followspots and the rest of the lighting (something that may not be possible if the difference is too great). The most common practice for using followspots in musical theatre involves using

Figure 15.8 Light plot from 2016 Springer Opera House production of *The Who's Tommy* (FOH and Overheads only)

Figure 15.9a A production shot from the 2001 University of Georgia production of *The Who's Tommy* a. Holiday scene

Credit: photo courtesy University of Georgia, Department of Theatre and Film Studies

Figure 15.9b Pinball Wizzard

Credit: photo courtesy University of Georgia, Department of Theatre and Film Studies

Figure 15.9c See Me . . . Feel Me . . . .
Credit: photo courtesy Springer Opera House

Figure 15.9d Sensation
Credit: photo courtesy Springer Opera House

them in solos and ballads to bring a sharp focus to the principal(s) while the rest of the lights are dimmed. This dimming is often to a full or partial **blackout.** I prefer to dim the stage to a variation of the existing lighting or some version of a **blueout** rather than a full blackout at these times.

Followspots are frequently used in pairs, and if they are located to either side of the house, the **pickups** should be assigned so that the spots crossover one another at the center of the stage as much as possible—meaning that a followspot mounted in the stageleft house should pick up performers entering from stageright. This provides an angle that places more light on a performer's face for a larger portion of an audience. If at all possible, a pickup by followspots from both sides works best because not only does the light from the two spots cover the front of a performer's face, but also each side of the face will also be lit. While designers will vary the size of spot for a variety of reasons, a typical body shot usually tries to light the performer to about knee level. If there is a natural line, such as the bottom edge of a skirt, this will often be taken as the place to draw the iris to. In the case of a duet where the performers are relatively close together, it is usually better to open the iris up a bit to cover both performers with each of the spotlights. If the pair starts to pull so far apart that the size of the pools get so large that they become a distraction, one spot should shift back to each performer using the traditional cross-over conventions. Most musicals are designed using two to four front followspots, while others, as in opera, may add additional followspots from a relatively steep location somewhere directly to the side and upstage of the proscenium from light bridges or towers erected elsewhere backstage. Regardless of how many or where the spots are located, followspots are a classical element of musical theatre.

Musical theatre tends to be associated with one of the most presentational forms of entertainment lighting, not only because of the manner in which the plot is created or its heavy reliance on followspots, but also due to the way in which it is usually cued. Cueing in musical theatre is typically complex and follows the rhythms, emotional qualities, and momentum of the music. Mood and focus are critical elements of cueing for musical theatre. The look and the manner of transitioning or getting between the different images are all important. More than a few good lighting designs for musicals have been wrecked because the designer was not sensitive to the musical transitions. In addition, a stage manager who can't **call a show** can destroy an otherwise great design. In these cases, either the person calling the cues will need to be replaced or the cueing will have to be simplified. Once again, it is best if a lighting designer can follow the score of a production, but since most musicals are published with a libretto it is still fairly easy for a designer who doesn't read music to cue a musical. If a designer is cueing from a libretto, it is important to find an alternate manner of documenting and cueing any portions of the musical that aren't based on the text (e.g., overtures, entr'actes, dance sequences, and dance breaks). Precueing and the development of a solid **cue synopsis** comprise an extremely important step in the design process for designing musicals. I use a recording of a musical's soundtrack to assist in precueing every musical that I design. The best part of this process is that it allows me to work on sections of the lighting over and over again, outside of the theatre, until I am finally satisfied with the sequences. There are a variety of special cueing techniques that are associated with musical theatre productions. While these aren't limited to musical theatre, they have become characteristic of this type of designing. Sidebar 15.2 provides a description of several of these cueing techniques.

Ballyhoo   A theatrical use of a followspot(s) to create sweeping movements in a figure-eight pattern that pans across an audience or stage.

Blackout   A cue where all lighting intensities are changed to zero in a zero count.

Build   To add intensity to a scene. Often used in association with the building music as a song moves towards its climax and finale.

Bump   A cue done on a zero count.

Button   A dramatic cue (usually with a zero count) that is executed on a specific beat of music. This is usually done to add visual emphasis to the music. Popular examples include shifting the color of the cyc or shifting the lighting's focus with the final cutoff of a song.

Button-in   A variation of button cue that pulls the lights into a tighter focus (e.g., using the button to pull the lights and focus to the principal character(s).

Button-out   A variation of button that opens the focus of the lighting back out to a larger portion of the stage (if not the entire stage).

Chase Effect   A variation of cueing often done as an effect that automatically sequences a series of individual light changes. The simplest chase is a progression of two or three individual looks and would include something like the chasing lamps in a marquee effect. This technique can be expanded to include any progression of cues such as alternating the colors of a cyc.

Fade to Black or All Fade   A cue where all intensities are faded to zero. The count can be anything.

Pile-on   To add additional lights, an effect, or a second cue on top of a cue that already exists on the stage.

Pull Down   In most cases, an overall drop in intensity over the entire stage. Often done to establish focus to a featured performer in a followspot or special. It might also refer to pulling focus to a given performer or subject.

Restore   Returning to a previous cue. Many times variations of a look will be created on stage with a common look separating them. The best example would be in creating a common look for each chorus of a song with different variations or looks for each of the verses.

Rolling Cues   A variation of chase-like effect that creates a repeating sequence such as a series of repeating color changes in a cyc or other wash system. The sequence is typically programmed to roll by itself with predetermined timings for both the duration of the entire sequence and the time between each step in the sequence. Each step is typically timed to change to the beat of the music.

Musical theatre can represent a significant challenge for a lighting designer because of the complexity that these shows bring to the theatre. Speed, preplanning, and efficiency are three important principles for succeeding in this design environment. Organization needs to be done thoroughly and preplanning is central to working in this area of performance. Anything that can be decided or committed to prior to loading into the theatre should be done ahead of time while the designer is fresh. In this way, valuable time isn't wasted making decisions that could have been made earlier in the design process and without the effects of being tired from spending numerous hours in a dark theatre. Speed and efficiency are extremely important for working successfully in this area of lighting design. You don't have vast amounts of time to tweak cues like you might have while lighting a play because the cues come at you so quickly. It is especially hard for an inexperienced designer to make the transition into this field because of the constant threat of becoming overwhelmed. The best method to begin working into this particular area of design is to observe and work with designers who have mastered this design format. Watch how they create a plot, look at how they structure cues, observe their preparation, watch how they build cues, and most importantly watch how they handle stress and work through the tech/dress process of building and tweaking their designs. This can be done from performing any role where you can observe a master designer in action—being a design assistant, board operator, master electrician, or even running a followspot. Regardless of the challenges and stress, lighting musicals can be extremely fun and an immensely rewarding design avenue to pursue. It is also important to note that even though the lighting can form a significant element of the overall spectacle and style of these productions, you still have to take care that you don't upstage the entire performance—to do so is still a disservice to a production. My personal reputation is predominantly connected to musical theatre, and I can honestly say that I find it to be one of the most personally rewarding areas of design that I work in.

For Further Reading

Palmer, Richard H. *The Lighting Art: The Aesthetics of Stage Lighting Design.* 2nd ed. Englewood Cliffs, NJ: Prentice Hall, 1994.

Pilbrow, Richard. *Stage Lighting Design: The Art, the Craft, the Life.* New York: Design Press/Quite Specific Media Group, Ldt., 1997.

Rosenthal, Jean and Lael Wertenbaker. *The Magic of Light.* New York: Theatre Arts Books/Little, Brown and Company, 1974.

Watson, Lee. *Lighting Design Handbook.* New York: McGraw-Hill, 1990.

CHAPTER 16

NON-TRADITIONAL LIGHTING DESIGN APPLICATIONS

IN THIS CHAPTER, I introduce a number of entertainment lighting specialties that employ lighting professionals and designers outside of the more traditional areas of theatrical lighting. Many of these specialties are closely related to theatrical design, with the most significant difference being simply one of scale. Others are variations of entertainment lighting, like concert and film /video lighting, which have a number of unique qualities and techniques as well as specialized equipment associated with them. Finally, there are additional areas of lighting that fall outside of entertainment design where theatrically trained lighting designers are also finding gainful employment. In these areas, the equipment and specific lighting techniques may vary quite significantly from those found in the entertainment industry but the essential principles of designing with light still hold true and form the foundations of how one works in these other industries. Display, architectural, landscape, themed and virtual lighting form examples of these other lighting specialties. This chapter will introduce several essential elements related to each of these specialty areas of lighting.

BRANCHING OUT INTO OTHER FIELDS OF LIGHTING

During the last 50 years, many lighting professionals have come to work not only within theatrical lighting but have also provided design services in a variety of other lighting disciplines on a fairly regular basis. Many of these—such as concert, film/video, and architectural lighting—were mentioned in the introduction to this chapter. The broadening of our horizons helps us secure more design projects. Some lighting professionals dabble within several different areas of lighting design while others establish themselves as specialists in a given niche such as lighting televised programs or special events, restaurants, retail, landscape lighting, etc. Several of the most noteworthy differences between these areas of lighting and theatrical lighting include project schedules, permanence of a design, codes and safety regulations, and financial incentives (both in terms of project budgets as well as design fees). In some cases, the applications are quite similar to those found in theatrical design and the shift is fairly simple; in others there is quite a bit of additional knowledge that a designer must acquire in order to make the transition into these other areas of design (i.e., architectural or film/video lighting).

I have thought for some time that it has become necessary to provide more of an introduction to these disciplines than to simply mention that they are areas of lighting that are alternatives to working in the theatre. In this chapter I provides an introduction to many of these lighting areas as well as a series of sidebars with brief biographies of lighting designers who have established a reputation within particular specialties of the lighting industry (full designer profiles and interviews with each of these and other specialty designers are found in *Stage Lighting: Design Applications and More*). On the other hand, these lighting areas are specialties in themselves: entire books have been written in regard to the specific needs, equipment, and design practices that are characteristic of any given lighting application. The depth of information required to provide a full reference for someone who has taken on a project in these areas is well beyond an introductory book like this and can't be dealt with here. However, in *Stage Lighting: Design Applications and More* I provide a series of follow-up chapters that present additional material on each of the specialty areas that are introduced here. While those chapters also can't present all that a designer needs to know in regard to a lighting specialty, the more detailed information should provide a solid bridge between a designer's theatrical experience and the more specialized materials that are related to a particular lighting discipline. The specific topics of the chapters in *Stage Lighting: Design Applications and More* are characterized by the headings that are found in this chapter: The Music Scene (Revues, Clubs, and Concert Lighting); The Spectacle Performance; Trade Shows, Industrials, and Corporate Events; Film and Video Basics; Display/Retail and Exhibit/Museum Lighting; Architectural Lighting; Landscape Lighting; Themed or Specialty Design; and Virtual Lighting (Renderings, Virtual Reality, Gaming, etc.). In addition to more detailed information, these chapters also provide a listing of more topic-specific references that can be used as a starting point for assisting anyone needing further information on a given area of lighting specialty.

THE MUSIC SCENE (REVUES, CLUBS, AND CONCERT LIGHTING)

The musical areas of entertainment are some of the most cutting edge and challenging yet rewarding disciplines in which a lighting designer may find employment. Production styles associated with these forms of entertainment are commonly stylized and frequently contain many theatrical and presentational elements. Like opera, the scale of these events is often quite large, providing a larger-than-life experience for both the performers and audience. Spectacle plays a significant role in these productions and a designer often has a fair amount of latitude in responding to the performers and their music. The bottom line lies in finding a balance between heightening the experience so that it enhances the performer(s) and their music while at the same time creating a stimulating visual environment that brings interest to a show, especially for patrons who are in the most distant seats from a stage. Lighting is a primary component of most concerts and is a major element of a typical concert experience. Mood and focus play especially important roles in this type of lighting and in most cases the lighting is dominated by relatively bold design choices. Saturated colors, extreme contrasts, distortion, and visual effects are not only common but frequently dominate these performances. Cueing plays

an extremely important role in these designs and it is quite rare for cues to remain on stage for more than a minute or even seconds at a time. Subtlety is relatively rare and the transitions between cues are usually very apparent to an audience—often to the individual beats and tempo of the music. Even though a designer is given an immense amount of freedom, choices must still be motivated by the music and the performing artists. It can be easy for a lighting designer to get swept up in the emotion of a performance and care must be taken to not misdirect an audience's focus by either upstaging the artists or losing track of the rhythmic elements of the production. The top designers who work in these areas usually have some form of music in their backgrounds and a keen sense of rhythm and timing. Bad cueing in these events is much more noticeable than in more traditional areas of lighting and can therefore have a greater impact on the overall success of a performance.

Musical Revues

A **musical revue** is a production based on a collection of songs and dances (usually from a variety of shows) that are performed in much the same manner as in a traditional musical—with the exception that the **book scenes** are removed or replaced with brief elements of narration. Many revues showcase the work of a particular time period or artist, such as a choreographer, director, or songwriter: for example, *Jerome Robbins on Broadway* presents the choreography of Jerome Robbins, while *Side by Side by Sondheim* showcases the musicals of Stephen Sondheim. A revue may also showcase a particular theme or talent. The *Follies* programs that are associated with the show girl productions in Las Vegas or the performances by the Rockettes at Radio City Music Hall form examples of these revues. *Tintypes* is an example of a musical revue based on the music and events of a particular time period (that of Charlie Chaplin and Theodore Roosevelt and the late 1800s to early 1900s) while *Sugar Babies* is a tribute to vaudeville and burlesque performances.

Most revues are presented by an ensemble of performers who take on the many roles represented by the musicals or other source materials that are used throughout the revue. Revues are created as a means of presenting the most memorable song and dance numbers of a particular interest. The storyline, if there is one, is often weak because the primary reason for the show's existence is simply the performance of a variety of song and dance routines, not necessarily connecting them together. This produces a wide range of performances that alternate between ballads and small intimate numbers, medleys that link a half-dozen or so songs together, and large production numbers that involve the entire company (traditionally the opening and closing numbers for each act). The lighting of musical revues isn't that different from lighting traditional musicals since nearly all of the performance elements come from musicals. However, there are several unique issues that a lighting designer must consider in order to create effective lighting for this type of entertainment. First, unit set designs are quite popular for these productions because of the amount of variety that must be included in these settings. It is also quite common to place the musicians or band on stage as part of the show. Due to issues like these, the lighting takes on a more central role in creating the variety that is required for each of the many routines. Lighting is also used as the primary vehicle for creating an appropriate atmosphere or mood and unique image for any given song or dance. Additionally, lighting plays a critical role in moving an audience through the transitions that occur between the musical numbers and cueing becomes a major component of these productions. The **cyc** is also frequently used as a major element of these designs. Finally, visual effects like **strobe lights, blacklight, fog** or **haze,** and **chase lights** also find their way into the lighting of many musical revues.

Nightclubs and Dance Club Lighting

These areas of lighting are unique in that the major focus isn't always on the performer or band but can shift to the audience, which is also usually lit. Contact with the audience and even full audience participation may be encouraged. The primary difference between a **nightclub** and **dance club** lies in whether a dance floor is present and whether or not dancing is encouraged while a band is performing. Nightclubs tend to provide a lounging area with tables for drinks and snacks and conversation along with a stage for the performers. Audience members are usually not encouraged to participate too fully in the event other than through applause and clapping along to the music at various points in a performance. On the other hand, a dance club will still have table and seating areas but the club's activities are centered around a dance floor(s). Dance clubs are meant to achieve the full participation of the patrons, encouraging them to become immersed in the music and dancing. A significant amount of the lighting equipment is typically focused onto the dance floor so that its effects can be played over the dancing patrons. Many clubs have live entertainment performing on a stage that faces a dance floor, which allows patrons to alternate between dancing to the band's live music and recorded music that a DJ plays while the band is on break—maintaining the best of both worlds.

In most clubs, a stage is part of the permanent facility and is equipped with a basic selection of lighting and sound equipment. The artists traditionally provide their own instruments and personal amps, while the venue uses a repertory plot and house sound system to provide for the primary lighting and sound needs of the performers. Typical club lighting rigs provide a series of washes from several different directions (such as front and back lighting) along with some specials and a short-throw followspot. In the smallest clubs or lounges, this may be as limited as having several different colored PAR-38s focused to each member of the band. As clubs grow, so do their lighting rigs—many to the point of providing a reasonably well-equipped rig featuring PAR-64s for several different color washes of front and back light, automated fixtures, and even LED instrumentation. In the smaller venues a house employee typically designs and runs the lighting **on the fly** (or **busking**) while more established bands may have their own lighting designer who uses the club's rig to design the show. While the stages of many bars and nightclubs are lit primarily with theatrical equipment, dance floors are typically equipped with a wealth of specialized gear—virtually all of it relates to effects lighting that is designed to energize and stimulate the patrons. While some of the lighting illuminates architectural elements of the club, the majority is based on throwing moving patterns of light and color not only throughout the venue but most importantly on the guests who are out on the dance floor. Much of this specialized equipment and its layout are discussed in *Stage Lighting: Design Applications and More.*

Concert Lighting

Concert lighting is one of the most expressive areas in which a lighting designer can work. On the other hand, it comes with a number of demands that make it a particularly stressful area to work within. Because of the immense role that a lighting designer plays in the overall success of a concert, most designers are expected to tour with the performers and personally run the console during each performance. Also, the followspots for these performances are usually run by local crew members who are not familiar with the show. In addition, the lighting director typically **calls** or gives instructions to these operators throughout a performance. Even though there are a number of individuals who get beyond their 30s or 40s and can still handle the rigors of touring, once reaching this age, many designers move on to other areas of lighting so that they can settle into a more traditional lifestyle and spend more time with their families. In cases where a designer has been lighting a performer for many years, it is common for the designer to light the show and go out on tour for only a brief period (the **shakedown**) and then turn the tour over to someone else (typically a **lighting director**) who supervises and runs the lighting from one performance to another.

With the lucrative financial rewards of the music industry and strong touring emphasis comes the fact that these shows are rarely produced in properly equipped theatres. This is due to the unconventional artists and audiences associated with these events as well as the increased costs of producing shows in larger venues with more seats to help keep the costs of the individual tickets down. In the early days of concert production, the artists typically toured with only their instruments and amps (much as they had when performing the club circuit) and the burden of transforming a space such as a gymnasium or fair building into a performance venue was left to the local promoter. This frequently resulted in a range of successes (and failures) in terms of providing what was considered acceptable by the artists. As a result, the concert touring industry began as artists started to tour using their own or rented lighting and sound equipment. Lighting and sound companies rose to the occasion in fulfilling the specialized needs of the concert business and placed a special emphasis on developing equipment that was not only portable and could be set up with a minimal amount of effort and time, but which was also reliable and could hold up to the pace and rigors of touring. **Trusses, chain motors, automated lighting, rolling dimmer racks** and **power distributions, PAR units,** and **portable generators** are only a few of the more important innovations that were developed. In fact, many of the most significant innovations of the entire lighting industry can be attributed to solving problems that were initially faced by the concert touring industry.

Once bands began touring with their own or rented equipment they did not compromise their tour itineraries, often maintaining a schedule that required back-to-back performances on a daily basis. Likewise, the shows also grew in sophistication with bands wanting to include the latest technologies in their programs. Many bands averaged five or six shows at as many venues each week. These trends have not changed to this day. Even despite the larger technical demands, the **one night stand** still is the most popular form of concert touring. This puts great demands on the crews in regard to the speed and ease in which the gear can be transported and assembled on a new site for each performance. Speed is everything to the touring electrician; in response, the concert industry developed a number of innovative techniques for modifying stage equipment so that it could be set up, struck, and transported as efficiently as possible. A large degree of the speed of loading-in and loading-out this gear relates to prepackaging the lighting and sound equipment. Much of the equipment is modular, allowing many of the steps for the equipment's assembly to be done prior to moving into a venue. The bottom line in most concert applications relates to speed and flexibility. Conditions are constantly changing from venue to venue; a touring designer must be capable of quickly sizing up a situation and making decisions that keep the momentum of a show moving forward. It is important to learn the difference between when a compromise is necessary and when to push for a specific production requirement, because these are critical assessments that a touring lighting director must be capable of achieving.

PAR-64s for many years have been the workhorse luminaire in conventional touring rigs for much of the concert industry. They are generally laid out in circuits of different colors that wash the entire stage. Most are hung from trusses that are placed directly downstage and upstage of the band. Backlight is an especially important element of concert productions. Specials are also commonly added as back diagonals for the drum kit and lead vocalists or instrumentalists to provide additional accents and focus. Washes may come from the front, back, side, down, or front diagonal. In most cases, the washes are nothing more than a repeatable color sequence of PAR-64s that are arranged along the length of a truss. One unique quality of concert lighting is its heavy reliance on followspots. These allow the principal artists to be given focus at any given time while the rest of the stage is bathed in washes of color or effects. (In many traditional setups, the followspots formed the only lighting that came from directly in front of the band.) Designers may also choose to place followspots in the upstage trusses to produce steep-angled backlight from behind the performers. More recent concert rigs (especially those created for significant performers) often feature many automated lighting fixtures. Today, LED luminaires, lasers, and various forms of projection or video technologies play a popular role in concert design. Figure 16.1a illustrates a fairly traditional concert light plot, while Figure 16.1b is of a more contemporary concert plot where the trusses aren't arranged across the width of the stage. The second plot also features the more contemporary practice of adding automated lights to the PAR-64 washes. The current trend is to place even more emphasis on automated luminaires and effects systems such as linear LED sources that can chase and video displays. Some concert rigs may be composed entirely of automated lights.

Cueing is the most challenging yet rewarding aspect of lighting musical events. A designer has to get their head into the music and know the artists, their music, and their routines as well as they possibly can. The majority of a concert design is based on intuition; improvised lighting is popular even if the designer has already established a general series of cues for a song or entire event (what is known as **busking**). This element of improvisation comes not only from a lighting designer's perspective but also from the band and the nature of the concert experience itself. I've often experienced times when musicians go off on tangents with solos and jams that occurred simply because the crowd provided some good feedback and everyone got a bit more into the show. This is some of the fun of working the concert scene. I've also had experiences where I've had no warning, other than the lead-in, of a band

Figure 16.1a Light plots for concert lighting. a. A traditional plot with upstage and downstage trusses of PAR-64s.

Figure 16.1b A contemporary plot with reconfigured trusses and automated lighting

launching into a song that wasn't even on the **set list** but was pulled from the band's repertory—one that they may not have played in days or weeks. A concert lighting director must be able to go with the flow when things like this happen and should try to enjoy the spontaneity of a performance. If you panic when an extra chorus gets played or a set list gets switched around, this is probably not the business for you. There are also a fair number of occasions where I have been the house man or have run lights for festivals where I had never worked with—or, for that matter, even heard of—any of the music from the bands that I was lighting. In these cases, you learn to use a number of standard looks and effects to improvise along with the band. By not doing anything too drastic a designer can usually run an effective show by simply busking along with the music. When working in situations where the designer is not familiar with the artists or their work, it is good to hesitate a few seconds while a band breaks into another number to evaluate where the song is heading before doing anything too drastic with the lights.

Lighting plays a major role in any concert event, and while there may be a significant amount of stress associated with mounting and running these productions, this career can also provide very valuable and fulfilling experiences for anyone who works in this area of lighting. The pace is fast and the challenges can be demanding, but very few forms of lighting allow the work of a lighting designer to have such a significant role and impact on a performance as that found in lighting concerts. For a much more detailed treatment of concert lighting, I urge you to examine Chapter 2 in *Stage Lighting: Design Applications and More* and then go on to explore Jim Moody's book, *Concert Lighting: Techniques, Art, and Business*. This book, in its fourth edition, and now with co-author Paul Dexter, is one of the primary references for concert lighting and working in the concert industry. Moody is one of the pioneers of concert lighting design and provides thorough discussions and examples relating to his work and experiences throughout this book. Dexter continues this practice and brings the most current equipment and techniques into the discussions.

Sidebar 16.1 DESIGNER PROFILE

James L. Moody

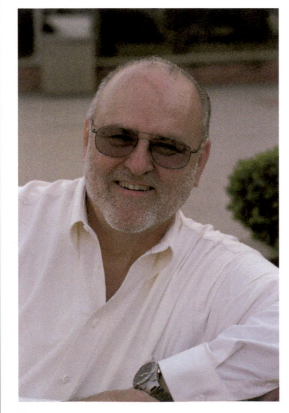

Credit: photo courtesy Beatrice Huguet

James L. "Jim" Moody is Professor Emeritus and Head of Technical Theatre and Design at The Theatre Academy at Los Angeles City College. He is a truly diversified lighting designer with credits in concert, television, theatre, Las Vegas shows and reviews, corporate productions, and film. He has designed more than 250 productions at Regional Equity theatres as well as for a number of college and universities as a guest artist. Jim is considered one of the founders of concert lighting and received the very first Concert Lighting Designer of the Year Award. Several of the concert acts and tours that he has designed include those for America, David Bowie, John Denver, The Eagles, The Fifth Dimension, Dolly Parton, Kenny Rogers, Linda Ronstadt, Rod Stewart, The Supremes, and Stevie Wonder. Also active in television lighting, he has earned two Emmy nominations and one team win for his lighting for video. He served for 10 years as Director of Photography on *Entertainment Tonight* and then switched to *Jeopardy!* and *Wheel of Fortune* for 12 years. He has also lit a number of corporate productions; his client list includes Apple Computer, Sony, Wendy's, The Sunkist Growers Association, Epson, Goodyear, Disney, Mercedes-Benz, Coca-Cola, Federal Express, and Bank of America. He has also designed architectural lighting including the Nevada Stater Museum in Las Vegas, which used the first all-LED lighting system. In addition to the

Emmys, his designs have earned him numerous other awards, including the USITT Distinguished Achievement in Lighting Award, Drama Logue Awards, and IESNA Achievement Awards. He has written many articles for a variety of lighting publications and two books, *The Business of Theatrical Design, 2nd Edition* (Allworth Press, 2013) and *Concert Lighting: Techniques, Art, and Business* (now in its fourth edition—Taylor and Francis, 2017).

Jim holds a BS degree from Southern Illinois University and an MFA in Theatre Lighting Design from the University of California, Los Angeles, and has completed his doctorate in Educational Management. After college, he needed work and began his lighting career in manufacturing as the assistant to the president of a rather small lighting manufacturing company while designing theatre at night. His venture into concert lighting is best told in his own words:

"After 10 years, I left a good-paying job to try full-time professional theatre, but it just didn't pay much. Concerts were new back then and I had a music background, so when I was offered a chance to do one I tried it and liked it. I made a lot of contacts very quickly and started going on the road with bands within the year. My first tour was with Rod Stewart and Small Faces, which had Ronny Lane as the guitarist before he joined the Rolling Stones. My second tour was for David Bowie and the Spiders from Mars on his first American tour."

When asked about how he prepared for working in the concert industry, Jim relates that he had no advanced preparation for concerts because nothing existed at the time—it was a brand-new medium:

"That is why Bob See, Tom Fields, Bill McManus, and I are considered by many as the founders of the concert lighting style. We all helped "teach" each other. The Las Vegas shows came with my concert artists being signed to do shows in the casinos and I went with them."

His crossing into film and television came later

"I worked in LA on non-union shows between tours and built up my knowledge of working in these mediums on the job and eventually got my International Alliance for Theatrical Stage Employees (IATSE) local #600 Director of Photography card. Corporate and Las Vegas shows are so much like theatre musicals that the transition to designing for them was pretty easy."

Once he became a full-time professor, his responsibilities to his department took the majority of his time, but he continues to design professionally, with his work being about 70% theatre, 10% architectural, 10% television, and 10% concerts.

Jim credits two individuals with helping him break into the business. First, Joe Tawil (president of GAM Products), the man he went to work for when he finished college, would become a real mentor and friend to him. Second, Joe would introduce him to famed Broadway lighting designer Julies Fisher, whom he later assisted for two shows: "That was my second big break. Julies is a great teacher as well as designer and really 'trained' his assistants—not just demanded that they go for coffee and pick up the laundry." One of several unique considerations of designing for concerts, as well as for Las Vegas revues and corporate shows, is that a sense of timing (musicality) is more critical than that needed in theatre. Jim claims that working in this area is great training for theatre because of the time pressure that is imposed on these designs: "Theatre now seems to me like we are walking at half-speed because I got used to the much tighter scheduling of concerts." In designing for film and television, he says:

"You have to give up the notion that you, as the Lighting Director, control what the audience will see and accept that the director determines which shots will be used. In multi-camera setups, the DP must allow each of the angles to be lit properly, not just one angle. Film and television lighting also require a heightened awareness of the needs of a director and an ability to be two steps ahead of them. Finally, knowledge of the technical requirements of the media, such as light levels and contrast are a must."

Unique considerations of working in the concert industry relate primarily to time:

"Scheduling, load-in, focus, calling the show, and strike all have to happen in 12–14 hours. Staying on top of everything and total advance planning are some of the keys to a designer's success. Not being afraid to make a decision when things are moving very quickly is another must-have skill."

What he likes most about concert lighting is the immediate gratification:

"Decisions must happen on the spot and the ability to think on your feet is essential. You must never be wed to a single idea. Be flexible and keep a clear vision of what your end design wants to be and then focus on getting as much as you can under the time, space, and financial constraints."

What he dislikes about the business is hardly anything. "Sometimes the inability of a booking agency to layout the tour far enough in advance or incomplete advance work can cause headaches. Worse, dates and venue styles can change at the last minute, such as from an arena to a few mixed dates in theatres. That can cause a situation where your rig won't work as you planned and you have to make quick decisions on what to drop or modify in a design." Jim believes that remaining totally *flexible* is the most important rule to consider when working in these areas: "You must have a plan and that plan must be open enough to have options that have already been considered so that when a change is necessary you are ready." He also suggests being bold: "There is no right or wrong way to light concerts—those who are successful are the ones that take chances."

In closing, Jim shares that

"I am a great believer in learning about *all* areas of lighting because cross-pollinated ideas from other media help make the most creative decisions possible. The added exposure will give you access to more creative tools. Even if you have no desire to work in these alternate media, the broader aspect of knowledge will always serve you well."

THE SPECTACLE PERFORMANCE

The term "spectacle performances" usually refers more to the scale and number and types of effects used during a performance than to anything else. The size of a facility that an event is produced within, the lavishness of its design elements, the size of the budgets, the number of cast members, and the technological sophistication of a show also play into the degree of spectacle. While scale is one of the most common means of attaining spectacle, it is not the sole measure of spectacle. There are many technologically advanced spectacle performances that take place in relatively small venues. The numerous Blue Man Group productions that are appearing in many cities provide examples of these spectacle productions that are often presented in more intimate environments. At the other extreme are huge extravaganzas like the half-time shows for the Super and Orange Bowl celebrations or the opening and closing ceremonies of the Olympic

Games. Spectacle raises the expectations and experience of an audience. There should be elements of surprise and some element of "wow" factor connected with these performances. Selective use of spectacle becomes an ever-important element of designing these events, yet a designer should show some restraint and not go overboard by simply producing one effect after another. Too much **flash and trash** can become nothing more than flashing lights and will fail to make any positive contribution to a performance. In fact, such techniques can have a detrimental effect by creating issues such as misdirection of focus, lighting that doesn't appear to be in sync with a show, or not providing enough variety within a performance. As usual, too much of anything—such as simply panning the automated lights around or spinning gobo effects solely because you can do so—can lead to problems.

Headline Acts

Headline acts are shows built around a given artist(s), typically those who have risen to superstar status. The act may be an individual or a group of performers such as a rock band, and the performance can be mounted in a traditional theatrical venue or in a concert-like setting such as in arenas or stadiums. In many ways headline acts provide a good transition between musical revues or concerts and some of the mega-productions that are examined in the following paragraphs. In many cases, these acts are presented in theatres that have been especially equipped to handle a given show. Some people in the business refer to these theatres as **showrooms.** The casino shows that feature Las Vegas acts like Bette Midler, Barry Manilow, or Cher (for your parents), and Mariah Carey or Celine Dion (for the younger crowd) form popular examples of these productions. The majority of these events are music acts, although magic and other popular forms of entertainment may also be represented in this format. Siegfried and Roy (remember the tiger attack?) along with Penn and Teller are two popular magic acts that perform regularly in casino hotels in Las Vegas. Other popular acts include comedy acts by Jerry Seinfeld, Martin Short and Jeff Dunham (the ventriloquist).Other popular casino cities that produce headline acts include Atlantic City, Reno, Lake Tahoe, and Branson, Missouri. These productions are frequently treated as permanent installations, and shows are presented on a regular basis—often daily, with two shows in a single evening.

In regard to lighting design, every choice should showcase the headliner, even though effects and spectacle are often major components of these shows. In addition, the spectacle elements should not distort or make the artist look unattractive in any way. Although many acts are billed around a single artist, most have accompanying vocalists, dancers or chorus members, and an orchestra that must also look attractive to an audience. At the same time, focus needs to be clearly maintained on the star performer. Followspots and color washes play an essential role in this form of entertainment. Figure 16.2 represents a plot designed for a touring revue of Rat Pack impersonators. Outside of the larger scale and the need for establishing a strong primary focus, most of the remaining elements of lighting these events follow the same principles that concerts and musical revues might use. Some of the larger effects that might be built into these shows include pyro-techniques, elaborate scenic elements, and lifts. The annual Christmas tour/show of the Trans-Siberian Orchestra that is frequently performed in a Las Vegas showroom features not only an elaborate light show, lasers, and pyro effects but also aerial lifts that take two of the lead guitarists out over the audience.

Arena Productions and Stadium Productions

The term "arena and stadium productions" refers more to a physical space for mounting a production than to an actual entertainment event. Once an event grows to a size at which it is no longer profitable to produce it in even the largest theatres, other venues need to be secured that allow for a greater number of audience members. This ultimately keeps the ticket prices more affordable. Rather than spreading the costs over a 3,000-seat auditorium, the audience for a single event can be increased to 5,000, 10,000, 50,000, or more. Much of Chapter 2

in *Stage Lighting: Design Applications and More* deals with concert tours where shows are produced in arena or stadium environments. Once concert promoters had the proper equipment and knew how to produce their shows in arena formats, other large-scale productions like circuses and children's productions (e.g., Disney ice shows and *Sesame Street Live*) also began to move into these venues, using the same techniques that had been perfected by the concert industry. The most popular method of producing these events is by trucking your own or rented equipment to a facility and setting the show up in the arena for a limited period of time. This may be for a single performance or could stretch to two or three weeks. In most cases, the performance period is restricted to only a couple of days and the production spends about a week in a given city and venue. Once again trusses, chain motors, rolling dimmer racks, PARs, and automated luminaires are common elements of these productions. The equipment is usually rigged from the steelwork or superstructure of the building and can be assembled and struck in a matter of hours. A concert in a sports arena on one evening can be followed by a basketball game the next day. In addition to concerts, many ice shows, children's programs, and even televised awards programs are conducted in these arena formats. In general, arena programs are lit with much fewer luminaires than what would be used in a concert, and more care is taken to provide a series of washes that cover the performance space in a variety of tinted colors. Throw distances are typically fairly long, which results

Figure 16.2 A light plot for a headliner revue

in the beam angles of many of the luminaires being relatively small. Followspots are frequently used to draw focus and once again form a significant element of these productions.

Stadium productions raise the level of expectation and spectacle still further by providing an even larger venue and audience—audiences of 60,000 to 100,000 people or more are quite common. Events that characterize this type of spectacle include the very largest concert events like The Rolling Stones or Garth Brooks concerts and other special events like the half-time celebrations associated with the Orange or Super Bowl and the opening and closing ceremonies of the Olympic Games (Figure 16.3). Scale once again becomes a major factor that drives these productions. Choices must be bold and a significant amount of the lighting is used to emphasize the bodies of the performers. Washes are commonly used to provide general area coverage for the event, while focus and the lighting of the stars is best done through followspots, often aided with large-format projection screens and live camera feeds using **I-MAG** technologies. These events often contain not only spectacle lighting and performance qualities but also audience participation, pyro and fireworks displays, and even laser shows. In the largest of these events, celebrity performers, hundreds of dancers, and thousands of audience members might participate. These events are nearly always televised and therefore involve yet another layer of complexity.

There are also issues in addition to scale that relate to lighting a production in the exterior environment of a stadium. While inclement weather may become an obvious concern, there are other factors that can actually have an even more profound effect on a performance. It is usually more difficult to light events at dusk through

Figure 16.3 Spectacle production of Vancouver 2010 Winter Olympics opening ceremony

Credit: photo in the public domain (US Army)

twilight than after the sun has dropped below the horizon due to the relative high level of ambient light that exists in these facilities. Deep shadows will form in these venues due to the specific location of the sun, which can cause contrast problems in different areas throughout the stadium. In addition, there are no rigging points in a stadium: all overhead gear must be rigged with either ground-supported systems or some sort of crane device. Mounting luminaires along the front tiers of the seating areas may provide alternative hanging positions. Due to the shortage of mounting positions typically associated with these venues, moving lights have become an especially attractive element for these events because of their ability to move and the fact that their physical parameters can be adjusted with the use of a lighting console. Often, these events tend to be some of the most costly events that we produce.

Sidebar 16.2 DESIGNER PROFILE

Jeff Ravitz has been involved in lighting for more than 30 years and entered the profession through designing concerts. He was introduced to video lighting through both adapting his live shows for a television audience and following his concert clients to light their music videos. His reputation is now based primarily in lighting television studio and live events for broadcast and music-based entertainment. Several notable clients that he has lit for broadcast specials and concert tours include Bruce Springsteen, Cher, Usher, Shania Twain, Rush, and the Superbowl XXIX Halftime Show. His lighting has won awards including a Primetime Emmy Award and second Emmy nomination plus nine regional Emmys. His program credits include comedy specials

for Kevin Hart and Dave Chappelle; the Writers Guild Awards; the game shows *Caesars Challenge*, *Personals*, *Wheel of Fortune* and *Jeopardy!*; ice shows; a specialty scene for a feature film, *The Manchurian Candidate*; and a number of infomercials and other special events. Jeff is a frequent guest lecturer about his art, craft, and techniques.

Jeff holds a theatre degree from Northwestern University but points to 30 years of experience as an important element of his training: "Trial and error, taking risks, learning from mistakes, observing the masters, and endless conversations and debates with friends, colleagues, and teachers are all important to my learning and staying current in the business." After college, he embarked on a theatre career but

Jeff Ravitz

Credit: photo credit: Jeff Ravitz (intensityadvisors.com)]

found that he missed his days as a musician. When an ad appeared in a local paper seeking a lighting designer for a local recording artist he applied and landed the job. He states that, "I had the time of my life combining my theatre, lighting, and music skills and found myself at the ground floor of an exploding new area in entertainment production." After several years, Jeff was exposed to the emerging field of music videos as well as lighting live concerts for broadcasts:

"I watched the crews and production teams that were brought in to create the videos and TV specials for my concert clients and learned much of the process. When it became common to have I-MAG projection of our shows onto large screens for the benefit of the audience seated farthest from the stage I had the opportunity to see the effects of lighting for the camera while I watched the results of the live action compared with the images that appeared on the screens. I got a sense of what worked, or didn't, and developed my own style and standards. With a few lucky breaks and the confidence of my clients, I was eventually given the opportunity to be the television LD (lighting designer) on a few

shows, and my resume and reel began to take form."

Jeff's next break came when he partnered with renowned designer James Moody to form a design firm. Moody had already made the transition from theatre to concerts and then into television lighting:

"Jim often had multiple opportunities (that is to say, he was frequently double and triple booked!), and I had the chance to sub for him on shows like *Wheel Of Fortune* and *Jeopardy!* as well as for sitcoms and newsmagazine shows. Jim is a most generous teacher and shares his experience and knowledge liberally. This partnership brought me to a new level of skill and confidence, and with the purchase of some really good meters I had the impetus to seek work as a lighting designer specializing in televised entertainment."

An event that really shaped Jeff's career was his televised lighting of the Bruce Springsteen E-Street Band reunion at Madison Square Garden. The show was shot in high-definition video, which was new at the time, and they spent a lot of time adjusting the show's lighting so that it was balanced for the camera while retaining the excitement of the original touring design:

"The resulting show was broadcast on HBO and I was honored with the Primetime Emmy for Outstanding Lighting Design along with my tour lighting director, Gregg Maltby. This gave me credibility as a TV lighting designer and I soon began to get more chances to design shows for live broadcasts and to adapt other designers' shows for the camera."

Jeff suggests becoming an active member of professional organizations that serve special areas of the lighting industry when crossing into other disciplines of lighting:

"I have been an avid member of the International Cinematographers Guild, the American Society of Lighting Designers, the United Scenic Artists, and the Illuminating Engineering Society of North America (IESNA). These organizations hold seminars and workshops that allow for person-to-person exchanges of ideas and experiences. I have also taken courses in architectural lighting and read everything that I have time for: trade publications, books, and articles."

Jeff also believes that maintaining a dialogue with your peers is important, from crew members to directors, producers, and senior members of the design community: "Talking to these people and sharing experiences continues an oral tradition of passing information along." Finally, he notes that just *doing* it is the most important way to improve and develop: "Trying out the newest equipment or techniques and doing your best to squeeze the most out of them is the best way to learn and grow."

Jeff shares that the main thing that separates television lighting from theatrical lighting is the wide gap between the sensitivities of the human eye and the camera: "The ability of the eye to simultaneously see many things of vastly different intensities and to assimilate them comfortably into a whole picture is far superior to that of a camera." Another major difference is in the camera's tendency to put the viewer in the front row or even nose-to-nose with the subject:

"The live audience sees a full frame from one end of the stage to the other and a lighting designer draws attention to the most important elements in a way that is similar to how a cinematographer goes from a wide shot to a close-up. However, the closest that a live audience member ever gets to a subject is still a minimum of 20 feet away. Things simply look different and the detail is not the same as when you view someone's face from one foot away as it would appear in an extreme close-up, where you see every subtle shadow. More importantly, the techniques that a lighting designer uses to make things look good, dimensional, and visible in a large venue for a live show create exaggerated shadows and other features that would appear somewhat grotesque if you were to suddenly change camera angles from a wide shot to a close-up. In lighting for the camera, there is much more emphasis on using lighting angles that flatter the face."

He also shares that, in live performances, it is not unusual to allow areas of the stage to fall off into darkness, which can be a problem in camera work. Multi-camera productions must be especially careful in paying attention to the different angles that can be simultaneously captured:

"From a tight close-up to a wide shot, from a view of what is behind the talent to a view of what is off to their side in the far distance—it all has to be considered. That is why we spend a lot of time analyzing the wings in TV production and how they will look in the background of certain side- or cross-shots. We also tell our clients that it is our mission to make the show on the screen appear as close to the live show as possible. But, in order to accomplish this, we also tell them that we will have to make some changes to the live show that might alter the experience for the in-house audience—though they may not even realize it."

Although the technical limitations of the camera can sometimes be challenging, he enjoys the new advantages that the medium poses and states that they have kept his approach fresh while allowing him to cross-pollinate between different parts of the lighting industry:

"There is no doubt that my TV lighting style is greatly affected by my years as a live show designer. I can draw from things that work—or don't—from each area and can then use them to extend my palette and broaden my tool chest."

Dedicated Venues

Dedicated venues are facilities in which an entire performance space has been created around the needs and artistic demands of a particular show or performance group. The best examples of this include the many Cirque du Soleil productions that have been mounted in cities like Las Vegas. These productions cost millions of dollars and months (if not years) to produce. The scale is huge, and monumental production elements like fantasy costumes, elaborate set pieces, and gymnastic apparatuses are characteristic of these shows. An immense amount of time is spent on creating a fully spectacle world around the performers. One of Cirque du Soleil's productions, *O*, is conceived around a playing space that is formed predominantly by a huge pool. Another,

KA, makes use of an immense wall that can pivot into nearly any position and degree of steepness and a pit that extends several stories below the stage. Performers use both of these as elements of the performance. Lighting is unique for all of these productions, and care is taken to produce a design that not only speaks to the individual acts/performers but also connects to the themes of a show as a whole. Stunning visual images have often been associated with these productions. The lighting is very specific, even to the point of adding hanging positions as specifically required by the designer.

Additional Areas of Spectacle

Two final areas of spectacle include events like the fountains used in **dancing water displays** and **aerial shows** in which light is projected into the air and sky. Fountain shows are frequently found in the gardens or atriums of upscale hotels and malls, while aerial shows are often associated with community festivals or celebrations. In both cases, specialized luminaires are used to project light onto the surfaces of either water or clouds (smoke in the case of fireworks) and other large-scale structures such as building facades. Most dancing water displays contain water fountains with a variety of water jets, sprays, and fountain heads to create artistic displays of pulsating water that are timed and choreographed to a musical soundtrack. In order to add more theatricality to the event, the fountains are lit and programmed to change color in response to the music and fountain choreography. In aerial shows, light is played off of clouds and smoke that is produced through fog and haze machines or even fireworks. More sophisticated techniques might include the aerial displays like those associated with an event like the Super Bowl or an outdoor celebration like the rededication of the Statue of Liberty. Just outside of Atlanta, there is a park called Stone Mountain that produces an event that combines choreographed lights, fireworks, and lasers in nightly shows throughout much of the summer. It has the reputation for being the largest aerial laser show in the world. On a more somber note, the memorial that was created for the Twin Towers attacks in New York City, which produced two shafts of light upwards from Ground Zero, was yet another example of aerial spectacle. In this example, two grids of narrow-beamed luminaires were directed skyward in two columns that were symbolic of the former towers. As a final example, the 2017 Super Bowl Half-Time Show made use of aerial lighting effects when Lady Gaga appeared on the roof of the stadium and was accompanied by a fleet of aerial drones that flew towards the stadium and that were lit and positioned to create various aerial displays (i.e., the United States flag and the Pepsi logo).

Trade Shows, Industrials, and Corporate Events

Many professionals refer to productions or events for trade shows and corporate events as **corporate theatre**. The lighting of these events follows design practices that are similar to those used in many other lighting applications. In some cases, such as in trade shows, the designs are more in line with what you might expect for a display or exhibit in a retail environment, while other corporate events are so driven by theatricality and spectacle that they can be compared to theatrical events that rival Broadway shows. Examples include product showcases associated with trade shows and other special events like press conferences, new product introductions, and business meetings. Political conventions (Figure 16.4) also are examples of these types of events. Because many

of these events are conducted in hotel ballrooms and convention centers or arenas, much of the equipment and production practices come directly from the concert industry. The majority of the companies that produce corporate events produce only one, or at most just a few, of these events each year. Due to this, virtually all of the equipment for these productions is rented from local theatrical rental houses. The annual car and boat shows that introduce the latest model cars and boats or the seasonal fashion shows produced by premier clothing designers are examples of these events. Although trade shows and corporate events may be open to the public, many are created and reserved for a select audience (i.e., employees who are members of a company's regional or national distribution system, sales representatives, or members of a specific profession).

Corporate Mentality

Whether lighting trade shows, industrials, or any other type of corporate event, the most important element for working successfully in this type of programming is making the product and its corporate sponsors look as good as possible. Because these events are produced predominantly by sales and commercial representatives, there are several important differences in how a designer is expected to work in this area of production. Probably the most significant difference lies in the fact that your producer is the company and that the people who are responsible for working with the design team often have limited backgrounds in theatrical production. This can lead to a number of situations where decisions are made by individuals who do not understand the ramifications of their choices. The best corporate producers have some background in the theatrical business and know how to be involved in the process while trusting their designers

Figure 16.4 The 2004 Republican National Convention (lighting by Bill Klages)

Credit: photo courtesy Bill Klages

to create the most effective presentation possible. Finding an effective way of communicating with those who aren't versed in theatrical terminology or practices is an important task for any designer working in corporate theatre. Illustrations and photographs are important; they can go a long way toward creating an understanding of what you intend to produce for a particular event. Another issue lies in the question of who is really in charge of a corporate production. While the production team may have worked extensively with an individual or team that represented the company throughout the planning stages of a project, someone further up the executive chain like a vice president or board chairman who has not been a part of the process may come in at the last minute and make demands of the event and its designers. Such situations can be frustrating and can add an incredible amount of stress and expense to an event as designers scramble to accommodate the changes being demanded by these people. I know of corporate shows where designers had to re-color and re-cue significant parts of a production due to revisions in a script or move entire stages and their related lighting rigs to different locations within a venue. I have even heard of an occasion where all of the lighting fixtures and trusses were repainted a different color just hours before the beginning of an event—all on the insistence of a corporate player further up the company ladder.

Corporate image is a final distinction between these areas and designing for more traditional theatrical venues. Where jeans and T-shirts are an unquestioned wardrobe for concert designers, a designer working in a corporate setting must fit in with the clients whom they are serving. While you may dress less conservatively than the typical suit and tie associated with most corporate dress codes, you do need to dress appropriately for the occasion and corporation for which you are working. This often requires a dress shirt and slacks or skirt, dress, or pant suit that gives a professional image. With some clients, this dress code could still include a coat and tie or other business attire. Being well-groomed (with no distracting body piercings or tattoos) is also part of this professional image. The corporate image should be presented at every occasion in which a designer is dealing with the client, which includes not only design meetings but also at all times when you are in the venue dealing with the company and general public. A designer's communication skills should also reflect those used in the business world and are yet another important element of working successfully in this niche of lighting design. Speaking with the language of a truck driver is only going to work with the drivers and crew; it will most likely make a designer look unprofessional when working with clients and other reps who are involved with a corporate event. Professional manners and paying attention to details as well as the client's needs are just as important in a small ballroom event as they are in a large multi-day event that takes place in a large arena hall or convention center.

Sidebar 16.3 DESIGNER PROFILE

Betsy Adams began her lighting career in theatrical design. She is a graduate of Smith College and assisted Tharon Musser for several years in the mid-1980s. She went on to design lighting for a number of regional and New York City productions before moving into corporate lighting, where she is a founding partner of the corporate design/production firm of Blue Hill Design. She continues to be active in both areas. She has notable theatrical credits with The Guthrie, Denver Center, Mark Taper Forum, Arena Stage, and Paper Mill and La Jolla Playhouses in addition to many others. Opera companies that she has designed for include the Seattle and San Diego opera companies, among others. A few of her more prominent clients in the corporate world include Saturn, Pfizer, IBM, Gillette, Ford, Kodak, Canon, and Pepsi-Cola.

Betsy had gained a number of professional design credits at reputable theatre companies across the United States and was well on her way to a very successful theatrical career when an incident occurred that would change her professional life. A company that had contracted her to light four productions folded on the night before she was to begin techs for the first production. This left her with a large hole in her immediate design schedule and employment. She contacted everyone she knew who might be able to send some design work her way. One friend introduced her to the head of the staging department at a company that produced corporate events, and that led immediately to work drafting for several technical directors in the company. After a short period of time she was given the opportunity to light her first corporate production, which ultimately led her to a whole new area of lighting design. While the percentage of corporate versus theatrical projects varies from month to month, she consistently finds that corporate events typically form about half of her design work in any given year. She notes that the state of the economy has a bigger impact on corporate projects: when the economy slows down, there are fewer corporate events, and those that exist tend to have smaller budgets.

When asked to discuss several of the significant differences between designing for corporate and

---

Betsy Adams

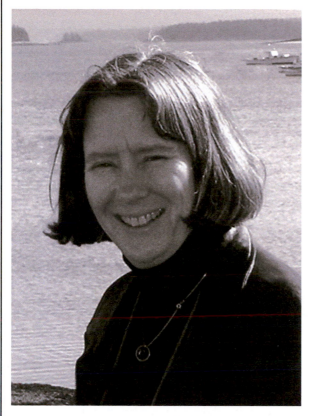

Credit: photo courtesy Robert Murphy

more traditional forms of theatre, Betsy singled out venue and schedule:

> "Most corporate events are produced in hotel ballrooms or convention centers. There is a lot more rigging involved, and lighting positions are dictated by rigging points. There is also a lot of creative truss design that goes hand-in-hand with the lighting design of corporate events. Once you get past the mechanical aspects, the design process is very similar in both worlds. Adjusting to the corporate world has more to do with getting used to the speed at which these events happen and expanding one's vocabulary."

She also emphasizes preparation and being able to deal with stress effectively. "The time pressure in corporate events is severe; one of the significant differences is that a corporate event has no previews and often only one rehearsal. The pressure of putting together a successful show is magnified many times."

Betsy goes on to add several additional tips that are fairly unique to working in corporate theatre. The design needs to work with the theme graphics of an event, which calls for close attention to both color and template choices:

> "You must know each company's corporate colors. Ford blue, Gillette blue, and IBM blue are all different. If you don't have the ability to change color with color-mixing equipment you must choose your colors with extreme care. It is also useful to know the color of the competition; this way you will not end up using Fuji green in a Canon show unless it is to support a moment where it is used to make a point or to get a laugh."

Video is often a part of corporate presentations through I-MAG (Image Magnification). If I-MAG is being used, the lighting must work for the camera as well as for the audience. A single person at a lectern is often projected onto a screen that is 7 × 15 feet or larger. Backlight is important, while downlight is rarely used because the shadows are much more apparent to the camera than to the naked eye. The background also needs to be visible. While a black velour drape behind a speaker may be perfectly acceptable to a live audience, on screen, the speaker will appear as a floating head if no light is placed on the dark background.

On the positive side, budgets and fees are larger than they are in the theatre and often give a designer an opportunity to try new equipment long before it becomes affordable in the theatre. It is also important to remain abreast of changes in the profession:

> "Keep in touch with colleagues, read the trades, go to rental houses or manufacturers' open houses to see demos of new equipment. It is a very small world, and we have all survived in it because we are good at what we do. There is a confidence and camaraderie that grows out of this type of work that I really enjoy."

On the downside, schedules are extremely tight, and there is rarely enough time to really polish your work. When asked what she believes to be the most important principle for lighting within the corporate environment Betsy states

> "Rule #1—Make the client happy. The lighting must support the structure of the event, whether that means a smooth opening sequence, an exciting awards segment, or a flawless speech by the CEO. The design process is all about being well-prepared when you walk into the venue and being able to do your job well and fast under high pressure on site. You have to think on your feet, adapt to changes, stay calm, and keep your sense of humor."

E-mails create an important paper trail regarding the progression of corporate events and messages must be returned promptly. This also holds true for phone messages. You should have a cell phone and must subscribe to a good voice messaging system. All messages that you place on your answering service for incoming calls should have a professional quality and you must get into the habit of checking your services at least once or twice daily—even when on the road or in rehearsals/performances. Messages should be checked even more often if you are expecting or are expected to provide important information to a client. Any e-mails that you create should also reflect a professional image and the slang and abbreviated language that one might use while e-mailing or texting friends should be avoided.

Corporate Production

On the whole, most corporate events are produced very quickly and time is an important limitation of these productions. A fashion show may load into a ballroom or mall location on a given morning and can be presenting shows as early as 10:00 or 11:00 a.m. On the other hand, organizational, design, and production meetings for many corporate events can occur months ahead of the actual production. Some companies may even have a division of full-time staff that deals with their corporate productions and may begin to work on future productions shortly after completing their current show. Regardless of amount of planning, the physical load-in of an industrial typically follows an abbreviated work schedule. While the number of days in a venue are kept to a minimum, the time is well-organized and a flurry of activity can occur at virtually any time of the day or night during the actual production of these events. Ballrooms are expensive, and companies frequently don't want to pay the additional rent and labor costs associated with providing time for an extended load-in and rehearsal process. These are often one-time events and it is hard to justify the costs associated with several days of load-in and rehearsals for a single 1- to 2-hour show. In many smaller productions, the load-in occurs in the morning and the event takes place later that day or evening. Often events are presented and quickly followed by a few hours of setting up and rehearsing for the next event, which is then presented and followed by yet another period of preparation before moving on to the next event in the production schedule. You are paid to be quick and efficient throughout the load-in and design process. You are also not done designing a corporate production until the final performance is over. Perhaps more importantly, you must create a certain amount of flexibility in these lighting rigs so that when changes are demanded, you can quickly adapt to the new needs of your client. As a rule, you should always make sure that you cover yourself with a couple of backups or options so that you can

react to the new demands that are bound to develop with corporate productions. Again, visual images that are presented to a client before you get into actual production can help ensure that you are on the same page as the client when you put everything together in the venue. Pre-show visualization tools like wysiwyg, Martin Show Designer, and LD Assistant are extremely beneficial for this type of work because you can pre-cue and run animated sequences to illustrate your lighting to the client.

Another important issue relates to money. Most corporate producers are used to dealing with corporate budgets that are much larger than the shoestring budgets (comparably) that theatrical productions typically must adhere to. As a result, they are often quite happy to spare little expense in producing as effective of a show as possible. Design fees and production budgets can be very attractive in comparison to those found in theatrical circles. The amount of money that marketing teams are used to spending on ad campaigns and the promotion of their products far exceeds what most of us would associate with theatrical budgets and by comparison can be considered very generous. This is especially true when comparing the number of performances that each type of production is associated with. Many corporate events are conducted for a single performance. Even if they are connected to a series of events, it is rare for these productions to last more than a week at a given location. Also, even if a show is moved between different regions of the country, like those associated with regional sales meetings, most corporate events are produced in fewer than half a dozen locations.

FILM AND VIDEO BASICS

Though the basic principles of lighting remain the same, film and video lighting can vary significantly from that of live theatrical production. These distinctions can be large or small. Since these forms of entertainment produce their images indirectly, many professionals like to refer to both film and video as **media.** One of the most significant differences between lighting for film or video and other forms of entertainment lighting is that you are lighting for a camera and not the human eye. This affects not only the manner in which a designer must approach a project, but also the type of equipment that is used in a design. Nonetheless, many of the concepts of good lighting that one learns in theatrical applications are applicable to these areas of lighting as well. One of the more significant differences between designing for media and designing for live theatrical events lies in the philosophical differences between the aesthetic and artistic forces that drive traditional forms of entertainment and the often more commercially driven requirements of film and video production. This is not to say that creating good art is not important in these media, but that much of the film/video industry is centered on a more commercial attitude. This is primarily due to the increased costs of producing these productions and the significantly larger audiences that they serve, especially within the area of television. A design team needs to not only produce satisfactory results from an artistic perspective but also must do so efficiently under time and cost restraints. In addition, although video and film productions aren't typically produced as frugally as most theatrical productions, consideration must still be given to the scheduling and rental rates of a studio or sound stage, the size and **calls** of crews, and any number of special issues like transportation of the crews and equipment for when a project is shot **on location.**

Even though they both design and control light, **directors of photography (DP)** (through **gaffers,** or **head lighting technicians)** and **lighting directors (LD;** through **electricians)** they deal with it in a rather indirect fashion, having to rely not on what they see on set but how the image appears on screen for film or on the master monitor for video. (Note that even though the term "gaffer" is used, these professionals are usually now called head lighting technicians. Both are affiliated with the film industry.) While the DP generally has the overall vision for a film's lighting, the head lighting technician is responsible for the majority of the lighting decisions and deals with the selection and placement of the equipment along with maintaining the desired intensity levels. Another group of professionals, the **grips,** are comparable to theatrical stagehands. Grips are responsible for setting up and assembling most of the equipment that will be used on a shoot, including scenery and camera equipment (e.g., dollies, cranes, and booms), as well as rigging and setting up many of the stands, reflectors, and other accessories that are associated with the lighting. DPs are concerned with camera positions and angles, lens choice, exposure settings, and the overall look of a scene. In reality, they provide the broad vision for the lighting and describe it (direction, intensity, character, mood, ambiance, etc.) to the gaffer, who translates this information into an image by selecting and placing the appropriate equipment. This forms a sense of collaboration between these professionals, with one of the most important jobs of a gaffer being simply anticipating the needs of the DP.

Lighting directors are traditionally associated with video work and have responsibilities and a role in productions that are quite similar to that of the lighting designer in theatre. They work with the **video engineer** or **video controller (VC)** to produce good-quality images for a program. Together they work to ensure that no scenes are under- or overexposured and that issues like color balance, exposure requirements, contrast ratios, and image matching are accounted for when shifting between different shots and cameras. One of their most important responsibilities is being accountable for image resolution and the contrast ranges of the images. The VC's main monitor displays what the final image will look like when broadcast or captured to tape or DVD. It is because of this need to work so closely together that the lighting director and VC generally sit next to one another in the control room for many studio productions like game shows and sitcoms, music videos, or live events. This is especially true when multiple cameras are used. The lighting director is also quite involved with the technical elements of lighting a video project—choosing luminaires, coloring, making determinations of intensity levels, contrast ratios and ranges, etc.

In the rest of this section I discuss key video/film concepts and provide brief overviews of how these topics are important to media production as well as how these areas of lighting differ from other areas of lighting design. These discussions are greatly expanded upon in *Stage Lighting: Design Applications and More,* in which I present additional materials related to specific topics such as exposure techniques, special considerations of lighting for the camera, studio and lighting setups, and equipment used in film and video lighting.

Light and the Camera

Film and video cameras are pretty similar in regard to the principles with which they function. Both make use of lenses and apertures to focus and control the light and images that they capture. Film cameras focus an image onto a photosensitive substance **(film)** made up of chemical emulsions, or layers, that are applied to the surface of a plastic material (which was celluloid in the past). The emulsions respond to different wavelengths (red, blue, and green) as the film is exposed to light. Once developed or processed, the film becomes a record of the associated images. A video camera works in much the same way with the exception that the film is replaced by photoelectric sensors that convert the light into a series of electronic signals. While films record the various wavelengths on emulsions, a video camera captures three separate video signals—once again, each associated with a different primary color of light. Until the advent of digital video, the electronic signals of a video camera were converted to a broadcast television signal or to magnetic impulses that were recorded onto video tape. Now, video images are recorded as bytes and pixels that are either broadcast or stored digitally on media such as hard drives and DVDs. The overall exposure recorded by a camera is a result of three different factors: the sensitivity of the film or video sensors, length of time that an image is exposed, and the amount of light allowed to enter the camera at any given time.

Film and video cameras impose a unique set of requirements upon lighting. Cameras see light in a different way than the human eye. A lighting designer must be aware of several properties that may change between the lighting that is observed by the eye in a studio or location setup and how it actually appears in the media as a final image. To make matters more difficult, many of these changes can be detected only with experience or with the aid of special equipment such as light meters. Several considerations unique to working with a camera include color temperature (known as white balance), color rendering, speed of exposure, and aperture or f-stop. Chapter 5 in *Stage Lighting: Design Applications and More* provides a detailed discussion of these and several other factors that can have an impact on a film or video image. All of these provide specific controls in how light is captured by a camera.

Two of the most important considerations when working with cameras relate to producing lighting levels that fall within the sensitivity ranges of a film or video camera's electronic sensors. The intensities must be strong so that the event is recorded (the **threshold exposure**) while not being so strong as to overexpose the image. In addition, it is important to produce appropriate **contrast ratios** in an image. Contrast ratios simply refer to the ratio between the brightest and darkest parts of an image or picture. Video cameras and film are not as sensitive as the human eye and cannot respond to contrast ranges or ratios that are too wide. On the other hand, a camera may also pick up variations in intensity that we cannot perceive with our human eyes. Trying to expose a camera's sensors or film to too great a contrast ratio results in parts of the image either going into extreme darkness or becoming so bright that they are overexposed and appear burned out.

Contrast ratios can also be described in terms of the relationship between the intensity of the **key light** and that of the base or **fill light** for a given scene. This tie to key and fill is quite popular in video production, and a lighting director often refers to **lighting ratios** when making comparisons between the intensities of the key and fill lights. If the key light for a scene is measured to be 100 footcandles and the fill is metered at 50 footcandles the contrast ratio will be 100:50 and therefore 2:1, or a one-stop difference between the light levels. This represents a fairly flat, or even, lighting ratio. A more dramatic contrast ratio would include a two-stop or 4:1 ratio. Sometimes professionals working in video will speak of high key and low key lighting. **High key** relates to images in which there is little difference between the intensity levels of the key and fill light—those with a small lighting or contrast ratio (1:1, 2:1, or 3:1). **Low key** is more dramatic, reflecting higher contrast ratios and a greater difference between the two lighting levels (5:1, 8:1, 10:1, etc.). Lighting ratios approaching 9:1 or greater tend to make the difference so drastic that the fill-lit areas may appear to be in complete darkness. A bright sunlit day can often have contrast ratios along this order. The famous film noir movies of the 1940s and '50s are great examples of low-key lighting. At the other extreme are the 2:1 lighting ratios that are fairly common for many television talk and news programs. Contrast ratios may be great or small, but the larger the degree of contrast, the more dramatic the image will appear and the greater the potential for encountering problems in the overall exposure settings.

Key and Fill Light

The system of key/fill lighting had its beginnings in the film and television industries and is now utilized throughout the entire lighting industry. This approach was introduced in the discussion of theatrical lighting in Chapter 10. In its initial inception, **key light** was associated with the primary or most intense light for a scene and was usually equated with the scene's motivating light source. In the early days of video and film lighting, cameras and film had very low light sensitivities. If the intensity levels fell too low, areas of the image would appear dark and unlit. Luminaires had to be capable of creating a high-enough threshold of illumination simply for objects to be seen by the camera or film. Just as on a stage, where there is little or no ambient light, cameras have a problem seeing into shadow areas that are not lit by the key light. More importantly, since cameras have a limited range of contrast ratios, they frequently have significant problems recording scenes where there is a significant difference between the darkness of the shadow areas and the areas that are illuminated by the key light. To compensate for this, additional luminaires (**fill lights**) are added to fill in or soften the effect of these shadows. This additional lighting provides a base level of illumination that prevents portions of the subject from going completely dark when seen through a camera. In the early days of video lighting this was sometimes referred as **base level lighting** or **base light.** If fill is not used carefully, though, too much fill light can also produce low-contrast lighting that will ultimately create a flat uninspired image.

Once a relationship has been established between the distribution angles of the key and fill light, the pattern is re-created through a series of adjoining lighting areas, just as is typically done in area lighting for the stage. However, unlike theatrical area lighting, this repetition is often limited to a small portion of a studio (e.g., the anchor desk for a news program). It is rare that an entire studio will be lit in this fashion. Lighting systems are also based on the camera placement and angles that will be used during a filming or taping sequence. Film and video designers need to be more conscious of the contrast ratios that exist between the key and fill light of a scene than do theatre lighting designers. Today, most film and video lighting makes some use of key/fill principles and lights the subject from at least two different directions. Each pair of luminaires creates a key/fill relationship that provides an indication of light coming from a given direction, with enough shadow illumination to sustain visibility throughout a scene. The McCandless Method is a specific variation of a key/fill application. While today's cameras have become much better at capturing low-light recordings and working with greater contrast ratios, a designer must still take care not to exceed the limits of the media that they are using.

Control Elements

Historically, dimmers have not been used that heavily in film or video lighting due to the combined effects of **amber shift** on a lamp's color temperature and the fact that these media are especially sensitive to color temperature changes. The number of luminaires that use ballasts and arc sources in film and video lighting has also contributed to the lack of dimmers that have been used in these industries. In addition, due to the lack of exposure sensitivity in older cameras, much of the lighting for film and video in the past was concerned with simply providing a base level of illumination that cameras could record. Rather than using dimmers, many luminaires used in film and video lighting make use of "**hot**" or **continuous light sources** that are simply plugged into a power source and turned on. These luminaires may be equipped with multiple lamps or lamps with several filaments that can be turned on or off in different combinations to control how much light a luminaire produces. Wattage of the light sources is yet another manner in which intensities may be controlled for film and video lighting, with higher wattage luminaires being used for greater intensities. In the past, most luminaires used in film and video lighting were powered by high-wattage light sources (incandescent or arc), but these are now being replaced with a variety of LED sources. Variations of LED panels that produce a nice, soft wash of light are particularly popular now in the industry. Another manner of varying the intensity of the light is related to the placement of a luminaire. Gaffers frequently adjust the distance between the lighting instruments and a subject as a manner of controlling a light's intensity.

A head lighting technician may also use one of several accessories to modify the intensity of a luminaire, including **scrims, silks, diffusers**, and **mechanical dimmers**. Most of these accessories alter the intensity of light that is shined through or reflected off them. Film is especially sensitive to color temperature variations as a result of dimming, and it is often desirable to not use dimmers at all in these applications. However, video setups—especially in studio production—often use dimmers. Initially they were used primarily for controlling ganged light sources rather than for dimming, but they are now often used to adjust contrast ratios and to balance or boost/drop intensity levels and draw focus to particular subjects in a scene. **Scrims** are made of a screen mesh (usually metal) of different densities and are

slipped into the front of a luminaire in a frame where the gel would be located. The light that passes through the scrim will drop in intensity by a given proportion without the lamp's color temperature being affected. The higher the density of the scrim, the more light it will absorb and the greater reduction it will have in a unit's light output. These scrims are quite similar to the dimming screens that are used in museum and exhibit lighting. Scrims are not specified so much by their density as by the number of f-stops by which they reduce the light. A single scrim reduces the light by half an f-stop while a double reduces the light by a full stop. A color system allows a scrim to be quickly identified by the color of its frame (green for a single and red for a double). Scrims are often grouped into a kit or pouch containing a basic selection of different densities that fit a given luminaire, and the entire kit is hung on or near the unit. **Neutral density filters (ND** or **NDF)** are used in the same way as scrims. These filter media are similar to gel except that the light's intensity is dropped without affecting the color temperature or overall spectral composition of the light. Each of the gel manufacturers makes a range of neutral density filters. Finally, indirect light may be introduced to a scene by reflecting light off panels or fabrics like silks (Figure 16.5).

Gels aren't used to the same degree in television or film lighting as they are in theatrical lighting. In fact, a significant amount of shooting is done with little or no color except for the use of color correction filters. While there are occasions when the use of more saturated colored filters are appropriate (linking the light to a specific motivational light source or for theatrical effects), they are usually the exception rather than the norm. Perhaps the most important aspect of working with filters in lighting for film and video relates to a series of specialty filters known as **color correction** or

Figure 16.5 Diffusion and reflector equipment Chimera panel kit (a selection of frames and C-stands as well as diffusion and reflective cloths)

Credit: photo courtesy Chimera Lighting

conversion filters. The most common use for these filters is in correcting the color temperature of a luminaire or light source so that it matches all the other light sources in a setup or matching the source's light with the particular needs of the video camera or film stock that is being used. Unmatched color temperatures of light sources in a scene can result in the color balance of a film or video being distorted and shifts in color within the final images. A gaffer or lighting director will typically match the color temperatures of the different luminaires throughout a setup by selecting correction filters that match or color-correct all the sources to the same color temperature. A common example of this might include shooting an interior daytime scene where the exterior light coming through a window is quite different from that of the room's interior. In this case, the interior lights and most likely all the production luminaires will be lit to an interior color temperature based on tungsten-halogen sources (approximately 3,200° K), while the daylight would have a color temperature more on the order of 5,600° K or higher. This will cause exposure problems between the differences in color temperature of these two sources. The typical solution for this is to simply place a specialty filter over the window surfaces to correct the daylight color temperature to that of the interior lighting. Specifically, this would call for a **CTO (color temperature orange) filter.** Likewise, when interior sources or luminaires with low color temperatures need to be raised to match a high color temperature source a **CTB (color temperature blue) filter** can be used to correct the color temperature of the light. These are also called correct-to-orange and correct-to-blue filters. In addition to the standard sheets, color correction filters come in sizes as large as 4 by 8 feet and in rolls. This allows the filters to be fit to large surfaces like windows and glass doors. A number of different CTO and CTB filters are available that allow sources of different color temperatures to be corrected to a standard color temperature like tungsten or daylight. These additional filters are indicated by values such as 1/4 CTO, 1/8 CTB, or 1/2 CTB, etc.

Key Elements in Film/Video Illumination

As discussed earlier, video and film cameras have a different way of "seeing": the image produced by a camera can be significantly different from what is seen by the native eye on a set or in the studio. Another set of differences refers to the proximity of the lighting and camera equipment for shooting film or video setups. Unlike theatrical situations where audiences have full view of the entire stage, a video or film shoot is staged only to the scale that encompasses the viewpoint of the camera angles that will be used for a scene. If a setup consists of close-ups, then the lighting will be placed close to the **talent** and just out of view of the cameras. Due to

this, the manner of providing general illumination can vary significantly in film or video shoots, being dependent on the type of action, distance to talent, and camera angles that a scene will require. Also, when camera angles change, the lighting needs to appear as though it is consistent from angle to angle. Sources that appeared to be in front of the talent must appear as if they have remained in the original location and that only the camera has changed position.

In addition to key and fill light we also speak of hard and soft light in film or video lighting. This is sometimes called **coherence. Hard light** is often associated with the key light for a scene and is quite directional. It is usually responsible for producing the strong highlights and sharp, well-defined shadows in a scene. **Soft light** is associated with diffuse illumination and does not produce any prominent shadows. It is often used as a fill light to soften shadows that may have been created by the key light, and it frequently provides a base level of illumination for the shadow areas of a subject. Hard light is frequently created by compact light sources that produce a very concentrated directional beam while soft light is produced by luminaires that create a soft, widely distributed pattern of light. Soft light, because of its relatively large source, also tends to wrap around a subject and fill in shadows that would be associated with the surface texture of the subject—something that is a real benefit when a performer's skin might have wrinkles or other imperfections. Many video and film lighting professionals prefer to shoot with soft light unless there is a specific need for the more dramatic shadows of a hard-lit scene. Soft light also allows a camera to be opened up a bit more, allowing more light to pass through its lens, which gives more control over the **depth of field** (the range in which objects remain in focus) of an image. Whether a light source is perceived as a hard or soft source generally comes down to a combination of two variables. Most important is the relative size of the light source in comparison to the size of the subject (soft sources are large). Also significant is the distance between the source and the subject. In reality, even though we may refer to hard or soft light luminaires, a luminaire could actually become either one depending on the specific combination of how large the light source is and how far away from the subject that it is placed. The key to producing soft light is to create diffuse light from a relatively large light source, which creates parallel rays that wrap around the surfaces of a subject. In fact, a soft light could in effect become a hard light if the source is placed far enough away from the subject so that the rays would no longer appear parallel.

Distribution in video and film lighting follows the same principles as in other areas of the lighting industry, with two minor adjustments. First, the camera is not always as sensitive to the directionality of the light as human eyes may be, and second, lighting professionals

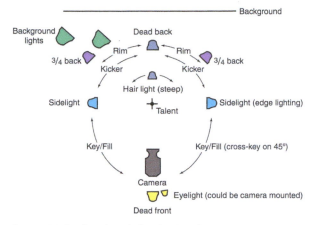

Figure 16.6 Directional distribution for a camera

their positions are shifted slightly to the side and around more of the subject. They also tend to wrap around the face of a subject, while **rim lights** have a higher elevation that edges (rims) the subject rather than wraps around it. Rim lights are often used to help separate a subject from the background. **Background lights** don't light the subject at all but instead wash the background behind it. These are used to maintain a proper balance and establish an appropriate contrast between the subject and the background. An additional form of lighting that may or may not focus on a subject is **effect lighting,** which is used to produce effects such as the projections of patterns like windows or doors, accents for fire light or moonlight, or any other lighting effect.

have given unique names to a number of specific lighting angles that are used in film and video lighting (Figure 16.6). These angles are based on the camera's location and are referenced from the camera being placed directly in front of the subject or talent. Lighting with a single directional source is quite rare in video or film setups: cameras have traditionally struggled with the extreme contrast created between those areas of the subject that are lit brightly and those that fall into shadow. As additional luminaires are introduced to a scene, the lighting director must become concerned with the contrast or lighting ratios that exist on each of the illuminated surfaces that are revealed by the lighting instruments. Typical distribution angles for video and film production include **dead front** and **dead back, sidelight, cross key** positions on the front diagonals, **3/4 back** on the back diagonals, and **offset angles** that fall just off the dead front and back positions. A sidelight can also be aimed so that it grazes the surface of a subject and produces extended shadows that emphasize the texture of a subject's surface **(edge lighting). Backlight** is an important element of camera lighting because of the need to separate subjects from the background. This usually comes from directly behind the subject. Other important angles that produce specific effects include **face** or **eyelight,** which is relatively flat light coming from about the same angle as the camera (and is often camera mounted) that enhances the performer's face and brings life or sparkle to their eyes. **Hair light** is used to add highlights to the talent's hair (it is a variation of steep backlight). The **kicker** and **rim light** are more confusing because they can mean different things depending on who you talk to. Most professionals agree that they are both variations of backlight that are shifted to the side to provide more modeling than a straight backlight. The **kicker** is a backlight that is offset to one side, but it can come from any direction above or below the subject (it is often used to simulate motivated sources and to produce dramatic effects). Kickers are often called **3/4 backlights** because

Bill Klages

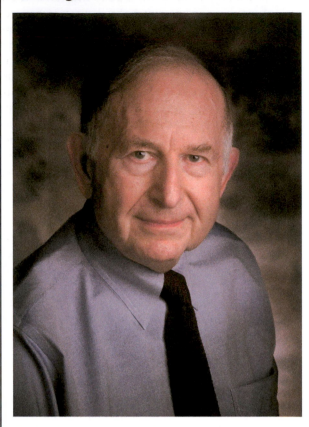

Credit: photo courtesy Bill Klages

inducted into the Television Academy of Arts and Sciences Hall of Fame, the only lighting designer to receive this honor. In 2015, he was inducted into the Alumni Hall of Fame of Rensselaer Polytechnic Institute, the nation's oldest technological research university.

In part, Bill's entry into television lighting can be attributed to simply being at the right place at a time when the industry was in its beginnings. He never had any formal training in lighting because people coming to work in the broadcast industry at that time came from electrical engineering backgrounds. "Lighting director" was the term that was first used for the individual that is now better described today as a "lighting designer." It took many years to erase this incorrect designation. Bill recounts his entrance into television through a series of opportunities that emerged early in his career:

“My career in television started very early (1948 to be specific). I was hired by NBC in New York as a result of having an Electrical Engineering degree, a requisite at the time. I was heavily involved in the technical aspects of television broadcast, which was then in its infancy.”

After a year or so, he moved to the operating group as a video control engineer, where he developed an interest in lighting and the manner in which visual quality was obtained in this (then) mysterious new medium: "As a result of this interest, and a set of unusual circumstances that could have only transpired at the time, I became a lighting director." His first show was *Playwrights 56,* the largest-budget live drama series that NBC had presented to date. The year was 1955:

“My only training for the job was from observing and analyzing from the video control position how the Lighting Directors practiced their craft at that time and how they obtained images that I either liked or didn't like. It was with the confidence of youth and my inexperience that I believed that I knew how it should be done and could prove it. Thankfully, there were disappointments and reverses along the way that humbled and matured this view.”

Bill believes that the abilities that define a person as a lighting designer are not confined to one lighting discipline. For example:

“I have been able to work in many areas: feature films, facility design, traditional theatre, architectural lighting as well as my primary field, television production. All that the designer must do is discover what unique technical requirements or techniques make the unknown discipline different from his own familiar and more comfortable discipline. This is illustrated when a theatrical lighting designer is asked to adapt and translate his efforts to a video production. If the designer exercises his imagination and observations, he will immediately be aware that the two audiences require rather different lighting methods and that his "bag of tricks" may fail in a very disappointing way when used for the television medium. He will also have to make the difficult decision about which discipline will take precedence (theatre or video audience).”

On the other hand, "The great joy is seeing an end result that is even better than what you had in your mind. The worst is when the end result does not meet your expectations." We are bombarded with trade publications and press releases that help us remain abreast of industry developments in all the lighting disciplines. However, he also suggests "swallowing your pride and watching other talented designers' efforts as well." He continues:

> "Lighting for a camera is much more complicated as a result of all the numerous changes of state that might be present (optical, electrical, and chemical, as well as heavy manipulation of the electrical signals before the final display of a visual image). Characteristic elements of the lighting system will demand techniques that cannot be as simplified as say, using a warm/cool approach (although it has been tried). Predicting the end result may be difficult and must be learned, but is not impossible if this skill is approached open-mindedly."

If Bill had to offer a cardinal rule, it would relate to creating proper exposure and the balance of values ("brightnesses") that are found between all of the elements in each camera view. When he got his break, there were no established methods:

> "Everyone was learning, known rules were few, and those that we assumed to be true were not necessarily true. Every day could bring not only a new revelation but also a different job experience. The personal associations made at this time would continue and expand like an enormous family tree throughout my entire career."

He recalls that even in the early days he was obsessed with the idea of how to obtain images on video that duplicated what he saw in feature films: "It has taken more than 50 years for the video system to finally get to a point where this is actually possible. The end result of having video acquisition replace film is a very practical reality of today."

Three-Point and Following Source Lighting

One common method of creating general illumination for a video or film shoot involves **three-point lighting.** Though the basic system may be modified, the essence of the three-point system lies in providing several luminaires that are placed around the subject. This is a simple approach that is treated in much the same manner as the McCandless Method in theatrical productions. In fact, critics of the system believe that it has produced many of the same negative influences in the film and video industry that the McCandless Method brought to the theatrical community—namely, that it has led to uninspired lighting when such an approach hasn't been necessary, especially with the sensitivity of today's cameras and films. Figure 16.7 illustrates a typical three-point lighting setup. The basis of the system lies in providing a key light that is from the front and

offset to one side of the subject and camera, a second light (the fill light) placed on the opposite front side of the subject, and a third unit used as a backlight placed directly behind the subject (often in line with the camera). The backlight is used to separate the subject from the background and a fourth light is often added to light the background itself. The method is quite adequate for producing basic illumination but at the same time can come off as uninspired and mechanical. With today's video cameras and films a lighting designer or head lighting technician can create their own variations of a three-point system by shifting the units around to some degree which then provides a unique solution to a particular setup. In fact, there are other popular lighting formulas based on variations of this system that use four or more lamps per area. In one system the units are oriented approximately 45° from one another and provide a variation of key/fill light for virtually any angle in which a camera might be placed. Some variation of three-point lighting is often used to light the talent or performers that are found on a set. More importantly, decisions regarding the key light placement should be based more on the motivational lighting elements of a scene than on a standard approach that is now somewhat dated. A newer technique of linking the lighting to motivational sources and a more dramatic quality of lighting is called **following source;** it is a direct result of the improved contrast ratios that have come to camera designs since the 1980s. Since then, the industry has steadily been shifting towards low-key lighting as the capacity for sensing larger ranges of intensity

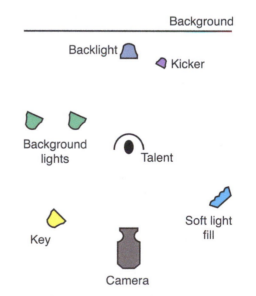

Figure 16.7 Three-point lighting (video variation): this formula lighting approach is actually a misnomer because the three basic angles (key, fill, and backlight) are frequently supplemented with additional units like background lights and kickers

and contrast ratios have improved. Following source has also brought more effective use of shadowing and stronger dramatic qualities to the lighting of today's film and video productions. With high-definition (HDMI or High-Definition Multimedia Interface) cameras and video screens now becoming so popular, following source has become an even more popular method of lighting for film and video productions. However, regardless of how inexperienced a lighting director is, the three-point-system remains a safe place to start from and will produce satisfactory results in most situations.

The remaining sections in this chapter introduce specialties that employ lighting professionals outside of the traditional areas of the entertainment lighting industry, although elements of entertainment design may still be present in some of these applications (e.g., themed design). Many of these specialties have not been around for much more than 50 years or have typically been designed by individuals whose backgrounds are quite different from that of entertainment lighting designers. This is because these designs are often based on more of an engineering perspective than theatrical design. These specialties require specialized equipment and specialized training—more so than what most theatrical designers are familiar with. Many of the lighting professionals who work in these areas are trained as **illuminating engineers,** who approach lighting designs from a more quantitative perspective than theatrical lighting designers would. Despite this, these specialties use the same controllable qualities and functions of light as theatrical lighting—it's just that they are used in somewhat different ways from how they might be used in entertainment applications. The design practices of these specialties and theatrical lighting have also moved much closer together during recent times and as a result, more theatrically trained lighting designers are entering these other disciplines.

Like the preceding sections, the rest of this chapter provides an introduction to some of the more unique elements of working in these lighting applications. Once again, there are sidebar introductions to lighting designers with established reputations in these specialties. For more specific information on a given discipline, the best place to begin is with the chapter that can be found on each topic in *Stage Lighting: Design Applications and More* and then move on to an examination of the *IESNA Lighting Handbook* and particular (Illuminating Engineering Society of North America (IESNA) guidebooks or recommended practices for a particular type of project

Retail and Museum Lighting

Retail lighting and museum lighting are unique because they contain elements of both entertainment and architectural lighting, yet the subject (a product, artwork, or artifact) cannot be displayed in a way that is too theatrical or that distorts its appearance. There are a number of architectural lighting principles found in display (or retail) and exhibit (or museum) lighting. Despite this, display and exhibit lighting can still be very creative areas in which a lighting designer might find work. Traditionally, the lighting in these disciplines fell to illuminating or electrical engineers. However, in recent years these industries have moved toward more creative lighting treatments that emphasize the thematic and aesthetic aspects of displaying an object rather than simply illuminating it. Some notable comparisons between retail or museum lighting and entertainment lighting are based on the fact that the approach to lighting these areas is usually more subtle than that of entertainment lighting. Colors must be chosen more carefully, movement cannot distract or distort a subject, and intensities and other lighting elements must be manipulated to reveal the subject in the best way possible. Throw distances are small compared to those found in entertainment and architectural applications. The smaller distances, sometimes smaller than 1 foot, result in these luminaires typically having lower wattages and larger beamspreads than those used in other applications. Care must also be taken not to harm the subject through exposure to excessive heat or other forms of electromagnetic radiation that can come from the light sources.

Lighting Layers

Both retail and museum lighting are based on the principles of **layering.** This refers to creating several different lighting systems that provide a variety of functions within a given space. In many ways, these systems aren't that much different from those developed in entertainment lighting—in fact, many of the same principles apply here too. The heart of lighting most stores and museums lies in the development of two different lighting systems. These include the **primary** or **general circulation** and **secondary** or **accent lighting systems.** The primary system may also be called the **ambient lighting system.** The primary lighting aids visitors in moving around in a store or museum and creates basic visibility throughout a space; the secondary systems accent or draw focus to displays or exhibits. In nearly all situations, several different lighting layers must be created due to the various visual tasks that are performed in these environments. For example, even though a jewelry store's merchandise is best displayed with cool-colored light, which enhances gems and silver, this particular light is unflattering to skin tones. A designer should also provide some form of incandescent lighting where potential customers can wear the jewelry and evaluate it. While the secondary systems are primarily associated with accent lighting, other types of lighting can be broken down into more specific functions. When evaluating the lighting for architectural and display or exhibit applications we worry not only about providing a given quantity of light on flat surfaces like table tops (**lighting the horizontal plane**), but we are also concerned about the quantity of light hitting vertical surfaces like walls and shelving or display units (**lighting the vertical plane**). Both are measured by the amount of light that strikes a surface (in footcandles or lux). In many stores, lighting the vertical plane may be more important than lighting the horizontal plane because most products are arranged along vertical shelves and displays. Also, many luminaires used in retail and museum lighting are decorative, and there are thousands of designs that can bring a unique character to an environment.

While dimmers are used in accent lighting, it is usually preferable to adjust lighting intensities by selecting lamps of different wattages rather than through using dimmers. The main reason for this lies in avoiding **red** or **amber shift** as lamps are dimmed. On the other hand, when a store or museum uses dimming, it is common for those dimmers operating at the highest levels to seldom run at over 90%, resulting in a color shift that creates an appropriate ambiance for an environment. This also saves energy and increases lamp life. Wire mesh screens (**dimming screens** or **reducing screens**) of various densities may also be placed over the front of a fixture to reduce the light output of a given lamp. This lowers the intensity without having an effect on the color temperature of the light. Dimming screens work in essentially the same way as the **scrims** that are used in the film and video industry. Figure 16.8 provides several examples of dimming screens. Accent lighting, through intensity control, is a primary element of display and exhibit lighting because these systems direct customers and visitors to merchandise and exhibits where subjects can be examined more closely.

Figure 16.8 Dimming screens

Credit: photo courtesy Philips Lighting

Essentials of Retail and Museum/Gallery Lighting

Since both retail and museum/gallery lighting are variations of architectural lighting, at least some, if not all, of the elements that make up a design are subject to various code guidelines and enforcement. Areas that need to be specified by a lighting designer or electrical engineer with training in these specialties include elements like **general circulation systems** (area or ambient lighting), **specialty areas** and **accent systems** for proper illuminance levels, **electrical distribution,** and **power densities.** You will find further details regarding these and other architectural lighting practices in *Stage Lighting: Design Applications and More*. Museums tend to have fairly permanent displays and are often designed by lighting specialists, while retail installations typically have the overall lighting systems designed by specialists, with the individual displays lit by the sales staff. In many cases, the professionals who do the general display or merchandising work for a store are trained in basic retail lighting and often light their own displays. Occasionally a store will have lighting specialists who light the majority of its displays and who may even travel regionally to light displays in similar stores as part of a retail chain. However, the day-to-day modification of a design that accommodates the routine changes of exhibits and displays often falls to members of a retail or museum staff, who produce mixed results because they have not received sufficient training in lighting. In these situations, it isn't uncommon to walk into an establishment to find luminaires like track lighting fixtures aimed at what appears to be open space due to a display being relocated without the lights being refocused. Galleries also tend to use their own staff to work with the curators and artists to light specific shows, while permanent exhibits or collections are often designed by lighting specialists. A cardinal rule in retail lighting is to illuminate a product or display in a way that enhances its features without causing any exposure damage. This type of lighting should reference an object's color rendition, texture, and detailing. The two most important issues relating to lighting a retail environment are drawing attention to the products and revealing them in the best way possible.

Museum and gallery environments are lit in much the same way as retail establishments. However, several principles of lighting these areas are quite different from those of retail lighting. Perhaps the most important difference relates to protecting the artifacts and artwork from being lit with too much exposure to radiant energy (visible light, ultraviolet radiation, and heat). This is critical when lighting one-of-a-kind artwork, artifacts, and rare or historic objects. Another significant difference is in the attention that is placed on determining the circulation patterns or visitor flow in museums and gallery settings. Rather than crowded sales floors, a series of individual galleries, halls, or exhibit chambers are set up throughout a museum or gallery that are each lit appropriately. The illuminations of the general lighting layers are kept much lower in museum and gallery designs—some designers even argue that an ambient layer isn't even necessary in some museum applications. Also, unlike retail environments that use more horizontal displays, the majority of museum and gallery exhibits consist of vertical displays that are hung along walls or in cabinets. Finally, mood and ambience play a large role in museum layouts, which also tend to be lighted in more dramatic styles than galleries or retail establishments (Figure 16.9). Galleries tend to approach lighting from a neutral perspective, creating an environment that reveals the artwork in a natural manner that lets the work speak for itself. Museums tend to have different lighting levels from one exhibit space to another, and a lighting designer must work to ensure that proper **transition zones** are created between spaces with large variations in their lighting levels.

Figure 16.9 Hall of Dinosaurs museum exhibit (Carnegie Museum of Natural History)

Credit: photo courtesy Christopher Popwich/C&C Lighting, LLC

Sidebar 16.5 DESIGNER PROFILE

Cindy Limauro designs lighting for theatre, opera, dance, and architecture. In addition to designing professionally, she leads the lighting program at Carnegie Mellon University and recently held a visiting professorship with the Higher Institute of Architectural Sciences, Henry van de Velde, in Antwerp (Belgium). She is a member of United Scenic Artists (USA) and the International Association of Lighting Designers (IALD), and was named a Fellow of the Institute by USITT. Several notable companies that she has designed for include the Pittsburgh Opera, Opera Columbus, Burt Reynolds Theatre, the Pittsburgh Public Theatre, the Cincinnati and Pittsburgh ballets, and the Barter Theatre in Virginia. Her international credits include work with Teatro Vascello in Rome and a series of architectural installations throughout Prague coordinated with a group of international lighting design students. Her movement into architectural lighting has produced a business partnership called C&C Lighting with her husband, Christopher Popowich (also a lighting designer), that has produced such creations as the lighting of the Gulf Tower, the Randy Pausch Memorial Bridge, the Hunt Library and the Hall of Dinosaurs exhibit at the Carnegie Museum of Natural History.

Cindy's formal training includes a BA in theatre from the University of Michigan and an MFA in lighting design from Florida State University. She became interested in theatrical lighting when Arthur Miller visited her undergraduate playwriting class (she originally majored in creative writing):

> ❝I also found an emotional connection to storytelling in the lighting course that I took and became a double major in English and Theatre. I was so mesmerized by the power of lighting and how it impacted an audience's experience that I chose to become a lighting designer after graduation.❞

Following graduation, she worked a couple of years and then went to graduate school, where she was introduced to the worlds of dance and opera. "I developed a love for all three areas and vowed that my career would follow this passion." After graduate school she primarily lit theatre and dance. Her first opportunity in lighting opera came from an artistic director who saw her dance work. Years later, her introduction to architectural lighting came from architects who saw her theatre

Cindy Limauro

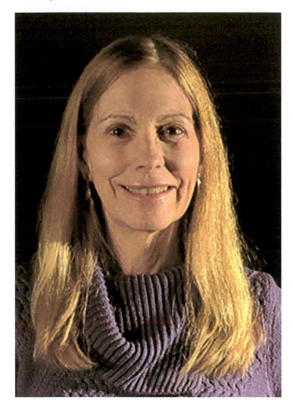

Credit: photo courtesy C&C Lighting

work and wanted a more dramatic approach to lighting one of their projects. She estimates her current design work to be about 60% theatre, opera, and dance, and 40% architectural lighting.

While Cindy continues to both work and teach in a number of areas of lighting, she has found that her skills readily transferred from one discipline to another. Even with the larger shift into architectural lighting she relates:

❝It was a natural transition going from theatre to architecture. The design process is very similar. I did take an IES workshop on architectural lighting but it mostly dealt with technical issues like lighting calculations and daylighting. My theatrical training has served me well in crossing over.❞

In discussing the similarities and differences between lighting for theatre and architectural projects she feels that the processes aren't that different from one another:

❝As a designer I ask the same questions. What kind of mood am I trying to create? Where is the focus? How do I create contrast and visual interest? In the theatre, I'm trying to reinforce

the director's vision. . . . In architecture, it's the architect's vision. Space is about people whether it is characters in a play or people in the real world. How is the space being used? Both disciplines also require collaboration and everyone working towards a common goal. The only real difference is that theatre lighting is temporary, while architectural lighting is permanent, and you have to be aware of additional issues like codes. While the lighting principles are the same, there are different fixtures and lamps in architectural lighting, but this, again, is something that a lighting designer can easily adapt to.❞

Several other unique considerations of architectural and display lighting relate to the specific conditions that you must work within:

❝Every city is different in regard to code issues. Also, if you are lighting a historic landmark there will usually be very strict rules about what you can and cannot do. Architectural lighting designers must also strive for energy efficient designs and need to think about issues like sustainability.❞

What Cindy likes most about working in the theatre is that it is a live event with an audience: "You never know how they are going to respond or if a show will run flawlessly." What she likes most about working in architecture is the permanence of the work. In all areas, she loves the collaboration with different people. What she dislikes most are the time and budget constraints facing today's arts: "While lighting technology is getting more and more sophisticated, the amount of time necessary to create a polished design is becoming less and less in the theatre. As a designer, you often have to work with speed and efficiency rather than enjoying a process of experimentation." What she likes least about working in architecture is how slow the process can be: "Projects require a much longer design period, and budgets can be cut at any time in the process."

Cindy remains current by attending both LDI (Lighting Design International) and Lightfair (the architectural and display lighting professionals' equivalent to USITT) trade shows and conferences and reading many of the lighting industry trade journals. In offering a bit of advice she suggests, "Whether working in theatre or architecture, always start from a black void. Add the first light and ask is this enough? If not . . . What do I need to add next? Too often people overlight." She also has a strong interest in bringing students from different cultures together and wants them to be involved in the communities where they live. These ambitions have been realized through projects like the Antwerp experience where students researched and created a design presentation for a museum and neighborhood for an architectural lighting installation. They did full-scale mock-ups and made a presentation to the city and museum staff, who were impressed enough that the design was actually installed that summer. Past student projects in Pittsburgh include working to create a Master Plan of Light for the Carnegie Mellon campus and collaborating with the Pittsburgh Cultural Trust on branding the downtown area with light. Cindy's passion for teaching architecture students about light has now become a partnership with the Nuckolls Education Fund. Together with her design partner, she has received grant funding to teach architectural lighting workshops at universities around the United States.

Two specialty areas of retail lighting are unique because they combine elements of theatrical production and retail design. These are **retail shows** and **themed stores**. In retail shows, actual performances or some variation of a production are created around a product, product line, or corporate/sales event. **Fashion shows, trade shows**, **product unveilings,** and **corporate sales meetings** are examples of these events, which are considered examples of corporate theatre/productions or industrials (discussed earlier in this chapter). These projects usually take place outside of the retail environment and are frequently presented in ballrooms and conference or convention centers. They are known for their spectacle and sizable budgets. Themed stores are a specialty area of retail design where customers are immersed in a designed environment. Building decor, layout, displays, music and sounds, and even costumed sales clerks can contribute to this immersive experience. Retailers that make use of heavily themed stores include the Disney Store, Build-a-Bear Workshop, and LEGO stores. Restaurants often make use of themed environments as well. Themed design will be discussed in more detail later in this chapter.

ARCHITECTURAL LIGHTING

Architectural lighting refers primarily to lighting buildings and structures. We often break this into several different, more specialized, areas of lighting design. The two most common specialties are **interior** and **exterior lighting.** Although these make up the most obvious specializations, others such as **landscape** lighting and **street** or **roadway lighting** have also emerged as specialties in this part of the lighting industry. Many architectural lighting designers work in several of these or even narrower specialties like **residential, hospitality** (hotel and restaurant), **healthcare, office,** and **house of worship** (church) design. **Themed lighting** goes further and brings a unique blend of architectural and entertainment design into a specialty that some call **architainment.** We also look at architectural lighting as a fairly permanent solution to an illumination problem that can be expanded to include the lighting of public monuments and statuaries, roadways and parking lots, and bridges as well as buildings.

Most lighting designers approach the lighting of buildings from one of two perspectives. The first approaches a design from a quantitative perspective in which minimal visual standards are determined based on the visual **task** (type of activity or work being done) and the specific needs of an environment. From this information, a design is developed by creating a lighting system that delivers the required level of illumination to the environment in which the task is to be completed. The second method is based more on aesthetics and is less concerned with specific illumination levels. In reality, every project draws on a combination of both approaches. The first can be quite complex and is often planned by individuals with mostly electrical-engineering backgrounds (**illuminating engineers**), while the second brings people into the design process from a variety of backgrounds like interior design and the theatrical professions. Even though there are illuminating engineers, most individuals coming from an engineering background design lighting as only one element of all of a building's electrical systems.

Unique Qualities and Demands of Architectural Lighting

Unlike entertainment lighting, most architectural lighting is permanent. In fact, a significant problem is that many installations are not properly maintained and once-beautiful designs are destroyed through issues like burnouts and dirty luminaires. Other common problems include burnouts being replaced with lamps that don't follow the original specifications or **fixtures** not being refocused once a subject has been moved or a lamp has been replaced. It is also important to note that design decisions related to architectural lighting are in a sense etched in stone. Fixture placements require that conduit runs and electrical boxes be placed within ceilings or walls where construction materials like drywall or plaster are built around a unit's housing. A mistake in calculating a mounting position or beam specification can result in lighting that is either too dim, misplaced, or mismatched to a given application. This can lead to safety issues, a costly fix, or a permanently mismatched luminaire-to-design application. Another important difference lies in the timeline of architectural projects: while entertainment projects are designed over a period of weeks and months, an architectural project typically takes months, if not years, to complete. While there is collaboration in architectural lighting, the collaborators come from a variety of professions. The lighting designer is usually employed by a client who is either the architectural firm designing the project, the **end user,** or the owner of a building. Other collaborators can include interior designers, planning and space consultants, electrical engineers, and engineers of specialty building systems like plumbing or heating, ventilation, and air-conditioning (HVAC) systems. Once a project has been put out to bid, the lighting designer will also work with the general and electrical contractors that are hired to install a design.

Another difference from entertainment projects lies in the immense variety of fixture designs that are available in architectural lighting. The next section identifies several popular ways of classifying these luminaires. Also, because of the fixtures' extended operation, reliability, maintenance, and efficiency are major factors in architectural applications. Additionally, the fixtures must be aesthetically pleasing because they are frequently in full view and may even bring decorative elements to a project. Finally, since most fixtures are mounted with a single purpose that will rarely change, the units are specified and manufactured to tolerances based specifically on what each fixture must accomplish for a particular task. All of this has led to manufacturers creating thousands of very tightly specified luminaires with a large variety of decorative designs and finishes for architectural lighting. This is very different from the few general-purpose luminaire designs that are associated with entertainment lighting.

Architectural Luminaire Classifications

One way that architectural luminaires are classified is by application. Applications might include **wall-washers, task lights, downlights,** etc. Wall washers create a wash of light over the surface of a wall, while task lights place light in a localized area where a specific task is completed (e.g., a desk, table, or reading lamp). Luminaires are also distinguished by their light source (**incandescent, arc or HID, LED, fluorescent,** etc.). With the ban-the-bulb movement and the change in energy usage codes and attitudes, LEDs are overtaking the architectural market by leaps and bounds. Two other methods of classifying architectural luminaires are based on their mounting arrangements and beam distributions. The five categories of fixtures named by IESNA that are based on mounting arrangements (Figure 16.10) include

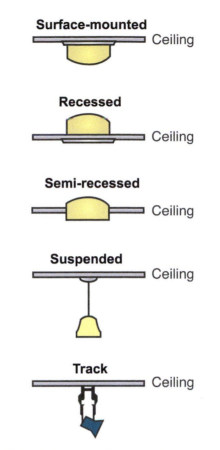

Figure 16.10 IESNA mounting classifications of architectural lighting fixtures

surface-mounted (mounted directly to walls and ceilings), **suspended** (luminaires hung below a ceiling from a **pendant,** wire, or other device), **recessed** (mounted within a wall or ceiling with the face of the fixture being flush with the surface), **semi-recessed** (mounted partially within a wall or ceiling cavity), and **track** luminaires (mounted to an electric path/rail or raceway) that are suspended below an architectural surface. IESNA has also defined fixture classifications that are based on the distribution pattern of a light source (Figure 16.11). These classifications assume that a fixture is mounted directly downward and include the following: **direct luminaires,** where 90–100% of the light is directed downward; **indirect luminaires,** where 90–100% of the light is directed upward and reflected off of the ceiling; **direct-indirect,** where light is directed both upward and downward roughly equally; **semi-direct,** where a significant amount of light is directed upward (10–40%) but the majority of the light is directed downward (60–90%); **semi-indirect,** where 10–40% of the light is directed downwards while 60–90% is directed upwards; and **general diffuse,** where light is directed outward in virtually all directions.

Direct luminaire

90% or more downlight

Indirect luminaire

90% or more uplight

Direct-indirect

40%–60%

40%–60%

Semi-direct luminaire

10–40% uplight

60–90% downlight

Semi-indirect luminaire

60–90% uplight

10–40% downlight

General diffuse

Figure 16.11 IESNA distribution patterns of luminaires

Key Elements in Architectural General Illumination

The process of lighting architectural spaces is largely based on perception and how **occupants** are affected by the way in which an environment is revealed to them. All architectural lighting is designed in order to provide several different functions within a lighted environment. This is essentially the same layered approach to lighting that was discussed for retail and museum design—one in which each layer provides a different function. Variations of this approach have been discussed in many other areas of lighting already presented throughout this book. The concept of providing a base level of illumination over an entire area and adding simple **accents** or additional work lights to specific areas is a popular example of this layered approach—with the assumption that each of these functions will most likely be satisfied by a different group of luminaires. While a project may have several different layers of lighting, the most important aspect of any architectural project is the **task lighting.** This is the lighting that provides the critical level of illumination for a specific job or task. In areas where more critical activities take place, a higher level of illumination is called for and specified. Illumination levels may also vary throughout a facility. Hallways and stairwells are not lit to the same levels as locations where more critical activities take place. One

significant difference between architectural applications and other areas of lighting is that the illumination levels for most architectural applications are dictated by specific building codes and recommendations. Another type of architectural lighting is the **ambient lighting** or **general illumination** that is provided throughout a space. Some designers call this **fill light,** while others may refer to it as **general lighting** or **base level lighting.** It is typically diffuse and provides a basic level of illumination for a space. It is also common for the task and ambient lighting to be created by the same luminaires in many environments.

The challenges of designing general lighting systems for architectural projects can be quite complex even though the basic manner of laying out an architectural design is quite similar to creating the area lighting for a stage. The major difference is primarily that luminosity levels must be calculated for the task(s) that will take place in an architectural space. Considerations are also made for visual acuity, reflectance levels of the surface materials, and the fact that luminosity levels are measured precisely rather than taken from general observations. Once the illumination levels are calculated, the lighting designer goes on to match luminaires and their beam patterns to the layout of a room in much the same way that stage lights are assigned to a stage. Through this, fixture layouts (**lighting plans** or **lighting layouts**) are generated in much the same way as theatrical light plots are created. A lighting layout for a condominium lighting project is illustrated in Figure 16.12. The general lighting for an architectural application is more complex not only in that the luminaires must deliver a prescribed quality and quantity of light, but also because the luminaires need to be considered from an aesthetic point of view. They must also be arranged neatly and should reduce effects like spill and glare.

Even though it is common for architectural spaces to be lit almost exclusively by task lighting systems, other elements are often added on top of a basic lighting design. Lighting may be used to direct attention and draw focus to a building's architectural features, lure occupants throughout a space, and/or establish a particular mood for an environment. Other lighting elements may be used solely in decorative ways like modifying the appearance of a building's architectural features (e.g., grazing a wall surface to add texture) or being a design element in itself (a chandelier or wall sconce). Luminaires can also bring visual interest, like sparkle, to an environment. A variety of specific lighting techniques are used to light architectural environments. Several of these include task and ambient lighting (discussed previously), as well as **accent lighting, cove lighting, decorative lighting, grazing, space manipulation,** and **wash lighting.** Chapter 7 in *Stage Lighting: Design Applications and More* provides a significant discussion regarding each of these lighting classifications.

Figure 16.12a A lighting design for a condo project. a. Lighting layout for the project.

Figure 16.12b A lighting layout for the project with circuiting and control specifications indicated

The Architectural Lighting Design Process

In the last 75 or so years we have become much more energy conscious, resulting in some of the first true elements of architectural lighting being instituted to maximize lighting efficiency and to conserve power. The popularity of fluorescent lighting in commercial buildings is a direct result of this. This economical influence continues to play an ever-increasing role in architectural lighting as we are now in the midst of once again shifting to even more economical light sources—this time in the form of LED luminaires. However, a second significant influence is in the philosophical shift of lighting spaces in a more aesthetic rather than quantitative manner. This movement began roughly in the 1970s. The argument of **quantity versus quality** has since led to a rethinking in how the lighting of most buildings is conceived and designed. This approach has expanded to include nearly every area of architectural lighting and is now considered not only as a functional building system but also as an integral part of a building's total design. This has led to the introduction of numerous carefully designed and highly visible lighting fixtures, especially for public spaces like municipal buildings, stores, hospitality properties, corporate headquarters, and churches.

Even though there's much more consideration of aesthetics in a lighting design, and the design solutions are more strongly based on the unique needs of an individual project, maintaining minimal illumination standards and following a set of general guidelines are still very much a part of the process of architectural lighting design. The newer approach has, however, resulted in a modified use of design guidelines for the architectural lighting community since 2000. The ninth edition of the *IESNA Lighting Handbook* addressed these changes and incorporated them into the design process, while still providing the required recommendations on illumination levels for any visual task. The 10th edition (released in 2011) has gone even further and has made a significant effort to readdress the specification process—placing a substantial emphasis of the design process on lighting quality (not quantity) and efficiency of design solutions. The IESNA also publishes design-specific guidelines that address unique areas of the lighting industry in a series of booklets called **recommended practices.** These provide guidance on the special needs and concerns of particular types of lighting installations. Recommended practices have been written and published by the IESNA for topics like hospitality design (hotels and restaurants), healthcare facilities, museums, schools and other educational buildings, as well as for offices and many other special areas of lighting design.

Regardless of application, many of the general principles of architectural lighting can be used for virtually all of the specialized architectural lighting applications that have emerged. Many of these are presented and discussed in a fair amount of detail in *Stage Lighting: Design Applications and More*. Specific lighting areas that are addressed there include residential lighting, hospitality lighting, public buildings, houses of worship, commercial and industrial lighting, lighting for educational and healthcare facilities, and exterior structures. Identification of the principal tasks, layering, and a solid use of basic lighting practices can result in the creation of energy-efficient lighting that satisfies the needs of any application while bringing visual interest to a project (see Figure 16.13). In many instances, several different lighting tasks may be addressed through a single lighting system—and a number of lighting environments often contain as few as one or two layers. This practice helps avoid issues like **ceiling clutter.** Sidebar 16.6 lists several lines of questioning that can be asked of almost any architectural project. Public and commercial buildings will also have additional lighting systems like **worklights** (for after-hours cleaning) and **emergency lighting** systems that become active when the principal lighting systems fail.

Figure 16.13a Architectural lighting. a. Accenting the reception area with multiple layers of luminaires

Figure 16.13b Revelation of both exterior and interior as part of the "total" design

Sidebar 16.6 LIGHTING DESIGN QUESTIONS

How does the lighting relate to the architecture and interior design?

Does the design satisfy the aesthetics and primary needs of the client?

Does the lighting contribute to the ambience or mood of the room or project?

Are appropriate illumination levels created by the lighting?

Does the design satisfy the needs of the primary visual task? Secondary? . . . etc.

Is there an appropriate level of control for the lighted environment?

Does the lighting enhance the architecture and other elements of a space?

Do the luminaires and other fittings blend in with the rest of the design elements?

Are different levels of focus or accents established appropriately?

Does the design comply with all applicable codes (building, safety, power densities, etc.)?

How does the design satisfy lighting economics and energy use?

Does the design satisfy the budgetary needs of the client?

The actual method of designing the lighting for an architectural project can vary considerably from one designer to another. While designers may refer to these steps differently (or recognize additional steps), there are essentially four steps that a lighting designer completes for most architectural projects. These are as follows:

1. Determine the design needs.
2. Determine the luminaires (light source, photometrics, and actual luminaire selection).
3. Create the layout.
4. Provide the control system(s) for the design.

It should be noted that these steps relate only to the design of the lighting, which is different from working through the construction phases of a project. Just as a lighting design for a theatrical production requires a concept, an architectural project requires a lighting concept. Many in architectural circles call this a **lighting scheme,** which is nothing more than the architectural equivalent of a lighting concept. As an architectural lighting designer makes choices in specific luminaires and where to place them, they develop a scaled plan (**lighting layout**) that functions in much the same way as a theatrical light plot. A variation of the lighting layout may also specify control data such as switch locations and circuiting information that identifies which luminaires share a common circuit. Once the lighting layout has been completed, additional forms and tables are developed that provide essentially the same types of schedules and control/fixture information that a theatrical designer's hookup and instrument schedule would provide.

Sidebar 16.7 DESIGNER PROFILE

Robert Shook

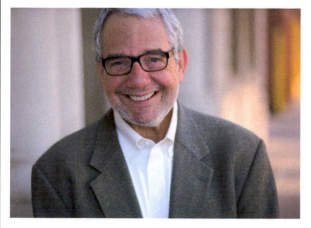

Credit: photo courtesy Leslie Schwartz

Robert "Bob" Shook began his career in theatrical lighting but was introduced to lighting architecture when he was asked to consult on a couple of architectural projects by Chicago architects who had seen his theatrical designs. He now works almost exclusively in architectural lighting and partnered with fellow lighting designer Duane Schuler in 1986 to form the architectural lighting firm of Schuler Shook. Bob holds the Fellow of the International Association of Lighting Designers designation and has consulted on numerous architectural lighting projects throughout the world. Several high-profile projects he has designed include O'Hare International Airport, the Chicago Downtown Lighting Master Plan, Wrigley Field, The Historic Water Tower (Chicago), John G. Shedd Aquarium (Chicago), Cathedral of the Immaculate Conception (Ft.

Wayne), Second Street Bridge (Columbus, Indiana), and numerous university projects (Rice University, Northwestern University, University of Notre Dame, Princeton University, and University of Chicago,). His lighting has won many awards (IESNA Int'l Illumination Design Awards, IESNA Illumination Design Awards, an IESNA Int'l Illumination Design Award of Distinction, IALD International Illumination Design Awards, and a GE Edison Award of Excellence).

Bob was trained in theatrical lighting design and received a BFA from the Goodman School of Drama and an MFA from Ohio University. He was working in the Chicago theatre scene following his graduate work when he was first approached to offer advice on how to light architectural projects: "My reputation as a theatrical lighting designer in Chicago led some clients to call me to help them with architectural lighting challenges. As a theatrical lighting designer, I welcomed the opportunity to design lighting that would be more permanent." His initial break came when Chicago architect John Vinci hired him for several small lighting projects—this being before he had established a reputation in architectural lighting. This introduction to the field of architectural lighting was extremely helpful in gaining entry to other projects with additional architects throughout Chicago. In 1980, he met his future business partner Duane Schuler while working for the Chicago Civic Theatre and Duane was resident lighting designer for the Lyric Opera of Chicago. They worked together consulting on a number of architectural projects and eventually formed their own lighting firm.

Bob's preparation for architectural lighting came primarily through his participation in the many educational seminars that are conducted through IALD and IESNA. Even with many years of designing architectural lighting, he tries to attend as many educational opportunities as possible: "The IALD and IES offer excellent seminars that are sources of information to help you remain up-to-date in the discipline, particularly with evolving technologies." In describing several unique differences between lighting for theatre and lighting for architecture he points out:

> "Architectural lighting design differs from theatrical lighting primarily by its permanence. In most cases, once luminaires are installed in an architectural environment, there's no moving them around or adding or subtracting to make corrections or refinements in a design. There's also no rehearsal process and little opportunity to test ideas. A lot more up-front research and calculation must be done to assure that the design will meet the client's requirements and expectations."

He also shares that "Architectural lighting must conform to local and national energy codes, so designs must utilize energy-efficient sources, primarily LEED. Designs must be tested for energy usage in addition to illumination levels, architectural integration, and artistic concept."

What Bob likes best about designing in architectural lighting is that every project is completely different in regard to the artistic requirements that it will have. He also likes the collaboration that takes place over the lifetime of a project and believes that "Lighting designers must discover how best to relate lighting to each architect's personal artistic process." This attitude also ties into what he considers to be one of the most essential principles of working in this area of lighting: "The lighting must be completely integrated into the architecture and that the lighting and architecture must be seen as one complete design."

Daylighting

All of the light sources discussed to this point in this chapter have been artificial or man-made: where light has been manufactured by converting one form of energy into another. Daylight, in contrast, is natural—and while we can't create it, it can be manipulated to enhance or supplement the lighting of an environment. It can also have detrimental effects on an environment as well. **Daylighting** uses natural sunlight to illuminate a space. Although sunlight isn't a typical consideration in entertainment lighting, it's becoming an ever more important element of architectural lighting. While there are aesthetic considerations for using daylighting as a supplemental light source for a project, energy conservation is a major factor in the increased role that daylighting is playing in many architectural lighting designs.

There are two daylight components. The first relates to **direct sunlight,** while the second relates to the effect of light scattering in the atmosphere and sky. This scattering creates a diffuse source of illumination called **skylight.** Direct sunlight is usually more of a problem than a benefit to architectural projects due to issues such as the extreme contrasts and glare that it can produce. It also produces a greenhouse heating effect when it is trapped in an interior. Sunlight is also fairly unreliable due to the extreme variation that it displays, and

Figure 16.14a Exterior lighting of Hunt Library in Pittsburgh, Pennsylvania (C&C Lighting, LLC). a. A single color setting for the building's facade.

Credit: photo courtesy C&C Lighting, LLC

Figure 16.14b A rainbow color setting for the building's facade

Credit: photo courtesy C&C Lighting, LLC

is therefore usually only considered as a supplemental light source for a building. Skylight is more consistent and has an overall predictability that direct sunlight does not. Just a few of the many daylight factors that have an impact on a building's daylight exposure include time of day, geographical location and orientation of a building, seasons, weather, and cloud cover.

Lighting Green and Lighting Economics

From the energy crisis of the 1970s on, lighting professionals have searched for ways to reduce the need for power, examined alternative energy sources, and looked to a variety of technologies for conserving and protecting our resources and environment. One of the programs in the construction industry that emphasizes environmentally friendly building practices is the **Leadership in Energy and Environmental Design (LEED)** certification program. This program provides certification of a building by tracking qualifying points earned by practicing environmentally sound building practices. Lighting is only one area that affects the certification process—but it can earn more than a dozen points toward the certification score of a particular project. While other parts of our society focus on conserving gas, commuting, recycling, and eliminating waste, the lighting industry focuses on issues like energy conservation, luminaire and power efficiency, and elimination of hazardous materials in its daily practices. While much of the interest in conservation is tied to making the earth a better place to live, an even larger part of the effort is economically based and related to finding methods to reduce a client's power and lighting maintenance bills as electricity and other sources of energy become more expensive.

Unlike entertainment lighting systems, architectural lighting systems are in operation for many hours a day. In the case of a commercial building this may mean that a considerable amount of power is consumed as the lights perform their daily tasks. This becomes even more significant as buildings get bigger and expand into large square-footage or multilevel structures like warehouses, industrial complexes, and high-rise apartments or office towers. Most economical concerns that relate to lighting are aimed at either reducing the power demands of an installation or making determinations of how long it takes for the savings of an investment in new lighting equipment to pay for itself. These issues are addressed through a series of practices that are called **energy management** and **lighting economics.** Energy management refers to finding ways of reducing a building's power demands while causing a minimal loss in quality to the lighting and other building systems. In large commercial buildings, lighting is often one of the most energy-demanding systems to operate. It can also have serious impacts on other building systems. For instance,

using more light sources can raise the temperature of a room and force the air-conditioning units to work harder. Power conservation has become so important that there are now energy codes that dictate how much power a lighting design may use over a given time period. This is expressed in **power densities** that refer to the watts/square foot that a building system consumes. The most widespread energy code that specifies power densities is **ASHRAE/IESNA 90.1**, which dictates the maximum number of watts per square foot that a lighting design may use for a given application. This and other energy codes increase or decrease the allowed power density specifications based on the activities that take place in a given environment. The maximum power density for a hospital is higher than one allowed for a hotel, while the power density allowed for a school or office building is higher than those of an adjoining parking garage. Nearly every building or renovation project must now be in compliance with these power density requirements. Several states, like California and New York, have much more stringent power codes than other parts of the country. Power codes may also be set by municipalities such as cities. In lighting economics, we are concerned with an issue called **payback,** where the costs of installing and operating lighting systems are compared to one another. The basic principle involves adding up all of the costs of installing (costs of the equipment and labor) and maintaining a lighting system (electrical use, lamp replacement, and maintenance costs such as cleaning, etc.) to make a determination of how long it will take for a system to pay for itself through the energy savings that are created by operating the system on a daily basis.

In addition to power consumption, lighting green also refers to recycling lighting resources: raw materials are returned to use instead of taking up space in a landfill, and hazardous materials are disposed of in a safe, environmentally friendly manner. Several specific ways in which the lighting industry recycles include the conversion of old luminaire housings to scrap metal or retrieving copper wiring and cables from old installations. Many older luminaires and wiring have hazardous materials like asbestos that must be removed and disposed of in specific ways. An even larger problem lies in the disposal of fluorescent lamps, which frequently contain mercury (a hazardous material). While lamp manufacturers now make mercury-free versions of these lamps, many fluorescent lamps used in commercial applications still contain mercury and should be disposed of in a prescribed manner.

LANDSCAPE LIGHTING

Landscape lighting is a special discipline of architectural lighting in which the lighting of a building's exterior and surrounding grounds combine to enhance a property's appearance. Items that are typically lighted as part of a landscape design include the vegetation (trees and plants), pathways, sculptures, water (pools and fountains), exterior building surfaces, and other architectural features of a property. Landscape lighting has been around for a number of years but has often been limited to commercial or high-end residential applications. Now, with advances in low-voltage equipment, landscape lighting is flourishing. Corporations often draw the public to their buildings by creating an inviting image that begins with viewing their property and its buildings from the street. Homeowners use landscape lighting to create curb appeal that increases the value of their homes while also making their yards usable for more activities over a greater portion of the day and year.

Lighting Landscapes

Landscape lighting provides a number of functions that are important to a building owner, and many go well beyond creating an aesthetic response or providing greater use of a property's outdoor spaces. A unique element of landscape lighting relates to the fact that the primary subjects of these designs are usually a property's plants and trees. This is very different from lighting for a building's occupants and creates several special considerations that must be examined while completing these projects. Despite this, lighting for particular types of visibility is still an important element of these designs. Many refer to this as lighting for **safety.** The most common form of safety lighting, **walkway** or **pathway lighting**, allows people to navigate successfully throughout a space after dark through placing luminaires along sidewalks and other paths. Another important function of landscape lighting falls to providing **security** for a property. While some security lighting is provided by simply flooding a property with floodlights, a more desirable approach often provides a more creative solution to security lighting than simply flooding an area with light. In the end, prowlers are usually more concerned with the absence of light than the way in which a property is lit.

There are two additional issues that a landscape lighting designer must contend with that are unique to this area of lighting. Both are related to the special needs of the luminaires that are used. First, the fixtures are exposed to the natural elements. Extreme shifts in the weather, prolonged exposure to ultraviolet radiation, exposure to moisture from rain and irrigation systems, and even harm from careless landscapers all have detrimental effects on these luminaires. Second, the means of powering these systems can be either **line-voltage** (120 volt) or **low-voltage** (most commonly 12 volt). Line-voltage systems deliver plenty of power but are more dangerous and require special safety practices in their installations. Low-voltage systems have issues related to **voltage drop** where the wires to the fixtures farthest from the power source undergo additional resistance that causes their lamps to glow more dimly than those located closer to the power source. Though the majority of low-voltage systems are powered by transformers, solar-powered luminaires are also quite popular in many residential installations. These are gaining even more popularity with the increased use of LED sources in landscape luminaires.

Essential Approaches to Lighting Landscapes

Unlike many other forms of lighting design, appropriate landscape lighting intensities are a relative rather than absolute determination from one installation to another. As a rule, the intensity levels of garden or landscape lighting are relatively low when compared to most other lighting applications. The overall intensity levels of a project are partially determined by the relative amounts of light associated with the neighboring properties and environment. Excessive **glare** should be avoided since people circulating throughout a property might be blinded by poorly aimed luminaires. For the most part, landscape lighting is best handled by creating **accents** that focus on specific elements of a landscape, not on creating uniform lighting throughout an entire space. The selective use of darkness brings contrast and visual interest to a design. Landscape lighting is also not limited to lighting trees and plants. In fact, many of the more effective elements of these designs involve lighting objects other than foliage. Pools and water features such as fountains are popular subjects for landscape lighting. The plants or growing elements are called **softscape,** while architectural features like footbridges, pathways, and sculptures are called **hardscape.**

Landscape lighting is usually designed from several different perspectives. While there's often a prominent view, there will also be features that are highlighted for those who see a project from other directions. The lighting from within a property must also be considered. Many restaurants offer choice seating where windows provide views of the landscaping and surrounding areas. Finally, landscape lighting designers must design with the idea of planning for the future. The vegetation is constantly growing and the lighting must evolve as the landscape matures and changes. Lighting saplings from below with in-ground fixtures will work nicely for a couple years but only until the branches of the trees extend beyond the beams of the fixtures. To correct this, the fixtures have to be refocused or moved to extend their coverage of the maturing branches.

There are a number of distribution patterns and functions that landscape lighting can provide for a property. Just a few of these include **area** and **pathway lighting, accent lighting, security lighting, spotlighting,** and even **contour** and **background lighting.** Some landscape lighting is based on familiar techniques like **cross lighting, grazing, uplighting,** and **downlighting,** while others like **shadowing, mirroring, perspective lighting, moonlighting,** and **vista lighting** are unique to this specialty. These are all discussed in *Stage Lighting: Design Applications and More.* Uplighting and path lighting are illustrated in Figure 16.15a, while Figure 16.15b shows an example of moonlighting and area lighting.

Principles of Landscape Lighting

There are many ways that a lighting designer can use light to create a unique exterior environment that is suited to the specific needs and tastes of a client. Many of these variables are based on factors like the personal preferences of a property owner, the types of plants being lit, and the intended use for the exterior

Figure 16.15a Landscape lighting projects. a. Lighting leading to a building's entrance lobby by uplighting trees and path lighting along a sidewalk

Figure 16.15b An example of moonlighting with area and path lighting along the flower beds

spaces. Contrast plays an important role in landscape lighting designs. This is most apparent when comparing **soft light,** which is generally more diffuse and less defined, and **hard light,** which has a hard, clean edge that produces relatively sharp shadows. Hard light is typically created from point light sources that are often used to direct focus and add sparkle to a scene. In pathway lighting (especially in public areas), issues like the base or minimum intensity level of a project may be dependent on local governance. A designer should also consider the effect of how much **light trespass** or spill is coming from other properties and the immediate neighborhood. On the flip side, a designer must be considerate of light trespass onto neighboring properties. While an uplight may be perfect for lighting a tree near a property line, you could create a problem if the spill or glare from that light enters a neighbor's bedroom.

Perhaps the most important element of the design process, as with architectural lighting, is getting to know the client and understanding their likes and dislikes, how they intend to use the exterior environment, and the items that they want to feature. After gaining an understanding of the client's expectations, the designer moves on to looking at the property and landscaping features or **site plans** to develop a concept and eventual **lighting plan** or **layout** for the project (Figure 16.16). Control and fixture schedules are also completed as part of the design package. The lighting layout is the equivalent of a light plot. It not only provides the luminaire specifications and locations but also the location of the circuiting, power sources (like transformers), and control devices (like timers).

THEMED DESIGN AND SPECIALTY LIGHTING

Themed design refers to creating some form of entertainment experience for patrons who share in an event. While theme parks are the most obvious example of themed designing, it should be noted that theming techniques have moved into many areas of our lives. Several of the more popular applications include the design of hotel and resort attractions, many upscale restaurants, and a host of retail establishments. In the purest sense, themed design seeks to create a story-like experience for anyone who is exposed to the themed event or environment. A truly themed attraction is organized and designed around a more significant experience and attempts to involve the guests in a story, even to the point of being participants in the action. There are many elements of our lives that are influenced by some form of theming, even though they may not be truly themed experiences in themselves. One only has to go to the nearest mall to find restaurants like Outback, Cracker Barrel, and Red Lobster or stores like The Disney Store, Build-a-Bear Workshop, LEGO Imagination

Figure 16.16 A site plan with landscape lighting indicated

Center, and Bass Pro Shops to see the effects of themed design. There's even a grocery chain in Connecticut (Stew Leonard's) that places **animatronic** animals and games throughout its stores. Many restaurants, especially in tourist areas, make use of themed design. Popular examples include Planet Hollywood, Rainforest Café, Cracker Barrel, and Chuck E. Cheese restaurants. On a smaller scale, themed design can appear in retail displays such as the room settings of furniture stores like Rooms to Go or the Ralph Lauren or Christie Brinkley clothing displays in department stores. While this area of lighting has traditionally been called **themed lighting,** professionals are now referring to this type of lighting as **specialty lighting.**

The Story

One of the most critical considerations that must be examined when completing a themed design is the story that is developed for a project. Not only is the story important in its own sense, but it also becomes the mechanism for connecting guests to the attraction on an emotional level. The story is used to define the event, and every design decision should be evaluated on how well it supports or ties into the story that is being told. Without it, a project simply becomes a ride or attraction with no greater experience for the participant.

Designers of themed events (especially themed attractions) try to create an all-encompassing experience that immerses the guests in an event. Universal Studio's E.T. Adventure doesn't simply take guests on an aerial bicycle ride—it places them in the same chase sequence as the boys who help E.T. escape from the authorities in the film. The ride tells a story while introducing the guests to additional adventure with E.T. A truly themed attraction attempts to bring as many of a participant's senses into the experience as possible. While sight and sound are the primary senses that are stimulated in these attractions, touch and motion are also addressed by creating vibrations and blasts of heat or air, using motion simulators, and using water and spray technologies to create mists or to otherwise get the guests wet. Disney and other park operators have even gone to the extent of introducing smells to some attractions. The initial interaction with an attraction begins as guests first approach the structure or building that houses the attraction and as they stand in the **queue** waiting for the actual ride. One technique for disguising excessive lines involves designing queues that lead from one chamber to another while revealing parts of the story (**exposition**) that lead up to the point where a ride actually begins. Some popular attractions with elaborate queues like The Amazing Adventures of Spiderman or Men in Black Alien Attack (Islands of Adventure/Universal Studios) and The

Pirates of the Caribbean (Disney) have mazes of tunnels and a half dozen or more chambers that entertain guests while they wait. The queue for Men in Black includes being led past a creature break room, a central control/processing area, and a weapons room before entering the staging area where guests are loaded into the vehicles for the actual ride. All of these areas are designed and lit appropriately. Figure 16.17 features a chamber from a themed attraction based on a Halloween horror attraction.

There are a number of examples beyond theme parks where strong storylines are worked into themed environments. Historical sites like Williamsburg and Mystic Seaport re-create entire villages based on themed environments where casts take on the roles of craftspeople who perform re-enactments of life in an earlier time. Museums and special exhibits are also gravitating towards more theming in their overall designs and the manner in which they create exhibits. The *Titanic* touring exhibit goes to the extent of issuing boarding passes to guests containing one of the names of the original passengers, which are compared to a survivor list at the end of the exhibit. Some people refer to this type of designing as **edu-tainment.** Regardless of the nature of the event, the story becomes the most important theme in driving the rest of the design decisions. Ultimately, it becomes the primary element that determines the success of a project.

Development of a Themed Project

One of the most challenging aspects of themed projects is found in the schedule that they follow. Even a fast-developing project can take six months to several years to complete: most of an attraction's development is based on original concepts and equipment that has never been created before. Attractions are also treated as construction projects rather than theatrical ventures and

Figure 16.17 A scene from a themed attraction that is part of a Halloween horror attraction

Credit: photo courtesy of Rick Clark and ID3 Group

are subject to the more stringent demands of building codes and other time-consuming construction practices. Another significant difference comes in that the equipment that makes a show possible often must be engineered as part of the design process. In fact, the show or ride, with all of its equipment, is usually designed before the building that houses the attraction. This ensures that the attraction is not compromised due to having to work within limitations of a predetermined space.

Most themed projects begin with brainstorming—what is called **blue sky development.** After this, a concept is developed and the team works out the project's details. In addition to entertainment value, there are also concerns regarding economics (budgets, schedules, etc.), volume of visitors per hour or day, duration of an event, crowd control, and engineering requirements that are unique to a project. For the lighting designer, this is the point where a formal **light plot** or **lighting layout, control schedule,** and other aspects of the lighting are finalized. The luminaires are also often mounted on scenic structures and may have to be placed by the designer personally. Finally, much of these installations are permanent, and the layouts must be accurate so that circuit boxes and conduit runs can be placed correctly by the electrical contractor. At some point, after the majority of the equipment is installed, the lighting team **aims** or **focuses** the luminaires and cues the attraction. The lighting, as well as all other elements of the attraction, is then tested and refined over an extended period of time (**shakedown**).

Considerations of Themed (Specialty) Lighting Design

Lighting in most theme parks or any other themed environment must ultimately operate on several levels. The solution to a design is also a factor of the nature of a project. An attraction in a theme park will have more flexibility in the way that it is lit than what can be expected in a themed restaurant, which in turn will have fewer limitations than lighting a collection of products in a themed retail environment. One thing that is almost certain is that the specific lighting for any attraction will almost always be unique since most themed projects are one-of-a-kind creations.

Much of the lighting in themed attractions goes back to the concept of creating layers of light, each with a particular purpose. The first layer, which is probably the most important, usually relates to lighting the story elements of an attraction. It should be lit first. What does a guest have to see? How should the focus be directed? What is the dominant mood of each setting? Questions like these refer to how the lighting designer contributes to telling the story of an attraction. Because of the amount of control that many of these tasks require, it's common for theatrical luminaires and control equipment to be used for many aspects of an attraction's lighting design. Some even refer to this as the **theatrical lighting** for an attraction. Contrast ratios are especially important in an attraction's lighting because they become the primary means of directing the guests' attention. The lighting equipment associated with much of this illumination is frequently off-the-shelf theatrical equipment that is mounted and wired in a permanent fashion. The most common practice is to run conduit and junction boxes from the dimmer racks to where the units are mounted and wired directly to their associated circuits. While theatrical gels are often used, the extended use requires their replacement on a regular basis—something that often gets ignored until the lighting becomes dismal. Because of this, many designers are specifying dichroic filters as a long-term solution to the gel problem. Maintaining the fixtures (lamp burnouts, cleaning, refocusing, etc.) is another concern for keeping these designs in their best condition.

Once the primary elements of an attraction have been lit there are additional features that will also need lighting. This is done through developing supplemental lighting for elements like the interior and exterior features of the building that houses an attraction. This is commonly called the **architectural lighting** element of an attraction. Even though this lighting is predominantly architectural, it doesn't prohibit these units and equipment from being used for theatrical functions, or vice-versa. This lighting typically provides general illumination for various building components and supports tasks like guest circulation (e.g., lighting building approaches, queues, and waiting areas), illuminating the exterior of the building, and lighting the attraction's landscaping. Often these systems are used in queues to help guests make the transition from the bright exterior sunlight to the much darker interiors of an attraction. Typically, these parts of an attraction's lighting use architectural and landscaping fixtures rather than theatrical luminaires. The architectural systems should also move beyond simple illumination and are frequently used to create moods, set off a building's features, illuminate signs, and make other statements about the attraction.

The final layer of an attraction's lighting design involves **effects lighting** and is used to create special effects throughout an attraction. Gobos can create textured light like that associated with being in the woods; LEDs can be used to create a shimmering water effect; chase and flicker effects are useful for fire effects;, and strobe sequences, fiber-optic effects, and black light (with day-glow paints) all form additional lighting effects that are popular in many attractions. These installations will also have **emergency** and **worklight** lighting systems that will also have to be designed and specified, although they are not used as part of the themed lighting.

Sidebar 16.8 DESIGNER PROFILE

Tom Ruzika

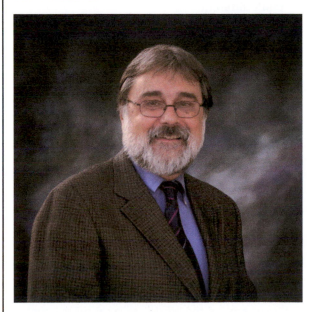

Credit: photo courtesy Donna Ruzika

Tom Ruzika has a career that reflects a project list with credits in many areas of lighting design. His designs have been seen on Broadway, in national tours, major regional theatres, and national and international dance and opera companies. He's designed more than 90 productions for the South Coast Repertory Theatre with design credits at other leading companies that include Coconut Grove Playhouse, Hollywood Bowl, Ford's Theatre in Washington, DC, the Laguna Playhouse, Los Angeles Civic Light Opera, Opera Santa Barbara, Berkeley Repertory Theatre, and the Mark Taper Forum. More uniquely, he has designed the lighting for numerous attractions associated with theme parks in six different countries, and architectural projects that include prestigious hotels, casinos, restaurants, and retail centers covering several continents (including North America, Asia, and Europe). His entertainment lighting can be seen at theme parks in six countries and his architectural lighting can be seen across the nation and in multiple Asian and European countries. Just a few of his themed projects include Backdraft, Earthquake, and Back to the Future (Universal Studios, Hollywood); the Main Street Emporium and renovation of the Disneyland Hotel Grand Ballroom (Disneyland); Batman Forever and Maverick shows at Movie World Australia (Warner Brothers); Seuss *Landing* at Universal's Islands of Adventure in Orlando; as well as five theme parks in Japan and additional attractions at Knott's Berry Farm and other parks. Several of his more visible architectural projects include Seminole Hard Rock Hotels and Casinos in Florida; casinos in Philadelphia, Pittsburgh, Des Plaines, Indiana, Oklahoma, California, and Las Vegas; the Hard Rock Hotel San Diego; South Coast Plaza; the Los Angeles Music Center; and Universal CityWalk. He has also consulted on more than 90 performance facilities and created an extensive master plan for lighting the exterior facades of 104 historic buildings in downtown Los Angeles. His lighting has won many awards across multiple areas of the industry, including numerous Critics Circle Awards, the Lifetime Achievement Award in Lighting from the Los Angeles Drama Critics Circle, Lighting Dimensions Designer of the Year Award, California State Polytechnic University, Pomona Alumni of the year, and a number of national and international architectural lighting design awards.

Tom's formal training includes a BS in Drama from California State Polytechnic University, Pomona, and an MFA from University of California, Irvine. More interestingly, his introduction to theatre came through his playing the organ for choirs in his high school auditorium: "Being backstage, this experience led to my interest in stage lighting. I learned theatrical lighting in high school 'by doing' and continued my training in college." His education in architectural lighting came about when he was asked to light a shopping mall parking garage to help make women look more attractive. He learned themed entertainment lighting when he was asked to light a portion of a theme park in Japan. He names several people who helped him break into each of the specialty areas of lighting in which he now works: Tharon Musser and Ken Billington (stage lighting), Pat Maloney of Universal Studios Hollywood (themed entertainment lighting), and Henry Segerstrom with the South Coast Plaza Mall project (architectural lighting). Since there are relatively few options for being trained in much of this type of lighting, most of his training came from "developing knowledge of all styles of lighting via projects that came through my design studio and being in the business for over 30 years." Currently, his design work is comprised of approximately 50% architectural and specialty lighting, 10% themed

entertainment, 35% theatre consulting, and about 5% theatrical performance designs.

Tom states:

"I love everything about working with light. There is great satisfaction in revealing something in an exciting, vibrant way, making it stand out no matter what it is . . . an actor, or a building. This is especially true today with the many new light sources that are available. Our imagination can really soar because we can achieve so many exciting compositions of light."

Several unique conditions of working in architectural and themed lighting include the considerations involved in picking the light sources and luminaires and where you ultimately put the lighting fixtures:

"You need to collaborate with the architects in the early phases of the design; there is no lighting plan with specific hanging positions like in a theatre, so you have more freedom, but at the same time you have more constrictions due to building codes, energy restrictions, construction techniques, lamp choices, and the stylistic nature of the architecture that you are illuminating."

On the other hand, Tom also shares:

"All lighting design is based on the same principles; what makes the difference is in the question of what are you lighting? An actor, a building, piece of art, cartoon characters; the principles are all the same—it's the equipment that's different."

When asked to respond to what he considers to be "Rule #1" for lighting within any of these disciplines, Tom replies that it has to be about "providing high quality 'selective visibility' to a project or environment—be it an actor, building, or themed scenic element." He also comments on the lack of time that can exist on these projects as well:

"You don't always have time for creative or reflective thought on a project. With today's computer-aided systems, we get projects on a Friday afternoon and are told that initial design drawings must be finished by Monday. We are given less time to actually design!"

Like many other designers, Tom reads the trade magazines, goes to LDI, and observes what other designers around the world are creating as a means of remaining on top of the technology and business. One final thought that he shares speaks to how he has done so well in such a range of disciplines throughout the lighting industry: "Good lighting design practice is based upon knowledge, skill, and collaboration. It is also in accepting challenges, problem solving, talent, and bringing a sense of fun and adventure to a project."

In contemporary society, there is a wide range of design projects that have some form of themed elements contained within them. While theme parks and their associated attractions are obvious examples of these special areas of design, other areas like restaurants, hotels, and retail stores comprise additional niches where the concepts of themed lighting are put into regular practice. The most extreme forms of themed lighting can be found in the spectacle productions that form the closing events that are found nightly in many of the theme parks. These productions contain a story, music, large numbers of performers, and often fireworks, pyro, lasers, and other effects that are viewed from various locations throughout the park. In some cases, a specific performance area or pavilion may be constructed to house these events. One of the best examples of this type

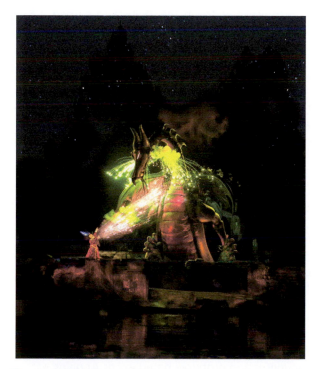

Figure 16.18 Mickey Mouse as the Sorcerer's Apprentice battling a dragon in *Fantasmic!* at Disneyland Park in the Disneyland Resort (Anaheim)

Credit: photo courtesy ©Disney

of event are the Disney productions of *Fantasmic!* that are produced nightly at both the Anaheim and Orlando Disney parks. Chapter 9 in *Stage Lighting: Design Applications and More* provides detailed discussions of several different forms of themed projects and how their lighting might be approached by a lighting designer.

VIRTUAL LIGHTING (RENDERINGS, VIRTUAL REALITY, GAMING, ETC.)

Virtual lighting refers to lighting within the simulated or digital worlds of computers and other electronic devices like video games and smart phones. Since the appearance of the personal computer (PC), many areas of design have seen the potential for using specialized software to present and communicate information to other design professionals and their clients. Entertainment designers, architects, and interior designers all make use of virtual designing in their professions. The best comparison to virtual design is creating a scenic model that is placed in a model light lab where it can be illuminated. All objects that are contained in a virtual environment are created (**modeled**) to simulate three-dimensional elements. While the creation of the initial model is usually quite time consuming, the advantage that computer modeling brings to a project is in the flexibility with which a design may be presented. In traditional rendering, a single viewpoint is taken of a design with a specific perspective view that is then painted or illustrated in a manner that reflects a choice of materials and lighting for a given scene. This rendering is good for a single combination of features only; if a team wants to make comparisons between different materials, colors, viewing angles, or any other design elements like lighting, additional renderings must be made—each one beginning from scratch. Digital designs allow a single model to be created and saved as a master file that is then used to generate a number of additional images based on different combinations of materials, views, colors, and lighting conditions. These images are typically called **computer renderings** or **visualizations.** Computer rendering allows many of the repetitive tasks of creating a rendering to be eliminated since only one model is required for exploring the many options. These computer visualizations have evolved from primitive images to scenes that can illustrate the same amount of detail as a photograph. Design visualizations that depict this amount of detail are often called **photorealistic** or are said to display a high degree of **photorealism.** Due to the speed at which computers can produce new images, they can easily create animated sequences that follow the changing position of a virtual camera or alter variables such as the materials, colors or lighting in the models themselves. In some cases, the new images are created **on the fly,** in real time, allowing an observer to move through a virtual world (**walk-through** or **flyby**) as environments are rendered around them (e.g., computer action games). A walk-through takes much more computational power because the viewer is free to look and move through the virtual world as they please while a flyby takes a viewer along a predetermined path that is determined by the project's creators and thus requires much less computational power to render.

Virtual Design

Virtual design depends on the electronic files generated by computer programs. In effect, everything created in a virtual design is an assemblage of formulas and mathematical data. The image is a representation of specific values and color associations for a collection of points known as **pixels.** The smaller the pixels, the more **resolution** or detail an image can display. However, the more pixels used to create an image, the more calculations a computer must make to generate an image, the more time needed for this process, and the more data that is stored in an image file. In the end, a designer must consider the tradeoff between rendering speed and file size versus the amount of detail and resolution that will be depicted in a final image. If a single photorealistic image

of an architectural rendering is desired, it would make sense to use a very high resolution for its rendering. However, if the same image were part of an animation, it would be better to lower the resolution so that the sequence could be rendered more quickly. The average viewer will not see the difference in quality as the animation is played. With computer processors getting faster and the amounts of RAM increasing, we can now use much higher resolutions than even a few years ago. This allows us to create more detailed animations that are rendered more quickly. The final images are bigger and look better, but expectations have also gotten higher. What took a long time to render for the look that we produced at one time still takes a long time to render today because of the higher levels of detailing that we now expect in current images.

A variety of special applications in virtual design are presented in Chapter 10 of *Stage Lighting: Design Applications and More*. Several of the specific topics presented there include using virtual lighting as a tool for visualization, creating virtual design elements for film and video production, and virtual game design. A detailed discussion of the different rendering processes is also presented.

Sidebar 16.9 DESIGNER PROFILE

Chris Wells

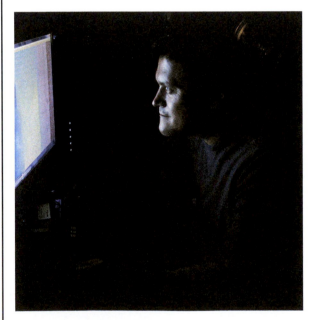

Credit: photo courtesy Chris Wells

Chris Wells is a digital animation and visual effects expert who has been working in digital effects and lighting for more than 20 years. He began college

in technical theatre in the 1990s and earned a BA degree from the University of Georgia, where he discovered the world of digital (computer-generated, or CG) graphics early in his student career. He was one of the first students to forge a path in the study of digital design. His training led to experiences in both filming and digital arts. Chris began his professional career at a small Atlanta-based company, where he worked for several years developing the skills that allowed him to transition to a more established company based out of New York. During that time, he spent several years working mostly on commercials and television. Later, he moved to Los Angeles to work not only in these forms of digital media but also on motion pictures. Since then, he has helped create or supervise the lighting and effects for numerous projects. Several of his more familiar credits include *The Curious Case of Benjamin Button, Take Shelter, Looper, The Incredible Hulk, 300, Live Free or Die Hard, The Fantastic Four, X-Men: The Last Stand*, and *The Day After Tomorrow*. Currently, he is an independent visual effects supervisor and producer based in Los Angeles.

Chris's earliest interests in lighting were in theatrical lighting, which is what he began studying in college. But after taking an introductory animation class as an independent study and being mentored by one of his professors (Mike Hussey), he was "able to translate my enjoyment of stage lighting into a digital art back in the days when digital classes were almost nonexistent." Chris began his work in the animation industry by working in all areas of computer animation. Even while attending college he "showed a particular knack for replicating photorealistic imagery in his computer animations." While in school, he learned basic skills in both digital imaging and lighting. After graduation he spent several years honing his craft: "From there I started working on projects in the smaller markets but was constantly recruited into the feature film market." Through his work in these markets, Chris emerged as a digital artist who specializes in lighting and visual effects:

"In my particular profession I get to sit down and light digital scenes for movies, but my main job is to work with other artists to make sure that they are hitting their aesthetic marks, whether that is matching a pre-existing image or creating their own concept for a film."

As for training beyond the classroom, Chris states:

"I had to learn about photography. It's good to know how to light a small area or enclosure, but it's better when you know how light in the real world works. Photography allows you to study light and to develop an understanding of how it behaves."

When Chris was asked to respond to how this area of lighting is different from other lighting areas, he identified several important observations, the most important probably being "it's fake." You can do things in the digital world that are impossible to create in nature, but this can have a cost:

"The biggest problem I've noticed with myself and other digital artists is that you have so much creative freedom that it's hard to stay focused on what's important. You don't just "make light," you also create the surfaces that are being lit. I constantly remind myself that composition is just as important as the world that I'm lighting or creating."

He adds: "Even though the lighting may be fake, the concepts of how you work with light are the same—instead of wearing gloves and climbing ladders, you sit at a desk and turn on the computer."

What Chris likes most about designing in this area of lighting are the challenges and freedoms that come with most projects: "I really enjoy watching and being part of the evolution of a project." This freedom can also have a downside. "Some projects can be mentally exhausting and I've had to work on some projects for months, looking at the same images over and over again." In order to remain current he suggests observing both nature and other people at work:

"Since we work in visual effects, I always encourage people to "go outside" and see the world. The more you see, the more you'll train your eye for future projects. Things are always changing so it's good to watch what other people are doing to see if their ideas might help you in your future work. There are still many things in the digital world that aren't physically accurate, so we learn tricks to accomplish the same look. Over time, people are figuring out how to make the physics work with newer software that, along with subtle changes, helps make higher-quality images possible."

His most important advice is to "know what you want, whether it's a photo-real object or an abstraction—always have a plan for what it is that you want to accomplish."

Virtual Light Sources

Virtual lighting makes use of several unique groups of virtual light sources with distinct properties that make them different from one another. These lights can be altered or manipulated in a number of ways (color, intensity, falloff, etc.) that make each source unique in a given setting—much in the same way that traditional luminaires may be controlled. In addition to normal parameters like being able to adjust intensity or color, some of these sources can go on to produce effects that are impossible to create in the real world. Perhaps the most unique of these is the ability to create a negative lighting effect where a virtual light source can be pointed in a given direction and used to actually remove light from a target area. Also, virtual lights do not necessarily cast shadows (the shadows can be turned on and off as desired), which allows for effects like shining a light directly through one object onto another without producing a shadow (Figure 16.19). More specifics regarding the classifications of virtual lights are presented in *Stage Lighting: Design Applications and More*. Some virtual lights have names and properties that are similar to several of the classifications of traditional luminaires,

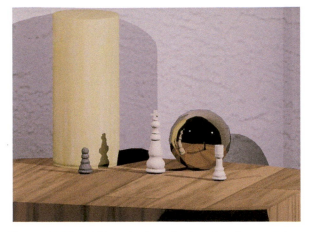

Figure 16.19a Faking shadows in virtual reality; note how objects have highlights but may or may not have cast shadows. a Key light with cast shadows turned on.

Figure 16.20 Virtual lighting for an animation: Waterwitch animation project with naturalistic virtual lighting (CG supervisor: Michael Hussey)

Credit: photo courtesy University of Georgia, Department of Theatre and Films Studies for Perpetual Motion Films and Port Columbus National Civil War Naval Museum

Figure 16.19b Key light with cast shadows turned off (fill light shadows have been left on)

like **ambient lights** and **spotlights,** while others (such as **point** or **omnidirectional lights** and **global illumination**) are unique to virtual environments.

Lighting Techniques for Virtual Lighting

Lighting for virtual scenes is often based on the same principles of illumination as other forms of lighting design. However, there are a couple of interesting twists in virtual lighting that allow a designer some extra freedom to create lighting that is impossible to create under real-world circumstances. Here, a designer uses software to manipulate the lighting so that the final image displays the effects that they want, whether the result can actually be produced in the real world or not. Several of these cheating techniques in virtual design have already been discussed. However, one additional quality of

virtual lighting that is especially interesting comes in the sense of establishing the **falloff** or **attenuation** of a light source. While the intensity of light in the real world follows the Inverse Square Law and rapidly drops off as it moves away from its source, the attenuation of a virtual light can be set to the whims of a lighting designer. The intensity can even be set to increase as it moves away from its source or might be set to fluctuate if it fits the needs of a project. In most cases, virtual lighting follows one of two models. The first tries to replicate the real world and is used in simulations like architectural renderings where a designer is trying to predict the appearance of a subject and its lighting as accurately as possible (Figure 16.20). The second is commonly associated with animations and is based more on the practices used in film and video lighting. **Three-point lighting** has come to be a staple in many animation sequences, but here, too, the industry is moving away from a standard approach to lighting and is shifting towards lighting based on the sources and **motivational** needs of a project. Another unique quality of this form of design is that a scene can often be lit with a single light that is representative of a specific source, and it is not necessary to duplicate a series of **lighting areas** (as it is in theatrical lighting). This reinforces the illusion of a single source producing a scene's lighting because it eliminates issues like overlapping light pools and multiple shadows from additional lights.

FOR FURTHER READING

Brown, Blain. *Motion Picture and Video Lighting*. 2nd ed. Amsterdam; Boston: Elsevier/Focal Press, 2008.

Box, Harry C. *Set Lighting Technician's Handbook: Film Lighting Equipment, Practice, and Electrical Distribution*. 4th ed. Oxford; Boston: Focal Press, 2010.

DiLaura, David L., Kevin W. Houser, Richard G. Mistrick, and Gary R. Steffy. eds. *Illuminating Engineering Society–the*

Lighting Handbook Tenth Edition: Reference and Application. New York: Illuminating Engineering Society, 2011.Illuminating Engineering Society of North America. *IESNA Lighting Education 100 (Fundamental Level).* New York: Illuminating Engineering Society of North America, 1993.

Gordon, Gary. *Interior Lighting for Designers.* 5th ed. Hoboken, NJ: John Wiley and Sons, Inc., 2014.

Illuminating Engineering Society of North America. *IESNA Lighting Education 150 (Intermediate Level).* New York: Illuminating Engineering Society of North America, 1993.

Illuminating Engineering Society of North America. *IESNA Lighting Ready Reference.* 4th ed. New York: Illuminating Engineering Society of North America, 2003.

Illuminating Engineering Society of North America. *An Introduction to Light and Lighting (ED 50).* New York: Illuminating Engineering Society of North America, 1991.

Karlen, Mark and James Benya. *Lighting Design Basics.* 2nd ed. Hoboken, NJ: John Wiley and Sons, Inc., 2012.

Millerson, Gerald. *The Technique of Lighting for Television and Film.* 3rd ed. New York and London: Focal Press, 2013.

Moody, James L and Paul Dexter. *Concert Lighting: Techniques, Art, and Business.* 4th ed. Oxford; Boston: Focal Press, 2017.

Moyer, Janet Lennox. *The Landscape Lighting Book.* 3rd ed. New York: John Wiley and Sons, Inc., 2013.

Rae, Mark. ed. *IESNA Lighting Handbook.* 9th ed. New York: Illuminating Engineering Society of North America, 2000.

Schiller, Brad. *The Automated Lighting Programmer's Handbook.* 3rd ed. Amsterdam; Boston: Elsevier/Focal Press, 2017.

Watson, Lee. *Lighting Design Handbook.* New York: McGraw-Hill, 1990.

APPENDICES

APPENDIX A

LIGHTING PERIODICALS

ENTERTAINMENT LIGHTING DESIGN

American Cinematographer (www.theasc.com)
Filmmaker Magazine (www.filmmakermagazine.com)
Lighting and Sound America (www.lightingandsoundamerica.com)
Live Design (www.livedesignonline.com)
Projection, Lights and Staging News (PLSN; www.plsn.com)
Theatre Design and Technology (TD & T; www.usitt.org)
Videomaker Magazine (www.videomaker.com)

ARCHIVAL ENTERTAINMENT PUBLICATIONS (OUT OF PRINT)

Lighting Dimensions
Theatre Crafts
Theatre Crafts International

ARCHITECTURAL AND DISPLAY LIGHTING DESIGN

Architectural Lighting (AL; www.archlighting.com)
AL LED, a supplement to Architectural Lighting (www.archlighting.com)
Architectural SSL (www.architecturalssl.com)
Contract Lighting (www.contractlighting.net)
Hospitality Design (www.hospitalitydesign.com)
Illuminate: Lighting Architectural Spaces; a supplement to Architectural Products (www.arch-products.com)
Interiors and Sources (www.interiorsandsources.com)
Lighting Design and Application (LD + A; www.ies.org)
Metropolis Magazine (www.metropolismag.com)
Mondo* Arc (www.mondoarc.com)
Residential Lighting (www.residentiallighting.com)
VMSD (www.vmsd.com)

ONLINE RESOURCES

eLumit (www.elumit.com)
Design Guide (www.designguide.com)
Light Search (www.lightsearch.com)

* Many of these trade publications offer both online and print versions.

LIGHTING EQUIPMENT MANUFACTURERS

The companies listed here comprise a sampling of manufacturers that produce a variety of lighting equipment. Some of these companies specialize in theatrical or entertainment equipment, while others are representative of other specialized areas of lighting, such as architectural or display lighting equipment. The URL for each company's website is provided so that students can access the most current information regarding a variety of lighting products. There has been no attempt to create a comprehensive list of manufacturers, only enough to aid students in beginning the task of researching quickly evolving equipment. Many companies contribute products in more than one of the categories but are listed in only one area to save space. One final note: manufacturers of lighting equipment frequently appear/disappear and change corporate partners. Though the contacts presented here were accurate at publication, some of this information may have changed.

LUMINAIRE AND CONTROL EQUIPMENT

ACT Lighting (www.actlighting.com)
Acclaim Lighting (www.acclaim-lighting.com)
AC. Power Distribution, Inc. (www.acpowerdistribution.com)
Action Lighting (www.actionlighting.com)
Alkalite/Elation Lighting (www.elationlighting.com)
Altman Lighting Company (www.altmanltg.com)
ADJ (www.adj.com)
Applied Electronics (www.appliednn.com)
Avolites (www.avolites.org.uk)
Barco (www.barco.com/en)
Chauvet Lighting (www.chauvetlighting.com)
Clay Paky S.p.A. (www.claypaky.it)
Compulite Systems (2000) Ltd. (www.compulite.com)
DmxSoft (www.dmxsoft.com)
Dove Lighting (www.dovesystems.com)
Electronic Theatre Controls (ETC) (www.etcconnect.com)
Galaxia Electronics Co. Ltd. (www.winvision.co.kr)
High End Systems (www.highend.com)
Inner Circle Distribution ICD-Coemar USA (www.icd-usa.com)
Johnson Systems, Inc. (www.johnsonsystems.com)
Lehigh Electric Products, Co. (www.lehighdim.com)
Leprecon (www.leprecon.com)
Leviton/NSI/Colortran (www.leviton.com)
Lex Products Corp. (www.lexproducts.com)
Lighting and Electronics, Inc. (www. ledlinc.com)
Lightronics, Inc. (www.lightronics.com)
Lycian Stage Lighting (www.lycian.com)

Martin Professional/Harman (www.martin.com)
Moonlight Illumination Co. (www.moonlightusa.com)
Philips/Color Kinetics (www.colorkinetics.com)
Philips/Strand Lighting (www.strandlighting.com)
Phoebus Lighting and Manufacturing/Strong Lighting (www.phoebusmanufacturing.com)
PixelRange (www.pixelrange.com)
Robe Lighting (www.robelighting.com)
Selecon North America–Philips (www.seleconlight.com)
Spotlight S.R.L. (www.spotlight.it)
SSRC (www.ssrconline.com)
Strong Lighting Equipment (www.strong-lighting.com)
Swisson of America Corp. (www.swisson.com)
Techni-Lux, Inc. (www.techni-lux.com)
TMB Production Supplies and Services Worldwide (www.tmb.com)
Vari-Lite–Philips (www.vari-lite.com)

Peripheral Equipment and Accessories

Apollo Design and Technology, Inc. (www.apollodesign.net)
Birket Specialty Lighting (www.birketspecialtylighting.com)
City Theatrical, Inc. (www.citytheatrical.com)
Doug Fleenor Design (www.dfd.com)
GAMPRODUCTS, INC. (www.gamonline.com)
GOBOLAND (www.goboland.com)
GoboMan, Inc. (www.goboman.com)
Goddard Design Company (www.goddarddesign.com)
INLIGHT GOBOS (www.inlightgobos.com)
Lee Filters (www.leefiltersusa.com)
RC4 Wireless/Soundsculpture Inc. (www.theatrewireless.com)
Rosco Laboratories, Inc. (www.rosco.com)
SeaChanger by Ocean Optics (www.oceanoptics.com)
SSRC (www.ssrconline.com)
Tempest Lighting (www.tempestlighting.com)
Wybron, Inc. (www.wybron.com)

Lighting Software

AGi32 Software (www.agi32.com)
AutoDesk (www.autodesk.com)
CAST Software (www.cast-soft.com)
FocusTrack (www.focustrack.co.uk)
Future Light, Inc. (www.future-light.com)
LD Assistant (www.ldassistant.com)
LTI Optics (www.ltioptics.com)
John McKernon Software (www.mckernon.com)
Stage Research, Inc. (www.stageresearch.com)
Vectorworks Spotlight by Nemetschek North America (www.vectorworks.net)

Lamps and Light Sources

GE Lighting (www.gelighting.com)
Philips Lighting (www.philips.com)
Osram Sylvania (www.sylvania.com)
USHIO America, Inc. (www.ushio.com)

ARCHITECTURAL EQUIPMENT

AC Electronics (www.ace-ballast.com)
Acuity Lighting (www.acuitybrands.com)
Advance (www.advance.philips.com)
Bartco Lighting (www.bartcolighting.com)
Dreamscape Lighting, Inc. (www.dreamscapelighting.com)
Eaton (http://eatonlightingsystems.com)
Edge Lighting (www.edgelighting.com)
Elliptipar Lighting (www.thelightingquotient.com)
Focal Point (www.focalpointlights.com)
Halco Lighting Technologies (www.halcolighting.com)
Hubbell Lighting (www.hubbelllighting.com)
LEDtronics, Inc. (www.ledtronics.com)
Leviton Manufacturing Company, Inc. (www.leviton.com)
Lighting Control and Design (www.acuitybrands.com)
Lightolier/Philips (www.lightingproducts.philips.com)
Lutron Electronics, Co., Inc. (www.lutron.com)
Neo-Neon (www.neo-neon.com)
Prescolite (www.prescolite.com)
Pure Lighting (www.purelighting.com)
Revolution Lighting (www.rvlti.com)
SPI Lighting (www.spilighting.com)
Times Square Lighting (www.tslight.com)
Universal Lighting Technologies, Inc. (www.unvlt.com)

FILM/VIDEO AND PROJECTION EQUIPMENT

Airstar America, Inc. (www.airstar-light.com)
American Grip, Inc. (www.americangrip.com)
ARRI, Inc. (www.arri.com)
Barco (www.barco.com/en)
Christie (www.christiedigital.com)
Daktronics/Vortek (www.daktronics.com)
Gerriets International, Inc. (www.gerriets.com/us/)
Green Hippo Ltd. (www.green-hippo.com)
Harkness Screens (USA) Ltd. (www.harkness-screens.com)
Mole Richardson Company (www.mole.com)
Pani Projection and Lighting (www.pani.com)
Photon Beard (www.photonbeard.com)
Robert Juliat (www.robertjuliat.com)
Sunray Mfg. (www.dadcopowerandlights.com)
The Tiffen Company, LLC (www. lowel.tiffen.com)

RELATED EQUIPMENT AND MANUFACTURERS

Bad Dog Tools (www.baddogtools.com)
Clark Transfer, Inc. (www.clarktransfer.com)
Clear-Com Communication Systems (www.clearcom.com)
Columbus McKinnon Corp. (www.cmworks.com)
Global Truss (www.globaltruss.com)
HME (www.hme.com)
James Thomas Engineering (www.jthomaseng.com)
J.R. Clancy, Inc. (www.jrclancy.com)

Laser Production Network (www.lasernet.com)
Look Solutions USA, Ltd. (www.looksolutions.com)
MDG Fog Generators (www.mdgfog.com)
Prolyte Products Group (www.prolyte.com)
Skjonberg Controls, Inc. (www.skjonberg.com)
Telex Intercom Headsets (www.telex.com/)
TOMCAT USA, Inc. (www.tomcatglobal.com)
Total Structures (www.totalstructures.com)
Ultratec Special Effects Inc. (www.ultratecfx.com)
Vortek/ETC (www.vortekrigging.com)
Wenger—JR Clancey (www.performance.wengercorp.com)
Union Connector Co., Inc. (www.unionconnector.com)
Universal Manufacturing Corp. (www.universaltruss.com)

PROFESSIONAL ORGANIZATIONS AND UNIONS

The American Association of Cinematographers (ASC; www.theasc.com)
Entertainment Technician Certification Program (ETCP; http://etcp.esta.org)
Entertainment Services and Technology Association (ESTA; www.esta.org)
Illuminating Engineering Society of North America (IESNA; www.ies.org)
International Organization of Lighting Designers (IALD; www.iald.org)
International Alliance of Theatrical Stage Employees (IATSE; www.iatse-intl.org/home.html)
National Council for Qualifications for the Lighting Profession (NCQLP; www.ncqlp.org)
Organistion des Scenographes, Techniciens et Arcitects de Theatre (OISTAT; www.oistat.org)
Professional Light and Sound Association (PLASA; www.plasa.org)
United Scenic Artists Local 829 (USA; www.usa829.org)
United States Institute for Theatre Technology (USITT; www.usitt.org)

USITT LIGHTING GRAPHICS STANDARD

USITT RP-2, Recommended Practice for Theatrical Lighting Design Graphics - (2006)

Preamble

The original Graphics Standards Board noted that a standard is an example for comparison and an authority, which serves as a model. It should be noted that this model cannot hope to cover all possible situations encountered during the drafting of a light plot or section and thus should be viewed as a guide that theatrical lighting practitioners use to create their drawings. This document, therefore, represents a "recommended practice." The terms *instrument* and *luminaire* are used interchangeably throughout the document to designate lighting luminaries while other equivalent designations may also include *fixture, unit* and *lantern*. This document also does not seek to represent a specific manufacturer of lighting equipment but suggests common instruments in general use. The result is a group of generic instrument types that can be adapted to specific uses as necessary rather than an attempt to present a symbol for each luminaire available.

The purpose of this document is to establish a standardized language among lighting designers and anyone else who needs to understand or execute such a design. In practical terms, this document is intended to provide guidelines so that anyone, ranging from technicians who hang the luminaires to other members of the production team, can clearly understand the intent of the lighting designer.

1.0 Introduction

Legibility and consistency should determine the graphic choices made in the drafting of both CAD and hand-drafted drawings. USITT, or modified ANSI three-line thickness standard drafting practices, may be employed as set forth in the USITT Scenic Design and Technical Production Graphic Standard of 1992 (reissued April 15, 1999). Complex drawings may require the use of three- or four-line thicknesses. Luminaire outlines should take visual precedence over other information on the lighting design drawings.

The graphical representation of a lighting design normally consists of two categories of documents: the Light Plot and the Lighting Section. Preferably, the documents are produced in 1/2" = 1'-0" scale. Other scales, such as 1/4" = 1'-0", 3/8" = 1'-0", 1:25 or 1:50 (if working in SI or metric) may be used after considering the size of the architectural space, the overall size of the document and reproductions, the number of individual luminaries, and the desired legibility of their text and numeric attributes. A complete lighting design requires additional paperwork such as channel hookups and shop orders not addressed in this document. Generally, the light plot should include all information necessary to assure clear understanding of the designer's intentions.

1.1 Special Considerations for CAD drawings

Computer assisted drawings should follow the same recommended practice as those drawn by hand. However, several additional considerations should be made. Layer, class designation, line weight, and color assignment must be coordinated with other members of the production team who are using the same document to create other drawings. This avoids confusion between the draftspersons or the end users. When a lighting graphic symbol is created with "labels," attention must be paid to the relative orientation of both the symbol and its associated text. When a symbol is inserted into a drawing, the associated text should be properly oriented with the rest of the text in the drawing. The luminaire symbols that are included in some computer applications may be specific to various manufacturers' equipment rather than the generic symbols provided in this document. Nevertheless, the size and designation of the luminaires used should follow these generic symbols as closely as possible.

2.0 The Light Plot

The Light Plot is a composite plan drawing that provides the most descriptive possible view of the luminaries so that the production staff can most efficiently execute the design intent. It may consist of more than a single plate; however, all plates should be the same size to facilitate reproduction. Distances between front of house hanging positions and the playing area can be compressed in a light plot.

2.1 Information contained in the Light Plot

Normally, the light plot should include all information necessary to assure clear understanding of the designer's intentions. The location and identification data of every luminaire, accessory, and specialty unit should be represented on the light plot, along with the following information:

- The centerline
- A lineset schedule when appropriate
- A ruler or some other indicator of distance left and right of ceterline in scale
- A ruler indicating on-stage distances up and down stage (or the 90° axis to centerline) in scale
- A drawn representation of the edge of the stage where applicable
- A drawn representation of the edge of the playing area where applicable
- Basic scenic elements
- All scenic masking
- All architectural and scenic obstructions
- The proscenium arch, plaster line, smoke pockets, or other architectural details necessary to orient the lighting design in flexible spaces
- Trim measurements for movable mounting positions should read from the stage level surface (or other common point of reference) to the pipe (or mounting position)
- Trim heights to boom positions measure from bottom of the boom base to the side arm or clamp
- Identification (label) of hanging/mounting positions
- The legend or instrument key designating symbol type and notation in the light plot
- The title block (see Section 4)
- Sightlines

© 2006

Additional information may include:
- Lighting areas
- Template key
- Color key
- Liability disclaimer
- Union stamp

2.2 Luminaire symbol information

The luminaire symbols used on the light plot should represent the approximate size and shape of the luminaires in scale (except where computer applications supply more specific symbols). The symbol should be placed so that its location reflects its exact hanging point. Unless otherwise noted, the default spacing between typical fixed focus luminaires is 18" (or 45 cm) to allow for adequate focus range of each luminaire. When the symbols are placed in relative locations other than the default, dimension lines or other measuring notations should be added between the symbols to indicate the distance and to facilitate mounting the luminaires. It is acceptable to visually orient the angle of each drawn luminaire to either focus points or 90° axes.

Normally, each symbol should be accompanied by the following information:
- Luminaire number
- Indication of focal length or beam spread as part of the symbol (where appropriate)
- Indication of any accessories such as templates, irises, scrollers, top hats, barn doors, etc.
- Channel (or control designation)
- Axis notation for PAR lamps

Additional information may include:
- Focus
- Wattage
- Circuit and/or dimmer number or space for the electrician to add this information
- Indication of "two-fers"
- Color notation
- Color notation for scrollers
- Template notation

2.3.1 Designation and numbering of conventional mounting positions
- Front of House (FOH) positions begin numbering from the position closest to plaster line.
- Onstage electrics number from downstage to upstage.
- Onstage booms number from downstage to upstage.
- All hanging locations not intersecting centerline are subnamed by their location relative to centerline. Ladders, box booms, booms, and such are divided between stage left and stage right; stage left listed first.

2.3.2 Numbering luminaires within conventional mounting positions

Each luminaire receives a unique whole number. If a luminaire has an attachment that alters the beam of an instrument, the attachment will often not receive its own whole number but rather the host instrument's number. Luminaires that are inserted between previously numbered fixtures are assigned the lower luminaire's unit number plus an additional letter (e.g., 3A or 3B). At the designer's discretion, decimal or letter suffixes may also be added to a luminaire's number. In common practice, multi-circuited luminaries such as striplights will be assigned a letter with a corresponding number for each circuit (e.g., A1, A2 and A3 while luminaries with multiple control channels or attributes will often be represented through a whole number designation of the unit number followed by a decimal point and number representing specific attributes for the luminaire (e.g., 23.1, 23.2 and 23.3).
- Luminaires on hanging positions perpendicular to centerline (e.g., battens) are numbered from stage left to stage right.
- Luminaires on onstage booms or other vertical hanging positions are numbered from top to bottom, downstage to upstage.
- Luminaires mounted on FOH positions parallel to centerline should number starting with the units nearest to plaster line.
- Luminaires mounted on FOH positions non-parallel to centerline (box booms) should number starting with the units closest to centerline.

2.3.3 Designation and numbering of mounting positions in non-proscenium venues
- Pipe grid positions should be designated by numbers on one axis of the grid and by letters on the other axis.
- Other atypical mounting positions may be designated by compass points or numbering in a clockwise manner.
- Mounting positions that repeat should be numbered from a consistent starting point.
- Other atypical hanging positions should be designated in a fashion that is sensible to the electricians. Luminaires hung in these positions should be numbered in an intelligible fashion compatible with other luminaire designations on the plot.

3.0 The Lighting Section The Lighting Section is a sectional view in which the cutting plane intersects the theatre, typically along the centerline but may intersect any plane that best illustrates the mounting positions. This drawing provides the most descriptive view of the hanging positions relative to the architectural and scenic elements of the production. While it may be appropriate to compress distance (horizontal or vertical) in a presentational section, doing so in the working version reduces its effectiveness.

3.1 Information contained in the Lighting Section The purpose of the lighting section is to communicate spatial information and relationships of all other elements relative to the lighting design. The following information should be represented on the lighting section:

- Definition of where the section is "cut"
- Stage floor, deck, or "vertical zero" location (indication of which one is being used as reference zero)
- Proscenium, plaster line, smoke pocket, or the "horizontal zero" location
- Back wall or upstage limitation of the performing space
- Vertical audience sight points and/or sightlines
- Downstage edge of stage floor and/or edge of playing area
- Architectural details necessary to orient the lighting design in non-proscenium spaces
- All hanging positions including side elevation of booms, ladders, etc.
- Trim height for all hanging positions that can change height
- Identification of all lighting positions
- Architectural and scenic obstructions
- Sectional view of scenery
- All masking
- Title block (See Section 4)
- Scaled representation of the luminaire that determines batten height mounted in each position.
- Human figure (or "head height") in scale

Additional information may include:
- Vertical ruler in scale
- Horizontal ruler in scale
- Defined distance to other elements not shown on the drawing (to follow spot booth, other sightlines, etc.)
- Liability disclaimer
- Union stamp

4.0 Title Block
Acceptable locations for the title block are:
- Lower right hand corner of the drawing
- Vertical banner on the right side of the drawing

4.1 Information contained in the title block
To be placed in the order deemed most important by the lighting designer:
- Name of the producing organization
- Name of the production
- Name of the venue
- Drawing title
- Drawing number (i.e., "1 of 4")
- Predominant scale of the drawing
- Date the plate was drafted
- Designer of the production
- Draftsperson of the drawing

Additional information may include:
- Location of the venue
- Director of the production
- Other members of the production team
- Lighting assistant and/or Master Electrician
- Date and revision number
- Approval of the drawing

- Contact information (telephone and fax numbers, e-mail addresses)

5.0 Legend or Instrument Key
Placement is acceptable in any location that does not conflict with other information.

5.1 Information contained in the legend or instrument key:
- Pictorial representations (symbols) of all luminaires and devices shown on the plot with identifying descriptions of each.
- Beam spread (in degrees or focal length) for each luminaire type if the numeric value is not part of the luminaire's name
- Designation of all notations associated with each luminaire.
- Color manufacturer designation (e.g., R = Rosco, L = Lee, G = Gam, etc.)
- Template manufacturer designation (when applicable)
- Wattage (total luminaire load) and/or ANSI lamp code
- Symbols for any accessories – templates, irises, color scrollers, top hats, barn doors, etc.

Additional information may include:
- Luminaire manufacturer • Representation of "two-fers"
- Indication of voltage

6.0 Symbol Guidelines
These guidelines represent a selection of standard generic symbols that approximate the size and shape of stage luminaires. Further differentiation or notation may be necessary to distinguish between luminaires of approximately the same size. This may include shading the symbol, making the "front" of the symbol a heavier line, and other individual techniques. As manufacturers introduce new luminaries and accessories that are not specified by the current Recommended Practice, a designer may either create new symbols or make variations in existing symbols that approximate the silhouettes and optical qualities of the new equipment. In this case, a clear indication of the new symbol must be included within the Instrument Key. Detailed luminaire symbols specific to each manufacturers' products and supplied by computer drafting programs may be substituted, provided they allow the specialized markings needed to exactly specify the luminaire and provided they are properly explained by the instrument key (see Section 5).

These symbols are presented as a guideline. Specific choices should be considered to differentiate between different manufacturers of the same type of luminaire. It is USITT policy not to specify any manufacturers in the Symbol Guidelines.

Because of the number and complexity of attributes in automated fixtures, each designer must determine a logical notation system for the luminaire used.

6.1 Ellipsoidal Reflector Spotlights

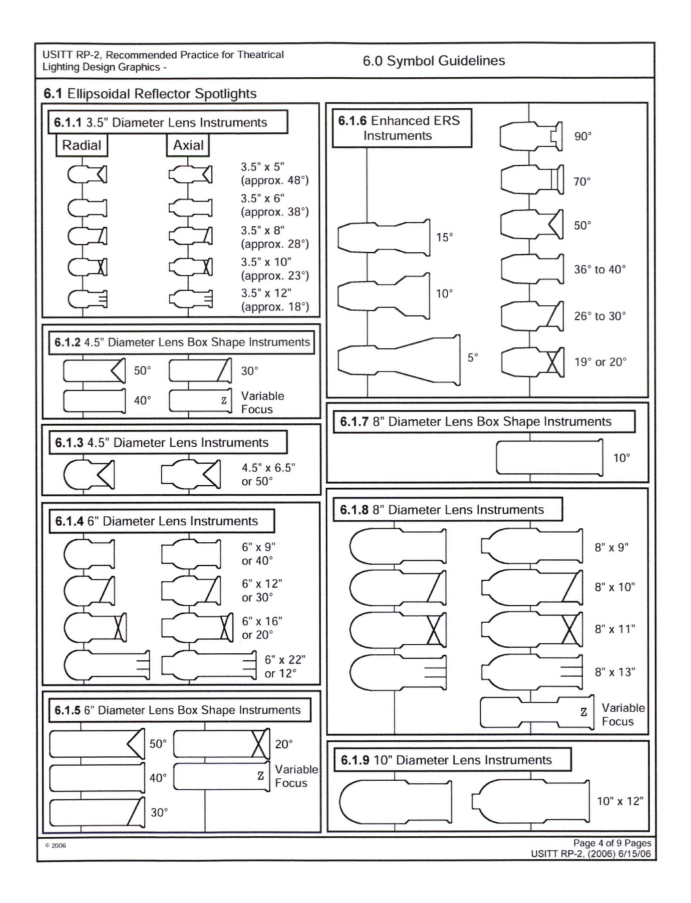

6.1.1 3.5" Diameter Lens Instruments

Radial   Axial

3.5" x 5"
(approx. 48°)

3.5" x 6"
(approx. 38°)

3.5" x 8"
(approx. 28°)

3.5" x 10"
(approx. 23°)

3.5" x 12"
(approx. 18°)

6.1.2 4.5" Diameter Lens Box Shape Instruments

50°   30°

40°   z Variable Focus

6.1.3 4.5" Diameter Lens Instruments

4.5" x 6.5"
or 50°

6.1.4 6" Diameter Lens Instruments

6" x 9"
or 40°

6" x 12"
or 30°

6" x 16"
or 20°

6" x 22"
or 12°

6.1.5 6" Diameter Lens Box Shape Instruments

50°   20°

40°   z Variable Focus

30°

6.1.6 Enhanced ERS Instruments

90°

70°

50°

36° to 40°

26° to 30°

19° or 20°

15°

10°

5°

6.1.7 8" Diameter Lens Box Shape Instruments

10°

6.1.8 8" Diameter Lens Instruments

8" x 9"

8" x 10"

8" x 11"

8" x 13"

z Variable Focus

6.1.9 10" Diameter Lens Instruments

10" x 12"

© 2006

6.1 Ellipsoidal Reflector Spotlights

6.1.10 10" Diameter Lens Box Shape Instrument

10°

6.1.11 Variations on Standard ERS Symbols

ERS with radial reflector

ERS with axial reflector

ERS with a single lens

Variable Focus (Zoom ERS) — Z

Variable Focus (Enhanced Zoom ERS) — Z

ERS with a template or gobo — T

ERS with an iris — I

ERS with gobo rotator — R

ERS with double gobo rotator — RR

6.2 Fresnel Lens Instruments

3" Fresnel

6" Fresnel

8" Fresnel

12" Fresnel

Oval Beam Fresnel

6.3 PAR Lamp Instruments & Designations

6.3.1 PAR Instruments

MR-16 Birdie

PAR 38

PAR 46

PAR 56

PAR 64

Axial PAR or Enhanced PAR

Variable Focus PAR Lens — Z

Beam spreads for Axial, Enhanced, or multiple PARs use the designations shown for PAR 64 examples.

6.3.2 PAR Designations

Extra Wide Flood (XWFL)

Wide Flood (WFL)

Medium Flood (MFL)

Narrow (NSP)

Very Narrow (VNSP)

Lamp axis orientation

(Used to indicate where beam lands or filament orientation)

6.4 Beam Projector Instruments

10" Beam Projector

12" Beam Projector

16" Beam Projector

Enhanced Beam Projector

6.5 Ellipsoidal Reflector Floodlights

10" Scoop

12" Scoop

14" Scoop

18" Scoop

6.6 Cyclorama Instruments

6.6.1 T-3 Cyclorama Instruments

Focus Direction Example

1 circuit T-3 Unit

2 circuit T-3 Unit

3 circuit T-3 Unit

4 circuit T-3 Unit

6 light T-3 Unit

9 light T-3 Unit

6.6.2 Cyclorama Instruments

1 Cell

2 Cell

3 Cell

4 Cell

4 Cell

The symbol for multiple cyclorama instruments approximate an accurate size & shape.

6.7 Striplight Instruments & Mounting Designations

6.7.1 Striplight Instruments

Overall length of the instrument dependent on number of lamps. Measure the instruments.

MR-16 Striplight

R40/PAR 38 Striplight

This symbol is used for either of these lamps. Label the lamp type in the instrument key.

PAR 56 Striplight

PAR 64 Striplight

6.7.2 Striplight Mounting Designations

Pipe Mounted (Hung)

Trunion Mounted (Ground row)

6.7.3 Fluorescent Instruments

6.7.3 Fluorescent Instruments

Overall size of the instrument dependent on size and number of tubes. Number of circuits vary per unit. Be specific.

T-10 2 Tube 2 Circuit

Option 2

4 Foot 2 Tube

5 Foot 3 Tube   Option 1

6 Foot 1 Tube

6.8 Automated Luminaires

Symbols for Automated Luminaires should approximate size, shape, and swing radius.

6.8.1 Fixed Bodies

Moving mirror instrument

6.8.2 Moving Yokes & Heads

Moving Yoke (Shown with Enhanced 19°)

Moving Head Wash Luminaire

Moving Head Spot Luminaire

Zero Reference Point as specified by Designer

Moving Head Spot Luminaire

External Moving Mirror Device

6.9 Practicals & Special Units

Practical Luminaire

35 mm Slide Projector

The symbol for Special Effects instruments approximates an accurate size & shape.

6.10 Follow Spot

Follow Spot

6.11 Symbols for Circuitry

Two-fers

6.12 Symbols and Layout for Lighting Booms

Hatch or shade acceptable for top view of boom

Floor Plate

Boom Base

Flange Mount

Option 1

Yoke out; (no sidearm)

8'-0"
4'-0"
2'-0"

8'-0"
4'-0"
2'-0"

1
2
4 3

• Layouts may not be to scale
• Choose only one type of layout per plot

Option 2

Shown are different examples of indicating height designation

8'-0"
3'-0"
1'-6"

1
3
2
5
4

6.13 Accessory & Ancillary Symbols

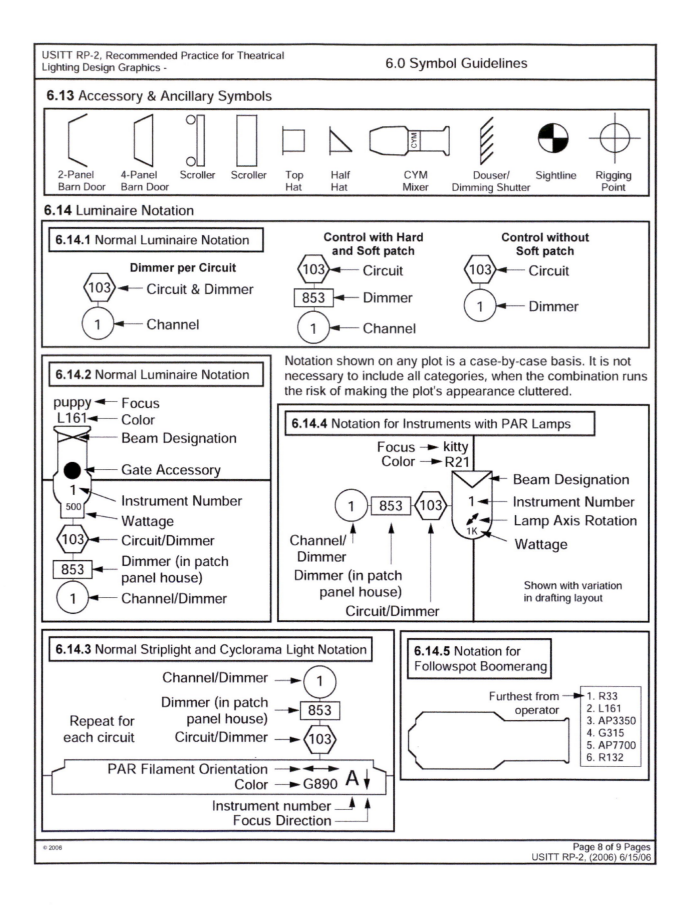

| 2-Panel Barn Door | 4-Panel Barn Door | Scroller | Scroller | Top Hat | Half Hat | CYM Mixer | Douser/ Dimming Shutter | Sightline | Rigging Point |

6.14 Luminaire Notation

6.14.1 Normal Luminaire Notation

Dimmer per Circuit

103 — Circuit & Dimmer
1 — Channel

Control with Hard and Soft patch

103 — Circuit
853 — Dimmer
1 — Channel

Control without Soft patch

103 — Circuit
1 — Dimmer

6.14.2 Normal Luminaire Notation

puppy — Focus
L161 — Color
— Beam Designation
— Gate Accessory
1 — Instrument Number
500 — Wattage
103 — Circuit/Dimmer
853 — Dimmer (in patch panel house)
1 — Channel/Dimmer

Notation shown on any plot is a case-by-case basis. It is not necessary to include all categories, when the combination runs the risk of making the plot's appearance cluttered.

6.14.4 Notation for Instruments with PAR Lamps

Focus → kitty
Color → R21
— Beam Designation
1 — Instrument Number
— Lamp Axis Rotation
1K — Wattage

1   853   103
Channel/ Dimmer
Dimmer (in patch panel house)
Circuit/Dimmer

Shown with variation in drafting layout

6.14.3 Normal Striplight and Cyclorama Light Notation

Channel/Dimmer → 1
Dimmer (in patch panel house) → 853
Repeat for each circuit   Circuit/Dimmer → 103
PAR Filament Orientation →
Color → G890 A
Instrument number
Focus Direction

6.14.5 Notation for Followspot Boomerang

Furthest from operator →
1. R33
2. L161
3. AP3350
4. G315
5. AP7700
6. R132

© 2006

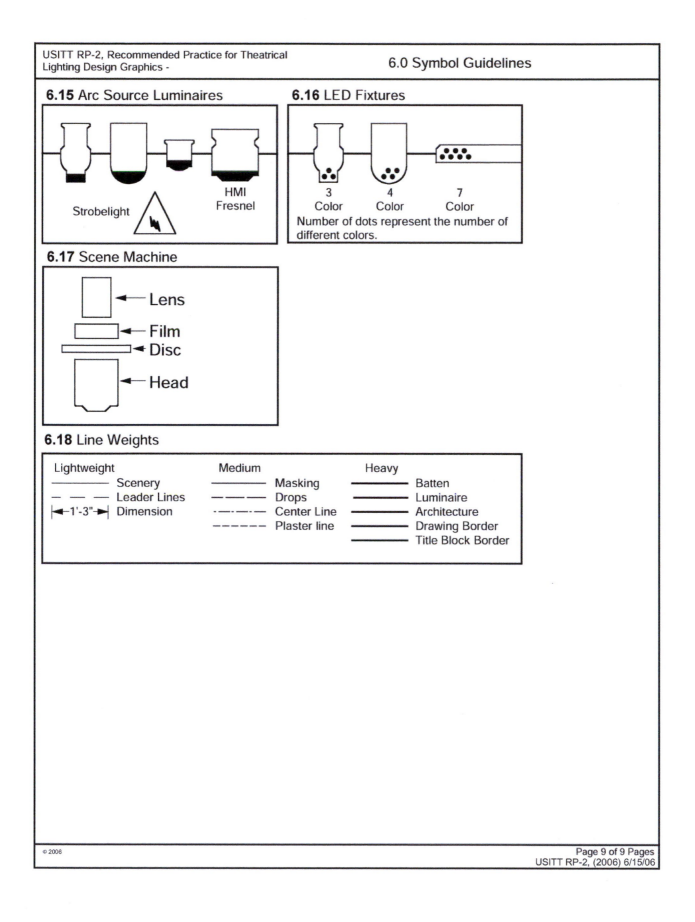

6.15 Arc Source Luminaires

Strobelight

HMI
Fresnel

6.16 LED Fixtures

3
Color

4
Color

7
Color

Number of dots represent the number of different colors.

6.17 Scene Machine

← Lens

← Film

◄ Disc

← Head

6.18 Line Weights

Lightweight		Medium		Heavy	
———	Scenery	———	Masking	———	Batten
— — —	Leader Lines	— — —	Drops	———	Luminaire
◄—1'-3"—►	Dimension	-—·—·—	Center Line	———	Architecture
		— — — —	Plaster line	———	Drawing Border
				———	Title Block Border

APPENDIX E

IESNA LIGHTING GRAPHICS

SAMPLE LIGHTING LAYOUT PLAN SYMBOLS

- ○ Downlight
- ◎ Indirect
- ◐ Wallwasher
- ◀○ Accent
- ✦ Steplight
- ☐ Downlight
- ⊢☐ Sconce
- Punch Wallwasher
- ◉ Pendant or Chandelier
- ⊗ Exit (2 Faces)

⊢━━━┤ Fluorescent Strip

▭ Linear Luminaire

▭ Linear Indirect

▭ Wraparound

▭ Linear Pendant

━━━ Track

━━━ Linear

▭ 2x4 Troffer

▦ Troffer (w/Louvers)

✳ Chandelier

⊕ Table/Floor Lamp

**Symbols Should Reflect Actual Shape and Size of Luminaire
(Fixtures are Surface Mounted Unless Noted)

MODIFIERS

▱ RECESSED

☐ RECESSED ⊘

⊢☐ +72° MOUNTNG HEIGHT

◉ PENDANT/SUSPENDED

⊶ TRACK (w/orientation)

▱ IDENTIFIER
A₁ (Luminaire Type A w/Variation 1)

▭ IDENTIFIER
B (Luminaire Type B)

▭ IDENTIFIER
B2 (Luminaire Type B2)

▭ IDENTIFIER
2c (Circuit 2/Switch c)

▭ IDENTIFIER
3a / E2 (Circuit 3/Switch a) (Luminaire Type E2)

CONTROL

- S Switch
- S_D Dimmer Switch
- S_{OS} Occupancy Sensor Switch
- S_3 Three-Way Switch
- S_4 Four-Way Switch
- S_{DF} Fluorescent Dimmer Switch
- S_{D3} Three-Way Dimmer Switch
- S_L Switch w/Pilot Light
- S_{DM} Dimmer Master/Preset Panel

GLOSSARY

Absorption A process by which light (and its associated wavelengths) is absorbed by a material and usually converted into heat.

Abstraction (stylization) Expressing artistic style in a way that is in opposition to realism. Stylization is more abstract and symbolic, while realistic styles emphasize duplication of the natural environment.

Accent (secondary) lighting A form of lighting associated with architectural and museum or retail lighting that provides focus to specific subjects or displays. It's also found in landscape lighting, where it is used to provide sparkle or establish focus. In concert lighting, accent lighting refers to the color accents that come from the backlight and sidelights.

Accent light A luminaire used to draw focus or attention to a given feature or subject. In entertainment design it is often used to supplement practicals or to suggest other sources that are lighting a scene.

Adaptation A process where the eye narrows its response to a limited brightness range to become more efficient and sensitive within a narrow range of intensities. The eye accepts this as normal and tends to ignore brightnesses outside of this range.

Adapter A short cable with different connector types mounted on each end.

Additive Color Mixing When different wavelengths or colors of light are combined to produce another color. The process requires different colored light sources illuminating or falling on the same surface.

Add-on A specialty program that is installed on top of a CAD program. The application works within the original program and provides a host of extra tools that are designed for the specific area of design.

Addressing The process by which control/channels are assigned to specific dimmers and the attributes of other lighting/specialty equipment such as automated lights.

Advance To visit a performance venue prior to a scheduled load-in to survey the space.

Aerial Show An exterior spectacle production that typically includes lighting effects, lasers, and fireworks.

After Hours (Cleaning/Maintenance) Lighting See *Worklight*

Afterimages The illusion that appears following the removal of a disproportionally high color saturation or high-intensity light source or other image/stimulus that remains unchanged for an extended period of time.

Aim To focus landscape and architectural luminaires or fixtures.

Air Light A reference to lighting in which the actual beams of light become visible due to the effects of haze and smoke (first associated with the concert lighting industry).

Aircraft Landing Lights (ACL) Narrow-beamed lamps adapted from their use in airplanes for theatrical purposes. They are often low-voltage sources that must be used in conjunction with a transformer.

Alignment A manner of adjusting the orientation/relationship between a luminaire's reflector and lamp in order to achieve maximum light output.

All Fade A cue in which all of the lights are dimmed out, typically to a count that is greater than 1 second.

Alternating Current (AC) A type of electricity developed through electromagnetism that results in the voltage constantly changing both direction and level (voltage) over a period of time.

Amber Drift See *Red Shift*

Ambient (General Circulation or Primary) Lighting 1. General non-directional background light that is a result of scattering and indirect reflections. 2. A retail/museum and architectural lighting system that provides a blanket of general illumination over an environment.

American National Standards Institute (ANSI) A standards organization that regulates codes and measurement standards.

American Society of Cinematographers (ASC) Professional organization for directors of photography.

American Society of Lighting Designers (ASLD) A society of the film and video industries that represents lighting directors and gaffers.

Americans with Disabilities Act (ADA) An act that prohibits any form of discrimination based on disabilities. In the entertainment and construction industry this relates to providing accessibility to those with disabilities and we speak of buildings and shows being ADA compliant.

Amperage (A) The measurement of electrical flow that relates to the rate of electrons flowing through a point at any given time. Its unit of measure is the ampere.

Analog Control A control format where the console creates a constant low-voltage signal that is proportional to the voltage being made available to a circuit.

Angle The direction from which light comes from and strikes an object. Various responses in mood and other overall lighting qualities are associated with the directionality of light.

Angstrom (Å) A unit of measurement for light wavelengths. It is equal to 1/254,000,000 of an inch.

Animation Disk A moving wheel accessory that is placed in front of a spotlight to create simple motion effects.

Applause Button A console button, similar to a blackout button, that bumps the intensities of all the lights to full rather than out.

Arc A very bright, high color temperature light source created by an electrical spark that jumps between two electrodes.

Architainment A variation of design that combines elements of architectural design with entertainment. It is another name for themed design.

Architectural Lighting Lighting the interiors and exteriors of buildings. It can also refer to the architectural lighting elements of a themed design or other structures.

Architectural Luminaires A classification of exterior lighting fixtures that are used to bring focus to entryways or other significant features of a building.

Architecture for Control Networks (ACN) A lighting control protocol that primarily addresses the formatting of control communications over an ethernet network. It covers several specific protocols that are packaged together as a unit or suite. This protocol supports bi-directional data flow between a console and any networked gear. ACN may also be used as an acronym for Advanced Control Network.

Area Control Creating general or area lighting so that there is an ability to pull into smaller portions of the stage or lit environment. Greater area control allows more specific area selection while less area control is more general and less defined.

Area Lighting (General Illumination) A means of bringing overall visibility to an environment. This usually means providing a system of luminaires that creates a consistent even coverage across an environment, giving the appearance of being lit by a single distant light source. In landscape lighting this refers to lighting an area with enough illumination that a given task can be performed.

Area versus Color Control A choice in area or general lighting where specific control of the luminaires is based on whether more specific control is designed into the number of areas that the luminaires light or by the different colors that are lighting an environment.

Aria A solo that is performed (usually by a principal character) in an opera.

ASA (ISO) An index of how sensitive or fast a film reacts to light. Values are based on a standard by the American Standards Association (now ANSI—American National Standards Institute) or International Organization of Standardization (ISO). The higher the rating, the faster the film speed and more quickly it can capture an image.

ASHRAE/IESNA 90.1 A document that guides energy codes and the manner in which power densities are determined and specified for architectural lighting.

Aside A performance technique in which a performer addresses the audience. Asides are often performed downstage and frequently present a character's inner thoughts.

Assistant House Electrician The electrician who is second in command of the electrics crews for a performance facility.

Assistant Lighting Designer (ALD) A personal assistant to the lighting designer whose duties may vary considerably from one situation to another but whose primary task lies in the organization and documentation of a lighting design.

Assistant Master Electrician (AME) An electrician who is directly under the master electrician and is usually charged with specific aspects of coordinating the electrics crews both for a performance as well as the load-in and strike of a production.

Associate Lighting Designer An individual who operates at a level of authority just below the lighting designer. The responsibilities of an associate lighting designer can vary considerably but are more along the lines of providing artistic input and assistance to the lighting designer. Associate designers often cover various responsibilities for a lighting designer who cannot be present at various meetings or work calls.

Astronomical Clock A control device or computer used in architectural and landscape installations that executes a timing program that instructs lighting equipment to turn on and off at predetermined times.

Atmospheric Effects A classification of special effects that involves introducing various particles into the air for a production. Fog, smoke, and haze form the most popular examples of these effects.

Attenuation (Falloff) The property by which a light's intensity drops off as it moves farther away from its source.

Attribute A control function of a luminaire or lighting accessory. The most common examples involve automated lights, with attributes like pan, tilt, color, etc. In CAD light plots, attributes refer to notation data like color and channel numbers.

Attributed Block A library symbol (block) used in CAD software that not only contains the basic symbol but also a means of tailoring the data associated with a symbol to the specific block. Lighting often uses attributed blocks to insert luminaires into a drawing while modifying attributes like color, unit number, and channel to the specific unit that is being inserted.

Autofader A variation of crossfader or splitfader that has a timing device. Times are preset and run at the assigned times once the cue is initiated.

Automated Color Changers See Scrollers

Automated Lights (Automated Luminaires) Fixtures that have multiple control features/attributes that allow elements of a luminaire like its pan and tilt to be changed through control commands. Also called intelligent, wiggle, and moving lights.

Autotransformer A dimmer that harnesses the technology of AC currents and their ability to induce magnetic fields to create a back-EMF that in turn regulates the voltage/intensity of a circuit.

Averaging Meter A reflective light meter that records the average light level throughout the entire field of a camera. These meters are good for determining overall exposure.

Awning An architectural feature that is placed over windows and other glazed surfaces that provides shade and helps block direct sunlight from entering a window.

Axial ERS A version of the ellipsoidal reflector spotlight (ERS) that places the lamp directly on the back of the housing (on the optical axis) where it is inserted into the center of the reflector. These units were developed in the 1970s and are much more efficient than earlier ERS designs.

Back Diagonal A direction of lighting distribution that comes from behind and to the side of an object and gives a rimming type of effect.

Background Lights or Lighting Luminaires in film and video shoots that light the background behind a subject and are used to maintain a proper balance between the subject and background. Also used as a concept in landscape lighting where more distant or perimeter areas are lit while other subjects are lit in the foreground.

Backing off the Rods See Ballet Dim

Backlight An angle that comes from behind a subject and helps to separate and push the subject forward, away from the background. It can produce a rim/halo effect.

Backlot A collection of many exterior locations that are scenic constructions used for filming movies.

Baffle (Egg Crate) An optical accessory typically added to architectural luminaires and soft-lights that creates a network of box-like dividers over the face of a fixture. They help block the viewer from direct lamp and reflector glare.

Balance A consideration of the intensity or illuminance levels between different objects or surfaces. Also a concept in an electrical system where the demands of the entire service are evenly distributed on each of the power legs.

Balcony Rail A hanging position located across the front face of a theatre's balcony. It provides a relatively flat lighting angle and is often used for washing a stage.

Ballad A slow, often romantic or sentimental, song that is usually performed as a solo or duet.

Ballast A transformer-like device that is wired in series with a fluorescent, arc, or HID lamp and regulates the current and voltage to the lamp. It also provides the initial voltage needed to start the arc process.

Ballet Dim (Backing off the Rods) The use of a followspot in such a subtle manner that the audience may not be aware that a followspot is being used. Designers use ballet dim to draw focus without drawing attention to the light itself.

Ballyhoo A way of sweeping spotlights (followspots or automated luminaires) throughout a venue. A ballyhoo may be done over the stage or audience.

Barn Doors An accessory that provides folding flat panels which are placed at the front of a luminaire that can be rotated and tilted inward or outward to block glare and spill of unwanted light.

Base An element of a lamp that supports the lamp in its proper orientation within a luminaire and provides the electrical contacts that lead to the lamp's filament.

Base Cue A cue that has the predominant elements of the lighting for a given scene or setting established. This is often returned to and then recalled and modified as needed for additional cues.

Base Light or Base Level Lighting Another name for fill light used by some lighting directors and directors of photography. Light added to a scene to bring shadow areas to an intensity level that the camera can record. Some refer to the process as base level lighting. Also used to define the ambient light in an architectural application.

Basic Retail Environment A low-end, economical store or retail environment. Lighting is designed predominantly from a visibility or functional point of view.

Batten A pipe that is located and flown from directly above the stage. Battens are used as temporary mounting positions for lighting instruments, maskings, and scenery.

Batten Tapes A piece of scenic webbing that is secured along a batten and marked with a centerline and additional marks or labels for every luminaire hung on the associated electric. They are frequently used in touring and eliminate the need for measuring the distance from each unit to centerline.

Beacon A specialized fixture that produces a moving effect based on the same effect as the rotating light on emergency vehicles.

Beam A hanging position of horizontal pipe mounted in the ceiling above an audience that runs across the width of an auditorium.

Beam Angle The angle representing the beam distribution of a luminaire where the intensity has fallen off by no more than 50% of the initial intensity.

Beam Projectors A luminaire that uses a parabolic reflector. This is the only spotlight that does not contain a lens. Beam projectors produce a very harsh intense beam of nearly parallel rays of light.

Beam Spread The amount of coverage that a luminaire creates as a distribution pattern. Beam angle and field angle are two specific ways of expressing beam spread.

Below Grade A manner of mounting architectural or landscape luminaires in a vault or waterproofed box where only the lens (if that) projects above the ground's surface.

Bend A property of rear projection screens where image intensities drop off and are not seen as well by people who are to the sides and outside of a critical viewing angle.

Best Boy The electrician, in video and film production, who is the gaffer's assistant.

Bidding A construction phase where contractors are provided with documents and make offers for providing the lighting equipment and its installation for a set price.

Bi-directional Data Digital control information that is exchanged in both directions between lighting consoles and sophisticated devices like automated luminaires.

Binning Refers to the practice of sorting LEDs into groups based on color that provide the best color match of light output between LEDs of the same color. This is done due to the inconsistencies that exist in the LED manufacturing process.

Birdies Small PAR luminaires that are designed around MR16 lamps.

Black Box Theatre (Blackbox Theatre) A theatre facility that allows complete flexibility in assigning staging arrangements. Black box theatres are typically painted completely black and have a lighting grid over the entire room.

Blacklight A specialized luminaire or form of light that has the majority of its spectral composition in the ultraviolet range. Special dyes and bleached objects will glow (usually in psychedelic colors) when activated by this light.

Blackout A fade to complete darkness that is done to a zero count (instantly).

Blackout Button A push-button switch that allows a control board or console to instantly lower every channel to zero intensity.

Blackout Check A blackout cue that is loaded just prior to opening the house so that a venue can be checked for complete darkness.

Bleed Out Diffused light that smoothly fades out at the edge of a beam.

Blind (Blind Mode or Preview Mode) Programming or writing lighting cues without the benefit of observing the actual lights, environment, or subject(s). Also, a console mode that displays channels and their associated levels for previous or upcoming cues. This allows a designer to work on the cues while another cue is on stage.

Block A pre-designed symbol stored in the invisible background of a CAD drawing that allows simple insertion of the symbol into a drafting. Blocks contain the outline of the luminaire along with a host of other information regarding the unit and how it is to be equipped (color, focus, wattage, control channel, etc.).

Block Cues (Hard Blackouts) Cues that are entered into a console with all channels assigned to a level of zero to create points that stop any tracking instructions.

Blocking Notation A means of drawing graphic diagrams to record or notate the movements and positions of the performers.

Block Matrix Lights A variation of LED luminaire that is similar to a blinder design. This creates a block or grid-like arrangement of high-intensity LED sources into a 4 × 4 or 5 × 5 arrangement that can be used for a variety of washes or effects. Each chamber can be controlled individually/pixel mapped and the units can be combined to produce larger composite digital images.

Blood Pressure Cue A very subtle lighting cue that is created with the intention of being unnoticed by an audience as a means of preventing visual fatigue and its consequences.

Blueout A special type of fadeout in which all of the lights fade to a deep blue as opposed to complete darkness. This assists crews in scene changes and can also make these shifts more interesting from an audience perspective.

Blue Sky Development A form of concept development where a team is given a blank slate and simply brainstorms themes for an attraction.

Board Operator A crew member who helps the designer program the light board and executes the cues as ordered by the stage manager during performances.

Body (Hood or Housing) The actual enclosure of a luminaire. The housing provides for the proper mounting and orientation of all the optical components and accessories of a unit.

Bollard A special form of post light that is frequently used to mark pathways and entrances. They are usually around 3 feet in height and typically have the luminaire and its lenses incorporated into the design of the post.

Book Scenes A type of scene associated with musicals where the mode of delivery shifts to traditional acting without an emphasis on singing or dancing.

Boom Base A heavy (50 pounds) metal plate of cast iron that forms the floor base that supports the vertical pipe of a boom.

Boomerang (Color Boom) A device that allows followspot operators to quickly change a spotlight's color. Most color booms contain six different colors or gels.

Booms (Trees) Pipes extending upward from the stage floor that allow luminaires to be mounted vertically rather than horizontally.

Borderlights Banks of permanently wired striplights that stretch across the width of a stage. These were popular before the use of spotlights for general illumination and contained three or four circuits of colored roundels (typically red, blue, and white, although circuits of canary or green were often substituted for white).

Borders An overhead masking that stretches across the width of a stage and prevents audience view of the flyspace and any scenery or lighting equipment above the stage.

Bounce Drop A drop that is placed behind another drop (either a translucent drop or one with translucent elements) and to which light is focused and reflected towards the back of the first drop.

Bow Cue A cue used for curtain calls. They are usually fairly bright in intensity and cover most if not all of the stage.

Box Boom A hanging position that historically came from a boom mounted in the box seats of a proscenium theatre. The position provides front-diagonal lighting, and we now often refer to any position coming from the side walls of a theatre as box boom positions, box seats or not.

Box-Spot (plano-convex spotlight or P-C Spotlight) Luminaire representing one of the earliest forms of theatrical spotlight and is quite similar to a Fresnel spotlight. It consists of a spherical reflector, light source, and single plano-convex lens. It is still popular throughout Europe and other parts of the world.

Bracketing A photographic technique of taking multiple exposures to increase the chances of obtaining a successful image—one at the exposure suggested by a light meter and then a second and third exposure shot one f-stop on either side of the recommended exposure.

Branch Circuits Individual circuits, with their own circuit protection, that lead from a distribution panel to electrical equipment like lights and outlets.

Break-in An adapter for the male end of a multi-cable that interfaces the cable with other cables or electronic hardware like a dimmer rack. It separates the multi into individual male connectors for each circuit.

Break-out An adapter for the female end of a multi-cable where the cable interfaces with other cabling. The break-out separates the multi into individual female connectors for each circuit.

Brightness Perception A consideration of all the variables that determine the brightness of an object—the amount of light falling on the object, optical sensitivity, and the degree of reflectivity are all factors in the perceived intensity of an object.

Broad A linear light source used in television and film production that features thin tubular lamps. They are generally considered and used as a soft light.

Brute A multi-light or cluster light used in film and video that uses an arrangement of nine lamps in a rectangular array.

Buhl Projector An enhanced Ektagraphic Slide Projector where the standard lamp is replaced with a high-wattage one along with a system of heat sinks and high-powered fans for extra cooling. These projectors have superior lenses.

Build To increase the intensity by either raising the intensity levels of the individual dimmers or by adding additional lighting instruments into a cue.

Bulb The glass envelope of a lamp that creates the appropriate atmosphere for the lamp.

Bullet Lights A landscape luminaire that is used for both flood and spotlighting. The unit has an inverted-cone shape that has its socket and electrical fittings in the tip of the housing while the lamp's face is exposed through the wider opening.

Bump (Flash) Buttons A momentary switch/button associated with a controller or submaster that can instantly bump its level to full regardless of the actual controller setting.

Bump Focus A method of focusing electrics when they can't be reached by a ladder or lift (this often occurs with raked or heavily platformed stages). The batten is lowered to within reach, the lights are rough focused and then the batten is flown to trim height where the focus is observed. The process is repeated until the focus of all the lights is correct and their shutter cuts are adjusted properly.

Bundle A number of individual cables or circuits that are simply tied together as they run along a hanging position. They are created for hanging positions like electrics and booms as a way of pre-packing the circuits and facilitating a faster hang while touring. Bundles are often used as an alternative to multi-cables.

Burning-Off Drying out the moisture left in luminaires after a rain by heating the lamps up slowly through powering them up in increments of approximately 10–15% over a period of time.

Burnout The breakdown of a gel or filter from continued exposure to light and heat. The gel eventually fades in the center and may even melt completely through. Also used to identify a failed lamp.

Bus Bars Metal bars that are used in large-capacity applications for moving electricity from one location to another instead of using heavy wires or cables.

Busking A term often associated with a form of improvised lighting where a designer has a number of pre-programmed presets, effects and automated lighting moves that are selected and played back as a show evolves. Busking is especially popular for designing music festivals.

Butterflies (Nets or Silks) Large diffusers used in the video and film industry that are made of translucent muslin or silk-like fabric mounted on large folding frames. Smaller versions are mounted on simple frames held in stands that are placed in front of a luminaire. Sizes and materials will vary, which results in a variety of names being associated with these diffusion accessories. Nets are made of a mesh material (bobbinet), while butterflies and silks are made of translucent material.

CIE Chromaticity Chart A chart that indicates the wavelengths of color radiation given off at various temperatures of a black body radiation. The importance to lighting designers lies in its depiction of the relationships between each of the three primary colors and that fairly accurate color predictions can be made for resultant colors that are formed through mixing different colored light sources.

Cable (Jumper) Technically refers to combining several insulated wires into a single shield or jacket. It is also used synonymously with jumper to describe a two/three conductor cable with a male connector on one end and female on the other.

Cable Lighting A variation of track lighting where the track is replaced by decorative cables that also function as conductors for the low-voltage electricity.

CAD (Computer-Aided Drafting) Software programs that are designed for drafting. While initially developed for drafting needs, the software has evolved to include full modeling and visualization.

Call A work period for crew members. A call time is when individuals report to work.

Call a Show Providing the cueing commands (i.e., sound or lighting cues) to the crews during a rehearsal or performance. This is usually done by the stage manager.

Camera Rehearsal A rehearsal in film and video setups that would be similar to a dress rehearsal in the theatre. Lighting, costumes, actors, and cameras are all rehearsed and tweaked before the actual shooting takes place.

Camera-Lights (Obie) A variety of portable luminaires used in film and video shoots that are mounted to a camera in order to produce good front fill over a subject.

Camlock (Cam-lock) A heavy-duty connector that is used on each individual cable of feeder cables, dimmers, and other power distribution equipment.

Candlepower (Candela) Distribution Curve A representation of photometric data that allows comparisons to be made between luminaires. These data represent a graphical representation of the measured light output (intensity) of the luminaire at various angles to either side of the centerline of a luminaire.

Carbon-Arc Spotlight A spotlight (often a followspot) that has a carbon-arc light source.

Cast Shadow A shadow that is produced in the silhouette image of an object by a given light source.

C-Clamp A type of mounting hardware that secures a lighting instrument's yoke to a batten or other hanging position or pipe.

Ceiling Cavity (Plenum) The void between the decorative ceiling and the bottom of the overlying floor or ceiling joists. It hides equipment like ducts, conduit, and pipes.

Ceiling Clutter A reference to an unsightly, disorderly arrangement of lighting fixtures on a ceiling of a retail, commercial, or other architectural lighting project.

Cell An individual lamp or reflector along with its associated housing in a cyclorama (cyc) light or far cyc. Each cell is gelled and wired independently of the others. Cells are often bolted together and hung from a common yoke. Typical units contain three or four cells that are often colored in the three primary colors.

Centerline An imaginary reference line that passes through the center of a stage, room, or building. Most side-to-side measurements are based on the centerline.

Centerline Section (Section) A sectional drawing that is drawn as if cutting through a facility on a plane along the centerline of a stage. It is a side view of the building/stage along this plane and is used to determine vertical heights and trim settings.

Certified Lighting Designer (CLD) A certification program specifically designed for lighting designers that was sponsored by the IALD in 2015. Like the NCQLP certification, it is earned by exam and then renewed though retaking the exam or by completing a given number of educational activities to remain current in the field. It has a recertification period of five years.

Chain Hoist (Chain Motor) A winch or hoist that is specifically designed for overhead rigging. They are used to support trusses, speaker assemblies, and scenic components, most extensively in the touring industry.

Change Order A contract document used in specifying permanent installations that outlines a revision and amends the original construction documents.

Changeover The time given to making changes from one production to another. While it may refer to the transfer between new productions, it is more commonly associated with the daily changes being made between repertory productions.

Channel A control assignment that provides the actual identity of control that a console recognizes as a base element for assigning control voltages. Channels are typically assigned intensity levels that fall between 0–10 and 0–100%.

Channel Check (Dimmer Check) A check done at various points in the load-in and before each performance where each dimmer or channel is brought up to make sure that every lamp is both operational and hasn't lost its focus.

Channel Schedule A form of designer paperwork that presents all of the luminaire data of a light plot in a table format. It is a form of the hookup that organizes the data by channel number.

Chase (Chase Lights) A programmed effect that produces a rapid sequence of cues/steps that are each associated with a given set of luminaires. Theatre marquees form an example.

Cheat Sheet A table that lists all of the control channels in order and then provides additional information relating to the purpose and color associated with each channel. It performs the same function as a magic sheet.

Check Cues Cues that are placed in a console for checking/verifying that various tasks have been completed. An example would be glowing any circuits that have been repatched at intermission to ensure that they have actually been reassigned.

Chicken Coop/Space Light A film and video soft light that is typically suspended from above and used to create a general level of fill or area lighting over an area. They are built around the concept of a soft reflective canopy using several light sources. The chicken coop is built around a rectangular arrangement of lamps, while the space light is cylindrical and uses multiple lamps in a circular arrangement.

Chief Lighting Technician (Gaffer) A video or film crew member who is the equivalent to a master electrician in theatrical production. Gaffers work with the lighting director or director of photography to provide the specified equipment, filters, and power for each shot. They also supervise the lighting staff during production.

Chimera A soft light used in film and video work that is built around the concept of creating a soft reflective canopy containing one or more light sources. Chimeras are usually mounted on a stand and used to produce horizontal fill light. They have collapsible hoods of diffuse material that are adjusted to a given situation.

Chinese Lanterns A soft light that is similar to the larger lighting balloons where lamps are placed within a circular lantern-like sphere to create a soft, diffuse light for a film or video setup.

Choke A coil that is wired in an electronic dimmer (usually SCRs) to reduce electronic interference generated by the dimmer.

Choreography The movement patterns and gestures that are established for a dance or other movement-based performance.

Chroma (Saturation) The purity of a color. The more saturated the color, the more specific and limited the range of wavelengths associated with it.

Chroma Key A form of composite or matte photography in which an electronic image of one scene is projected onto a neutral surface in another. The most popular versions are based on the colors of these surfaces and are known as blue-screen or green-screen techniques.

Chromatic Aberration (Color Fringes) An effect of an unwanted prismatic or rainbow effect at the edge of a beam of light. It is usually due to inferior lenses.

Cinch-Jones Connector A special multi-conductor connector that is used for connecting analog control cables to one another and to control gear like light boards and dimmer packs.

Cinebach Projector A variation of Linnebach projector where the sides and slides have been curved to accommodate the shape of a curved cyclorama.

Cinematographer (Director of Photography, or DP) Individual who is responsible for creating the entire visual environment for a video or film. Although the director of photography is responsible for the lighting they also have responsibilities in choosing location, determining camera angles and range of an individual shot, and selecting the camera lenses and film speeds.

Circuit A complete cycle of electron flow that follows a pathway from a source, through a device, and back to the source.

Circuit Breaker Electrical device that is designed as the weakest link in a circuit and meant to trip or "blow" if the circuit encounters a short or is overloaded. A circuit breaker can be reset once it has blown.

Circuit Layout A floorplan that includes all of the information found in a typical floorplan plus an indication of all the circuits and their locations.

Circuit/Control Schedules Paperwork used in landscape lighting that organizes the data by circuit/control assignments (similar to theatrical dimmer schedules).

Circulation Lighting A form of architectural or themed lighting that provides enough visibility so that people can move around safely within an environment.

Cleaning/Maintenance (After Hours) Lighting See Worklight

Closed Fixture A landscaping luminaire in which a lens and protective gasket are placed over the front of the luminaire to prevent water from entering the unit.

Closed-Backed Window A display window that has a back and is shut off from the store that is behind the window.

Closing-in A method of making a proscenium opening smaller through lowering the borders and bringing the legs farther onto the stage.

Cluster Mounting A mounting method used in street and roadway lighting where several fixtures are mounted from a single pole.

CMY Mixing See CYM Mixing

Cobra Head A luminaire used with HID lamps in roadway and street lighting that has a distinct shape that resembles the head of a cobra. Most high-pressure sodium, mercury, and metal halide street lamps are of this particular type of luminaire.

Coefficient of Utilization (CU) A factor that relates to the overall efficiency of a luminaire within the Lumen Method calculation. CUs are determined by luminaire manufacturers and are found in tables that make a correlation between the CU, reflectance of a room's surfaces, and the RCR for a given situation.

Coherence A means of describing the overall quality of light in film and video lighting. It is usually associated with the hardness or softness and diffusion of the light.

Cold-Cathode A lamp that produces light as a glow from the discharge of electrons within an enclosed tube. One of the more popular versions gives off a cold cobalt blue light that is often used in cove lighting applications. The tubes can be bent to follow the contour of architectural elements and come in a variety of colors.

Color A controllable quality of light. A perception based on how specific wavelengths of light stimulate the photo sensors in our eyes. Light will have an associated color based on the specific collection of wavelengths being present in its makeup.

Color Adaptation Distortion in color perception when the eyes are overstimulated due to being under the influence of lighting conditions that have remained unchanged for an extended period of time. This results in the perceived color being distorted until the cones become fully functional.

Color Boom See Boomerang

Color Constancy A quality of perception that allows us to accept that an object's color is constant despite variations in the color of the light that it is illuminated by.

Color Contrast Comparisons in hue and relative warmth/coolness either within or between scenes.

Color Correction (Color Conversion) Filters A special type of color media that filters a light source to change its color temperature. These are extremely important to the film and video industry where it is imperative that light from different sources be modified so that they appear to share common color temperatures.

Color Depth Refers to the number of colors that a video screen or projector can effectively create. The simplest screens display 8-bit data, which translates to 256 different levels for each of the three primary colors or a total of 16.7 million different colors. A 16-bit screen, on the other hand, can create 65,000 color levels in each of the primaries, for a total of 275 billion colors.

Color Extender An accessory that looks like a top hat and has internal slots that allow a luminaire's gel to be placed farther away from a light source.

Color Frame (Gel Frame) A thin square of folded sheet metal with a large hole located in its center used to hold gel at the face of a lighting fixture.

Color Fringes See Chromatic Aberration

Color Key A figure that illustrates the approximate angles and color of light that surround a subject. A lighting key may be developed for any moment of a production but is usually used to illustrate the full wash systems of a stage.

Color Media Materials that either filter or modify the light produced by a source or fixture. Gel and color filters are popular names given to color media.

Color Organ A popular entertainment device of the 1970s with audio sensors that could be tuned to specific frequencies which, upon activation, could flash lights to a musical beat.

Color Palette In automated lighting, the color settings used to create a given color are preset so that a previously defined color can be brought back through use of a simple recall or library system.

Color Rendering The ability of a light source to accurately render or light a variety of colors without distorting the natural colors of an object.

Color Rendering Index (CRI) An index number that refers to the color-rendering ability of a source and how accurately it can depict an object's true color. Sources with high CRIs have more individual wavelengths in their composition and enhance a larger range of colors. The maximum CRI possible is 100.

Color Scroller A lighting accessory that places an assembly of color filters (12 or more) in a scroll-like configuration that is then rolled into various positions to change the color of the light.

Color Temperature A comparison of the sum of all the individual wavelengths of a light source with the color emitted from a black box radiation for a given temperature. Every color of radiant energy can be equated to a referenced temperature on the Kelvin scale, where absolute zero equals 0° Kelvin or –273° Celsius.

Color Temperature Meter Directors of photography and lighting directors use a special light meter to measure the color temperature or overall color output of light. These measure light along two different scales: the first measures red/blue present, while the second measures the magenta/green content of the light.

Color Wheel 1. An accessory that is mounted in the color holder of a luminaire that moves a motorized disk of colored filters through a unit's light. 2. A diagram that illustrates the primary and secondary colors and their relationships to one another.

Color-Compensation Scale A specialized scale (actually two scales) used in connection with a Color Temperature Meter to correct the color temperature of a light. They are used to make a selection of color/gel correction that will make the light appear white on film.

Colorist The person who adjusts the color and development of a film to ensure proper contrast exposure and color continuity between different takes and setups.

Combination Circuits Circuits that contain both series and parallel components. A common combination circuit contains several lights wired together in parallel placed under the control of a single switch that is wired in series.

Commission Starting up the lighting systems in architectural lighting, which involves completing any aiming and programming the levels for an installation as the design team turns the building over to the occupants.

Communications Workers of America (CWA) An umbrella union representing workers primarily within the telecommunications and media industries such as the National Association of Broadcast Employees and Technicians (NABET), but also includes other affiliates such as flight attendants, newspaper and publishing professionals, and public service employees.

Compact Fluorescent A form of fluorescent lamp that combines the lamp with a ballast in a single unit. These lamps are often used as retrofits for traditional incandescent lamps because of their efficiency.

Compact Iodide Daylight (CID) Lamp A special variation of metal halide lamp that makes use of a specific mixture of gases and metal halides to produce a cleaner, brighter light source.

Compact Source Iodide (CSI) Lamp Another variation of metal halide lamp that make use of a specific mixture of gases and metal halides to produce a characteristic quality of light.

Company Switch (Road-tap) A specialized distribution panel or disconnect box that provides the power (typically 200–800 amps of three-phase power) that a touring lighting system or other equipment may be connected to.

Complementary Color A color that lies directly across the color wheel from a color.

Complementary Tint Theory A lighting technique of the stage that is associated with creating a fairly naturalistic style of lighting. The effect is produced if two fixtures containing complementary tints are hung on opposing 45° angles from one another. The lights are to be hung 45° to each front/side of a subject (splitting centerline) with a vertical angle of 45° for each light. The method is credited to Stanley McCandless and is often called a McCandless Method or hang.

Composite (Matte) Photography An image created through a combination of several individual shots or settings. Blue- or green-screen technology form popular examples of an electronic insertion of one shot into another.

Composition A function of lighting that relates to combining all of the elements of a scene, stage, or environment together into a complete unified visual package.

Compound Reflectors A reflector shaped with more than one principal shape along its surface. This is a more efficient way of directing light in a primary direction.

Computer Rendering An image of a subject or environment that is created through creating a virtual model, coloring/texturing it, and lighting it through using a computer and specialized software.

Concave Lens A lens in which one of the surfaces is curved inward towards the center of the lens.

Concept A manner or method of approach to creating meaning in a production. It refers to an approach to a design problem and addresses the themes, style, and conventions that will be used in a production.

Concept Development The first design phase of a project, in which a team first lays out the general ideas, concepts, and parameters of a project.

Conductors Materials that allow electron movement easily and have little resistance to electrical flow. Metals are usually the best conductors.

Conjugate (Secondary) Focal Point The second focal point of an ellipsoidal reflector to which all light is reflected from a source placed at the primary focal point. Any light or image that passes beyond the conjugate focal point is reversed.

Connectors Electrical hardware that allows for the easy connection and disconnection of multi-wired cables. Connectors may be male or female.

Conservation A process of providing limited lighting exposure to materials that are subject to heat and light damage, especially ultraviolet radiation. This is especially important in retail and museum or gallery lighting design.

Construction Documents A set of documents that contain all the plans (lighting layouts, reflected ceiling plans, details, etc.) and specifications for a design.

Content The source material for digital images and projections.

Continuity 1. Observing details in video and film shooting to ensure that no discrepancies occur between camera angles and that every take is lit in exactly the same way, providing consistency from one angle to another. 2. In electrical theory, continuity relates to providing a complete wiring path with no breaks in a circuit.

Continuous Fire A dimming state where an SCR blows in the on position and the dimmer remains at full intensity despite any changes in the control signal.

Continuous Light Sources (Hot Light Sources) Luminaires used in film and video production that are not dimmed and are designed to simply plug into a power source.

Contour Lighting Lighting that follows contours or lines. One of the most obvious cases of this is when people line their walkways or pathways with luminaires.

Contract Document Phase An architectural design phase where the contract documents are created and assembled. The specification of the lighting equipment and installation requirements are done at this point in the design process.

Contract Rider (Rider) An addendum to the contract for a touring company, band, or artist that lists the production needs that must be provided by the local promoter

Contrast Ratios A range of intensity variations that compare the brightest to darkest elements within a frame or image. Contrast ratios are especially important to film and video production and refer to these proportional intensities. A camera with a large contrast ratio is capable of capturing a more extreme range of intensities.

Contrast Viewing Glasses A set of specialty glasses that are used to view a scene through a tinted filter. They allow quick identification of the highest- and lowest-intensity areas and help in setting the lighting/exposure levels of a scene.

Control Usually used to reference brightness or intensity modifications and control but also refers to determining which luminaires are circuited and wired together. In architectural applications this can also refer to focus and beam control as well.

Control Cable A low-voltage signal cable in electronic dimming systems that provides communication between a console and the dimmers or other devices.

Control/Circuit Schedules Schedules in landscape designs that organize the design in manners such as by circuit or control assignments. These are very similar to the dimmer and instrument schedules used in entertainment designs.

Control Schedule An architectural version of the hookup or channel/dimmer schedule.

Control Specification A design document that is based on the lighting specification of a project from a control perspective.

Controller The actual slide switches or faders found on a lighting console. Controllers may control individual channels or dimmers, submasters, or even the grand master. Controller assignments range from 0–10 or 0–100% in intensity.

Conventionals A term used to reference traditional luminaires or lighting instruments when they are combined in a rig that has automated luminaires.

Conventions An approach or use of dramatic techniques that an audience accepts as a means for a playwright and production to present a dramatic event. These are theatrical techniques (e.g., blue light is accepted as darkness) that allow the team to present the story to an audience.

Convergence An association where the ground between the lighting and video designer is becoming increasingly blurred through digital images, automated luminaires, and projection techniques that are bringing the two disciplines closer together.

Converging Rays When light rays are redirected in such a manner that they are focused towards one another and a common point.

Convex Lens A lens in which one of its surfaces curves or flexes outward away from the center.

Cookie (Cucaloris or Gobo) These were developed in the film and video industry and are custom-made flags or panels (with holes or patterns cut into them) that are placed between a light source and a target. Originally, it was meant as a "go between" and often called a gobo. While this, too, forms a shadow projection it is quite different from placing a template in an ERS as in the case of a theatrical gobo.

Cool Colors Light that has an abundance of blue, green, and lavender wavelengths and tends to produce psychological responses of calm, contentment, or melancholy.

Corporate Theatre (Corporate Sales Meeting) A special area of performance events that are produced by corporations to increase sales or to introduce new products.

Corridor A distribution pattern associated with dance lighting that forms a pathway extending from an extreme upstage position straight downstage.

Count The timing of a cue, usually based on seconds.

Cove (Slot) A lighting position that replaces the box boom position. A vertical cut located in the side walls of an auditorium where a boom or ladder-like device is located behind the wall for mounting front-diagonal light sources.

Cove Lighting A form of architectural lighting where wash luminaires are hidden behind a masking along the edges of a room or perimeter of a tray or other architectural feature. It creates a decorative wash around the perimeter of a room.

Cross Lighting A lighting technique in which two lights are aimed at a subject from opposite directions. This adds dimensionality to an object while also providing a slightly more diffuse lighting treatment.

Crossfade To evenly shift from one lighting cue or scene to another.

Crossfader A specialized fader that allows a board to shift or fade between two or more presets. In one extreme position one preset will be live while in the opposite position a second preset will become live while the first is faded out.

Cross-Key Lighting A variation of film and video lighting in which the camera is located essentially in a frontal position with two luminaires mounted roughly in opposing 45° front-diagonal positions.

CRT (Cathode Ray Tube) Projector The first widely used projector, which essentially projected three overlapping images of red, blue, and green light onto a common screen and had a relatively low intensity.

C-Stand A folding stand that is fully adjustable and used for mounting luminaires and grip equipment that is associated with location shooting.

CTB (Color Temperature Blue) Filter A filter used to correct the color temperature of light sources or luminaires with low color temperatures that need to be raised to match the higher color temperature of an exterior light source.

CTO (Color Temperature Orange) Filter A filter typically placed over window surfaces to correct the daylight color temperature to that of interior light sources.

Cucaloris See Cookie and Gobo.

Cue (Cueing, Look or State) A static lighting image or look that creates a given combination of lights and their angles, intensities, and overall mixing. Cueing refers to establishing the looks and recording them so that they can be duplicated from performance to performance.

Cue Blocks A method of numbering cues as a group based on their having similar functions. A common cue blocking technique includes grouping cues from individual dances of a dance repertory into blocks of cues that begin with specific numbers like 10, 20, 30, etc.

Cue List (Cue Stack) A series of cues that are stored in a console that can be pulled up and initiated by a programmer at will.

Cue Only Mode A console mode by which any changes made in a cue are performed on that cue only and will not have any impact on any other cues.

Cue Stack See Cue List

Cue Synopsis Design paperwork that functions as a guideline for the creation of a production's cues. It assigns a cue number to each cue and then goes on to describe specific information related to the cues. Cue numbers, counts, execution points, and a visual description of the cues are included in this information.

Cue-In (Set Levels) The cue-writing session where cues are created through a selection of luminaires, their colors, and intensities. Transitions are also determined during these sessions. Also known as level setting or writing cues.

Cue-Writing Session (Level-Setting Session) See Cue-in.

Curtain Warmer A lighting cue typically done when the main or show drop is in for presets, intermissions, or scene changes where the drop or curtain is glowed with a wash of low-intensity frontlight. Sometimes the lights that form this wash are called curtain warmers.

Cut 1. A film and video editing technique in which changes are made in what an audience sees through making switches between camera angles or scenes. 2. To strike or drop something from a production.

Cut List A listing of the number of cuts/frames of a particular gel color that will be required in each frame size for a production.

Cut Sheet Reference literature that provides specification data for a piece of lighting equipment. Examples of this data might include photometric data, mounting specifications, voltage/lamp requirements, and control channel capabilities, etc.

Cut-Off A quality of roadway luminaire design that refers to controlling how much light spills above a horizontal plane. Luminaires are characterized in regard to how much glare and spill that they allow above a given reference point.

Cyc Light (Far Cyc) A floodlight that has a significantly large distribution pattern and produces a smooth wash over a large area. Its soft edges allow it to be easily blended with adjoining fixtures. Far cycs are often used as a multi-colored wash luminaire where several cells are gelled differently from one another.

Cycle The voltage fluctuation that occurs throughout a single revolution of a generator. Also used to describe frequency comparisons in electromagnetic radiation.

Cyclorama (Cyc) A large, flat, scenic surface used as a neutral background for stages and television studios. The wrapped or curved cyc curves around the upstage corners of a stage or studio and extends back downstage at its sides.

CYM Mixing (CMY Mixing) A technology found in many automated luminaires that allows a designer to manipulate three dichroic filters (cyan, yellow, and magenta) to mix light of virtually any desired color.

Dailies (Rushes) The first prints of film that was shot during a given day. Dailies are often developed during the late afternoon and evaluated after the evening meal or the next day.

Daisy-Chain (Straight Run) A popular landscape wiring technique that forms a single chain of luminaires that are wired in parallel along an entire circuit/run. While being simplest to install, it also experiences the greatest effect of voltage drop.

Damper A set of shutters in a followspot that allow an operator to quickly cut the light across the top and bottom beam edges.

Dance Breaks The portion of a song and dance number in musical theatre where the performer(s) stop singing and go into a featured dance routine.

Dance Club A particular type of nightclub in which dance by the patrons is the primary element of entertainment.

Dance Tower A variation of boom that uses a metal truss-like structure to support the sidelights.

Dancing Water Display A performance event that features fountains with a variety of choreographed jet sprays and colored lighting, which are set to music.

Dark Ride A themed ride in which vehicles move through a darkened environment where only accent lighting is used on given features of the ride. The vehicle passes from one chamber to another through doors that it "bumps" open.

Day-for-Night A filming technique where a filter is placed over a camera's lens that filters the daylight to give the illusion of the scene being shot at night.

Daylighting A consideration of architectural lighting that uses the natural effects of daylight to provide supplemental illumination to an interior space.

Dead Refers to a circuit not having power.

Dead Back A reference to a light that is mounted directly behind a subject.

Dead Front A reference to a light that is mounted directly in front of a subject.

Dead Hang To tie-off or hang something like a batten directly from the grid.

Deck Electrician An electrician who works backstage to connect and disconnect temporary circuits, shift equipment, and make new circuit assignments throughout a show.

Decorative Lighting Luminaires with the primary function of adding to the decor of a space. They often bring glitter and sparkle to an interior design and are illustrated by chandeliers, wall sconces, and floor or table lamps.

Dedicated Controller A lighting console that is designed specifically for operating lighting equipment.

Dedicated Venue A performance facility that is specifically designed around the event that it houses. Cirque du Soleil programs often make use of dedicated venues.

Delay/Wait A manner of placing a hold on part of a segment of a cue's transition times. The actual nature of each is dependent on the specific console.

Depreciation A reduction in the light output of a lamp or luminaire over time. Factors that cause depreciation might include temperature effects, place in life cycle, dirt and grime, etc.

Depth of Field A range of focus located on either side of the focal point where objects remain in relatively good focus.

Design Development A design phase that represents a point at which the team comes to a basic agreement on the design, works out the details, and moves toward finalizing their designs.

Design Meeting A meeting between the director and all of the designers. Concepts are presented and the team collaborates and refines ideas regarding the designs for a production.

Design on the Fly A design mode in which a lighting designer runs a console predominately in a manual mode while creating original cues during an actual performance. This is a manner of improvising along with the performers.

Design Packet An information packet that a lighting designer sends to the venue ahead of their arrival that includes all the information that the crew will need to hang the design. It contains the light plot, other draftings related to the electrics department, the lighting schedules, and inventory or shop orders.

Design Paperwork (Paperwork or Schedules) A set of standardized lighting forms that organize all the information presented in the light plot in table formats. Each schedule is organized around a given type of lighting data. Instrument and channel schedules or hookups form the most commonly used schedules.

Design Phase A step in design development that refers to making a determination of the actual image of light. The initial phase relates to developing a concept, while later stages deal with translating this image into practical choices like fixture selection and mounting positions that support this vision.

Desk (Lighting Console) A computer or automated lighting control device. It is preferred over older terms like light board.

Diagonal A distribution pattern associated with dance lighting that form(s) diagonal pathways that extend from a downstage corner to the opposite upstage corner of the stage.

Dichroic (Cold Mirror) Reflectors A recent innovation that permits heat and low-wavelength electromagnetic radiation to pass through the reflector to the back of the instrument while the shorter wavelengths (light) are reflected.

Dichroic Filter A glass color filter that works on the principle of reflecting unwanted wavelengths of light rather than by absorbing them.

Diffuse A quality of light that is generally associated with a soft even distribution that does not produce sharply defined shadows.

Diffuse Reflection A type of reflection where light is scattered in numerous directions.

Diffuser A piece of glass, plastic, or other material that is placed over the front face of a luminaire to scatter and soften light while also preventing view of the light source.

Diffusion Media (Frost) Media similar to gel that is used to alter the quality of the light (to soften, as a rule). Film and video designers tend to use more diffusion due to the closer proximity that the luminaires have with the subject.

Digital Control A control protocol where a burst or packet of information (channel numbers and intensities) is sent to the dimmers and other equipment at a time when a change is required in the channel levels.

Digital Light A new generation of automated lighting instruments that in addition to having all the functions of any other automated fixture also have the ability of projecting still and video images.

Digital Projection Projection techniques that make use of computer or digital images/files and projectors rather than traditional techniques such as film or shadow projection.

Digital-to-Analog Converter (Multiplexers) A piece of equipment that acts as an interface for translating the digital signals of a control console to the analog control voltages used by older dimmers.

Dimmer A control device that adjusts the intensity of the lights. In most cases, a dimmer varies the voltage to control the brightness of the lights.

Dimmer Check See Channel Check.

Dimmer Doubling™ (Multiplexing) A trademark for ETC technology that allows designers to add additional control to a lighting system through adding specialized hardware to an existing dimmer. These additions effectively convert the single dimmer into two separately controlled dimmers.

Dimmer Plate (Plate) The physical dimmer assembly in resistance and autotransformer dimming. It contains the coils, mounting plate, electrical contacts, and shoe mechanism.

Dimmer Schedule A specific form of paperwork or hookup that presents all the luminaire data of a light plot in a table format. It organizes the information by dimmer number.

Dimmer-per-Circuit (DPC) A specialized form of dimming in which every lighting circuit is hardwired to its own dimmer.

Dimming Changes in intensity of a luminaire. Dimming may be both raised (dimming up) and lowered (dimming down).

Dimming Curve A relationship between how smoothly or proportionally a dimmer controls its load as it progresses from off to full.

Dimming Screen (Reducing Screen) A lighting accessory with a metal screen that is used in architectural and display lighting to lower the intensity of a luminaire without having an effect on the lamp's color temperature. Different screen densities provide a variety of intensity drops.

Dip To lower the intensity of a lighting fixture or entire cue.

Direct Component An element of lighting considered by illuminance at a point calculations for the line-of-sight measure of light coming directly from a luminaire to a particular point on a surface

Direct Current (DC) Electricity in which the voltage remains steady and relatively constant throughout time. Batteries produce DC current.

Direct Luminaires An IESNA classification of luminaire based on a distribution pattern where 90–100% of the light is directed downward.

Direct Sunlight One of the components of daylighting. This refers to the effect of sunlight shining directly into a space or facility.

Direct-Indirect Luminaires An IESNA classification of luminaire based on a distribution pattern in which the light is directed equally well in both the upward and downward directions.

Director of Photography See Cinematographer.

Director's Concept A statement presented by a director that addresses issues such as themes, meaning, character analysis and associations, and a specific interpretation of a script. The degree of realism or stylization and any symbolism may also be presented in a concept. The statement provides the context within which the production is to be created and becomes the guideline that shapes all of the interpretations and decisions connected with producing the project.

Disconnect Box A distribution panel that provides a power source for easy connection to supplemental equipment like a touring dimming rack. A company switch or road-tap are common examples of disconnect boxes.

Display Lighting An area of lighting that refers to lighting displays associated with retail and museum lighting as well as any other types of displays.

Dissolve Effect An effect that smoothly fades from one photographic image to another.

Distortion A series of properties by which a projection may be deformed. The most common form of distortion relates to keystoning.

Distributed Dimming A form of dimming that uses solid-state electronics to shorten individual cable runs through placing the actual dimmers in locations where the circuits would be located.

Distribution A controllable quality of light. Most lighting designers relate distribution to two specific lighting properties: angle or direction and quality.

Distribution Amplifier A device placed on a DMX control line to strengthen the control signal.

Distribution Panels Secondary electrical panels located throughout a building that are fed from the main switchboard and further distribute the power into branch circuits that lead to specific electrical equipment like lights and outlets.

Divergence When light rays are redirected in such a manner that they are focused away from one another and a common point.

DMX 512 The original universal control protocol for digital dimming. It provided a common control signal that allowed control and dimming equipment from a variety of manufacturers to work together. A newer variation of the control protocol was updated in the 1990s and is known as DMX512A.

Dots (Flags and Fingers) In film and video lighting these are opaque objects that are placed between the source and the target to block light from an unwanted area. Each variation relates to a different shape and variety of sizes.

Double Rotator A variation of gobo rotator that allows two gobos to be stacked to produce a composite gobo effect. Both gobos may be rotated in either direction at a variety of speeds.

Double-hang A manner of providing additional variety by duplicating lighting instruments representing a given wash or function. The most common example is in providing a second color system for a given lighting angle.

Doughnut An accessory placed in the color frame of a luminaire that consists of a metal plate with a hole cut at its center. They are used to sharpen the image of gobos.

Douser A mechanical dimmer used to dim lighting fixtures that cannot be dimmed electrically. They are found on followspots and other units that use arc sources.

Downlight A distribution angle that comes from directly above a subject and tends to produce distorted or heightened shadows that can have the effect of shortening or squashing a subject.

Dramatic Form (Structure) The manner in which a play is crafted with specific elements of its structure being presented to an audience at given points in its performance.

Dramatic spine (major dramatic question) The element or action that will form the major conflict of a play. Examples might include whether a particular social injustice is righted, if a particular relationship is restored, or if the boy ends up with the pretty girl.

Drop boxes A circuit distribution box that is lowered from a stage's grid and provides from three to 12 or more circuits to a new hanging position. Six additional circuits form a fairly common standard.

Drop Focus When a luminaire's focus setting slips due to not being tightened down sufficiently or through other factors such as vibrations in a venue which results in the focus falling lower than originally set by the designer.

Dry Run (Walk-Through) A film or video first rehearsal in which the actors arrive for a blocking rehearsal and the director establishes their movement patterns.

Dry Tech (First Tech and Technical Rehearsals) A rehearsal that is often associated with the actual cue-writing process or first evaluation of the cues by the director. It focuses on the technical elements of a production, not the performers. Lighting, sound, and scenic elements are introduced and integrated into the production at this time. Performers are usually not called unless there are especially complex sequences involving them.

Dumping a Show When a computer lighting console loses its memory and all of the cues and their related data is lost.

Edge Lighting A type of film or video lighting that uses a variation of sidelight to graze a subject's surface to produce extended shadows that emphasize its texture.

Edit Cues Making revisions or changes in the cues.

Educational Facilities Lighting Lighting that is associated with the illumination of schools and college or university facilities along with other educational buildings.

Edu-tainment A form of themed entertainment that is often used in museums. This uses entertainment and themed design elements as a method of teaching.

Effect Lighting 1. Video or film lighting that doesn't directly affect the subject but is used to produce specific effects in a scene (projection patterns, accents, etc.). 2. Lighting in a themed attraction that exists only for effect (strobes, black light, etc.).

Effects 1. Lighting that generates some form of optical effect (fire effects, water reflections, lightning, etc.). 2. A set of menus found on computer lighting consoles that allow a designer to create elaborate cue sequences into pre-programmed effects.

Effects Module A pre-programmed effect like a chase sequence that can be assigned to specific control channels. Operators can usually vary the speed and intensity of the effects.

Effects Projector A projector that is equipped with a series of modular motion effects that can be used to create moving effects like rain and fire.

Egg Crates See Baffles.

Egg-Crate Grid A lighting grid that consists of a series of portholes that are created in a regular grid pattern directly above a stage. The portholes, or wells, are fashioned into the structure of the ceiling (2 to 3 feet square) and contain a pipe or other hardware for mounting luminaires.

Electric A hanging position for lighting that is found directly above the stage and consists of a pipe or batten that runs across the width of a stage. Many facilities have permanent electrics equipped with raceways and larger counter-weight arbors.

Electrical Contractor The company (or individual), in architectural applications, that is contracted to acquire and install the lighting equipment according to the designer's specifications and building codes.

Electrical Distribution The electrical pathway in which electricity flows from its power source through a series of cables or wires and electrical hardware to its final destination and devices that use it, like luminaires.

Electrical Mastering A form of control in which individual dimmers are assigned or wired together with dimmers of a larger capacity for easier mastering.

Electrical Potential A difference in energy levels at two different points. It comes through the addition or gathering of electrons at one of the points and represents a potential for electrical flow.

Electricians Crew members who work around electricity and are primarily associated with the preparation and execution of the lighting for a production. In architectural applications electricians are licensed and install all of the electrical equipment.

Electrics Crew The crew that is responsible for all of the electrical requirements of a production. Their work focuses on lighting and sound but they also provide power to effects, lifts, hydraulic pumps, winches, and other electrical equipment.

Electromagnetic Radiation Energy in the form of electromagnetic waves or radiant energy.

Electromagnetic Spectrum A continuum representing a collection of different levels of radiant energy, like visible light, that are specified by different wavelengths. The longer wavelengths (radio, television, and electricity) relate to lower energy levels, while the shortest (gamma and cosmic rays) relate to higher energy levels.

Electromagnetism A physical phenomenon in which an electrical current can be produced or induced by moving a wire through a magnetic field.

Electronic Control A form of lighting control using semi-conductor electronic hardware in which a low-voltage control signal is used to proportionally regulate the line-voltage that determines the brightness of the lights.

Electronic Dimming A form of dimming in which a low-voltage control signal is created at a light board/console, which in turn regulates a line-voltage power supply that provides proportional power to a circuit and luminaires.

Electronic Mastering A low-voltage form of mastering that became possible through electronic dimming. Electronic mastering provides presetting and a host of other dimming features that aren't possible with manual control systems.

Ellipsoidal Reflector A reflector based on the shape of an ellipse. A unique property of this reflector is that through placing a light source at the primary focal point, the light is focused to and passes through a conjugate or secondary focal point.

Ellipsoidal Reflector Floodlight (ERF or Scoop) The simplest floodlight in use. It creates an extremely wide distribution pattern of soft, diffuse light. The edges are soft and easily blend with adjoining fixtures.

Ellipsoidal Reflector Spotlight (ERS) The most extensively used spotlight, with optics that are superior to other luminaires and produces a crisp, even pool of light. Most ERSes have very sharp, well-defined edges as well as the ability to shape the light through accessories like shutters or gobos.

Emergency Lighting Lighting that comes on and gives a base level of illumination when there is a power outage. It is powered by a battery or generator.

Encapsulated Arc Sources A variation of short-arc lamp in which the arc is enclosed in a glass envelope. In film and video setups, these lamps have very high color temperatures (approximately 5,500° K) and are often used to supplement daylight.

Encoder A knob or rotary control found on control consoles that is particularly friendly for programming the attributes of intelligent fixtures.

End User The individual(s) who will actually be inhabiting (working within or experiencing) the lit environment. The lighting is specified according to their tasks.

Energy Management Reducing a building's power demands while producing a lighting system that is designed and used in a way that is energy efficient and doesn't have an adverse effect on lighting quality or other building systems.

Enhanced Definition Lens Tube (EDLT) A lens barrel developed by ETC for the Source Four Spotlight that has superior optics.

Enhanced Ellipsoidal Reflector Spotlight (ERS) An improved variation of the ellipsoidal reflector spotlight (ERS) that was developed in the early 1990s by ETC. Its improved lamp, shutters, and reflector design produces far superior light than traditional ERSes. It is becoming the luminaire of choice for most designers.

Enhanced PAR A PAR luminaire that is designed around the newer HPL lamp. The light is similar in quality but superior to a traditional PAR, and beam angles are varied through the replacement of lenses rather than by using different lamps.

Entertainment Services and Technology Association (ESTA) An organization of theatrical manufacturers and dealers that provides resources to the commercial areas of the entertainment community as well as a venue for establishing many of the standards of the industry.

Entertainment Technician Certification Program (ETCP) A certification program that helps to ensure that individuals have an established level of competency as a professional (rigger or electrician). Certification is granted through passing an exam every three years or going through a series of educational programs.

Establish a Scene A function of lighting in which light is used to communicate specific information about the environment that is being created (time of day, season, geographical location, etc.).

Evaluation Phase A phase of construction that takes place after a client has taken occupancy and where the designer checks client satisfaction, performs fixes or modifications as needed, and helps the client understand how to maintain and operate a design.

Exit Lighting A special lighting system that powers signage that identifies exit routes and doorways in public buildings.

Expendables (Perishables) Lighting materials such as gel, tie-line, and gobos that must be purchased and cannot be returned once used.

Exposure 1. Amount of light used to sensitize or produce an image on film or video. 2. The detrimental effect of heat, visible light, and ultraviolet radiation coming from light sources (of particular concern in retail and museum or gallery lighting). It can also come from natural sources like daylight.

Exposure Ratios A variation of contrast ratios for video lighting where a comparison is made between the lighting intensities of any two objects or areas in an image.

Extended Service Lamps with longer lamp lives than normal lamps.

Exterior Lighting Lighting of the outside of a building and its entrances. Many make a distinction between exterior lighting and lighting the surrounding grounds (landscape lighting).

Extrude A virtual modeling technique in which a two-dimensional shape/plane is stretched along a length that is perpendicular to itself to produce a three-dimensional object. An example would be extruding a circle into a solid tube or cylinder.

Eyelash (Half Hat) A variation of a top hat that masks only half the cylinder.

Eye-Light A type of front fill used in film and video work that comes in at a low angle from the front (often mounted on the camera) and provides good facial light while bringing sparkle to a subject's eyes.

Face-Light A frontal source used in film and video that comes in at a low angle and provides good facial lighting. Eye-light is a special type of face-light.

Faders The actual slide switches found on a lighting console.

Falloff Refers to a light's intensity dropping off as you move away from its source. Falloff is directly related to the Inverse Square Law.

Far Cycs See Cyc Lights.

Far-Side Key Placement of the key light in film and video so that it is on the side of a performer's face that is away from the camera. Far-side key is usually preferable.

Feeders (Feeder Cables) Large-gauge wires that deliver high capacity power to distribution panels and other dimming/electrical equipment.

Female Connector A connector with one or more receptacles for making quick connections between electrical devices and cables. The female connector provides the source of the power.

Fiber Optics An assemblage of very thin glass or plastic tubes that transport light. There are two popular forms: end-emitting fiber, which conducts light throughout its length where it emerges at the end of the fiber; and side-emitting fiber, which radiates light along its sides that glow like a neon tube.

Field Angle The angle representing the beam distribution of a luminaire where the intensity has fallen off to 10% of the intensity at the center of the beam. Field angles are inclusive of beam angles.

Filament The part of an incandescent lamp that contains the highly resistant material that is heated to produce the actual light source.

Filament Sing (Lamp Sing) A side effect of early electronic dimmers where the dimmers caused the filaments of the lamps to vibrate and actually produce harmonics that could be heard.

Fill Light Light that is the result of diffusion or scattered reflections; in many cases, this is ambient light. In entertainment and film or video lighting, fill light is an additional source that adds light to the areas of an object that would be associated with shadows or achieves a base level of illumination that the cameras can record. In architectural and landscape lighting, fill light is a low-level light that provides an overall ambience to an area while tying all the other sources together.

Film A medium in which photosensitive emulsions are exposed to light to record images.

Filtering Placing a material in front of a light source that selectively removes frequencies or wavelengths of light.

Filters A material through which light passes where certain wavelengths are filtered out (absorbed) while others pass directly through. Gel is a generic name for filters.

Fingers See Dots.

Fires Refers to the moment of switching on or the sampling point of an SCR dimmer.

Firmware Software that is downloaded to a console, automated light, or other computer peripheral and improves or updates the equipment's performance.

First Team The primary or actual performers in a film or television production.

First Tech See Dry Tech Rehearsal.

Five Times Rule A rule for establishing the validity of using the Inverse Square Law in lighting calculations—the law is less accurate at close distances. It states that the distance between the source and target should be at least five times the largest viewed dimension of the source to provide accurate luminance calculations.

Five-Point Lighting A system for area lighting design that is based on five luminaires. The most common practice involves placing four units at roughly 90° from one another and adding a fifth downlight to an area.

Fixed Capacity An association in which a dimmer (generally resistance) must be fully loaded in order to achieve complete dimming.

Fixture A name given to a luminaire, but more specifically designating a luminaire that is permanently installed or mounted.

Fixture Library A collection of data regarding automated luminaires and their attributes. These can be downloaded and stored in a console to eliminate programming that would be required for setting the units up in a console.

Flags See Dots.

Flash and Trash A reference from the concert industry that alludes to simply flashing lights without any clear thought or consideration towards a lighting design.

Flash Buttons See Bump Buttons.

Flat Angle A lighting angle that is relatively low and straight-on.

Flat Field A beam distribution pattern in which the intensity of the beam remains fairly consistent and even throughout the entire field or pool of light.

Flat Field Luminaires Newer enhanced spotlights developed since the early 1990s that have relatively flat fields and more efficient light production.

Flatted Reflectors A variation of mirrored reflectors that have a series of prismatic faces over the reflector surface.

Flicker Device An animation device that produces a flicker effect, which is created through placing a motorized disk with open areas in front of a spotlight's beam of light.

Flood Focus A setting for a Fresnel spotlight in which the lamp is moved closer to the lens, which causes divergence and results in the light being spread out.

Floodlight A luminaire that has a soft, diffuse light with undefined edges that washes over a large area evenly. Floodlights do not usually contain a lens.

Floodlighting A type of lighting that creates a soft, evenly distributed light over a large area.

Floor Mount A lighting instrument that sits or is mounted to the deck or floor.

Floor Pocket A theatrical distribution box located in the stage floor that contains several independent circuits.

Floorplan (Groundplan) A scaled top view of a performance area or environment that provides an aerial view of a facility as if the roof had been removed.

Flown Truss (Flying Rig) A truss supported from above by winches or chain hoists.

Fluorescent Bank Luminaires used in the video and film industry that contain a group of fluorescent lamps (often with special properties) that are housed together and used as economical wash luminaires. They can be either a soft or hard light source depending on what other units are used in a setup. Kino Flo units are popular examples of these luminaires and come in a variety of sizes and lamp configurations.

Fluorescent Lamp A lamp that works on the principle of energizing a field of low-pressure gas between two electrodes. Unlike arc sources, whose light comes from the arc, this arc is in the ultraviolet range and energizes another material like phosphorous that glows and actually creates the light.

Flyby A tool used in visualization programs that permits a viewer to experience a virtual world through following a view along a predetermined path.

Flying Rig See Flown Truss.

Focal Length A measurement taken from a given point of a lens (its optical center) to its focal point.

Focal Point A point of focus along the optical path of a lens or reflector that coincides with the location from which light rays will be directed to produce parallel light rays. The reverse (where parallel light rays are directed to a focal point) is also true.

Focus 1. A lighting function that refers to drawing attention to various elements of an environment. 2. Aiming and adjusting the beam quality of a luminaire.

Focus Chart A table that documents the focus characteristics of each luminaire in a design. Most importantly, it documents the unit's location of the hotspot and focus as well as the focus settings (hard/soft), spot/flood settings, and shutter positions.

Focus Palettes (Focus Points) Reference points to which automated lighting fixtures have pre-assigned pan and tilt positions. This allows a programmer to quickly move a light to predetermined positions.

Focusing (Focus Call) A crew call in which the lighting crews aim and adjust each light for optimum performance under the direction of the lighting designer.

Focusing Spots Location luminaires that are relatively small and designed to be mounted on portable stands. They can be open-faced or may contain a lens. In some cases, the reflector may also be changeable.

FocusTrack A specialized device that is used where a lift or ladder cannot be used due to obstructions to their movement on the deck or over an audience. It essentially places a movable boatswain's chair on a track that is mounted on or near a neighboring electric or truss. An electrician sits in the chair and is moved along the position at trim height to focus lights across the position without having to deal with the obstructions that are below.

Follow Cue A cue that is launched automatically without a "go" instruction by a preceding cue. For instance, Cue 12 brings up a special on a performer, which is then automatically followed by Cue 13, which is a 300-count sunset fade that is launched with a pre-programmed time after Cue 12 has been initiated.

Following Source A video or film technique in which the lighting is based predominantly on motivational lighting elements.

Followspot A spotlight that is used to follow performers around a stage or performance area. Most have controls for easy modification of the shape and color of the light.

Followspot Operator An individual who operates a followspot. They typically control pan and tilt, color, and size and sharpness of the beam of light that strikes the performers.

Footcandle A measure of illuminance that is based on the illuminance level found at a one-foot distance from a candle.

Footlights A lighting position at the very front edge of the stage at floor or stage level that provides a wash of uplight onto the performers.

Four-Point Lighting A system for general lighting that is based on four luminaires being placed at roughly 90° orientations with one another. This is a popular approach for thrust and arena lighting design.

Four-way Barn Door A control device that is placed in the front of a luminaire and has four individual panels that can be rotated into the beam of light to block or control spill.

Four-wire System (Wye) An electrical service connection where a power utility provides three different hot wires and a common neutral to a given site.

Framing To shape the light around a subject using shutters or other devices. Framing is often associated with architectural, retail, and museum applications.

Framing Projector A smaller variation of ERS that is often box-shaped and contains superior optics along with shutters and other accessories for manipulating the shape of the light. Framing projectors are used in retail and architectural design, but are more commonly associated with museum, gallery, and landscape lighting.

Frequency A method of measuring waves based on the number of oscillations per unit time.

Fresnel Lens A variation of plano-convex lens that has portions of the convex surface removed. A dimpled texture on the plano surface adds a diffusing effect that masks the concentric rings found on its front surface.

Fresnel Spotlight Named for the inventor of the Fresnel lens, Augustine-Jean Fresnel, the essential elements include a lamp, spherical reflector, and Fresnel lens. Light from Fresnels is moderately harsh, while the edges are soft and not clearly defined.

Front Diagonal A distribution angle that places a light approximately midway between a front light and a sidelight angle. It offers the best of both angles in regard to revelation of a subject.

Front End The portion of a control system that contains the console or light board.

Front Light A lighting angle that comes from in front of a subject and helps provide visibility and visual clarity. At the same time, it can flatten and reduce the effect or appearance of three-dimensional textures and forms.

Front of House (FOH) A reference to lighting positions that are downstage of the proscenium or are in the audience area (house).

Front Projection A form of projection where the projector and source material are placed in front of the screen or projection surface.

Frost See Diffusion Media.

Frosted Finish A bulb finish that contains a natural diffuser to soften the light that a lamp produces.

F-Stop The size of the aperture/opening of a camera lens, which is expressed through a set of numbers that relate to one another logarithmically. Every drop in f-stop equates to allowing twice as much light into a lens.

Funnel A tapered or cone-shaped snoot or top hat.

Fuse An electrical device that is designed as the weakest link in a circuit and meant to trip or "blow" if the circuit should become overloaded. Unlike a circuit breaker, most fuses cannot be reset.

Gaffer See Chief Lighting Technician.

Gain A way of characterizing a screen or projection surface's ability to reflect or transmit light. The higher the gain, the better the material performs as a screen.

Gaseous Discharge A form of arc light source where the arc is placed in a specific atmosphere of gases. Fluorescent lamps are an example of this light source.

Gate The area of an ERS that is located roughly at the unit's secondary (conjugate) focal point. This is the location where the light is most concentrated and where shutters, gobos, and other accessories are placed.

Gating The process in electronic dimming in which a low-voltage signal is used to control or sample the high-voltage output of a dimmer through triggering an SCR so that it fires or turns on at a given point in a cycle.

Gauge A measurement of the thickness or diameter of a wire. The larger the gauge (number), the smaller the diameter of the wire and the less current or load that it can safely carry.

Gear A term often used by entertainment professionals for lighting equipment.

Gel A color filter originally made from animal gelatin that was tinted to produce different colors. As fixtures improved, gel could no longer stand up to the temperatures of the newer light sources and has been replaced by plastic filters.

Gel Frame See Color Frame.

Gelstring A sequence of gels that have been taped together to form a scroll of adjoining colors for a color scroller. Gelstrings typically contain 12 or more colors.

General Circulation Lighting See Ambient Lighting.

General Diffuse Luminaire An IESNA classification of luminaire based on a distribution pattern in which light is directed equally well in nearly all directions.

General Illumination See Area Lighting.

General Lighting See Area Lighting.

Generator A device that allows mechanical motion to be transferred into electrical potential or power by moving electrical coils through a magnetic field. Portable generators that are used on location shoots for film or video may be as small as lawnmower engine or as large as truck or trailer-mounted units. A generator is often called a "Genny" by people in the business.

Genie-Lift (Genie Tower and Super Lift) Ground supports for trussing that are adaptations of lifts that were designed for the construction industry.

Genny Operator (Generator Operator) The individual who operates and monitors the generator(s) on a location or remote shoot.

Ghost Light (Ghost Load) 1. An additional load of lamps placed on a resistance dimmer to bring it to full capacity while also allowing a full range of dimming for a circuit. 2. A bare bulb lamp placed on a stand and left glowing when a theatre is not in operation. This prevents people from being harmed when entering the space.

Ghosting 1. A dimming condition in which a full out cannot be achieved by a dimmer, despite having a setting that should produce no light. 2. Placing very low levels of intensity on a stage, such as during a near blackout for a scene change or to check if a lamp is working.

Glare The presence of distracting light within a viewer's field of vision. This may come about as the result of an unusually high level of reflectance (snow on a bright afternoon) or when an observer is forced to look directly into a light source.

Glazing The clear or translucent material used on windows and building facades.

Glitter (Sparkle) A positive element of glare. We may want to create a limited amount of glare to add visual interest and perhaps some focus to a scene or object.

Global Illumination A special form of virtual lighting that creates a uniform light throughout an environment.

Goal Post Grip equipment used in location shooting that connects two vertical stands like C-stands with a horizontal arm or batten to which luminaires and other grip equipment can be mounted.

Gobo (Pattern or Template) 1. A metal or glass pattern that is inserted into the optical path of a luminaire to create a texture or designed image in light. 2. The film and video industries identify gobos as custom-made flags or panels (with holes or patterns cut into them) that are placed between a light source and a target. See Cookie and Cucaloris.

Gobo Rotator An accessory that generates a rotating motion for gobos.

Grand Master An intensity fader that provides a mechanism in which the entire system's intensity can be controlled by a single fader.

Gray Card A poster-like reference card that is printed in a middle gray and used for white balancing cameras and color temperature calibrations for shooting video under a given set of lighting conditions.

Gray Scale A reference scale used in film and video lighting that rates light reflectivity and value on a scale of 0 (black or total absorption) to 10 (white or total reflection). It is used for color balancing and exposure settings.

Grazing Light played across the surface of an object at an extreme angle. This angle is used to enhance the texture of a surface.

Green Bed (Greenie) A catwalk system of platforms that are hung from the rafters of a sound stage at about 4 feet above a set. They are arranged along the outline of a set and have a series of holes along their edges for mounting luminaires along their perimeters. Power is dropped down to the platforms from above and distributed to the lights as needed.

Green Power Using conservation methods or "thinking green" as a way of lowering the energy demands of a project and ultimately saving our natural resources.

Grid A structure at the top of a theatre's flyspace that supports all the blocks and rigging hardware for all the flying equipment (battens, scenery, maskings, and electrics). Also short for lighting grid—a series of pipes hung over a performance space for hanging luminaires and other objects.

Grip Truck A truck used on location shoots that holds and transports lighting and grip equipment for location production. Studios rent grip trucks that are equipped with a predetermined inventory of lighting and grip equipment for a standard fee.

Grips The crew members for film and video shoots who are responsible for the movement and setup of any equipment required for a production. They are also responsible for the installation and operation of camera gear like dollies and cranes.

Ground A point that represents the lowest potential for an electrical charge (earth or absolute ground) and toward which all electricity strives to flow. In electrical services, the ground is a safety path or wire that leads from a device to an earth ground and becomes the emergency path for any unwanted electrical flow.

Ground Fault Circuit Interrupter (GFCI) A device that detects any flow of electricity between the neutral and earth ground. If it detects any, it trips in the same way as a circuit breaker trips. They are typically installed in areas where there is a higher risk of shock and are often found in kitchens, bathrooms, and exterior locations.

Ground Row A collection of luminaires (usually striplights) that are floor-mounted across the width of the stage that illuminate a drop or cyclorama from below.

Ground Supported Truss A truss that is supported from below by towers or lifts.

Groundplan See Floorplan.

Group Relamping A method of relamping in which lamps are replaced together as a group on a regular schedule. The schedule is based on the number of hours that the system is in operation and the rated lamp life of the lamps. This is especially efficient when luminaires are hard to reach.

Groups A manner of combining channels or dimmers into larger elements with less specific control when using an electronic control system.

Hair Light A form of film and video lighting (a variation of steep backlight) that is used to add highlights to the talent's hair.

Halation An effect where there is a slight scattering of light around the edges of a beam or projected images (such as a gobo) that prevents a sharp well-defined edge to be produced.

Half Hat See Eyelash.

Halogen Metal Iodide (HMI) Lamp A special variation of HID lamp that makes use of metal halides to produce an arc light source with better color rendering capabilities than other arc sources.

Hanging and Circuiting Placing or hanging the luminaires and wiring them according to the specifications of the lighting designer.

Hanging Cards A partial copy of a light plot that contains the information that an electrician needs to hang a single lighting position. They can be mounted on laminated cards or cardboard so that they can stand up to the abuses of touring.

Hanging Irons Specialized hardware, with an attached C-clamp, that are used to hang striplights. Two are required for each stripligh—one for each end.

Hanging Position A permanent mounting position for luminaires located throughout a performance venue. They also usually have permanently wired circuits running to them.

Hanging Section A portion of a light plot that provides the location and labeling of all the battens/linesets that are hung from above the stage.

Hard Blackouts See Block Cues.

Hard Light A classification of light in film and video lighting that is often associated with the key source for a setup. It is quite directional and generally the primary source responsible for producing strong highlights and sharp, well-defined shadows in a scene. In landscape lighting, this is the higher contrast light and is marked by clear well-defined shadows.

Hard-Lights A classification of film and video luminaires that produce a sharp light with shadows. The luminaires are often focusable and have a reasonable degree of control. They form strong shadows and are good directional light sources, making them a logical choice for key lights.

Hardscape The architectural and sculptural elements of a landscape.

Haze A low-grade fog or smoke that lightly charges the atmosphere with particles that permit the beams of light to be seen.

Hazers A piece of equipment that is similar to an atmospheric fog machine that lightly charges the air with a haze rather than filling the air with fog or smoke.

Head An accessory that is added to a projector to create a specific projection effect.

Head Gaffer The individual who supervises the entire lighting department for a television or film production.

Healthcare Lighting Lighting associated with the needs of the medical industry. It is one of the more complex areas of architectural lighting and relates to lighting hospitals, long-term care facilities, and medical offices or labs.

Heat Shield A special form of clear, gel-like material that filters ultraviolet radiation. It is inserted at the front of a unit, between the lamp and gel (leaving a gap for airflow between them) and can help extend a gel's life.

Heat Sink A metal fin-like assembly for mounting and cooling SCRs and other electronic equipment.

High Key A lighting condition in video lighting in which there is little difference between the lighting levels of the key and fill light, meaning that there is a small lighting/contrast ratio (1:1, 2:1 or 3:1) and a less dramatic image.

High-Bay A variation of luminaire commonly found in "big-box" stores and warehouses that provides a wash of general lighting from relatively high mounting heights.

High-Density Dimmers Small, compact dimmers that can be packaged into a limited amount of space (high-density racks). Today's high-density dimmers are small enough that nearly 200 of them can be mounted in a single rack.

High-End Retail Environment A retail market in which the customer enters an environment where they are made to feel comfortable and catered to as they go through the purchasing process.

High-Intensity Discharge (HID) Lamps. Highly efficient sources that use an enclosed arc to produce light. These lamps require a ballast and have a warm-up period of up to 10 minutes. They are common to architectural applications with mercury, high pressure sodium, and metal halide forming the most common examples.

Highlights Flashes of reflected light that represent areas that are directly illuminated by a light source.

High-Mast Lighting Mounting street and roadway luminaires on poles over 60 feet tall.

High-Pipe-Ends (HPE) Luminaires that are hung on the extreme ends of the electrics for high-angled sidelight.

High-Power LEDs (HPLEDs) A second generation of LEDs that produce a much higher light output than traditional LEDs. They are very efficient and produce enough light to be used as an actual light source. They are often combined into arrays or clusters of multiple HPLEDs that can produce enough heat to require a heat sink.

High-Pressure Sodium Lamp A variation of HID lamp that uses sodium as its primary lamp fill and is often used for street lighting. It is very efficient and can be recognized by its pinkish-orange color.

High-Resolution Mode A mode associated with the degree of control that an attribute has in an automated luminaire. High-resolution modes are associated with 16-bit/two-channel operation of an attribute. Resolution modes are frequently associated with pan/tilt functions where fine and course adjustments are available for these movements.

Hologram An advanced projection effect that is produced through a combination of laser and film effects. The unique quality of holograms is that they can produce an illusion of a three-dimension image.

Home (Homing) A process that automated luminaires go through as part of a startup sequence where the stepper motors are referenced to specific points so that the luminaires share a common reference for their attributes with every performance.

Home Run (Spidering) A manner of theatrical circuiting in which luminaires are wired directly from their hanging position all the way back to the dimmers. This is popular for touring and is often done in road houses and rental facilities.

Hood (Body) 1. The actual enclosure of a luminaire. It provides for the proper mounting and orientation of all the optical components while also providing a way for mounting the luminaire and its accessories. 2. An optical accessory for architectural luminaires that fits over the face of a fixture and helps block viewers from direct glare coming from a lamp or reflector.

Hookup Design paperwork that presents all of the information contained in a light plot in a table format. The data is organized by control (channel or dimmer number).

Hospitality Lighting A variation of architectural lighting that refers to the hotel and restaurant industries.

Hot Light Sources See Continuous Light Sources.

Hot Wire Wire that leads to the power source for a circuit.

House Electrician Typically a master electrician assigned to a specific theatre or performance space, which is common in both union and road or touring houses. This term is also used to distinguish between a local and touring electrician on work calls.

Houses of Worship (Church) Lighting A specialized area of architectural lighting that refers to lighting churches, temples, and other religious structures.

Housing See Body.

Hub A computer networking device that allows multiple Ethernet connections to be connected together through a special interface.

Hues The generic name for a color (e.g., red, blue, orange, etc.). Hues become a familiar means of communicating basic color information from one person to another.

Illuminance The density of light that has struck an object's surface and is then reflected. Two measurements of illuminance include the lux (one lumen per square meter) or the footcandle (one lumen per square foot).

Illuminance at a Point A lighting calculation used for determining the illuminance at a specific location rather than the average illuminance over an area. This method of calculation can be used for both horizontal and vertical surfaces and is best utilized for single light sources. It is particularly helpful for determining the illuminance in applications involving wall surfaces like displays and bulletin boards.

Illuminating Engineer An individual who designs the lighting for architectural projects who comes from an electrical engineering background.

Illuminating Engineering Society of North America (IESNA or IES) A professional society that provides services to lighting professionals and the lighting industry. Publications, training, and controlling specification standards and recommended practices for the industry are a few of the responsibilities of this organization.

Illumination Engineering A specialized field of electrical engineering that relates to the design and specification of architectural and other permanent lighting installations.

Illuminator The equipment that provides the light source for a fiber optics bundle.

I-MAG (I-mag or I-Mag) A video projection system used in large venues in which live camera feeds are sent to large-format screens that allow the most distant audience members to see the artists more closely.

Image of Light (Lighting Scheme/Concept or Point of View) A vision of the lighting for a project. All other tasks related to a lighting design ultimately go back to this initial step in the process.

Imagineers The unique creative team of Disney that forms the primary leadership in the development of Disney's themed attractions. They come from a creative background that is part artists and part engineers.

Incandescence The most popular method of light production, which is represented by the common light bulb. A metal filament is heated to the point that it gives off electromagnetic radiation and glows.

Incident Light Meter An exposure type of light meter that is used by standing in the location of the subject and pointing the meter back towards the camera and light source. It measures the level of light striking a subject.

Independent Master A special form of controller that allows those channels assigned to it to function independently from any other mastering on the board.

Index of Refraction The relative speed of light moving through translucent materials expressed as a proportional ratio to the speed of light moving through a vacuum.

Indexing Rotator A gobo rotator that allows gobos to be stopped at precise locations.

Indirect Illumination A form of illumination in which light is reflected off another surface before being used as a source of illumination. Many architectural designs use the ceiling to create indirect illumination. Film shoots use large reflector panels to soften a light source and to provide indirect illumination to a scene.

Indirect Luminaire An IESNA classification of luminaire based off of a distribution pattern in which 90–100% of the light is directed toward the ceiling, where it is reflected back into the room.

Induced Current The current that is created in a wire from the pulsations of a magnetic field, as in the case of a transformer.

Industrial Lighting Lighting facilities that are involved in the manufacturing process.

Industrials A type of corporate theatre where large spectacle presentations combining performers, theatrical gimmicks like presentational lighting and pyro effects, and large-screen video projections build enthusiasm for a product or company service.

Inky The smallest version of Fresnel spotlight (a 3-inch variety).

In-one A plane or zone that forms a pathway across the width of a stage. It is associated with the area between the proscenium opening and the first set of legs. Additional planes include in-two, in-three, etc.

Instrument A luminaire. The term "instrument" is more commonly used in the theatrical and entertainment areas of lighting while fixture or luminaire is more popularly used in architectural applications.

Instrument Schedule Lighting paperwork that organizes the data contained in a light plot by hanging position and instrument number.

Insulated Gate Bipolar Transistor (IGBT) A solid-state component of the newer sine wave dimmers that has the capability of sampling an AC current several hundred times throughout each half cycle of a dimming cycle, which produces a more accurate sampling of the AC voltage than traditional SCRs.

Insulation Highly electrical resistant material used to cover conductors such as wires.

Insulator A material with high electrical resistance that forms a barrier to electrical flow.

Intelligent Lights See Automated Lights or Moving Lights.

Intensity A quality of light associated with the brightness of light.

Interconnection Panel (Interconnection Pachbay) See Patchbay.

Interference Patterns. A laser image in which the laser is distorted by passing through an irregular piece of material like glass or plastic which causes its individual waves to become scattered or knocked out of phase with one another. The technique produces colored patterns of light that form simple or more complex organic patterns that are capable of being transported over long distances.

Interior Lighting An area of lighting that refers to lighting building interiors.

Interlocking Handles A form of mechanical mastering done through connecting banks of dimmers (resistance or autotransformer) to common shafts and control handles that can be locked together through spring-loaded pin mechanisms.

Intermediate Colors (Tertiary Colors) An unequal mixture of primary colors.

Intermediate Retail Environment A retail environment that falls between the high-end and basic retail markets. It contains elements of both markets and would best be characterized by department stores where different departments are lit differently.

International Alliance of Theatrical Stage Employees (IATSE) The union that represents the lighting and stagehand crews for theatre, video and film, and other production houses and facilities. It is common to hear this union called the IA or local.

International Association of Lighting Designers (IALD) A professional society that is similar to the IESNA but whose membership is restricted to lighting designers.

International Illumination Design Awards (IIDA) Design awards that are given annually for exceptional examples of architectural lighting design.

Inverse Square Law A law that states that the illuminance of a light source is inversely proportional to the square of the distance from the source. $E = I/D^2$.

Iris (Iris Kit) 1. A mechanical device or accessory that allows light to be shuttered in a circular pattern that permits an operator to narrow or expand the diameter of the light. 2. The colored part of the eye that adjusts the amount of light entering the eye (also found in cameras).

Irons A category of hanging hardware and accessories. Items like C-clamps, sidearms, and hanging irons form examples of irons.

Island Window A window display that is surrounded by glass on all sides and allows customers to walk around it to examine merchandise.

ISO See ASA

Jewel Lighting A variation of the zone lighting formula in which an emphasis is placed on higher intensity levels and the low-angled sidelight that is hung primarily from booms positioned along the sides of the stage and the front diagonals. In addition to the basic washes, jewel lighting adds accents and specials to bring visual interest to a design, and characteristically lights a subject from many angles.

Jones Box A lighting accessory that connects all of the individual control cables of analog dimmer packs to an interface of the digital to analog converter.

Jones Connectors (Cinch-Jones Connectors) A special connector associated with analog control cables that provides low-voltage connections between the control cable and the console or dimmers.

Jumper (Cable) A cable containing two or three insulated conductors that has a single male and female connector on each end. It is often used synonymously with cable.

Junction Method A landscape wiring technique that attempts to eliminate voltage drop through wiring every lamp back to a single point in the circuit.

Key 1. A portion of the light plot that indicates the specific choice of luminaire with an associated symbol or accessory. 2. The key light or luminaire that provides the key light.

Key and Fill A system for creating general lighting in which one source (the key) is associated with the primary or apparent source and another (the fill) provides enough illumination to suggest any ambient light required for general visibility. It originated in the film and television industry where cameras required minimum levels of illumination to prevent shadow areas from going completely dark.

Key Light The light that is the primary source responsible for lighting a scene. It is associated with the source of the lighting and produces the strongest highlights and shadows.

Keystone Effect A distortion effect that occurs when a projection surface and projector's slide and resulting image are not oriented properly along the same axis. Keystoning causes lines and surfaces to spread outward in a radiating rather than parallel manner.

Kicker A form of lighting distribution in film and video lighting in which a backlight is offset to one side but can come from any direction above or below a subject.

Knock-Offs A substitute fixture provided by a contractor for architectural installations that is less expensive than those originally specified and often only meets the specifications minimally. They are used to increase profit margin and are undesirable in most situations.

Ladder A hanging position that performs the same function as a boom but is hung from above. Ladders often look similar to an extension ladder and allow sidelight to be added while avoiding ground support that gets in the way of traffic on the deck.

Lamp A device that produces artificial light.

Lamp Alignment Adjusting the orientation or relationship between the reflector and lamp of a luminaire to achieve maximum light output.

Lamp Flicker An unwanted flicker effect that can appear in film and video images when using arc sources (most notably HMI) which is caused by not having the power of the camera and lamp's ballast synchronized properly.

Lamp Life The average number of hours that a lamp will burn before failing. It is based on trials in which light production drops off by 80% or more.

Lamp Sing See Filament Sing.

Lampholders A socket and adjustable fitting that is used to mount flood and spot lamps like PAR-38s from the face plate of a junction box.

Landscape Lighting Lighting exterior grounds and its plantlife.

Laser A special form of light that contains a limited or even single wavelength of light that is emitted in a concentrated, narrowly defined direction. A laser emits light in a synchronized or stepping manner that increases its intensity or energy.

Latitude The range of darkness to brightness that a film's emulsion or video camera is capable of capturing. Latitude is often expressed in terms of f-stops.

Law of Reflection The angle of incidence is equal to the angle of reflection. An essential physical property that determines the behavior of light with reflectors.

Law of Refraction (Snell's Law) As light passes into a more dense material, the light is bent toward a normal angle at the surface boundary between the materials, while light passing from a more dense material into one of less density is bent away from the normal angle with the surface.

Layered Design Approach A design approach connected primarily with architectural design (but also used elsewhere) in which different visual tasks are solved through providing several different lighting solutions on top of one another, each one solving the needs of a particular task.

Layering A technique of using contrast to superimpose one or more lighting systems on top of each other (e.g., creating a base level illumination over an area and placing accent specials on various subjects in that space).

LCD (Liquid Crystal Display) Screens and Projectors A projection technique in monitors and screens that are constructed of a matrix of liquid crystals that form an image by having their individual reflectances or light outputs varied through a small control voltage. These units can be assembled into screens of almost any size. LCD projectors are different from traditional projectors in that an LCD panel is located within the projector, where a high-intensity light source is placed behind the display, which then projects the image onto another surface.

Leap-Frog A method of touring in which a producer elects to duplicate some of the equipment so that the duplicated gear only plays at every other stop. This occurs when a tour is so large that it cannot be set up in the time allotted between stops and gives the crew an extended period of setup time.

Learning Education Units (LEUs) A unit of course instruction that is given for a specified number of classroom hours of continuing professional education. LEUs are frequently used to maintain certifications like the LC Certification by NCQLP.

LED (light-emitting diode) A solid-state device that produces light through a process in which electricity is applied to a crystal or diode material in a given direction or manner. The result of this creates light in a very limited range of wavelengths.

LEED (Leadership in Energy and Environmental Design) A program in the construction industry that emphasizes environmentally friendly building practices.

Leg (Phase) One of the power sources or hot wires of an electrical power service.

Legs A masking of vertical fabric that is hung to either side of the stage to block audience view of the stage's wings.

Leko See Ellipsoidal Reflector Spotlight (ERS).

Lens An optical device that makes use of refraction to consolidate and redirect light. If a point light source is placed at the focal point of a lens the associated light will be redirected into parallel rays.

Lens Barrel The focusing portion of a spotlight, which consists of a moveable assembly containing the fixture's lenses.

Lens Flare An effect created when backlight accidently hits a camera's lens. It usually causes an undesirable effect through producing internal reflections of the light in the camera but can also be used intentionally for dramatic effect.

Lensless Spotlight A location luminaire that is nothing more than a housing containing a roughly spherical reflector and small tubular tungsten-halogen lamp. It has a wide distribution pattern and provides a good, economical source for the limited power that it consumes.

Level-Setting Session See Cue-Writing Session.

Library Cues Cues in a memory board that may not necessarily be part of a cue sequence but are stored for safekeeping. Storing base cues or an old version of a cue that a designer may wish to go back to form examples of library cues.

Life Cycle Costing A calculation that predicts how much a lighting system will cost to install, operate, and maintain over its projected life span.

Lift 1. A mechanical device (usually with electric or pneumatic power) that is used, like a ladder, for elevating electricians and other crew members to the heights where they can troubleshoot and focus luminaires in their hanging positions. 2. A mechanical device that is used to support lighting gear like trusses from below (the deck).

Light A specific form of electromagnetic radiation that corresponds to the wavelengths of radiant energy that are visible to the human eye. It is commonly known as the visible spectrum.

Light Attic A chamber found in display cases (particularly museum cases) that is added to the top of a cabinet that houses the lamps, diffusers, baffles, or other optical accessories used for illuminating a case. This gives protection through separating the lighting elements from the artifacts or other case contents.

Light Bridge A winched catwalk that contains several lighting pipes (often with pre-wired circuits) that is flown directly over and across the width of the stage.

Light Center Length (LCL) A measurement from the center of a lamp's filament to a specified location on its base. This base location depends on the style of a lamp but remains consistent between all bases of a given style.

Light Grid A network of perpendicular pipes that are hung at regular spacings (3 to 5 feet apart) above a stage or studio. It is used to hang luminaires and scenery from above a performance area.

Light Jockey The operator who improvises a light show on the dance floor for a club.

Light Lab A layout of lighting fixtures and a pipe/grid system that allows fixtures to be hung, wired, and experimented upon in a limited small-scale setting, usually with a height of only 6–12 feet. The lab is used for experimentation prior to completing a prototype or actually lighting of a project.

Light Loss Factor (LLF) A factor in lighting calculations that deals with properties that inhibit the delivery of light to an application. This represents factors like the effects of ambient temperature on a luminaire, heat exchange, voltage factors, ballast efficiency, lamp depreciation, burnouts, and the amount of dirt or cleaning that impairs or improves a luminaire's efficiency.

Light Mapping A visual representation of an architectural lighting design created by making an indication of the location of each luminaire on an overlay (acetate, vellum or tissue) of the associated floorplan while adding a shading of color (typically in the color of the light; i.e., yellow for incandescent fixtures) that represents the distribution patterns of the associated lighting fixtures. The density of the color is varied in proportion to the projected intensity of the associated light.

Light Plot (Lighting Plan) A drafting that communicates all of the information that a crew will need to execute the hanging and circuiting of a design. Typical information contained in a light plot includes choice of type and number of fixtures, hanging locations, gel colors, and control or wiring information.

Light Pollution A condition in which reflected and misdirected light or glare causes scattering and a general ambience of unwanted light in an area. This can be as limited as spilling light onto a neighbor's property or as large as the loss of a nighttime view of the stars by city glow.

Light Shelf A passive solar device placed outside window surfaces that is used to reflect sunlight upward through the window and into the room, where it is reflected off of the ceiling as an indirect light source.

Light Trespass A condition in which light spills into an unwanted area or causes unwanted glare. This is a particular issue when light causes problems with neighboring properties.

Light-Emitting Diode See LED.

Lighting Area A smaller portion of an environment or stage created by dividing a larger area into a series of smaller spaces that are each illuminated in a similar manner.

Lighting Balloons An aerial balloon used in exterior location lighting that is flown above a set and contains one or more internal HMI light sources that provide diffuse light to the areas below.

Lighting Calculations A process of using a variety of formulas to determine various lighting properties for an architectural installation. A determination of illumination levels (Lumen Method and Point at a Source) form the most common calculations, but power efficiencies and economic calculations like payback or maintenance costs are also done for most projects.

Lighting Certified (LC) A professional certification for architectural lighting designers by the National Council for Qualifications for the Lighting Profession (NCQLP). To earn the LC certification an individual must pass an exam and/or participate in educational activities on a three-year cycle.

Lighting Concept (Lighting Scheme, Image of Light or Point of View) A mental image or plan that creates a framework that drives the individual decisions for any lighting project. The concept addresses issues such as style, mood, and transitional patterns as well as specific environmental qualities such as location, geographical setting, and time frame. Lighting concepts are more typically associated with theatrical and entertainment lighting projects. Also see Lighting Scheme.

Lighting Console See Desk.

Lighting Designer (LD). The individual who is charged with the overall design of the lighting of a production, event, or environment. A lighting designer produces an artistic vision for the lighting of a project.

Lighting Director The individual who has overall charge of the lighting and its design for a film or video.

Lighting Economics Using calculations to determine the actual costs of installing and maintaining a lighting system. These calculations are also used to determine maintenance and relamping schedules.

Lighting Green To design lighting using environmentally sensitive practices. Lower power densities and consideration toward disposal of hazardous materials (e.g., mercury) form several examples of these considerations.

Lighting Instrument See Luminaire.

Lighting Key A visual representation of the primary lighting angles and colors that would be used as part of a general or overall lighting scheme for a scene or project.

Lighting Kit A selection of approximately a half-dozen location luminaires, along with their accessories (scrims, barn doors, flags, etc.), and portable stands and mountings that are packaged as a group in a shipping case.

Lighting Layout (Lighting Scheme or Lighting Plan) The architectural equivalent of a light plot. It identifies the type and location of the luminaires and also often illustrates the wiring and switch locations that are specified by a lighting designer.

Lighting Plan See Light Plot.

Lighting Pole A pole used in studio setups that helps a studio electrician pull the luminaires down from the lighting grid (pantographs) to their working heights while also focusing and adjusting them from the studio floor.

Lighting Ratios In video production, a variation of contrast ratio that is based on the relationship between the reflected intensity of the key light to the base or fill light.

Lighting Scheme (Image of Light or Point of View) A vision or image of the lighting for a given project. It is the architectural equivalent of a lighting concept.

Lighting Score A manner of illustrating specific lighting qualities found on stage at any given moment. The lighting score is a table that indicates specific moments or scenes across the various columns and a variety of lighting functions or properties for each scene that are identified and characterized across each row.

Lighting Specification An architectural contract document based on a specification of the luminaires that will be used on a project. It is organized from a luminaire perspective.

Lighting Stands Portable stands used in film and video lighting (particularly location work) to mount luminaires and accessories from the floor.

Lighting System (System) A group of luminaires that perform similar functions and work together as a group. Washes form popular lighting systems in which a group of lights share qualities like color, hanging angle, and basic instrument type while being focused to different areas of the stage.

Lighting Template 1. A specialized stencil used to draw proportionally scaled lighting instruments on a light plot, section, or lighting layout. 2. See gobo or pattern.

Lighting the Horizontal Plane Measuring the quantity of light striking flat surfaces (the workplane) that are parallel with the ceiling (e.g., a desk or countertop).

Lighting the Vertical Plane Measuring the quantity of light striking flat surfaces that are perpendicular to the ceiling (e.g., shelving units and walls).

Lighting Unit See Luminaire.

Limelight An antiquated luminaire that contained a block of lime that was heated by a gas flame to the point that it created a bright source of light for the stage.

Linear (Wash Light) Light sources and fixtures that have a long narrow source like a fluorescent tube and are used to create smooth, even washes over an area.

Lineset A batten and its associated rigging hardware.

Line-Voltage A reference to electric systems that are operated on normal household currents of 120 volts AC.

Linnebach Projector A variation of lensless or shadow projector that was developed in the early 20th century by Adolph Linnebach, a stage engineer from Germany. The projector has a single light source placed at the rear of its housing, while large acetate or glass slides are designed to cover the entire front of the fixture.

Live 1. Refers to a circuit having power or current within it. 2. A performance mode where cues are actually on stage and being executed during a performance.

Load The total capacity requirements of a circuit. It contains the power requirements (amps or watts) of every device contained on a circuit.

Load-In The process by which all of the technical elements and equipment (scenery, lighting, sound, etc.) is transported and set up in a performance venue. In lighting, this usually refers to the hanging, circuiting, and focusing of the luminaires.

Lobster Scope A visual effect that produces a strobe-like property. This was developed during the vaudeville era and before strobe lights. It was produced when a followspot operator rapidly passed an opaque panel like a piece of cardboard back and forth in front of the light to produce a flicker effect.

Local See IATSE.

Lock the Unit Down A command given by a lighting designer to an electrician during a focus call that indicates the designer is pleased with the pan and tilt adjustments of a light and that the electrician should tighten down the appropriate set-bolts.

Long-Throw Followspots Followspots used in large venues like auditoriums, arenas, and stadiums.

Look (Cue or State) A static lighting image or look that creates a given combination of lights and their angles, intensities, and overall mixing. Cueing refers to establishing the looks and recording them so that they can be duplicated from performance to performance.

Look and Light A method of lighting associated with studio lighting in which the designer simply goes into a studio and picks lighting from whatever instrumentation is already hung. Commercials are frequently shot in this manner.

Loop System A low-voltage landscaping lighting technique that reduces voltage drop by having all the luminaires wired in a daisy-chain with both ends of the cable or circuit wired to the transformer.

Louvers An optical accessory with baffles or concentric rings that is placed over the face of a fixture to block the viewer from direct glare.

Low Key A lighting condition in video/film lighting that is more dramatic than normal and reflects higher contrast ratios (5:1, 8:1, 10:1, etc.) and greater difference between the intensities of the key and fill lights.

Low-Capacity Dimmer A dimmer with a relatively low-wattage or load rating, frequently 1,200 watts or less.

Low-Pressure Sodium Lamp A variation of HID lamp that can be identified by its deep yellow color (like a bug light). It is very efficient but has very poor color rendering.

Low-Resolution Mode A mode associated with the degree of control that an attribute has in an automated luminaire. Low-resolution modes are associated with 8-bit/one-channel operation of an attribute and do not have the same degree of control (fine-control) as high-resolution modes of control.

Low-Voltage Lighting systems that are operated on a voltage of approximately 12 volts (AC or DC), although other voltages are also used, such as 24 volts. Display and landscape lighting systems often use low-voltage power.

Lumen A measurement of light that refers to the luminous flux of a light source.

Lumen Maintenance A consideration of how quickly the light output of a lamp drops over the time that it is in operation or ages.

Lumen Method (Zonal Cavity Method) A specific manner of calculating and specifying average illumination levels or lumen density for an architectural lighting application. Properties such as volume of the environment, physical properties of the luminaire, mounting heights, condition of the room's reflective surfaces, and visual tasks all play a role in the illumination levels that are calculated by using this method.

Lumen Output The amount of light that is delivered by a lamp or luminaire.

Luminaire The lighting fixture. A luminaire contains a light source, reflector, housing, and many times a lens(s). Other names for luminaire include lighting units, fixtures, instruments, and lamps.

Luminance The source's intensity divided by the surface area of the source as observed by the viewer. A directional function that is dependent on the relationship or viewing angle of the viewer.

Luminous Exitance A measurement of intensity that refers to the total amount of light either reflecting off or leaving a surface. It is not direction-dependent like luminance. Reflection/transmission factors are introduced to the metric based on the reflective/transmitting qualities of the source or object.

Luminous Flux A measure of the actual flow of energy from a light source. The most common unit of measure is the lumen.

Luminous Intensity A measurement of the ability of a light source to produce intensity in a given direction. It is usually measured in candela.

Magic Lantern The forerunner of traditional projectors. Development of the magic latern is generally credited to Jesuit Father Athanasius Kircher in the late 1600s. Although crude in comparison to today's standards, it provides the principal method by which most traditional projectors are still designed. Light sources could be oil or limelight.

Magic Sheet A type of paperwork that designers use when they set levels or program a show's lighting. It is an abbreviated form that is often created in a visual format and contains only the information that a designer will need to set levels (typically only channel, color, and purpose/focus).

Main Feeders Heavy-duty cables that connect a main switchboard to the distribution panels that are located throughout a building.

Main Switchboard The primary distribution center for a building. It is connected directly to the power source that comes from outside the building.

Maintained Illuminance The average amount of light that reflects off of a given surface (usually horizontal).

Male Connector A connector with one or more pins/blades for making quick connections between electrical devices and cables. The male connector taps into the source of power.

Manual Control or Dimming A form of dimming in which electricians are responsible for physically moving various components or hardware to regulate the lighting intensities. All cues must be executed in a live state.

Mark Cue (Move Cue) A cue that is created for presetting a moving light attribute or other DMX function so that the move is done without the knowledge of an audience.

Married When circuits and their associated cables are run from one electric or batten to another. This is usually done by running the circuits off the end of one batten onto the same end of a second batten and forming a loop of excess cable between the two pipes. The battens must be flown together when moving either batten.

Maskings Drapes, flats, or other scenic materials that are used to prevent view of the backstage and fly areas by an audience. Legs and borders are common examples of maskings that are found on many stages.

Master Electrician (ME) The technician who plays the most important supervisory role for the lighting installation. MEs are charged with making sure that the lighting and other electrical equipment is installed and operated in an efficient safe manner.

Mastering A manner of having multiple dimmers or other lighting controls controlled together. There are essentially three types of mastering: mechanical, electrical, and electronic.

Matte Photography See Composite Photography.

McCandless System (The Method) A method for providing relatively naturalistic lighting for general stage illumination based on the teachings of Yale professor Stanley McCandless in the 1930s. His technique, often called "The Method" (McCandless did not intend this), is based on dividing a stage into areas that are around 8 feet in diameter, with each area being lit by two luminaires containing complementary tints hung at 45° both above and to each side of an area.

Meat Rack A rolling rack containing a series of pipes from which lighting instruments are transported and hung for storage.

Mechanical Mastering A form of mastering in which some form of physical device is used to mechanically link the control handles of individual dimmers.

Media 1. A reference that is usually made to film or video, where the performance is often recorded in some manner. 2. Projection Content.

Media Server A computer that allows a designer to create and edit digital content for many forms of digital screens and projectors, including digital lights. Material is developed in the media server and transferred to the projectors or screens. These devices come pre-loaded with a diverse collection of video and animation files that can be edited or used directly, but more importantly, content can be imported from collections found on CDs, DVDs, or digital video and animation clips that are downloaded from the web or provided by the media designer.

Medium Base A specifically sized lamp base (1 inch in diameter).

Memory Control Lighting consoles that actually store cues in some type of memory (long or short term). Computer consoles form the most notable examples.

Mercury Lamp A variation of HID lamp that is cost-effective and used in many security and highway lighting applications. It is recognized by its bluish-green to white light.

Metal Halide Lamp A form of HID lamp that is very efficient and becoming fairly common in retail environments. The lamps contain various combinations of metal halides in addition to the traditional mercury and argon gases. These additional materials produce a better quality of light that is associated with better color rendering and a crisp quality of fairly high color temperature.

Metamerism An effect of perception where objects that appear to share the same color under one light source will appear differently under another light source. This is due to the spectral composition of the two light sources being different, and it has become a more significant issue with the appearance of LED light sources. The metamerism index relates the percentage of reflectance that a light source has within different colored wavelengths.

Metaphor A means of representing specific meanings where an object or series of words is used figuratively or symbolically to represent or make comparisons or meanings between objects.

Middle Gray A reference on the gray scale for video/film lighting that represents the midpoint of the perceived value of white/black as well as an 18% overall reflectance.

MIDI (Musical Instrument Digital Interface) Control A control format that allows one device to trigger actions in another through various digital instructions, such as using a light console to trigger various effects devices or having the lighting controlled by a soundtrack. Two variations of this include MIDI Show Control (MSC) where the triggers are controlled by events, and MIDI Time Control (MTC) where the triggers are based on a timing code.

Mids Luminaires mounted on a boom at head height as a special form of sidelight.

Miniature Base A specifically sized lamp base (approximately 3/8 inch in diameter).

Miniature Reflector (MR) Lamp A miniature lamp that is similar to a PAR lamp in that it has a reflector (flatted) built into the lamp's construction.

Mini-Striplight A revision in striplight design that is about half the width and height of traditional striplights and based on the MR-16 low-voltage lamp.

Mired (Micro-Reciprocal Degrees) A scale used in film and television production that relates the difference between perceived and actual color temperature by dividing the light's measured degrees in Kelvin by 1,000,000. Mired factors are used to calculate the proper color correction that must be applied to a source.

Mirror Board A special type of reflector or shiny board used in film and video lighting in which the surface of the panel is covered with a mirrored surface.

Mirror Lighting A technique of lighting water features in a landscape project where the water is purposefully kept dark so that the nearby lit structures and related activities can be reflected on the water's surface.

Mockup Used to create an experimental situation for architectural lighting applications. Mockups use actual design elements like the wall and floor materials or finishes and furniture in a limited fashion so that luminaire choices and design solutions can be examined in a limited but full-scale setting. A mockup may even involve testing luminaires on site.

Modeling A function of lighting that uses light for enhancing the three-dimensional qualities or form of an object. Also known as revelation of form or sculpting.

Modeling Programs A variation of CAD software where three-dimensional virtual models are created in a computer with realistic materials and lighting that produce a reasonably accurate image or rendering of the virtual object(s) or scene.

Modeling/Sculpting Systems A lighting system or collection of luminaires characterized by washes of back and side light that enhance depth perception throughout a stage.

Mogul Base A specifically sized lamp base (1-1/2 inch in diameter).

Moment A point where all of the elements of a stage picture are frozen and recorded, as if a snapshot were taken of the stage composition.

Monopole A telescoping pole used to mount luminaires in a studio grid that allows a lighting unit to be quickly brought down to a lower height (from its stored position) for use, or for creating flatter angles.

Mood Refers to creating a specific emotional response. Architectural spaces also project moods, much of which can be directly attributed to their lighting.

Moonbox (Shadow Box) A specific type of shadow box that is created to simulate a moon. Shadowboxes are boxes with enclosed light sources that have a translucent front and are used to produce a lighting effect that actually transmits light. Signs are often produced as shadowboxes.

Moonlighting A special form of down-lighting that simulates natural moonlight by mounting mercury vapor lamps in the tops of trees or poles so that the shadows and cool color provide a suggestion of moonlight.

Motion Detectors (Occupancy Sensors) An energy-saving switching device that extinguishes lights in areas like stairwells and restrooms that have not been occupied for a set amount of time. They can also be used to restore lighting when someone enters the space.

Motivated Lighting Often used synonymously with motivational lighting, but refers to light coming from both actual and apparent sources (sources not actually visible to the observer). It is represented by sunlight streaming through a doorway, a room being lit from an imaginary fixture like a chandelier, or a field being lit by the sun from somewhere above and behind the audience.

Motivating Light (Motivating Sources) A special form of motivational lighting in which the actual light source is seen on stage. Examples include placing candles or lanterns on stage, flashlights, a fireplace or fire, or having sconces, table lamps, or chandeliers on a stage.

Motivational Accents Luminaires and washes that are used to provide an indication of a specific or suggested motivational light source.

Motivational Lighting Light that is linked to an apparent source such as sunlight, a given lamp or chandelier, or an effect like a fireplace. It is presented in a realistic style and attempts to approach the lighting from a perspective that represents how light would appear in a natural setting.

Mounting Height The height at which an architectural fixture is mounted. It's used in the same way that throw distances are used in entertainment luminaires.

Move Cue See Mark Cue.

Movement One of the controllable qualities of light. It suggests changes in the lighting by: seeing the actual light source move on stage (carrying a flashlight), seeing light but not the actual source move (the effect of a follow-spot), and seeing changes in the lighting over time (running cues).

Moving Head A variation of automated luminaire in which the body of the luminaire swivels to complete pan and tilt motions.

Moving Lights See Automated Lights.

Moving Light Operator See Programmer.

Moving Mirror (Scanner) A type of automated luminaire in which a moving mirror is placed at the front of a unit to reflect or direct the light to different locations.

Moving Mirror Accessories An accessory that provides an alternative to expensive moving mirror luminaires/scanners and allows movement to be introduced to conventional luminaires. This accessory and its control components are placed in the gel frame at the front of a luminaire and allow the focus to be redirected by a moving mirror.

Moving Yoke An accessory that allows a conventional luminaire's focus (pan and tilt) to be repositioned.

M-speed A control attribute of many automated fixtures that uses a speed function to even out any jerky motions that a fixture might display while moving a light or its attributes during a cue transition.

Multi-cable (Multi) Cables that are manufactured with a number of independent conductors that terminate in individual male and female connectors corresponding to the number of circuits that are contained in a cable.

Multi-lights A luminaire used in film and television lighting that consists of an array of lamps mounted in a fixed arrangement on a panel or as groups of lamps mounted in frames that allow several lamps to be focused together. Individual lamps may be turned on or off independently or as a group. One of the most popular multi-lights is the nine-light, which combines nine PAR lamps into a three-by-three grid arrangement. This particular unit may also be called a brute, while other variations are based on the size of the lamps (e.g. a maxi-brute uses PAR-64s).

Multiple-Feed System A landscape lighting technique where individual cable runs are run from different junction points that in turn have multiple luminaires wired to each junction point (daisy chained or junctioned).

Multiplexers See Digital to Analog Converter.

Multiplexing See Dimmer Doubling™.

Multiplying Factor A numerical factor multiplied by the throw distance to calculate an approximate pool diameter for light associated with a given luminaire.

Musco Lights A popular aerial platform that adds supplemental television lighting to sports arenas. These truck-mounted cranes are used to surround a stadium in order to place an array of around a dozen luminaires (one array per truck) high enough above the stadium to shoot over the walls onto the playing field.

Museum Lighting An area of lighting that involves lighting artifacts and artwork associated with museum collections.

National Association of Broadcast Employees and Technicians (NABET) A union in the broadcasting industry that represents directors of photography and lighting directors along with other engineers and technicians like cameramen.

National Council for Qualifications for the Lighting Profession (NCQLP) A professional certification agency used primarily for architectural lighting designers who must pass a comprehensive exam. If successful, the individual is "Lighting Certified" and may use the LC behind their name.

National Electrical Code (NEC) A construction code that provides a set of standards for guiding the specification and installation of electrical equipment like lighting packages.

Naturalism A school of style that represents an extreme form of realism.

Near-Side Key A form of lighting in film and video setups in which the key light is placed on the side of the performer's face nearest the camera.

Neon A lighting effect in which neon gas is placed in a glass tube that is bent into designer-determined shapes. The gas is energized by a transformer, causing the entire tube to give off light. Neon gives off an intense red light while other gases produce other colors like yellow, blue, and white.

Nets See Butterflies.

Neutral The wire that provides the return path for electricity in a circuit.

Neutral Density Filter (ND or NDF) A media that is similar to gel but is instead used to drop the overall intensity of a lamp. More importantly, it drops the intensity without having an impact on the color temperature of the source.

Nodes Termination points in a lighting control network that become the points where an ethernet signal is converted to DMX ports.

Non-Motivated Lighting Lighting that is not tied to an apparent light source, with which the designer creates an image based on emotional responses, mood, or symbolic elements for a production or project.

Non-Tracking Console A lighting console in which cue edits or changes can only be made a single cue at a time and where a modification cannot be incorporated into future cues.

Notation 1. A portion of the light plot that indicates the meaning of any data such as color, unit number, and channel assignment that is attached to the luminaires (it is sometimes called "typical"). 2. A way of recording blocking and performer movements through a series of sketches.

Notes When it is not possible to make a change or to edit a cue immediately (on the fly), a designer makes a list of any problems that need to be fixed by the next rehearsal or performance. Technical notes require a crew and physical action (gel/focus changes, inoperable lamps, etc.), while board notes relate to console programming.

Obie See Camera-Lights.

Objective Lens An assembly of high-quality optical lenses that are placed in front of a slide in a traditional projector. They are used to focus the image precisely onto a projection surface.

Occupancy Sensors See Motion Detectors.

Occupants The people that will occupy or use an architectural space or environment.

Office Lighting Architectural lighting that refers to lighting offices and business centers.

Off-line Editor A simulator provided by most console manufacturers that replicates their console for a desktop computer or laptop. Off-line editors allow a designer to pre-program or edit a show without using the actual console.

Ohm's Law Relates resistance to the voltage and amperage of a circuit. $I = E/R$.

Omnidirectional Light A virtual light that creates light in all directions and that moves away from the light source.

On Location Shooting a film or video in a natural setting; the actual setting or a place similar to where the action is to be set.

On the Fly 1. Making and recording cue changes live or as the performance or rehearsal is in progress. In many live events, such as in concert lighting, a number of the cue sequences and much of the designing are completed on the fly. 2. Being able to render virtual images in actual time—such as in computer gaming.

One-Night Stand A form of touring in which a production is loaded-in, performed, and struck in a single day.

One-to-One Patching A condition where all dimmers and channels share the same number assignments.

Online Catalogs Product catalogs of cut sheets and other product literature that are created and distributed in electronic formats. The most popular forms are found on company websites though some of this literature may still be distributed by CDs.

Onstage 1. Anything that is located in audience view. 2. A reference to come toward centerline. 3. Luminaires or hanging positions that are located on or above a stage.

Open Fixture A landscaping luminaire in which no attempt is made to shield the lamp and its related components from the elements.

Open-Backed Window A display window that has no back and is open to the store behind the window.

Optical Density An expression of the relative ability of light to move through a material and the effect that it has on the speed of the light transmitted through it.

Opto-Isolator A device placed on the control line to protect a console and other components from a power surge. The device forms a junction where the electrical impulses of the control signal are converted to a light source (usually an LED) and then back again to an electrical impulse.

Organistion des Scenographes, Techniciens et Arcitects de Theatre (OISTAT) An international organization of theatrical designers and technicians that is affiliated with USITT.

Out-of-town Tryout A production (with an intent to go to Broadway) that is initially produced in a theatre away from Broadway as a means of lowering production costs. If successful, the show then transfers to Broadway.

Overheads A term used to reference the lighting units that are hung above the stage.

Overhire Hiring theatrical crew members on a temporary or per-show basis.

Pack (Stack) A reference to loading and storing theatrical equipment and scenery. Equipment can be stacked or packed in the trucks, wings, or almost anywhere as needed.

Page A utility device on computer consoles that allows controllers to be assigned to different functions. This allows them to be reassigned throughout a production.

Painting with Light The design aesthetic of creating the lighting images or looks/cues for a production. The process produces an image through a combination of individual lights and their colors, angles, intensities, and overall mixing.

Palettes A series of functions that are assigned to a lighting console's encoders, submaster/channel controllers, and group displays that provide an operator with a means of organizing the data required for programming a show. Common palettes are nothing more than a selection of presets that are stored, easily accessible, and organized by categories like focus points, color, gobo patterns, etc.

Pan A pivoting adjustment of the side-to-side focus of a luminaire's orientation.

Pantograph A studio accessory with scissor-like telescoping arms that is used to mount luminaires from a studio grid. It allows luminaires to be quickly pulled down to a lower height.

Paper Tech A meeting completed prior to the first tech, during which cues and their placement are discussed by the director, designers, stage manager, and other personnel.

Paperwork See Design Paperwork.

PAR Can (PAR Fixture) A luminaire using a PAR lamp as the basis of its design. These fixtures are durable and easily hung and focused, but they have no beam-shaping qualities other than through the selection of a specific lamp. The light produced by PAR cans is harsh and crisp, with relatively soft edges that allow adjoining units to easily blend with one another.

PAR Lamp (parabolic aluminized reflector) A lamp that contains a pre-defined lens, reflector, and filament. It is unique in that it is a complete fixture within a lamp.

Parabolic Reflector A reflector that is very similar to a spherical reflector, with the exception that it is flattened to some degree. Due to its shape, light that strikes it after leaving the focal point is reflected in a way that creates parallel rays of light.

Parallel Circuit A circuit that differs from a series circuit in that each device is wired directly to the power source. This results in components like lamps having access to the full amount of power despite any other lamps that might be wired into the circuit. Any breaks in the circuit will only have an effect on those units that are directly wired to that part of a circuit.

PAR-Bar An assemblage of PAR fixtures (usually six) that are rigged along with their circuiting into a module along a single pipe or section of unistrut (A U-shaped channel fabricated from steel). These modules are then mounted into trussing or lighting towers for a production.

PARNel A relatively new fixture design by ETC that combines the light quality of a PAR with the spot/flood capabilities of a Fresnel. It is designed around the 575-watt HPL lamp and by turning a knob an electrician can vary the fixture's beam from a spot to flood setting.

Pastel Tints Lightly colored gels or light that have a fair amount of most of the individual wavelengths and produce essentially white light that is tinted slightly in favor of a particular hue.

Patch To assign a specific circuit to a dimmer or a dimmer to a channel.

Patchbay (Patch Panel, Interconnection Panel, or Interconnection Patchbay) A piece of electrical hardware that allows circuit and dimmer assignments to be made in a theatre or studio where there are a limited number of dimmers. Plugs representing circuits are plugged into outlets that are associated with the assigned dimmers.

Pathway Lights Landscape luminaires that are used to line sidewalks and driveways.

Pattern See Gobo or Template.

Payback Determining the point in time where a lighting system saves enough money in maintenance and power savings costs to pay for itself.

Peaked Field A beam pattern in which a concentrated hotspot is formed near the center of a spotlight beam.

Pendant A classification of architectural luminaire where the unit is suspended from below a ceiling by a cord, chain, or other similar device.

Penetration In daylighting, the depth to which light extends into a room from its exterior walls and windows.

Penumbra Effect A problem associated with lensless projectors in which the filament size or surfaces are too large or numerous to produce a single image. It causes fuzzing or blurred edges in any images created by the projector.

Pepper's Ghost A famous projection effect that uses mirrors and transparent materials like glass or plexiglass to reflect images of an object or "ghost" to new locations.

Performer Specials Luminaires that are designated specifically to light a performer at a given moment(s) within a performance.

Perimeter Lighting Lighting that is designed to light the top wall surfaces that extend around the perimeter of a store or public building.

Perishables See Expendables.

Personality A series of settings for an automated luminaire or other device that allow specific parameters of the unit to be set for an individual application or preference. Sample settings might include placing the unit in an audio sensory mode, reversing the pan and tilt settings, or putting the unit in a power-saving mode.

Perspective Lighting Landscape lighting that creates an illusion of distance either by placing the light sources in a set of skewed lines that follow a perspective projection or by using lower-wattage sources at distances further from the viewer.

Phase See Leg.

Photo-Electric Sensor (Photosensor) An electrical control device that switches circuits on and off by sensing light intensity levels.

Photometrics The study of the quality and quantities of light.

Photopic Vision That portion of vision attributed to the cone receptors that are responsible for both our color and detail vision within typical interior and exterior lighting illuminance ranges.

Piano Board A dimming package that contains a framework with a collection of individual dimmer plates (six, 12, or more dimmers) along with their associated handles and mastering levers.

Pick Point (Pick) Any location along a truss or other structure where a cable is supported from overhead by some form of rigging such as a chain motor.

Pickup 1. A followspot coming on and lighting a specific target. 2. Location where a flown object is supported by an overhead cable, rope, etc.

Pigtail A 12–24-inch cable that terminates in a female plug from a circuit along a raceway or distribution box. It can also refer to the lead wires and male plug coming from a luminaire.

Pile-On A cueing function in which additional lights or effects are added or layered on top of whatever lighting already exists on the stage.

Pin Matrix A pinned plugging system on "rock and roll" preset consoles that was laid out as a grid to electronically assign control channels to submasters, which in turn featured bump/flash buttons.

Pinspots A nickname that many designers have given to ERSes, which are based on a 3 1/2-inch diameter lens. The name doesn't match the optical characteristics of these fixtures. Club owners also use pinspots, but these are small spotlights that produce an intense shaft of light through the smaller filaments of DC lamps.

Pitch A screen property that refers to the size or spacing of the smallest elements of a display (i.e., the spacing between the clusters of LEDs that define a pixel for the screen). Pitch is important because it determines a screen's resolution and optimal viewing distance or range.

Pitting A form of corrosion in landscape luminaires that causes the metal finish to become rough and pitted.

Pixel The smallest degree of resolution in a digital image. If an image or projection is enlarged beyond this point, the squares representing this resolution simply get larger with no further development in details.

Pixel Mapping Using control of digital projectors or individual LEDs in larger LED arrays and screens or other devices to produce digital patterns and images (projection or video) on or over two-dimensional surfaces.

Pixelation An effect in digital imaging. An image is enlarged beyond a point where the individual pixels become separated and distort the image.

Plane (Zone) A distribution pattern associated with dance lighting based on movement patterns along pathways across the width of the stage (between each set of legs).

Plano Lens A lens with essentially two flat sides.

Plano-Convex Lens The most popular lens used in the lighting industry. One side is flat, while the other is convex.

Plano-Convex Spotlight (P-C spotlight) See Box-Spot.

Plant and Sing An older opera practice where a featured singer would come downstage and simply sing the aria or other featured solo with very little physical action.

PLASA (Professional Light and Sound Association) An international organization of theatrical manufacturers and dealers who provide educational resources and set professional and industry standards.

Plasma Lamp A relatively new form of solid-state lighting where a mixture of ionized gas is energized by radio frequencies in order to form a field of plasma energy that produces nearly full-spectrum light. The light from these lamps is comparable to short-arc sources but at the same time is very efficient and with lamp lives that are especially long.

Plasterline A reference line for measuring distances in the upstage/downstage directions that is based on an imaginary line across the width of the proscenium located between the furthest upstage edges of the proscenium wall.

Plate See Dimmer Plate.

Plenum See Ceiling Cavity.

Pleasure Gardens The earliest form of amusement parks. Pleasure gardens appeared in the 1500s in Europe. They were a variety of gardens that also provided simple rides and attractions.

Plot and Light A method of film and video lighting where a lighting director actually selects and plots the lighting for a studio or shoot in the same way that theatrical designers design a light plot.

Plotter A large-format printer used in printing large-scaled drawings like light plots.

Plotting Service A company that owns a large-format plotter for printing CAD files or draftings for a fee.

Point Illuminance Method An architectural lighting calculation that determines illuminance at a specific point through an examination of light as both a direct component and various indirect components from a given source(s).

Point Light Source The principle by which luminaire and lamp manufacturers strive to create the smallest light source possible by concentrating the majority of the light at a focal point, which makes any associated lens or reflector all the more efficient.

Point of Purchase A base for sales personnel. It is where sales are conducted and typically contains cash registers and counters for completing the paperwork and packaging of a transaction.

Point of View See Image of Light, Lighting Scheme, or Lighting Concept.

Port A hanging position above an audience that provides the same function as a beam, with the exception that these are openings in the ceiling that only house four to six lighting instruments each.

Portable Generator See Generator.

Portrait Lamp A fixture usually placed directly above or below a frame that uses a tubular incandescent lamp and shade on an adjustable arm.

Post Lights A luminaire mounted on a post or pole (e.g., a streetlight, bollard, or lamp post).

Post-Occupancy Evaluation A process that takes place after a client has taken occupancy of a space that checks client satisfaction, fixes or modifies any issues that may have developed, and helps the client understand how to maintain and operate an installation.

Power (P) The rate of doing work. In the case of lighting, it is usually expressed in wattage, which refers to how much power it takes over time to produce a given amount of light.

Power Density A determination of how much energy is consumed per unit area of a building (watts per square foot). Many municipalities limit a building's power density based on factors like the type of tasks required and its location.

Power Formula Relates Power (P) or wattage to the voltage (E) and amperage (A). $P = I \times E$

Power Grid The networked system of wiring that delivers power from a generating plant to a customer.

Power-Con Connector A specialty connector that is often used to daisy-chain power from one LED luminaire to another. These connectors typically have a blue casing and positive locking mechanism that operates in a twisting motion. These connectors are also used in sound systems for speaker connections.

Practical A working fixture on a set like a table lamp, chandelier, or wall sconce.

Preset A specific "look" for the lighting that can be called up on a repeated basis. In cue terminology, it refers to a lighting cue that is used prior to the start of a show or act and is present for when the audience is gathering.

Preset control An electronic dimming method in which duplicate sets of controllers (presets) are provided for each channel/dimmer. Operators shift between presets for different cues, alternating live presets with those used for upcoming cues.

Preview Mode See Blind and Blind Mode.

Primary Coil One of several coils found in a transformer. This coil is associated with the source voltage and will induce a current in a secondary coil(s).

Primary Colors Basic elements of light (red, blue, and green) that are used in various combinations to produce every other color of light. Primary colors also exist in pigment (red, yellow, and blue).

Primary Focal Point A point associated with a reflector or lens that refers to where light is focused to or from.

Primary Focus The area or subject with the strongest focus in a room or on a stage.

Primary Lighting See Ambient Lighting.

Prismatic Glass (Variegated Glass Filters) A type of plastic or glass that contains a textured surface that refracts and diffuses any light that passes through it. These accessories are placed in the gate of a luminaire in much the same way as a gobo is used to produce various visual effects.

Product Unveiling A specific type of corporate production where a "show" is about introducing a new product for the very first time.

Production Meeting A meeting between the designers, director, and department heads that is used to check progress between departments and to discover and resolve any issues that might develop between departments.

Production Number A large-scale song and dance piece that typically involves most, if not all, of the company of performers in a highly spectacle musical number. They are often found as opening and finale numbers for the different acts of a musical.

Profile Spotlight A variation of the ERS that is in popular use throughout Europe. European designers tend to call all ERSes "profile spots."

Programmer (Moving Light Operator) The person responsible for the programming and operation of a console that controls moving lights. The title has evolved to include anyone who programs a lighting console (both conventionals and movers).

Programming (Programming Phase) 1. Placing the lighting commands (intensity levels, cues, moving light instructions) into a console. 2. The first phase of architectural projects, in which fact finding is used to determine the client's needs.

Project Manager The individual on architectural projects who is assigned to a project and becomes the liaison between the designer and construction crews.

Projection Booth (Spotlight Booth) A room located near the back of an auditorium that houses projection and control equipment, followspots, and their crews.

Projection Mapping Using digital projections to map an image or video over three-dimensional surfaces. Examples of this include the large-scale video sequences projected onto the facades of buildings.

Projector A piece of equipment that is used to project an image to another location or surface/screen.

Projector Bay A cubby-hole set into the upstage wall of a stage that gives projectors an increased throw distance.

Proportional Patch Provides a method for channels or dimmers to be locked into a maximum intensity setting that is lower than 100%.

Prototype (Template) A master CAD drawing that contains all of the major elements of a space or facility. Prototypes eliminate redrawing features that are shared by many drawings (title blocks, facility outlines, reference lines, keys, etc.).

Pull Down A lighting cue that draws the focus to a particular character, object, or location on the stage. The areas around this are typically lowered in intensity.

Punchlist A list of items that are damaged, forgotten, or incorrectly installed on an architectural or permanent installation. It ensures that a contractor is aware of and fixes problems.

Pyro Technician (Pyro Tech) A crew member who specializes in special effects that involve fire and explosives. These technicians are typically both certified and licensed for this type of work within the entertainment industry.

Quantity of light See Quantity versus Quality.

Quantity versus Quality A lighting philosophy where architectural designers strive to create quality-driven rather than simply quantity-driven lighting designs (footcandle requirements). While intensity is still factored into lighting a particular situation, there are now other elements like color, angle, and glare that are also factored into the overall quality of the design.

Quartz Lamp See Tungsten-Halogen Lamp or TH lamp.

Queue A waiting area in theme parks that gives the appearance of a shortened line by arranging the line in a series of rows that turn back on one another while also leading to additional staging areas or chambers with more queues and waiting times.

Rack A metal cabinet used to house electronic components. Sound components and dimmers are the most common racks found in the entertainment industry. Racks may be portable or permanently installed in a facility.

Radial ERS The earliest version of the ERS, which made use of lamps that burned in a base up configuration with their lamp housings being located on the top back of an instrument.

Rain Curtain A theatrical drape of highly reflective metallic material like mylar that is slit into strips approximately 1/4 inch wide. When treated with light they sparkle and shimmer. The most popular ones are silver and take on the color of any light that strikes them.

Rate A control that allows for modifying the timing of a cue. Rate settings allow operators to speed up or slow down cueing during a performance.

Ray-tracing A special feature of visualization programs that calculates the effect of a vast number of light rays from each light source in a project. The calculations are quite specific and time consuming but result in an image that often approaches photorealism in detail.

Rear Projection A form of projection where the projector(s) are placed behind a translucent screen or projection surface.

Rear-Projection Screen (RP screen) A screen made from special materials that are translucent and allow an image to be projected from behind the screen while remaining visible on its surface.

Recessed Luminaires A classification of architectural luminaires based on a mounting position that is mounted within a wall or ceiling.

Recommended Practice A set of design guidelines that represent common techniques and practices in special areas of architectural lighting design. These are not codes and are not subject to regulation, but they represent what most designers would consider appropriate practices for a given application.

Red Shift (Amber Drift) The effect of a light changing color as the intensity of a lamp is dimmed (becoming more red/amber).

Reducing Screen See Dimming Screen.

Reflected Ceiling Plan An architectural drafting that indicates the layout of a ceiling with peaks, trays, domes, etc. Lighting designers use this to locate their luminaires and often simply add the lighting information directly to the plate, converting it into a form of light plot or lighting layout.

Reflected Radiation Component (RRC) A component used in calculating horizontal illuminance that expands illuminance calculations to account for various reflected elements. The calculation is essentially the same as the Lumen method with the coefficient of utilization being substituted with this additional factor.

Reflection A method in which light waves or an image are redirected off of a surface.

Reflective Light Meter An exposure light meter that is used by standing near a subject and measuring the light that reflects off of it. This is an accurate means of measuring exposure since it measures the amount of light actually leaving the surface of the subject.

Reflector An optical device that uses reflection to gather and redirect light.

Reflector Lamp See R-Lamp.

Reflector Unit, Panel or Board, Shiny Board Frames or panels used in video and film production that are covered with reflective materials to reflect light into a scene. The source can be a luminaire that is hung nearby or a distant source like the sun.

Refraction A physical property in which light is bent while passing through materials of different densities.

Remote Device Management (RDM) A relatively new control protocol that provides bi-directional communication along with plug-and-play features to lighting consoles and equipment. Once plugged into a network, the console locates and determines the type and number of fixture attributes for a unit while also assigning control channels to each attribute.

Rendering An image of a project that is created by a designer. These are often done by a computer in lighting applications and illustrate how the lighting will appear on an imaginary setting. In reality, it offers only an approximation of the final image but may approach photorealism if taken to an extreme.

Rental House A company specializing in the rental and sale of theatrical equipment.

Re-patch To reassign/re-plug circuits during a performance or rehearsal.

Repertory Light Plot A light plot that supports several different productions. While many of the general systems are shared, specials, recoloring, and refocusing are often used to address specific needs of each of the individual productions.

Request for Information (RFI) A formal request for information or a conflict resolution sent by the general contractor or subcontractor to a designer through the architect. The lighting designer formally responds to the RFI to either resolve the conflict, clarify the information, or answer any other questions that may have developed.

Residential Lighting Lighting the interiors and exteriors of homes and private residences.

Residuals A weekly fee paid to designers on a long-running show that is based on a percentage of the box office receipts.

Resistance (R) An electrical property that relates to a material or object creating a barrier to electrical flow.

Resistance Dimmer A specific form of dimmer in which electrical resistance is introduced to a circuit to regulate the intensity of the lights. It is an especially wasteful form of dimming and requires dimmers to be loaded to full capacity.

Resolution The degree of detail that is displayed in a projected or digital image.

Restore Cue A cue that is repeated from an earlier time in a production.

Retail Lighting Lighting associated with sales displays and retail stores.

Retrofit A variation of lamp that is a TH lamp replacement for an earlier lamp design. Retrofit lamps have a smaller bulb but maintain the same base and LCL of the lamp that they are replacing.

Revealing Form A function of lighting that refers to enhancing dimensionality or revealing the sculptural or three-dimensional elements of a subject.

RGB (Red, Green, and Blue) 1. A digital signal format used on screens, monitors, and projectors. This is a composite signal that combines separate inputs of each of the primary colors for video or digital images. 2. A form of additive color mixing.

Rhythm A function of light that refers to lighting movement and transitions. As tensions mount and resolve, the lighting should underscore the dramatic action and may appear to be very subtle or dramatic to an audience.

Ride Vehicle A car or motorized vehicle that carries guests in a theme ride or attraction.

Rider See Contract Rider.

Riding the Plot When an electrician or lighting assistant makes constant reference to the light plot and guides the progress of a focus through calling out the channels of the luminaires as they are needed.

Rim Light A variation of backlight used in film and video lighting that is offset to the side of a subject and tends to have a higher elevation than kickers. It produces a wrapping effect that models or edges (rims) a subject and helps to separate them from the background.

Rim Lighting Light or a lighting systems that etches or rings(rims) a subject from the side and back, particularly the backlight system.

Ring Top A piece of hardware consisting of a metal loop that is screwed to the top of a boom pipe and provides the connection for a tie-off rope.

R-Lamp (Reflector Lamp) A lamp that contains a reflector and diffuse lens that allows the light to be concentrated in a pool that spreads gently away in a single direction. It is similar to a PAR Lamp.

RMS Voltage (VRMS) A measurement of the overall average voltage across legs of a multi-phase power system. It may also be called the Root Mean Square Voltage.

Road Case A special shipping case used for transporting sensitive lighting and sound gear that is made of durable materials and lined with specially fitted foams to protect the case's contents.

Road House A theatre that typically presents touring productions.

Road-tap See Company Switch.

Roadway Lighting Lighting that provides illumination to highways and streets.

Rods 1. The pencil-sized electrodes that are used in arc light sources like followspots. They are made out of carbon and have a copper sheathing over them. 2. Optical sensors in the eye that respond to a wide range of light sensitivities and are responsible for our scotopic vision.

Rolling Dimmer Rack A portable dimmer rack that is fashioned like a road case with wheels and is used for touring.

Room Cavity Ratio (RCR) A volume associated with the Lumen Method calculation that relates the volume (height and area) of an entire room to the portion of the room with which we are concerned regarding illumination levels. It is also used as one of the variables that determine the efficiency of a luminaire and design solution.

Rooster Mount A method of mounting a luminaire in which the unit is spun up so that it is mounted directly above the pipe.

Root Mean Square Voltage See RMS Voltage (VRMS).

Ropelight A decorative effect that places miniature lamps (often of several different circuits or colors) in a flexible plastic tube. The tube is then used to outline structures.

Rotary Dimmer A dimmer (usually an autotransformer) that is often self-contained and operated from a knob or handle attached to a rotary shaft that extends through the center of the dimmer.

Roundels Circular glass filters that are installed in many striplight fixtures.

Rover A portable boom that is relatively short (usually less than 4 feet), contains very few luminaires (often only one or two), and is equipped with dollies so that it can be easily moved around as needed.

Run A circuit or cable that leads from one location to another. It can also be related to the cable distance that lies between two electrical devices.

Run the Barrel A focus command in which the lens barrel of a lighting instrument is set in the all the way forward position which is usually associated with producing the softest beam edges.

Run-through A type of rehearsal in which a segment of a play, musical, etc. is run or rehearsed without interruption. This may be as small as a few pages or a scene to as much as the entire play.

Rushes See Dailies.

Safety Cable A segment of 1/8 inch aircraft cable (about 2 feet long) equipped with a loop and special snap fitting that allows lighting instruments to be further attached to a hanging position and prevents a unit from falling due to failure of a yoke or C-clamp.

Safety Lighting Landscape or street lighting that is used primarily for visibility. It directs people to different parts of a property while also helping them to avoid hazards and navigate through a space safely.

Saturation See Chroma.

Saturation Rig A special type of lighting rig or grid used in film and video studios in which the grid is pre-hung and cabled heavily with a variety of luminaires and accessories. The lighting director simply chooses the gear from what they see is available, patches and focuses the units, and makes them work for the particular setup. Saturation rigs are popular in studios that are rented on a daily basis (e.g., taping commercials).

Save 1. To record a show and all of its cue information into the console or backup system. 2. To turn off a unit that is no longer needed (when the focus of the unit is complete or it is no longer desired in a cue).

Scanner (Moving Mirror) 1. A type of automated luminaire in which a moving mirror is placed at the front of the unit to direct the light to different locations. 2. A form of laser projection in which a laser beam is rapidly moved along a path. We cannot distinguish this movement, and through perception, connect the points and see the image as a series of lines that lie along the path of the laser. We use scanning to trace or draw basic images.

Scene Machine An effects projector by GAM that combines superior optics and a more intense light source with a series of modular motion effects that can be used to produce a desired image and motion.

Scenic Breakdown A listing of the specific scenes, locations, and time frames that occur in a script or performance event.

Scenic Floorplan A variation of floorplan that in addition to providing information about a facility also provides specific information about the scenic design for a production.

Scenic Specials A lighting instrument that is focused specifically to a scenic element of a production (e.g. a light focused to a sculpture or picture frame, a wall decoration, a tree, or scenic surface).

Schedules See Design Paperwork.

Schematic Development The second phase of architectural design development, in which the initial concepts are refined and developed into the foundations that will set the tone for the rest of the project. It sets the major parameters and starts to lock the team into some basic ideas.

Sconce A decorative luminaire that is mounted to a wall surface.

Scoop See Ellipsoidal Reflector Floodlight (ERF).

Score The sheet music or orchestration of an opera, musical, or other music-related event.

Scotopic Vision That portion of vision attributed to the rods' photoreceptors that are sensitive to light across a wide range of wavelengths and luminous levels. It is responsible for our sight at levels of low illumination and our peripheral vision.

SCR (Silicon Controlled Rectifier) An electronic component used in electronic dimming that is turned on and off (fired) through a low-voltage signal current to selectively sample or control the high-voltage output of a dimmer.

Screen A specially treated surface that is used as a projection surface. Screens come in a variety of sizes, colors, and shapes and perform with varied degrees of success. They may be used for both front or rear projection.

Scrim 1. A special type of scenic fabric with a loose weave that when treated with relatively steep-angled front light appears opaque but becomes transparent when lit from behind. 2. In film and video lighting scrims are metal meshes that are placed in front of light sources to drop the intensity of a lamp; different densities drop the intensity by various increments. Scrims lower the intensity while having no effect on color temperature, which cannot be achieved in dimming (red shift).

Scrim-Through A combined lighting/scenic effect in which a scrim that is front lighted and appears opaque is made transparent to reveal a scene behind it through lighting the objects behind the scrim. The reverse process is known as a scrim-back.

Script Analysis A careful study of a script. It gives the first indication of themes, plot, characters, settings, mood, style and specific lighting requirements of a play.

Scrollers (Automated Color Changers) An automated color changer that uses individual filters taped together to form a scroll. The scroll is rolled back and forth to specific positions that correspond to the different colors.

Sculpting/Modeling Systems A lighting system or collection of luminaires characterized by washes of back and side light that enhance depth perception.

Seasonal Affective Disorder (SAD) A form of seasonal depression that is due to the individual not being exposed to enough sunlight.

Second Team A group of stand-ins in television and video shoots who are used for lighting and camera rehearsals to replicate the blocking while the real actors (first team) are getting into costume and makeup.

Secondary Coil A coil in a transformer that has the induced voltage produced in it. This voltage is proportional to that of the primary coil and is dependent on the relative number of turnings in each coil.

Secondary Colors A combination of equal mixtures of any two primary colors. In light, these are magenta, cyan, and amber. In pigment they are orange, green, and violet.

Secondary Focus An area or object that has focus brought to it but which does not have the primary focus.

Secondary Lighting See Accent Lighting.

Secondary Panels (Panel Boards) Circuit boxes fed through feeder cables from a building's primary distribution center that bring power to all of the branch circuits in a given area of a building.

Secondary Service Conductors Heavy-duty cables that carry the main power supply into a building and to the main switchboard.

Section (Sectional View) A drafting representing a room or performance venue from a side view. The section is typically drawn as if you were to cut through a facility along the centerline of the stage and is used to determine beam coverage, lighting angles, approximate throw distances, and masking sightlines.

Security Lighting Lighting systems that make a property more visible and less shadowed to discourage prowlers and other criminal activities.

Selective Visibility Revealing to an audience only what they need to see in order to gain an understanding of an event.

Semi-Direct Luminaire An IESNA classification of luminaire based on a distribution pattern in which a significant amount of light is directed upward (10–40%) but the majority is still directed downward (60–90%).

Semi-Indirect Luminaire An IESNA classification of luminaire based on a distribution pattern in which a significant amount of light is directed downward (10–40%) but the majority is directed upward (60–90%).

Semi-Recessed Luminaire A classification of architectural luminaires based on a mounting position being partially contained within a wall or ceiling.

Series Circuit A circuit in which the leads of each device are sequentially connected together in a daisy-chain with the first and last devices being connected to the power supply.

Service The actual power configuration or number and capacity of wires brought into a building from a power utility.

Service Entrance The point where the electrical service enters a building.

Set Levels See Cue-In.

Set List (Play List) A listing of the order of the songs that will be performed for music related performances like concerts.

Set Mount A lighting instrument or practical that is mounted directly to the scenery.

Set Wireman The individual on a film or video crew who is in charge of wiring and maintaining all of the practicals that are mounted on a set.

Setup (Shot) An element of television and film production based on the filming of a scene and individual camera placement. Each camera angle along with its adjustments for lighting and other production elements comprises an individual shot.

Shadow Box (Moon Box) 1. A lighting effect in which lamps are enclosed in a light-tight box having a designed pattern or image cutout of its front panel. Gel is used to color the cutout, while scrim may be put across its front to mask the design when not in use. Moon boxes and simulated neon signs are often created in this manner. 2. A small window display (often as small as a foot square) that is placed at eye level.

Shadowing A method of casting shadows in landscape lighting in which a luminaire is placed in front of the plants and trees where it will not only light the subject but also cast its shadow onto the background as an element of the design.

Shadows Shadows are represented by either the area of an object that is not lit or the pattern of darkness that is cast by an illuminated object (cast shadow).

Shakedown The initial period of a tour (often a week or so) during which the production is tested out and tweaked. This can refer to design items (the cues, staging, and lighting itself), the load-in and strike process, arrival order and stacking of trucks, size of crews (touring and local), etc.

Shielding A method of constructing roadway luminaires so that their light is forced downward and not to the sides or upward. It protects drivers from glare.

Shins (Shin Buster/Shin Kicker) A luminaire that creates low-angled sidelight that is mounted at floor level at the base of a boom.

Shiny Board See Reflector Unit or Reflector Panel/Board.

Shoe A part of a mechanical dimmer that contains an electrical contact that is moved across the dimmer to sample voltage at different points over a dimmer's coils.

Shoebox Design An ERS design in which the housing or body is based on a rectangular (shoebox) shape rather than the traditional cylinder of most ERS designs.

Shop Order An inventory of all the materials and equipment that will be required to complete a lighting design.

Short-arc Lamp Modern arc sources commonly used in followspots, projectors, and other high-intensity units like moving lights. The lamp makes use of a heavy glass bulb with electrodes permanently built into the lamp. On operation, an arc forms between the electrodes with no need for trimming or adjustment.

Short-Circuit Creating an accidental flow of electricity. When two hots come into direct contact with one another, or a hot wire makes accidental contact with the neutral, or ground which commonly results in shocks, sparks, or a possible fire.

Short-Throw Followspots Followspots designed with a range of beamspreads that are appropriate for a small venue. These throw distances are optimally between 25 and 50 feet.

Shot See Setup.

Show Control A manner of linking several different control systems together so that all events/cues can be triggered by a single console. Lights, pyro, and other effects are often triggered by the soundtrack of a performance.

Showcase Lamp A special version of incandescent tube lamp that is long and thin, and has been designed specifically for shelf lighting. It is also popular in cabinet lighting and frequently used in both retail and museum applications.

Showroom Special theatres often associated with cruise lines and casino or nightclubs that have well-equipped fly houses, lighting equipment, and stages but where the audience areas are more like ballrooms. The houses often include tables and bars in addition to traditional theatrical seating. The ceilings are usually relatively low, which can result in overall flat lighting from the front of house. Las Vegas singers and comedy acts frequently perform in these facilities.

Shutter Speed A camera setting that indicates how long film is exposed to light.

Shutters The most important controls in an ERS. They are four metal plates that are inserted into the field of light to flatten or shape a spotlight's beam.

Sidearm An iron or hardware item that provides a method of mounting lighting fixtures to the side of a batten or boom while keeping the pan and tilt adjustments in their standard orientations.

Sidelight A lighting distribution angle that comes from the side and helps to model and give three-dimensional form to a subject.

Silhouette Lighting Lighting the background behind an object rather than the object itself.

Silicon Controlled Rectifier See SCR.

Silks See Butterflies.

Sine Wave Dimmers A recent innovation in dimming technology that makes use of IGBT dimming to produce a more effective, less noisy (electronically) dimmer by using a much higher sampling rate of the AC current than traditional SCR dimmers.

Single-Source Lighting (Single-Source System) A form of general illumination in which either an actual single light source is used to illuminate the stage or a series of individual instruments are used in such a way as to give the illusion that light is coming from a single source.

Site Plan A drafting that contains all the buildings, walkways, and landscape features of a property. A landscape lighting designer uses this to plot the design.

Site Survey A visit to the location where a lighting installation or design will actually take place. It is an opportunity to observe the facility, take measurements, and to seek out any unique concerns that may not be readily observed in the plans.

Skydrop Essentially the same scenic background as a cyc, with the exception that it is colored a light tint of blue.

Skylight 1. An important component of daylighting. It refers to the more consistent overall diffuse glow of the sky as a lighting element (a result of scattering and general diffusion in the atmosphere). 2. A window-like architectural feature that is mounted in a roof or ceiling and allows daylight to enter a building.

Slide A source of original artwork for a projection. In most cases slides are made of translucent or transparent materials that allow light to pass through them.

Slide Patch A special type of patch panel where all of the circuits are arranged in rows along one axis (horizontal or vertical) while all of the dimmers are arranged along the opposing axis. A sliding contact is assigned to each of the circuits or dimmers along one of these axes and is moved along the axis and snapped into position over the corresponding circuit or dimmer to which the assignment is going to be made.

Slot See Cove.

Slow Blow A fuse or circuit breaker failing due to excessive heat in a circuit. The breaker often appears to trip for no reason. Slow blows are most often due to conditions like excessive resistance being created in a circuit by extralong or under-sized jumpers, loose connections, or a slight overload of a circuit.

Smart Preset Boards The first memory boards. These were special variations of a preset board that had features that could store cues in a temporary memory.

Snell's Law See Law of Refraction

Snoot (Top Hat) An accessory that blocks spill by preventing light from opening up or spreading too quickly once leaving a luminaire. It is also used to control glare from backlights. Video and film professionals prefer to call it a snoot, while theatrical professionals use "top hat."

Society of Motion Picture and Television Engineers (SMPTE) A professional organization associated with technicians of the film and television industries. The organization sets the standard for synchronizing various production elements (sound, lights, pyro, machinery, etc.) through its SMPTE show control.

Socopex (Socapex) Cables A popular form of multi-cables used in entertainment applications. These multi-cables have special electrical fittings on each end for adapters (break-ins and break-outs) to be connected to their ends, which separates the cable into individual male and female connectors for each circuit.

Soft Light A type of light associated with the film and video industry characterized by diffuse illumination that does not display any prominent shadows. It is often associated with fill light and is used to soften any shadows created by a key light.

Soft-Lights A classification of luminaires in the film and video industry that produce a nice shadowless light over a large area. The fixtures lack a lens system and are often outfitted with diffusion media to ensure a soft, shadowless source of illumination.

Soft Patch Assigning dimmers and other control attributes to specific channels or controllers on a lighting console. Since the assignments are done electronically, the actual load of the dimmers does not factor into these assignments.

Softscape The growing elements or plants, foliage, and trees of a landscape design.

Solid Core Conductor A type of wire in which the conductor is a single piece of solid copper or metal.

Sound Stage A large, warehouse-like facility that is used for large-scale film and video productions. It is a larger version of a studio and contains lots of open space and a flexible lighting system that is easily modified to the many scenes and productions that may share the floor at any given time.

Sound Wing A stack of speaker cabinets stacked on either side of a concert stage. The sound wings supply the general PA or sound for the audience.

Space Light See Chicken Coop.

Space Manipulation Using architectural lighting to alter an occupant's perception of a space.

Spacing Criteria A set of conditions such as illuminance levels and mounting heights that are used to determine how far apart architectural luminaires may be spaced from one another.

Sparkle See Glitter.

Special A luminaire that is used for a specific need or function.

Special Visibility Lighting in which luminaires or lighting are assigned to a particular need of visibility that cannot be achieved by the general illumination or area lighting.

Specialty Areas A variation in area lighting that creates additional lighting areas that mimic the actual lighting areas but are based on special needs like a variation in height or hanging restrictions. They are lit to give the appearance of being part of the same lighting environment.

Specialty Lighting (Themed Lighting) Lighting that is associated with themed design. It is a combination of traditional and entertainment based lighting design. Now more often called specialty lighting rather than themed lighting.

Specify A manner of identifying and providing documentation (on paper) of the exact performance and installation requirements of an architectural or other lighting installation or design.

Specular Reflection A type of reflection created from materials that have a shiny or mirrored surface that follows the Law of Reflection quite specifically.

Spherical Reflector A reflector based on the shape of a sphere that reflects light back through the focal point of the reflector.

Spidering See Home Runs.

Spike (Surge) A very sudden increase in voltage that can create a safety hazard or may damage equipment. A surge will typically last for less than a second.

Spill Stray or unwanted light. Spill is due to scattered reflections or the continuation of light beyond a target onto objects that a designer does not want to light.

Spill Rings A video and film lighting accessory that functions the same way as an egg crate, with the exception that they are used on circular-faced luminaires.

Spin the Bottle To rotate a PAR lamp to orient the axis of the lamp's filament.

Splitfade A cue in which the lights coming up in a cue will do so at one speed while the lights coming down or out will do so at another speed.

Splitfader A variation of crossfader that includes a second fader (wired in opposition to the first) to allow a board to fade between different presets with different up and down rates and proportions.

Spot Focus The position in a Fresnel spotlight where the lamp or reflector assembly is moved toward the back of the unit that causes the light to converge over a central point and into a tighter spot setting.

Spot Luminaire An automated fixture that is used as a spotlight and has beam edges that can be focused to a sharp edge. These luminaires often contain effect devices, several manners of producing color, and one or two gobo wheels that can each hold up to five or more gobos, as well as moving attributes like pan and tilt.

Spot Meter A reflective light meter that measures light through a very narrow portion of a camera's field. Spot meters are good for measuring contrast ratios between areas of high and low illumination within a camera frame.

Spot Relamping A manner of relamping that requires maintenance workers to replace lamps as burnouts occur.

Spotlight A luminaire that has well-defined edges and a fairly narrow distribution pattern, which is often used for creating accents. As a rule, spotlights contain lenses.

Spotlight Booth See Projection Booth.

Spotlighting A form of lighting where specific objects or performers are pointed up or given focus through creating an accent on them. This may be achieved by adding intensity, sharpness, different colors, or other contrasting features to the light.

Spotting Light (Spotting Lamp) A low-wattage lamp (usually red) that is placed at the rear of an auditorium to aid dancers in keeping their orientation (facing front) while making pivoting movements.

Spread Reflection A type of reflection in which most light from a source is reflected off a surface as predicted by the Law of Reflection, but due to an uneven surface this is not as specific or directional as a specular reflection.

Spud A pin-like fitting that slips into a receiving piece of hardware and allows a film or video luminaire to be quickly mounted to a stand or other support device.

Stack See Pack.

Stage Mode A console mode that displays the channels and their associated intensity levels that are actually live and on stage.

Staging the Story A function of lighting where we consider the techniques of producing a production by finding theatrical mechanisms for presenting the story or event to an audience (e.g., manner of achieving scene changes).

Stair Light A special architectural luminaire that is designed to be mounted or recessed directly into the structure of stairs and directs light downward onto the treads.

Starting Address The first channel of any DMX-controlled device. It represents the first attribute and is the one that a fixture's addressing switches will be set to.

State (Cue or Look) A static lighting image or look that creates a given combination of lights and their angles, intensities, and overall mixing. Cueing refers to establishing the looks and recording them so that they can be duplicated from performance to performance.

Step Lens A less popular version of the plano-convex lens that removes elements of the plano surface, leaving the convex surface intact. This lens produces a series of concentric rings in the beam of many spotlights and is no longer used in the lighting industry.

Step-down Transformer A transformer that is used to lower an AC voltage. The primary coil will be larger or contain more windings than the secondary coil.

Stepper Motors Small motors used in the movement of automated lighting attributes that create motion by rotating through a series of steps that refer to an attribute's position. This motion can appear jerky, especially at slow speeds.

Stepping Effect The effect by which a laser emits energy, in which the corresponding wavelengths of each waveform are in sync with all other waveforms, with the effect producing a higher amplitude and energy level.

Step-up Transformer A transformer that is used to raise an AC voltage. The secondary coil will be larger or contain more windings than the primary coil.

Stiffener An accessory that is mounted to a batten and taped to its associated lift cables to prevent a pipe from spinning. It is very similar to a sidearm, which may be used in its place.

Storyboards 1. Simple drawings that give an indication of each camera shot for film or video production along with the visual composition of each shot. 2. In theatrical applications, the storyboard is used as an informational sketch that indicates the lighting composition and qualities for a given moment.

Straight Run See Daisy-Chain.

Stranded Conductor A type of wire in which a number of individual strands of copper or other conductive wire are woven together to form a larger conductor.

Street Lighting A variation of roadway lighting that not only lights the street but also the sidewalks and surrounding buildings, adding security and safety to an area.

Strike 1. Take down and remove all of the equipment used in a production. 2. Turning on or "striking" an arc light source.

Striplight A luminaire that uses multiple lamps arranged in a side-by-side fashion that form a "strip" of light. A typical unit contains three or four circuits in which every third or fourth lamp is wired and colored separately as a common circuit.

Strobe Light (Strobe) A special xenon lamp that can be set for especially rapid on-off sequences and can produce stop-action motion.

Structure See Dramatic Form.

Studio A production facility for film and video production that is similar to a black box theatre and contains a large open area and lighting grid.

Style A function of lighting that relates to creating visual qualities that produce a characteristic overall quality for a production. The degree of realism may be used as a means of comparing styles. Style is specifically determined through the collaboration and discussions of the production team.

Stylization See Abstraction.

Subject The object or individual that is being lit.

Submaster A dimming control that provides for an assignment of several individual dimmers or control channels that function together as a unit.

Subtractive Color Mixing A method of color mixing that occurs when various wavelengths of light are removed. All materials selectively absorb (or reflect) different wavelengths, which defines an object's natural color.

Subtransmission Lines Relatively high-voltage lines from substations that first reduce the voltage from transmission lines which in turn run to other substations that reduce the voltage even further so that it is safer to run into neighborhoods.

Sun-gun A battery operated hand-held lamp that is used on location shoots for film and video. It is similar to a spotting lamp.

Supertitles A line-by-line translation of an opera text that is typically projected onto a screen located directly above the proscenium opening of a stage.

Surface-Mounted Luminaires A classification of architectural luminaires based on a mounting position that is mounted directly to a wall or ceiling.

Surge See Spike.

Suspended Luminaires A classification of architectural luminaires based on a mounting position below a ceiling, from a pendant or other device.

Suspension Grid (Tension Grid) A lighting grid found in many black box theatres that consists of a mesh of woven aircraft cable that permits electricians to walk directly above the theatre on the grid.

Swatch Book A booklet that provides a sample of the actual color filter, transmission charts, and other information for each filter in a manufacturer's specific series or product line of filters or gels. Samples of color correction, diffusion, and reflective materials are also frequently contained in swatch books.

Switch A device used to control the flow of power in a circuit. Open switches prevent the flow of electricity, while closed switches allow the current to flow.

Swivel Socket An accessory inserted into a standard socket that permits a lamp to be swiveled and focused in many directions.

Symbol Libraries A collection of CAD symbols or blocks that are created or purchased by the designer and stored for future use.

System (Lighting System) The combined use of multiple luminaires and washes that have similar if not identical functions to provide a unified appearance throughout an entire lit environment.

Tabbing-in Moving the torms of a larger stage in towards centerline. The practice is common for touring productions, which can then always play within a standard-sized proscenium opening.

Tag A label or identifier placed on a lighting layout along with a luminaire symbol (in architectural projects) that provides a reference to additional information relating to the fixture with which the tag is associated. This information might include the luminaire model number and manufacturer, finish, control information, lamp specification, etc.

Tail Down The practice of hanging a pipe below an existing batten or grid so that the luminaires can be hung from a lower trim height.

Take A shooting segment in film and video production. It involves a given setup, set of actions, and camera shot.

Talent The subject or performer that is to be lit in a video or film setting.

Tap A device that breaks either one or two phases of service off of a three-phase service.

Task A visual requirement or job that must be performed successfully within a given set of lighting conditions in architectural applications.

Task Light A somewhat portable light that can be moved into position to provide specific illumination to a limited area for completing a given task.

Task Lighting Specification calculations and recommendations that are used to calculate minimum illumination levels for architectural applications representing a given visual task (function) or application requirement.

Tech with Actors (Wet Tech) A rehearsal that focuses on the technical elements of a production but also includes the performers so that the performers and cues can be integrated with one another.

Technical Rehearsal A rehearsal in which the focus of the work is placed on the integration of the technical elements of a production. Light, sound, scene shifts and special effects are typically worked out in these rehearsals. Performers may or may not be part of these rehearsals.

Template 1. A sheet of rigid plastic that is stamped with a variety of symbols that provide scaled silhouettes of lighting instruments and other architectural details that are traced onto a drafting or light plot. 2. A master CAD file that is used as a base drawing for more specific draftings like floorplans or light plots (also known as a prototype). 3. See gobo or pattern.

Tension Grid See Suspension Grid.

Tentative Hookup A preliminary hookup that allows a lighting designer to work out the dimmer or channel assignments of a lighting design.

Tenting Placing a surround of diffusion material most of the way around a subject or setup to produce an evenly diffused lighting environment around the subject.

Terminator A hardware device or accessory that is plugged into the last unit of a DMX control line or run that helps prevent erroneous data from confusing the equipment along the data run.

Tertiary Colors See Intermediate Colors.

Theatrical Lighting In themed attractions, the part of the lighting installation that is supplied by theatrical luminaires, control, and related lighting equipment.

Theme An area of analysis where the playwright and director try to convey a message to an audience. Themes often refer to the social message(s) or meanings of a play.

Themed Design (Themed Entertainment) A form of design in which an environment is created along a specific theme and some form of entertainment is also achieved. A visitor or viewer is immersed in an interactive environment that has some form of story associated with it. Popular themed projects include restaurants, stores, and theme parks.

Themed Lighting (Specialty Lighting) Lighting that is associated with themed design. It is a combination of traditional and entertainment based lighting design. Now this is more often called specialty lighting.

Thinking Green A philosophy of designing buildings and lighting that are efficient and conserve natural resources while limiting byproducts that harm the environment.

Three-fer An adapter with three female plugs wired to a single male connector that allows lighting instruments to be combined together onto a common circuit.

Three-phase Power A form of power distribution in which three separate legs or hot wires are provided to a facility or piece of equipment.

Three-Point Lighting (Three-Point System) A common method of illumination for video and film that involves three light sources that create a variety of contrast ratios around a subject, which in turn emphasizes the modeling or sculpted qualities of a subject. It's also a common standardized approach to lighting thrust and arena productions.

Three-way Switch A special type of switch that allows a circuit to be controlled through using one of several switches that are placed in different locations.

Three-wire System An electrical service that provides two hot wires (legs) and a common neutral.

Threshold Exposure The lowest exposure or light level setting at which a camera or film can record an image.

Throw Distance The line-of-sight distance measured from the luminaire to a target.

Tight Specifications Writing design specifications that are so specific that only the equipment desired by the designer can fulfill the requirements of a project.

Tilt An adjustment of a luminaire's beam in an upward or downward direction.

Timecode A series of signals that are placed at specific points in a soundtrack to automatically trigger light cues or other effects or events at a specific time. In effect, the timecode simply tells the console to execute a given cue number much like an operator would tell a console to execute a cue by hitting the "go" button.

Timer A switching device that makes use of an internal clock that turns electrical devices on and off at predetermined times. An astronomical clock or timer is often used in architectural applications and is based on a 24-hour clock, which automatically adjusts for seasonal fluctuations and other factors like daylight savings time.

Tint A color that is combined with either white light or a mixture of other wavelengths that produce a softer, less saturated version of the original hue.

Title Block A segment of a drafting plate that provides essential information regarding the drafting. Information often found in the title block includes: production or project title, the producing organization or firm, theatre or building name, identification of the designer, scale, and date of the drafting.

Toning Accents A wash of luminaires or lighting system that modifies or tones the color of a space or object over a broad area.

Top Hat See Snoot.

Topper A special form of flag used in the film and video industry that is used specifically to block the upper portion of a luminaire's beam.

Torm A name given to the first vertical sidelighting position that is just upstage of the curtain line on a proscenium stage. Some designers name torms in the same manner as booms.

Track Luminaires A classification of architectural luminaires based on a mounting position being an electric path/rail or raceway.

Track Sheets A record of the individual channel levels for every cue contained in a production. Each cue's count information is also fully documented along with any effects or other control information related to the show.

Tracking Making a hard copy of all the channel levels and count information associated with each cue of a production.

Tracking Mode A console mode in which changes made in one cue are copied or "tracked" through future cues. A lighting console that provides for tracking is often called a tracking console.

Trade Show A corporate event in which a number of products and services (usually from a variety of companies with related products/services) are presented to a select group of potential customers, clients, or professionals.

Transfer Circuits/Transfer Panels Permanent circuits that are run to a location where they can be reassigned. Transfer circuits are common in road houses where the FOH circuits terminate at an interface where they can be assigned to either the house lighting system or a touring company's dimmers.

Transformer An electrical device that uses coils and magnetism to modify voltages. They can either step-up or step-down the voltage depending on the relative number of turnings in the primary and secondary coils.

Transformer Schedule A schedule used in landscape lighting that is similar to a conventional dimmer schedule. This schedule organizes the equipment by transformer assignments and their associated circuits/loads.

Transition Zone (Transition Area) An area or zone created in museum and gallery lighting where additional exhibits and transitional lighting are designed with the primary purpose of providing an area and time for a viewer's eyes to adjust to the lighting levels between adjoining areas.

Transitions Refers to the process and visual changes that occur while advancing from one cue to another.

Translucence A property that allows light to pass through a material and will allow a viewer to observe light and shadows but at the same time obscures the ability to see directly through the material.

Transmission Refers to the lighting wavelengths that pass through a gel, diffuser, or other material. Transmission refers to the percentage of radiant energy that continues beyond the filter and can be expressed as a total output across all wavelengths or as an output within specific wavelengths. Transmission rate refers to the percentage of light that actually passes through a material like a gel. More saturated gels have lower transmission rates.

Transmission Lines The heavy-duty power lines that are used to transfer power over long distances.

Transmission Rate See Transmission.

Transmission Substation A network of heavy metal cables, insulators, mast-like structures, and transformers that are used to either boost or lower the voltage of electricity as it is transported from a power plant to a customer. Those near a power plant that boost the voltage are called transmission substations, while those in neighborhoods that lower the voltage are called distribution substations.

Traveler A drapery that parts at the center and opens and closes across the stage.

Trees See Booms.

Triac An electronic component in electronic dimmers that functions in essentially the same way as SCRs.

Tri-colored Luminaires that use arrays of three different colored LEDs as a light source. The LEDs are in the three primary colors of red, blue and green with each color controlled by an individual control channel. In theory, additive mixing can be used with these to produce nearly any color, but in reality, many of the colors are compromised due to poor spectral coverage.

Trim 1. The height of a hanging or mounting position, like a batten, measured from the stage floor to its working height. 2. The range settings of a dimmer from the point where the load goes out (low trim) to the point at which the load comes to full intensity (high trim).

Trimming 1. Adjusting the movements and relative positions of the rods in a carbon-arc unit for optimal performance. 2. An adjustment of a dimmer's voltage so that full movement of the dimmer corresponds to both a smooth/even and complete range of intensities.

Triple-hang A manner of providing a third alternative in color or focus for a general lighting system or area.

Troffer A popular architectural luminaire based on the use of fluorescent tubes and housings that fit as flat panels within standard drop-ceiling grids.

Trombone A zoom/focus assembly found on followspots that allows the beam angle and focus range of the spotlight to be easily modified.

Trunions Hardware that is used to mount striplights as floor units (one per side).

Truss A framework of reinforced metal tubing that becomes the support mechanism for lighting, sound, and other theatrical elements. These modular structures are popular in the touring industry because they are simply bolted together and often have all the lighting equipment already pre-hung within them.

Tungsten-Halogen Lamp (TH lamp or Quartz Lamp) A special version of incandescent lamp that uses a mixture of halogen gas and the tungsten-halogen process to create a more efficient and longer lasting light source.

Tungsten-Halogen Process The halogen in a TH lamp results in tungsten particles being deposited on the hottest portion (filament) of the lamp rather than the cooler bulb, creating a recycling effect that increases lamp life while also preventing the cloudy buildup on the bulb that affects the performance of traditional lamps.

Tweak A process of making refinements in the lighting cues and design throughout the rehearsal process.

Two-fer An adapter with two female plugs wired to a single male connector that allows lighting instruments or cables to be combined together.

Two-Way Barn Door An accessory that is placed in the front of a luminaire (frequently Fresnels) with two moveable panels that can be adjusted into the beam of light for controlling spill or glare.

Two-wire System An electrical service that provides a single hot wire and neutral.

Unified Production A production in which all of the design and performance elements reinforce one another to form a cohesive whole in which nothing appears to be out of sync or place with the other elements.

Unistrut A channel of steel that is essentially U-shaped with flanged edges used to hang stage equipment like luminaires with bolts or other specialized hardware. PAR-bars are often fashioned from unistrut.

United Scenic Artists (USA) The union that represents lighting, scenic, sound, and costume designers, along with scenic artists and most recently, projection designers. It is now affiliated with IATSE.

United States Institute for Theatre Technology (USITT) An organization that represents designers and technicians across all disciplines of stagecraft throughout the entertainment profession.

Universe A unit of control based on a single control cable and its associated 512 individual channels of control.

Uplighting An unnatural angle where objects are lit from below. It is a dramatic angle and is often used for drawing focus or creating a special effect.

Valence Lighting Lighting that is used to light vertical displays and walls in which the luminaires (often using fluorescent tubes) are hidden behind a linear panel while the light is distributed upward and downward.

Value A component of color used to describe a color's overall lightness or darkness based on a gray scale.

Value Engineering Refers to using lower-quality equipment and installation practices than originally specified in order to increase a contractor's profit margin or to lower the overall costs of the installation for the client.

Variegated Glass Filters (Prismatic Glass) A form of plastic or glass with a textured surface that refracts and diffuses any light that passes through it. These accessories are placed in the gate of a luminaire in much the same way as a gobo is used.

Vectorscope An instrument that breaks a video signal down into its composite colors or wavelengths and plots the individual color signals in a radial format on an electronic screen. White is found at the center of the circle, while each of the primary and secondary colors are located at various points around the radius. The further from the center that a signal is plotted, the more saturated the color.

Veiling Reflections Unwanted reflections of light sources such as sunlight, windows/skylights, and luminaires onto viewing surfaces such as computer screens that obscure the view of the desired object(s). Reflections that obscure window displays form another example.

Verdigris (Verdi Green) An anodized finish that is used to retard the corrosion of metal landscape luminaires. It resembles a black and green marbleized effect.

Vertical Toning Strips (VTS) Striplights that are mounted on booms in a vertical orientation. Dance companies will sometimes make use of this technique to produce their sidelight washes.

Video Assist System An in-lens video camera used to capture a film camera's framing and to provide immediate feedback for what has been filmed.

Video Controller (VC) or Video Engineer A control system (and person) that controls the video output for a production. The VC controls all elements of the image on the master monitor, which becomes the final signal that is broadcast or recorded.

Video Mapping A projection technique in which a digital video signal is sent to a display device where each pixel or primary element of the image is displayed by individual control signals by various projection or LED devices that together form a composite video image.

Video Wall A composite wall of tiled LCD panels or video monitors that together produce a large-scaled screen or video display. Each tiled panel may display either an independent image or a small portion of a larger image.

Video-Tiling A projection technique in which multiple projectors are used to project a select portion of a larger image over a large surface like a building façade.

Virtual Design Any design that is created by computer simulation.

Virtual Lighting Lighting that is created for a virtual environment within a computer.

Visibility The principle of using light to reveal or illuminate objects. It's the primary function of lighting.

Visible Spectrum That portion of the electromagnetic spectrum to which the human eye is sensitive and where individual wavelengths of light are visible. It is found approximately in the range of 400 (violet) to 700 (red) nanometers.

Vision of Light Another manner of referring to a lighting concept or lighting scheme.

Vista Lighting A form of landscape lighting that provides supplemental lighting of an area that has a panoramic view of a distant landscape.

Visual Acuity Being able to manipulate the visual stimulus and environment so that a visual task may be completed. It is a function of factors like the size of the subject, distance between subject and viewer, surface reflectivity, amount of illumination, and the sensitivity of the sensors.

Visual Comfort Probability (VCP) A lighting calculation based on the angle between an observer and a light source and survey data that enables a designer to determine the degree of offensiveness of glare and other negative impacts that a luminaire and mounting position can have on an occupant.

Visual Fatigue A process by which a viewer's eyes grow tired due to certain optical sensors being overstimulated by an unchanging visual environment.

Visual Task A visual skill or job that requires an appropriate level of visibility in order to perform the job successfully.

Visualization The use of a computer and specialized software to design, pre-program and simulate a production or architectural design. It produces images that approximate what the final design might look like under actual lighting conditions.

Voltage (E) A measurement of the electrical potential difference that exists between two points and is measured through a unit known as the volt. We may also refer to voltage as electromotive force (EMF).

Voltage Drop A measured drop in voltage that occurs as electricity is conducted through greater distances as the resistance in a circuit gets larger.

Vomitory (Vom) An aisle found in thrust and arena theatres that is typically placed on the corners of adjoining audience sections.

Walk-through 1. A film or video first rehearsal of a setup where the actors arrive for a blocking rehearsal and the director establishes their movement patterns. In this context, designers may also call this a dry run. 2. A tool in some visualization programs that permits a viewer to manipulate their view to complete a simulated exploration of a virtual space.

Walkway Lighting A form of landscape lighting that illuminates and often lines sidewalks and paths.

Wall Pack A classification of wall-mounted luminaires in which a grazing light is cast away from the fixture along the wall while a decorative shade shields the viewer from the light source.

Wall Pocket A theatrical distribution box containing three to six circuits that is located along the perimeter walls of a stage.

Wall Reflected Radiation Component (WRRC) A component used as a factor in calculating vertical or wall illuminance that expands the illuminance calculations to account for various reflected elements. The calculation is essentially the same as the Lumen Method, with the coefficient of utilization being substituted with this additional factor that represents vertical illuminations.

Wall Sconce A decorative luminaire that is mounted to the surface of a wall.

Wall-Washer An architectural luminaire that is typically mounted as a surface or recessed ceiling mount whose light grazes or washes a vertical surface like a wall.

Warm Colors Light that has an abundance of red, yellow, and orange wavelengths. They produce responses of tension or action and appear to advance towards us.

Warming Current A small current used to pre-heat lamp filaments so that a sudden surge like bringing a dimmer to full won't over stress a lamp.

Wash Using several luminaires to cover a significant portion of scenery, stage, or other area designated by a designer. The individual fixtures are blended from one unit to another to give the appearance of being lit by a single light source.

Wash Light See Linear Light.

Wash Luminaire Automated fixtures that have soft edges so that a series of them can be blended together to produce a wash. Another significant difference between wash luminaires and spot luminaires is their lack of features like patterns/gobos and other features like shutters that make more controllable forms of light.

Wash System A group of luminaires that share common characteristics (e.g. angle and color) and operate together to produce an even coverage over an area that is larger than what a single spotlight can cover. The individual units work together (each covering a portion of the area) to produce a uniform coverage over the entire area.

Washed Stage A lighting approach for general illumination that dates back to wash variety luminaires and light sources that were typically candle or lantern flames. Horizontal strips of luminaires were typically hung above and across the stage, while additional luminaires were placed on stands to the sides of the stage. This lighting was often characterized by a strong use of footlights to help soften the shadows that were cast on the performers by the overhead lights.

Watt (P) A measurement of the rate of doing work and can be thought of in terms of how much power that a task might be using or consuming.

Wavelength A manner of measuring and describing waves that correlates to the distance between the points in which a wave undergoes a complete cycle (often measured peak to peak).

Well Lights Landscape luminaires that are nothing more than a cylinder containing a lamp and its electrical components, buried so that the face of the lamps are about even with the surface of the ground.

West Virginia Formula Based on the Power Formula, it relates the wattage of a circuit to the voltage and amperage. $W = V \times A$ (Watts = Volts $\times$ Amps)

Wet Tech See Tech with Actors.

Wheel A mechanical control device that allows a board operator to manually adjust any channel levels or rates that are placed under its control.

White Balance A process where video cameras are adjusted for overall color temperature sensitivity through registering what the camera sees as white light. This process ensures faithful overall color reproduction.

Wiggle Lights See Intelligent Lights, Moving Lights, Automated Lights, and Luminaires.

Window Well An architectural feature that sets a building's windows deeper into a wall surface, providing additional protection from the effects of direct sunlight.

Wing Panel An accessory that provides a set of manual faders to a control console or computer running software that converts the computer into a lighting control system.

Wire A component for conducting electricity that contains a metal conductor covered by insulation that shields it from other conductors. A wire by definition only contains one conductor.

Wireless Dimming A relatively new form of control in which information such as a DMX signal is transmitted through dedicated radio frequencies. Similar to the manner in which wireless mics are controlled, a receiver is addressed and then assigned channel information just as any other soft-patching is done. Some of these systems may also include a power supply so that there are actually no control or power wires leading to the circuit at all and are useful for placing lighting in costumes or on scenic pieces that must remain mobile.

Wish List A worksheet that lists all of the functions that a lighting designer intends to create throughout a design. It is then used to determine the number and type of luminaires, number of control channels or dimmers required, etc., but more importantly is used to prioritize this list and to determine ways in which the uses and associated lights can be consolidated, re-patched, or cut in order to make the design practical.

Work Notes Notes that refer to technical or mechanical issues that require a crew and need to be fixed by the next rehearsal or performance (e.g., burned out gel or lamps, adding a unit, or dropped focuses are common examples of work notes).

Working Trim The trim or height at which a hanging position is flown to and from where the lights are actually used for a production and focused from.

Worklight (After Hours or Cleaning/Maintenance) Lighting A lighting system that is used after hours by maintenance and cleaning staff in restaurants, nightclubs, or other facilities that operate under low illumination levels during normal business hours. In the theatre, worklights are used for general illumination for load-ins and load-outs, rehearsals, and work calls where the stage lighting is not required.

Workplane In lighting calculations, the plane in which a visual task is completed. In most cases it represents a horizontal plane that extends across an entire room. For instance, a plane representing the height of all the desks in a classroom or office.

Writing a Show Blind Preprogramming a show in a remote location without the benefit of being able to see the stage and the effects of light on it.

Wye See Four-wire System.

Xenon Lamp A special form of short-arc lamp that is used in followspots and other luminaires.

Yoke A U-shaped bracket that supports the actual body of a theatrical luminaire that is then attached to a hanging position by a C-clamp. Tilt adjustments are made by setting the bolts or handles that attach the yoke to the luminaire while pan adjustments are made by setting the bolt that attaches the yoke to the C-clamp.

Yoking Out Spinning the C-clamp around a pipe so that a luminaire is mounted somewhere between straight down and 90° upward. This variation in hanging is used to help shoot around obstructions like adjoining luminaires or stretching a bit more height out of a low hanging position.

Zonal Cavity Method See Lumen Method.

Zone See Plane.

Zone Lighting A lighting formula for general illumination that represents a variation of the washed stage and is often used where a layered effect (wing and drop setting) might be created through the scenery. It is especially popular in dance productions. Zone lighting makes use of wash luminaires that are used primarily to light the scenery from above but is then supplemented by high-angled sidelight (the most dominant lighting angle), backlight, and a limited amount of front fill.

BIBLIOGRAPHY

Albers, Josef. *Interaction of Color, 50th Anniversary Edition*. New Haven, CT: Yale University Press, 2013.

Allen, Kevin Lee. Vectorworks *for Entertainment Design: Using* Vectorworks *to Design and Document Scenery, Lighting, and Sound*. Burlington, MA: Focal Press, 2015.

Alton, John. *Painting with Light (Reprint)*. Berkeley and Los Angeles: University of California Press, 2013.

Ball, David. *Backwards and Forwards: A Technical Manual for Reading Plays*. Carbondale and Edwardsville: Southern Illinois Press, 1983.

Barbizon Lighting Company. *Electricians Pocket Book*. Ver. 4.0. New York: Barbizon Lighting Company, 2007.

Bartlett, Brandon, Jesse K. Miguel, Phillip Miller, Adam Nobel, Todd Peterson, and Martha Rowlett. *3D Studio Architectural Rendering*. Indianapolis, IN: New Riders Publishing, 1996.

Beard, Richard R. *Walt Disney's Epcot: Creating the New World of Tomorrow*. New York: Harry N. Abrams, Inc. Publishers, 1982.

Bellman, Willard F. *Lighting the Stage: Art and Practice*. 3rd ed. Louisville, KY: Broadway Press, 2001.

Birn, Jeremy. *[Digital] Lighting and Rendering*. 3rd ed. Indianapolis, IN: New Riders Publishing, 2013.

Bowers, Brian. *Lengthening the Day: A History of Lighting Technology*. Oxford: Oxford University Press, 1998.

Box, Harry C. *Set Lighting Technician's Handbook: Film Lighting Equipment, Practice, and Electrical Distribution*. 4th ed. Oxford and Boston: Focal Press, 2010.

Boylan, Bernard R. *The Lighting Primer*. Ames: Iowa State University Press, 1987.

Brady, Susan and Nena Couch. eds. *Documenting: Lighting Design*. New York: Theatre Library Association, 2007.

Brandston, Howard M. *Learning to See: A Matter of Light*. New York: Illuminating Engineering Society of North America, 2008.

Briggs, Jody. *Encyclopedia of Stage Lighting*. Jefferson, NC: McFarland and Company, Inc., Publishers, 2003.

Bright, Randy. *Disneyland: Inside Story*. New York: Harry N. Abrams, Inc. Publishers, 1987.

British Broadcasting Company (BBC). *Low Energy Lighting Guide for TV Productions*. Oxford: BBC Publications, 2011.

Brooker, Darren. *Essential CG Lighting Techniques*. Oxford and Boston: Focal Press, 2003.

Brown, Karen M. and Curtis B. Charles. *Computers in the Professional Practice of Design*. New York: McGraw-Hill, 1995.

Brown, Blain. *Motion Picture and Video Lighting*. 2nd ed. Amsterdam and Boston: Elsevier/Focal Press, 2008.

Cadena, Richard. *Electricity for the Entertainment Electrician and Technician*. 2nd ed. Oxford and Boston: Focal Press, 2014.

Cadena, Richard. *Automated Lighting: The Art and Science of Moving Light in Theatre, Live Performance, Broadcast, and Entertainment*. 3rd ed. Oxford and New York: Taylor & Francis/Routledge, 2018.

Cadena, Richard. *Lighting Design for Modern Houses of Worship*. Las Vegas, NV: Timeless Communications, 2008.

Carson, Verne and Sylvia E. Carson. *Professional Lighting Handbook*. 2nd ed. Stoneham, MA: Butterworth-Heinemann, 1991.

Caruso, James R. and Mavis E. Arther. *Video Lighting and Special Effects*. Englewood Cliffs, NJ: Prentice-Hall, Inc., 1991.

Carver, Gavin and Christine White. *Computer Visualization for the Theatre: 3D Modeling for Designers*. Amsterdam and Boston: Elsevier/Focal Press, 2003.

Claiborne, Vickie. *Media Servers for Lighting Programmers: A Comprehensive Guide to Working with Digital Lighting*. Oxford and Boston: Focal Press, 2014.

Davidson, James. *Garden Lighting: Contemporary Exterior Lighting*. New York: Sterling Publishing Company, Inc., 1999.

DiLaura, David L., Kevin W. Houser, Richard G. Mistrick, and Gary R. Steffy. eds. *Illuminating Engineering Society– The Lighting Handbook Tenth Edition: Reference and Application.* New York: Illuminating Engineering Society, 2011.

Dillon, Maureen. *Artificial Sunshine: A Social History of Domestic Lighting.* London: National Trust Enterprises, Ltd., 2002.

Dong, Wei and Kathleen Gibson. *Computer Visualization: An Integrated Approach for Interior Design and Architecture.* New York: McGraw-Hill, 1998.

Dunlop, Beth. *Building a Dream: The Art of Disney Architecture.* New York: Harry N. Abrams, Inc. Publishers, 1996.

Elenbaas, W. *Light Sources.* New York: Crane, Russak and Company, Inc., 1972.

Essig, Linda. *Lighting and the Design Idea.* Fort Worth, TX: Harcourt Brace College Publishers, 1997.

Essig, Linda. *The Speed of Light.* Portsmouth, NH: Heinemann Press, 2002.

Ferncase, Richard K. *Film and Video Lighting Terms and Concepts.* Newton, MA: Focal Press, 1995.

Fielder, William J. and Frederick H. Jones. *The Lit Interior.* Oxford: Architectural Press, 2001.

Fitt, Brian and Joe Thornley. *Lighting by Design: A Technical Guide.* Oxford and Boston: Focal Press, 1992.

Fitt, Brian and Joe Thornley. *Lighting Technology: A Guide to the Entertainment Industry.* 2nd ed. Oxford and Boston: Focal Press, 2002.Flanigan, Steven R. *Lighting, HD, Film and Business: A Maverick's World.* Colorado Springs, CO: Self-Published, 2010.

Friedel, Robert and Paul Israel. *Edison's Electric Light: Biography of an Invention.* New Brunswick, NJ: Rutgers University Press, 1986.

Gazillo, Eric. *Projection Design and Production for Live Entertainment.* New York: Focal Press, 2017.

Geraghty, Katie (Certification Director). *ETCP Candidate Handbook (Entertainment Electrician).* New York: Entertainment Services and Technology Association, 2006.

Gerhard, Mark, Jefferey M. Harper and Jon McFarland. *Mastering Autodesk* 3ds Max *Design 2010.* Indianapolis, IN: Wiley Publishing, Inc., 2009.

Gillette, J. Michael and Michael McNamara. *Designing with Light.* 6th ed. New York: McGraw-Hill, 2014.

Gloman, Chuck B. and Tom Letourneau. *Placing Shadows: Lighting Techniques for Video Production.* 3rd ed. Oxford and Boston: Focal Press, 2013.

Gordon, Gary. *Interior Lighting for Designers.* 5th ed. Hoboken, NJ: John Wiley and Sons, Inc., 2014.

GTE Products Corporation. *Sylvania/GTE Lighting Handbook for Television, Theatre and Professional Photography.* Danvers, MA: GTE Products Corporation, 1984.

Hart, John. *Lighting for Action.* New York: Amphoto, 1992.

Hays, David. *Light on the Subject.* New York: Limelight Editions, 1989.

Holshevnikoff, Bill. *ARRI Lighting Handbook: How to Get the Most from Your New ARRI Kit.* Blauvelt, NY: ARRI, Inc., 2000.

Huntington, John. *Control Systems for Live Entertainment.* 3rd ed. Amsterdam and Boston: Elsevier/Focal Press, 2007.

Illuminating Engineering Society of North America. *IESNA Lighting Education 100 (Fundamental Level).* New York: Illuminating Engineering Society of North America, 1993.

Illuminating Engineering Society of North America. *IESNA Lighting Education 150 (Intermediate Level).* New York: Illuminating Engineering Society of North America, 1993.

Illuminating Engineering Society of North America. *IESNA Lighting Ready Reference.* 3rd ed. New York: Illuminating Engineering Society of North America, 1996.

Illuminating Engineering Society of North America. *IESNA Lighting Ready Reference.* 4th ed. New York: Illuminating Engineering Society of North America, 2003.

Illuminating Engineering Society of North America. *An Introduction to Light and Lighting (ED 50).* New York: Illuminating Engineering Society of North America, 1991.

Illuminating Engineering Society of North America. *Museum and Art Gallery Lighting (RP-30–96).* New York: Illuminating Engineering Society of North America, 1996.

Illuminating Engineering Society of North America. *Recommended Practice for Lighting Merchandising Areas (RP-2–01).* New York: Illuminating Engineering Society of North America, 2001.

Illuminating Engineering Society of North America. *Recommended Practice for Museum Lighting (RP-30–17).* New York: Illuminating Engineering Society of North America, 2017.

Ingham, Rosemary. *From Page to Stage.* Portsmouth, NH: Heinemann, 1998.

Jackman, John. *Lighting for Digital Video and Television.* 3rd ed. Amsterdam and Boston: Elsevier/Focal Press, 2010.

Jacques, David Martin. *Introduction to the Musical Art of Stage Lighting Design.* 4th ed. Long Beach: David Martin Jacques, 2017.

Johnson, David. ed. *Universal Studios Islands of Adventure (Special Supplement to Entertainment Design).* New York: Intertec Publishing, 1999.

Johnson, Glenn M. *The Art of Illumination: Residential Lighting Design*. New York: McGraw-Hill, 1999.

Kalay, Yehuda E. *Architecture's New Media: Principles, Theories, and Methods of Computer-Aided Design*. Cambridge, MA: MIT Press, 2004.

Karlen, Mark and James Benya. *Lighting Design Basics*. 2nd ed. Hoboken, NJ: John Wiley and Sons, Inc., 2012.

Keller, Max. *Light Fantastic: The Art and Design of Stage Lighting*. New York: Prestel Verlag, 1999.

Kook, Edward F. *Images in Light for the Living Theatre*. New York: Edward F. Kook, 1963.

Kramer, Wayne. *The Mind's Eye: Theatre and Media Design from the Inside Out*. Portsmouth, NH: Heinemann, 2004.

Kundert-Gibbs, John. ed. *Maya: Secrets of the Pros*. Alameda, CA: Sybex, Inc., 2002.

Kundert-Gibbs, John and Dariush Derakhshani. eds. *Maya: Secrets of the Pros*. 2nd ed. Alameda, CA: Sybex, Inc., 2005.

Kurtti, Jeff. *Since the World Began: Walt Disney World, the First 25 Years*. New York: Hyperion, 1996.

Landau, David. *Lighting for Cinematography: A Practical Guide to the Art and Craft of Lighting for the Moving Image*. New York: Bloomsbury, 2014.

Laseau, Paul. *Architectural Representation Handbook: Traditional and Digital Techniques for Graphic Communication*. New York: McGraw-Hill, 2000.

Lindsey, Jack L. *Applied Illumination Engineering*. 2nd ed. Liburn, GA: The Fairmont Press, Inc., 1997.

Livingston, Jason. *Designing with Light: The Art, Science and Practice of Architectural Lighting Design*. Hoboken, NJ: John Wiley and Sons, Inc., 2014.

Lowell, Ross. *Matters of Light and Depth*. New York: Lowell-Light Manufacturing, Inc., 2000.

Lyver, Des and Graham Swainson. *Basics of Video Lighting*. Oxford and Boston: Focal Press, 1995.

Marling, Karal Ann. ed. *Designing Disney's Theme Parks: The Architecture of Reassurance*. New York: Flammarion, 1997.

Maulkiewicz, Kris. *Film Lighting: Talks with Hollywood's Cinematographers and Gaffers*. Revised ed. New York: Touchstone Publishing, 2012.

McCandless, Stanley. *A Method for Lighting the Stage*. 4th ed. New York: Theatre Arts Books, 1958.

McCandless, Stanley. *A Syllabus of Stage Lighting*. 5th ed. New Haven, CT: Yale University Press, 1941.

McCarthy, David, Ste Curran, and Simon Byron. *The Art of Producing Games*. Cambridge, UK: The Ilex Press Limited, 2005.

McMills, Anne E. *The Assistant Lighting Designer's Toolkit*. Oxford and Boston: Focal Press, 2014.

Millerson, Gerald. *The Technique of Lighting for Television and Film*. 3rd ed. New York and London: Focal Press, 2013.

Mills, Kenneth H., Judith E. Paul, and Kay B. Moormann. *Applied Visual Merchandising*. 3rd ed. Englewood Cliffs, NJ: Prentice-Hall, Inc., 1995.

Mobsby, Nick. *Practical Dimming*. Cambridge, UK: Entertainment Technology Press, 2006.

Mobsby, Nick. *Practical DMX*. Cambridge, UK: Entertainment Technology Press, 2006.

Moody, James L. *The Business of Theatrical Design*. 2nd ed. New York: Allworth Press, 2013.

Moody, James L and Paul Dexter. *Concert Lighting: Techniques, Art, and Business*. 4th ed. Oxford; Boston: Focal Press, 2017.

Morris, Dave and Leo Hartas. *Game Art: The Graphic Art of Computer Games*. New York: Watson-Guptill Publications, 2003.

Mort, Skip. *Stage Lighting: The Technicians' Guide: An On-the-Job Reference Tool with Online Video Resources*. 2nd ed. New York: Bloomsbury Methuen Publishing, 2015.

Moyer, Janet Lennox. *The Landscape Lighting Book*. 3rd ed. New York: John Wiley and Sons, Inc., 2013.

Mumm, Robert C. *Photometrics Handbook*. 2nd ed. Louisville, KY: Broadway Press, 1997.

Narboni, Roger. *Lighting the Landscape*. Basel, Switzerland: Birkhauser, 2016.

NFPA (National Fire Protection Association). *NFPA 70: National Electrical Code (NEC) 2008*. Quincy, MA: National Fire Protection Association, 2017.

Novitski, B. J. *Rendering Real and Imagined Buildings: The Art of Computer Modeling from the Palace of Kublai Khan to Le Corbusier's Villas*. Gloucester, MA: Rockport Publishers, Inc., 1998.

Omura, George. *Mastering 3D Studio VIZ 3*. Alameda, CA: Sybex, Inc., 2001.

Palamar, Todd. *Mastering Maya 2016*. Indianapolis, IN: John Wiley and Sons, Inc., 2007.

Palmer, Richard H. *The Lighting Art: The Aesthetics of Stage Lighting Design*. 2nd ed. Englewood Cliffs, NJ: Prentice Hall, 1994.

Parker, W. Oren, R. Craig Wolf, and Dick Block. *Scene Design and Stage Lighting*. 9th ed. Boston: Wadsworth, 2009.

Pegler, Martin M. and Anne Kong. *Visual Merchandising and Display: Studio Instant Access*. 7th ed. New York: Fairchild Publications, 2018.

Penzel, Frederick. *Theatre Lighting Before Electricity*. Middletown, CT: Wesleyan University Press, 1978.

Pilbrow, Richard. *Stage Lighting Design: The Art, the Craft, the Life*. New York: Design Press/Quite Specific Media Group, Ltd., 1997.

Portas, Mary. *Windows: The Art of Retail Display*. New York: Thames and Hudson, Inc., 1999.

Rae, Mark. ed. *IESNA Lighting Handbook*. 9th ed. New York: Illuminating Engineering Society of North America, 2000.

Rafferty, Kevin. *Imagineering: A Behind the Dreams Look at Making the Magic Real*. New York: Hyperion, 1996.

Reid, Francis. *Lighting the Stage: A Lighting Designer's Experiences*. Oxford and Boston: Focal Press, 1995.

Rhiner, James L. *A Complete Guide to the Language of Lighting*. Elk Grove Village, IL: Halo Lighting Division, McGraw-Edison Company, 1983.

Robbins, Claude L. *Daylighting: Design and Analysis*. New York: Van Nostrand Reinhold Company, 1986.

Rosenthal, Jean and Lael Wertenbaker. *The Magic of Light*. New York: Theatre Arts Books/Little, Brown and Company, 1974.

Russell, Sage. *The Architecture of Light*. La Jolla, CA: Conceptnine, 2008.

Sandström, Ulf. *Stage Lighting Controls*. Oxford and Boston: Focal Press, 1997.

Sapsis, Bill. *Heads Up and Tales*. Lansdowne, PA: Sapsis Publications, 2007.

Saxby, Graham. *Manual of Practical Holography*. Oxford and Boston: Focal Press, 1991.

Schiller, Brad. *The Automated Lighting Programmer's Handbook*. 3rd ed. Amsterdam and Boston: Elsevier/Focal Press, 2017.

Shelley, Steven Louis. *A Practical Guide to Stage Lighting*. 3rd ed. Oxford and Boston: Focal Press, 2014.

Simpson, Robert S. *Lighting Control: Technology and Applications*. Oxford and Boston: Focal Press, 2003.

Smith, Fran Kellogg and Fred J. Bertolone. *Bringing Interiors to Light: The Principles and Practices of Lighting Design*. New York: Whitney Library of Design, 1986.

Steffy, Gary. *Architectural Lighting Design*. 3rd ed. New York: John Wiley and Sons, Inc., 2008.

Steffy, Gary R. *Time-Saver Standards for Architectural Lighting*. New York: McGraw-Hill, 2000.

Steffy, Gary R. *Lighting the Electronic Office*. New York: Van Nostrand Reinhold, 1995.

Szenasy, Susan S. *Light: The Complete Handbook of Lighting Design*. Philadelphia, PA: Running Press Book Publishers, 1986.

Tharp, Twyla. *The Creative Habit: Learn It and Use It for Life*. New York: Simon & Schuster, 2003.

Thomas, James. *Script Analysis for Actors, Directors, and Designers*. 4th ed. Oxford and Boston: Focal Press, 2009.

Turner, Janet. *Designing with Light: Public Spaces*. New York: Watson-Guptill Publications, 1998.

Vasey, John. *Concert Sound and Lighting Systems*. 3rd ed. Woburn, MA: Butterworth-Heinemann Press, 1999.

Viera, Dave. *Lighting for Film and Electronic Cinematography*. Belmont, CA: Wadsworth Publishing Company, 1993.

Walne, Graham. *Projection for the Performing Arts*. Oxford and Boston: Focal Press, 1995.

Warfel, William B. *The New Handbook of Stage Lighting Graphics*. New York: Drama Book Publishers, 1990.

Warfel, William B. and Walter R. Klappert. *Color Science for Lighting the Stage*. New Haven, CT: Yale University Press, 1981.

Watson, Lee. *Lighting Design Handbook*. New York: McGraw-Hill, 1990.

Weishar, Peter. *Digital Space: Designing Virtual Environments*. New York: McGraw-Hill, 1998.

Whitehead, Randall. *The Art of Outdoor Lighting: Landscapes with the Beauty of Lighting*. Gloucester, MA: Rockport Publishers, Inc., 2001.

Whittaker, Ron. *Video Field Production*. 2nd ed. Mountain View, CA: Mayfield Publishing, Company, 1996.

Winchip, Susan M. *Fundamentals of Lighting*. 3rd ed. New York: Fairchild Books, 2017.

Wojtowicz, Jerzy. *Virtual Design Studio*. Hong Kong: Hong Kong University Press, 1995.

INDEX

Note: *Italicized* page numbers indicate a figure and page numbers in **bold** indicate a table on the corresponding page.